ROAST
REVOLUTION

ROAST REVOLUTION

**CONTEMPORARY RECIPES FOR
REVAMPED ROAST DINNERS**

KATHY KORDALIS

photography by Mowie Kay

RYLAND PETERS & SMALL
LONDON • NEW YORK

CONTENTS

INTRODUCTION 6

HOW TO ROAST 8

CLASSICS 12

FAST 30

SLOW 52

MERRY 82

WEEKENDS 100

SIDES 120

TREATS & TIPPLES 134

MENU SUGGESTIONS 156

INDEX 158

ACKNOWLEDGEMENTS 160

INTRODUCTION

Roasting is one of the oldest cooking methods, and one which remains popular for a number of reasons. A hot oven alone can bring out the deep, robust flavours of almost any ingredient, rendering it perfectly crisp or tender. Its spacious proportions mean that it lends itself well to creating plentiful meals for sharing just as well as smaller meals for one or two. It is truly one of the easiest, yet most impressive ways to cook.

So why the need for a roast revolution? With a kitchen technique that is so traditional, it is easy to get stuck in a rut. In this book, I aim to shake up your roasting repertoire and show you how to incorporate ingredients and flavours from around the world, create healthier, lighter roasts, whip up quick mid-week roasts and create show-stopping indulgent dishes that will wow your family and friends.

An important part of the roast revolution is the realization that meat, fish and vegetables can all be equally worthy of star-ingredient status. As roasted meat is rich in protein, minerals and vitamins, it was traditionally considered a feasting meal and eaten more seldomly than it is today. Increasingly, people are returning to eating less meat or not at all, and to consider the provenance and welfare of animals.

I love a roasted vegetable centrepiece, and can show you that vegetables are anything but boring when you manage to cook them just right. Many people have trouble judging what makes the difference between soft, caramelized glory and plain mush – the recipes in this book and tips in the following pages will help you master the technique.

Whatever your central ingredient happens to be, the important thing is to start with the best quality piece of meat, fresh fish or vibrant bunch of vegetables you can find – it will make the end result infinitely more delicious. Particularly if you are looking for something special, speak to your butcher, fishmonger or greengrocer about what will be best on the day. If you are cooking meat, something on the bone looks impressive and makes for a succulent meal.

The best part about roasting, for me, is the flexibility and versatility it allows. Throughout this book, there are ample opportunities to mix and match mains with sides and challenge conventional ideas of what makes a good roast.

Get started with the selection of classic recipes, which combine simplicity with small, fresh twists – try Roast Beef with Beetroot, Blood Orange & Horseradish Salad & Cumin Pumpkin Whip. Fast-cook dishes make use of the quickly transformative power of a hot oven with recipes such as Gochujang Roasted Aubergine Steaks and Soy & Sesame Baked Monkfish. Slow-roasting is an easy and satisfying way to cook, sample the Sticky Plum-roasted Cabbages or Stuffed Porchetta. If you are looking for spectacular celebration dishes, there are plenty, try Truffle-roasted Cockerel with Hasselback Squash, Carrots & Kale with a Sausage & Freekeh Crumb. Crowd-pleasing Rum Ribs with Twice-baked Stuffed Potatoes or Salt-crusted Sea Bass are ideal for weekend dining. Finally, take your pick from the selection of sides, desserts and cocktail recipes to beautifully finish off your feast. Use the menu suggestions at the back of the book to help you create unique combinations perfectly suited to you.

HOW TO ROAST

MEAT & HEAT

Roasting is an excellent cooking technique for a wide variety of meats and fish. It is especially suited to poultry and leaner cuts of lamb, pork and beef. More fatty or sinewy cuts of meat need a little extra time, but fabulous results can still be achieved.

Meat is primarily a muscle, and different muscles do different things in the body. Muscles that work more in the animal will be tougher than those that are used less. Parts of the animal that tend to work the most are the shoulder, neck, and legs, hence these can often be tougher cuts of meat. The parts of the animal that work less are found in the back and especially towards and including the small of the back. The muscles that work less are more tender and suited for dry-cooking quickly in a very hot oven. Tougher cuts of meat require some sort of liquid, like the braising liquid in a pot roast, or low, slow cooking, which tenderizes tough muscles.

ON OR OFF THE BONE?

There are different advantages to buying meat both on and off the bone. Boneless joints are easy to carve but won't always have the flavour which comes from the juices released from the bone marrow. However, you can always ask your butcher for some bones to roast your meat on top of. You can also ask your butcher for your joint of meat to be chined – they will cut the bone from the meat but leave it on the joint.

CUTS OF MEAT

BEEF

Beef comes in many different cuts, so once you have identified the cut, you can work out the cooking method to get the most out of it. The general rule is, if it is lean, cook it fast, and if it is fibrous, cook it slow.

Rib of beef This is a lovely thick, rich, on-the-bone cut, perfect for roasting. It tends to have a lot of flavour and always looks impressive to serve, though can be more difficult to carve.

Fillet of beef/tenderloin If you are looking for the ultimate in luxury, this is a boneless joint with a fantastic flavour. It is the centre cut of the fillet on the back of the cow which does very little work and is therefore very lean, with little fat and fibres. It is best cooked rare and served in thin slices.

Brisket This is a flat piece of muscle on the underside of the animal. Great for braising, this muscle does a lot of work and requires long, slow cooking to tenderize it.

LAMB

Joints of lamb can be prepared to be cooked on or off the bone. With a few exceptions, it is usually preferable to cook joints of lamb on the bone to keep the meat moist and to infuse more flavour.

Leg of lamb Most commonly cooked on the bone, this generous cut is probably the archetypal family lamb roast. You can also buy legs of lamb boned or partially boned, which are easier to carve.

Rack of lamb The rack of lamb is a bone-in joint cut from the rib section. It is often French-trimmed to remove excess fat and clean along the top, making it an impressive looking joint. The rack of lamb doesn't take very long to roast and yields tender, juicy meat.

Shoulder of lamb Most often served deboned and rolled, this more humble cut is usually deemed less tender, so is better suited to slow cooking. However, it is full of flavour and makes a decent carving roast.

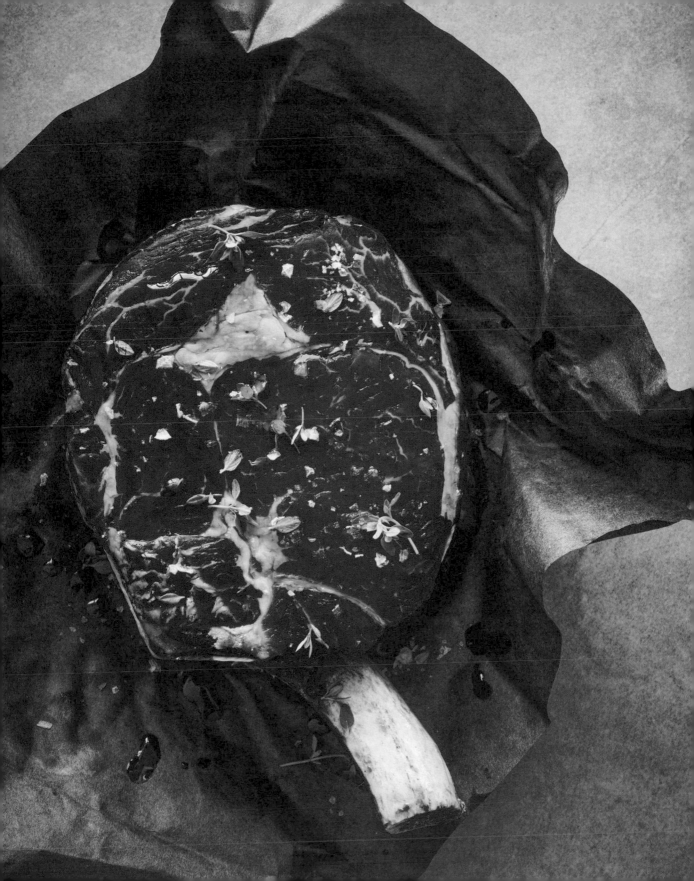

PORK

Pork has always been an economical meat – but no less delicious. It has a high water content, therefore is well known for its juiciness and is ideal for dry-roasting. Unless you are making pulled pork, it often doesn't require extra moisture. Joints with properly scored rind are good for the crackling.

Rolled pork shoulder The most common pork joint for households, this is not the leanest of meats, but it is a very tasty cut – the fat that runs through the joint adds to the flavour when it is cooked.

Pork loin The pork loin is considered to be a prime cut, equivalent to sirloin of beef. Loins are where we cut chops from, but left whole, this is a lean and tasty joint. It can either be left on the bone and chined or deboned and rolled for easy carving.

POULTRY

Whether you choose standard, free-range or organic is a matter of personal choice, but if possible, go for the best bird you can afford.

Chicken Alongside pork, chicken is the most widely consumed meat in the world. It is easy to cook and a safe choice for a roast. Chickens are available in small, medium and large sizes. Choose a bird with plump breasts, dry skin and no bruising or blood spots.

Poussin are very young chickens usually between 4–12 weeks old. Best served as a single portion.

Cockerel These are large male chickens which range from between 3–5 kg/6½–11 lb. As they are left to mature longer, they have a strong flavour.

Turkey The traditional Christmas or Thanksgiving meal, turkey is as popular now as it has ever been.

Ducks are generally aged between 7–9 weeks and have a large amount of subcutaneous fat that should be rendered when cooked, and skin that should be roasted until perfectly crisp. Duck is a very strongly flavoured bird, which stands up well to strong sauces.

FISH

Fish is delicious when roasted – whether you choose a whole fish for a centrepiece or small fillets for a quick supper. Cooking a whole fish on the bone looks really impressive, but it means that your guests need to work harder. If serving a whole fish, always make sure you have removed the small bones in the flesh, or alternatively, have your fishmonger fillet the whole fish for you. Follow these tips when buying fresh fish:

If buying whole fish, check the eyes, they should be bright, shiny and full; cloudy sunken eyes mean that the fish has been sitting around for too long.
Take a look at the skin and scales, the fresher the fish, the brighter and more metallic its skin will be.
Touch the fish The fish should be nice and firm, and it should spring back to the touch.
Make sure the gills are clean and a bright red; as a fish ages, its gills will dull and start to turn brown.
When buying fillets, check the flesh to make sure it is firm, smooth and intact, not flaky.

MAKING VEGETABLES THE STAR

The flavour of roasted vegetables is equally as stunning as meat or fish – even for those who are not keen on the taste of boiled or steamed veg, a golden roasted vegetable is an entirely different specimen.

Large vegetables roasted whole, such as butternut squash or cauliflower, make stunning centrepieces to be carved up and shared round. Serve them marinated, with a flavourful sauce or stuffed, just like you would a joint of meat. Smaller vegetables such as aubergines/

eggplants or artichokes are just as satisfying and perfect for serving in individual portions.

For the best browning, be generous with the oil on your vegetables. Tossing the veggies in a bowl with oil before roasting is a good way to ensure an even coating. To further encourage crispy, golden exteriors, always pop your roasting pan into the oven to preheat.

Never crowd vegetables in the oven as they'll release steam and turn soggy. Leave room for the hot air to circulate and use more than one tray if needed.

When roasting more than one type of vegetable at a time, cutting your vegetables to the right size is key. If you are mixing thicker vegetables, like potatoes and carrots, with more delicate ones like Brussels sprouts and onions, be careful that the more delicate ones don't burn, while the stockier ones need to be tender in the middle. So cut the delicate vegetables into larger pieces or put them in to roast later.

Low-moisture vegetables tend to go crisp and caramelized in the oven, whereas moist vegetables, such as tomatoes, will be tender with a great flavour, however, take special care not to overcook these as they will turn to mush.

TIPS & TRICKS FOR PERFECT ROASTS

- Start by preheating your oven for at least 20 minutes to make the most of the dry, indirect heat that's great for cooking large items.
- Never take the ingredients straight from your refrigerator to the oven – bring them to room temperature first.
- Use a wide, open roasting pan or a baking dish to allow ingredients to roast evenly. A rack helps increase the circulation of hot air. If you don't have a rack, put vegetables underneath the joint.
- Trussing meat helps to keep the roast at the same thickness, which means it cooks more evenly.

Never remove the string before cooking.
- Cover the roast with oil or butter to help the salt and pepper stick.
- After cooking, keep meat covered with foil and rest to let the juices sink back in.
- For leaner meats, it's best to baste with the cooking juices during the cooking process. For slower roasts, keep the cooking juices topped up and the roast tightly covered.

TIMES & TEMPERATURES

Test your meat with a meat thermometer 30 minutes before the recipe says it should be done. Insert the thermometer into the thickest part. If there's a bone, avoid it or the reading could be inaccurate. If it's not done, put the meat back into the oven. When you've hit the right temperature, let the meat rest. The temperature will increase by 5–15°C (40–60°F) after resting, so take the meat out of the oven a few degrees before it hits the ideal internal temperatures below:

Beef, lamb and venison rare: 52°C (126°F), medium: 60°C (140°F), well done: 75–80°C (167–176°F)
Pork 75–80°C (167–176°F)
Poultry 75–80°C (167–176°F)

Chicken must be thoroughly cooked before serving, with no pink meat. Pierce the thickest part of the thigh with a skewer and let the juices run out. If they are clear, then it's cooked, but if they still look pink, return to the oven for 15 minutes, then test again.

When fish reaches the proper cooking temperature, it becomes opaque and flakes. To test if fish is cooked, poke the tines of a fork into the thickest part at a 45-degree angle, then gently twist the fork and pull up some of the fish. Undercooked fish resists flaking and is translucent.

CLASSICS

These recipes have classic elements at their heart which have stood the test of time. Sometimes, it only takes one extra spice, herb or little treat to breathe new life into a traditional dish. The twist on a modern roast, for me, is all about adding a fresh and crisp touch.

ROAST BEEF ON THE BONE
WITH BEETROOT, BLOOD ORANGE & HORSERADISH SALAD
& CUMIN PUMPKIN WHIP

What I love about this combination is that it takes the traditional elements of classic roast beef to a much lighter place. All three of these separate dishes hold up well on their own (if you want to mix and match them with other things) but together they are an incredible flavour match! Perfect served warm or cold.

1 x 2.5-kg/5½-lb. beef rib with 3 bones, fat trimmed and removed from fridge 1 hour before cooking
1 tbsp vegetable oil
20 g/1½ tbsp butter, softened
2 red onions, skins cleaned but left on, quartered
1 tsp beetroot/beet powder (optional)
sea salt and freshly ground black pepper

Preheat the oven to 200°C (400°F) Gas 6.

Place the beef on a rack in a large roasting pan. Mix together the oil and butter and smear all over the beef, then season very well with salt and pepper. Add the red onions to the pan around the beef.

Roast the beef in the preheated oven for 10–15 minutes, then turn the temperature down to 170°C (325°F) Gas 3. Cook for a further 12–15 minutes per 500 g/18 oz. for rare, 15–18 minutes per 500 g/18 oz. for medium and 20 minutes per 500 g/18 oz. for well done.

Rest on the rack for at least 15–20 minutes before carving. Sprinkle with beetroot/beet powder (if using) and serve with the Cumin Pumpkin Whip and Beetroot, Blood Orange & Horseradish Salad.

CUMIN PUMPKIN WHIP

500 g/18 oz. pumpkin, peeled, deseeded and chopped
1 white potato, peeled and chopped
½ tsp cayenne pepper
2 tsp olive oil, plus extra for drizzling
1 tsp ground smoked cumin
2 garlic cloves, peeled
3 tbsp tahini
sea salt and freshly ground black pepper
toasted pumpkin seeds/pepitas, to serve (optional)

Place the pumpkin and potato in a saucepan and cover with cold water. Bring to the boil over a high heat, then simmer for 15 minutes or until the vegetables are tender. Drain well.

Blend the pumpkin and potato with the rest of the ingredients, except the pumpkin seeds/pepitas, in a food processor until smooth.

When ready to serve, return the pumpkin whip to a saucepan over a low heat and reheat, then serve warm, drizzled with olive oil, sprinkled with toasted pumpkin seeds/pepitas (if liked) and plenty of freshly ground black pepper.

BEETROOT, BLOOD ORANGE & HORSERADISH SALAD

1 bunch each purple and golden beetroot/
    beets, scrubbed, skins left on
2–3 candy beetroot, scrubbed, skins left on
2½ tbsp olive oil
1 tbsp butter
3 blood oranges, peeled and sliced into
    rounds
200 g/7 oz. baby spinach
½ bunch fresh chives, halved
20 g/2 tbsp pumpkin seeds, toasted
    (optional)

HORSERADISH DRESSING
2 tbsp creamed horseradish
50 ml/3½ tbsp buttermilk
sea salt and freshly ground black pepper
pinch of fresh thyme, to garnish

Preheat the oven to 180°C (350°F) Gas 4.

    Place the beetroots/beets in a roasting pan and fill with 1 cm/⅜ inch of hot water. Drizzle with 1½ tbsp of the oil and season with salt and pepper. Cover the pan with foil and roast in the preheated oven for 45–50 minutes, turning occasionally, until tender. The cooking time will vary depending on the size of the vegetables. Peel and chop the beets into quarters and set aside.

    Meanwhile, warm the remaining 1 tbsp olive oil and the butter in a saucepan over a medium-high heat. Add the blood orange slices and cook for 1–2 minutes on each side until caramelized, then remove and set aside. Add the spinach to the pan, season with salt and pepper and allow to gently wilt.

    Place the wilted spinach and blood oranges on a platter, then top with the roasted beetroot/beet quarters, chives and pumpkin seeds/pepitas (if using).

    To make the dressing, in a small bowl, mix the creamed horseradish with the buttermilk and season with salt and pepper. Sprinkle with thyme to garnish. This dressing works equally well on the salad and as a condiment with the beef.

LEMON & OREGANO ROAST CHICKEN
WITH CARAMELIZED HONEY & CHILLI LEMONS

Super lemony, super tasty and super simple! Nothing beats a roast chicken, whether it's part of a meal to share or whether you roast a bird to eat throughout the week. Delicious served with these caramelized lemons and a crisp mixed salad.

10 g/2 tsp butter
10 g/⅓ oz. fresh oregano leaves, finely
    chopped (or 1 tsp dried oregano)
3 tbsp extra virgin olive oil
1 lemon, zested and halved
1 x 1.8-kg/4-lb. whole chicken
1 whole garlic head, unpeeled, halved
    widthways
4 sprigs fresh oregano (optional)
100 ml/⅓ cup plus 1 tbsp chicken stock
sea salt and freshly cracked black pepper
mixed salad and dill sprigs, to serve
    (optional)

large roasting pan, lightly greased

Preheat the oven to 200°C (400°F) Gas 6.

Mix together the butter, chopped oregano, oil, lemon zest and some salt and pepper. Place the chicken in the prepared roasting pan and rub with the oregano butter. Fill the chicken cavity with the lemon halves, half the garlic and 1 sprig of the oregano (if using).

Scatter the rest of the oregano (if using) and the rest of the garlic cloves around the pan and pour in the chicken stock. Roast in the preheated oven for 20 minutes, then turn the heat down to 180°C (350°F) Gas 4 and roast for a further 1 hour 20 minutes, basting occasionally. Make sure the skin is golden, the flesh is no longer pink and the juices run clear when the chicken is pierced. Cover and rest the chicken for 5 minutes, then carve and serve with a mixed salad, dill sprigs and the Caramelized Honey & Chilli Lemons.

CARAMELIZED HONEY & CHILLI LEMONS

2 lemons
3 tbsp runny honey (or more, to taste)
1 tsp chilli flakes/hot red pepper flakes
1 tbsp extra virgin olive oil

Preheat the oven to 200°C (400°F) Gas 6.

Cut the lemons into 8 wedges each and place in a bowl. Add the honey, chilli flakes/hot red pepper flakes and the extra virgin olive oil and tip into a roasting pan. Roast in the preheated oven for 40 minutes, basting with the cooking juices every 10 minutes.

NOTE these are not for the faint-hearted! You must like the taste of lemon. When I want the strongest flavour, I eat them with the bitter skin, for a more subtle taste I eat only the lemon flesh, and for a mild tart chilli/chile flavour, I simply squeeze them over my food.

PERFECT CRACKLING ROAST PORK
WITH BAKED SAGE & CALVADOS APPLES

These flavours, for me, bring back memories of long Sunday lunches. This easy recipe allows you to roast everything in one tray, with just a few little additions that bring a new spark to an old classic. You can then serve simply with a salad and some crusty bread or whip up a gravy with the pan juices and add some greens and a potato side dish (see pages 122–125).

1.8 kg/4 lb. piece of pork loin, rolled, removed from the fridge 1 hour before cooking
1 tbsp olive oil
2 tsp sea salt flakes

BAKED SAGE & CALVADOS APPLES
4 small sweet red apples, skins left on, halved horizontally
30 g/scant ¼ cup hazelnuts
6 shallots, peeled and halved horizontally
1 bunch fresh sage leaves
150 ml/⅔ cup Calvados
100 ml/⅓ cup plus 1 tbsp vegetable stock
2 tbsp double/heavy cream (optional)
sea salt and freshly ground black pepper

Preheat the oven to 200°C (400°F) Gas 6.

Place the pork in a roasting pan and use a paper towel to pat dry all over. Use a very sharp knife to make long slashes at about 5 mm/¼ inch width apart across the skin, making sure you don't cut through to the meat underneath. (You can always ask your butcher to do this bit for you if you like.) Massage the olive oil into the skin followed by the sea salt flakes, pushing them down inside the cuts.

Scatter the apples, hazelnuts, shallots and sage around the base of the pork. Pour in the Calvados and the vegetable stock, then season to taste with salt and pepper. Roast in the preheated oven for about 30 minutes or until crackling starts to form, then reduce the heat to 180°C (350°F) Gas 4 and cook for a further 35 minutes per 500 g/18 oz., plus 35 minutes.

Rest the roasted pork for 5 minutes, then carve into thick slices and serve with the roasted apples, hazelnuts, shallots and pan juices. If you want a richer sauce, stir the cream through the warm pan juices just before serving.

LAMB CUTLET RACKS
WITH PEA & OLIVE PISTOU & OVEN-DRIED & ROASTED TOMATOES ON CHARCOAL FLATBREADS

When serving this dish, I like to lay the flatbreads on a platter and place the warm lamb racks with the dried and roasted tomatoes on top, so that the cooking juices from both soak into the bread. For sharing with all your favourite people!

6 double lamb cutlets, French trimmed
40 ml/scant 3 tbsp olive oil
sea salt and freshly ground black pepper

ovenproof frying pan

Preheat the oven to 180°C (350°F) Gas 4.

Season the lamb cutlets generously with salt and pepper. Heat the olive oil in the ovenproof frying pan/skillet and cook the cutlets, fat-side down, over a medium-high heat for 5–7 minutes until golden, then for a further 1–2 minutes each side until brown. Transfer to the preheated oven and roast for 5–7 minutes for medium-rare or until cooked to your liking. Cover with foil to keep warm until ready to serve.

CHARCOAL FLATBREADS

250 g/1¾ cups strong white bread flour, plus extra for dusting
230 g/generous ¾ cup Greek yogurt
10 g/⅓ oz. activated charcoal powder (available from health food shops)
2 tbsp olive oil, plus extra for brushing
2 tsp baking powder
2 tsp sea salt

Pulse all the ingredients in a food processor until a dough forms. Turn out onto a lightly floured surface and knead until smooth. Divide the dough into 6, then cover with clingfilm/plastic wrap and rest for 10 minutes.

Roll out each piece of dough to 3 mm/⅛ inch thick and brush with olive oil. Heat a large frying pan/skillet over a medium-high heat and cook the flatbreads in batches for 1–2 minutes on each side, turning once, until puffy and lightly charred.

ROASTED TOMATOES

4–6 large tomatoes on the vine
3 tbsp olive oil, plus extra to serve
pinch of saffron
30 ml/2 tbsp white wine
1 tsp chilli flakes/hot red pepper flakes
1 tbsp runny honey
2 garlic cloves, unpeeled
6 sprigs fresh thyme
2 sprigs fresh tarragon

For the roasted tomatoes, preheat the oven to 180°C (350°F) Gas 4.

Place the tomatoes on their vine on a baking sheet and drizzle with the 3 tbsp olive oil. Mix the saffron into the white wine and drizzle over the tomatoes. Add the chilli flakes/hot red pepper flakes, honey and garlic. Roast in the preheated oven for 10 minutes, then lower the oven temperature to 150°C (300°F) Gas 2, add the thyme and tarragon and cook for 30 minutes more, until the tomatoes are soft but still hold their shape.

Reserve the tomato cooking juices to serve alongside the lamb and drizzle the roasted tomatoes with a little extra olive oil just before serving.

OVEN-DRIED TOMATOES

2 plum tomatoes, thinly sliced
2 tsp sea salt

To make the dried tomatoes, place the tomato slices on the dehydrator tray and sprinkle lightly with the salt to help draw out the liquid. Arrange the tomato slices at least 1.5 cm/½-inch apart on dehydrator trays and leave 2.5–5 cm/1–2 inches between the racks to allow for good air circulation.

Dehydrate for 6–12 hours, turning the tomatoes and rotating the racks as needed to promote even drying. Watch closely towards the end of the process, they should turn deep red and be totally dry yet still pliable (not crisp). They should not feel tacky to touch. Remove each tomato as it's ready, leaving the thicker ones to finish drying. Store in an airtight container until ready to serve.

PEA & OLIVE PISTOU

1 garlic clove, peeled and crushed
150 ml/⅔ cup olive oil
150 g/1 cup fresh or frozen peas,
 blanched
50 g/1¾ oz. Nocellara olives, pitted
 and chopped
3 sprigs fresh mint, leaves picked
1 sprig fresh tarragon, leaves picked
freshly squeezed juice of ½ lemon

Pulse the garlic, a pinch of sea salt and 100 ml/⅓ cup plus 1 tbsp of the olive oil in a food processor. Add the peas, olives, mint, tarragon and lemon juice. Check the consistency (it should be similar to pesto) and add the extra oil if needed. Adjust the seasoning and serve with the lamb. The pistou will keep in the fridge for 2 days.

ULTIMATE VEGGIE ROAST
WITH POMEGRANATE KETCHUP

Served with a slightly tart pomegranate ketchup, this show-stopping vegetarian roast contains many delicious layers of flavour. It can also be a great recipe to feed a family for a few days – a lot of vegetables and goodness packed into one meal!

1 red onion, roughly chopped
200 g/7 oz. mixed peeled butternut
    squash flesh and sweet potato, diced
200 g/7 oz. chestnut mushrooms,
    roughly chopped
1 red (bell) pepper, deseeded and diced
6 garlic cloves, unpeeled
4 tbsp olive oil, plus extra for brushing
1 x 400-g/14-oz. can butter/lima beans,
    drained and rinsed
250 g/9 oz. mixed nuts, toasted
30 g/1 oz. dried porcini mushrooms,
    soaked and drained
3 fresh rosemary sprigs, leaves picked
1 bunch fresh thyme, leaves picked,
    reserving some to garnish
1 bunch fresh parsley, leaves picked
100 g/3½ oz. pitted green olives,
    roughly chopped
4 spring onions/scallions, finely chopped
50 g/⅓ cup mixed raisins
20 g/2 tbsp capers, drained (optional)
2 tbsp soy sauce
60 g/generous 1 cup fresh breadcrumbs
freshly squeezed juice of ½ lemon
sea salt and freshly ground black pepper
pomegranate seeds, fresh sage leaves
    and purple basil to garnish (optional)

TO LINE THE PAN
1 large or 2 small aubergine/eggplants,
    thinly sliced lengthways
2–3 courgettes/zucchini, thinly sliced
    lengthways

griddle pan/grill pan
20-cm/8-inch, deep springform baking
    pan, lightly greased with oil and
    base-lined with baking parchment

Preheat the oven to 200°C (400°F) Gas 6.

Toss the onion, butternut squash, sweet potato, chestnut mushrooms and red (bell) pepper with the garlic and 2 tbsp of the oil in a large bowl. Spread out in a large roasting pan and roast in the preheated oven for 25–30 minutes, until soft, turning once.

Meanwhile, prepare the pan lining. Preheat the griddle pan/grill pan over a medium-high heat. Brush the aubergine/eggplant and courgette/zucchini slices with the remaining oil and season with salt and pepper. Griddle for 1–2 minutes on each side until lightly charred, then set aside to cool until needed.

Add the roasted vegetables and garlic to a food processor and pulse to a chunky purée. Set aside in a large mixing bowl.

Place the butter/lima beans, nuts, re-hydrated porcini mushrooms and herbs in the food processor and pulse to roughly chop. Add to the bowl with the roasted vegetable purée along with the olives, spring onions/scallions, raisins, capers (if using), soy sauce, breadcrumbs and lemon juice. Season with salt and pepper and mix together until well combined.

Preheat the oven to 160°C (325°F) Gas 3.

Line the base of the prepared baking pan with alternating slices of courgette/zucchini and aubergine/eggplant, overlapping slightly, until the base and sides are totally covered. Pile the vegetable filling in and pack down gently. Place the remaining grilled vegetable slices over the top to completely cover the filling, tucking in or trimming untidy edges. Brush with oil and scatter with the reserved thyme. Cover the pan with foil and roast in the preheated oven for 40 minutes, uncovering 10 minutes before the end of the cooking time until the top turns golden.

Rest for 5 minutes in the pan, then loosen the edges with a knife and carefully turn out onto a serving plate. Garnish with pomegranate seeds, sage and purple basil leaves, if liked, before serving.

POMEGRANATE KETCHUP

3 onions, peeled and quartered
4 celery sticks, roughly chopped
4 tbsp olive oil
3 garlic cloves, thinly sliced
1 tsp ground coriander
½ tsp ground cinnamon
1 tsp ground allspice
½ tsp freshly ground black pepper
4 x 400-g/14-oz. cans chopped tomatoes
3 tbsp tomato purée/paste
200 ml/generous ¾ cup red wine vinegar
200 g/1 cup light brown soft sugar
4 tbsp pomegranate molasses

Put the onions and celery into a food processor and pulse to finely chop. Heat the oil in a very large saucepan over a low heat, add the onions and celery, cover, then cook for 5 minutes to soften. Uncover, then add the garlic and cook, stirring, for 5 minutes more. Tip in the spices and cook, stirring, for 1 minute. Stir in all the remaining ingredients and bring to the boil. Simmer, uncovered, for 1 hour until the liquid has reduced significantly. Blitz with a stick blender until smooth, then strain into a bowl. The ketchup will thicken a little when it cools, but if yours seems runny, cook a little longer, stirring often, until reduced. The ketchup will keep in an airtight container in the fridge for up to 3 months.

ROASTED HAKE NICOISE-ISH SALAD
WITH TARTARE DRESSING & GARLIC BREAD SHARDS

This revamped classic French salad is all roasted in one tray for ease. Served with garlic bread and tartare dressing, you simply can't go wrong with these flavours.

500 g/18 oz. boiled baby new
    potatoes, halved
4 garlic cloves, peeled
5 tbsp olive oil
100 g/3½ oz. cherry tomatoes
    on the vine
300 g/10½ oz. green/French beans,
    trimmed
50 g/1¾ oz. pitted Kalamata or
    French olives
4 skinless hake fillets
flaked sea salt and freshly ground
    black pepper
8 anchovies, to serve
mini purple basil, to garnish (optional)

TARTARE DRESSING
100 g/scant ½ cup mayonnaise
100 g/scant ½ cup Greek yogurt
3 tbsp capers, drained and chopped
3 tbsp drained and chopped gherkins/
    dill pickles
1 small shallot, finely chopped
grated zest and freshly squeezed juice
    of 1 lemon

Preheat the oven to 190°C (375°F) Gas 5 and place a large, rimmed baking sheet on the central rack to warm.

Toss the potatoes with the garlic and 3 tbsp of the olive oil in a large bowl and season to taste with salt and pepper. Arrange the potatoes and garlic in an even layer on the preheated baking sheet and roast in the preheated oven for about 10 minutes. After 10 minutes, add the tomatoes to the pan, turn the potatoes and roast together for another 10 minutes until the potatoes are browned.

Meanwhile, in another bowl, toss together the beans and olives with 1 tbsp of the oil. Season with salt and pepper and set aside.

Mix all the ingredients for the tartare dressing together in a small bowl, adding a little water if needed, until you reach a pouring consistency. Season to taste and set aside.

Season the hake fillets, then coat them with the remaining 1 tbsp oil. Remove the baking sheet from the oven (leaving the oven on) and push the potatoes and tomatoes slightly to one side so that they take up about a third of the pan. Place the fish on another third, then the green/French bean mixture in the remaining space.

Roast in the preheated oven for about 8–10 minutes or until the fish is cooked through. Serve topped with anchovies, drizzled with the tartare dressing and garnished with mini purple basil, if liked.

GARLIC BREAD SHARDS

1 x 30-cm/12-inch sourdough baguette,
    cut into slices diagonally
70 g/⅔ stick unsalted butter, softened
3 garlic cloves, crushed
1 tbsp finely chopped fresh parsley
1 tbsp finely chopped fresh basil
sea salt and freshly cracked black pepper

Preheat the oven to 180°C (350°F) Gas 4.

Place the slices of baguette on a baking tray. In a bowl, mix together the butter, garlic and herbs and season with salt and pepper. Spread the garlic butter onto the slices of bread. Bake in the preheated oven for 8–10 minutes.

Serve with the Roasted Hake Nicoise-ish Salad.

FAST

Roasting need not be just for the
weekend. These speedier recipes are
ideal for mid-week suppers or when
you have an impromptu get-together.
The type of deep flavour-punch that
might otherwise take hours can be
achieved with a very hot oven instead.

OVEN-CHARRED CURRIED PORK CHOPS
WITH GREEN CHILLI & COCONUT SAMBAL

The spicy, fresh flavours in this speedy meal provide a new take on curry night, and you might just find you start serving this life-changing sambal with everything. Paired with cooling herb and mango-topped yogurt and poppadoms, it's just bliss!

4 pork chops, excess fat trimmed
2 green chillies/chiles, left whole
4 spring onions/scallions, left whole
a pinch dried curry leaves

MARINADE
2 tsp ground cumin
2 tsp ground coriander
80 g/⅓ cup Greek yogurt
30 ml/2 tbsp flavourless oil
freshly squeezed juice of ½ lemon
2 garlic cloves, crushed
2 tsp grated fresh ginger
2 tsp curry powder
1 tbsp chilli/chili powder
sea salt and freshly ground black pepper

TO SERVE
plain yogurt topped with diced mango
freshly chopped mint, coriander/cilantro and spring onions/scallions
poppadoms

Preheat the oven to 200°C (400°F) Gas 6 and the grill/broiler to high.

For the marinade, toast the ground spices in a small, dry saucepan over a medium-high heat for about 30 seconds until fragrant. Place in a food processor with the yogurt, flavourless oil, lemon juice, garlic, ginger, curry powder and chilli/chili powder and blend until smooth. Season to taste with salt and pepper. Combine the marinade with the pork chops in a large bowl, turning them to make sure the meat is coated on all sides. Set aside, uncovered, at room temperature and leave to marinate for 10 minutes.

Place the chops in a roasting pan with the whole chillies/chiles and spring onions/scallions and sprinkle over the dried curry leaves. Grill/broil for 5 minutes until the chops take on some nice colour, then roast in the preheated oven for 20–25 minutes, depending on the thickness of the pork, until the meat is nice and charred.

Serve with cooling yogurt topped with mango, mint, coriander/cilantro, spring onions/scallions and poppadoms and the sambal.

GREEN CHILLI & COCONUT SAMBAL

50 g/scant ¾ cup coarsely grated fresh coconut flesh
1 bunch fresh coriander/cilantro, coarsely chopped
2–3 long green chillies/chiles (to taste), thinly sliced
1 tbsp finely chopped banana shallot
1 tbsp finely grated fresh ginger
1 garlic clove, finely chopped
3 spring onions/scallions, roughly chopped
sea salt and freshly ground black pepper
1 lime, cut into quarters, to serve

Blend all the ingredients (apart from the lime) in a food processor to make a paste. Season to taste with salt and pepper and refrigerate until required. Serve with the fresh lime wedges on the side.

ROSEMARY LAMB NECK FILLETS
WITH HERBY GRAIN BOWLS & CHARRED TOMATO YOGURT DRESSING

To solve your midweek meal conundrum, here is a tasty, healthy take on roast lamb. Lamb neck cooks quickly and you can make the grain bowls in advance.

600-g/1 lb. 5-oz. (2–3) lamb neck fillets
3 large garlic cloves, crushed to a paste
   with a little sea salt
1½ tbsp smoked paprika
1 tbsp runny honey
1 tsp dried marjoram
1 tsp tapenade
4 tbsp extra virgin olive oil
freshly squeezed juice of ½ lemon
2 red Romano peppers, halved and
   deseeded
2 red chillies/chiles, halved
3 sprigs fresh rosemary
sea salt and freshly ground black pepper

griddle pan/grill pan

Preheat the oven to 220°C (425°F) Gas 7.

Rub the lamb neck fillets with the garlic paste, paprika, honey, marjoram, tapenade, 3 tbsp of the oil and some black pepper.

Heat an ovenproof frying pan/skillet or griddle pan/grill pan over a high heat and, when it is hot, pour in the remaining 1 tbsp oil. Sear the lamb fillets on all sides for about 4 minutes.

Remove the pan from the heat and squeeze over the lemon juice. Add the peppers, chillies/chiles and rosemary to the pan. Roast in the preheated oven for 15 minutes, then cover with foil and rest for 5 minutes. The lamb should still be slightly pink inside.

Slice the neck fillets into thin rounds and divide between the Herby Grain Bowls. Top with the Charred Tomato Yogurt Dressing and serve.

HERBY GRAIN BOWLS

300 g/1¾ cups red quinoa, rinsed
1 red onion, finely chopped
200 g/2¼ cups pomegranate seeds
85 g/½ cup shelled pistachios, toasted
   and roughly chopped
handful each fresh coriander/cilantro,
   flat-leaf parsley and mint, roughly
   chopped
freshly squeezed juice of 3 lemons
1 tsp agave syrup
sea salt and freshly ground black pepper
watercress, to garnish

Cook the quinoa following the pack instructions until just tender. Drain and spread over a platter to cool.

Stir through all of the remaining ingredients and season to taste with salt and pepper. Divide between four bowls and garnish with watercress to serve.

CHARRED TOMATO YOGURT DRESSING

200 g/7 oz. cherry tomatoes
2 tbsp olive oil
1 garlic clove, crushed
1 tsp chilli/chile jam (optional)
150 g/generous ⅔ cup Greek yogurt
sea salt and freshly ground black pepper

Drizzle the tomatoes with the oil and season with salt and pepper. Grill/broil the tomatoes under a high heat in a cast-iron frying pan/skillet or grill basket for about 4 minutes until lightly charred.

Mix the other ingredients into the yogurt, followed by the charred tomatoes.

WHOLE ROASTED CAULIFLOWER

WITH CHIMICHURRI SAUCE, FARRO & COURGETTE SALAD
& PISTACHIO LABNEH

A fusion of flavours, with both Middle Eastern and Argentinian influence, this special meal makes a whole roasted cauliflower the star of the table.

1 large or 2 small whole cauliflowers
3 garlic cloves, crushed
2 tbsp extra virgin olive oil
10 g/2 tsp butter, softened
grated zest of 1 lemon
1 tbsp wholegrain mustard
1 tsp celery salt
sea salt and freshly ground black pepper

CHIMICHURRI SAUCE

½ bunch fresh flat-leaf parsley
½ bunch fresh coriander/cilantro
3 sprigs fresh oregano, leaves picked
1 garlic clove, crushed
80 ml/⅓ cup olive oil
1 tsp smoked paprika
1 tsp ground cumin
1 tsp ground coriander
freshly squeezed juice of 1½ lemons
1 green chilli/chile, finely chopped
  (optional)

In a food processor, blend all the chimichurri ingredients together to make into a chunky paste.

Preheat the oven to 220°C (425°F) Gas 7.

In a large steamer basket set over a pan of gently simmering water, cook the cauliflower(s) for 6–8 minutes, until just tender when pierced with a knife. Alternatively, cook the cauliflower(s) for 5–6 minutes in a saucepan of boiling water until just tender, then drain well and pat dry with paper towels.

Meanwhile, stir together the garlic, olive oil, butter, lemon zest, mustard and celery salt with a little salt and pepper to make a paste, and set aside.

Place the cauliflower(s) in a roasting pan and spread all over with the paste. Season well with salt and pepper. Roast in the preheated oven for 20–25 minutes, basting with the cooking juices halfway through, until golden.

Serve on a bed of the Farro & Courgette Salad (see page 38), drizzled with some Chimichurri Sauce and with the Pistachio Labneh on the side.

PISTACHIO LABNEH

500 g/2⅓ cups Greek yogurt
2 tsp sea salt
100 g/⅔ cup shelled pistachios, toasted
  and chopped
grated zest of 1 lemon, to garnish

Combine the yogurt and salt in a bowl. Spoon into a sieve/strainer lined with muslin/cheesecloth over a bowl. Cover with clingfilm/plastic wrap and refrigerate for 12 hours or overnight until thick and the liquid has drained. Discard the liquid and refrigerate the labneh until required.

Stir in the chopped pistachios and garnish with lemon zest just before serving. It is also good topped with a little Chimichurri Sauce.

FARRO & COURGETTE SALAD

250 g/1¼ cups farro
200 g/generous 1½ cups broad/fava
   beans, podded
2 courgettes/zucchini, spiralized
20 g/¾ oz. barberries, soaked in water
   and drained (or dried sour cherries)
4 spring onions/scallions, finely chopped
100 g/3½ oz. marinated artichokes,
   drained and quartered
handful fresh flat-leaf parsley, roughly
   chopped
small handful each fresh dill and fresh
   chives, thinly sliced
sea salt and freshly ground black pepper
large handful of pistachios, to garnish

DRESSING
2 garlic cloves, crushed
100 ml/⅓ cup plus 1 tbsp extra virgin
   olive oil
50 ml/3½ tbsp red wine vinegar
½ tsp ground sumac

Cook the farro in a saucepan of boiling salted water until al dente following the packet instructions. Drain and spread on a tray to cool.

Meanwhile, briefly submerge the broad/fava beans in a large saucepan of boiling salted water for 15 seconds, then plunge straight into a bowl of iced water (this makes them easier to peel). Drain, then slip the beans out of their skins.

Combine the beans in a bowl with the cooked farro, courgettes/zucchini, barberries, spring onions/scallions, marinated artichokes and herbs.

For the dressing, in a small bowl, stir together the garlic, olive oil, vinegar and sumac and season to taste. Pour onto the salad and toss to combine. Scatter with the pistachios to garnish.

MOJO CHICKEN
WITH ADOBO BLACK BEANS

A casual but tasty meal, this Cuban-style citrus-spiked chicken with Mexican beans is full of exciting, zingy flavours and can be achieved with very little effort.

6 skin-on, bone-in chicken thighs
2 (bell) peppers, deseeded and sliced
    into rounds
1 orange, sliced into rounds
1 large red onion, sliced into rounds

MARINADE
4 tbsp extra virgin olive oil
handful fresh coriander/cilantro
grated zest and freshly squeezed juice
    of 2 oranges
freshly squeezed juice and grated
    zest of 1 lime
1 tsp dried oregano
1 tsp ground cumin
½ tsp smoked paprika
4 black garlic or smoked garlic cloves,
    peeled
1 tsp sea salt
½ tsp freshly ground black pepper

Place all the marinade ingredients in a food processor and blend until the coriander/cilantro is finely chopped. Pour the marinade over the chicken in a large bowl and mix to make sure every piece is coated. Cover with clingfilm/plastic wrap and leave in the refrigerator overnight to marinade.

The next day, preheat the oven to 180°C (350°F) Gas 4.

Spread the sliced (bell) peppers, orange and onion out evenly in a large roasting pan. Scrape the residual marinade off the chicken and dot around the roasting pan. Place the thighs, skin-side down, in the roasting pan. Roast in the preheated oven for 30 minutes.

After 30 minutes, turn the chicken and baste with the pan juices. Roast for a further 20 minutes or until the chicken skins are nicely browned. Rest the chicken for 5 minutes before serving with the roasted fruit and veggies from the pan and the Adobo Black Beans.

ADOBO BLACK BEANS

2 tbsp olive oil
1 x 400-g/14-oz. can black
    beans, drained and rinsed
2–3 chipotle chillies/chiles in
    adobo sauce (or use 1–2 tsp
    chipotle paste)
2 tsp ground cumin
100 ml/⅓ cup plus 1 tbsp
    vegetable stock
1–2 avocados, peeled, pitted
    and sliced
1 tbsp basil seeds (optional)
handful fresh coriander/
    cilantro
3 spring onions/scallions, sliced
crème fraîche, to drizzle

Warm the oil in a frying pan/skillet over a low-medium heat. Add the black beans and chillies/chiles in adobo sauce and simmer gently, using the back of a spoon to crush some of the beans and chillies/chiles. Add the cumin and vegetable stock and cook down for about 5–10 minutes to create a thick, chunky sauce. Serve with the sliced avocado sprinkled with basil seeds (if using), coriander/cilantro, spring onions/scallions and crème fraîche.

STUFFED & ROASTED BUTTERNUT SQUASH

This recipe takes advantage of the sturdy yet tender texture of butternut squash when baked. Presented stuffed, it makes a great centrepiece for the table and looks great cut into slices. The sweet, mellow flavour of the squash is complemented by salty feta, tangy sun-dried tomatoes and earthy walnuts and grains.

1 medium butternut squash
3 tbsp olive oil, plus extra for drizzling
1 small red onion, thinly sliced
2 garlic cloves, crushed
100 g/3½ oz. cooked Puy lentils
100 g/3½ oz. cooked mixed grains
150 ml/⅔ cup vegetable stock
3 sprigs fresh thyme, leaves picked
1 tbsp Dijon mustard
50 g/1¾ oz. feta or vegan cheese, crumbled or chopped
30 g/⅓ cup sun-dried tomatoes, chopped
2 tbsp chopped walnuts
1 fennel bulb, thinly sliced (optional)
small handful freshly chopped parsley
sea salt and freshly ground black pepper
steamed Tenderstem broccoli and Marsala gravy (see page 85), to serve (optional)

cooking string

Preheat the oven to 180°C (350°F) Gas 4.

Cut the butternut squash in half lengthways. Scoop out and discard the seeds, then put both halves in a roasting pan, cut-side up. Drizzle 1 tbsp of the olive oil on top of each squash half and rub around to coat. Roast in the preheated oven for 20–25 minutes until the squash is just tender when pierced with a fork. The timing may vary a little depending on the size of your squash. Be careful not to overcook the squash as it will be cooked again when assembled.

Remove the squash from the oven and leave to cool long enough so that you can handle it. Scoop out and set aside the flesh in the centre of both halves, leaving about a 2.5-cm/1-inch border all around so that the vegetable keeps its shape. Roughly dice the removed squash flesh and set aside for a moment.

In a large frying pan/skillet, heat 1 tbsp of the oil over a medium-high heat. When hot, sauté the onion and garlic for about 10 minutes until softened and beginning to brown. Add the cooked Puy lentils and cooked grains, then add the vegetable stock and cook for a further 5 minutes, stirring occasionally.

Remove the pan from the heat and add the thyme leaves, mustard, feta, sun-dried tomatoes, walnuts and fennel (if using). Season with salt and pepper and mix well. Finally, stir in the chopped squash flesh and parsley. Stuff the mixture into both sides of the roasted squash, packing it down so that you can fit in as much as possible.

Pick up one squash half and quickly and carefully turn it upside-down on top of the other half. Use the kitchen string to tie up the squash to keep it together. (You can now choose to let the squash cool, cover with foil and store in the fridge for up to 3 days until ready to cook, or you can roast it straight away.)

When ready, lightly brush the squash with the remaining 1 tbsp oil. Bake in the preheated oven for 20–35 minutes to heat through.

Delicious served with Tenderstem broccoli and the Marsala gravy (see page 85) made with veggie stock and omitting the pan juices.

GOCHUJANG ROASTED AUBERGINE STEAKS
WITH VEGETABLE EGG FRIED RICE

This is a real favourite of mine, I love how the gouchujang paste melds with the aubergine/eggplant to create an umami, savoury yet sweet and succulent vegetable 'steak'. The egg fried rice and dressing just help to bring it all together.

2 round aubergines/eggplants
sea salt and freshly ground black pepper

GOCHUJANG MARINADE
4 garlic cloves, crushed
1 thumb-sized piece of fresh ginger,
    peeled and chopped
80 ml/⅓ cup dry sake
4 tbsp gochujang (Korean chilli/chile
    paste)
80 ml/⅓ cup mirin
60 ml/¼ cup flavourless oil

Cut the aubergines/eggplants into 4-cm/1½-inch thick slices.

Preheat the oven to 180°C (350°F) Gas 4.

Put the marinade ingredients in a blender and blend to a purée. Set 60 ml/¼ cup of the marinade aside and refrigerate.

Put the aubergine/eggplant steaks in a roasting pan and season with salt and pepper. Add the remaining 60 ml/¼ cup marinade and turn the vegetables to coat on all sides. Roast in the preheated oven for 10 minutes.

Take out of the oven and brush each side with the reserved marinade. Return the aubergines/eggplants to the oven for a further 20 minutes or until cooked through and golden.

Meanwhile, in a small saucepan cook down any remaining marinade for 20 minutes to make a sauce to serve on the side.

VEGETABLE EGG FRIED RICE

200 g/1 cup mixed white and
   wholegrain rice
3 tbsp peanut/groundnut oil
4 eggs, lightly beaten
1 small red onion, finely chopped
25 g/1 oz. fresh ginger, peeled and
   finely chopped
200 g/7 oz. baby corn, sliced in half
   lengthways
200 g/7 oz. mangetout/snow peas,
   sliced widthways diagonally
1 tbsp Shaoxing wine
1 tbsp light soy sauce
1 tsp Chinese black vinegar
½ tsp sesame oil
2 spring onions/scallions, thinly
   sliced
100 g/⅔ cup fresh peas
100 g/1¾ cups beansprouts

DRESSING
1 tbsp chopped garlic
4 tbsp Chinese black vinegar
1 tbsp caster/granulated sugar
1½ tsp sesame oil
3 tbsp light soy sauce
1½ tsp mirin
1 tsp sesame seeds
1 spring onion/scallion, chopped

Cook the rice according to the packet instructions, drain (if necessary) and leave to cool.

Heat 2 tbsp of the peanut/groundnut oil in a hot wok until the surface shimmers, then add the beaten eggs and cook over a high heat without stirring until beginning to set. Fold the egg in onto itself and cook for 30 seconds, then repeat folding until almost set. Drain on paper towels and set aside until needed.

Add the remaining 1 tbsp oil to the wok, then add the onion and ginger and stir-fry over a high heat for 30–60 seconds until softened. Add the baby corn and mangetout/snow peas and stir-fry for 1 minute. Add the Shaoxing wine, soy sauce, black vinegar and sesame oil and cook the sauce mixture for 30 seconds.

Add the rice and stir to coat in the sauce, then cook without stirring for 2–3 minutes until a light golden crust forms on the rice at the bottom of the wok.

Add the spring onions/scallions, peas and reserved omelette and stir-fry everything together for 1 minute, breaking up the egg mixture. Remove the wok from the heat, then quickly toss in the beansprouts and stir through before serving.

Mix all the dressing ingredients together and serve alongside the Vegetable Egg Fried Rice, Gochujang Roasted Aubergine/eggplant Steaks and sauce made from the gochujang marinade.

SALMON INFERNO
WITH KAREDOK SALAD

Here, hot and spicy Asian salmon is paired with a fresh and fragrant Indonesian-style salad. Saltiness and crunch are provided by a peanut dressing and prawn/shrimp crackers served on the side. This dish can work well as a shared appetizer or light lunch, but it is also perfect for a quick evening meal during the week.

600-g/1 lb. 5-oz. salmon fillet
1 tbsp olive oil
2 garlic cloves, finely grated
2 tbsp fish sauce
freshly squeezed juice of 2 limes
2 tbsp sambal oelek (or other hot chilli/chile paste)
1–3 tbsp palm sugar/jaggery
1 tbsp peanut/groundnut oil

TO SERVE
lime wedges
fresh Thai basil, mint and coriander/cilantro
prawn/shrimp crackers
sweet chilli/chile sauce

large roasting pan, lined with baking parchment or foil

Preheat the oven to 200°C (400°F) Gas 6.

Brush the salmon skin with the oil and place it, skin-side down, in the prepared roasting pan.

In a bowl, mix together the garlic, fish sauce, lime juice, sambal oelek, palm sugar/jaggery and peanut/groundnut oil. Spread this mixture evenly over the salmon flesh.

Roast in the preheated oven for about 20 minutes or until the salmon is cooked through – check by poking a knife into the thickest part of the fillet and making sure the fish flakes easily.

Serve directly from the pan or use a couple of fish slices to carefully lift the salmon onto a serving platter. Serve the fish with lime wedges for squeezing over, Karedok Salad, fresh herbs, prawn/shrimp crackers and sweet chilli/chile sauce.

KAREDOK SALAD

200 g/7 oz. fine green/French beans, cooked and cut into 3-cm/1-inch lengths
1 small Chinese cabbage, thinly sliced (on a mandoline if you have one)
1 large cucumber, cut into julienne
100 g/1¾ cups beansprouts
a handful fresh Thai basil
4 shallots, thinly sliced into rounds

DRESSING
2–3 tbsp peanut/groundnut oil
150 g/1¼ cups unsalted peanuts, toasted
1 tsp galangal paste
1–2 red chillies/chiles, chopped
2 garlic cloves, roughly chopped
freshly squeezed juice of 2–3 limes
2 tbsp palm sugar/jaggery
2 tbsp light soy sauce
½ tsp shrimp paste

Gently toss all the ingredients for the salad together and serve on the serving platter or in the pan with the salmon.

In a food processor, pulse together all the ingredients for the dressing until coarsely blitzed, and serve drizzled over the salad.

QUICK ROAST BEEF FILLET
WITH PARSNIP & POTATO OVEN FRIES, PEPPERCORN SAUCE & ROCKET

Steak and chips is elevated to another level with this simplified but sophisticated take on the popular classic. Buttery-soft roasted fillet steak is served with crispy baked parsnip and potato fries and a quick creamy peppercorn sauce – just delicious!

1 x 1-kg/2 lb. 4-oz. middle
    fillet of beef
30 g/¼ stick butter, softened
2 tbsp flavourless oil
6 garlic cloves, unpeeled
sea salt and freshly ground black
    pepper
rocket/arugula, to serve

Preheat the oven to 220°C (425°F) Gas 7.

Rub the fillet of beef with plenty of salt and pepper, then the butter and the 2 tbsp oil. Heat a large frying pan/skillet over a high heat until very hot. Sear the beef on all sides until browned, then transfer to the centre of a roasting pan. Arrange the garlic cloves around the beef and drizzle with a little oil.

Roast in the preheated oven for 23–25 minutes for medium-rare. It should feel springy when lightly pressed. When the beef is cooked to your liking, transfer to a warm platter, cover with foil and allow to rest for 10–15 minutes before serving.

Carve the beef into slices and serve with a rocket/arugula salad garnish and one roasted garlic clove per serving, for guests to squeeze over while eating.

PARSNIP & POTATO OVEN FRIES

2 parsnips
2 sweet potatoes
2 tbsp extra virgin olive oil
4 sprigs fresh thyme, leaves picked
sea salt and freshly ground black
    pepper

Preheat the oven to 200°C (400°F) Gas 6.

Clean the skins on the parsnips and sweet potatoes and slice them into thin strips. Put the strips in a bowl, add the olive oil, season with salt and pepper and toss together. Spread out in a single layer on a baking sheet and bake in the preheated oven for 25 minutes or until golden brown, flipping over halfway through the cooking time.

Sprinkle generously with thyme leaves, and season with extra salt and pepper to serve.

PEPPERCORN SAUCE

1 tbsp flavourless oil
1 banana shallot, finely chopped
1 garlic clove, crushed
100 ml/⅓ cup plus 1 tbsp beef stock
2 tbsp brandy
1 tbsp Worcestershire sauce
1 tbsp Dijon mustard
150 ml/⅔ cup double/heavy cream
   (or half-fat crème fraîche)
2 sprigs fresh green peppercorns
   (or use ½ tsp crushed black
   peppercorns)
2–3 sprigs fresh tarragon, leaves
   picked and chopped
¼ bunch fresh chives, chopped
sea salt

Heat the oil in a sauté pan over a medium heat and add the shallot. Cook until softened, then add the garlic and beef stock and simmer for 3 minutes.

Add the brandy, Worcestershire sauce, mustard, cream (or crème fraîche) and peppercorns. Stir and bring to the boil over a high heat. Season to taste with salt and simmer for about 6–8 minutes until the sauce reaches the consistency of pouring cream. Stir in the herbs and serve.

SOY & SESAME BAKED MONKFISH
WITH A SEAWEED CRUMB & GREENS IN CARAMELIZED TAMARI BUTTER DRESSING

Monkfish is great for roasting as it's substantial and takes heat well. Here it is served with vegetables dressed in caramelized tamari butter for a stylish yet fuss-free meal.

1 x 1.5-kg/3 lb. 5-oz. monkfish tail fillet (skin and bone removed – you can ask your fishmonger to do this)
1 thumb-sized piece of fresh ginger, peeled and Julienned
1 lime, cut into thin wedges
2 spring onions/scallions, halved lengthways
2 garlic cloves, thinly sliced

MARINADE
4 tbsp soy sauce
2 tbsp sesame oil
1 tbsp runny honey
1 garlic clove, finely chopped
1 thumb-sized piece of fresh ginger, peeled and finely grated

grated zest and freshly squeezed juice of 1 lime
1 tbsp black sesame seeds

SEAWEED CRUMB
2 tbsp wasabi peas, coarsely blitzed in a food processor
1 tbsp dried seaweed, crumbled
1 tbsp black sesame seeds

TO SERVE
200 g/7 oz. cooked soba (buckwheat) noodles
thinly sliced spring onions/ scallions
pickled ginger
sliced daikon radishes
lime wedges

baking sheet, lined with baking parchment
cooking string

Preheat the oven to 180°C (350°F) Gas 4.

Lay the monkfish tail on the prepared baking sheet. Fill the cut where the bone used to be with the ginger, lime wedges, spring onions/scallions and garlic. Tie the fish up securely with the cooking string in rounds spaced evenly widthways along the length of the fish.

In a bowl, mix together all the ingredients for the marinade. Drizzle the marinade over the fish and bake in the preheated oven for 25–30 minutes or until cooked through, basting with the cooking juices halfway through cooking.

Meanwhile, for the seaweed crumb, mix together the ground wasabi peas, seaweed and black sesame seeds and set aside.

Sprinkle the baked fish with the seaweed crumb just before serving with the noodles, spring onions/ scallions, pickled ginger, daikon radishes, lime wedges and the greens in their tamari butter dressing.

GREENS IN CARAMELIZED TAMARI BUTTER DRESSING

50 g/3½ tbsp butter
2 tbsp tamari or soy sauce
1 red chilli/chile, finely chopped
2 garlic cloves, crushed
200 g/7 oz. Tenderstem broccoli
4 baby pak choi/bok choy

Melt the butter in a frying pan/skillet over a medium heat. As the butter melts, it will begin to foam. The colour will progress from yellow to golden to, finally, a toasty-brown. As soon as you see the colour change and smell that nutty aroma, add the tamari or soy sauce and chilli/chile, then turn the heat to low and cook for 1 minute.

Finally, stir in the garlic and keep warm while you cook the vegetables.

Cook the broccoli in a large saucepan of boiling water for 2 minutes. Add the baby pak choi/bok choy to the same pan and cook for 1 minute more. Drain the vegetables well.

Dress the vegetables in the caramelized tamari butter and serve alongside the baked monkfish.

SLOW

Some things just taste better given more time. There's something so comforting about slow-cooking, you combine the ingredients, let the oven work its magic and come back to a fragrant, tender dish. In this chapter, find delicious, melt-in-your-mouth recipes that are well worth the wait.

SPICED SLOW-ROASTED BEEF BRISKET BUNS
WITH RUSSIAN-ISH SAUCE & SAUERKRAUT

This recipe is completely inspired by my recent stay in New York. It is my take on the amazing Reuben sandwich served at Katz's Deli, which is overflowing with sauerkraut and Russian dressing. Yes, the deli is from *When Harry met Sally!*

2 tbsp coconut oil
1.8-kg/4½-lb. piece of lean beef brisket
8 shallots, peeled and halved
   lengthways
6 garlic cloves, peeled but left whole
8 fresh thyme sprigs
sea salt and freshly ground black pepper

EARTH SPICE RUB
2 tbsp smoked paprika
2 tsp coarsely crushed black peppercorns
1 tsp cayenne pepper
1 tsp ground turmeric
1 tsp fennel seeds
1 tsp ground cumin
1 tsp celery seeds
1 tsp dried oregano
1 tsp sea salt

TO SERVE
4–6 crusty bread rolls
½ portion Sauerkraut
1 beetroot/beet, peeled and grated
1 portion Russian-ish Sauce
½ bunch fresh parsley

large, flameproof roasting pan

For the earth spice rub, grind all the spices and herbs together in a food processor. Stir in the sea salt and set aside.

Preheat the oven to 180°C (350°F) Gas 4.

Rub the coconut oil all over the brisket, then season with salt and pepper. Place the large, flameproof roasting pan over a high heat. Sear the meat for about 3–4 minutes until browned on all sides. Remove from the heat and transfer to a large board. When cool enough to handle, rub the brisket all over with the spice rub.

Place the shallots, garlic and thyme sprigs in the roasting pan in a single layer and sit the brisket on top. Pour in 375 ml/1⅔ cups water and roast the brisket in the preheated oven for about 20–25 minutes until the shallots and garlic are amber brown.

Reduce the heat to 150°C (300°F) Gas 2 and cover just the brisket with a piece of wet baking parchment. Tightly cover the whole pan with a double layer of foil and continue to cook for another 4 hours, basting and adding water according to the following schedule: after 1 hour baste the meat with the juices, after 2 hours add 100 ml/⅓ cup plus 1 tbsp water and baste again. After 3 hours, add 100 ml/⅓ cup plus 1 tbsp water and baste, after 3½ hours add 80 ml/⅓ cup water and baste again.

Increase the oven temperature back up to 180°C (350°F) Gas 4. Uncover the meat, baste once more, and then roast, uncovered, for a final 15–20 minutes until the meat is a deep, dark golden brown on the outside. The basting and addition of moisture should make the meat very tender and stop the base from burning. Remove from the oven and rest for 15 minutes covered with foil, before carving the meat into thick slices to serve. Stuff the meat into crusty bread rolls with the roasted shallots, Sauerkraut, the raw beetroot/beet stirred through the Russian-ish Sauce and a little fresh parsley.

SAUERKRAUT

**450 g/1 lb. Savoy or white cabbage
(about ½), core removed and thinly
sliced**
1 tbsp sea salt
1 tsp caraway seeds

1 x sterilized litre/quart jar

Put the cabbage, salt and caraway seeds into a bowl
and toss to combine, then massage the salt and spices
into the cabbage briefly. Leave to stand for about 30
minutes until the cabbage starts to wilt. Transfer to
the jar and press to pack the cabbage down. Pour in
water to just cover the cabbage and top with a small
plastic sandwich bag filled with water to keep the
cabbage submerged. Put the lid on the jar and set
aside at room temperature for 1–2 days until bubbles
appear on top, then refrigerate, covered with clingfilm/
plastic wrap with a hole pierced in the top for 3 days
before using. The sauerkraut will keep in the fridge for
about 1 month; the flavour will get stronger as it ages.

RUSSIAN-ISH SAUCE

**200 g/scant 1 cup good-quality
mayonnaise**
1 tsp good-quality tomato ketchup
1 tsp Sriracha (or to taste)
1 tsp Dijon mustard
4–5 cornichons, roughly chopped
1 tsp Worcestershire sauce
½ tsp smoked paprika

In a bowl, mix together all the ingredients.
Serve with the brisket buns.

BRAISED BEEF CHEEKS
WITH OLIVE & CORN-TOPPED POLENTA & SALSA CRIOLLA

Richly flavoured beef cheeks pair beautifully with creamy polenta, a salty olive and corn topping and tangy salsa criolla. Serve with a simple salad to freshen the dish.

50 ml/3½ tbsp olive oil
1 onion, finely chopped
1.5-kg/3 lb. 5-oz. beef cheeks, trimmed
1 tbsp each ground cumin and ground coriander
2 tsp Earth Spice Rub (see page 54)
1 tsp dried oregano
1 tsp chilli/chili powder (or to taste)
6 garlic cloves, finely chopped
1 tbsp tomato purée/paste
1 x 400-g/14-oz. can chopped tomatoes
300 ml/1¼ cups lager/beer
1 tbsp balsamic vinegar
1 tbsp brown sugar
handful fresh oregano, leaves picked
simple side salad, to serve
chilli/chile sauce, to serve (optional)

large, ovenproof casserole dish

Preheat the oven to 140°C (275°F) Gas 1.

Heat half the olive oil in the ovenproof casserole dish over a medium heat. Sauté the onion, stirring occasionally, for around 12–15 minutes until golden and tender. Transfer the onion to a bowl and set aside.

Add the remaining oil to the casserole dish, then add the beef cheeks in batches and brown for 2–3 minutes on each side. Return all the meat to the pan and add the spices, oregano, chilli/chili powder and garlic and stir. Stir in the sautéed onion, tomato purée/paste, canned tomatoes, lager/beer, vinegar and sugar. Cover the pan with a lid, then braise the meat in the preheated oven for 4½–5 hours until just tender.

Remove the lid and continue cooking over a medium heat on the hob/stove-top for about 20–30 minutes until the liquid has reduced and the meat is very tender. Leave to cool slightly, then break the meat into pieces with a fork. Serve the beef on a bed of the Olive & Corn-topped Polenta with the Salsa Criolla, a simple side salad and chilli/chile sauce, if you like.

SALSA CRIOLLA

1 small red onion, thinly sliced (on a mandoline if you have one)
1 tbsp coarsely chopped fresh coriander/cilantro
2 red chillies/chiles, cut into julienne
freshly squeezed juice of 1 lime
generous pinch of sea salt

Soak the onion in iced water for about 5 minutes until crisp. Drain well, then place in a bowl with the coriander/cilantro and julienned chillies/chiles. Squeeze over the lime juice, then add the salt and toss to combine.

OLIVE & CORN-TOPPED POLENTA

400 ml/1¾ cups chicken or vegetable
  stock
250 g/scant 1¾ cups polenta/cornmeal
100 g/1 stick minus 1 tbsp unsalted
  butter
150 g/2¼ cups finely grated Parmesan
1–2 tbsp buttermilk
sea salt and freshly ground black pepper

CORN & OLIVE TOPPING
2 tbsp/¼ stick butter
175 g/6 oz. baby corn, thinly sliced into
  thin rounds
30 g/1 oz. green olives, pitted and
  roughly chopped
popcorn sprouts, to garnish (optional)

Combine the stock with 1 litre/quart
of water and bring to the boil in a
saucepan. Season with salt and pour
in the polenta/cornmeal in a slow
stream, whisking constantly, until
incorporated. Reduce the heat and
simmer gently for about 40 minutes,
stirring occasionally, until soft.

  Towards the end of cooking, stir
in the butter, Parmesan, buttermilk,
black pepper and more salt, if needed.

  To make the topping, melt the
butter in a frying pan/skillet. Add the
corn and sauté over a medium heat
until browned. Stir in the olives and fry
for 1 minute. Top the polenta with the
olive, corn and butter mixture and
garnish with popcorn sprouts, if liked.

GARLIC-INFUSED SLOW ROAST
LEG OF LAMB & LAYERED POTATOES
WITH CHARRED LETTUCE & SOUSED CUCUMBER

Here the lamb juices, flavoured with garlic and harissa, melt into the potatoes as they cook. The soused cucumber and charred lettuce add brightness to the dish.

1.5 kg/3 lb. 5 oz. waxy potatoes
   (such as Charlotte), unpeeled,
   and thinly sliced lengthways
2 large onions, thinly sliced
1 bunch fresh lemon thyme, leaves
   picked, plus extra to garnish
1 whole garlic head (6–8 whole cloves)
   3 cloves unpeeled in the potatoes,
   the rest peeled
1 x 2-kg/4½-lb. leg of lamb
2 tbsp olive oil
3 tbsp harissa paste
½ tsp ground sumac (optional)
600 ml/2¼ cups chicken stock
sea salt and freshly ground black pepper

Preheat the oven to 160°C (325°F) Gas 3.

Mix the potato slices with the onions, thyme leaves and 3 unpeeled garlic cloves in a bowl and season with salt and pepper. Roughly layer the potato mixture in a roasting pan and put the lamb leg on top, skin-side up. Use a knife to pierce the skin all over. Rub the oil, then the harissa paste and sumac into the skin and insert the peeled garlic cloves into some of the holes. Pour the chicken stock over the potatoes and roast in the preheated oven for 4½–5 hours, until the lamb and potatoes are tender.

In the last 30 minutes of cooking, transfer the cooking juices into a saucepan on the hob/stove-top over a medium heat and let reduce down to make a sauce while the potatoes are crisping up.

Cover the lamb and potatoes with foil and rest for 20 minutes. Carve the lamb and serve with the sauce, potatoes garnished with lemon thyme, Soused Cucumber and Charred Lettuce.

SOUSED CUCUMBER

100 ml/⅓ cup plus 1 tbsp white balsamic
   vinegar
50 g/¼ cup caster/granulated sugar
6 black peppercorns
½ cucumber, cut into 3-mm/⅛-inch slices
½ bunch fresh mint, leaves picked

Heat the vinegar and sugar in a small saucepan over a low heat for about 3–4 minutes, until the sugar dissolves.

Add the peppercorns and pour the liquid over the sliced cucumber in a bowl. Set aside for 30 minutes at room temperature to pickle. Garnish with the mint leaves to serve.

CHARRED LETTUCE

2 Cos/Romaine lettuces, halved
   lengthways
1 tbsp flavourless oil
1 tsp icing/confectioners' sugar
sea salt and freshly ground black pepper
1 lemon, cut into wedges, to serve

Put the lettuce halves in a bowl, drizzle with the oil and season with salt and pepper, making sure that the leaves are evenly coated. Lay the lettuces, cut-side up, and sprinkle evenly with the icing/confectioners' sugar.

Heat a large frying pan/skillet over a high heat and place the lettuce halves, cut-side down, in the pan. Allow to char before turning over to char on the back. Serve with the wedges of lemon.

STUFFED PORCHETTA
WITH PICKLED VEGETABLES, CELERY, FENNEL & MUSTARD

I have updated this traditional Italian dish for you to make at home. My favourite way
to eat this is with English mustard, fresh and pickled vegetables and crusty bread.

2-kg/4½-lb. boneless pork sirloin,
    butterflied and rind scored at
    1-cm/³⁄₈-inch intervals (you can ask
    your butcher to do this)
1 tbsp extra virgin olive oil
4 garlic cloves, finely chopped
2 tsp roasted fennel seeds, crushed
    with a pestle and mortar
½ bunch fresh flat-leaf parsley,
    finely chopped
2 tbsp pine nuts
1 tsp chilli flakes/hot red pepper flakes
    (optional)
1 tsp celery salt
grated zest of 1 lemon
500 ml/2 cups plus 2 tbsp white wine
coarse sea salt and freshly ground
    black pepper

TO SERVE
1 fennel bulb, shaved into thin slices
3 celery stalks, shaved into thin slices
celery leaves
English mustard
crusty bread

cooking string
small roasting pan lined with
    baking parchment

Place the pork, rind-side up, on a wire rack in the sink, and carefully
pour boiling kettle water over the skin to help the score marks open,
then leave to stand for 10 minutes to dry. Pat dry with paper towels.

Preheat the oven to 220°C (425°F) Gas 7.

In a bowl, stir together the oil, garlic, crushed fennel seeds,
parsley, pine nuts, chilli flakes/hot red pepper flakes (if using),
celery salt and lemon zest. Season to taste with salt and pepper.

Lay the pork out on a board, rind-side down, and rub the stuffing
mixture over the flesh. Carefully roll up the sirloin widthways, then
tie tightly with a piece of string in the middle. Tie at either end,
about 1 cm/½ inch in, then at intervals along the length of the roll.
If filling escapes, push it back in.

Place the porchetta, skin-side up, in the lined roasting pan and
pour the wine into the base. Season the rind generously with sea
salt and roast in the preheated oven for about 35–40 minutes or
until the skin starts to crackle and brown.

Reduce the oven temperature to 180°C (350°F) Gas 4 and roast
for another 40 minutes until the pork is tender when pierced with
a sharp knife. Cover and leave to rest for 20 minutes, then thinly
slice and serve with the Pickled Vegetables, a light salad of shaved
fennel, celery stalks and leaves, English mustard and crusty bread.

PICKLED VEGETABLES

300 ml/1¼ cups white wine vinegar
150 g/¾ cup caster/granulated sugar
1 tbsp sea salt
½ tsp celery seeds
1 small green cabbage
1 red (bell) pepper
1 carrot
1 cucumber

Mix together the white wine vinegar, sugar, salt and celery seeds
with 150 ml/²⁄₃ cup water in a medium bowl and set aside.

Trim and core the cabbage and cut into very thin slices (using a
knife or adjustable-blade slicer) and put in a large bowl. Core, deseed
and thinly slice the (bell) pepper; peel and thinly slice or julienne the
carrot; thinly slice the cucumber. Add all the vegetables to the
cabbage in the bowl.

By this time, the sugar and salt in the pickling liquid should have
dissolved. If not, whisk a few times. Taste and adjust the seasoning,
if needed. Pour the pickling liquid over the vegetables and cover the
bowl with clingfilm/plastic wrap. Refrigerate for 1 hour or up to 1
week – the vegetables will become more pickled as they rest.

CIDER PORK BELLY
WITH KUMQUAT RELISH & RHUBARB PICKLE

The sweet and sour kumquat relish and rhubarb pickle both cut beautifully through the rich saltiness of the pork in this dish. It would also pair well with the Sesame Kale with Zingy Dressing (see page 131) and the Classic Roasties (see page 122).

1.8-kg/4-lb. boneless pork belly, skin
    scored
1 tbsp fine sea salt
3 garlic cloves, unpeeled and bruised
1 bunch fresh thyme
3 fresh bay leaves
200 ml/generous ¾ cup dry cider

Preheat the oven to 170°C (325°F) Gas 3.

Using papers towels, pat the pork rind dry. Rub the pork rind all over with the sea salt, pushing it into the scored lines. Put the pork into a roasting pan and scatter round the garlic cloves, thyme and bay leaves. Pour the cider around the pork, not over the rind. Roast in the preheated oven for 2 hours 40 minutes.

After this time, increase the oven temperature to 220°C (425°F) Gas 7 and cook for a further 30–40 minutes to crisp up the crackling, checking often to ensure that it is not burning. You want crunchy crackling and tender meat underneath.

Remove the meat from the oven, then cover with foil and rest for 10 minutes. Carve the pork into thick slices and serve with the Kumquat Relish and Rhubarb Pickle.

KUMQUAT RELISH

200 g/7 oz. unpeeled kumquats
100 g/¾ cup sultanas/golden raisins
2 shallots, peeled and halved
200 g/1 cup caster/granulated sugar
200 ml/generous ¾ cup apple cider
   vinegar
20 g/¾ oz. fresh ginger, peeled and
   cut into julienne
20-cm/8-inch piece of fresh turmeric,
   peeled and cut into julienne
1 red chilli/chile, halved lengthways
   or 1 tsp dried chilli flakes/hot red
   pepper flakes
1½ tsp yellow mustard seeds
1 tsp sea salt

1 x sterilized 500 ml/17 fl oz. jar

Put the kumquats into a saucepan with enough water to cover them. Bring to the boil over a medium-high heat, then turn down the heat and simmer for 3–5 minutes until tender. Drain, then leave to cool. Cut the kumquats in half lengthways, then remove and discard the seeds and set aside.

Stir together the sultanas/golden raisins, shallots, sugar, vinegar, ginger, turmeric, chilli/chile (or chilli flakes/hot red pepper flakes), mustard seeds and salt in a saucepan over a medium-high heat until the sugar has dissolved. Add the kumquats and simmer for 20–30 minutes until the mixture reaches soft setting point. Spoon into the jar, then seal and leave cool to room temperature. The relish will keep for up to 3 months refrigerated.

RHUBARB PICKLE

4–6 large rhubarb stalks
   (about 400 g/14 oz.)
1 tsp mustard seeds
2 tsp pink peppercorns
3 cloves
5 star anise
200 ml/generous ¾ cup apple cider
   vinegar
250 g/1¼ cups caster/granulated sugar
½ tsp pink Himalayan sea salt

2 x sterilized 700-ml/24-fl oz. jars

Trim the rhubarb stalks down so that they are able to fit into the jars. If the stalks are too broad, slice them lengthways in half too. Set aside. Divide the mustard seeds, peppercorns, cloves and star anise between the two prepared jars. Pack the trimmed rhubarb pieces into the jars above the spices. Set aside.

In a small saucepan, combine the apple cider vinegar with 250 ml/1 cup plus 1 tbsp water, the sugar and salt and bring to the boil, then simmer, stirring, until the sugar and salt have dissolved.

Pour the pickling liquid into the jars over the rhubarb, leaving a 1.5-cm/½ inch gap at the top. Tap the jars gently to dislodge any air bubbles. If the liquid level has dropped, add some more pickling liquid to top up. Seal the jars and leave to pickle for at least 48 hours before eating. The pickle will keep for up to 2 weeks refrigerated.

NOTE If you want to seal the jars to give your pickle a longer shelf life, wipe the jar rims, apply the lids and rings and process the full jars in a boiling water bath canner for 10 minutes. When the time is up, remove the jars from canner and set them to cool on a folded kitchen towel. When the jars are cool enough to handle, remove the rings and test the seals. If the jars are sticky, wash them to remove the residue. Sealed jars can be stored in the pantry for up to 1 year.

S PLAKI
ND, OREGANO & LEMON CRUMB

oy my Greek roots and adoration for octopus, this recipe simplifies what
em daunting to some. The octopus is surprisingly delicate in flavour and pairs
nderfully with the Mediterranean flavours of tomatoes, lemon and oregano.

1-kg/2 lb. 4-oz. octopus*, head removed
2 desiree potatoes, skins left on and
    thinly sliced on a mandoline
1 tsp dried oregano
60 ml/¼ cup extra virgin olive oil
2 whole garlic heads, halved
6 medium vine tomatoes, halved
sea salt and freshly ground black pepper
100 g/3½ oz. blanched broad/fava beans,
    podded and peeled, to serve
mini pea shoots and fresh dill, to garnish
    (optional)

ALMOND OREGANO & LEMON CRUMB
100 g/¾ cup whole almonds, toasted
3 sprigs fresh oregano, leaves picked
grated zest of 2 lemons

Preheat the oven to 180°C (350°F) Gas 4.

Put the octopus in a large baking dish and season with salt
and pepper on both sides, rubbing it in well.

Combine the potato slices in a bowl with some salt and pepper,
½ tsp of the oregano and 2 tbsp of the olive oil and toss to coat.
Arrange the potatoes around the octopus in the baking dish.

Arrange the garlic and tomato halves around the dish. Season
all the ingredients to taste with salt and pepper and the remaining
½ tsp oregano. Drizzle the remaining oil over the top of the octopus.

Put the baking dish in the preheated oven and cook for 1 hour,
until the tops of the potatoes are golden brown.

Meanwhile, combine all the ingredients for the almond,
oregano and lemon crumb in a food processor and blitz to crumbs.

Serve the octopus plaki warm from the baking dish, scattered
with the almond, oregano and lemon crumb, blanched broad/fava
beans and some mini pea shoots and dill to garnish, if liked.

NOTE To ensure that the cooked octopus is tender it needs to
be pre-tenderized. If you buy it frozen from the fishmonger, the
freezing process will have tenderized it. If you buy the octopus
fresh, it will need to be pre-boiled to tenderize. To do this, place the
octopus in a large saucepan with 240 ml/1 cup white wine, 1 lemon
cut in half and three peeled garlic cloves. Cover with water, by about
2.5 cm/1 inch over, and bring to the boil over a medium heat. Reduce
the heat to a simmer and cook for about 60–90 minutes, depending
on the size of the octopus, until it is tender when pierced with a
sharp knife. Drain the octopus and allow it to come to room
temperature before roasting straight away as instructed.

STICKY PLUM-ROASTED CABBAGES
WITH GREEN BEANS & GLAZED CASHEWS & TOFU CHIPS

Deliciously sticky and juicy – who would have thought that cabbages could taste this good? Perfect served with glazed cashews, green beans and crunchy tofu chips.

½ green cabbage, cut into thick slices
½ red cabbage, cut into thick slices
5 plums, pitted and cut into wedges
2 red onions, cut into wedges
2 tbsp flavourless oil

PLUM SAUCE
1 thumb-sized piece of fresh ginger, peeled and finely grated
150 g/¾ cup soft light brown sugar
150 ml/⅔ cup apple cider vinegar
1 tbsp freshly squeezed lemon juice
1 tsp sea salt
1 tsp Chinese five-spice powder
½ tsp chilli flakes/hot red pepper flakes

2 baking pans, lined with baking parchment or foil

Preheat the oven to 180°C (350°F) Gas 4.

Combine all the plum sauce ingredients in a small saucepan over a low-medium heat, stirring occasionally, for 10–15 minutes until the sugar and spices have dissolved and you have a smooth sauce.

Arrange the cabbage slices, plums and red onion on the prepared baking pans and drizzle evenly with the oil and then the sauce, reserving a little sauce to serve on the side of the dish.

Roast in the preheated oven for 25–30 minutes. The cabbages should be browned and sticky but still have some bite when cooked. Serve with the reserved plum sauce on the side, the Tofu Chips and Green Beans & Glazed Cashews.

TOFU CHIPS

2 x blocks 200 g/7 oz. firm tofu, drained and excess water pressed out
cooking oil spray
2 tsp sea salt
1 tsp onion powder
1 tbsp Sichuan pepper
pinch of cayenne pepper
½ tsp chilli/chili powder

baking sheet, lined with baking parchment

Preheat the oven to 150°C (300°F) Gas 2.

Slice the tofu into very thin pieces, no more than 3-mm/⅛-inch-thick. Lay out the slices on the prepared baking sheet. Lightly mist the slices with a little cooking spray.

Bake in the preheated oven for about 25 minutes or until golden brown and crisp.

Mix together the remaining ingredients in a small bowl and sprinkle on the tofu chips to taste, then serve.

GREEN BEANS & GLAZED CASHEWS

300 g/10½ oz. green/French beans, trimmed
150 g/generous 1 cup raw cashews
1 tbsp soy sauce
4 tbsp rice vinegar
1 garlic clove, crushed
1 thumb-sized piece of fresh ginger, peeled and grated
1 tsp toasted sesame oil
1 tsp white sugar
sea salt

Bring a large pan of salted water to the boil. Add the green/French beans and bring back to the boil, then simmer for about 3–5 minutes until just tender. Drain and plunge straight into a bowl of ice-cold water to stop the cooking process. Drain the beans well and dry with paper towels. Set aside.

Dry-toast the cashews in a small frying pan/skillet over a medium heat, shaking the pan to make sure they don't burn. Once toasted, turn the heat up to medium-high and add the soy sauce. Toss to coat and cook for about 30 seconds until the liquid has evaporated. Leave to cool completely.

In a large bowl, whisk together the rice vinegar, garlic, ginger, sesame oil and sugar. Add the green/French beans to the dressing and stir to coat. Serve topped with the soy-glazed cashews.

IMAM BAYILDI ROASTED AUBERGINES
WITH HERBY TAHINI YOGURT & HONEY
& SESAME FRIED SAGANAKI CHEESE

An Ottoman delicacy brought to Greece many years ago, my Grandma used to make this aubergine/eggplant dish for me, and here I have updated it with the addition of capers and raisins. Served with herby tahini yogurt and fried sagnaki cheese, every time I eat it I am transported to family meals in the Greek mountains.

4 medium aubergines/eggplants
5 tbsp olive oil, plus extra for brushing
2 red onions, halved and thinly sliced
3 garlic cloves, thinly sliced
1 tsp ground cinnamon
pinch of ground nutmeg
100 ml/⅓ cup plus 1 tbsp white wine
1 x 400-g/14-oz. can crushed tomatoes
1 tsp runny honey
20 g/⅛ cup sultanas/golden raisins
20 g/2 tbsp capers, drained
1 handful fresh oregano leaves
1 tsp chilli flakes/hot red pepper flakes
sea salt and freshly ground black pepper
handful fresh parsley, to serve
2 tbsp pine nuts, dry-toasted, to serve

Preheat the oven to 200°C (400°F) Gas 6.

Use a knife to make a deep slit lengthways in each aubergine/eggplants (taking care not to pierce all the way to the bottom). Fit the aubergines/eggplants into a roasting pan, slit-side up, and brush with a little oil. Roast in the preheated oven for 30 minutes.

Meanwhile, make the sauce. Heat 3 tbsp of the olive oil in a frying pan/skillet over a medium heat. Add the onions and fry until soft and translucent. Add the garlic and fry for another minute or two. Stir in the cinnamon and nutmeg, then cook off for another minute. Increase the heat to medium-high, add the wine and let it reduce for 5 minutes. Add the tomatoes, honey, sultanas/golden raisins, capers, oregano, chilli flakes/hot red pepper flakes. Season with salt and black pepper and cook for another 20 minutes, stirring occasionally, until the ingredients are starting to caramelize. Add water if the mixture begins to stick.

After the 30 minutes, remove the aubergines/eggplants from the oven and leave in a colander over a sink to cool and let the moisture drain. Reduce the oven temperature to 180°C (350°F) Gas 4.

Scoop out and reserve some of the cooled aubergine/eggplant flesh to make room for the stuffing. Finely chop the flesh and add to the tomato sauce mixture. Fry off over a medium heat for 5 minutes until the sauce amalgamates with the aubergine/eggplants.

Place the aubergines/eggplants in a baking dish and lightly sprinkle the inside of each with ½ tsp sea salt, then spoon the tomato sauce mixture into the cavity of each. Drizzle the remaining 2 tbsp olive oil and 3 tbsp water around the aubergines/eggplants and cover the tray with foil. Roast in the preheated oven for about 45 minutes, uncovering for the last 20 minutes. Serve the aubergines/eggplants warm or at room temperature, sprinkled with fresh parsley and toasted pine nuts, with the Herby Tahini Yogurt and the Honey & Sesame Fried Saganaki Cheese.

HERBY TAHINI YOGURT

3 garlic cloves, crushed
1 bunch fresh coriander/cilantro
1 bunch fresh flat-leaf parsley
1 tsp ground coriander
150 g/²⁄₃ cup tahini
100 g/scant ½ cup Greek yogurt
grated zest and freshly squeezed
    juice of 1 lemon
sea salt and freshly ground black pepper
micro herbs, to garnish

Add all the ingredients, except the
lemon juice and micro herbs, to a food
processor and blitz. With the motor
still running, gradually drizzle in 175
ml/¾ cup water and process until the
sauce is light green and about as thick
as sour cream (you may need to add
extra water). Season with salt and
pepper and lemon juice to taste.
Garnish with micro herbs.

HONEY & SESAME FRIED SAGANAKI CHEESE

200-g/7-oz. block of Saganaki cheese
    (or halloumi is a great alternative)
1 tbsp runny honey
1 tsp sesame seeds
fresh lime wedges, to serve
1 small red chilli/chile, thinly sliced,
    to garnish
1 tbsp freshly chopped coriander/
    cilantro, to garnish

If it hasn't come ready-sliced, slice
the cheese into thin triangles. Fry the
cheese slices in batches in a frying
pan/skillet over a medium heat until
golden. Drizzle over the honey and
scatter over the sesame seeds.
Serve with lime wedges for squeezing
over and garnish with chilli/chile and
freshly chopped coriander/cilantro.

INDIAN SPICED SLOW-COOKED DUCK
WITH EGG HOPPERS & CRISPY OKRA

If you are looking for a roast with an exciting array of Asian-fusion flavours and ingredients, then this is the one for you. Crispy tamarind and Indian spice-glazed whole roasted duck is served with Sri Lankan egg hoppers and crispy okra.

1 whole duck, about 1.75 kg–2 kg/
   3¾–4½ lb.
sea salt, for sprinkling

GLAZE
1 tsp ground cumin
100 g/3½ oz. tamarind paste
2 tbsp soft light brown sugar
1 tsp ground ginger
½ tsp black Indian salt
1 tsp chilli/chili powder

Preheat the oven to 160°C (325°F)
Gas 3.

Pull any fat away from the duck cavity and trim off the excess. Sit the duck on a rack over a roasting pan. Sprinkle salt all over the skin, then roast the duck in the preheated oven for 1½ hours.

Meanwhile, mix together the glaze ingredients. After 1½ hours, brush some of the glaze over the duck. Return to the oven and roast for 1 hour more, brushing more glaze over the duck a couple more times as it cooks.

Remove from the oven, cover with foil and rest for 10 minutes before carving into thin slices or shredding with two forks to serve with the Egg Hoppers and Crispy Okra.

EGG HOPPERS

200 ml/generous ¾ cup coconut cream
5 g/2 tsp fresh yeast
1 tsp caster/granulated sugar
250 g/2 cups rice flour
1½ egg whites
1 tsp sea salt
6 eggs
vegetable oil, for frying

Put the coconut cream, yeast and sugar into a large bowl, stir to combine, then cover with clingfilm/plastic wrap and stand in a warm place for about 45 minutes until the mixture is slightly risen and frothy.

Sift the rice flour into the yeast mixture and whisk to a smooth batter. You may need to add between 150–200 ml/⅔–generous ¾ cups water to achieve a pouring consistency. Cover the bowl with a damp kitchen cloth and stand in a warm place for 3–4 hours until the batter mixture has doubled in size. The warmer the room, the quicker the batter will rise.

Just before cooking, lightly beat the egg whites with a fork until foamy, then stir into the coconut mixture with the salt. Heat a small, deep, non-stick frying pan/skillet (or wok) with a lid over a medium heat. Coat the hot pan with 2 tsp oil, pouring out any excess. Add about 125–150 ml/½–⅔ cup batter to the pan and, working quickly, swirl the batter around so it coats the sides and bottom in a thin layer. Pour any excess back into the bowl.

Cook for 1 minute or until the edges start to colour, then crack an egg into the middle of the hopper and put the lid on. Cook for 3 minutes or until the egg white is cooked but the yolk is still runny. The hopper should be soft in the middle and crisp at the edges.

Carefully tip the pan and slide the hopper onto a plate. Repeat with the remaining oil, batter and eggs to make six hoppers and serve immediately.

CRISPY OKRA

500 g/18 oz. okra
100 g/¾ cup chickpea/gram flour
½ tsp ground turmeric
½ tsp chilli/chili powder
1 tsp ajwain/carom seeds
   (or substitute dried thyme)
4 tsp chaat masala
sea salt, to taste
flavourless oil, for deep-frying
pinch of panch phoran (Bengali
   five-spice), to serve (optional)

Wash the okra and dry very thoroughly. Remove the stems, then chop each okra diagonally into thin slices. Put the okra slices into a mixing bowl and sprinkle over all the dry ingredients, except the salt. Toss together to coat.

Preheat some oil over a medium heat in a wok or heavy-based saucepan. Drop a grain of rice into your hot oil, if the rice comes back to the top and starts cooking, your oil is hovering around the correct temperature of 180°C (350°F).

Season the okra with salt and toss again just before frying.

Deep-fry the okra in small batches, until crisp. Remove with a slotted spoon and drain off the excess oil on paper towels. Sprinkle with a tiny pinch of panch phoran to serve, if liked.

MIDDLE EASTERN SPICED VENISON SHAWARMA
WITH GRILLED WATERMELON & FETA SALAD &
SPINACH & RAISIN DIP

The perfect sharing platter! This is a modern take on the traditional Levantine shawarma, which normally refers to meat roasted on a spit. Here, the venison has simply been rolled around a filling of cinnamon sticks, onions and an array of Middle Eastern spices before being roasted. Venison is a lean meat and perfectly suited to carrying strong flavours. Serve with the salad and dip, stuffed into lavash breads, if you can get them, or pitta breads.

60 ml/4 tbsp olive oil
2 red onions, thinly sliced
2 tsp qalat daqqa (Tunisian five-spice –
    a blend of ground black peppercorns,
    cloves, grains of paradise, ground
    nutmeg and ground cinnamon)
3 garlic cloves, crushed
2 bay leaves
2 cinnamon sticks
1 tsp ground cardamom
1 tsp sea salt, or to taste
½ tsp freshly ground black pepper
750 g/1 lb. 11 -oz. venison haunch,
    deboned, fat and sinews well-trimmed

TO SERVE
pickled chillies/chiles
lavash breads or pitta breads

cooking string

Preheat the oven to 180°C (350°F) Gas 4.

To make the filling, heat half the oil in a frying pan/skillet over a medium heat. Add the onions and half the qalat daqqa (Tunisian five-spice) and sauté, stirring, for 8–10 minutes until soft. Stir in the rest of the ingredients (apart from the venison and pickled chillies/chiles) and sauté, stirring, for 3 minutes more until fragrant. Remove the mixture from the heat and leave to cool sightly.

Spread the venison haunch flat on a board, flesh-side up, and pack the cool filling where the bone would have been in an even layer. Roll the meat around the stuffing. Tie the rolled up joint at 2.5 cm/1-inch intervals with cooking string as neatly as possible. Rub the remaining qalat daqqa (Tunisian five-spice) evenly over the prepared venison.

Heat the remaining oil in a large frying pan/skillet and sear the meat until browned on all sides. If you want meat that is still a little pink in the oven, put the meat in a roasting pan and roast in the preheated oven for 12 minutes per 500 g/18 oz. for medium-rare or 10 minutes per 500 g/18 oz. for rarer. Alternatively, you can cook the venison low and slow at 140°C (275°F) Gas 1 for 2 hours until super tender and falling apart.

Remove from the oven, cover with foil and rest for 20 minutes. Slice the meat, remove the cinnamon sticks and serve with pickled chillies/chiles, the Grilled Watermelon & Feta Salad, Spinach & Raisin Dip and store-bought lavash breads or pitta breads.

GRILLED WATERMELON & FETA SALAD

cooking oil spray
1 x 10-cm/4-inch x 4-cm/1½-inch chunk
    watermelon, skin and seeds removed
½ lemon
½ bunch fresh flat-leaf parsley leaves
¼ bunch fresh mint leaves
30 g/1½ cups wild rocket/arugula
300 g/10½ oz. mixed tomatoes,
    quartered
extra virgin olive oil, to drizzle
100 g/3½ oz. feta, cut into thick slices
sea salt and freshly ground black pepper

griddle pan/grill pan

Grease a griddle pan/grill pan with cooking oil spray and place over a high heat. Grill/griddle the watermelon and ½ lemon, flesh-side down, for about 2 minutes.

Carefully turn the watermelon on its side and cook for a further 2 minutes. Remove the lemon from the pan and set aside. Repeat the turning and cooking process on the other side of the watermelon so that all sides are charred.

Combine the herbs, rocket/arugula and tomatoes in a bowl. Drizzle with a little olive oil and toss to coat. Season with salt.

Place the grilled watermelon onto a plate, top with the feta slices and the herb salad. Season with salt and pepper and serve the grilled lemon on the side for squeezing over.

SPINACH & RAISIN DIP

2 tbsp sultanas/golden raisins, chopped
1 tbsp olive oil
2 large shallots, finely chopped
¼ tsp ground turmeric
250 g/4 cups spinach leaves
200 g/1 scant cup thick natural yogurt
squeeze of fresh lemon juice
sea salt and freshly ground black pepper

Soak the sultanas/golden raisins in warm water for 15 minutes, then drain.

Heat the oil in a heavy-based frying pan/skillet over a medium heat. Fry the shallots until soft and translucent. Stir in the turmeric and sultanas/golden raisins and fry for 2–3 minutes. Remove from the heat and let cool.

Bring a saucepan of salted water to the boil and blanch the spinach for 20 seconds. Plunge into ice-cold water to refresh, then squeeze out as much liquid as you can. Finely chop the spinach, then mix into the yogurt with the raisin mixture. Season to taste with salt, pepper and lemon juice.

ROASTED MUSHROOMS
WITH WARM FREGOLA SALAD & PARMESAN CRISPS

SERVES 4

These slow-roasted mushrooms are warming, comforting and super delicious!
Leftovers with the salad actually make a brilliant lunch the next day too.

700 g/1 lb. 9 oz. mixed Portobello and
  Portobellini mushrooms
5 golden shallots, thinly sliced
3 garlic cloves, thinly sliced
45 ml/3 tbsp extra virgin olive oil
50 g/3½ tbsp butter, coarsely chopped
30 g/¼ cup lightly toasted hazelnuts,
  coarsely chopped
8 fresh thyme sprigs, plus extra to serve
30 ml/2 tbsp hazelnut oil
sea salt and freshly ground black pepper

Preheat the oven to 200°C (400°F) Gas 6.

Place the mushrooms in a single
layer in a roasting dish. Season to taste
with salt and pepper, then scatter over
the remaining ingredients. Cover with
foil and roast in the preheated oven
for 1 hour, uncovering for the last
20 minutes, until just tender. Serve
scattered with extra thyme sprigs.

WARM FREGOLA SALAD

300 g/10½ oz. fregola
2 tbsp olive oil
1 onion, finely chopped
3 garlic cloves, crushed
200 ml/generous ¾ cup white wine
350 ml/1½ cups vegetable stock
2 bay leaves
2 tbsp sun-dried tomato paste
1 bunch fresh basil, leaves only
200 g/7 oz. wild rocket/arugula
freshly squeezed juice of 1 lemon
drizzle of extra virgin olive oil
sea salt and freshly ground black pepper

PARMESAN CRISPS

100 g/3½ oz. Parmesan cheese, finely
  grated
100 g/3½ oz. Parmesan cheese, coarsely
  shredded
2 baking sheets, lined with baking
  parchment

Preheat the oven to 200°C (400°F) Gas 6.

In a medium bowl, stir together the cheeses.

Spoon heaped tablespoons of the mixture onto the prepared
baking sheets, spacing them at least 5 cm/2 inches apart. Slightly
flatten each mound with the back of a spoon.

Bake in the preheated oven for 8–10 minutes until the crisps
are golden brown. Allow the crisps to cool completely on the baking
sheets before carefully removing with a spatula – they may break
if you try to move them while still warm.

Serve with the Roasted Mushrooms and Warm Fregola Salad, or
store in an airtight container at room temperature for up to 3 days.

Cook the fregola in a large saucepan of boiling salted water for
about 6–8 minutes until almost al dente. Drain the fregola but
do not rinse, reserving 250 ml/1 cup plus 1 tbsp of the cooking liquid.

Heat the oil in a saucepan over a medium heat. Add the onion
and sauté, stirring, for 5 minutes. Add the garlic and sauté for a
further 3–5 minutes until soft. Add the wine and simmer for about
5 minutes until the pan is almost dry.

Add the stock and bay leaves and bring to a simmer again.
Add the partially-cooked fregola and simmer for about 5 minutes,
stirring, until the fregola is tender and the broth has thickened.

Season with salt and pepper and add some reserved cooking
liquid, if needed, to moisten. Turn down the heat and stir through
the sun-dried tomato paste. Before serving, stir through the basil,
top with rocket/arugula and drizzle with lemon juice and olive oil.

MERRY

A year is filled with many special occasions – from Christmas, Thanksgiving and Easter to birthdays, anniversaries and long-awaited reunions. Wow your friends and family on these memorable days and celebrate with home-cooked masterpieces full of love.

TRUFFLE-ROASTED COCKEREL
WITH HASSELBACK SQUASH, MARSALA GRAVY, ROASTED CARROTS & KALE WITH A SAUSAGE & FREEKEH CRUMB & BREAD SAUCE

Cockerel has a great flavour and is my go-to Christmas roast. This is my take on the classic English Christmas dinner, a side of bread sauce is a must!

1 x 3-kg/6¾-lb. cockerel (ask your butcher to truss or see method)
1 black truffle (around 50 g/1¾ oz.), finely shaved
1 whole garlic head, sliced in half widthways
2 onions, unpeeled, halved
1 bunch fresh thyme sprigs
1 bunch fresh rosemary sprigs
4 fresh bay leaves
40 g/3 tbsp butter
2 bergamot oranges (or use lemons), halved
sea salt

cooking string (optional)

Preheat the oven to 180°C (350°F) Gas 4.

Insert your fingers between the skin and breasts of the cockerel to create pockets. Place 4–5 large slices of truffle on each breast underneath the skin. Pull the skin back over to secure. Place half the garlic head and 2 halves of onion inside the cockerel cavity, along with a third each of the thyme and rosemary and 2 bay leaves.

If your bird has not been trussed by your butcher, tuck the wings beneath the cockerel and tie the legs together with cooking string.

Rub the cockerel with 2 tbsp of the butter and season well with sea salt. Line a roasting pan with a generous bed of the remaining thyme, rosemary and bay leaves. Nestle the remaining garlic, onions and the orange halves (or lemons) into the herbs. Sit the cockerel on top and roast in the preheated oven until cooked through and the juices run clear. For a cockerel that weighs less than 4.5 kg/9 lb. 15 oz., roast for 45 minutes per kg or 18 minutes per lb. plus 20 minutes. Baste the meat with juices every 30 minutes to stop it drying out.

Rub the cooked cockerel with the remaining 1 tbsp butter, then remove it from the pan and cover with foil and a kitchen cloth. Rest in a warm place for at least 30 minutes until ready to serve. Use the pan juices for the Marsala Gravy recipe, if you like (right).

HASSELBACK BUTTERNUT SQUASH

4 tbsp/½ stick butter, softened
4 large freshly chopped sage leaves, plus about 6 small sage leaves for stuffing the slits
1 garlic clove, finely grated
½ nutmeg, freshly grated
1 large butternut squash
4 fresh bay leaves
4 sprigs fresh lemon thyme
sea salt and freshly ground black pepper

Preheat the oven to 180°C (350°F) Gas 4.

In a bowl, mix together the butter, chopped sage, garlic and nutmeg and a pinch each of salt and pepper.

Peel the squash, cut in half lengthways and remove the seeds. Place the squash halves, cut-side down, on a chopping board with a wooden spoon either side. Cut slits 3-mm/⅛-inch apart down each squash half, using the spoon handles to avoid cutting all the way through. Insert a few small sage leaves, the bay leaves and lemon thyme sprigs in the slits. Season and brush each with ½ tsp of the butter mixture. Roast in the preheated oven for 65–75 minutes, brushing on more butter every 10 minutes, until tender.

ROASTED CARROTS & KALE WITH A SAUSAGE & FREEKEH CRUMB

300 g/10½ oz. baby carrots with tops, scrubbed
3 garlic cloves, unpeeled
3 tbsp olive oil
½ tsp ground cumin (optional)
2 tsp runny honey
½ tsp Himalayan pink sea salt
200 g/7 oz. cavolo nero, roughly chopped

CRUMB
3 large herby pork sausages, roughly chopped
1 tbsp olive oil
100 g/3½ oz. freekeh, cooked and cooled
1 sprig fresh rosemary, leaves chopped
6 freshly chopped sage leaves
sea salt and freshly ground black pepper

Preheat the oven to 180°C (350°F) Gas 4.

Place the carrots and garlic cloves in a roasting tray and drizzle with the olive oil. Sprinkle over the cumin (if using), honey and pink sea salt and toss to mix. Roast in the preheated oven for 10–15 minutes.

Meanwhile, fry the chopped sausages in the oil in a frying pan/skillet over a medium heat until browned, breaking up with a spoon as they fry. Add the cooked freekeh and herbs and season to taste. Continue to cook until the freekeh is crisp and slightly browned.

Meanwhile, cook the cavolo nero in a large saucepan of boiling water for 2–3 minutes, then drain.

Put the kale on a serving plate and toss with the roasted carrots and sausage and freekeh crumb.

MARSALA GRAVY

30 g/¼ stick unsalted butter
1 small onion, chopped
2 sprigs each rosemary and thyme
1 garlic clove, peeled
1 tbsp plain/all-purpose flour
250 ml/1 cup plus 1 tbsp chicken or vegetable stock
80 ml/⅓ cup Marsala wine
cooking juices from the cockerel roasting pan (optional)

BREAD SAUCE

20 g/1½ tbsp butter
1 tbsp olive oil
½ onion, finely chopped
1 small garlic clove, peeled and bruised
1 dried bay leaf
4 cloves
300 ml/1¼ cups chicken stock
200 ml/generous ¾ cup milk

200 g/4 cups fresh breadcrumbs (keep 1 tbsp for topping)
1–2 tbsp sour cream
sea salt and freshly ground black pepper

CRISPY TOPPING
1 tbsp breadcrumbs (from above)
1 tbsp butter
¼ tsp grated nutmeg

Heat the butter and oil in a large saucepan over a medium heat. Add the onion, garlic, bay leaf and cloves and sauté for 10–15 minutes until the onion is soft.

Add the stock and milk and bring to a simmer, then reduce the heat and simmer gently for 5–6 minutes.

Stir in the breadcrumbs and simmer for 4–5 minutes until the liquid has been absorbed. Remove the bay leaf, cloves and garlic and then process the mixture in a blender until smooth.

Stir in the sour cream to taste, season well with salt and pepper. (You can add more milk at this point if you prefer a thinner sauce.) Warm the sauce through again gently on the hob/stove-top, if needed, to serve.

For the topping, fry the breadcrumbs in the butter in a small frying pan/skillet until brown and crispy. Stir in the nutmeg and use to top the bread sauce.

Melt the butter in a saucepan over a medium heat. Sauté the onion in the butter for 5 minutes or until starting to colour, then add the herbs and garlic. Add the flour and stir continuously for 30 seconds over the heat to cook out, then stir in the stock, Marsala and cooking juices (if using). Bring to the boil, then simmer over a low heat for 5 minutes. Keep chilled, then warm over a medium heat and remove the garlic to serve.

MAPLE & GINGER TURKEY CROWN
WITH SWEET POTATOES & DEVILS ON HORSEBACK

This recipe is perfect for an easy Thanksgiving or celebration meal. It would go well with the Brussels sprouts side (see page 130) or simple crunchy slaw (see page 133).

2.3 kg/4½ lb. turkey crown

1 tsp olive oil

4 sweet potatoes, peeled and cut into wedges

1 whole head garlic, sliced in half widthways

3 red onions, peeled and cut into wedges

4 bay leaves

3 sprigs fresh rosemary

sea salt and freshly ground black pepper

MAPLE & GINGER GLAZE

2 banana shallots, peeled and finely chopped

1 x 5-cm/2-inch thumb of ginger, peeled and grated

4 garlic cloves, peeled and crushed

2 tbsp olive oil

grated zest and freshly squeezed juice of 1 orange

2 tbsp kecap manis (Indonesian sweet soy sauce)

2 tbsp soy sauce

4 tbsp maple syrup

Preheat the oven to 190°C (375°F) Gas 5.

Put the turkey crown into a large roasting pan with plenty of space around the sides. Drizzle with olive oil and season with salt and pepper. Cover the turkey with foil and put into the preheated oven to roast for 20 minutes per kg or 12 minutes per lb. plus 1 hour 10 minutes. Halfway through cooking, add the sweet potatoes, garlic, onions, bay leaves and rosemary to the pan and season. Return to the oven to finish cooking while you make the glaze.

Put the shallots, ginger, garlic and olive oil in a small, heavy saucepan and cook over a low heat for about 5–7 minutes, stirring occasionally, until softened. Add the remaining ingredients, then bring to the boil and cook, stirring, for 3–5 minutes. Reduce the heat to medium and simmer for 10 minutes until thickened. Strain out the onion, ginger and garlic and finely mince using a sharp knife, then stir back into the glaze. Remove from the heat and leave to cool to room temperature. Cover and refrigerate the glaze until needed.

When the turkey has 20 minutes left, carefully remove from the oven, remove the foil and brush with the maple and ginger glaze. Add the devils on horseback to the pan now, if using. Return the turkey to the oven (uncovered) for the remaining 20 minutes.

Check that the turkey is cooked through by piercing the thickest part with a knife – the juices should run clear. Transfer the cooked turkey to a warm serving plate but keep the veggies and devils on horseback warm in a low oven. Cover the turkey with foil and rest for at least 10 minutes before carving and serving.

DEVILS ON HORSEBACK

12 pecan nuts

extra virgin olive oil, for drizzling

12 prunes, pitted

12 Parmesan shavings

6 pancetta slices, halved widthways

sea salt

Season the pecans with sea salt and drizzle with oil, then stuff one inside each prune where the pit would have been (using a knife to make a larger incision if needed) with a shaving of Parmesan.

Wrap each stuffed prune in a piece of pancetta and set aside until ready to cook with the turkey. Alternatively, bake separately in an oven preheated to 190°C (375°F) Gas 5 for 20 minutes.

MISO & UMEBOSHI BAKED PUMPKIN
WITH COURGETTE PANCAKES & QUICK
ASPARAGUS & CARROT KIMCHI

A vegetable-centric dish worthy of the main event! I like to serve this pumpkin
on a courgette pancake with some kimchi and a spoonful of Japanese mayonnaise.

1 kabocha pumpkin or 3 small pumpkins
bunch of spring onions/scallions
4 tbsp flavourless oil
2 tsp sesame oil
4 tbsp white miso paste
2 tbsp soy sauce
4 tbsp mirin
4 tsp umeboshi paste

cooking string (optional)
roasting pan, lined with baking
   parchment

Preheat the oven to 180°C (350°F) Gas 4.

Cut the pumpkin(s) in half
lengthways and deseed. Cut the
pumpkin(s) into 5 cm/2-inch thick
wedges and tie loosely together with
cooking string. Nestle the spring
onions/scallions between the wedges
and place in the prepared roasting pan.
(Alternatively, you can spread the
wedges and onions in a roasting pan
without tying.)

Mix together the remaining
ingredients in a small bowl with 2 tbsp
water to make a marinade and brush
generously all over the pumpkin slices.

Roast in the preheated oven for
30–40 minutes for 1 medium pumpkin
(or 30–35 for 3 smaller) turning over
halfway through until tender. Shake
the pan to coat the pumpkin pieces in
the sticky marinade and remove to a
serving plate.

QUICK ASPARAGUS & CARROT KIMCHI

200 g/7 oz. asparagus, shaved
    into ribbons
200 g/7 oz. carrots, peeled and
    shaved into ribbons
1 tbsp sea salt
1 tbsp sugar
5 spring onions/scallions, cut into
    5-cm/2-inch lengths
1 tbsp gochugaru paste (coarse
    Korean red chilli/chili pepper
    powder) or 1 tbsp chilli flakes/hot
    red pepper flakes, finely ground
2 garlic cloves, crushed
1 tbsp fish sauce
1 thumb-sized piece of fresh ginger,
    peeled and grated

In a large bowl, toss together the sliced asparagus, carrots, salt and sugar.

Add the spring onions/scallions, gochugaru paste (or crushed chilli flakes/hot red pepper flakes), garlic, fish sauce, and ginger and toss well to coat.

Serve immediately or cover with clingfilm/plastic wrap and leave at room temperature for 2 days to allow fermentation to begin before refrigerating. This kimchi will keep for only a few days in the fridge as it is a quick version.

COURGETTE PANCAKES

250 g/1¾ cups plus 2 tbsp plain/
    all-purpose flour
2 eggs
500 g/18 oz. green and yellow
    courgettes/zucchini, coarsely
    grated, salted and moisture
    squeezed out
1 tbsp flavourless oil, plus extra for
    frying
3 spring onions/scallions, finely
    chopped
½ tsp Chinese five-spice powder
    (optional)
sea salt and freshly ground black
    pepper

Put the flour and a big pinch of salt in a bowl and whisk in the eggs. Whisk in 200–250 ml/¾–1 cup plus 1 tbsp water (as needed) to make a thick batter. Leave to rest at room temperature for 10 minutes.

Add the grated courgettes/zucchini, the oil, spring onions/scallions, Chinese five-spice (if using) and some black pepper to the batter and mix thoroughly.

Heat a little oil in a large frying pan/skillet and, when it's very hot, ladle in enough mixture to cover the base of the pan completely. Cook over a medium heat for about 2–3 minutes until the underneath is set, then slide it out onto a plate and invert it back into the pan to cook the other side. Keep the cooked pancakes warm in a low oven while you use up the batter. Using a large frying pan/skillet, you should get 4 thick pancakes.

EASTER POUSSINS
WITH WHITE WINE SAUCE, MAXIM POTATOES
& ASPARAGUS IN LEMON & CAPER BROWN BUTTER

This is a light and elegant meal, perfect for a spring time or Easter celebration after a long winter. Plating a whole poussin each will make your guests feel rather special.

4 oven-ready poussins
4 garlic cloves, unpeeled
2 lemons, halved
1 bunch fresh thyme, divided into 4
40 g/3 tbsp butter, softened
8–11 vine leaves, brined and rinsed
 (available from Greek food specialists)
100 ml/⅓ cup plus 1 tbsp white wine
sea salt and freshly ground black pepper
Asparagus in Lemon & Caper Brown
 Butter (see page 133) to serve

WHITE WINE SAUCE
2 shallots, finely chopped
1 tbsp plain/all-purpose flour
200 ml/generous ¾ cup white wine
200 ml/generous ¾ cup chicken stock
15 g/1 tbsp butter
1 tbsp freshly chopped chives

Preheat the oven to 220°C (425°F) Gas 7.

Season the inside of each poussin with salt and pepper, then stuff each with a garlic clove, lemon half and the thyme. Smother the skins with the butter and season with salt and pepper.

Lay two vine leaves out widthways side-by-side, slightly overlapping on a work surface. Place one poussin on top at the breast end, leaving the legs extended past the leaves. Fold the leaves up around the sides. Repeat with the remaining poussins and leaves.

Sit the birds in a shallow roasting pan. Pour the wine into the pan around the birds. Roast in the preheated oven for about 40 minutes or until cooked through. Baste with the juices a few times during the cooking process. Remove from the pan, cover with foil and set aside to rest while you make the white wine sauce.

Place the pan with the cooking juices on the hob/stove-top over a medium heat, add the shallots and cook, stirring occasionally, for 8 minutes. Add the flour and cook for 2 minutes, stirring. Turn up the heat, add the wine and simmer for 2 minutes. Add the chicken stock and cook for 8–10 minutes until thickened. Take off the heat, mix in the butter, season to taste with salt and pepper and stir through the chives to finish. Serve with the Poussins, Maxim Potatoes and Asparagus in Lemon & Caper Brown Butter.

MAXIM POTATOES

500 g/18 oz. baking potatoes, peeled
100 g/7 tbsp organic ghee, melted
sea salt and freshly ground black pepper

a round 5-cm/2-inch cookie cutter
baking sheet, lined with baking
 parchment

Preheat the oven to 160°C (325°F) Gas 3.

Slice the potatoes into 2–3-mm/⅛ inch-thick pieces on a mandoline (do not rinse them or put in water as the starch is needed). Use the cutter to cut out 48 discs (12 per person). Arrange the 12 discs in an overlapping symmetrical ring on the prepared baking sheet and brush with melted ghee. Repeat for each serving, cover with baking parchment and a baking sheet. Roast in the preheated oven for 15–20 minutes, checking after 10 minutes.

Remove the top baking sheet and parchment and reduce the oven heat to 120°C (250°F) Gas ½. Cook for a further 20 minutes until the potatoes are golden brown. Season to taste and serve.

ROASTED ROOT VEGETABLES & OVEN-DRIED PERSIMMON
WITH SAFFRON & DATE PILAF TOPPED WITH MINT & SPINACH YOGURT

A real flavour sensation, this meal makes the most of lots of wonderful jewel-bright vegetables. Perfect for piling onto a sharing platter and letting everyone dig in.

1 romanesco broccoli, sliced
   lengthways into 'steaks'
6 garlic cloves, peeled and bruised
2–3 heritage carrots, peeled and cut
   into large batons
2 beetroots/beets, peeled and cut
   into wedges
4 medium tomatoes on the vine
150 g/5½ oz. padrón peppers
3 tbsp olive oil
sea salt and freshly ground black
   pepper

OVEN-DRIED PERSIMMON
4 ripe but firm fuyu persimmons
1 tbsp freshly squeezed lime juice
2 tbsp runny honey mixed with
   2 tbsp hot water
3 cardamom pods, smashed
2 tbsp/¼ stick unsalted butter, cut
   into small pieces

*3 baking sheets, lined with baking
   parchment*

For the persimmons, preheat the oven to 160°C (325°F) Gas 3.

Peel the persimmons, cut them in half lengthways and then slice them into 2.5-cm/1-inch-thick wedges. Arrange the slices in a baking dish, drizzle them with the lime juice and sprinkle with the honey mixture, cardamom and butter. Roast in the preheated oven for 40 minutes, basting occasionally, until tender. Set aside.

Increase the oven heat to 180°C (350°F) Gas 4.

For the roasted vegetables, place the romanesco and 2 garlic cloves on the first prepared baking sheet, the carrots, beets and 2 garlic cloves on the second and the tomatoes and padrón peppers on each side of the third prepared baking sheet with the remaining garlic. Drizzle everything with oil and season. Put all three trays in the preheated oven for 10 minutes.

After 10 minutes, increase the oven temperature to 200°C (400°F) Gas 6 and remove the peppers and set aside. After 20 minutes, remove the tomatoes. Roast the other two trays for another 20–25 minutes or until the vegetables are caramelized. Remove from the oven and stir through the oven-dried persimmon to serve with the Mint & Spinach Yogurt and the Saffron & Date Pilaf.

MINT & SPINACH YOGURT

3 tbsp Greek yogurt
2 tbsp olive oil
2 handfuls of baby spinach
freshly squeezed juice of 1 lemon
1 handful fresh mint, leaves picked
sea salt and freshly ground black
   pepper

In a food processor, blitz all the ingredients together into a smooth dressing and season to taste. Serve on the side of the pilaf and vegetables or drizzle over everything as you prefer.

SAFFRON & DATE PILAF

2 tbsp olive oil
1 red onion, thinly sliced
1 garlic clove, crushed
200 g/generous 1 cup wild rice
90 g/½ cup red quinoa, rinsed
500 ml/generous 2 cups vegetable
  stock (or more if needed)
pinch of saffron threads
3 medjool dates, pitted and chopped
grated zest and freshly squeezed
  juice of ½ lemon
1 x 400-g/14-oz. can chickpeas,
  drained and rinsed
1 tbsp olive oil
sea salt and freshly ground black pepper

large, heavy-based casserole
  dish with a lid

In the large, heavy-based casserole dish, heat the olive oil and sauté the onion over a medium heat for 8–10 minutes until soft.

Add the garlic and cook for a further minute, then add the wild rice and quinoa and gently stir. Add the vegetable stock and stir through the saffron and chopped dates.

Cover with the lid and simmer gently for 35–45 minutes or until the rice and quinoa are cooked, adding more stock if the pan is looking dry.

Uncover, remove from the heat and stir through the lemon zest and juice, chickpeas and olive oil. Season to taste with salt and pepper before serving.

LOVER'S POT ROAST CHICKEN WITH ANCHO CHILLIES, CHORIZO & BLACK BEANS
WITH PICKLED JALAPEÑOS, CORN & NECTARINE SALSA & TOSTADAS

The perfect meal for a night in with a cooling glass of beer, this spicy, enticing pot roast chicken dish serves two lovers with leftovers or four loved ones.

1 x 1.6-kg/3½-lb. free-range chicken
2 tbsp olive oil
1 large onion, thinly sliced
200 g/7 oz. cooking chorizo,
   cut into chunks
1 tbsp smoked paprika
1 tbsp smoked ground cumin
2 dried ancho chillies/chiles
200 ml/generous ¾ cup chicken stock
2 x 400-g/14-oz. cans cherry tomatoes
2 x 400-g/14-oz. cans black beans,
   drained and rinsed
pinch of sugar, if needed
sea salt and freshly ground black pepper
2 tbsp freshly chopped coriander/
   cilantro, to garnish
freshly squeezed juice of 1–2 limes,
   to serve

*heavy-based casserole dish (big enough
to fit your chicken inside) with a lid*

Preheat the oven to 220°C (425°F) Gas 7.

Put the chicken in a roasting pan and rub with 1 tbsp of the oil. Roast in the preheated oven for 30 minutes until the skin is golden.

Meanwhile, add the remaining 1 tbsp olive oil to the casserole dish over a medium heat. Fry the onion and chorizo for 10 minutes.

When the chorizo has taken on some colour, stir in the smoked paprika, cumin and whole dried chillies/chiles. Cook for 30 seconds, then pour in the chicken stock and canned tomatoes. Simmer gently for 5 minutes. Once the chicken is golden brown, remove it from the oven and place it on top of the sauce. Cover the dish with the lid. Reduce the oven temperature to 180°C (350°F) Gas 4. Place the casserole dish in the oven and roast the chicken for 1 hour.

After 1 hour, remove from the oven, take the chicken out and place on a board and cover with foil to rest for 10 minutes.

Place the sauce on the hob/stove-top over a medium heat and add the black beans. Allow them to warm through, season with salt and pepper and a pinch of sugar, if needed. Garnish with the coriander/cilantro and squeeze over lime juice to taste. Serve with the chicken, Corn & Nectarine Salsa, Pickled Jalapeños and Tostadas.

CORN & NECTARINE SALSA

2 corn cobs/ears, husks and silks
    removed
2 nectarines, pitted and cut into
    thick wedges
1 yellow (bell) pepper, deseeded
    and thinly sliced
1 avocado, peeled, pitted and thinly
    sliced
2 spring onions/scallions, chopped
sea salt and freshly ground black pepper
fresh coriander/cilantro, roughly
    chopped, to garnish
Tabasco sauce, to serve
lime wedges, to serve

griddle pan/grill pan

Heat a barbecue or griddle pan/grill pan on a medium-high heat and grill the corn, turning occasionally, for about 5–8 minutes until charred and just cooked through. Set aside to cool briefly.

Char the nectarine wedges on the barbecue or griddle pan/grill pan for 1–2 minutes on each side.

Slice off the charred corn kernels and place in a bowl with the remaining ingredients and charred nectarines. Toss to combine and season to taste. Garnish with coriander/cilantro and serve with Tabasco sauce and lime wedges for squeezing over.

PICKLED JALAPEÑOS

650 ml/2¾ cups white wine vinegar
60 g/⅓ cup caster/granulated sugar
1 tbsp sea salt flakes
1 tsp coriander seeds, coarsely crushed
1 tsp black peppercorns
1 garlic clove, peeled and bruised
500 g/18 oz. (about 12) green or red
    jalapeños, halved

large sterilized jar with a lid

Combine all the ingredients, apart from the jalapeños, with 650 ml/2¾ cups water in a saucepan and bring to a simmer over a medium heat. Stir until the sugar has dissolved and set aside to cool to room temperature.

Put the jalapeños in the jar, add the liquid, cover with the lid and refrigerate for 2 days before eating. These will keep for 2 months in the fridge.

TOSTADAS

vegetable oil, for shallow-frying
6–8 small plain wheat or cactus tortillas
sea salt

Heat the vegetable oil (about 2 cm/¾ inch deep) in a large frying pan/skillet over a medium-high heat.

Fry the tortillas, one at a time, for 1–2 minutes on each side, turning once, until golden and crisp (be careful as the hot oil will spit).

Transfer to a tray lined with paper towels as each one finishes cooking. Season to taste with sea salt and serve.

WEEKENDS

Here are some very special roasts for
those long, lazy weekend days when
you have a bit of extra time and want
to indulge. Still easy, but comforting
and impressive. It's all about
letting the oven do the work
and using those extra hours
to your advantage.

ASIAN FIVE-SPICED LAMB SHANKS
WITH MUSHROOM STICKY RICE & SMASHED SICHUAN CUCUMBER

This certainly is a revolutionary Sunday roast! I also like to serve it with a fresh salad of lettuce, peanuts and chillies/chiles to complement all the other flavours.

2 tsp Chinese five-spice powder
1 tsp chilli flakes/hot red pepper flakes
3 star anise
1 cinnamon stick
1 tsp Sichuan peppercorns
60 ml/¼ cup soy sauce
130 ml/generous ½ cup Chinese cooking wine
1 tbsp tamarind paste
1 tbsp palm sugar/jaggery
8-cm/3-inch piece of fresh ginger, peeled and julienned
8-cm/3-inch piece of fresh turmeric, peeled and julienned
2 garlic cloves, peeled and halved
6 small round shallots, peeled and halved
300 ml/1¼ cups vegetable stock
4 lamb shanks, French-trimmed

Preheat the oven to 180°C (350°F) Gas 4.

Dry-fry the Chinese five-spice, chilli flakes/hot red pepper flakes, star anise, cinnamon and Sichuan peppercorns in a small frying pan/skillet over a medium heat for 1–2 minutes, stirring, until fragrant.

Stir the spices with the soy sauce, wine, tamarind, sugar/jaggery, ginger, turmeric, garlic, shallots and vegetable stock in a large jug/pitcher.

Place the lamb shanks in a large roasting dish and drizzle with the spice mixture. Roast the lamb shanks in the preheated oven, turning occasionally, for about 2–2½ hours until the lamb is almost falling off the bone.

Remove the shanks from the dish and cover with foil to keep warm. Skim away excess fat from the juices, then strain into a saucepan and simmer over a medium heat on the hob/stove-top for 5 minutes to reduce and warm through for a sauce to accompany the lamb.

SMASHED SICHUAN CUCUMBER

2 large cucumbers
2 garlic cloves, peeled and smashed
1–2 tsp chilli/chile oil
2 tsp sesame seeds
fresh coriander/cilantro, to serve

DRESSING
1 tsp sea salt
1–2 tsp Sichuan peppercorns, crushed (to taste)
2½ tsp white sugar
2 tsp sesame oil
1 tbsp soy sauce
1 tbsp rice vinegar

Combine the dressing ingredients in a small bowl and stir until the salt and sugar have completely dissolved. Set aside.

Wash the cucumbers and pat them dry with a clean kitchen cloth. On a cutting board, lay a large knife flat against a cucumber, and smash it lightly with your other hand. The cucumber should crack open and smash into four sections. Repeat along its full length and with the other cucumber. Cut the smashed cucumbers into angled bite-sized pieces.

In a large bowl, mix the cut cucumber with the dressing, garlic and chilli/chile oil, and toss together well.

Divide the smashed cucumber and dressing into smaller serving bowls and garnish with the sesame seeds and coriander/cilantro. Serve immediately so that the cucumber still has some bite.

MUSHROOM STICKY RICE

200 g/generous 1 cup Thai sticky rice,
 rinsed a few times, then soaked
 in water for at least 40 minutes
1 packet banana or bamboo leaves
 (if frozen, rinsed under hot water
 to clean and thaw)
1 onion, finely chopped
1 tbsp flavourless oil
1 garlic clove, finely chopped
200 g/7 oz. shiitake and/or mixed
 mushrooms, chopped
1 green chilli/chile, chopped
1½ tbsp fish sauce
1½ tbsp soy sauce
3 spring onions/scallions, thinly sliced
extra fish sauce or fresh lime juice,
 to serve (optional)

bamboo steamer with a lid

While the rice is soaking, line your steamer with two layers of banana or bamboo leaves so that the leaves extend out over the sides. Place the steamer over a large saucepan filled with a little water (at least 2.5 cm/1 inch) and have a tight-fitting lid ready.

Cook the onion in the oil in a frying pan/skillet over a medium heat, stirring, for 5 minutes or until translucent. Add the garlic, mushrooms and chilli/chile. Turn the heat to medium-high and stir-fry for 1–2 minutes, until fragrant.

Reduce the heat to low and stir in the drained sticky rice, plus the fish sauce, soy sauce and half the spring onions/scallions.

Transfer the rice to your prepared steamer. Cover with the lid and steam over a high heat for 40–55 minutes. (Check and top up the water halfway through, if needed, and fluff up the rice.)

When ready, remove from the heat and stand with the lid on for 5 minutes. The rice should be soft, sticky and slightly translucent. If there are any hard grains, steam for another 5 minutes.

Taste and sprinkle over a little more fish sauce if more saltiness is needed. If too salty, add a squeeze of lime juice and gently stir in.

Garnish with the remaining spring onions/scallions and serve straight from the steamer with the Asian Five-spiced Lamb Shanks, lamb sauce, Smashed Sichuan Cucumber and extra salad with peanuts and chillies/chiles, if liked.

CHARRED CHICKEN
WITH COGNAC PRUNES & VELVET POMME PURÉE

Brining the chicken overnight and then charring it before roasting adds an amazing tenderness and depth of flavour to this roast. It would be divine served with the Sautéed Brussels with Pancetta & Hazelnuts (see page 130).

1 x 1.5-kg/3 lb. 5-oz. chicken

OVERNIGHT BRINE
small bunch fresh bay leaves
2 tbsp black peppercorns
150 g/¾ cup rock salt
175 g/¾ cup plus 2 tbsp brown sugar
250 ml/1 cup plus 1 tbsp malt vinegar
3 litres/quarts water

FOR ROASTING
2 carrots, peeled and coarsely chopped
2 onions, coarsely chopped
15 g/1 tbsp butter, melted
1 tbsp olive oil
12 pitted prunes
4 sprigs fresh thyme
130 ml/generous ½ cup Cognac
1 heaped tbsp plain/all-purpose flour
500 ml/generous 2 cups chicken stock
sea salt and freshly ground black pepper

griddle pan/grill pan
cooking string

To make the brine, place the bay leaves, peppercorns, salt, sugar, vinegar and water in a big saucepan (large enough to fit your chicken) over a high heat. Bring to the boil and cook, stirring, for 4 minutes or until the salt and sugar have dissolved. Remove from the heat and set aside to cool completely.

Place the chicken, breast-side down, in the brine. Cover with the lid and refrigerate overnight or for a minimum of 12 hours.

When you are ready to cook the chicken, preheat the oven to 180°C (350°F) Gas 4. Scatter the carrots and onions in a small roasting pan and set aside.

Remove the chicken from the brine and pat the skin dry with paper towels, using a very large sharp knife, cut lengthways down the centre of the chicken to spilt it into two halves.

Warm the griddle pan/grill pan over a high heat and griddle/grill the chicken halves, skin-side down, for 6–8 minutes each until the skin is nicely charred all over.

Place the chicken halves on top of the vegetables in the roasting pan. Brush the chicken skin with the melted butter, drizzle with the olive oil and season with salt and pepper. Scatter the prunes and thyme sprigs around the chicken and pour in 100 ml/⅓ cup plus 1 tbsp of the Cognac. Roast the chicken in the preheated oven for 1 hour until the juices run clear and the chicken is cooked through.

Transfer the chicken halves and roasted prunes to a plate and cover with foil to rest for 10 minutes.

Put the roasting pan on the hob/stove-top over a medium heat. Break up all the cooking bits, including the roasted onions and carrots, and add the remaining Cognac and the flour and cook for 3 minutes, stirring. Stir in the chicken stock and cook for about 10 minutes until the gravy has thickened. Serve with the chicken, reserved prunes and Velvet Pomme Purée.

VELVET POMME PURÉE

1.5 kg/3 lb. 5 oz. potatoes, such as Desiree
100 g/1 stick minus 1 tbsp butter, cubed
300 ml/1¼ cups milk
6 tbsp double/heavy cream
sea salt and freshly ground black pepper
drizzle of truffle oil, or to taste

Peel the potatoes and cut into even cubes. Boil in a large saucepan of salted water for about 12–15 minutes until tender.

Drain well, then return to the pan and dry-cook for 1–2 minutes over a medium heat.

Turn off the heat and mash the potatoes or press through a ricer back into the pan – they should be totally lump-free. (Don't use a food processor as it will make the potatoes gluey.)

Gradually beat the butter into the potato purée until shiny.

Heat the milk and cream in a small saucepan until just boiling, then slowly mix into the potato purée with some salt and black pepper (you may not need all the milk mixture). The potato should become a soft velvety purée. Mix in the truffle oil and more seasoning to taste. Keep warm until required or cool and chill. When reheating, add extra creamy milk to soften and/or extra butter.

SLOW-ROASTED SHIN OF VEAL
WITH WARM WINTER SALAD & HERB & WALNUT DRESSING

A whole shin of veal takes a long time to slow-cook, but it is a thing of beauty. Paired with this warm winter salad and herb and walnut dressing, it is a comforting dish. Serve with the Gnocchi 'n' Blue cheese (see page 126) for extra comfort on top.

2 large or 3 small shins of veal
200 ml/generous ¾ cup white wine
2 carrots, peeled and halved if large
3 celery stalks, halved
1 fennel bulb, cut into large wedges
1 bunch fresh sage
1 bunch fresh rosemary
4 fresh bay leaves
1 whole garlic head, sliced in half widthways
100 ml/⅓ cup plus 1 tbsp chicken or vegetable stock
sea salt and freshly ground black pepper

Preheat the oven to 140°C (275°F) Gas 1.

Season the shins of veal with salt and pepper and place in a large, deep heavy roasting pan. Brown the meat over a medium heat on the hob/stove-top, then remove the meat and set aside.

Deglaze the pan with the wine and add the vegetables, herbs, garlic and stock. Return the veal to the pan, cover with foil and place in the preheated oven for 20 minutes. Turn the heat down to 110°C (225°F) Gas ¼ and cook for a further for 6–8 hours until very tender.

Remove from the oven and transfer the cooking juices to a small saucepan over a medium heat on the hob/stove-top. Re-cover the meat to keep warm while you reduce the juices for 10 minutes to make a sauce to serve with the veal and Warm Winter Salad.

HERB & WALNUT DRESSING

6 tbsp walnut oil
35 g/¼ cup walnut halves, toasted
1 garlic clove, crushed
3 tbsp sherry vinegar
½ tsp maple syrup
1 tbsp freshly chopped parsley leaves
1 tbsp freshly chopped basil
sea salt and freshly ground black pepper

Combine the walnut oil, walnut pieces and garlic in a saucepan over a low heat for a few minutes until fragrant. Stir in the sherry vinegar and maple syrup. Remove from the heat, then season with salt and pepper and whisk to bring everything together. Stir in the parsley and basil and use to dress the Warm Winter Salad.

WARM WINTER SALAD

1 cauliflower, cut into florets
7 tbsp olive oil
2 red onions, cut into wedges
4 garlic cloves, smashed
3 sprigs fresh rosemary
2 lemons, thinly sliced into rounds
2 radicchio, cut into wedges
1 400-g/14-oz. can butter/lima beans, drained and rinsed
a pinch of ground sumac
sea salt and freshly ground black pepper

Preheat the oven to 200°C (400°F) Gas 6.

Toss the cauliflower with 3 tbsp of the olive oil and some salt and pepper in a bowl. Transfer to a roasting tray and cook in the preheated oven for 15 minutes.

Stir in the red onions, garlic, rosemary and lemon slices. Drizzle over the remaining 4 tbsp oil and roast for a further 10 minutes.

Add the radicchio wedges and cook for a further 5 minutes.

Place onto a serving dish, add the butter/lima beans and top with a pinch of sumac to finish.

ROASTED ARTICHOKES
WITH HERBY SCONES, TALEGGIO SAUCE,
AGRODOLCE SAUCE & QUAILS' EGGS

Based on a classic French dish, this recipe makes enough to serve four as a main meal or eight as an appetizer. It would be perfect for a light al fresco lunch. The flavours of the delicate eggs, artichokes, scones and two sauces balance really well.

8 globe artichokes, top 2.5-cm/1-inch, chokes and stems removed
freshly squeezed juice of 2 lemons
6 tbsp olive oil
6 garlic cloves, peeled
sea salt and freshly ground black pepper
soft-boiled quails' eggs, peeled, to serve

Preheat the oven to 180°C (350°F) Gas 4.

Place the artichokes, stem-side down, in a bowl and drizzle with the lemon juice, reserving the lemons.

Slightly separate the artichoke leaves on each one with your hands. Insert a knife blade into the centre of each artichoke to create a garlic clove-sized space. Drizzle the artichokes with the olive oil, then press 1 garlic clove into the centre of each where you made the hole and season with salt and pepper. Tightly wrap each artichoke twice with heavy-duty foil.

Place in a roasting dish with the squeezed lemon husks and roast in the preheated oven for 60–80 minutes until sizzling.

Serve the roasted artichokes with the quails' eggs, Taleggio Sauce, Agrodolce Sauce and the Herby Scones on a serving platter.

HERBY SCONES

200 g/1½ cups self-raising/self-rising flour, plus extra for dusting
50 g/3½ tbsp butter, at room temperature
25 g/¼ cup rolled/old-fashioned porridge oats
75 g/⅔ cup grated Cheddar cheese
150 ml/⅔ cup whole milk
½ bunch fresh chives, finely chopped
½ bunch fresh chervil, finely chopped

4-cm/2-inch round plain cookie cutter

Preheat the oven to 220°C (425°F) Gas 7.

Place the flour in a large mixing bowl, then rub in the butter with your fingers. Stir in the oats and the grated cheese, then the milk and herbs. If the mixture feels like it might be too dry, add a touch more milk and bring together into a soft dough.

Roll out the dough on a lightly floured surface no thinner than 2 cm/¾ inch. Use the cookie cutter to firmly stamp out rounds – try not to twist the cutter as this makes the scones rise unevenly. Re-roll the trimmings and stamp out more until all the dough has been used up.

Transfer to a non-stick baking sheet and dust with a little more flour (or grated cheese). Bake in the preheated oven for 15–18 minutes until well risen and golden. Serve warm.

TALEGGIO SAUCE

150 ml/⅔ cup whole milk
200 g/7 oz. Taleggio cheese with rind,
 coarsely chopped
sea salt and freshly ground black pepper

Bring the milk to the boil in a
saucepan. Remove from the heat
and stir in the cheese until it begins
to melt, then blend with a hand-held
blender until smooth. Season to taste.
Taleggio sauce will keep refrigerated
for up to 3 days and can be reheated
gently before serving.

AGRODOLCE SAUCE

180 ml/¾ cup white wine vinegar
50 g/¼ cup soft light brown sugar
1½ red onions, finely chopped
50 g/⅓ cup currants
60 g/½ cup pine nuts
2 lemons, segmented
½ bunch fresh dill, to garnish

Combine the vinegar and sugar in a
saucepan and simmer over a medium
heat, stirring, until the sugar has
dissolved. Place the onions in a bowl
and pour over the vinegar. Add the
currants and let steep for 5 minutes.
 Preheat the oven to 160°C (325°F)
Gas 3.
 Toast the pine nuts in the
preheated oven for 4–6 minutes until
golden. Stir into the onion mixture
along with the lemon segments.
Garnish with dill sprigs and serve.

RUM RIBS
WITH TWICE-BAKED STUFFED POTATOES

Ideal for that movie night or relaxed meal at the weekend. Your friends and family will love you for cooking this, but beware, things will get messy! Great served with the Cabbage, Apple & Celery Slaw (see page 133).

2-kg/4½-lb. pork ribs
1 tbsp sea salt
2 tbsp brown sugar
3 tbsp Earth Spice Rub (see page 54)
 Cabbage, Apple & Celery Slaw
   (see page 133), to serve (optional)

MARINADE
4 tbsp runny honey
3 tbsp soy sauce
2 tbsp sesame oil
100 ml/⅓ cup plus 1 tbsp dark rum

GLAZE
3 tbsp treacle/molasses
2 tbsp soy sauce
100 ml/⅓ cup plus 1 tbsp apple
   cider vinegar
6 whole allspice berries
1 tsp ground ginger
2 tbsp freshly chopped thyme leaves
4 tbsp runny honey
200 ml/generous ¾ cup orange juice
1 cinnamon stick
100 ml/⅓ cup plus 1 tbsp dark rum

baking pan, lined with foil with
   a grill rack inside

Prepare a large plastic fridge bag or other container that will fit the ribs. (If your racks of ribs are too large, you can cut them in half along one of the bones, but try not to disassemble them too much, as they will cook best left as whole as possible.) Rub the ribs with the salt, sugar and earth spice seasoning.

Stir together all of the marinade ingredients in a small bowl. Place the ribs in the plastic bag or container, then cover evenly with the marinade and refrigerate for at least 2 hours or overnight.

Preheat the oven to 150°C (300°F) Gas 2.

Arrange the ribs on the grill rack in the prepared baking pan and cover them with foil.

Cook in the preheated oven for 2 hours, turning the meat over halfway through.

Meanwhile, make the glaze. Combine all the ingredients, except the rum, in a saucepan and bring to the boil. Reduce the heat and simmer gently for 30–45 minutes, until the glaze has thickened.

Stir the rum into the glaze, simmer for 1 minute, then remove from the heat and keep warm.

Once 2 hours have passed, uncover the ribs, flip again, and brush with some of the glaze. Put them back in the oven, uncovered, for 1 more hour. Flip and re-glaze the ribs at the final 30-minute mark.

Remove the ribs from the oven and place on a chopping board to rest for 5–10 minutes. Cut the ribs into portions along the bone so that each individual rib has plenty of meat and place on a large platter. Serve with a bowl of the remaining warm glaze on the side, for dipping, the Twice-Baked Stuffed Potatoes and Cabbage, Apple & Celery Slaw (see page 133).

TWICE-BAKED STUFFED POTATOES

2 large baking potatoes, scrubbed
3–4 tbsp whole milk
30 g/2 tbsp unsalted butter
2 tbsp sour cream
1 tsp Dijon mustard
1 tsp Worcestershire sauce
small handful freshly snipped chives,
    plus extra to garnish
100 g/1 generous packed cup grated
    strong Cheddar
sea salt and freshly ground
    black pepper

Preheat the oven to 180°C (350°F) Gas 4.
    Prick the potatoes with a fork. Bake
in the preheated oven on the oven rack
for 1–1½ hours until tender. Leave to cool
for 10 minutes but leave the oven on.
    Halve the potatoes lengthways,
and scoop the flesh into a medium
bowl. Add the milk, butter, sour cream,
mustard, Worcestershire sauce, chives
and three-quarters of the cheese.
Season with salt and pepper.
    Scoop the filling back into the
potato skins and place in a baking
dish just large enough to hold them.
Sprinkle with the remaining cheese.
Bake in the preheated oven for 15–20
minutes to heat through.
    Garnish with chives before serving.

SALT-CRUSTED SEA BASS
WITH BRANDADE & GREEN QUARTET WITH CAPER DRESSING

This meal is the perfect pescatarian spread – the fish is substantial, the brandade is intensely flavoured and the green quartet adds bountiful freshness. Wow your guests by taking the salt-crusted sea bass to the table and cracking it open in front of them.

1.5-kg/3 lb. 5-oz. whole sea bass
2 lemons, sliced
½ bunch fresh parsley
½ bunch fresh dill
2–3 kg/4½–6½ lb. coarse sea salt

Preheat the oven to 200°C (400°F) Gas 6.

Wash and dry the fish well. Stuff the cavity with the lemon slices, parsley and dill. Sprinkle a layer of salt in a roasting pan for the fish to sit on, about 1-cm/¼-inch deep. Place the fish on the salt and pour the rest of the salt over and around the fish so most is covered; it is fine if the head and tail are not completely covered.

Roast the fish in the preheated oven for 30 minutes. Remove from the oven and allow to rest for about 10 minutes. You can test if the fish is cooked through either by using a meat probe to test the internal temperature (it should read at least 50°C/122°F by this point) or by inserting a metal skewer to feel if it is piping hot. The fish will continue to cook inside its salt crust during the resting time.

To serve, crack the salt and pull it away from the fish – it should take the skin with it. The fish can then be served whole or the flesh removed to a serving platter. Serve with the Brandade and Green Quartet with Caper Dressing.

BRANDADE

400-g/14-oz. piece of salt cod
    (pre-soaked in cold water in the
    refrigerator for 24 hours, changing
    the water 3–4 times)
1 tbsp freshly squeezed lemon juice
2 sprigs fresh flat-leaf parsley
1 dried bay leaf
8 black peppercorns
2 garlic cloves, finely chopped
2 slices of white bread, crusts removed,
    soaked in water for 1 minute, then
    squeezed dry
200 ml/generous ¾ cup whole milk
100 ml/⅓ cup plus 1 tbsp olive oil
sea salt and freshly ground black pepper
1–2 tbsp capers, drained, to garnish
toasted rustic-style bread, to serve

Drain the salt cod and place in a wide saucepan with the lemon juice, parsley, bay leaf, peppercorns and enough water to cover. Bring to the boil over a high heat, then reduce the heat to low and simmer, covered, for 15 minutes. Drain the cod, cool slightly, then remove and discard the skin and bones. Break up the flesh into coarse flakes.

Process the flaked fish, garlic, bread milk and oil in a food processor until well combined. With the motor running, gradually add the olive oil in a thin, steady stream and process until well combined and smooth, then transfer the mixture to a bowl.

Season to taste with sea salt and freshly ground black pepper and combine well. Scatter with capers to garnish and serve warm with slices of toasted rustic-style bread.

GREEN QUARTET

- 100 g/3½ oz. mangetout/
  snow peas, trimmed
- 100 g/3½ oz. sugar snap peas,
  trimmed
- 100 g/3½ oz. green/French beans,
  trimmed
- 100 g/¾ cup frozen peas, defrosted
- fresh sea rosemary, to garnish
  (optional)
- sea salt

Boil all the vegetables, apart from the peas, in a large saucepan of salted water for 3–4 minutes. (I like my vegetables crunchy, but cook them longer if you like.) Drain and then add the defrosted peas – just to heat them. I like to have these quite raw. Top with the caper dressing and sea rosemary to garnish, if you like.

CAPER DRESSING

- grated zest and freshly squeezed
  juice of 1 lime
- grated zest and freshly squeezed
  juice of 1 lemon
- 1 tbsp capers, drained and rinsed
- 1 garlic clove, crushed
- 1 tsp wholegrain mustard
- 1 tbsp finely chopped flat-leaf parsley
- 3 tbsp extra virgin olive oil
- 1 tbsp almonds, toasted and chopped

Prepare the dressing by simply whisking all the ingredients together in a small bowl.

SIDES

All the sides and more — from comforting potatoes, Yorkshire puds and cheesy bakes to light and zingy salads and veggies. These dishes are designed to be versatile, so mix and match away with the mains to your heart's content.

POTATOES 4 WAYS

Everyone loves a potato side dish, and here are my favourite four! They are all deliciously different, so you can mix and match at least one of these with pretty much any roast in this book.

CLASSIC ROASTIES SPICED WITH BAHARAT

1 kg/2¼ lb. Maris Piper or Russet
    potatoes, peeled and cut into
    3–4 pieces each, depending on size
100 ml/⅓ cup plus 1 tbsp olive oil
    (or your choice of fat)
2 tsp plain/all-purpose flour
2 tsp baharat spice mix
    (see recipe below)
sea salt

BAHARAT
2 tbsp freshly ground black pepper
1 tbsp ground coriander
1 tbsp ground cinnamon
1 tbsp ground cloves
1½ tbsp ground cumin
½ tsp ground cardamom
2 tbsp ground nutmeg
2 tbsp paprika

To make the baharat, simply mix all the spices together. The spice mix will keep for up to 6 months stored in an airtight container.

For the potatoes, preheat the oven to 180°c (350°F) Gas 4 and place a large roasting pan in the oven to warm up.

Place the potatoes in a large saucepan and cover with water. Season with sea salt, then bring to a rolling boil.

When boiling, reduce the heat to medium and simmer the potatoes fairly vigorously, uncovered, for 2 minutes.

Meanwhile, put the oil (or fat) into the hot roasting pan and return to the oven for a few minutes until very hot.

Drain the potatoes in a colander, then shake the colander a few times to fluff up the outsides. Sprinkle the potatoes with the flour and shake again so they are evenly and thinly coated.

Carefully transfer the potatoes to the hot fat (it will sizzle), then turn to coat in the oil. Spread the potatoes out evenly in a single layer. Roast in the preheated oven for 30 minutes, turning halfway. Turn once more and roast for a final 10–20 minutes until golden and crisp. Season to taste with salt and baharat spice mix and serve.

LEMON & HERB POTATO WEDGES

1 kg/2¼ lb. Cyprus potatoes or Yukon
    Gold potatoes, peeled and cut into
    thick wedges
4 tbsp olive oil
freshly squeezed juice of 2 lemons
2 tsp sea salt
1 tsp dried oregano
½ tsp freshly ground black pepper
250 ml/1 cup plus 1 tbsp chicken or
    vegetable stock

Preheat the oven to 200°C (400°F) Gas 6.

Put the potato wedges into a large bowl. Drizzle with the olive oil and lemon juice and toss to coat. Add the salt, oregano and black pepper and toss again. Spread the potato wedges out in a deep roasting pan and pour the stock over.

Roast in the preheated oven for about 50 minutes until the wedges are tender and golden.

SMOKED BABY POTATOES WITH PAPRIKA AIOLI & CRISPY CAPERS

600 g/1 lb. 5 oz. baby new potatoes
3 fresh thyme sprigs
1 garlic clove, peeled and bruised
1 fresh bay leaf
sea salt
melted butter, to serve

PAPRIKA AIOLI
2 garlic cloves, crushed
2 egg yolks
1 tbsp Dijon mustard
300 ml/1¼ cups oil (half flavourless oil and half olive oil)
1–2 tsp smoked paprika, to taste, plus extra for sprinkling
1 tbsp white wine vinegar
sea salt and freshly ground black pepper

CRISPY CAPERS
1 tbsp capers, drained
½ tbsp olive oil

handful of hay
large casserole dish or saucepan, lined with foil

Combine the potatoes, thyme, garlic and bay leaf in a large saucepan and cover generously with cold water, add a little sea salt, then bring to a rolling boil. Once boiling, reduce the heat to low-medium and simmer, uncovered, for 25–30 minutes until just tender when pierced with a skewer. Drain and set aside.

Spread the hay in the base of the prepared casserole dish or saucepan and position a wire rack directly on top. Spread the potatoes on the wire rack, cover with a lid and place the dish or pan over a high heat for 3–4 minutes until the hay starts to smoke.

Reduce the heat to low and smoke for about 30 minutes until the potatoes are tender and well flavoured with smoke.

Meanwhile, for the capers, preheat the oven to 180°C (350°F) Gas 4. Spread the capers on a small baking sheet, drizzle with the oil and roast in the preheated oven for 20–25 minutes until crispy.

While the capers are roasting, make the aioli, put the garlic, egg yolks and mustard into a food processor. Blitz to a paste, then very slowly drizzle in the oil with the processor running to make a thick mayonnaise. Stir in the paprika and vinegar and season to taste. The aioli will keep covered in the fridge for up to 2 days.

Top the aioli with the crispy capers and an extra pinch of smoked paprika and serve with the hot smoked potatoes, drizzled with melted butter.

MARMITE SWEET POTATOES

1 kg/2¼ lb. sweet potatoes, peeled and cut into bite-size pieces
3 tbsp olive oil
4 tsp marmite/yeast extract
sea salt and freshly ground black pepper
2 spring onions/scallions, sliced diagonally, to serve

Preheat the oven to 180°C (350°F) Gas 4.

Spread the sweet potato pieces in a roasting pan, drizzle with the olive oil and season with salt and pepper. Roast in the preheated oven for 35 minutes, turning halfway through.

Mix the marmite/yeast extract into the cooking oil in the pan and give the potatoes a good shake to coat. Place back into the oven and roast for a further 10–15 minutes or until golden. Serve sprinkled with the spring onions/scallions.

CHEESY SIDES 3 WAYS

These delicious cheesy sides will raise the stakes at your dinner table.
Sometimes you just need some melted gooey goodness to feed the soul.

GNOCCHI 'N' BLUE CHEESE

**500 g/18 oz. ready-made fresh
gnocchi (I've used a mixed variety
with beetroot/beet and spinach
gnocchi)**
100 g/1¾ cups fresh spinach (optional)
100 g/½ cup crème fraîche
75 ml/⅓ cup single/light cream
4 tbsp grated Parmesan
100 g/3½ oz. soft blue cheese
freshly ground black pepper

Cook the gnocchi in a large saucepan
of boiling water according to the
packet instructions.

Plunge the spinach (if using)
into the same pan of boiling water
when the gnocchi is cooked, then
immediately drain the contents of
the pan through a colander, shaking
off the excess water.

Put the crème fraîche and single/
light cream in a ovenproof dish with
the grated Parmesan. Add the hot,
drained gnocchi and spinach (if using)
and stir well. Crumble the blue cheese
over and season with black pepper.

Preheat a grill/broiler to medium.

Slide the dish under the hot grill/
broiler for 5–7 minutes until the cheese
is bubbling. Serve straight away.

MAC 'N' CAULIFLOWER CHEESE

200 g/1⅔ cups dried macaroni
200 g/7 oz. cauliflower, cut into
  florets
2 garlic cloves, finely chopped
120 ml/½ cup dry white wine
2 tsp Dijon mustard
2 tsp freshly chopped thyme leaves,
  plus extra to serve
600 ml/2½ cups pouring/light cream
400 g/4¼ cups grated Cheddar
100 g/½ cup crème fraîche
1 tsp smoked paprika
100 g/3½ oz. Parmesan, grated
70 ml/⅓ cup olive oil
80 g/1½ cups coarse fresh sourdough
  breadcrumbs
grated zest of 1 lemon, plus extra
  to serve
sea salt and freshly ground black
  pepper
crisp-cooked pancetta slices,
  to serve (optional)

Preheat the oven to 180°C (350°F) Gas 4.

Start to cook the macaroni in a large saucepan of well-salted boiling water for about 6–7. Add the cauliflower to the same pan after 4 minutes. Drain, reserving 2 tbsp of the cooking water, then return both to the pan off the heat.

Stir in the garlic, wine, mustard and thyme. Add the cream, Cheddar, crème fraîche, paprika and half the Parmesan and oil. Season with salt and pepper, mix well, then transfer to four individual 450 ml/15 fl oz. baking dishes (or a large baking dish). Add a dash of cooking water if the mixture is looking too thick.

Mix together the breadcrumbs, lemon zest, remaining Parmesan and remaining oil in a bowl and season with salt and pepper. Scatter the crumbs over the pasta and bake in the preheated oven for 15–20 minutes until the filling is bubbling and the top is golden brown. Scatter with extra thyme and lemon zest and serve hot topped with the crispy cooked pancetta slices (if using).

MUSHROOMS 'N' CHEESE

100 g/3½ oz. feta, crumbled
50 g/1¾ oz. grated halloumi
100 g/scant ½ cup ricotta
6 Portobello or 8 Portobellini
  mushrooms
40 g/⅓ cup walnuts, chopped
6 fresh thyme sprigs, leaves picked
1 tbsp extra virgin olive oil
sea salt and freshly ground black
  pepper
1 tsp chilli flakes/hot red pepper
  flakes, to serve
1 tbsp runny honey, to serve
baby basil, to garnish (optional)

*baking sheet, lined with baking
  parchment*

Preheat the oven to 200°C (400°F) Gas 6.

Mix together the feta, halloumi and ricotta in a bowl. Arrange the mushrooms on the prepared baking sheet. Divide the cheese mixture between the mushrooms and sprinkle over the walnuts and thyme. Drizzle with the oil and season with salt and pepper.

Bake in the preheated oven for 15 minutes or until the cheese melts and the mushrooms are tender. Sprinkle with the chilli flakes/hot red pepper flakes and drizzle with the honey to serve. Garnish with baby basil, if you like.

YORKSHIRE PUDDINGS 2 WAYS

MAKES 12 INDIVIDUAL OR 1 LARGE

This basic Yorkshire pudding recipe works perfectly well on its own but if you feel you want to add an extra element, the grape or leek variations are delicious.

BASIC YORKSHIRE BATTER
250 g/1¾ cups plus 2 tbsp plain/
  all-purpose flour
150 ml/⅔ cup whole milk
4 eggs, beaten
2 tbsp sunflower oil
sea salt

*12-hole muffin pan, large roasting pan
  or ovenproof frying pan/skillet,
  greased well with fat or oil*

Sift the flour into a large bowl with a large pinch of salt. Combine the milk in a jug/pitcher with 150 ml/⅔ cup cold water. Make a well in the middle of the flour and add the eggs. Pour in a little milk and water, then whisk together into a smooth batter. Mix in the rest of the liquid, until you have a batter the consistency of single/light cream. Leave to stand at room temperature for at least 15 minutes.

Preheat the oven to 230°C (450°F) Gas 8 and put your chosen greased pan on a high shelf for 10 minutes to heat up.

If using a roasting pan or frying pan/skillet, take the pan out of the oven and place on the hob/stove-top over a medium heat while you pour in the batter. If using a muffin pan, simply quickly pour in the batter and return to the oven. If it doesn't immediately sizzle when added, return the pan to the oven to further preheat.

Cook the Yorkshires in the preheated oven for 15–20 minutes until well risen and golden. Watch towards the end of the cooking time, but don't open the door early or your puddings will sink.

BABY LEEK VARIATION

150 g/5½ oz. baby leeks, halved
  widthways and trimmed
5 fresh thyme sprigs
1 tbsp olive oil
1 x quantity Basic Yorkshire Batter
  (see above)

12-hole muffin pan, well-greased

Sauté the baby leeks with the thyme in the olive oil in a frying pan/skillet over a medium heat for 6 minutes. Preheat the muffin pan as instructed (above). Ladle in the batter, then quickly top each with the sautéed leeks and cook in the preheated oven as instructed above.

GRAPE VARIATION

150 g/5½ oz. red seedless grapes
1 tbsp runny honey
1 x quantity Basic Yorkshire Batter
  (see above)
sea salt and freshly ground black pepper

ovenproof frying pan/skillet, well-greased

Preheat the oven to 200°C (400°F) Gas 6 and put the pan/skillet in to warm for 10 minutes. Put the grapes into the hot pan/skillet, then drizzle with the honey and season with salt and pepper. Roast in the preheated oven for 8 minutes. Quickly pour in the batter and cook in the preheated oven at 230°C (450°F) Gas 8 as instructed above.

BRASSICAS 3 WAYS

This round up of brassica recipes is straightforward and flavour-packed, adventurous and a joy to serve. The cooking methods and additional ingredients are intended to bring out the inherently satisfying flavours of these vegetables.

SAUTÉED BRUSSELS WITH PANCETTA & HAZELNUTS

700 g/1 lb. 9 oz. Brussels sprouts
100 g/3½ oz. pancetta, thinly sliced
1 tbsp olive oil
50 ml/3½ tbsp white wine
50 g/⅓ cup hazelnuts, toasted
   and chopped
3 sprigs fresh lemon thyme, leaves
   picked
1 knob/pat butter
sea salt and freshly ground black
   pepper

Trim the stems of the sprouts and remove any yellow or spotted outer leaves. Coarsely shred the sprouts using the coarse shredding attachment in a food processor or using a sharp knife. Set aside.

Fry the pancetta in the oil in a frying pan/skillet over a medium-high heat until crisp. Remove with a slotted spoon to drain on some paper towels. Set aside, reserving the pancetta fat in the pan.

When ready to serve, reheat the fat in the pan until hot. Add the shredded sprouts and the wine. Sauté, stirring, for about 3–5 minutes until the sprouts are crisp-tender and bright green. Add the fried pancetta, the hazelnuts, thyme, butter and salt and pepper and toss to combine and melt the butter. Remove from the heat and serve.

SAVOY CABBAGE WEDGES IN KOMBU GARLIC BUTTER SAUCE

80 g/¾ stick butter
1 Savoy cabbage, cut into 6 wedges
2–3 garlic cloves, crushed, to taste
2 sheets vegetarian kombu, finely
   chopped
4 rehydrated dried shiitake
   mushrooms, finely chopped
1–2 tsp sherry vinegar, to taste
sea salt

large frying pan/skillet with a lid

In a large frying pan/skillet over a medium heat, melt 50 g/3½ tbsp of the butter and then add the cabbage wedges. Cook for 5 minutes, until browned on one side, then turn the wedges over and cover the pan with the lid. Cook for 10 minutes, until tender and a little browned. Just before serving, season lightly with salt.

Meanwhile, for the kombu garlic butter sauce, in a saucepan combine the garlic, kombu, mushrooms, vinegar and 225 ml/scant 1 cup water. Bring to the boil, then reduce the heat and simmer for 5 minutes.

Remove from the heat, and whisk in the remaining 30 g/¼ stick butter, a little at a time. Serve the warm cabbage wedges drizzled with the garlic butter sauce.

SESAME KALE WITH ZINGY DRESSING

2 bunches kale, ribs and stems
   removed, leaves torn
1 tbsp olive oil
2 tsp toasted sesame oil
sea salt and freshly ground black pepper
1 tbsp sesame seeds, to serve

ZINGY DRESSING
1 garlic clove, crushed
grated zest and freshly squeezed juice
   of 1 lemon
freshly squeezed juice of 1 lime
1 tsp yuzu juice
4 tbsp olive oil

large frying pan/skillet with a lid

Rinse the kale and then briefly shake
dry, leaving some water on the leaves.

Heat the olive oil and sesame oil
in the large pan over a medium heat.
Add the kale and season with salt and
pepper. Reduce the heat to medium-
low, then cover the pan with the lid
and cook, tossing occasionally, for
5 minutes until the kale is just tender.

To make the dressing, combine
the garlic, lemon zest, lemon, lime
and yuzu juices and oil in a small bowl.
Season with salt and pepper and whisk
together. Drizzle over the kale and
scatter with the sesame seeds to serve.

SUMMERY VEGETABLE SIDES 3 WAYS

Light, fresh and colourful, these sides all pair perfectly with many of the roasts. Try the slaw with ribs or beef brisket, the asparagus with a poultry recipe and the courgettes/zucchini with any of the more Mediterranean-sounding dishes.

CABBAGE, APPLE & CELERY SLAW

200 g/7 oz. white cabbage, core removed, finely shredded
200 g/7 oz. red cabbage, core removed, finely shredded
1 red onion, halved and thinly sliced
1 celery heart, base thinly sliced, stalks thinly sliced lengthways and placed in iced water, leaves reserved
1 Granny Smith apple, cored and cut into julienne

PARSLEY & APPLE CIDER DRESSING
80 ml/⅓ cup apple cider vinegar
60 ml/¼ cup apple juice
1 tsp maple syrup
2 tbsp extra virgin olive oil
3 tbsp freshly squeezed lemon juice
½ bunch fresh parsley, finely chopped
2 sprigs fresh tarragon, leaves picked and finely chopped
½ bunch fresh chives, chopped
sea salt and freshly ground black pepper

For the dressing, combine all the ingredients in a small bowl, whisk to combine and season to taste with salt and pepper. Set aside.

Place the slaw ingredients in a large serving bowl and toss to combine. Pour the dressing over, then toss gently to combine again and serve immediately.

SAUTÉED COURGETTES WITH BASIL & PARMESAN

2 tbsp olive oil
10 g/2 tsp butter
1–2 garlic cloves, to taste, finely chopped
3–4 courgettes/zucchini in mixed colours, cut into 1–2 cm/⅜–¾-inch slices on the diagonal
few drops freshly squeezed lemon juice (optional)
1 pinch ground sumac (optional)
1 pinch chilli flakes/hot red pepper flakes
30 g/1 oz. shaved Parmesan
20 g/¾ oz. fresh basil leaves
sea salt and freshly ground black pepper

Gently warm the oil and butter in a heavy-based saucepan over a low heat.

Add the garlic and courgettes/zucchini and cook, partially covered and stirring occasionally, until soft and starting to caramelize.

When the courgettes/zucchini are ready to serve, add a squeeze of lemon juice and pinch of sumac, if using. Place onto a serving plate and season with salt and plenty of black pepper. Top with the chilli flakes/hot red pepper flakes, Parmesan shavings and fresh basil leaves and serve.

ASPARAGUS IN LEMON & CAPER BROWN BUTTER

3 bunches asparagus, trimmed
80 g/¾ stick butter, diced
2 shallots, finely chopped
1 tbsp salted baby capers, rinsed and drained well
freshly squeezed juice of 1 lemon
sea salt
finely grated Parmesan, to serve
mini red chard, to garnish (optional)

Cook the asparagus in a large saucepan of salted boiling water for 2–3 minutes until just tender.

Drain, then transfer to a plate.

Put the butter in a frying pan/skillet over a high heat for 1–2 minutes until starting to turn nut-brown.

Remove from the heat, stir in the shallots, capers and lemon juice and spoon over the asparagus. Scatter over Parmesan, to taste, and mini red chard to garnish, if you like. Serve with the Easter Poussins, White Wine Sauce and Maxim Potatoes (see page 90).

TREATS & TIPPLES

These gorgeous desserts will satisfy your
sweet tooth and round off your roast. Whether
you want to make a treat for the family or give
your guests the perfect end to an evening, most
can be made in advance and finished just before
serving. The selection of tipples includes both
apéritifs and digestifs for those days when just
a nightcap is enough.

STICKY SPICED LOAF CAKE
WITH SALTED TOFFEE SAUCE & ROASTED PEARS

This loaf cake can be made in advance, then the dessert can be finished on the day with the freshly roasted pears and warm salted toffee sauce. The overall effect is reminiscent of sticky toffee pudding, but with added fruit and spice.

300 g/2¼ cups plain/all-purpose flour
1 tsp bicarbonate of soda/baking soda
  (dissolved in 2 tbsp hot water)
3 tsp ground ginger
½ tsp ground allspice
1 tsp ground cinnamon
150 g/¾ cup light brown soft sugar
100 g/⅓ cup black treacle/molasses
300 g/scant 1 cup golden/corn syrup
150 ml/⅔ cup whole milk
150 g/1¼ sticks unsalted butter
2 eggs, beaten
grated zest of 2 lemons

SALTED TOFFEE SAUCE
200 ml/generous ¾ cup double/heavy
  cream
60 g/½ stick butter, diced
80 g/scant ½ cup light brown soft sugar
¼ tsp ground allspice
½ tsp sea salt (or to taste)

*900-g/2-lb. loaf pan, greased and lined
  with baking parchment*

Preheat the oven to 160°C (325°F) Gas 3.

Combine the flour, dissolved bicarbonate of soda/baking soda and all the spices in a large mixing bowl and set aside.

Put the sugar, treacle/molasses, syrup, milk and butter in a medium saucepan over a low-medium heat and stir gently until the sugar has dissolved. Turn up the heat and bring the mixture to just below boiling point, then mix this straight into the bowl with the dry ingredients and allow to cool a little.

Beat in the eggs and lemon zest until the mixture is combined and it resembles a thick pancake batter. Pour this into the prepared loaf pan and bake in the preheated oven for 50–60 minutes, until a skewer inserted into the centre of the cake comes out fairly clean.

Leave the cake to cool completely in the pan before turning out.

Meanwhile, to make the toffee sauce, put the cream, butter, sugar and allspice in a saucepan over a gentle heat until the butter has melted and the sugar has dissolved. Turn the heat up slightly and let the mixture bubble, stirring, for 2–3 minutes until thick, toffee-coloured and silky. Stir in the sea salt to taste. Serve the warm toffee sauce poured over the cake with the Roasted Pears (below).

ROASTED PEARS

3–4 pears
2 tbsp white dessert wine
squeeze of fresh lemon juice
30 g/¼ stick butter, diced
2 tbsp caster/granulated sugar
thyme and shaved crystallised ginger, to
  decorate

Preheat the oven to 180°C (350°F) Gas 4.

Core the pears, cut into thirds and place in a baking dish. Drizzle with the wine and lemon juice and scatter with the butter and sugar. Roast in the preheated oven, turning occasionally, for 25–35 minutes until tender. Decorate with thyme and crystallized ginger.

YOGURT PANNA COTTAS
WITH APPLE & YUZU JELLY & PERSIAN CANDY FLOSS

Here is a simple, yet impressive looking and fresh-tasting dessert that can be prepared the day before and kept in the fridge overnight. This allows you to give the main course all your attention the next day and then wow your guests by whipping out these pre-made delights.

PANNA COTTAS
400 g/scant 2 cups Greek yogurt
200 ml/scant 1 cup double/heavy cream
5 tbsp runny honey (or to taste)
1 tsp vanilla paste
1 tsp yuzu juice
3 gelatine leaves, soaked in cold water for 5 minutes to soften

FOR THE APPLE & YUZU JELLY
250 ml/1 cup plus 1 tbsp good-quality apple juice (I like to use Golden Delicious)
1–2 tbsp yuzu juice, to taste
3 gelatine leaves, soaked in cold water for 5 minutes to soften

TO SERVE
Persian candy floss (optional)
Turkish delight squares

4 small wine glasses or wide, shallow glass tumblers

For the panna cottas, stir together the yogurt, cream, honey, vanilla and yuzu juice in a small saucepan. Warm through over a low heat until the mixture is hot but not bubbling. Remove the pan from the heat, then squeeze the water out of the gelatine leaves and stir in until dissolved.

Divide the mixture between the 4 wine glasses or tumblers. Leave to cool and then chill in the refrigerator for about 3–4 hours until set.

Meanwhile, make the apple and yuzu jelly. Put the apple juice into a saucepan and bring to a gentle simmer over a low heat. Remove from the heat and stir in the yuzu juice and squeezed-out gelatine until dissolved. Allow to cool, then transfer to a jug/pitcher and carefully divide between the tops of the set panna cottas in a fairly thin layer. Chill again for 3–4 hours until set, or until you are ready to serve.

Serve the yogurt panna cottas each topped with a little Persian candy floss, if you like, and with a few squares of Turkish delight on the side.

CHOCOLATE PASTRY TART
WITH CHOCOLATE CRÈME CHANTILLY, POACHED BERRIES
& SALTED HAZELNUT PRALINE

With chocolate pastry, creamy chocolate swirls, liqueur-poached berries
and praline, how else can I describe this dessert other than just sublime!

CHOCOLATE PASTRY
200 g/1½ cups plain/all-purpose flour,
   plus extra for dusting
60 g/½ cup icing/confectioners' sugar,
   sifted
30 g/generous ¼ cup cocoa powder
100 g/1 stick minus 1 tbsp cold salted
   butter, coarsely chopped
2 egg yolks

POACHED BERRIES
200 g/7 oz. blackcurrants or
pitted cherries (optional)
2 tbsp caster/granulated sugar
150 ml/⅔ cup crème de cassis
1½ tsp cornflour/cornstarch mixed
   with 1½ tsp water

SALTED HAZELNUT PRALINE
125 g/scant ⅔ cup minus 2 tsp caster/
   granulated sugar
40 g/⅓ cup roasted hazelnuts, warmed
   in a low oven
1–2 pinches sea salt

CHOCOLATE CRÈME CHANTILLY
200 ml/scant 1 cup double/heavy cream
30 g/4 tbsp icing/confectioners' sugar,
   sifted
scraped seeds of 1 vanilla pod/bean or
   1 tsp vanilla paste
250 g/1⅛ cups ricotta
200 g/7 oz. dark/bittersweet chocolate,
   melted and cooled a little

28-cm/11-inch loose-based tart pan
baking beans
baking sheet, greased with oil

For the chocolate pastry, blend the flour, icing/confectioners' sugar
and cocoa in a food processor until combined. Add the butter and
process until the mixture resembles fine crumbs, then add the egg
yolks and process to combine. Turn out onto a work surface and
bring the pastry together with the heel of your hand. Wrap in
clingfilm/plastic wrap and rest in the fridge for 1 hour.

Roll out the pastry on a lightly floured surface to 3-mm/⅛-inch
thick and line the tart pan, trimming the edges. Chill for 1 hour more.

Preheat the oven to 180°C (350°F) Gas 4.

Line the chilled pastry with baking parchment and fill with
baking beans. Blind-bake in the preheated oven for 15 minutes.
Remove the parchment and baking beans and bake for a further
8 minutes until dry and crisp. Leave the tart case to cool completely.

To make the poached berries, place the fruit in a saucepan with
the sugar and crème de cassis over a low heat for 3–5 minutes until
the sugar has dissolved. Stir through the cornflour/cornstarch
mixture and heat through until the fruit is coated in sticky syrup.
Leave to cool and then refrigerate until needed.

To make the salted hazelnut praline, stir together the sugar and
60 ml/¼ cup water in a saucepan over a medium-high heat until the
sugar has dissolved. Brush down the sides of the pan with a wet
pastry brush to remove any sugar crystals and simmer without
stirring, swirling the pan occasionally, for 8–12 minutes until the
mixture turns into a rich caramel. Stir in the warm nuts, then tip the
mixture onto the prepared baking sheet (be careful, as the caramel
will be very hot) and set aside for 20–25 minutes until set. Break into
pieces, then process to coarse crumbs in a food processor.

For the crème Chantilly, whisk the cream, sugar and vanilla
together in a bowl until soft peaks form; refrigerate until required.

To assemble the tart, swirl the ricotta with the melted chocolate
and crème Chantilly and dollop into the pastry case. Remove the tart
from the pan and top with the poached berries and praline.

COCONUT CHEESECAKE
WITH ROASTED PINEAPPLE & FRESH MANGO

Tropical sunshine meets classic cheesecake in this very easy to prepare dessert. With a roasted and fresh fruit topping, this summery treat would provide a perfect happy ending to a main course with spicy Asian, Carribbean or Mexican flavours.

650 g/3 scant cups cream cheese,
   at room temperature
110 g/½ cup plus 1 tbsp rapadura sugar
   (raw cane sugar)
3 eggs
300 ml/1⅓ cups coconut cream
finely grated zest and juice of 2 limes
1 tsp vanilla paste

COCONUT BASE
130 g/4½ oz. digestive biscuits/graham
   crackers
60 g/generous ¾ cup desiccated/dried
   shredded coconut
100 g/1 stick minus 1 tbsp butter, melted

ROASTED PINEAPPLE
190 g/scant 1 cup soft light brown sugar
1 fresh ripe pineapple, peeled, cored
   and cut into chunks
freshly squeezed juice of 2 limes
1 fresh firm mango, peeled, pitted
   and spiralized or grated, to serve
fresh mint leaves, to decorate

*23-cm/9-inch loose-based cake pan,
   buttered and base-lined with baking
   parchment*

Preheat the oven to 180°C (350°F) Gas 4.

First, make the coconut base. Blitz the biscuits/graham crackers to fine crumbs in a food processor. Tip into a bowl and mix with the desiccated/dried shredded coconut and melted butter. Press into the base of the prepared cake pan in an even layer and bake in the preheated oven for 7 minutes until golden.

Remove the base from the oven and leave to cool slightly. Reduce the oven temperature to 160°C (325°F) Gas 3.

Meanwhile, blend the cream cheese with the rapadura (raw cane sugar) in a food processor until smooth. Add the eggs, one at a time, processing after each addition to combine. Add the coconut cream, lime zest and juice and vanilla paste and process one last time until the ingredients are well combined. Pour the mixture over the baked coconut base and smooth over with a spatula. Bake in the preheated oven for 30–35 minutes until lightly golden on top and set around the edges with a slight wobble in the centre. Leave to cool to room temperature, then refrigerate for 2–3 hours until completely chilled.

Meanwhile, to make the roasted pineapple, preheat the oven to 180°C (350°F) Gas 4.

Spread the brown sugar in the base of a roasting tray. Add the pineapple chunks in a single layer. Roast in the preheated oven, turning occasionally, until the sugar has melted and the pineapple has become caramelized.

Remove the fruit to a bowl and strain the syrup from the pan into another bowl. Stir the lime juice into the syrup and refrigerate both the pineapple and syrup separately until chilled.

Serve the cheesecake topped with the caramelized pineapple and spiralized fresh mango. Drizzle with the syrup and sprinkle with fresh mint leaves to decorate.

MELON SALAD
WITH ORANGE BLOSSOM SYRUP &
HOMEMADE MANGO & PASSION FRUIT SORBET

The ultimate refreshing dessert, this is a simple but effective combination of tangy fruit, fragrant syrup and smooth, intensely flavoured sorbet.

200 g/7 oz. peeled seedless watermelon
   flesh, cut into fingers
150 g/5½ oz. peeled honeydew melon
   flesh, cut into wedges and/or balls
200 g/7 oz. seedless red grapes, halved
   lengthways
100 g/generous ¾ cup lychees,
   peeled and deseeded
50 g/⅔ cup pomegranate seeds
freshly squeezed juice of 1 lime
pulp from 1 passion fruit
edible flowers, to garnish (optional)

ORANGE BLOSSOM SYRUP
250 g/1¼ cups caster/granulated sugar
freshly squeezed juice of 2 blood
   oranges or normal oranges
2–3 tsp orange blossom water,
   or to taste

To make the orange blossom syrup, combine the sugar with 100 ml/⅓ cup plus 1 tbsp water in a saucepan and stir over a medium-high heat until the sugar has dissolved.

Brush down the sides of the pan with a wet pastry brush to prevent sugar crystals from forming, and continue to heat through for about 4–5 minutes until a light syrup has formed.

Remove from the heat and gradually add the orange juice (be careful as the mixture may spit). Return to the heat and stir to combine, then simmer until the mixture is syrupy. Remove from the heat and stir in the orange blossom water. Set aside to cool.

Meanwhile, prepare and slice the rest of the fruit for the fruit salad and divide between your serving bowls. Squeeze over the lime juice and scatter over the passion fruit pulp. Add a scoop of Mango & Passion Fruit Sorbet (below) to each bowl and drizzle with the cooled orange blossom syrup. Garnish with edible flowers, if liked.

MANGO & PASSION FRUIT SORBET

175 g/¾ cup plus 2 tbsp golden
   caster sugar
1 tbsp glucose syrup
2 fresh mangoes, peeled, pitted
   and chopped
pulp of 6 passion fruit
freshly squeezed juice of 2 limes

ice cream machine

Combine the sugar, glucose syrup and 175 ml/¾ cup water in a saucepan. Warm through and stir over a medium heat until the sugar has dissolved, then simmer for 3 minutes until syrupy.

Pour the syrup into a jug/pitcher and top up with cold water to make the total volume around 450 ml/scant 2 cups. Set aside.

Purée the mangoes in a blender and pass through a sieve/strainer into a bowl. Sieve/strain the seeds out of the passion fruit pulp. Stir the mango purée, passion fruit juice and lime juice into the jug/pitcher of syrup. Pour into an ice cream machine and then churn following the manufacturer's instructions.

Spoon the churned sorbet into a container and freeze until needed, removing it from the freezer 20 minutes before serving so that it can soften a little.

SPARKLING SORBET COCKTAILS 3 WAYS

Somewhere between a palate-cleansing dessert and a scrumptious cocktail, for those occasions when you want something sweet but a bit lighter, one of these is perfect. I can think of nothing more pleasant to sip on a warm afternoon!

PROSECCO PASSION

**1 tbsp passion fruit pulp, seeds removed
(fruit husks reserved to decorate)
15 ml/½ fl oz. peach liqueur
chilled Prosecco, to top up
1 scoop mango and passion fruit sorbet
(ready-made or see recipe page 144)**

Place the passion fruit pulp into the bottom of a Champagne coupe and then add the peach liqueur. Top up with Prosecco and gently drop the scoop of sorbet into the glass. Decorate with the reserved passion fruit husks, if you like.

POMEGRANATE SCROPPINO

**15 ml/½ fl oz. vodka
freshly squeezed juice of ½ lemon
chilled Prosecco, to top up
dash agave syrup, or to taste
1 scoop ready-made pomegranate sorbet
1 tsp pomegranate seeds, to decorate**

Place the vodka and lemon juice in a Champagne coupe and top up with Prosecco. Stir in the agave syrup. Gently drop the scoop of sorbet into the glass and decorate with the pomegranate seeds.

MARGARITA FIZZ

**30 ml/1 fl oz. tequila
chilled good soda water/club soda or
tonic water for a more bitter taste
dash agave syrup, or to taste
1 scoop ready-made lime sorbet
fresh lime slice, to decorate**

Pour the tequila into a Champagne coupe. Top up with soda water/club soda or tonic water, as preferred, and mix in the agave syrup. Gently drop in the scoop of sorbet and decorate with the slice of fresh lime.

MATCHA & LIME TRAYBAKE
WITH LIME CRÈME FRAÎCHE FROSTING
& MINI MERINGUES

A popular ingredient in Asian desserts, matcha powder is made from powdered green tea leaves. It makes this cake a very pretty green colour, especially when paired with snowy white meringues and pink petals. The green tea element in this moist cake is subtle and marries well with the lime and the lovely light frosting.

40 g/3 tbsp butter, softened
220 g/1 cup plus 2 tbsp caster/
    granulated sugar
140 ml/scant ⅔ cup vegetable oil
4 eggs
60 ml/¼ cup buttermilk
1 tsp vanilla paste
25 g/¾ oz. matcha powder, sifted
250 g/1¾ cups plus 2 tbsp self-raising/
    self-rising flour
grated zest of 3 limes
store-bought mini meringues or crushed
    large meringues, to serve
pale pink edible flower petals,
    to decorate

CRÈME FRAÎCHE FROSTING
100 g/½ cup crème fraîche, chilled
200 g/1 cup minus 2 tbsp full-fat
    cream cheese
50 g/3½ tbsp unsalted butter, well
    softened
150 g/1¼ cups icing/confectioners'
    sugar, sifted
freshly squeezed juice of 1 lime

18 x 30-cm/7 x 12-inch rectangular cake
    pan, buttered, base-lined with baking
    parchment and sides dusted with flour

Preheat the oven to 160°C (325°F) Gas 3.

Beat together the butter, sugar and oil in an electric stand mixer or using a hand-held electric whisk for about 2–3 minutes until pale. Add the eggs, one at a time, beating well between additions.

Gradually beat in the buttermilk, then the vanilla and matcha. Sift in the flour and add the lime zest and fold to combine. Pour the cake mixture into the prepared pan, then smooth the top and bake in the preheated oven for 25–30 minutes until risen and the centre springs back when lightly pressed. Leave to cool in the pan for 10 minutes, then turn out onto a wire rack to cool completely.

To make the frosting, beat together the crème fraîche, cream cheese, butter, icing/confectioners' sugar and lime juice until combined into a light and fluffy frosting. Spread over the cooled cake and decorate with mini meringues or crushed meringue and pale pink edible flower petals.

MARTINIS 3 WAYS

The perfect martini can be either shaken or stirred, dirty or dry, you name it, there are many variations on this classic. Whether you try the zesty lime, delicate rose or something different with the cool and dirty, these are bound to go down a treat.

LIME MARTINI

60 ml/2 fl oz. gin
30 ml/1 fl oz. dry martini
3 tsp triple sec
freshly squeezed juice of 1 lime
handful of ice
lime wedges and/or Thai basil,
   to garnish (optional)

Combine the gin, dry martini, triple sec and lime juice in a cocktail shaker or mixing glass with a handful of ice. Stir well, then strain into a martini glass. Garnish the drink with some lime wedges and/or Thai basil, if you like.

COOL & DIRTY MARTINI

½ cucumber, chopped
60 ml/2 fl oz. gin
30 ml/1 fl oz. dry martini
1–2 tsp olive brine
handful of ice
cucumber flower, to garnish (optional)
green olives and blue cheese, to serve

Muddle the cucumber in the base of a cocktail shaker or mixing glass, then add the gin, dry martini and olive brine with a handful of ice. Stir well, then strain into a martini glass. Garnish with a cucumber flower, if you like, and serve with green olives stuffed with blue cheese.

ROSE MARTINI

45 ml/1⅓ fl oz. gin
20 ml/⅔ fl oz. dry martini
3 tsp white crème de cacao (optional)
3 tsp good-quality rose syrup or 2–3
   drops rose water
handful of ice
edible rose petals, to garnish (optional)

Combine the gin, dry martini, crème de cacao (if using) and rose syrup or rose water in a cocktail shaker or mixing glass with a handful of ice. Stir well, then strain into a martini glass. Garnish with rose petals, if you like.

AFTER DINNER DRINKS 3 WAYS

 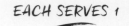

These sophisticated brandy-based cocktails are typically intended to remedy the effects of a hangover, but I think they are perfect for serving before a meal, especially on a Sunday just before a roast.

BRANDY BITTERS

30 ml/1 fl oz. brandy
squeeze of lemon juice
20 ml/⅔ fl oz. orange Curaçao
1 tsp simple sugar syrup
2 dashes Angostura bitters
soda water/club soda, to top up

Combine all the ingredients, apart from the soda water/club soda, in a cocktail shaker with ice. Shake, then pour into a tall glass over ice. Top up with soda water/club soda and stir.

CORPSE REVIVER

40 ml/1⅓ fl oz. brandy
dash grenadine
squeeze of fresh orange juice
Champagne, to top up
orange zest, to garnish

Pour the brandy, grenadine and squeeze of orange juice into a Champagne coupe. Top up with Champagne and garnish with orange zest.

BRANDY FIX

40 ml/1⅓ fl oz. brandy
20 ml/⅔ fl oz. freshly squeezed
    lemon juice
100 ml/3⅓ fl oz. pineapple juice
1 tsp simple sugar syrup
ice
a dash yellow chartreuse

Combine all the ingredients, apart from the yellow chartreuse, in a cocktail shaker with ice. Shake, then pour into a small tumbler over ice. Top with the dash of yellow chartreuse.

COFFEE NIGHTCAPS 3 WAYS

What more could you want at the end of a meal than one of these slightly boozy coffee cocktails? The perfect way to end an evening.

MEXICAN COFFEE

40 ml/1⅓ fl oz. tequila
20 ml/⅔ fl oz. kahlúa
240 ml/1 cup strong hot freshly
  brewed coffee
vanilla ice cream, to serve
chopped coffee beans and/or cocoa nibs
  and cinnamon sticks, to garnish
  (optional)

Combine the tequila, kahlúa and coffee in a jug/pitcher. Decant into small glass tumblers and top each with a scoop of vanilla ice cream. Garnish with chopped coffee beans and/or cocoa nibs and a cinnamon stick, if you like.

IRISH COFFEE

50 g/1¾ fl oz. instant coffee
50 ml/fl 1⅔ fl oz. Irish whiskey
2 tsp light brown sugar
60 ml/¼ cup double/heavy cream,
  lightly whipped to thicken
cocoa powder, to garnish (optional)

Make a pot of instant coffee and pour 400 ml/1¾ cups into a jug/pitcher. Add the whiskey and sugar and stir to dissolve. Decant into two tall Irish coffee glasses. Spoon the cream over each coffee, so that it sits on the top. Sprinkle with a little cocoa powder to garnish, if you like.

ESPRESSO GRANITA

150 g/¾ cup caster/granulated sugar
4 tbsp ground Arabica coffee

muslin/cheesecloth
shallow freezerproof container

Put the sugar and 150 ml/⅔ cup water in a small saucepan over a low heat. Stir to dissolve the sugar, then increase the heat and boil for 1 minute. Remove from the heat and leave to cool.

Put the ground coffee and 500 ml/generous 2 cups water in a saucepan over a high heat. Bring to the boil and boil for 1 minute. Remove from the heat and set aside until cold.

Strain the cold coffee mixture through a muslin/cheesecloth-lined sieve/strainer into the freezerproof container. Mix in the sugar syrup, then cover and freeze for 2 hours.

Gently scrape the frozen edges into the centre and break into smaller crystals with a fork. Freeze for a further 30 minutes, then repeat the freezing and breaking process 2–3 times, until granulated in texture with small ice crystals. Serve.

MENU SUGGESTIONS

Whether you go for the traditional three courses or serve a few platters for everyone to share, there are plenty of dishes in this book that can be mixed and matched to create your ideal menu. Here are some ideas to get you started!

FESTIVE FEAST

Slow-roasted Shin of Veal (*see page 109*)

Lemon & Herb Potato Wedges (*see page 122*)

Sautéed Brussels Sprouts with Pancetta & Hazelnuts (*see page 130*)

Baby Leek Yorkshire Puddings (*see page 128*)

Chocolate Pastry Tart with Chocolate Crème Chantilly, Poached Berries & Salted Hazelnut Praline (*see page 140*)

Irish Coffees (*see page 155*)

RELAXED SUMMER PARTY

Lemon & Oregano Roast Chicken with Caramelized Lemons (*see page 19*)

Whole Roasted Cauliflower with Chimichurri Sauce (*see page 36*)

Sautéed Courgettes with Basil & Parmesan (*see page 133*)

Coconut Cheesecake with Roasted Pineapple & Fresh Mango (*see page 143*)

Prosecco Passion Sparkling Sorbet Cocktails (*see page 147*)

SIMPLE DINNER PARTY

Cool & Dirty Martinis (*see page 151*)

Appetizer to share of Salmon Inferno With Karedok Salad (*see page 46*)

Quick Roast Beef Fillet with Parsnip & Potato Fries, Peppercorn Sauce & Rocket (*see page 48*)

Roasted Pears with Salted Toffee Sauce (*see page 136*)

FATHER'S DAY

Asian Five-spiced Lamb Shanks with Mushroom Sticky Rice (*see page 102*)

Miso & Umeboshi Baked Pumpkin (*see page 90*)

Savoy Cabbage Wedges in Kombu Garlic Butter Sauce (*see page 130*)

Matcha Tray Bake (*see page 148*)

Lime Martinis (*see page 151*)

MAY DAY CELEBRATION

Garlic-infused Slow Roast Leg of Lamb
on Layered Potatoes (*see page 61*)

Grilled Watermelon & Feta Salad
(*see page 77*)

Roasted Root Vegetables & Oven-dried
Persimmon (*see page 94*)

Melon Salad with Orange Blossom Syrup &
Homemade Mango & Passion Fruit Sorbet
(*see page 144*)

Brandy Fix Cocktails (*see page 152*)

WINTER WARMERS

Cider Pork Belly with Kumquat Relish
& Rhubarb Pickle (*see page 64*)

Classic Roasties Spiced with Baharat
(*see page 122*)

Sesame Kale with Zingy Dressing
(*see page 131*)

Sticky Spiced Loaf Cake with Salted Toffee
Sauce & Roasted Pears (*see page 136*)

Mexican Coffee (*see page 155*)

ROMANTIC VALENTINE'S DAY MEAL

Brandy Bitters apéritifs (*see page 152*)

Appetizer to share of Roasted Artichokes
with Agrodolce Sauce, Quails' Eggs, &
Herby Scones (*see page 110*)

Roasted Hake Nicoise-ish Salad with
Tartare Dressing & Garlic Bread Shards
(*see page 28*)

Yogurt Panna Cottas With Apple & Yuzu
Jelly & Persian Candy Floss (*see page 139*)

LAZY SUNDAY

Rum Ribs (*see page 114*)

Adobo Black Beans (*see page 39*)

Corn & Nectarine Salsa (*see page 97*)

Marmite Sweet Potatoes (*see page 125*)

Mushrooms 'n' Cheese (*see page 127*)

Mango & Passion Fruit Sorbet
(*see page 144*)

INDEX

A

adobo black beans 39
agrodolce sauce 111
aioli, paprika 125
almond, oregano & lemon crumb 66
apples: apple & yuzu jelly 139
  baked sage & Calvados apples 20
  cabbage, apple & celery slaw 133
artichokes, roasted 110
Asian five-spiced lamb shanks 102
asparagus: asparagus in lemon & caper brown butter 133
  quick asparagus & carrot kimchi 91
aubergines/eggplant: Gochujang roasted aubergine steaks 44
  imam bayildi roasted aubergines 70

B

baharat, classic roasties spiced with 122
beef 8
  braised beef cheeks 58
  quick roast beef fillet 48
  roast beef on the bone 14
  spiced slow-roasted beef brisket buns 54
beetroot, blood orange & horseradish salad 15
black beans: adobo black beans 39
  lover's pot roast chicken 96
blackcurrants: poached berries 140
bone, roasting on 8
brandade 116
brandy: hair of the dog 3 ways 152
bread: bread sauce 85
  charcoal flatbreads 23
  garlic bread shards 28
  lavash bread 76
  spiced slow-roasted beef brisket buns 54
broccoli: greens in caramelized tamari butter dressing 51
Brussels with pancetta & hazelnuts 130
butternut squash: hasselback butternut squash 84
  stuffed & roasted butternut squash 42

C

cabbage: cabbage, apple & celery slaw 133
  sauerkraut 55
  Savoy cabbage wedges 130
  sticky plum-roasted cabbages 68
cakes: matcha & lime traybake 148
  sticky spiced loaf cake 136
capers: caper dressing 117
  crispy capers 125
caramel: caramelized honey & chilli lemons 19
  salted hazelnut praline 140
carrots: quick asparagus & carrot kimchi 91
  roasted carrots & kale 85
cashews: green beans & glazed cashews 68
cauliflower: mac 'n' cauliflower cheese 127
  warm winter salad 109
  whole roasted cauliflower 36
charcoal flatbreads 23
cheese: gnocchi 'n' blue cheese 126
  grilled watermelon & feta salad 77
  herby cheese scones 110
  honey & sesame fried Saganaki cheese 71
  mac 'n' cauliflower cheese 127
  mushrooms 'n' cheese 127
  Parmesan crisps 80
  Taleggio sauce 111
  twice-baked stuffed potatoes 115
cheesecake, coconut 143
chicken 10
  charred chicken 106
  lemon & oregano roast chicken 19
  lover's pot roast chicken 96
  mojo chicken 39
  see also cockerel
chillies: green chilli & coconut sambal 32
  lover's pot roast chicken 96
  pickled jalapeños 97
  salsa criolla 58
chimichurri sauce 36
chips, tofu 68
chocolate pastry tart 140
chorizo: lover's pot roast chicken 96
cider pork belly 64
cockerel 10
  truffle roasted cockerel 84
coconut: coconut cheesecake 143

green chilli & coconut sambal 32
coffee: espresso granita 155
  Irish coffee 155
  Mexican coffee 155
corn: corn & nectarine salsa 97
  olive & corn-topped polenta 59
corpse reviver 152
courgettes/zucchini: courgette pancakes 91
  farro & courgette salad 38
  sautéed courgettes with basil & Parmesan 133
crackling 20
crème Chantilly, chocolate 140
crème fraîche frosting 148
cucumbers: smashed Sichuan cucumber 102
  soused cucumber 61
cumin pumpkin whip 14
curry: over-charred curried pork chops 32

D

dates: saffron & date pilaf 95
devils on horseback 88
duck 10
  Indian spiced slow-cooked duck 74

E

earth spice rub 54
Easter poussins 92
eggs: egg hoppers 75
  vegetable egg fried rice 45
espresso granita 155

F

farro & courgette salad 38
fish: roasting techniques 10
  see also monkfish; salmon etc
flatbreads, charcoal 23
freekeh: sausage & freekeh crumb 85
fregola salad, warm 80
fries, parsnip & potato 48
frosting, crème fraîche 148

G

garlic: garlic bread shards 28
  garlic-infused slow roast leg of lamb 61
gin: Martinis 151
gnocchi 'n' blue cheese 126
Gochujang roasted aubergine steaks 44
granita, espresso 155
grapes, Yorkshire pudding with 128

gravy, Marsala 85
green beans: green beans & glazed cashews 68
  karedok salad 46
green quartet 117
greens in caramelized tamari butter dressing 51

H

hair of the dog 152
hake Nicoise-ish salad 28
hasselback butternut squash 84
hazelnuts: salted hazelnut praline 140
  sautéed Brussels with pancetta & hazelnuts 130
herb & walnut dressing 109
herby grain bowl 35
honey & sesame fried Saganaki cheese 71
horseradish dressing 15

I

imam bayildi roasted aubergines 70
Indian spiced slow-cooked duck 74
Irish coffee 155

J

jelly, apple & yuzu 139

K

kale: roasted carrots & kale 85
karedok salad 46
ketchup, pomegranate 27
kimchi, quick asparagus & carrot 91
kumquat relish 65

L

labneh, pistachio 36
lamb 8
  Asian five-spiced lamb shanks 102
  garlic-infused slow roast leg of lamb 61
  lamb cutlet rack 22
  rosemary lamb neck fillets 35
lavash bread 76
leeks, Yorkshire pudding with 128
lemon: caramelized honey & chilli lemons 19
  lemon & herb potato wedges 122
  lemon & oregano roast chicken 19
lentils: stuffed & roasted butternut squash 42

lettuce, charred 61
limes: lime Martini 151
    matcha & lime traybake 148
lover's pot roast chicken 96

M
mac 'n' cauliflower cheese 127
mango, brown sugar
    pineapple & 143
maple & ginger turkey crown
    88
margarita fizz sorbet cocktail
    147
marmite sweet potatoes 125
Marsala gravy 85
Martinis 151
matcha & lime traybake 148
maxim potatoes 90
mayonnaise: Russian-ish sauce
    55
meat: roasting techniques
    8–10
    see also beef, lamb etc
melon salad 144
menu planner 156–7
meringues, mini 148
Mexican coffee 155
Middle Eastern spiced venison
    shawarma 76
mint & spinach yogurt 94
miso & umeboshi baked
    pumpkin 90
mojo chicken 39
monkfish, soy & sesame baked
    51
mushrooms: mushroom sticky
    rice 103
    mushrooms 'n' cheese 127
    roasted mushrooms 80

N
nectarines: corn & nectarine
    salsa 97

O
octopus plaki 66
okra, crispy 75
olive & corn topped polenta
    59
orange blossom syrup 144
oranges: beetroot, blood orange
    & horseradish salad 15

P
pancakes, courgette 91
pancetta, sautéed Brussels
    with 130
panna cottas, yogurt 139
paprika aioli 125
Parmesan crisps 80
parsnip & potato oven fries 48

passion fruit: Prosecco passion
    sorbet cocktail 147
pea & olive pistou 22
pears, roasted 136
peppercorn sauce 49
peppers (bell): mojo chicken 39
persimmon, oven-dried 94
pickles: pickled jalapeños 97
    pickled vegetables 62
    rhubarb pickle 65
pilaf, saffron & date 95
pineapple: brown sugar
    pineapple & mango 143
pistachio labneh 36
pistou, pea & olive 22
plums: sticky plum-roasted
    cabbages 68
polenta, olive & corn topped
    59
pomegranate: pomegranate
    ketchup 27
    pomegranate scroppino 147
porchetta, stuffed 62
pork 10
    cider pork belly 64
    over-charred curried pork
        chops 32
    perfect crackling roast pork
        20
    rum ribs 114
    stuffed porchetta 62
potatoes: classic roasties
    spiced with baharat 122
    garlic-infused slow roast leg
        of lamb & layered
        potatoes 61
    lemon & herb potato
        wedges 122
    maxim potatoes 90
    roasted hake Nicoise-ish
        salad 28
    smoked baby potatoes with
        paprika aioli 125
    twice-baked stuffed
        potatoes 115
    velvet pomme purée 107
poultry: roasting techniques 10
    see also chicken, turkey etc
poussins 10
    Easter poussins 92
praline, salted hazelnut 140
Prosecco sorbet cocktails 147
prunes: charred chicken 106
pumpkin: cumin pumpkin
    whip 14
    miso & umeboshi baked
        pumpkin 90

Q
quinoa: herby grain bowl 35
    saffron & date pilaf 95

R
relish, kumquat 65
rhubarb pickle 65
rice: mushroom sticky rice 103
    vegetable egg fried rice 45
    see also wild rice
roasting techniques 8–11
root vegetables, roasted 94
rose Martini 151
rosemary lamb neck fillets 35
rum ribs 114
Russian-ish sauce 55

S
saffron & date pilaf 95
salads: beetroot, blood orange
    & horseradish salad 15
    cabbage, apple & celery
        slaw 133
    farro & courgette salad 38
    grilled watermelon & feta
        salad 77
    karedok salad 46
    roasted hake Nicoise-ish
        salad 28
    warm fregola salad 80
    warm winter salad 109
salmon inferno 46
salsas: corn & nectarine salsa 97
    salsa criolla 58
salt cod: brandade 116
salt-crusted sea bass 116
salted hazelnut praline 140
salted toffee sauce 136
sambal, green chilli & coconut
    32
sauerkraut 55
sausage & freekeh crumb 85
Savoy cabbage wedges 130
scones, herby cheese 110
sea bass, salt-crusted 116
seaweed crumb 51
sesame kale 131
sorbet, mango & passion fruit
    144
sorbet cocktails 147
soused cucumber 61
soy & sesame baked monkfish
    51
spinach: mint & spinach
    yogurt 94
    spinach & raisin dip 77
squash see butternut squash
sticky spiced loaf cake 130
sweet potatoes: marmite
    sweet potatoes 125
    parsnip & potato oven fries 48

T
tahini yogurt, herby 71
Taleggio sauce 111

tamari butter dressing 51
tart, chocolate pastry 140
tartare dressing 28
tequila: margarita fizz sorbet
    cocktail 147
    Mexican coffee 155
toffee sauce, salted 136
tofu chips 68
tomatoes: charred tomato
    yogurt dressing 35
    dried tomatoes 23
    pomegranate ketchup 27
    roasted tomatoes 23
tostadas 97
truffle roasted cockerel 84
turkey: maple & ginger turkey
    crown 88

U
ultimate veggie roast 26–7

V
veal, slow-roasted shin of 109
vegetables: green quartet 117
    pickled vegetables 62
    roasted root vegetables 94
    roasting techniques 10–11
    ultimate veggie roast 26–7
    vegetable egg fried rice 45
    see also aubergines,
        tomatoes etc
velvet pomme purée 107
venison shawarma 76

W
walnuts: herb & walnut
    dressing 109
warm winter salad 109
watermelon: grilled watermelon
    & feta salad 77
    melon salad 144
whiskey: Irish coffee 155
wild rice: saffron & date pilaf 95
wine: Marsala gravy 85
    pomegranate scroppino 147
    Prosecco passion sorbet
        cocktail 147
    white wine sauce 90

Y
yogurt: charred tomato yogurt
    dressing 35
    herby tahini yogurt 71
    pistachio labneh 36
    yogurt panna cottas 139
Yorkshire puddings 128

Z
zingy dressing 131

Senior designer Megan Smith
Design assistance Emily Breen
Commissioning editor Alice Sambrook
Production manager Gordana Simakovic
Art director Leslie Harrington
Editorial director Julia Charles
Publisher Cindy Richards

Prop stylist Olivia Wardle
Food stylist Kathy Kordalis
Indexer Hilary Bird

First published in 2018 by
Ryland Peters & Small
20–21 Jockey's Fields, London
WC1R 4BW
and 341 E 116th St, New York NY 10029
www.rylandpeters.com

10 9 8 7 6 5 4 3 2 1

ISBN: 978-1-78879-027-7

Printed in China

NOTES
· Both British (Metric) and American (Imperial
plus US cups) measurements are included in these
recipes for your convenience, however it is important
to work with one set of measurements only and
not alternate between the two within a recipe.
· Ovens should be preheated to the specified
temperatures. We recommend using an oven
thermometer. If using a fan-assisted oven, adjust
temperatures according to the manufacturer's
instructions.
· All butter is salted unless otherwise specified.
· All eggs are medium (UK) or large (US), unless
specified as large, in which case US extra-large
should be used. Uncooked or partially cooked eggs
should not be served to the very old, frail, young
children, pregnant women or those with
compromised immune systems.
· When a recipe calls for grated zest of citrus fruit,
buy unwaxed fruit and wash well before using. If
you can only find treated fruit, scrub well in warm
soapy water before using.
· When a recipe refers to flavourless oil, use an oil
such as sunflower, rapeseed or vegetable oil which
won't overpower the other flavours in the dish.

ACKNOWLEDGEMENTS

Thank you to Mowie Kay for being a true gent and a super-talented photographer,
you are truly inspirational. Olivia Wardle, thank you for the beautiful props and
styling – it has been a treat to work with you! You added the most elegant touches,
which just elevated this project. Sarah Fassnidge, thank you for tasting and testing
all the recipes – your skills and opinion are invaluable to me. Evangeline Hardbury,
thank you for all your calm assistance and reassurance on set, and for just being a
pleasure to be around. To the wonderful Leiths team, who kindly offered their time
and talent, Sian Williams, Lauren Cartridge and Sophie Wyburd, thank you all!

At Ryland Peters & Small, the marvellous Megan Smith, thank you for your
counsel, vision and hilarious wit! You bring so much enjoyment to any project. Thank
you Alice Sambrook for your patience in checking, correcting and generally tirelessly
editing my work – what a gem! Thank you to Leslie Harrington and Julia Charles for
your guidance and encouragement and for always being available. To my publisher
Cindy Richards for giving me the opportunity to work on such a lovely project with
a great team.

Finally, thank you to my friends and family the world over for your support!

For Matthew, my favourite taster!

THE

MINDS

OF THE

WEST

THE

MINDS

OF THE

WEST

Ethnocultural Evolution in
the Rural Middle West, 1830–1917

Jon Gjerde

The University of North Carolina Press | Chapel Hill and London

Library of Congress Cataloging-in-Publication Data

Gjerde, Jon, 1953–

The minds of the West : ethnocultural evolution in the rural

Middle West, 1830–1917 / Jon Gjerde.

p. cm.   Includes bibliographical references and index.

ISBN 0-8078-2312-0 (cloth : alk. paper)

1. Ethnology—Middle West.   2. Middle West—Social conditions.

3. Acculturation—Middle West.   4. Immigrants—Middle West—

History.   5. Migration, Internal—Middle West—History.   I. Title.

F358.G58   1997   96-22213

306'.0978—dc20   CIP

01 00 99 98 97   5 4 3 2 1

For Ferne Sorenson Gjerde Aurand

CONTENTS

Acknowledgments xi

Introduction 1

Part One. The Region

1. The Prospects of the West: A Promise and a Threat 25

2. The Burden of Their Song:
Immigrant Encounters with the Republic 51

Part Two. The Community

3. We'll Meet on Canaan's Land: Patterns of Migration 79

4. You Can't Put All Your Horses in One Corral:
Conflict and Community 103

Part Three. The Family

5. Farming Is a Hard Life:
Household and the Agricultural Workplace 135

6. A Tale of Two Households: Patterns of Family 159

7. Mothers and Siblings among the Corn Rows:
The Individual Life Course and Community Development 187

Part Four. The Society

8. They Soon Abandoned Their Wooden Shoes:
Ethnic Group Formation 225

9. Teach the Children Domestic Economy:
Conceptions of Family, Community, and State 251

10. So Great Is Now the Spirit of Foreign Nationality:
Late-Nineteenth-Century Political Conflict 283

Epilogue 319

Notes 327

Index 411

Contents

TABLES AND FIGURES

Tables

3.1 First Place of Residence, Immigrants from Fortun, by Date of Emigration 95

4.1 Patterns of Intermarriage within Crow River's Regional Subcommunities, 1858–1899 121

7.1 Household Size by Age and Parentage of Household Head, Wisconsin, 1905 190

7.2 Children Ever Born by Parentage in 1900 to Married Women Born 1855 or Before 191

7.3 Differential Fertility between Immigrants and the Native-Born, 1900 and 1910 192

7.4 Indirect Mean Age at Marriage for Women by Background and Generation, Two Datasets Based on 1900 Federal Census 196

7.5 Marriage Prospects for Sons and Daughters by Birth Order, Children of Luster Immigrants 208

7.6 Proportions at Home by Age, Birth Order, and Sex, Two Norwegian American Populations, 1880 211

7.7 Age at First Marriage over Time, Two Middle Western Samples, 1830–1899 212

7.8 Marriage Prospects for Second-Generation Youth Based on Descendants of Immigrants from Luster, Norway 214

7.9 Proportions at Home by Age, Birth Order, and Sex, Two Norwegian American Populations, 1900 215

7.10 Households Augmented with Parents by Parent-Child Relationship of Male Household Head, Norwegian and Norwegian American Populations 216

10.1 Simple County-Level Correlations of Selected Variables in Relation to 1916 Iowa Suffrage Referendum 302

10.2 Simple County-Level Correlations of Selected Variables in Relation to 1882 Iowa Prohibition Referendum 306

10.3 Simple County-Level Correlations of Selected Variables in Relation to 1917 Iowa Prohibition Referendum 307

Figures

1.1 The Upper Middle West, 1890 6

3.1 Place of First Residence in the United States for Immigrants from Fortun, Norway 94

4.1 Norwegian Settlers in the Crow River Settlement by Region of Origin and Time of Arrival 120

Tables and Figures

ACKNOWLEDGMENTS

My mother is a daughter of the middle border. Born in 1908, she was reared by a Danish father and a Yankee mother on a farm in southwestern Minnesota. She cherishes still the memories of her Danish grandmother who lived with the family and remembers well being schooled in Methodist ways by her mother. When she came of age, she chose to marry the son of a Norwegian Lutheran pastor who had been raised in deeply rooted rural Norwegian communities of the American Northwest. It probably came as little surprise to her when her son some years later wed a German American Roman Catholic. In sum, she lived in a region where ethnic and religious identities were clearly defined but where interaction between people, at least by the twentieth century, was relatively common and boundaries were often breached. Her life is emblematic of the narrative of the rural Middle West that is the topic of this book, and it is to her that the book is dedicated.

The premise that it takes a village to raise a child is no less true in writing a book. No scholar works alone, and my debts are many. My research work was eased by the hospitality and efficiency of the staffs of a variety of archives throughout the Middle West. In particular, I would like to thank the State Historical Society of Wisconsin in Madison; the Minnesota Historical Society in St. Paul; the Iowa State Historical Division in Des Moines and Iowa City; the University of Iowa Library Special Collections; the Norwegian-American Historical Association at St. Olaf College; the Center for Dubuque History at Loras College; the Cedar Falls Historical Society; and the archive of the Dominican Sisters on the beautiful Sinsinawa Mound in southwestern Wisconsin. On the west coast, I have profited from the proximity of the Bancroft Library at the University of California at Berkeley. The opportunity to utilize these archives was made possible in part by grants and leaves from the University of California, including a Humanities Research Fellowship.

The path to this book's completion has been made simpler by friends and colleagues who have offered crucial advice along the way. My work at the California Institute of Technology over a decade ago enabled me to hone my skills in historical demography; James Q. Lee and J. Morgan Kousser have remained helpful colleagues. A year in Lund, Sweden, in 1991–92 allowed me to present my work at Lund University and Linköping University. More importantly, I got to know Bengt Sandin, Eva Österberg, and Kim Salamon and to experience firsthand life in the corporate society that is Sweden. During that year as well as at other conferences, I became reacquainted with other Scandinavians, including Ståle Dyrvik, Gunnar Thorvaldsen, Erik Helmer Petersen, Jette Mackintosh, and Øyvind Gulliksen, whose work I continue to respect. I have also benefited from the spirited intellectual community that characterizes the University of California at Berkeley. Graduate students, many of whom have since become professors, have assisted me with research tasks and read portions of the book. I would like to thank Robert Angres, Mark Cachia-Riedl, Lawrence Glickman, Gerd Horten, Steve Leikin, Jody Seim, and Lars Trägårdh. I am especially grateful to Heath Pearson, who was always ready to perform research tasks cheerfully and efficiently; Anne McCants, with whom I continue to work on issues of family history and historical demography; and Anita Tien, whose careful reading and candid assessments improved the manuscript greatly. Many of my colleagues read and criticized parts of the manuscript. Richard Abrams, Andrew Barshay, Robin Einhorn, James Kettner, Lawrence Levine, and Robert Middlekauff read sections of the book, offered advice, and improved the final product. I profited from informal discussions with David Hollinger and Gene Irschick and with Jan de Vries, who, like me, has never entirely left the Middle West behind.

Other scholars throughout the United States have helped me along the way. Kathleen Neils Conzen, a gracious scholar with keen insight, read parts of the manuscript and invited me to present a chapter at her Social History Workshop at the University of Chicago in 1993. Daniel Scott Smith and Olivier Zunz have kindly shared their work and advice over the years. Todd Nichol, Richard Johnson, and Peter Franson have tutored me on the intricacies of Lutheranism in the United States. Debbie Miller helped at critical moments to obtain details from the Minnesota Historical Society. Odd Lovoll has shared with me his knowledge of Norwegian America and his distinctive good humor. Robert Ostergren, as always, has been a cheerful ally; in particular, I thank him and the University of Wisconsin Cartographic Laboratory for their help in preparing the figures. My debt to Thomas G. Ryan extends back to my years as an undergraduate student, but here I want to thank him for his advice on the referenda in Iowa in the late nineteenth and early twentieth centuries. I never met the late Father J. K. Downing, but his translations of segments of *Die Iowa* and the *Luxemburger Gazette* aided me in examining the German newspapers in the region. Finally, the people at the University of North Carolina Press have been great. Lewis Bateman has been the careful and professional editor all historians hope for.

My most profound indebtedness is to my extended family, who represent the peoples of the Middle West. I am grateful to my in-laws in Iowa, who welcomed an outsider into their deeply rooted Roman Catholic community for countless summers as I conducted research. Many thanks to my siblings for their help in prodding me to finish the book. And I offer my deepest gratitude to Ruth, who is always there, and to Christine and Kari, who grew up with this book. The book is dedicated to Ferne Sorenson Gjerde Aurand, who taught me about the Middle West and instilled in me a belief that I should be respectful and understanding of the people with whom I interact and, by implication, the subjects whom I study. I hope the book reflects that advice.

THE
MINDS
OF THE
WEST

INTRODUCTION

everend Albert Barnes, a Presbyterian clergyman,
ascended pulpits in New York City and Philadelphia in 1849 to deliver a series of sermons on the
state of the nation at a time of tremendous change. Naturally, his attention was drawn westward, to the rich river valleys beyond the Appala-
chians that had been the locus of great change during the preceding few
decades. Amid this growth, Barnes associated the West with a heterogeneity of "minds." Whereas New England had historically been characterized by a "sameness" and homogeneousness of character, Barnes
observed, in the West, "nearly all the world has its representatives." The
historical moment was singular. In the West, "a strange and mighty
intermingling of minds of great power, under different propensities and
views," was producing "a population as the world has never before seen
on the settlement of a new land."[1]

The migration westward, Barnes affirmed, was not only unique but
also of pivotal relevance to the future of the United States. The "minds"
that he observed in the West were diverse in their "elements." On the one
hand, the "Puritan mind"—characterized by its love of civil and religious
liberty, hatred of oppression and wrong, and desire to promote the cause
of sound learning—infused the region. Barnes contrasted it with what he
called the "foreign mind," diverse with "little homogeneousness of character and views" and with myriad languages, faiths, and cultures. It was
a "mind mostly bred up under monarchical forms of government; little
acquainted with our republican institutions; restrained at home less by an
intelligent public sentiment than by the bayonet; tenacious of the forms
of religion in which it was trained; and to a large extent, having little
sympathy with the principles of the Protestant faith." Lesser intellectual
streams—including that of the "indolent" southerner—were also present,
but it was the foreign mind that most troubled Barnes, for the population
was "not yet . . . amalgamated" and its elements were to a great extent
"still embodying the sentiments which they cherished in the lands where
they were born."[2] Most ominously for Barnes, those "sentiments" were

1

often antithetical to the harmonious operation of the American Republic.

Barnes's lectures reflected a torrent of fears that swept over many residents of the United States at mid-century. His tone betrayed an Anglo-Saxon racialism that attached eternal truths to a romantic ethnic past.[3] His discourses also expose central elements of his idea of the West and the section of the American landscape that would soon be known as the "Middle West," the regional focus of this study. Due to an enormous westward migration, the region became a setting of great ethnic diversity. It was the kingdom of the Yankee West[4] and a place where immigrant families re-created new Europes.[5] As a result, the "foreign minds"—the cultural patterns of these westward-migrating groups—profoundly informed the development of the region from political, social, and cultural perspectives. The West was an environment where cultural differences both interacted and were contested. Throughout this book, middle western society will serve as a locale in which to explore this cultural diversity. Conduct, from electoral politics to patterns of land tenure, manifested a cultural signature stemming from the minds carried westward.

Yet it is Barnes's juxtaposition of the minds and the West that complicates the story and suggests the importance of the interactions between the cultures transplanted in the region and the possibilities of the West itself. As such, this juxtaposition neatly frames a series of issues that, though situated in the West, inform American history more generally. First, Barnes alluded to the meaning of the West for nineteenth-century observers. By Barnes's time, the "West" had already long been a metaphor for opportunity in the white American mind. Available land, after all, was the force that J. Hector St. John de Crèvecoeur argued in 1792 transformed Europeans from dependent peasants to American farmers.[6] A century later, Frederick Jackson Turner's West had retained a mythic quality since he depicted the frontier as a place where the independent producer was made free by an open environment, an environment central to the health of the American society and polity.[7] It is no coincidence that the West was often perceived to be a place where cultural differences were muted and where the concept of the American people was forged.

Yet Barnes's sermons, by underscoring the diversity of cultural traditions that were then being rerooted in the West, also demonstrated fears that these cultures did not share common understandings of state and society. Because the West was rich, it was alluring to immigrants of all stripes. Because many immigrants were unschooled in Protestantism or Republicanism, however, the future of the West, and perhaps the world, was at risk. In short, Barnes asked, what kind of society would be formed in a land rich in resources—a precondition of American strength—but peopled by cultures that did not understand, and perhaps did not agree with, American republicanism?

A second theme embedded in Barnes's sermon, then, was the likelihood that the region would be the setting for conflict between the minds. Even as he spoke, Barnes argued, the West was the locus of a "fierce intellectual conflict" in which each culture was "struggling for the mastery . . . to diffuse itself all over that great valley." The West, he affirmed, would continue to be "the great battle-field of the world—the place where probably, more than any where else, the destinies of the world are to be decided." He stated it simply yet ominously: "If this nation is to be free, the population of the [Mississippi] valley is to preserve and perpetuate our freedom; if it is to be enslaved, the chains that are to fetter us are to be forged beyond the [Appalachian] mountains."[8] It is telling that Barnes perceived the dangers of bondage as lying in the West—a region increasingly peopled by those of a "foreign mind"—rather than in the South, where chattel slavery actually existed. Barnes's myopia notwithstanding, cultural conflict between American-born Protestants and European immigrants and their descendants remained a common thread running through the nineteenth-century Middle West. To be sure, Barnes overestimated the threat of the "foreign mind" and the portent of the struggle. Perhaps it did not become the "great battle-field of the world," but the region was the site throughout the nineteenth century of political struggle that was informed by differentiated cultural patterns.

The conflict was muted in part because of a third theme implicit in Barnes's sermon: that the "minds" themselves were transformed as they were transferred to the West. In this context, the narrative of the "foreign mind" is particularly interesting. Immigrant traditions that were carried westward were reformulated in the West. Although the West provided a setting where secluded ethnic settlements were formed and where traditions were recast, it was also an intellectual and social context that was fluid and porous. Succinctly stated, a central fact of immigrant life in the West was the inherent tension between the centrifugal forces of new social patterns set in the context of an apparently open environment, on the one hand, and the centripetal attractions of nucleated settlement and cultural retention, on the other. Conflict between leader and laity, between parents and children, and among community members was based in large part on this crucial fact.

The critical relationship in this book, then, is the juxtaposition of cultural patterns—the minds—and environmental possibilities in a region diverse in cultural traditions and rich in resources—the West—that was replete with tension, conflict, even paradox. These interactions between cultural patterns and economic opportunities and constraints are, to be sure, fundamental to U.S. history generally. But the issues and events were magnified and isolated in the West, which, as Barnes suggested, was a locale that defined the American Republic but was peopled by the foreign mind. In sum, the vast tracts of land that contained the promise to transform the migrant simultaneously possessed the potential to nurture former cultural patterns. As we will see, both occurred in a complex interaction that informs the narrative of the immigrant in the United States and the story of the Middle West. In this introduction, I begin the discussion of the interactive relationship between the land—the West—and the cultures of the people—the minds—who came to inhabit it. In so doing, I will adumbrate the argument of the chapters to follow.

The "West"

The Middle region . . . was an open door to all Europe. . . . It had a wide mixture of nationalities. . . . In short, it was a region mediating between New England and the South, and the East and the West. It represented that composite nationality which the contemporary United States exhibits, that juxtaposition of non-English groups, occupying a valley or a little settlement, and presenting reflections of the map of Europe in their variety.
—Frederick Jackson Turner, "The Significance of the Frontier" (1893)

Writing a half century after Albert Barnes, Frederick Jackson Turner also understood the importance of the cultural diversity of the West. When he surveyed the "Middle region," he saw it as a district that both contained representatives of and mediated between the American cultural hearths of New England and the South and between the mature eastern and newly settled western regions of the United States.[9] He later observed that the upper regions of the Middle West were dominated at mid-century by migrants from the Middle States and New England.[10] Turner was also acutely aware of an outpouring of untold millions of immigrants, principally from Europe, who also settled mainly in the Upper Middle West. Coming of age in small-town Wisconsin, his life experience as well as his scholarship reflected a crucial fact: that the Middle West was a region of "composite nationality."

The significance of the European migration to the rural Middle West must be underscored. Americans pondering the nineteenth-century immigrant story today typically look to an urban experience of teeming ethnic neighborhoods in burgeoning eastern American cities. They tend to forget that a considerable number of Europeans moved to the region that would soon come to be known as the Middle West. During the two decades prior to the Civil War, the foreign-born dominated the westward march into the Old Northwest.[11] Until at least 1880, the proportion of residents of foreign birth in the middle western states roughly paralleled the proportion of the foreign-born in the urbanizing East.[12] More significant for our purposes is the fact that immigrants not only moved to the West but established farms as part of an immense settler immigration principally from Europe. By 1880, over one-half of all farmers in Wisconsin, Minnesota, and Dakota were foreign-born; about one-third of the farmers in Michigan, Iowa, and Nebraska and one-quarter of those living in Illinois had been born outside the United States.[13] Put differently, over two-thirds of all foreign-born farmers toiling the soil in 1880 lived in the Old Northwest and the states of Iowa, Minnesota, and Nebraska and the territory of Dakota to the west.[14] The 1890 census that declared the frontier closed also provides us with the raw material to reconstruct a landscape segmented among cultural groups rerooted from Europe and the eastern United States (see figure I.1).[15] The rural tracts of the Upper Middle West, therefore, were locales where the minds of the West were mingled and where perhaps they would clash.

That confrontation was made all the more likely by the changing character of immigrant origins as the nineteenth century progressed. Whereas American-born migrants were increasingly dominated by those with a Yankee past, roughly half of the immigrants to the United States between 1840 and 1879 were Roman Catholics.[16] A significant portion of the rest followed Lutheran, Reformed, or Anglican traditions; they were not "Papists," but neither were they "Puritans." And a sizable segment of these people eventually resided in the Middle West. Richard Jensen, in estimating the religious character of the Middle West in 1890, determined that the largest group was made up of Roman Catholics, followed by Methodists. Lutherans were the third largest, just ahead of Baptists and Presbyterians.[17] These religious convictions were not only diverse in character but also widely professed. Jensen notes that in 1890 more than 70 percent of middle westerners were church-affiliated.[18] The region, geographer Robert C. Ostergren has demonstrated graphically, was a "heavily churched landscape."[19]

The relationship between the land and the way migrants occupied it was critical in informing the meaning of the West for many Americans. For Turner and numerous others, the solution to problems posed by America's pluralism was in fact lodged in the capacity of the United States to assimilate its citizenry through the immense power of the American environment. This capability was tied to one strand of a narrative built upon the myth of the West: the rural expanses of land that beckoned to white migrants from the eastern United States and Europe were

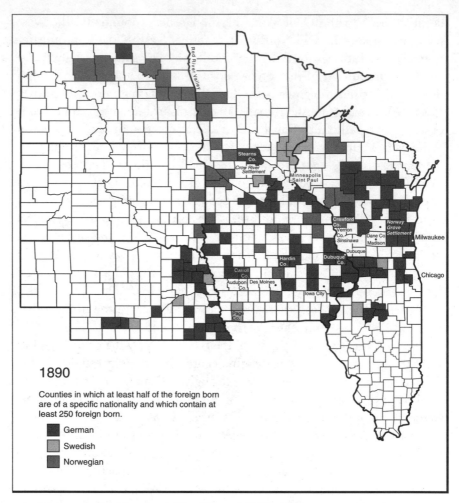

Figure 1.1. The Upper Middle West, 1890

perceived to be "free" in the sense that they were unoccupied and inexpensive. Freedom begot democracy. The precedents instituted in such acts as the Northwest Ordinance thus created an environment and a political structure in which conceptions of "freedom," in its many shapes, converged.[20] Here in the West, on the vast tracts of land that comprised the Northwest Territories and the expanses to the west of it, slavery was illegal and "freedom"—its inverse—allegedly was enhanced. Here "liberty" reputedly created a condition of opportunity.[21]

The hordes of Europeans that flocked westward, making the West one of the most ethnically and culturally diverse regions in antebellum America, were not a threat from this perspective. Since they were defined as "white," European immigrants could enjoy citizenship and rights

6   Introduction

denied to others. Unlike "nonwhite" peoples, who consistently faced citizenship restrictions, those who possessed a "foreign mind" could join the American Republic. Immigrants arriving to breathe the freedoms of American liberty and the opportunities identified with American wealth, according to this rationale, were acculturated in the process into a developing American tradition. Many northern Americans therefore perceived the West as a harbinger of American greatness. It was celebrated as the future center of American energy and wealth, a paragon of the freedoms viable in an American Republic based on immense natural wealth. For Turner, Barnes, and countless others, the Middle West was a place where quintessential questions concerning a plural nation would be addressed and presumably solved.

Yet events as they unfolded in the West gave rise to a competing narrative that was not as benign or as salutary. The West, with its vast cache of land, from this angle of vision, was actually a site of potential destruction. The western expanses were not as powerful a force as they appeared to Turner or Crèvecoeur. Rather, they were merely settings where foreign citizens were able to cordon themselves off from the developing American tradition. They were possible staging areas where practitioners of the foreign mind—Roman Catholics, in particular—could ultimately use the landed wealth and the republican tradition of the United States, ironically two of the linchpins of American greatness, to threaten the American state and society.

The West thus summoned different visions to different Americans. To some, it was a metaphor of American opportunity and wealth and a locus of a fluid society in a continual process of redefinition. To others, it represented cultural fragmentation that threatened to destroy the developing American tradition. Significantly, these two contradictory views were born out of similar objective facts of migration and immigration to a developing region. The very conditions that created the potential for greatness also provided the basis for fear.

European immigrants also tended to construct varied meanings of the West from similar objective observations that in some respects paralleled but in other respects crosscut the American narrative. They often accepted a rhetoric of American exceptionalism with as much certainty as their American-born counterparts. The United States, it was repeatedly suggested, was a land of freedom and opportunity when compared with their European homes." The West, with its vast tracts of available land, best exemplified this freedom. Yet the meaning of "freedom" was used in multifarious ways. The West could be a place where liberal individual freedoms were highlighted. Yet it was also perceived as a wide, open space where migrants could use apparent American freedoms to reestablish traditions segregated from the impurities of other cultural groups. The enormous opportunities to own land and to separate into ethnic communities provided migrating groups with the latitude to transplant cultural patterns as the nation expanded. The West perhaps did not create "the American, this new man," so much as provide the liberty to reestablish and embellish upon former patterns of life.[23]

The possibility of seclusion in the West was indeed realized in the profusion of culturally defined settlements that dotted the Middle West. Settlements of Europeans and eastern Americans, the result of innumerable individual decisions made within a community context, took root in the Middle West. These communities were typically centered on ethnic institutions that refabricated a basis for social ties as they created a forum to retain their members' faiths. Migration chains thus linked people and their cultural traditions across space. In these enclaves, institutions—most notably the family, the church, and the community—were formed that structured local society and the relationships within the community and the home. It is crucial to note that their formation was part and parcel of an opportunity distinctive to the United States, with its landed wealth and putative freedoms of belief.

In a very real sense, then, allegiances to the American nation and to cultural traditions carried across the sea could coexist. Indeed, they could be mutually supportive and self-reinforcing.[24] Immigrants celebrated life in the United States because it enabled them to retain beliefs that originated outside of it. They thus could develop a "complementary identity" that pledged allegiance to both American citizenship and ethnic adherence. Whereas Europeans argued that such a complementary identity strengthened allegiances to multiple affiliations, many of the American-born were not so sure. American critics pointed out that an identity whose essence was partly "foreign"—and here again they focused on allegiance to Roman Catholicism—jeopardized complete loyalty to the United States in the long run.

While the immigrant presence unnerved American observers, the multilayered identities of loyalty of immigrants to ethnic locality and nation also created challenges for the immigrant leadership. To be sure, the tension between civil society and more particularistic beliefs was a common issue in an era in which citizenship and nation were being created. Jean-Jacques Rousseau, after all, had puzzled over the relationship between public life and citizenship, on the one hand, and private enterprise and belief, on the other, as early as 1750 in his *First Discourse*.[25] The question, however, was especially perplexing for European immigrants who joined the United States in midstream. Although they applauded the rights they held in the United States, including freedom of religion—

"we have full liberty to regulate everything according to God's Word," wrote an early German Lutheran immigrant—they were forced to consider how those liberties would affect their families and religious communities.[26] How was their faith to be integrated into American society and how would it be changed as a result? The West provided the "freedom" to reproduce family patterns carried from Europe, but it also gave family members the liberty to bristle at patterns of intrafamilial inequality. Although they tended to celebrate uncritically their perceptions of American rights, immigrants likely did not entirely contemplate their full effect. The dynamic created out of competing yet complementary identities, in short, would continue to engender challenges for immigrants and their children throughout the nineteenth century and into the next.

The idea of the West, then, did not resemble a fixed template that framed the ways in which immigrants were transformed into Americans. Instead, it was more like a changing landscape that offered opportunity, even though the definition of opportunity varied. The Middle West was a location where notions of emerging American pluralisms were paralleled with a transplantation of cultural patterns from Europe. The region is an ideal site for the study of the interactions between environment and culture, a place where the vast power of the environment at once licensed cultural groupings to reestablish their institutions and retain their ideologies and authorized beliefs in the American myth of freedom and opportunity. It is an exemplary locale, as Turner recognized long ago, for the study of both cultural conflict between and cultural change within the "minds" under the umbrella of American culture.

The "Minds"

There was a most miscellaneous cluster of persons sticking upon their no less miscellaneous effects. . . . Square-built German fraus sat astride huge rolls of bedding, displaying stout legs, blue worsted stockings, and hob-nailed shoes. Sallow Yankees, with straw-hats, swallow-tailed coats, and pumps, carried their little all in their pockets; and having nothing to lose and everything to gain in the western world to which they were bound whittled, smoked, and chewed cheerfully. —Laurence Oliphant, *Minnesota and the Far West* (1855)

When Laurence Oliphant observed at mid-century an array of migrants waiting to board a ferry on their westward trek, he was struck by the differences in the outward appearance of the "hardy" American "pioneers" and the immigrants "who represented half the countries of Europe."[27] What he failed to note were the social and cultural differences of the migrants. Any full appreciation of cultural conflict and change in the West demands that we grapple with the intellectual and cultural antecedents of those who migrated to it. Given the enormous variety of cultural traditions carried westward, the task is formidable. Through painstaking research, historians have differentiated and detailed the patterns of society and culture among both the American- and European-born. They have explored the implications of traditions rooted in eastern American cultural hearths and have underscored their variations.[28] The myriad cultural traditions of immigrants from the European continent and the Celtic fringe in the nineteenth century—those whom Albert Barnes lumped together as progenitors of the "foreign mind"—were even more disparate.[29] In spite of, or perhaps because of, this diversity, we can profit by beginning with Barnes's two formidable minds—the Puritan and the foreign—carried westward by American pioneers and European immigrants.

Barnes's dichotomy of intellectual lineages was reinforced by patterns of migration. Immigration to the United States was weak in the first decades of the nineteenth century,[30] precisely at a time when social and intellectual developments in the United States and Europe diverged to create a cleavage that would have major implications for cultural development in the Middle West. In Europe, opposition to the eighteenth-century rationalism stemming from the Enlightenment profoundly informed religious practice in the early nineteenth century in different ways. It encouraged, on the one hand, a pietism that repudiated the influence of colorless religious leaders. Yet, on the other hand, it simultaneously induced social critics, Protestant and Catholic alike, to reconsider the proper construction of society and posit corporatist solutions for societal ills. Likewise, the rejection of rationalism and the tumult of European revolutions prompted religious leaders and theologians to retreat to confessional forms that focused on the body of true believers. Not only did this spur a seeming conservative drift within the church hierarchies and most notably within the papacy, but it privileged a particularist rather than a pluralist perspective.[31] Many groups of immigrants streaming westward were taught that they, as true believers, should segregate themselves from the godless throngs, a task that was made simpler in the West but was perilous for an American pluralism. These developments contrast with early-nineteenth-century evangelical movements in the United States that fostered a pietism that stressed the individual's quest for conversion and reaffirmed the promise of a democratic order established by the revolutions of the late eighteenth century. When European immigrant streams swelled in the 1830s, they mingled with those of Americans moving westward, but the intellectual contours of Europe differed dramatically from those that had evolved in the eastern United States.

Intellectual patterns of society and economy in the northeastern United

States were based, of course, on an English inheritance. Early colonial household patterns were informed by the patriarchalism of thinkers such as Robert Filmer, who in *Patriarcha* (1680) posited an organic unity that linked child to father and subject to king, a reproduction in broad outlines of older notions of kinship and family.[32] Yet they were increasingly influenced by the ideas of John Locke and the Scottish common sense philosophy. Locke, who argued that parental authority was temporary, was instrumental in pushing patriarchalism out of the mainstream of English natural law. By the mid-eighteenth century, Francis Hutcheson stressed not only the limits of parental authority but also the contractual nature of the family and the state. By then, Edwin G. Burrows and Michael Wallace argue, "contractualism" had triumphed over "patriarchalism" in English natural law.[33]

The Anglo-American world was further recast by a series of revolutions that altered arrangements in state and society. The most significant, of course, was the political reformulation stemming from the American Revolution. As Gordon S. Wood argues, the traditional character retained by British American colonial society well into the eighteenth century was transformed by a revolution that replaced the British monarchy with the American Republic.[34] In affirming the desirability of a republican form of government, American society was transfigured socially and culturally by the late eighteenth century, having jettisoned most of its corporatist elements.

This political reconfiguration was both informed by and accompanied by changes within society. Historians have noted the parallels between structures of authority in the state and those in the household. The ascendancy of contractualism in state relations was reflected in modifications in the home. On the one hand, contemporaries repeatedly remarked upon the waning of household authority illustrated by the increasing lack of control that parents had over their children.[35] On the other hand, the influence of government on the family intensified.[36] Perhaps it is an overstatement to argue, as does Wood, that whatever remained of "patriarchy was in disarray" at the dawn of the nineteenth century. Yet it is clear that tremendous social and political change had revolutionized American society and its family by that time.[37]

As the nation entered the nineteenth century, it moved with increasing velocity toward the creation of a social order that sanctioned and celebrated individual latitude. Many Americans stated quite explicitly that their society was based on countless individual relationships with the state rather than arrangements of a collectivity. They privileged the rights of the individual over the relationships between constituent parts of the society. And whereas nineteenth-century religion repudiated rationalist thought, its revivalist tradition endorsed an individualized, pietist approach. Swept up in an evangelical movement that Martin Marty argues "churched the West," many of those who participated in the Second Great Awakening believed that the individual sinner had been given the gift of achieving salvation independent of the priesthood. The American-born in the early nineteenth century thus participated in what Nathan O. Hatch calls a "democratization of Christianity." [38]

By mid-century, many white Americans unselfconsciously celebrated the genius of a developing tradition that fostered a "liberty" based on individual rights, democracy, economic growth, and progress. They sincerely argued that these characteristics endowed American society with a moral force that would knit the nation into a harmonious whole. [39] Considering that most people lived in localized neighborhoods that continued to rely on the community and many people, such as women and children in families or slaves on plantations, remained enmeshed in webs of inequality, it is remarkable that a rhetoric of liberty and freedom within the home, the community, and the society writ large was so vociferously proclaimed. Yet such proclamations were made—not surprisingly, principally by men—and they linked the speakers' Protestant faith to the republicanism of the nation.

In constructing their national mythology, these American-born also measured their advances against the cultures and beliefs of others. When they examined the cultural and religious backgrounds of European immigrants, they found them wanting in many ways. Like Barnes, Protestants from the northern United States—those who were of a "Puritan mind"—indicted the European, and especially the Roman Catholic, worldview for its hierarchical authoritarianism, which allegedly devalued humanity and shackled the individual. "The Papacy and all state churches," argued Edward Norris Kirk in 1848, "exalt the Hierarchy . . . at the expense of human nature. But [Protestant] Christianity places each soul before God, in its identity and distinct personality. We cannot fully appreciate how much its cardinal doctrines have exalted man." [40] "Republicanism, modified by Christianity," on the other hand, Kirk affirmed, "does indeed exalt the individual man." [41] Protestant American culture thus advanced a morality and maturity that enabled individuals to act responsibly in the operation of the government and to create a system that benefited the majority of the people. "The cardinal principle of the Latin Church," Kirk continued, "is, the destruction of man's individuality and manhood, in all the higher functions of his moral nature. He cannot think, judge, believe, choose, address God, or govern himself in the department of his religious interests." Rather, "it must be done for him, by a corporation," so that "the layman is ever an infant in religious matters." It was no surprise, he concluded, that when Roman Catholic nations attempted self-government, they failed.[42]

It is extremely significant that both American and European commentators linked the virtues of American Protestantism and American republicanism with specific forms of family, society, and government. "Protestantism is republican," wrote Frenchman Michel Chevalier simply, and "Catholicism is essentially monarchical." "Under the influence of Protestantism and republicanism," he continued, "the social progress has been effected by the medium of the spirit of individuality; for protestantism, republicanism, and individuality are all one." Using a vague metaphor of membership in a community, Chevalier underscored his sense of the progress made in the American Republic. Unlike the European peasant whose culture was permeated by "gross superstition," the American farmer had harmoniously merged great principles from scriptural traditions with "notions of political freedom." "He is one of the *initiated*," concluded Chevalier, in matters extending from domestic relations in the family to the "dignity of man" and was part and parcel of the unfolding of another stage in the "succession of progressive movements which has characterized our civilization ever since it quitted its cradle in the East."[43]

The cultural trajectory of those who would emigrate from Europe in the nineteenth century differed remarkably from that of the American-born they would meet in the West. European peasants typically had not been exposed to the notions of individualism that were so boldly proclaimed in the United States, and most of them, as Barnes suggested, continued to live in societies characterized by authority and hierarchy. Despite frequent expressions of discontent, they continued to defer to the local and state authorities to whom they paid their taxes and who administered their spiritual lives. Their households, moreover, were characterized by what William I. Thomas and Florian Znaniecki would later term "familial solidarity," a complex arrangement in which relationships were informed by inherent inequality within the home.[44]

To be sure, Europe, like the Americas, underwent a transformation punctuated by vast economic change and political revolutions that stemmed from the Enlightenment. Socialist and republicanist movements surged across the Continent and inspired a segment of the emigrants. Other emigrants seized on notions, animated by discontent at home, that the United States offered a freedom denied them in Europe. "Westward," went a Swedish song, "where the sun shines over the land of free men; westward, where no serfs are sickened by vile chains."[45] Some decades later, Thomas and Znaniecki argued that "democratic America" gave the immigrant "a feeling of importance" that was rare in Polish communal life, especially among children who did not acquire "the traditional attitude of familial solidarity but rather the American individu-alistic ideals."[46] Nils Wohlin, writing about Sweden, echoed the claims of Thomas and Znaniecki when he suggested in 1910 that the "lib-eral epoch's individualist conceptions had undermined the peasants' old worldviews [åskådningar] about the family community [familjegemenskapen] and the lineage's land [släktjorden]."[47]

Yet old habits died slowly. European immigrants were influenced by the "liberal epoch," but they also reinstitutionalized cultural practices in the rural Middle West that opposed those of their American-born neighbors. As agents of the innovative act that international migration embodied, some early emigrants, hewing to older systems of belief, even questioned whether emigration itself might be a sin.[48] And although they heralded the opportunity to live in freedom when they arrived in the United States, their families continued to display patterns of inequality similar to patterns that had existed in Europe. "Familial solidarity" did not in-stantly wither, but rather attempts were made to reinstate it on farms in the Middle West. It was possibly fostered among peasants who became landholders in the land-rich Middle West. By stressing an authority and discipline that were critical elements in a collective responsibility, familial solidarity also systematically disadvantaged specific members of the col-lective whole.[49]

As immigrants carried their peasant sensibilities to the United States, their communities also revealed the influences of contemporary intellec-tual movements in the nineteenth century that evolved in reaction to the excesses of decades of revolution and upheaval and the sterile rationalism and formalism of the Enlightenment. One expression was a flourishing pietistic opposition that encouraged, as in the United States, emotionally charged spiritual awakenings among the peasantry in Europe.[50] Signifi-cantly, this pietist sentiment was rerooted in the Middle West by Euro-pean immigrants who, in many cases, were able to fuse their religious convictions with social and political perspectives consonant with Ameri-can Protestantism. As Timothy L. Smith argues, this sentiment was cru-cial to a developing regard for "modern" goals, including autonomy and self-realization, that contributed to the mobilization of the peoples that would comprise the European immigration.[51]

But this European pietism was accompanied—and often opposed—by a flourishing religious culture beginning in the early nineteenth cen-tury that was not so "modern." Pietism was merely one avenue to protest the barren rationalism of the eighteenth century; another involved a re-awakening of theological themes that had been dominant prior to the Enlightenment and in many cases disparaged Enlightenment thinking. This movement contained two strains of thought that would influence many European religious communities in the United States and sustain the familial solidarity observed by Thomas and Znaniecki. The first was a tendency toward a particularism that reaffirmed the belief that one's religious confession and scripture represented the only true faith. Among Protestants, this outlook was related to a confessional revival in the mid-nineteenth century that stressed that the Scriptures and confessions were immune from literary criticism.[52] Within the hierarchy of the Roman Catholic Church, it found expression in a series of papal proclamations that were antiliberal in character. In 1864, the publication of the Syllabus of Errors seemed to place the church in opposition to the secularism and liberalism of the century. Six years later, the Vatican Council accepted papal infallibility.[53] These particularist tendencies complicated believers' attempts to integrate religious belief into a national community that contained nonbelievers. Even when they accepted and celebrated the American state, many continued to puzzle over its relationship to their confessional community. If those who confessed a particular theology were the only godly folk in society, how were they to interact with the heathens?[54]

The second tendency was toward a renewal of a corporatist theology that tended to support institutional structures such as a hierarchical family as it opposed the premises on which liberalism was based. Corporatist theory, which influenced Roman Catholic and Protestant traditions alike, was built upon organic conceptions of state and society that assumed that comparisons between the body or the organism and the politically organized community were informative.[55] Roman Catholic natural law assigned every being a place in the whole and every link was based on a divine decree.[56] Individuals, knit into a societal whole, were further constrained by the privileged position given to "natural" institutions such as the family, the church, and occupational organizations such as the guild. Enmeshed in this web of institutions, they were obliged to recognize virtues of justice and charity within an organic unity rather than simply their contractual relationship with the state. These were virtues that not only followed from natural rights but were required of members of a society that was an imperative of nature itself. Although natural law presupposed a fundamental equality of individuals, temporal society was arranged by a group life that was hierarchical and ascriptive. Human beings were not able to choose their parental relationships as they would membership in a voluntary organization. They were born into them.[57] Among Lutherans, grace within the spiritual community was contrasted with the rule of law and coercion in the secular one. Religion itself thus remained a matter of faith rather than of law. The irrational state was surfeited with power, and the believer's place in the world—his or her "calling"—was established by "a system of perfect sublimation of social function in a given static order."[58] Abstract political equality within society did not exist, only a functional equality in the form of occupational worth. As in Roman Catholic belief, society was "not an aggregate but an organism."[59]

Both Roman Catholic and Lutheran traditions thus emphasized the importance of institutions, positioned between the individual and the state, as a source of societal strength. The family, the church, and the guild were all perceived as junctions that provided society with institutional and "moral" order. The community, typically undergirded by the church, shielded its members from dangerous outside influences. The family, which remained an especially critical institution in rural society, was the basis of society. By knitting its members into one continuous whole that esteemed patriarchal power and the "moral capacities of the collectivity," the family was a building block upon which society was based.[60]

These formulations had widespread social and political implications for ethnic groups in the United States. In many religious traditions, they were carried westward and merged with native principles that tended to be more liberal and ecumenical. Among Roman Catholics, the Irish American clergy, which dominated the American Catholic hierarchy in the nineteenth century, were not the principal advocates of Catholic corporatism but rather were instrumental in promoting a liberal or "Americanist" perspective that was aimed at transforming ethnics into "Americans." Instead, the strongest proponents of a conservative, corporatist Catholicism were Continental members of the church.[61] Deeply influenced by the corporatism espoused by Roman Catholics in the nineteenth century and later stung by the German *Kulturkampf*, German Catholics in the United States, as Philip Gleason has shown, hewed to a Christian order of society based on its "natural" institutions. At the same time, they eschewed forces in the United States such as liberalism, socialism, and anarchism that they perceived to be individualistic, materialistic, and atheistic. Divisions within the Catholic Church would come to a head in the late nineteenth century when the conservative wing, which comprised the majority of the laity, confronted the liberal "Americanist" advocates.[62]

Immigrant Lutheranism and Calvinism followed a similar sequence from mid-century onward. The Lutheran Church in the United States had gravitated toward a liberal position known as "American Lutheranism" in the early nineteenth century, but its drift was arrested in part by the German Lutheran immigration at mid-century. Confessional German Lutherans left Europe because they saw "no possibility of retaining" the "pure and undefiled" faith of the Lutheran confessions and thus sought a country "where this Lutheran faith is not endangered."[63] The church bodies that were formed out of this immigration—the Buffalo

Synod (1845), Missouri Synod (1847), Wisconsin Synod (1850), and Iowa Synod (1854)—reestablished a confessional Lutheranism in the Middle West.[64] Scandinavian Lutherans, although they proved less inclined to accept particularist and corporatist thought than Germans, nonetheless were influenced by it.[65] Similarly, the first wave of Dutch immigrants in the nineteenth century maintained a pietism that had been expressed in the secession from the National Reformed Church in Holland in 1834.[66] Yet again, these beliefs were overlaid by another wave of Dutch migration in the late nineteenth century that brought a theology deeply colored by a Dutch Calvinist corporatism based on the thought of Abraham Kuyper, who lamented the course of events and development of thought in the postrevolutionary age.[67]

Religious thought among nineteenth-century European immigrants therefore not only opposed that of the "Puritan mind" but also tended, in notable cases, to be moving in directions opposite to those expressed by many American-born migrants streaming into the Middle West. It is thus not sufficient to claim simply that European immigrants came to the United States with more "traditional" or less "modern" perspectives. Rather, their intellectual worlds were evolving and infused with intellectual developments that posited remarkably distinct conceptions of salvation and grace that not incidentally informed their models of society and its institutional structure. The following chapters will consider the degree to which the laity would embrace these worldviews and will illustrate the degree to which they informed patterns of life, from family structures and intrafamily obligations to partisan expressions in political debate in the late nineteenth century. They will show how cultural conflict developed when corporatist configurations, for example, seemed to many Yankees to fly in the face of their liberal paean to American life whereas many members of European ethnic groups challenged the prudence of invasions of their family and community by state-run institutions. And they will depict the challenges that immigrant cultures encountered when they attempted to use an increasingly liberal state to defend their corporatist convictions. In short, distinct cultural premises, perceived by those such as Barnes in the decades before the Civil War, would continue to be a source of conflict. And the West would remain a principal locus of that conflict.

The Argument

These differences [between Germans and Yankees] never led to anything like enmities. There was room on the land for all of us on tolerable terms. And the

> Iowa Germans have assimilated. The present generation of these formerly
> ignorant and superstitious peasants are blessed with all the virtues and
> cursed with most of the faults of average Americanism.
> —Herbert Quick, *One Man's Life* (1925)

Writing three-quarters of a century after Albert Barnes and thirty years after Frederick Jackson Turner, Herbert Quick too seized on the relationships between the minds and the West. Reflecting the work of immigration scholars as diverse as Turner, William I. Thomas and Florian Znaniecki, and Oscar Handlin, he confidently emphasized the power of the environment to transform ignorant peasants into average Americans.[68] Yet although Quick suggested that the "room on the land" created economic opportunity that mitigated the potential for conflict that arises from scarcity, he knew that it also provided the possibility for segmentation that enabled cultural groups to segregate themselves from others. Quick's many works on the Middle West portrayed it as a place where the possibilities of the environment and the complexities of the transplanted cultures stood in stark contrast to one another. Although American society enabled immigrants to reroot foreign traditions, the Middle West was an environment tailor-made for the formation of isolated ethnic communities. Nowhere was the purported economic opportunity in the United States more obvious. Nowhere were the possibilities of the segregation of foreign cultures more viable.

The Middle West is the terrain we will use to explore the implications of the tensions created as the minds entered the West. Since the region is vast, the survey must be selective. We will concentrate on the Upper Middle West, where European and "Yankee" settlement was particularly prominent.[69] We will place particular emphasis on European immigrants, especially those whose perspectives conflicted with liberal ideologies and whose experiences are particularly instructive as a result. And we will use case studies to illustrate, in single communities, the conflict (Quick's contention notwithstanding, cultural persistence did lead to "enmities") that occurred throughout the region on the local level.

Our discussion begins with the idea of the West and its varied meanings to different inhabitants of the United States. Whereas some white Americans hailed the possibility of the West, others were wary of a region that might ultimately be dominated by a foreign mind whose alien ideas could be used to undermine the Republic (see Chapter 1). European immigrants turned this argument on its head. Because the American West was an environment where old beliefs and languages could be reestablished amid more sanguine economic prospects, it would foster an adaptation and loyalty to American traditions (see Chapter 2).

Yet the transplantation of former systems of belief was not as simple as it might have seemed. To be sure, the homes and settlements of the rural Middle West varied in the ways in which authority, hierarchy, and inequality were expressed. Household structures differed in complexity; labor prescriptions for wives and husbands, parents and children varied; the spiritual power of the priest or minister diverged. The essence of these variations, moreover, was located in the culturally defined arrangements of home and society carried to and reformulated in the West. Even if cultural patterns were not perfectly transplanted from Europe to the United States, the blending of theological constructs with cultural patterns of the European peasant community contributed to the creation of American homes distinctly different from those of their Yankee neighbors. Although immigrants professed to treasure the American inheritance of "freedom" and "opportunity," they continued to sanction household inequalities that had been customary at home.

Cultural patterns carried westward, however, were modified as they were transplanted. Settlements in the West were marked by a syncretism in both the community and the family as migrants grappled with the tensions and contradictions of gaining the freedom to refabricate their cultures. Chapter 3 illustrates how patterns of settlement created boundaries within which former religious and cultural forms could be re-created. In this sense, they became the basis of "communities" established on common pasts and located on common beliefs (see Chapter 4). Despite a complex matrix of migration patterns that typically resulted in densely settled rural communities, the "community" nonetheless was in many ways a reconfiguration of former ties that in turn became the basis for conflict. Although communities were based on similar backgrounds of language, faith, and nationality, membership in them was voluntary and fluid. Because boundaries *between* communities were often strictly defended, conflict *within* the communities was common.

Since communities were typically formed around religious institutions, moreover, conflict within them was often framed in spiritual terms. As such, religious conflict occasionally unmasked the uneasy relationship between allegiance to an American civil society and allegiance to a religious faith. Immigrants with varying religious birthrights often celebrated the freedom to practice their beliefs in the United States. Their clergy often argued that the voluntary nature of worship fostered by a separation of church and state was purer than the nature of worship in the state churches that dominated much of Europe. Yet again, however, the "freedom" to re-create religious and cultural traditions also provided the "freedom" to dissent from them. The laity therefore could—and did—object to the power of the clergy. They often argued that majority rule ought to determine religious doctrine. They claimed the right to secede from old religious systems. The freedom to re-create hierarchical and authoritarian religious structures fostered challenges to a church leadership that in many cases sought to maintain authority and hierarchy as bases of faith. The aspiration to nurture corporate communities evaporated as the community came to resemble a voluntary association.

The ambiguities of freedom and authority were also crucial within the household, another central institution in the rural Middle West. The family was critically significant for many reasons, not least because its members were the principal source of workers on independent farms in the Middle West. Men, women, and children toiled to build farms, to grow marketable commodities, and to provide for their own sustenance (see Chapter 5). Recent studies illustrate that families were central forms of organization within rural settlements in the Middle West regardless of their ethnic pasts.[70] Cultural patterns that defined the family and its internal relationships, however, varied across rural ethnocultural communities. Once again, the cultural frameworks carried to the Middle West influenced the roles and relationships within the household (see Chapter 6). Commentators—journalists, novelists, historians, sociologists, and anthropologists—surveying middle western rural communities repeatedly noted fundamental differences between immigrant and Yankee families with regard to land tenure, labor use, and family relationships. The varying orientations of power and influence within families served as a basis for criticism of particular groups and their families. American critics who perceived stricter patriarchal forms in immigrant homes often condemned what they considered to be the lack of affection between immigrant spouses. European antagonists who saw American homes as arenas characterized by a deficiency of proper respect for authority within the household disparaged American women and children and argued that the weaknesses within American homes boded ill for the nation's future.

Household arrangements informed the life chances of family members and thus tended to create pressures within the household systems themselves (see Chapter 7). This dynamic was especially hazardous in European household systems that were set in a demographic disequilibrium as they were transplanted in the Middle West yet were undergirded by a corporatist household ethic. The household was another instance in which life in the rural Middle West had created the freedom to reestablish hierarchical and corporate forms while at the same time giving the people living within them the independence to contest them. Whereas European households remained remarkably distinguishable from Yankee families, they were environments replete with conflict that was expressed more and more frequently as the nineteenth century progressed and that increasingly endangered the survival of those very household forms.

Whereas cultural diffusion that infused social change into ethnic communities illustrated internal friction, social interaction and political conflict revealed patterns of negotiation and division between the minds in the West. As localized traditions powerfully informed community life, they were at the same time integrated into and redefined by interactions with the larger society (see Chapter 8). Middle westerners were increasingly tied into broader collective identities that simultaneously augmented their sense of loyalty to American institutions and enmeshed them in other broader "ethnicized" institutional structures. Political parties, for example, were "American" institutions, but their memberships consisted of blocs of voters defined by ethnicity and class.

Broad "ethnicized" structures provided ethnic spokespeople and their followers with an entrée into American political institutions. They also gave them a forum to critique American society, a critique that became especially passionate in the late nineteenth century, when a perceived cultural malaise intensified the sense of urgency among the religious leaderships to address seeming societal decline. As new cultural patterns diffused into immigrant communities and families, their leaders utilized political and social debate to stress how "proper" community and family forms could temper a social breakdown as the century drew to a close.

The relative influences of corporatist and liberal thought on the minds of the West powerfully informed conceptions of state and society, individual and institution. These differences were illustrated by critics of American society who warned ominously of a moral decline in family and society in the late nineteenth century (see Chapter 9). Leaders influenced by corporatist ideas stressed the significance of institutions that mediated between the individual and the state, such as the family and the church community, which were deemed essential to the proper operation of society. These ideal structures were opposed by those who, in the wake of the revolutions of the late eighteenth century, magnified the importance of the individual in relation to the intermediate institutions of the family and the religious community. Although an increasing number of European immigrants shared this perspective, corporatists saw it as a tragedy worsening year by year. American materialism and individualism, they cautioned, were systematically weakening the family. Because the family was a natural brace upon which society was constructed, its ineffectiveness attenuated the vitality of society and ultimately the state.

By the late nineteenth century, the Middle West was the site of a series of political contests that illustrated these broad ideological differences (see Chapter 10). As various ethnic Americans maligned the materialism and individualism of American society, segments among the American-born questioned whether the ultimate allegiance of Roman Catholics was to nation or church. Debate concerning public schools, temperance, and woman's suffrage, moreover, became politically charged as the region was centralized and bureaucratized and as the interaction among ethnic groups increased. By exploring the content of the debate, we observe how it was concretely defined by fundamental differences between cultural groups in the region regarding the relative roles of family, community, and state in American society. As ethnic groups brought their conceptions of society into the political debate and modified it as a result, however, the American political system in turn influenced them. Immigrants who sought to use electoral politics to promote their beliefs concerning community and family were forced to enter an environment that was a liberal expression of the will of the electoral majority.

The narratives that pertain to the interactions, tensions, and conflicts among and between the minds in the West thus illustrate central features of American society during a century of migration prior to World War I. They reveal how localized migrant groups could relocate to a new milieu and re-create patterns of life practiced at home. Yet they also expose the problems spawned by efforts to adjust to a different economic environment and a new civil society. These accounts indicate how the ethnicized groups were encompassed under the canopy of a pluralist American society and how they used that entrance to become part of the political and social debate of the nation. They illustrate how in entering that debate, the groups brought oppositional beliefs that inexorably were discarded or altered by the political system to which they increasingly adhered. In the end, they exemplify the genius of an American tradition that used freedoms of belief to amalgamate its heterogeneous citizenry into a pluralistic whole.

PART ONE

THE REGION

CHAPTER 1

The Prospects of the West

A Promise and a Threat

The westward migration across the Appalachian range in the antebellum era was a phenomenon of singular importance to the development of the United States. Despite ebbs and flows in its rate of growth, the white population in the western territories increased inexorably from the onset of migration until the Civil War. At one time a frontier of minor consequence to the American Republic, the Middle West quickly became a region of central importance to the future of the United States. The white population of the Old Northwest, which was slightly more than a quarter of a million in 1810, had increased sixfold twenty years later to number about 1.5 million.[1] In the three decades prior to the Civil War, moreover, the five states in the Old Northwest expanded to nearly 7 million inhabitants, an increase, as William Petersen points out, that exceeded the white population growth in the two centuries between the founding of Jamestown and the Louisiana Purchase.[2] As new territories were opened up to white invasion, the journeys reached farther west. By 1860, Iowa and Minnesota contained nearly 1 million white inhabitants. The states in the region, the oldest of which was a mere fifty-seven years old, thus contained over one-quarter of the American population on the eve of the Civil War.

The bulk of this migration was predicated on the opportunities inherent in the western territories. As farmers moved west, they purchased parcels from a vast cache of land on which they planted crops or anticipated profits from speculation. During the frenzied buying between 1835 and 1837, 38 million acres of land—nearly 60,000 square miles—were alienated from government ownership. Twenty years later, amid the peak years of land acquisition, nearly twice as much land—65 million acres—

was transferred from the public domain to private hands.[3] The boom-bust economy and the vast national growth that occurred during the period can be traced to the land transactions in the antebellum era.

The economic possibilities of the trans-Appalachian West inspired an ambivalence among those who anticipated a continued unfolding of an exceptional American Republic. Time and again, this chapter argues, the expansion to the west was regarded as proof that the American nation was unique and destined to greatness. Yet the westward trek also created concern about the cultural ramifications of the redistribution of population. From one perspective, observers feared that the immensity of the movement might create a plastic society that would remold basic cultural patterns in a most regrettable way. The very language of the eastern press exposed underlying fears. As newspapers in the East and West dutifully calculated the immense volume of wagons and migrants,[4] they often marveled at the rapid construction of towns, if not "mature" communities. The county seat of Wapello County, Iowa, the *Cincinnati Chronicle* noted in 1843, was only one month old but contained about 5,000 inhabitants. Beneath the editor's amazement that "a county [was] born in a month," creating "a baby among nations a month old" in the West, the metaphorical subtext was clear: how could a "baby" perform the duties and undertake the responsibilities of mature citizenship in the Republic?[5] The metaphor of youth was often juxtaposed with one of deluge. The *Philadelphia Sentinel*, for example, wrote in 1836 that "the *torrent* which has for years past *flooded* to the West in one *vast, unbroken and increasing stream*, has this year transcended even its former volume, and is now *pouring* thousands on thousands of our best operatives into the prairies of the Northwest."[6] Visions of immaturity and inundation represented fears that, either through youthful naïveté or gradual submersion, an unpredictable societal foundation would be created in the West.

The shifting origins of the migrants made these fears all the more troubling to many Americans in the East. Happily for New England intellectuals, Yankee migrants with backgrounds common to their own were conspicuous. They arrived, according to one paper, "by the hundreds and thousands from the hills and valleys of New England, bringing with them that same untiring energy and perseverance that made their native states the admiration of the world."[7] This Yankee spirit was especially noticeable since specific settlement tracts were dominated by New England migrants. Such locales, Hezekiah Niles observed in 1834, constituted a veritable "'northern hive' [that] has already, perhaps, furnished about one-half the present population of New York, and of the western states, generally."[8]

Yet when Frederick Marryat traveled throughout the West about the same time, he met caravans of immigrants from the "sterile but healthy state" of North Carolina who were distinct from the "poor German or Irish settlers" he also encountered.[9] The diffusion of an emigration from throughout Europe created novelties such as the Norwegian immigrants, whose "picturesque costumes and strange physiognomy excited the curiosity of the passengers" traveling across the Atlantic.[10] Importantly, while the picturesque costumes created a colorful variability among the migrants to the West, a diverse cultural baggage was carried there as well. And although Yankees were characterized by their "untiring energy and perseverance," the cultural constitution of the migrants from Europe—especially Catholic Europe—was, to many American observers, more suspect.

The "West," a region whose very name suggested opportunity and growth to many, thus also became a potential symbol of fear. A territory rich in resources was developing swiftly—perhaps too swiftly. The very rapid growth of the region lured multitudes of immigrants whose contribution to the development of the American Republic might not be salutary. Indeed, many American cultural leaders were forced to confront a troubling irony that the very potential of the West might breed germs that would have deleterious results not only for the region but also for the future of the American nation as a whole. For many, the promise of the West was inextricably connected to potential threats to future American development.

The Promise of the West

We fellers workin' out back there got more 'n' more like *hands*, an' less like human beings. . . . I'd rather live on an iceberg and claw crabs f'r a livin' than have some feller passin' me on the road an' callin' me 'fellah!' . . . I consider myself a sight better 'n any man who lives on somebody else's hard work. I've never had a cent I didn't earn with them hands. . . . Well, so I come West, just like a thousand other fellers, to get a start where the cussed European aristocracy hadn't got a holt on the people.—Hamlin Garland, *Main-Travelled Roads: Six Mississippi Valley Stories* (1891; emphasis in original)

Behold, the Lord thy God hath set the land before thee: Go up and possess it, as the Lord God of thy Fathers hath said unto thee; fear not, neither be discouraged.—Deuteronomy 1:21

The vast tracts of open land in the West enchanted Euro-Americans who saw it as a haven for both the oppressed and the entrepreneur. Fredrika Bremer, from a European perspective, likened geographical landmarks of the nation to gates and seized upon the West as a new Eden. "Do not the Alleghany Mountains and Niagara stand as giant watchers at its entrance," she asked, "to open the portals of that new garden of Paradise, the latest home of the human race? The people of Europe pour in through the cities of the eastern coast. Those are the portals of the outer court; but the West is the garden where the rivers carry along with them gold." [11] Central to this "Paradise" was the land that would serve as a sort of elixir to maintain happiness and order. According to J. Leavitt in 1840, the "soil of amazing fertility" in the Old Northwest and in the tracts of land to the west still in Native American hands permitted the region to be "as well adapted to the residence, support, improvement, and happiness of man, as any equal portion of the globe." [12]

Although western land promised a new beginning for individual migrants, it was also perceived as a mainstay of the republican experiment in the United States. Americans postulated clear correlations between feudal land systems and monarchies in Europe on the one hand and free land and republics in the Americas on the other. Representative Orlando B. Ficklin of Illinois underscored the critical role of free land in the American Republic. "It is a cardinal and sound principle of political economy," he said from the floor of Congress in 1844,

> that, in a republican government, the people, the masses, should as far as possible, be encouraged in their laudable desires to become owners of the soil. The relation of landlord and tenant is not favorable to the growth or maintenance of free principles. The constant aim of monarchies is to build up a landed and moneyed aristocracy; to accumulate wealth and power in the hands of the few; to create distinctions and orders in society; to make the poor laborer a mere serf of his wealthy employer; and a policy precisely opposite to that should be adopted by us. The moment the citizen becomes a freeholder, his ties to his country and its institutions are increased. He has his home, his fireside, and his personal liberty and security, to protect and defend. [13]

James B. Bowlin, a historian and a U.S. representative, expanded the geographical sweep in 1846 when he suggested that the effect of the American land systems "was to inculcate ideas of independence in the great body of the people, elevating their moral sentiments, and arousing their innate love of liberty, until it resulted in stretching a line of republics from the St. Laurence to the Rio de la Plata." [14] Reformulating a Jeffersonian axiom, Bowlin argued that "the government is free or despotic, just in proportion to the number of its rulers, or participants in political privileges. If you wish to preserve and perpetuate its democratic form," he concluded, "you must pursue a policy tending to disseminate the lands amongst the largest possible number of people in the state."[15]

The certainty that free land strengthened the nation by guaranteeing the loyalty of its people to the commonwealth was complemented by the belief that it lessened class conflict and therefore the possibility of class war. If inequitable land laws introduced a landlord-tenant relationship in the West, Mississippian Robert J. Walker warned in 1837, "it will establish a relation of abject dependence on the one hand, and tyrannical power on the other. It will impoverish the many, and enrich the few. It will create a war of capital against labor, of the producer against the nonproducer, of the cultivator against the speculator."[16] Free land apparently kept both the people and their institutions and government free.

Despite the rapid alienation of land in the three decades before the Civil War, most people believed that the supply of land was almost unlimited and would continue indefinitely to reward the laborer who moved to the West. To an Iowa newspaper, only one "want" existed in the West, "which, if supplied, would produce results whose magnitude and importance would literally astonish the world. This want is Labor!"[17] The demand for workers created ideal opportunities for those who could move west. In response to the misery of a national depression in the 1830s, the *Iowa News* (Dubuque) posited a seemingly simple solution. "A few of the thousands of workmen and industrious mechanics who are out of business in the eastern cities and have not wherewith to get their next dinner," it declared, "should emigrate speedily to our Iowa District, where they can get not only employment and high wages but may very soon hope with ordinary diligence to place themselves beyond the reach of pressure."[18] Over twenty years later, another paper in the same city marveled at the great number of emigrant teams that filled the streets. "Let 'em come," it pronounced. "Our broad prairies are great enough to hold the poor devils who are dragging out a miserable life under the slavery of New England Capital, or the despotism of the Eastern Continent."[19] The dissimilarities in the levels of misery in the East and the West were illustrated by a promotional pamphlet comparing the incidence of pauperism in the two regions. Figuring that the rates of pauperism were about sixty times greater in New York and Massachusetts than in Iowa, "A Pioneer" concluded:

> The same disparity exists between Iowa and the East with regard to the useless members of society, the drones, vagabonds, beggars, and others who lived by their wits and sharp practices. The reason for this great disparity is, not that human nature is different in Iowa from what it is in the East, but that a small amount of labor will produce a larger amount of the necessities of life in the West than

in the East. A man who can make more by honest labor in the day time than he can by stealing at night, will not be a thief; and the same reason accounts for the comparatively small amount of paupers, beggars, and vagabonds.[20]

The promise of the West thus implied an equality that marked it off from eastern regions. Englishman Charles Augustus Murray, who traveled throughout the Americas in the mid-1830s, bemoaned the lack of "social republicanism" in the Atlantic cities. Yet "the West presents a much truer picture of republicanism, because the equality existing elsewhere in theory, exists here in fact."[21]

Such public paeans to the West were obviously inspired in part by boosterism, but they were corroborated—though oftentimes with less bravado—by private accounts. Myranda Underwood, writing to relatives in the East in 1847 from Wisconsin, admitted that "we are poor and expect to be and are reconciled to poverty but think that we can do better here with our limited means than we could back east."[22] European immigrants usually agreed. Sjoerd Aukes Sipma stressed to his relatives back home in Friesland that "wealth and splendor are not to be found here, but you can be sure of a simple, farmer's life. Do not count on gathering treasures here in the far West," he warned, "but you can be sure of a good and abundant life, and that without too much work."[23] John and Mary Thomson commented that "a man can do better in this cuntry by far than he can do" in Scotland in large part because "manual labour is so much hier."[24] A letter to Sweden in the late 1840s also underscored the material wealth of the western United States. "All our bread is white, being made from bolted wheat flour. We get two kronor [54 cents] for a day's work, and in harvest time four kronor and all you want to eat! This is surely the Promised Land!"[25] A Norwegian traveler to Wisconsin in the 1840s stressed a similar theme when he wrote, "I could easily put myself in the place of a farmer, who, as he ate his simple meal, patted himself on the stomach and exclaimed: 'I must say, the food here is fine; we never need to be afraid of starving.' That means a great deal. Hunger," he concluded to his Norwegian audience, "is an enemy from which many of our highlands in Norway never feel safe. . . . Just think what an impression it would make on a poor highlander's imagination to be told that some day he might eat wheat bread every day and pork at least three times a week!"[26]

In addition to material abundance, Europeans perceived a greater social equality in their new homes in the West. Writing to parents and siblings in Norway in 1849, an immigrant emphasized that in Wisconsin there were "no so-called elite people [*Storfolk*] as there are in Norway. A simple workingman is just as respected as any other man . . . and one's hat is not taken off his head for any man; in fact, it is not taken off any oftener than one eats."[27] "No one must take off his hat," a phrase repeated over and over by immigrants from nations throughout Europe, was part of an iconography that attested to perceptions of greater social equality in the United States.[28]

Given these opportunities, many of the American-born argued that it would be relatively simple for Europeans to translate their satisfaction with American life into loyalty to the United States. "And what shall we say," asked Edward Norris Kirk in 1848, "of the future swellings of [the great tide of foreign immigration]?" He answered:

> Europe is perhaps now passing through one of those convulsive processes, in which the vengeance and the mercy of God shall strangely commingle, to punish and to regenerate her guilty nations. . . . Her weary children are now dashing the bitter cup from their lips, and fleeing in thousands to this asylum. From Norway's arctic zone, to Italy's sunny shores; the rich and the poor, the villain and the upright, the industrious and the indolent—they are coming to share our great patrimony, to mould our national character, and to be moulded. And let them come. We welcome them. Our hearts shall outstrip the tardiness of law, and naturalize them at their land. They are Americans, if they come with that intention, the instant their feet touch our shores.[29]

A writer in the *Home Missionary* agreed. "The flying thousands who escape from French and German revolutions, and Irish penury and starvation," he wrote, "look to our land alone for refuge, never thinking of any other as promising them political liberty, intellectual elevation, or rewarded labor and sufficient food."[30] The American land had much to offer the downtrodden.

The potential of the immigrant multitudes, other writers argued, in turn would aid the United States. As early as 1832, Hezekiah Niles noted that a large number of Germans who were on their way to the "immeasurable west" would soon be joined by thousands more. "Let them come," he concluded. "They are an industrious and moral race, and will do well here. We rejoice that our country presents a haven, where the weary and oppressed even in this world may have a rest."[31] Some thirteen years later, Niles rephrased his paean to American opportunity and freedom. "What a restless, but enterprising spirit characterizes the American people!" he marveled in 1845. "They are ever ready to follow to the world's end the bright promises of ambition, of wealth, or charity. This restlessness, activity, and enterprise," he wrote, "are the characteristics of freemen—the result of free institutions which give an impetus to the human mind. . . .

Even the oppressed and down trodden of other countries seems here to receive new life," Niles concluded. "The countenance brightens, and hope beams from the eye, as they breathe our pure air, and drink in the spirit of our free institutions."[32]

As the oppressed inhaled the freedoms of the United States, their metamorphosis led some observers to forecast the creation of an improved American "race." Reiterating Crèvecoeur's views, these nineteenth-century commentators foresaw the emergence of a fortified American character especially in the independent West, where the various "races" interacted with one another. Michel Chevalier, during his visits to the United States, argued that "the fusion of the European with the Yankee takes place slowly, even on the new soil of the West." Nonetheless, enough "foreign blood has been mingled with the Yankee blood to modify the primitive character of the New England race, and to form a third American type, that of the West[, which] . . . is characterized by its athletic forms and ambitious pretensions." This new "race," in short, was "superior" to the others.[33] A southern paper, for its part, stressed the contribution of the South when it argued that increased intercommunication "will hasten the process of fusing and blending all elements [of ethnic diversity] together, and will prevent individual sections from cherishing to exclusion their peculiar or hereditary prejudices. The descendants of the puritan will mingle with the sons of the cavaliers. . . . The steady gravity and unyielding firmness of the German, harmonizing with the ardent and warm-hearted temperament of the Irishman will constitute the equilibrium of a noble character." Whereas the "antiquated sobrieties of the old world [have] exhausted their capability and their energy," the writer claimed, "the human race [in the United States] was about to start afresh, with new combinations of elements, from which spring an untried principle of vitality."[34]

The opportunities inherent in the West, then, were manifested in a cluster of salutary influences on the nation as a whole. Largely inspired by republican ideals, many Americans—and Europeans—saw the West as a region that would replicate, or even improve upon, the promise of the United States. The land provided prospects for individual independence that allegedly made settlers both more "honest" and more "American." As migrants—American- and European-born alike—celebrated the liberties inherent in their new condition, American observers found it simple to welcome them and proclaim the continued unfolding of a republican spectacle. Free land made men free. It created an environment where individuals and the Republic could achieve their fullest form.

The Threats Inherent in the West

Let no foreign Holy Alliance presume, or congratulate itself, upon the hitherto
unsuspicious and generous toleration of its secret agents in this country.
America may for a time sleep soundly, as innocence is wont to sleep,
unsuspicious of hostile attack; but if any foreign power, jealous of the
increasing strength of the embryo giant, sends its serpents to lurk within his
cradle let such presumption be assured that the waking energies of the infant
are not to be despised, that once having grasped his foes, he will neither be
tempted from his hold by admiration of their painted and gilded covering, nor
by fear of the fatal embrace of their treacherous folds. — Samuel F. B. Morse,
Foreign Conspiracy against the Liberties of the United States (1835)

Behold, therefore, I will bring strangers upon thee, the terrible of the nations;
and they shall draw their swords against the beauty of thy wisdom,
and they shall defile thy brightness. — Ezekiel 28:7

Although the abundant resources of the West were critical in sustaining
an antebellum ideology that proclaimed continued opportunity for white
residents of the United States, many observers were troubled by the fact
that the possibilities of the West were Janus-faced. From a slightly different angle of vision, the West's resources paradoxically could be viewed as
the cornerstones of a series of scenarios that led to the destruction of the
Republic. For although vast tracts of land that unceasingly lured millions
of migrants westward were palpable evidence of the superiority of the
young nation, they were also magnets that drew regressive forces toward
the nation like moths to a light. A question that haunted many American
critics at mid-century was whether the fragile Republic could control a
massive, seemingly chaotic migration predicated on land and liberty, two
linchpins in the maintenance of the American experiment.

This dilemma had troubled eastern Americans for decades. The vast
opportunities symbolized in the West likely would encourage a great migration that could in turn beget an inchoate society incapable of executing adequately the duties of citizenship. As the size of the West grew in
the nineteenth century, so did fears concerning its immaturity. The "vast"
West, Lyman Beecher noted, which contained 150,000 white settlers in
1795, was peopled by nearly 5 million people forty years later. "If no calamity intervenes," Beecher reasoned, the region would contain about 100
million residents by 1900 and perhaps 300 million inhabitants when it
was "fully peopled." [35] Beecher's figures were succeeded by more modest
yet still sizable estimates. Based on calculations of land availability and
European population densities, the *Home Missionary* figured in 1841 that
the 440,211 square miles of the ten western states might soon be the home

of nearly 50 million people. Illinois, Missouri, and Arkansas alone—each of which was equal in size to seven Massachusettses—could together soon contain nearly 20 million residents, 2 million more than the entire population of the United States at the time. As the United States conquered and annexed lands throughout the 1840s and the tracts in the West increased relative to those in the East, the ratio of population in the West compared to that in the East grew. Again using Massachusetts as the unit of measurement, Albert Barnes figured that "Texas alone could be divided into *forty-four* such states. The territory ceded by the late treaty with Mexico . . . would make *seventy-two* States of the same dimensions. . . . What a country!" he concluded. "What a field for Christian enterprise!"[36] Another clergyman, also concerned about the conversion of souls residing in the West, agreed; this region, he wrote, was "a broad, fertile land."[37]

This expansion would have enormous political and cultural repercussions not only for the West but also for the nation as a whole. As the region's population grew, its political representation in the federal government would also increase, which in turn would inescapably affect the East. One perspective, of course, was buoyantly optimistic that the "freedom" and "liberty" inherent in the West would reverberate eastward. "From the beginning of the century," complained a mid-century Iowa newspaper, "the middle and the northern states have perverted the legislation to selfish ends. It will not be long," however, "thank providence, ere the Valley of the Mississippi—the garden spot of the world—will wield a controlling influence in national affairs."[38] An opposite perspective, however, focused on the character of the migrants and the society they created. Leaders as diverse as Timothy Dwight and Thomas Jefferson, after all, had decades before belittled those who moved west.[39] The critique continued in the mid-nineteenth century. Conservatives feared a "refluent wave" that would inundate the East. As the population increased in the West, the *Home Missionary* warned, "the people of the Great Valley will outnumber those of the old states, and control the moral and political influence of this nation." If the West and its people were not properly controlled, "its turbid wave" would roll back upon the East. "If, then, *we* do not now mould the West," the journal concluded ominously, "it will soon mould *us*."[40]

Critics also feared that European immigrants who failed to consent to the intricacies of the republican gospel would replicate the behavior of American-born migrants to the West that so troubled eastern Americans. Liberty could lead to license. "Coming to a country like America, and hearing the most exaggerated stories of its ample freedom for all men, without a thought of their responsibility to the nation sustaining the fabric of this glorious freedom," Frederick Saunders and T. B. Thorpe stressed,

THE REGION

"they conclude that here the field of licence lies open, and that any sort of restraint is powerless and illegal against unbounded indulgence."[41] "Never having seen liberty," concurred Thomas R. Whitney, "they know not what it is, and with the first taste of its sweets, all restraints, civil and religious, become alike irksome to them. They soon begin to regard all laws as oppressive," he concluded, "whether they emanate from the edict of a despot, or the openly-declared will of a free people."[42]

Such a prospect was daunting because it was generally agreed that the West lacked the institutional framework to harmonize society. Migrants enjoyed the "freedoms" to move and to build societies, but members of the eastern elite feared that they might misuse their liberty and move not only themselves but society as well in a most unsalutary direction. "Liberty and lawlessness," Saunders and Thorpe reminded their readership in 1855, "are with them one and the same thing."[43] If those within the widening migrant streams abused liberty or were led in errant ways, they would fail to assent to the developing institutions of the American tradition that had blessed the nation. Therein lay the challenge.

Whereas eastern critics dreaded the consequences of settlements issuing forth from uninstitutionalized migrations to the West, they were increasingly troubled by a second scenario by the mid-nineteenth century. In addition to fearing inchoate societies in the West, Americans worried about the results of a migration of those fettered to "regressive" European institutions. The fears were rooted in a broad-based nativism that punctuated American life in the three decades prior to the Civil War.[44] Beneath a virulent anti-immigrant sentiment manifested in riots and powerful political movements was a relatively consistent critique of the cultural patterns of the immigrant and their impact on the developing American Republic. Within that critique, concerns about the future role of the West in the unfolding drama of the United States were embedded.

The promise of the United States, according to this critique, was based on a combination of economic opportunity, political equality, and a superior cultural foundation. The nation, to be sure, was blessed with material abundance, but material wealth could sustain the nation's promise only if society and the state maintained a progressive worldview that promoted intellectual and economic freedoms. That worldview had a glorious past. "Religion, patriotism, and morality, have been the foundation-stones of our success as a nation," maintained Whitney, "and our happiness and prosperity as a people." The "foundation-stones" were "laid upon the rock of a stern Protestant faith," Whitney concluded, mixing metaphors, "and their fruits have been all that our institutions promised—civil and religious liberty."[45] Providence would continue to unfold. "It is too important a truth for any of us to overlook," wrote Saunders and

Thorpe confidently, "that the American Republic is the home of Liberty, and the final hope of the world."[46]

The potential traps of providential liberty, however, were many. The Republic, after all, was a human construction and, as such, could be subverted by its citizenry. And regressive human forces were close at hand. The most obvious symbol of such forces for a large segment of mid-century northerners was the southern slaveowner who held his slaves and his region in bondage. Yet the specters of the despotic European monarch and the authoritarian Catholic priest were threats that at least prior to 1854 were much closer at hand in the West, threats that could also undermine and ultimately destroy the American experiment.[47] Significantly, the iconography of the Roman Catholic Church in this critique in many ways paralleled that of the slaveholder. The church was characterized as a hierarchical force that inhibited individual freedoms; it was "irrational"; it kept its victims in "slavery"; and it had vast implications for the development of the West and ultimately of the Republic.

Thomas R. Whitney was explicit in his correlations of liberty and slavery with republicanism and Romanism, "two isms . . . for all time." "Romanism," Whitney began simply, "is diametrically opposed to Republicanism." The opposition was due politically to the hostility of the Roman Catholic Church to "our free institutions." "The simple fact," Whitney argued, "that one is an *absolute* government, and the other a *popular* government, establishes the antipodal." The consequences of this "simple fact" were profound and wide-ranging. "American Republicanism" cultivated intelligence among the people and ensured the freedom of the press, whereas "Romanism" suppressed intelligence and silenced the press. "American Republicanism" extended "the full liberty of conscience to all its people," whereas Romanism pronounced "liberty of conscience to be a wicked heresy." "In a word," Whitney concluded ominously, "American Republicanism is FREEDOM; Romanism is *slavery*."[48]

Furthermore, these "two forms of government" had opposite effects on the degree of economic development. To Whitney, "American Republicanism is the parent of progress." It expanded the intellect and elevated "the standard of the individual man." As a result, locomotives were built, commerce was sustained, and the sciences were encouraged. Romanism, on the other hand, was "the open foe of progress." It "stifles the energies of its subjects, stultifies the intellect, and wraps the soul in a mantle of superstitions" that prostrated "all self-respect in the individual." Any interest in art, industry, or literature was pursued "only for the purpose of multiplying its own weapons against human freedom." In sum, "where Romanism prevails, there is stagnation and public lethargy.

Where American Republicanism prevails, there is industry, intelligence, energy, and public prosperity."[49] The outcome of the battle between the minds in America, in short, was of monumental significance.

It is obvious to the modern reader that this paean to freedom and progress was riddled with inherent contradictions and obvious omissions. Freedom and citizenship, for one thing, were predicated on a "whiteness" that excluded many Americans. Importantly for our purposes, however, because European immigrants were defined as white, they were placed within an arena that accorded them the rights of citizenship. Ironically, European immigrants, and especially Roman Catholic immigrants, perceived by many of the American-born as lacking the wherewithal to perform the duty of citizens, potentially were critical forces in the nation's political future. This appraisal of Catholicism and, by implication, of the effects of immigration was broad-based and wide-ranging. Many of its precepts could be linked to a classical republicanism that strove for a homogeneous and virtuous citizenry.[50] Yet by the mid-nineteenth century, many Americans who did not explicitly recognize an allegiance to classical republican doctrines defended the importance of a homogeneous America. Anti-Catholicism soon was linked to a free-soil ideology, to evangelical reform, and to a movement of moral uplift led by women.[51] In its variety of forms and expressions, moreover, nativism had diffused broadly across the political spectrum in the United States and would find expression in most major political party traditions as well as in the zealous nativism of the American (Know Nothing) Party.[52]

In addition to having a broad appeal, the nativist critique was also enduring. Americans long before the anti-immigrant Know Nothing movement of the 1850s—and long after it—grappled with the meaning of immigration in relation to the unfolding American nation. Yet nativism became particularly shrill in the two decades between the publication of the works of Morse and Beecher in 1835 and the flowering of the Know Nothing Party, during which, not coincidentally, immigration increased dramatically. Nativists, in no uncertain terms, pointed out the vast size of the immigrant stream at mid-century. Samuel Busey noted in 1856 that in the past sixteen years, 3.4 million immigrants had arrived on American shores, and he surmised (wrongly as it turned out) that an additional 2 million would immigrate before 1860. To illustrate the significance of immigrants' numbers in concrete terms, Busey calculated the demographic effects of the number of immigrants arriving in one year alone. If the immigrants of 1854 were spread over an area with the average population density of the United States, he calculated, they would settle 64,000 square miles, the equivalent of eight Massachusettses. If they were concentrated, they would nearly equal the number of people then living in North Carolina.[53]

These fears were exacerbated by anxieties that immigration would continue to increase well into the foreseeable future. "The future of the European nations," wrote Saunders and Thorpe in 1855, "is stormy and dark." Europe, they stressed, was "crowded with people, oppressed with poverty, containing much sterile land, and doomed to the horrors of complicated and obstinate wars." It surely would "long send vast and vaster yearly bands to share our free peace, our rich and boundless lands, and our quiet wealth."[54] To support their point, Saunders and Thorpe needed only to cite recent trends. The "great, steady, and increasing stream of Europeans" over three-quarters of a century had begun with a few thousand but by mid-century averaged 400,000. As this "exodus" continued to grow, Busey calculated, in "fifteen years the foreign will outnumber the native population."[55]

Although nativists feared immigration in general, specific apprehensions about the cultural effects of immigration were fixed principally on regions—such as the West—where European newcomers were especially numerous. In 1850, Busey calculated, nearly one-half of the voters in Wisconsin were foreign-born. The ratio in Iowa was one in four; in Illinois and Ohio, one in six. The West, Busey concluded ominously, was the region toward which "the tide of immigration is rapidly tending." The inference for the future was "clear and indisputable": "the territorial possessions will be settled by foreigners."[56]

Many western states, nativists complained, were in fact attempting to attract immigrants. Despite federal laws that required immigrants to live at least five years in the United States prior to naturalization, states such as Illinois permitted aliens to vote if they had arrived in the state at least six months prior to an election, federal or otherwise. The only ostensible motive for this policy, Whitney argued, was an attempt to induce settlement in "the tenantless lands of the great interior." Despite what he called the "intrinsically meritorious" sentiment of such a policy, Whitney stressed that it enfranchised those incapable of wielding the ballot for the good of the state. "What guarantee have our sister States of the West," Whitney asked rhetorically, "within whose fruitful borders the tide of European immigration is pouring like a living flood; what guarantee have they that their too liberal constitutions and laws will not melt like wax, before the consuming heat of imported opinions, and through the manipulation of foreign voters, be remodelled and made to assume new aspects, repulsive to rational liberty, subversive of religion, and hostile to the true interests of the State?" Indeed, the new regions of the West, Whitney concluded, would find "that they have encouraged a clannish sentiment among their foreign population" that would prove detrimental to state and nation.[57]

Fueled by visions of "slavery," concerns about the rush of European migration to the West were based not only on its volume but also on the palpable fear that liberties, an inherent component of the American mission, would not be maintained by the immigrant hordes. Because of the peculiar importance of the West in sustaining these liberties, the development of an immigrant culture there was especially vexing. The "great experiment," replete with its republican institutions, faced continual challenges, and as Beecher contended as early as 1835, "the *religious and political destiny* of our nation is soon to be decided in the West." Although the West represented "a young empire of mind, and power, and wealth, and free institutions, rushing up to a giant manhood," its people confronted frightening evils from the benighted masses flowing from Europe. Roman Catholics, in particular, represented not only unenlightenment but also a threat to the future of the American republican government. And Beecher believed that threat would be played out in the West, whose destiny would be determined by a conflict of institutions "for purposes of superstition, or evangelical light; of despotism, or liberty."[58]

As immigration from Europe continued to increase at mid-century, observers voiced misgivings about the shifting ratios of those who adhered to institutions characterized by "liberty" to those identified with "despotism." "How long," asked a Protestant in 1849, "will our remaining Puritanism bear the process of dilution and mixture with the heterogeneous ingredients which, willing or unwilling, we see daily poured into our cup? Here are these hundreds of thousands [of immigrants], with their full grown prejudices, and errors of every kind, to be won to such practical views of truth and liberty, as will make them safe and peaceable citizens and neighbors, and, if possible, evangelical Christians."[59] Like many other champions of the American Republic, this writer perceived the prospect of an immensely troubling irony: the very opportunities that created the potential for American greatness also encouraged myriad cultural groups to migrate there, which in turn held the seeds of the potential ruin of American liberties.

To be sure, many Americans clung to the belief that the inherent liberties of the young nation and the abundant opportunities of the West were elixirs that could transform the immigrant. The degree to which the immigrant posed a threat therefore was inversely related to the potential for the acculturation of immigrants to American beliefs. If immigrants could be "converted" to the American system, if they could be transformed into republicans *and* Protestants, they likely would shake off their Old World trappings just like other Americans before them. As new Americans, they could abandon their attachments to hierarchy and their inhibitions concerning individualism. They could then take part in and contribute to the American experiment.[60]

Yet even as it fostered a massive migration, the mighty empire of the West posed another challenge: it provided an arena in which ambiguous loyalties could be secluded and maintained. One of the greatest threats to the creation of a homogeneous nation was a "clannishness" promoted by patterns of residence in which groups of people clustered together. The broad expanses of the West encouraged such clannishness, thereby kindling fears that migrants to the western territories would not fuse into another "American" type or live in "American" communities. The concern was not focused exclusively on European immigrants. An early Illinois resident in 1831, for example, bemoaned the fact that colonies formed in the eastern states were migrating as groups into Illinois. "Not that we have any objection to emigration in itself," wrote James Hall, ever the booster. "On the contrary, few have done more than we, to encourage and promote it . . . and we care not from what point of the compass he may come; but wish to see them come to Illinois, with a manly confidence in us, and with the feelings, not of New Englanders, or Pennsylvanians, but of Americans."[61] In short, a new American could not be created in a milieu where old regional loyalties lingered.

The misgivings, however, were more pointed when directed at European immigrants who exploited the opportunities of the United States in clustered settlements that allowed them—paradoxically, in the minds of American nativists—to maintain their former social and cultural worlds. Whitney contended that immigrants nestled in their neighborhoods would experience an "interchange of old thoughts, old memories, and old associations" so that "the *home* sentiment will wrestle with the new influence." As a result, "a clannish spirit would grow up among them, and the recollections of the past will cluster tenaciously, and almost holily, about their hearts."[62]

The "old thoughts" that clustered tenaciously around immigrants' hearts represented not only thoughts of home but also cultural patterns that sprang from "despotic" and "authoritarian" regimes. Indeed, Samuel F. B. Morse argued as early as 1835 that the "ignorant" immigrants could "live surrounded by freedom, yet liberty of conscience, right of private judgment, whether in religion or politics," would be "effectually excluded by the priests, as if the code of Austria already ruled the land." However, "republican education, were it allowed freely to come in contact with their minds, would doubtless soon furnish a remedy for an evil for which, in the existing state of things, we have no cure."[63] Lyman Beecher, around the same time, concurred. "Catholic Europe is throwing swarm on swarm upon our shores," he argued. "Their embodied and insulated condition," moreover, "as strangers of another tongue, and their unacquaintance with protestants, and prejudices against them, and their fear and implicit obe-dience of their priesthood, and aversion to instruction from book, or tract, or Bible, but with their consent, tends powerfully to prevent assimilation and perpetuate the principles of a powerful cast." If they would associate with republicans, the powerful principles would wear away, concluded Beecher. "If they scattered, unassociated, the attrition of circumstance would wear off their predelictions [*sic*] and aversions."[64] Conversion and clannishness, to Beecher and many others, were antithetical.

For these reasons, Americans who perceived the centrality of the West to the future of the United States were troubled by a steady stream of re-ports that European immigrants were planning to establish self-contained colonies throughout the region. In 1832, for example, a committee repre-senting Rhenish Bavaria was formed to initiate talks with the government of the United States about the purchase of a tract of land to be settled by disaffected Germans. The tract, to be called "New Germany," would be-come the twenty-fifth state of the Union. According to the *Stuttgard [sic] Universal Gazette*, the new German state would "receive all those whose hopes and claims to liberty and right are disappointed in old Germany." Part and parcel of the potential of American freedom, the plan never-theless was anathema to American commentators. Niles's views resonate with a combination of republican, American, and Americanizing pos-tures:

> We shall give these, all such as these, from any and every country, a hearty welcome—but the idea of settling in a large and compact body, cannot be approved. In coming hither, they should expect that their children, at least, will become *Americans*, in habits, manners and feelings; and be *fully* incorporated into the body of the citizens. Most reflecting persons, we think, have regarded it as unfortunate, that, in certain parts of the United States, the *German*, *Irish*, or *French* population (so called, though the large majority may be *natives*) are so located as seemingly to have different interests, or at least dif-ferent views from the public good—remaining as *separated* classes of the people, and so liable to particular influences, which perhaps, are sometimes prejudicial to the "general welfare" and often excited to subserve peculiar purposes.

If the public good was maintained by creating a common American nationality, Niles concluded, "all . . . separations of the people into classes, using even different languages, must materially impede the for-mation of a national character, and the spread of useful knowledge."[65]

Despite repeated expressions of these fears, European plans for founding colonies increasingly punctuated the 1830s and 1840s. A society named "Germania," formed in New York City in 1835, for example, sent a memorial to Congress asking for land for German fugitives. After the request was denied, the society attempted to direct Germans to settle in a single state where they could gain political control, making it German de facto if not de jure. By 1847, Franz Löher decided that a German state could and ought to be formed in the Northwest. Since the Irish remained in the East and Americans were scattered throughout the nation, he argued, a planned colonization somewhere in the West could create a largely German society and state. Here, amid what was destined to become the "ruling center" of North America, Germans could, according to Löher, "form a German state, in which the German language is as much the popular and official language as the English is now, and in which the German spirit rules."[66]

Colonization schemes were especially distasteful to Americans when they were organized under the auspices of the Roman Catholic Church. In late 1842, for example, a pamphlet entitled *A Proposed Plan of a General Emigration Society by a Catholic Gentleman* was published in London and Dublin. The plan called for the investment of capital in large tracts of land in the Mississippi Valley that would be peopled by destitute Irish peasants. In return for a pledge of temperance and a commitment to work three years on the land, the peasant would receive passage to the Middle West and the prospect of ten acres of land after the contract was fulfilled. Whereas the *Freeman's Journal and Catholic Register* in New York City argued that the plan would "put an end to the evils which attend the desultory and unprotected emigration of the poor Irish,"[67] the nativist American response bordered on hysteria. An exegesis of the text of the pamphlet focused in particular on the settlement patterns. As the pamphlet stressed, the colonies would be located in the West—the region that "will become the heart of the country, and ultimately determine the character of the whole"—and organized around an institutional framework based on the priesthood. The immigrants were thus, according to critics, to be planted "in masses, in definite districts, subject to certain conditions," the most contemptible of which was the authority of the priest. By conflating two concepts dear to Americans, the commentator concluded, "even if no such foreign conspiracy against our *Protestantism* and *liberty* exists, there is, unquestionably, throughout the length and breadth of Europe a general sympathy in just such view and measures, as such a conspiracy would employ."[68]

Planned colonies, in fact, often elicited fears of a concerted conspiracy aimed at undermining the American Republic. Nativists observed as early as the 1830s that colonies not only retarded the immigrants' conversion to the American faith but also were staging grounds in which immigrants remained the dupes of foreign despotic and authoritarian powers attempting to destroy the Republic through deceit and trickery.[69] The authoritarian states in Europe, in concert with the Roman Catholic hierarchy in Europe and the United States, were not interested in simply settling European peasants in a more abundant material milieu. Rather, in the minds of many Americans, they ultimately intended to use these benighted peasants as political minions to destroy the American republican experiment.

Americans insisted that a republic was the most beautiful and progressive form of government, but they also knew that it was the most fragile. Its purity could easily be muddied by the concerted plans of those who did not have the commonweal of the citizenry at heart. For "no government," according to Beecher, "is more complex and difficult of preservation than a republic." The American Republic depended on the wisdom of an independent and virtuous citizenry, yet as time passed, the nation received "a rush of dark-minded" immigrants like never before. Combining agricultural and biblical metaphors, Beecher affirmed that "clouds like the locusts of Egypt are rising from the hills and plains of Europe, and on the wings of every wind are coming over to settle down upon our fair fields." Those who remained behind, "cheered by the news of [the immigrants'] safe arrival and green pastures, are preparing for flight in an endless procession."[70]

Nativists were quick to point out that the monarchists in Europe openly admitted and baldly celebrated the conspiratorial designs of the despots and their apocalyptic vision of America's future. Although the duke of Richmond felt that the government of the United States was "weak, inconsistent, and bad, and could not long exist," he argued that "so long as it exists, no Prince will be safe upon his throne." The sovereigns of Europe, the duke continued, thus understood that the infant republic would be crushed "*by subversion rather than conquest.*" The scenario was familiar to any well-read nativist. To begin with, "all the low and surplus population of the different nations of Europe will be carried into" the United States. These immigrants "will bring with them their principles," will adhere to them, and ultimately will become citizens with the right of suffrage. The stage was thus set: "The different grades of society will then be created by the elevation of a few, and by degrading many, and thus a heterogeneous population will be formed, speaking different languages, and of different religions and sentiments, and to make them act, think, and feel alike in political affairs, will be like mixing oil and water." Stemming from these heterogeneous sentiments, "discord, dissension, anarchy, and civil war will ensue, and some popular individual will assume the government, and restore order," after which "the sovereigns of Europe, the emigrants and many of the natives [would] sustain him."[71]

This calculated conspiracy was based on two central views. First, homogeneity was essential to a smoothly functioning republican society, whereas a heterogeneous, pluralist environment created weaknesses that could be exploited by the Republic's enemies. Immigrant enclaves in the West, in this scenario, were not simply examples of clannishness that would be difficult to penetrate; they were the sites that laid a foundation for the systematic subversion of the American Republic. Second, locales of great importance to Americans and to the Republic were also places of great risk. Although the West held promise, immigrant enclaves there were a threat. "Popery has directed a longing eye to that immense tract of land," wrote John Angell James of Birmingham, England, in reference to the western states, "and has already felt the inward heaving of ambition, to compensate herself for her losses in the old world, by her conquests in the new. The valley of the Mississippi has been, no doubt, mapped as well as surveyed by emissaries of the Vatican; and cardinals are exulting, in the hope of enriching the Papal See by accessions from the United States." Using a similar metaphor of military preparation, another observer contended that "at every important point on the Mississippi, the Romanists have commenced their work, and stationed their men." The war matériel—cannon fodder as well as monetary resources— was derived almost exclusively from foreign sources.[72] The West, a seat of progress and a grounding for the Republic, had become a site of conspiracy, most regressive and most authoritarian. Nativists were left to puzzle over a conundrum wherein a center of liberty could lead logically, almost inexorably, to a triumph of despotism.

The American Protestant Response

Now, I have to ask, if Catholics in Europe can afford to sustain men here, with
a view to *future influence*, so as to gain time and prejudice the public mind in
their favor, ought not the churches of New-England to station their men here,
on these outposts of Zion, to counteract this influence, and to strip off the mask
from those who transform themselves into angels of light?—"Romanism in
Iowa," *Home Missionary* (1842; emphasis in original)

The twin narratives of the West as a place of promise and as a threat to the nation had both short- and long-term consequences. The immediate problem in the mid-nineteenth century was the need to defeat what appeared to many to be an imminent immigrant peril. To be sure, many of the most distinct misgivings with regard to the immigrant were focused on the American city, a setting that was experiencing massive growth and increasing self-doubt.[73] Yet the West, that linchpin of American greatness, remained another arena of concern in which apocalyptic scenarios pointed to inevitable confrontation. "Two distinct nationalities [such as foreigners and natives] cannot exist together harmoniously under the same jurisdiction," Samuel C. Busey argued. Whether in cities or on the frontier, he wrote, "it is contrary to the laws of nature for any two people so unlike physically, mentally, morally, socially, and politically, to live together. . . . A conflict must come."[74]

American spokesmen put on a brave face about the onslaught of foreign colonies and voiced optimism about the outcome of the battle. At the very least, Beecher, with his Protestant progressive worldview, found it difficult to accept a reversal of providence. God had not brought their "fathers to this goodly land to lay the foundation of religious liberty," he argued, "only . . . to abandon his work."[75] He would not, according to a Protestant missionary, "abandon to the dominion of Antichrist, our schools, our republicanism and the living churches of the land."[76] Indeed, when "the West is filled with the Gospel," wrote yet another, it will send forth representatives who "will be, by choice, or by the constraint of a virtuous public sentiment, the advocates of righteousness."[77]

The promise of the West, with its inherent liberties and economic opportunity, moreover, unleashed forces that increased the difficulty of transplanting the garish trappings of the Old World. The "emigrant from the old world," Albert Barnes argued, had "broken away from a thousand influences in favor of a false religion in his own land." These "influences"—"the moss-grown cathedral, . . . pompous ceremonial, the long train of priests"—were "unseen where a man makes a western prairie his home." And even if they were brought to the West, they would have to be reproduced over a period of time during which the immigrant's "own mind, and more especially the minds of his children, shall be open to the better influence which grows out of our Protestant and Republican institutions."[78] The environment of the West perhaps would transform the immigrant. The battle would be long, most witnesses agreed, but a victory was in the offing.

It was widely believed, moreover, that such a victory ultimately would be won by creating a homogeneous, tractable western populace. Thomas Jefferson, as early as 1785 in *Notes on the State of Virginia*, predicted the ill effects of diversity. "The greatest number of emigrants" to the United States, he held, had grown up under the aegis of monarchy. As a result, they would "bring with them the principles of the governments they have imbibed in early youth; or if able to throw them off, it will be in exchange for an unbounded licentiousness." Since they would be vacillating between one extreme and the other, "it would be a miracle were they to stop precisely at the point of temperate liberty." They would share these principles with their children, and their families would play a role in the creation of law. In that enterprise, they would "infuse into [legislation] their spirit, warp and bias its direction, and render it a heterogeneous, incoherent, distracted mass."[79] From this perspective, incoherent heterogeneity needed to be replaced by harmonious homogeneity.

One avenue to create homogeneity was to restrict immigration or the rights of the foreign-born in the United States. Nativists thus advocated change in the land policy of the federal government that would tend to discourage immigration. Some of the land was "given to a few of our children who may move out west," complained the *Newark Daily Advertiser*, "but the bulk of it will be given to foreigners just landed—men who have no more claim on our charity than Chinese, Hindoos or Africans."[80] Others urged that legal changes be made to increase the required length of residence in the United States prior to naturalization or to prohibit naturalization altogether. Some ultimately concluded that the act of immigration itself ought to be restricted.[81]

Less pessimistic Americans, who decided that immigration for better or for worse was a fact of life, sought to maintain the centrality of what they considered the "American" creed. They recognized, however, that such a task would be difficult. Busey stressed that immigrants had "been reared under institutions hostile to personal liberty, to free institutions, and to a Republican government." They congregated to establish "*foreign* organizations" that "repudiated the fundamental principles of our government."[82] The daunting challenge was to help the immigrant discover the truth. That discovery would be facilitated by the chance to enjoy the opportunity and liberties in the West.

Yet for many in the northeastern United States, the forging of homogeneity, made difficult in the West simply because the region offered a haven where Old World loyalties could be fostered, was not to be left to chance. Ultimately, their proposals for dealing with the worst types of western migrants—the savage American pioneer and the clinging European Catholic peasant—and the establishment of the foundation of empire were one in the same: the creation of a succession of homogeneous settlements that would serve as staging areas for constant proselytization.[83] According to Beecher, "The integrity of the United States demands special exertions to produce in the nation a more homogeneous character, and to bind us together by firmer bonds." These "firmer bonds," to

Beecher, would be created by "pious, intelligent, enterprising ministers" who would "produce a sameness of views, and feelings, and interests, which would lay the foundation of our empire upon a rock."[84] Homogeneity thus meant only one type of sameness: the transplantation of societies that conformed to the cultural and political predilections of their associates in the northeastern United States.

Neither the plan nor the cultural hubris was new. Leaders in New England had long felt a responsibility to settle and proselytize the West to reestablish the Protestant foundations that underlay their region of birth.[85] Accordingly, they advocated the construction of religious and educational institutions that would re-create the manifest virtues existent at home. Beecher, ever inclined to hyperbole, echoed a decades-long fear: "that our intelligence and virtue will falter and fall back into a dark minded vicious populace—a poor, uneducated, reckless mass of infuriated animalism." As "the West is filling up as by ocean waves," he continued, without education the "millions of freemen on their fertile soil" in the region would suffer from "corrupting abundance." In an illuminating coupling of sin and virtue, Beecher argued that in areas without religious education, "vice and irreligion" overtake "thrift and knowledge." The population of the "great West," in short, demanded "for its moral preservation the immediate and universal action of those institutions which discipline the mind, and arm the conscience and the heart. . . . A nation is being 'born in a day,'" he concluded, "and all the nurture of schools and literary institutions is needed, constantly and universally, to rear it up to a glorious and unperverted manhood."[86]

The paradox that those who feared ethnoreligious divisiveness would prescribe a form of ethnic retrenchment in settlement and proselytization in the West was lost on them. In their minds, they, unlike their adversaries, *were* American. Armed with a Christian republican dogma, missionaries moved westward resolved to form small homogeneous communities that would create the building blocks for a good society.[87] They carried with them the self-imposed burden that the West, of such great importance to the nation and Christianity, had to be saved by Protestant New Englanders. As William Salter, a member of the Andover Band, a group of Congregational missionaries who attempted to church the frontier West, wrote in his diary, if a "good Common-Wealth" were to arise in the territory of Iowa, "it will have to be done in the main by Novo Anglo-Saxon men." They brought with them as well a hatred of less "progressive," less "republican" faiths.[88] The Protestant missionaries thus were religious in purpose but attentive to the secular importance of the West and the relationships between the sacred and the temporal. Indeed, the mission of God and that of America could not be disentangled. As Asa Turner, leader of the Andover Band, predicted, "sacred Republicanism" and "secular Republicanism" would "go hand in hand across the continent."[89]

The immediate prophesies made amid a red-hot antebellum nativism thus warned of enormous struggles between American republicans and European immigrants, between Protestantism and Catholicism, between "good" and "evil." As Beecher reminded his readers, this was not a simple "controversy about religion." Rather, the struggle was between two competing worlds, two competing cultures. "In all ages," Beecher contended, "religion of some kind, has been the former of man's character and the mainspring of his action." The question Beecher and those of his ken confronted, then, was monumental. Would American progress continue under the direction of a republican Protestant tradition? Or would it surrender to a wholly different religion, replete with different conceptions of the configuration of society? In Beecher's bifurcated world, past religio-cultural systems had "been the great agitator or tranquilizer of nations, — the orb of darkness or of light to the world, — the fountain of purity or pollution, — the mighty power of riveting or bursting the chains of men."[90] The future, to Beecher, was bifurcated as well. In the United States, the struggle between foreigners, a word that oftentimes indicated both non-American birth and unassimilable belief, and Americans would continue.

Over the long term, the nativist urgency ebbed and flowed across the decades, erupting periodically in revivals of hostile nativism and diminishing when the character of the immigrant was considered less problematic or when other political issues took center stage. In the rural West — later known as the Middle West — nativism was dampened in part because of perceptions that the rural, if not the urban, environment was indeed working its wonders and transforming immigrants into Americans.

Yet even in the Middle West, the perception that the behavior and beliefs of immigrants and their children were improper persisted throughout the nineteenth century. Although the political rights of European immigrants and their children remained assured, nativists continued to form and support political movements that attempted to control the behavior, influence the lives, and convert the beliefs of immigrants and their children. After all, adherents of the "foreign mind" remained a formidable force in the Middle West, ironically made even more imposing by their growing political clout. Later chapters will illustrate that concerns about converting the unwashed were voiced well into the twentieth century, even if the methods proposed for accomplishing this conversion began to differ. In debates over public schools and alcohol, many of those with Yankee pasts confronted time-worn anxieties about the impenetra-

THE REGION

bility of the immigrant community and the immigrant home with a new-found confidence in the effectiveness of state-led institutions. Although the rhetoric became muted, the basic questions outlined by antebellum nativists would continue to plague many Americans. The conflict was less fierce, but the antagonisms that divided the minds of the West endured.

CHAPTER 2

The Burden of Their Song

Immigrant Encounters
with the Republic

When Bishop Mathias Loras called upon a dying Irish immigrant on the Iowa frontier in the early 1840s, the feeble man's poignant plea to the priest was simple: "Like my ancestors in Ireland, I should like to repose in the holy ground under the shadow of the cross. The sanctified earth would be no longer to me a strange land and I should less regret the tombs of my country." Heeding the dying man's requests, Loras and the small Irish colony inaugurated a new sacralization of space by erecting a twelve-foot-high oak cross, which, according to the bishop, successfully served "to protect the land cultivated by our Christians and to stretch forth its arms to the savages who inhabit the neighboring forests."[1] Loras's work is emblematic of the prominent role played by Roman Catholic missionaries who early on made a cultural imprint on the Middle West. Working initially with Native Americans, Roman Catholic priests turned their attention to European settlers when waves of migrants entered the West. They soon became active in encouraging and directing migration and settlement.[2]

The story of these early missionaries parallels in some ways and cross-cuts in others the narratives of the American-born leaders who were simultaneously moving westward. As emigration from Europe swelled in the mid-nineteenth century, western Catholics, not unlike their Protestant adversaries, perceived the temporal and spiritual promise of the West. "I do wish," wrote Father Francis Pierz in 1855, "that the choicest pieces of land in this delightful Territory [of Minnesota] would become the property of thrifty Catholics who would make an earthly paradise of this Minnesota which Heaven has so richly blessed, and who would bear out the opinion that Germans prove to be the best farmers and the best Christians in America."[3] Loras arrived at similar conclusions. "No section of the country offered finer soil or climate," he wrote following his extensive travels throughout eastern Iowa, "or provided more favorable opportunities for an industrious agricultural population."[4]

One even discerns in the writings of the Catholic clergy a sense of providence regarding the West and America comparable to that expressed by the American-born. In 1844, Father Samuel Mazzuchelli thanked the Lord, "who is rich in mercy," for providing an effective means of spreading the "Truth" of Catholicism throughout the United States. Through the War of Independence, "the designs of Divine Wisdom" had freed the country from the domination of England, which in turn had precipitated an "emigration of many Catholic families from Europe," who could now live as Catholics in a more abundant environment.[5] The signs of providence were wondrous, even miraculous. "On the feast of the Epiphany," wrote Pierz in 1855, "there was seen here in Minnesota . . . a remarkable apparition of the holy cross in the sky. As the full moon arose at eight o'clock in the evening the holy cross appeared in yellowish hue and most heavenly brilliance upon the rising moon. . . . The cross was surrounded by a bright nimbus of the rarest and loveliest of colors. The whole phenomenon," he concluded, "was entrancingly beautiful and bright." Pierz divined the significance of the spectacle by noting that "the holy cross, seeming to rest on Minnesota's soil and to expand far and wide with the rising moon," was a clear symbol that the Minnesota Territory would soon be populated by Christians, undoubtedly Catholic and probably German.[6]

Besides providing better material conditions, this providential West also enabled isolated settlement, which Catholic leaders saw as a solution to the increasingly hostile nativism in the East. Loras, writing in an eastern Catholic paper, encouraged migration to the West for this very reason. "Many Catholics will certainly be induced to emigrate toward the western regions of Iowa," he predicted. "I persevere in the conviction that they can hardly do anything better [and] I speak chiefly of those who now live in that New England where Catholicity is so shamefully persecuted."[7] Other missionary bishops and priests flooded eastern newspapers, in particular Catholic journals such as the *Catholic Observer* and the *Boston Pilot*, with accounts of the advantages of western residence.[8] At the same time, they successfully appealed to Europe for funds that would enable a safer and larger Catholic emigration.[9]

Whereas both the foreign- and American-born could agree that the

West held material and spiritual promise, then, immigrants saw that promise as based in part on the opportunity to seclude themselves in isolated settlements sheltered both from direct nativist hostility and from "American" tutelage—precisely what the nativists feared most.[10] The fact that American nativists feared the specter of growing rural European settlements is dripping with irony. It was nativist hostility in the East, Catholic leaders observed, that served in part to encourage Catholic migration westward to the region that many of the native-born considered the key to the destiny of the American Republic. Moreover, it was the vast tracts of rich land uninhabited by American citizens—a central component of exceptionalist beliefs about the West—that enabled Europeans to seclude themselves and maintain their beliefs.

Yet American nativists largely misinterpreted the meaning of the European migration and misunderstood the challenges immigrant leaders faced. European immigrants, like their American-born counterparts, not only perceived the great promise of the West but also tended to accept, if somewhat uncritically, many of the tropes and myths of the American nation. Many applauded a spirit of "freedom" that seemingly had not existed at home. To be sure, the region was desirable in part because it fostered the potential for self-contained societies. Yet even here, it was the "freedom" to form isolated communities and maintain cultural patterns that was one of the reasons for celebrating life in the United States. Whereas Americans tended to view immigration to the West as a validation of others' faith in their Republic, Europeans viewed the promise of the Republic as an explanation for their immigration.

These predispositions ought not discount the challenges that a massive immigration posed to the immigrant community, its leadership, and the nation as a whole. The nation faced the unavoidable fact that the vast majority of immigrants had indeed previously lived as subjects. The United States thus was forced to grapple with the immigrants' transformation into citizens. The nation had to contend with questions concerning how to educate people who were previously tied to fundamentally different political systems in American government. Immigrants had to address issues involving how they could be schooled in the American system so that they could realize the promise immigration offered. In short, they had to "learn republicanism."

The process of learning republicanism was advanced and simplified, I argue in this chapter, by access to a citizenship that did not demand that immigrants forsake their cultural pasts. Indeed, a political environment that permitted immigrants to maintain their religious beliefs and converse in their home language worked to augment loyalties to the nation. Newspapers and printed tracts instructed non-English speakers in the precepts, responsibilities, and rights inherent in the Republic. Seen from this perspective, allegiances to ethnic subgroup and nation were mutually supportive. An ethnic pluralism sustained the American polity.

This self-reinforcing relationship between nation and ethnic subgroup was more problematic, however, when it involved religious organizations, with which most immigrants identified and which were typically institutional centers in the rural immigrant community. Immigrant spiritual leaders repeatedly affirmed their loyalty to American institutions and to the American republican system. They frequently celebrated the freedom to practice their religion in the United States and the fact that the American free church was an institution that fostered their Christian beliefs. Yet they were also forced to ponder the apparent inconsistencies between republican citizenship and spiritual guidance. They often expressed concerns that their flocks were learning the precepts of liberal democracy all too well, as immigrants left the faith or proposed electoral solutions to spiritual problems that could not be solved by majority rule. In sum, whereas they were comforted by freedoms of religion, many religious leaders feared the consequences when putatively "free" patterns of behavior and belief spread seemingly out of control and interfered with church, home, and community.

The "Complementary Identity" and Learning American Republicanism

One of the Swede's flaxen-headed boys wanted to know if the king of Minnesota was a good man, and on being told that the king was dead and the country was ruled by a gentleman hired for the purpose called the governor, the little boy replied that he was sorry to hear of the king's death, and he hoped that he had a fitting monument.
— *Stillwater (Minnesota) Gazette*, 18 May 1881

These [Irish immigrants] became more American than the Americans, and knew how to appreciate the blessing of civic freedom far better than the natives, who had always enjoyed such blessing. They looked up to the Fathers of the Republic as to *the saints.* — John Talbot Smith, *History of the Catholic Church in New York* (1905; emphasis added)

Americans in the mid-nineteenth century celebrated the many ways in which their Republic improved upon the tired systems of the old European states. As they invented an American nationality that allegedly reflected these advancements, they stressed the conviction that their nation was structured according to abstract notions of freedom, equality, and self-government. This was necessary, Hans Kohn argued, because Americans of British descent could be distinct from their British past only insofar as they evinced a commitment to the ideological constructs—such as "freedom" and "self-rule"—that were a basis of their rebellion.[11] Alexis de Tocqueville observed that "the sovereignty of the people is . . . the last link in a chain of opinions which binds around the whole Anglo-American world." For Americans, "though in practice a republican government often behaves badly," he averred, "the theory is always good, and in the end the people's actions always conform to it."[12] If nations are formed as "imagined communities," then, the United States as a nation was visualized by its citizenry in the early nineteenth century in ideological terms: the American past, according to Herbert Croly, was "informed by an idea."[13]

This intellectual framework simultaneously placed a great responsibility on the citizenry and enabled relatively simple access to citizenship for those defined as "white."[14] For them, as Carl Friedrich wrote some years ago, "to be an American is an ideal," compared to being a Frenchman, which was "a fact."[15] An immigrant to the United States could become a citizen merely by consenting to the political ideology that defined its citizenry. Significantly, although they were required to renounce loyalties to foreign governments, immigrants and their descendants were not forced to forsake the cultural baggage with which they had arrived.[16]

Many American nativists, as we have observed, believed these circumstances posed acute problems with regard to immigrants arriving from the benighted European lands. They doubted that immigrants could learn the lessons of freedom. "*Subjects*," wrote Thomas R. Whitney, "cannot become good *citizens* in a moment. Men must be *educated* to freedom."[17] Traits such as "independence of character," he commented, "were rarely found in one trained to submission." Told that "he inhabits a land of liberty and equality," the immigrant "gets a confused notion that a great change has taken place in his condition. . . . He has heard something about 'liberty' before, without knowing what was meant, but the word 'equality,' is not found in his lexicon, and he can't make out how it is that he is 'as good as other people.'" Engraved on his mind "by the hand of a stern artist" were "thoughts and fancies adapted to his former state—lessons . . . of low, slavish, abject submission," which "are difficult to rub out."[18] Immigrants, in short, were untrained in the responsibilities of citizenship. In learning the intricacies of republican citizenship, they needed to comprehend the dangers of the abuse of freedoms on the one hand and of servile dependence on the other. American nativists questioned whether the European mind could avoid either extreme, especially considering the indoctrination immigrants carried with them. Catholic immigrants were human beings, Samuel F. B. Morse admitted, but "oppression has blotted out their reason and conscience and thought." As a result, "their liberty, is licentiousness, their freedom, strife and debauchery."[19]

These complaints had some merit. Europeans often failed to comprehend the basics of American republicanism when they arrived in the United States. It is true that some had been instructed prior to their emigration by guidebooks that described life in the United States, including its government, and introduced them to concepts of an American exceptionalism. "The United States," explained Ole Rynning in his guidebook published for Norwegian immigrants in 1838, "has no king. Nonetheless, there is always a man who has almost a king's authority. . . . Here there are laws, government, and authorities as in Norway. But *everything*," he concluded, "is intended to maintain people's *natural freedom and equality*."[20]

Yet even when immigrants had this guidance, the learning process often took some time. Ole Munch Ræder wrote in the 1840s that Norwegian immigrants had "not reached beyond the first rudiments of a republican education." Not only were many ignorant of political party differences, but a few settlers still called the government price on land "the king's price," an example of the persistence of the use of European terms as frames of reference.[21] C. L. Clausen, editor of the Norwegian paper *Emigranten*, detected similar conditions in 1852 when he expressed his amazement "at the lack of interest of our people in the West regarding political matters." Referring to the approaching presidential election, Clausen feared that "if some farm work is to be done on election day, [Norwegians] will fail to go to the polls even though the work could easily be postponed. It is a sad situation," he concluded, for "it indicates that the Norwegian-American has no conception of what it means to be an American citizen." Yet he betrayed a hope that the immigrants would "acquire this training in citizenship," and he urged his countrymen to "try to create a little political instinct in ourselves!"[22] Circumstances were similar, suggested the *Dubuque National Demokrat* some years later, among German immigrant farmers. Shortly after their arrival, German immigrants presumed that the "government goes on without them." Only after some time did they realize that as citizens, they were "part of the system."[23]

Like nativist critics, moreover, some Europeans were also distressed by diminished social controls that resulted from abuses and misunderstandings about the meaning of concepts such as liberty. One Irishman, writing home in 1826, denounced the Irish as "the worst conditioned people in this Country." "On their first landing," he argued, "they are extremely mean and servile." Yet "after meeting a short time with their Countrymen and hearing that all men are here free and equal in respect to their rights," he observed, "they think that freedom consists in being at liberty to do as they please and they become intolerably insolent."[24] Father Joseph Cretin commented on a comparable spiritual degeneration following a confrontation with his parishioners. "I did not believe the Irish character susceptible to this kind of malice against their own pastors," he complained. After all, "they are so docile in Ireland under the absolute and often arbitrary empire of their high clergy."[25] Freedom and liberty obviously could be abused.

They could also be misunderstood. Europeans often affiliated with political organizations because of vaguely understood appeals. German immigrants became Democrats in the 1840s, wrote one German, simply because " 'Democracy' stood for '*Freiheit*.' "[26] The Democratic *Daily Wisconsin Banner* solicited German votes in 1850 by suggesting a similar, if more intricate, interpretation. " 'Democracy,' " the editor wrote, "is a glorious word. There are few other words, in any language, which can be compared to it. To the poor man it is peculiarly precious since he is aware that he owes to it his escape from the serfdom in which his oppressors held him, and can now look up into heaven and thank his God that he has ceased to be a serf."[27] Vaguely articulated terms rather than political platforms often had greater appeal to the unschooled immigrant.

As they were introduced to the rhetoric and institutions of American exceptionalism, immigrants showed an inclination to celebrate the American political and social system. As we have seen, mid-nineteenth-century European immigrants commonly praised the economic possibilities that defined the nation and especially the West. They were also predisposed to esteem the "natural freedom and equality" of the nation's political institutions. These identifications were powerful forces in encouraging recent arrivals to develop loyalties to the United States and to learn about its institutions. Certainly for some the initial contact with the democratic culture in the United States was unnerving. Democracy so pervaded all "national habits" in the United States, Michel Chevalier remarked, that "it besets and startles at every step the foreigner who, before landing in the country, had no suspicion to what a degree every nerve and fibre had been steeped in aristocracy by a European education."[28] Yet those immigrants who had been touched by the flames of republicanism in Europe or influenced by the pronouncements of American liberty and opportunity often eagerly embraced the rhetoric of American republicanism. "In America," trumpeted *Nordlyset*, "liberty advances as proudly and deliberately as its gigantic rivers. [In Europe,] absolute despots or kings are everywhere in power. . . . Just let them sit on their thrones, wearing their robes of sable, and oppressing mankind! Here in America at any rate, there is neither king nor tyrant."[29] "Liberty in Norway was merely a dead letter on the statute book," agreed the editor of *Folkets Røst*

Immigrant Encounters with the Republic 57

in an 1858 editorial. "How greatly different [it is] in this country [where] we can . . . in common with the native-born Americans settle the political questions of the country." Here, in short, was "unmistakable evidence that in this country, freedom and equality exist in reality."[30]

Johan R. Reiersen, who journeyed throughout the United States in 1843, agreed. The fact that the American government was unhampered by monarchical and aristocratic interests, he argued, promoted a "spirit of progress, improvements in all directions, and a feeling for popular liberty and of the rights of the great masses exceeding that of any land in Europe." As a result, the republican government would not fail, in large part because "the masses" would never be "reduced—through the power of individuals or of capital—to the same slavish dependence that supports the thrones of Europe. Personal freedom is something the people suck in with their mother's milk," he concluded. "It seems to have become as essential to every citizen of the United States as the air he breathes."[31] The letters of members of a Norwegian correspondence society likewise stressed the spirit of freedom in the United States, which, they maintained, contained "the secret of general equality."[32] A German immigrant, writing to his kin in Europe at about the same time, compared his former home to his new one. In Germany, "alas, common sense and free speech lie in shackles," he wrote. If his relatives wished "to obtain a clear notion of *genuine* public life, freedom of the people and sense of being a nation," he contended, they should emigrate. "I have never regretted that I came here, and never! never! again shall I bow my head under the yoke of despotism and folly."[33] Other immigrants writing in different languages used nearly identical imagery: one Norwegian wrote that his people enjoyed tasting "the satisfaction of being liberated from the effect of all yoke and despotism."[34] Decades later, American "freedom" remained a trope for Germans explaining their forebears' migration to the United States. "Discontent prevailed in all classes of German society," wrote R. Puchner. "There was a longing for free political and free religious ideas; the old institutions seemed rotten and sick unto death; there was . . . only the ocean in between them [and] the new land of promise, the mighty republican Empire of America."[35]

These examples do not prove, of course, that all immigrants were satisfied with their decision to emigrate. Immigrants often returned home unhappy with life in the United States. Others remained in America but were despondent over their prospects. Nor did all immigrants find the degree of freedom they had anticipated. "It sounds ridiculous to hear a man speak of freedom," wrote a German worker in 1886, "when he is still enslaved by a *Corporation* as he was not in Germany."[36]

This evidence does indicate, however, that immigrants' steady rhetoric about salutary encounters with American conditions tended to mute their criticism of the new land. Immigrants' predisposition to glorify the possibilities of American citizenship, oftentimes uncritically, likely worked to hasten their integration into American society. The writings of Russian populist Grigorij Machtet during a journey in Kansas in 1874 described how immigrants were changed and their criticism of the American nation was softened by their encounters with American life. To be sure, the "raw material" of immigrant peoples had to be "processed and mastered by America."[37] Clearly, "many dark aspects, many blemishes," marred the United States. But the "mass of immigrants, uncertainly seeking a different way of life," tended to observe their new home through rose-colored glasses. Thus, although many Americans viewed Europeans with "a mixture of scorn, offensive pity, and sympathy," wrote Machtet, they could anticipate a transformation of immigrants because of their predisposition not to criticize American society. "Out of this stalwart but downtrodden, fearful, and hesitant German," he concluded, "must be created a citizen who is both competent and free; out of this ever drunk, ever swearing, ever fighting, fanatical Irishman must be created not only a harmless person but also a competent and free citizen." Despite such worrisome character defects, within five years in the United States the immigrant was indeed "reborn": "it is as though he has become a different person, as though he has 'been born into God's world.'" Importantly, Machtet believed that a person's inclination to embrace the American system of government not only remade the person but also powerfully muted criticisms of the United States. As long as immigrant discourse presupposed the salutary influences of American freedoms, expressions that emphasized American "blemishes" would be tempered. And celebrations of American life would continue.[38]

The absorption of national myths, however, did not mean that cultural pasts were discarded. On the contrary, immigrants seized on common national, linguistic, and religious traditions as cornerstones for fashioning their ethnic collectivities. These ethnic groups created boundaries, oftentimes reconfiguring common pasts, that were instrumental to ethnic leaders in a pluralist society.[39] Ethnic institutions, based on common intellectual, geographical, or linguistic pasts originating in Europe, were created in the United States to support interest-group associations in the polity and society. This process of "ethnicization" also did not nullify the development of loyalties to the United States. Rather than competing, the dual loyalties to nation and subgroup, invented under the auspices of an American creed, could be complementary.[40]

The ideological underpinnings of citizenship that privileged "freedom" and "self-rule" in fact enabled immigrants to nurture simultaneously their bonds to nation and to ethnic subgroup. Tropes of "freedom" and "liberty," perhaps because their meanings were so pliant, proved to be malleable concepts that fostered an appreciation among immigrants of the responsibilities and rights of American citizenship. Yet the very concept of freedom could also nurture the maintenance of Old World ties. One sense of "freedom," after all, implied the liberty to maintain patterns of life that varied from those of native-born Americans. Immigrants became citizens of the United States and theoretically performed the obligations of citizens, but basic rights inherent in their citizenship status allowed them to retain ethnic and religious allegiances they carried from Europe. Ironically, then, immigrants and their children could simultaneously—in a complementary, self-reinforcing fashion—maintain allegiances to the United States and to their former identities outside its borders.

In this way, faithfulness to an ethnic subgroup within a "complementary identity" theoretically fostered a magnified loyalty to the United States. Ethnic allegiances encouraged affinities with nation.[41] As Samuel P. Huntington has argued, "Defining and maintaining an ethnic identity was an essential building block in the process of creating an American national identity."[42] The ideologically based national identity, on the other hand, enabled people to reformulate former beliefs and fostered the formation of ethnic groups in the United States. In its stable form, then, the complementary identity represented more than the opportunity to develop a dual identity to nation and ethnic subgroup: it was a self-reinforcing concept that powerfully promoted an allegiance to American institutions at the same time that it fostered a maintenance of ethnic forms. Pluralism was embedded within national loyalty.

Evidence from memoirs and newspapers indicates that mid-nineteenth-century immigrants almost intuitively understood this complementarity. "Americanization" typically had a very different meaning for the myriad ethnic communities in the United States than it did for American-born nativists.[43] The editor of *Den Swenske Republikanen*, for example, argued in 1857 that his paper indeed intended to "Americanize" its readers, which to him meant that it sought "to acquaint them with the republican institutions of America and make those institutions respected and loved."[44] Immigrants thus did not necessarily have to become "Americans" to be "Americanized." Nativists notwithstanding, other European observers argued that the American system *was* inclusive, pointing out that Europeans who pledged allegiance to their "American" refuge did not lose their old national culture. "The American character," wrote Ole Munch Ræder in the mid-1840s, "is not yet so fixed and established that it excludes all others. The Americans," he concluded, referring here to the native-born, "are satisfied with demanding a few general traits of political rather than of really national significance." Repeating a contention made decades earlier by J. Hector St. John de Crèvecoeur, Ræder argued that "under such lenient influences, the aliens are elevated and improved, rather than changed."[45] Immigrants, in short, could be loyal citizens of the United States and members of ethnic groups simultaneously. Many different immigrants found it simple to translate Carl Schurz's advice to his male German counterparts: "I love Germany as my mother. America as my bride."[46]

Ethnic Americans throughout the nineteenth century ingenuously conflated these multiple loyalties. Public celebrations of national holidays, for example, consolidated images of both the European past and the American present. Irish immigrants in Dubuque merged an 1883 Fourth of July celebration with advocacy of the Irish National Land League and of independence for Ireland.[47] Swiss Americans saw no incongruity in incorporating the history of Switzerland into their Fourth of July observance in 1876. Their centennial parade float contained representations of Helvetia and Columbia surrounded by images of the Swiss cantons with their coats-of-arms.[48] Members of a rural German community six years later celebrated American life by reading the Declaration of Independence and listening to a speaker discuss the role of Germans in the Revolutionary War, "a chapter in American history," reported a German-language newspaper, "too little known."[49] "The jewels of Isabella the Catholic," Bishop John Hughes reportedly observed, "would be an appropriate ornament for the sword of Washington."[50] Some years later, Cardinal James Gibbons, upon watching the American and papal flags carried side by side in a parade, observed, "I always wish to see those two flags lovingly entwined, for no one can be faithful to God without being faithful to his country."[51] And Roman Catholic newspaper mastheads juxtaposed portraits of George Washington and Pope Pius X, a clear illustration of the importance and compatibility of allegiance to both church and state.[52]

The private correspondence of immigrants, like their public displays, also illustrates the fusion of new and old loyalties. A German Catholic tenant farmer in 1886, for instance, noted that a farmer in Europe had to perform grinding labor every day of the week. "If we asked permission [of the landlord] to go to Church on Sunday, then the man abused us . . . every time and said: 'You won't always need to be running after the priest if you find yourselves in the alms house.' And so," he concluded, "I am going to America [where] on Sundays as many as wish to may go to church. My children shall not imitate my slavery."[53] American freedoms provided the opportunity to practice Catholic beliefs.[54]

This complementarity would endure well into the nineteenth century. A remarkable correspondence between historian Kate Everest and spokesmen for German communities in late-nineteenth-century Wisconsin time and again demonstrated that old and new loyalties were self-reinforcing, that indeed they strengthened both allegiances. Ernest Mayerhoff, writing from Juneau County, stressed that his neighbors "want to become good American citizens, make use of the english language and try to master it for themselves and for their children, but they wish to retain also the German language and the Lutheran faith." In this way, he noted, his people enriched the United States just as their new country bettered them. "They accommodate to the english manners and customs," he continued, "when they think it is for the good, but retain their German customs, when they think the english are bad ones." As a result, Mayerhoff concluded, "they have improved in America in every direction and have learned not to be servants of mankind, but servants of God; and to become true citizens and to take care of the welfare of the Country."[55]

Other respondents were more defensive about their place in the United States, but they continued to stress the value of dual loyalties. When asked if the German inhabitants intermarried with "Americans," a resident of Sheboygan County, Wisconsin, wrote that "there are not ENGLISH Americans here to intermarry with." As he continued writing, he revealed his impatience. "This question," he claimed, "seems to take for granted, that only English or Irish blood makes an American." His neighbors, he continued, desired to maintain their customs and beliefs, including their mother tongue, and it "would be a sad loss to them and the state if they didn't." "If to get rid of all these things . . . good [though] they may be, means *to become Americanized*," he surmised, "why I suppose they are still rude German barbarians." On the other hand, "they and especially their children are learning the English language, the History & Constitution of the U.S., they read the newspapers, quite a number of English ones; they are intelligent voters, peaceable and industrious citizens, many of them English teachers in the public schools. . . . If you call that Americanizing," he concluded, "why then they desire it."[56] Joh. Kilian, writing in German about his Dodge County, Wisconsin, neighbors, contended that "they are all good American citizens [who] hold true and firm to their old Lutheran beliefs and virtuous customs."[57] Kilian evinced no impression that his statement, which succinctly and simply fused American identity with the maintenance of European customs, was incongruous.

Participants in the complementary identity often found it simple to proceed one step further and stress that they were better Americans than the native-born who questioned the extent of their loyalty. "I am as good an American as the most blue-blooded Yankee can be," emphasized a German Catholic priest in defense of an association of priests to which he belonged. The association was "American above all" since it could only have been formed "in the atmosphere of our glorious American constitution, which guarantees liberty to all—liberty of thought . . . liberty of association, [and] liberty of religious worship." Indeed, he concluded, it was those who attempted to "infringe this liberty" to maintain Catholic organizations who were "truly un-American."[58]

Expressions reflecting a complementary identity with nation and subgroup were thus American in conception and origin. Immigrants and their leaders invented and continually modified both a sense of allegiance to an imagined community composed of Americans and a reified notion of a common preimmigration past.[59] These identities, when developed in tandem, modulated in relation to one another. Ethnic leaders therefore compared conditions in the United States with those in Europe and, using a biblical allusion, stressed that immigrants "had shaken the dust [of Europe] from their feet and have reached the shores of this continent to lead a dignified life once again."[60] Or they spoke of their old country as a "land of tyranny."[61] Yet their reverence for their new country and their "patriotism" were often based on their freedom to be ethnically and religiously distinct. The cornerstone of the edifice of a Catholic church in rural Iowa contained an inscription that is an apt example of a mature dual identity. The inscription, composed in Latin, was a reminder that "while our sacred religion has been viciously persecuted at home for ten years, we may enjoy in this rich and beautiful country a perfect peace and the most wonderful religious liberty." Yet it also asked descendants of the German immigrants "to remain Catholics and down-to-earth and upright Germans." It solicited "God's abiding blessing," which it trusted the church would receive since the large, tall-steepled church "will show the blasé and utterly materialistic Yankee what Catholic faith and German spirit of sacrifice can achieve."[62] Several decades earlier, a German-language newspaper reported that a Democratic Party rally manifested a "fire of patriotism" that "stirred the Americans up."[63] Patriotism, it was clear, was not dependent on being "American," nor was a European national identity dependent on remaining loyal to Old World governments.

Thus, as a layered array of allegiances that linked particular local identities to a national membership, a complementary identity could strengthen allegiances to both a national and an ethnic identification.[64] As such, it could be simultaneously acculturative while it facilitated the construction of a pluralist society. Kerby A. Miller argues, for example, that the Irish American leadership successfully used a reified Irish nationalism and a sanitized Americanism to gain "social and cultural hegemony" over its "lower classes" while it simultaneously sought acceptance from and access to the larger native institutions. A syncretic ethnic culture that joined Catholicity, Democracy, trade unionism, and loyalty to the cause of Ireland enabled the Irish leadership to assert that Irish immigrants were simultaneously "good Irish Americans" and "good Americans."[65]

While pluralist structures could evolve from a complementary identity, some contemporaries emphasized the assimilative properties associated with a complementary identity. As Machtet had noted, the tendency to glorify the United States, in part because of its freedoms, also prompted those dissatisfied with their experiences to mute their discontent. Yet there was more: the complementary identity provided immigrant communities with a certain amount of latitude, a sort of safety zone in which they could maintain their ethnic allegiance as they moved first to American citizenship and then to "American" behavior. As a prominent Roman Catholic leader pointed out, "Anything which makes immigrants more satisfied," which could include maintaining old beliefs, "also makes them better citizens."[66] Thus the tension inherent in the complementary identity could ultimately hasten the metamorphosis of immigrants from loyal and patriotic citizens to loyal "Americans." It permitted immigrants to identify with their ethnic past in the context of their adopted nation, and thus it granted them the leeway to celebrate both. In this sense, a dynamic occasioned by the complementary identity worked as many Americans hoped it would: it ultimately was acculturative.

Some immigrants confidently predicted this progression. C. L. Clausen, editor of *Emigranten*, wrote in English "to our American friends" in the premier issue of his paper in 1852. "We came here as strangers and friendless," he wrote, "ignorant of your institutions, your language and your customs." Nonetheless, "you extended to us the rights of citizenship and equal participation in your privileges." In response to this "friendly welcome," through the pages of the new paper, Clausen pledged to "hurry the process of Americanization of our immigrated countrymen" so that they could be "one people with the Americans" and "contribute their part to the final development of the character of this Great Nation."[67] Five years later, "Typo," also writing in English in *Emigranten*, argued that the Norwegian immigrants had experienced "progress." "When we first landed on the shores of this continent," he noted, "we knew no more of the English language than 'yes' and 'no.'" After a few years, most of the immigrants could conduct business with the American-born, and some worked in the "legislative halls of this country." "This," he concluded, "is decidedly Progress." Regarding the Norwegian-language press, "Typo" contended that its "duty" was to "assimilate the heterogeneous elements of society, and consolidate a great nation with a government of the people."[68]

Church leaders—including Roman Catholics—occasionally echoed the views of the secular press. Liberal Catholic Bishop Clement Smyth, for example, argued that the loyalty of Catholics during the Civil War had resulted in "the advancement of the interests of [the Catholic] church in this country." Whereas the church had once been looked upon "with suspicion and was considered even as hostile to republican institutions," Smyth argued, it now attracted "the attention of thinking Protestants" and "excited their admiration of its governing principles."[69] Such a hope undergirded the attitudes of the liberal "Americanizers" within the Catholic Church in the late nineteenth century. Cardinal James Gibbons in 1891 urged his flock to "glory in the title of American citizen. We owe our allegiance to one country, and that country is America. We must be in harmony with our political institutions" because the United States "is the land of our destiny." Since "patriotism is a sentiment commended by almighty God Himself," he concluded, "loyalty to God's Church and to our country" should be "our religious and political faith."[70]

The firmly held belief that contemporary conditions enabled one to be simultaneously a better American and a better Catholic or Norwegian or Irishman, however, was not without its risks for ethnic leaders. As immigrant society enjoyed and celebrated the American freedoms to be ethnic, a complementary identity tended to nudge such discussions into a bourgeois and liberal discourse that muted debates about class and culture.[71] In the political sphere, Amy Bridges argues, immigrants and their children were encouraged, in an arena of competing identifications under the rubric of American citizenship, to develop loyalties to new institutions, such as the political party, that challenged or reformulated former ethnic allegiances. Changing institutional affiliations threatened ethnic leaders as they regulated immigrant discourse. They represented both the potential to empower immigrants politically and socially, as in the case of urban American labor, and the potential to channel and constrain that power within such American institutions as the political party.[72] Editors of non-English-language papers for their part attempted to instruct their readership about life in the United States, but they obviously hoped that readers would continue to consult media written for a non-English-reading audience. And although Gibbons hoped to merge a "religious and political faith," he certainly did not contemplate that his followers would privilege citizenship over belief.

The structures of belonging in families and ethnic communities, moreover, did not always correspond to those of American citizenship. Whereas the relationship between the liberal state and its citizenry was perceived by many to be the sum of the individual contracts, it was complicated by connections within families and within ethnic communities that could rival the rights and duties of citizenship. Perhaps some saw families as miniature republics, as Michel Chevalier contended in 1839.[73] But for many families were not small building blocks of the state so much as institutional structures that competed with and in some cases theoretically superseded it. The complementary identity becomes complicated in this context when societies were conceived, as they tended to be among European immigrants, as more organic and less contractual, more corporate and less individually based.[74]

These quandaries were particularly salient for European religious groups. To be sure, religious leaders were predisposed to celebrate American life and the inherent freedoms of the Republic. They frequently noted that America gave them the freedom to worship on Sunday. Although the state enabled the practice of religious belief, however, religious belief itself was not subject to allegiance to the state and therefore was not connected to citizenship. Societal structures based on particular religious ideas, moreover, did not necessarily conform to liberal, republican notions that were the basis for citizenship in an evolving American polity. The next section of this chapter argues that religious leaders treasured the conditions that permitted freedom of belief. Yet they were challenged when asked to revere a liberal society that permitted them, among other things, religious freedom but also imperiled communal beliefs and practices because of the society's penchant for stressing individual rights and freedoms. Ultimately, they found that they somehow had to nurture a reverence for "freedom" without discarding moral postures that might be at risk to the logical outcome of American liberty.

The Immigrants' Critique of American Society

> The Americans are fond of the word liberty; it is indeed the burden of their song, their glory and their pride. In some respects this is praiseworthy—an essential ingredient in national honour and national greatness; but in my opinion it is carried too far when it enters the sanctuary. . . . And yet religion is only one, the gospel is only one; and consequently no two conflicting creeds can be both right.—Rebecca Burlend, *A True Picture of Emigration* (1848)

Beneath a veneer of consensus among immigrants that celebrated the Republic lay profoundly different interpretations of the possibilities of American citizenship and the meaning of its concepts of liberty and freedom. European critics remained mindful of the importance of a state and society that enabled them the freedom to practice diverse customs. Yet they also feared that the very freedom to maintain their faith could also propagate license among their peers that would erode the central beliefs that knit them together. "Freedom" was a malleable concept, and its practice could begin an insidious process whose intrusion into every arena of life would be difficult to impede, especially since it was accepted and celebrated in the abstract. Thus the Norwegian newspaper *Emigranten* could lecture its immigrant readership on the differences between "freedom under law and order" and "licence."[75] Many European leaders therefore concurred with their American adversaries: liberty could lead to a self-indulgence deleterious to society at large.

Yet immigrant leaders who sought to transplant their cultural systems from Europe encountered even more pressing challenges. The many European immigrant traditions—with their Roman Catholic, Reformed, Calvinist, and Lutheran components—that were resituated in the Middle West resembled what Ernst Troeltsch termed church-types—inclusive institutions into which, as in a family or community, one was born.[76] Stressing hierarchical structures, these churches were likely to be influenced by contemporary movements that emphasized a corporatism and organicism. Those influenced by these ideas saw individual freedoms and volunteerism in a liberal republic as potential threats to corporatist societal structures. It is true that some immigrant sects and communities of belief that had embraced a nineteenth-century pietist sensibility found it more practical to merge religious beliefs with American society. They often skirmished with the more corporate wings within their church organizations over these very issues. Influential segments within the Roman Catholic community argued that even their church hierarchy should be adapted to the American Republic.[77] They believed that their faith—a conversation across continents and over centuries—had adjusted to secular political societies in the past and would continue to do so in the future.

A significant segment of European American cultural leaders, however, remained leery of the legacy of the Enlightenment upon which republican experiments were based. They encountered the internal contradictions of their churches nested in a society whose religious structures were based on voluntary membership and sectarianism. At the very least, many of them worried that the increasingly liberal tone in nineteenth-century American society would create a society of excess, materialism, and individualism.[78] Ironically, they valued the freedom that permitted people to reestablish communities of belief in America, but they feared the logical outcome when those within such communities also claimed their individual freedoms. What if an individualism that grew out of liberalism was valued in society and polity but was inadvisable in family life, community structures, or religious belief? And why were some freedoms acceptable whereas others were to be rejected? Religious leaders were well aware in the early nineteenth century of what Walter Lippmann would later term the "acids of modernity."[79] In this sense, they were concerned that their people might lose track of what they themselves considered the real purpose of existence on this earth. Like Rebecca Burlend, many European immigrants and their leaders were troubled when love of American political culture superseded or came into conflict with more meaningful beliefs.

Thus one of the great differences between the Yankee mind and the foreign mind concerned the relationship between church and state. Americans seemed to envision "sacred Republicanism" as marching across the continent hand in hand with "secular Republicanism."[80] Tocqueville argued that "in America it is religion which leads to enlightenment and the observance of divine laws which leads men to liberty." He contended that "freedom sees religion as the companion of its struggles and triumphs, the cradle of its infancy, and the divine source of its rights. Religion is considered as the guardian of mores, and mores are regarded as the guarantee of the laws and pledge for the maintenance of freedom itself." "Despotism may govern without faith," he wrote, "but liberty cannot."[81]

Many European religious leaders, in contrast, saw their faith as not so much a vehicle for the social control necessary to a republic as a set of beliefs central to their existence independent of the state. They perceived tensions between religion and the state and were forced, as a result, to tread the fine line between celebrating freedoms to practice diverse faiths and countenancing excessive liberties that jeopardized their own beliefs. To that end, they often criticized the increased prerogatives of the individual at the expense of institutions such as the church and family that mediated between individuals and the state. European leaders foresaw a society spinning out of control as individuals were cut adrift from their moorings. A Norwegian Lutheran pastor thus could express his admiration for the American Republic at the same time that he confessed a fear of "men who embraced a false humanism and were intoxicated with the modern rage for 'natural and inalienable human rights,' who considered outward, temporal freedom *absolutely* necessary to human beings."[82]

These leaders, from very early on, tended to express concerns that their adopted society was characterized by political immoderation, economic excess, and inordinate individualism. They worried, first, that the American polity would incline its citizens toward political intemperance. The "democratic institutions are no doubt very beneficial," admitted Ræder in 1847. Yet even in constitutional monarchies, such as in Norway, "there is a constant clamor for more and more rights and a continual striving toward democratic government." Republics such as the United States, he continued, "soon [had] a tendency to run to still greater extremes." Political rights, which "awaken the intellect" and "cause us to look around," lead "in many cases . . . to practical results," Ræder concluded. But they also "lead us into meditations, sensible or foolish according to our understanding and temperament."[83]

Fears about political immoderation were coupled with concerns that economic excess would stem from a proclivity toward materialism that pervaded American life. Whereas admirers of the American Republic connected the freedoms of the political environment to the genius of economic growth, immigrants occasionally expressed concerns about the long-term results of economic development. They feared that economic freedom—the "Yankee spirit," as one called it—had led to an overemphasis on material prosperity at the expense of more purposeful secular concerns. "Here is neither art, poetry, nor science," wrote a Norwegian clergyman simply. "Here are dollars and steam—that is all."[84] Dollars and steam, moreover, did not necessarily create a better society, especially when its citizens acted out of avarice. It was clear, the editor of *Emigranten* argued in 1857, that the immigrant should not be like the American, "who conducts his 'business' not for the benefit of his fellow man or society, but selfishly to 'make money' with the most complete unscrupulousness."[85] As a result, wrote a Norwegian clergyman to his relatives in Europe, "there is truly so little honesty and authority that one shudders." "I really do not know how long I can endure living under these beautiful republican conditions," he concluded sarcastically, "where the American God 'Money' holds the scepter of righteousness and where law and order are held in lowest esteem."[86]

A land where money implied right was a place that would challenge spiritual leaders for decades. Reverend Anton H. Walburg, a German Roman Catholic, maintained in the late nineteenth century that the materialism inherent in American culture would prove detrimental to his flock and his church. Enticements to "assimilate" would "lead our simple, straight-forward, honest Germans and Irish into this whirlpool of American life, this element wedded to this world, bent upon riches, upon political distinction, where their consciences will be stifled, their better sentiments trampled under foot."[87] Norwegian immigrants, according to one of their clergymen, likewise should not allow "themselves to become so engrossed in their worldly occupations that they were carried away by a materialism murderous to all spiritual interest, with every earnest thought destroyed by the thirst for gold and the coveting of earthly happiness."[88]

At the root of these political and material excesses, for many European leaders, was an individualism that had dangerous implications for both the spiritual and secular spheres. Such concerns were especially urgent for Roman Catholic immigrant leaders, who maintained religious beliefs that emphasized a natural order that relied on a web of institutions, above the individual and antecedent to the state, to order society. To be sure, American Catholic leaders had been influenced by a Catholic Enlightenment in the late eighteenth century, but by the mid-nineteenth century, many feared a "spirit" of Protestantism based on a freedom of religion that made private spiritual interpretations commonplace.[89] Many Roman Catholics were concerned that the sum of competing individual beliefs had created a sort of marketplace of creeds. According to Father Samuel Mazzuchelli, a pioneer priest in Wisconsin, "Protestantism has degenerated into a purely negative doctrine founded on *individual caprice and understanding*, influenced by every human passion and frailty." As a result, "in America, where the spirit of personal independence is carried to the extreme," individual understanding and sectarian competition became a mean-spirited popularity contest. "Sectarians," Mazzuchelli argued, "are even more disposed to deny what others believe, in order to give free rein to the suggestions of pride, malice, self-interest, passions, fanaticism, and *individual delusions*." Truth was thus the ultimate loser as "the authority and teachings of all the ages are laid low before the defective and fallacious reasoning of every sectarian with the proud exclamation, 'I am free!'"[90] Freedom and majority rule, in short, which were proudly proclaimed in the political sphere, failed when they entered the sanctuary. Yet in the United States, "the political principle that the majority ought to rule," Mazzuchelli insisted, also regulated religious matters in every Protestant denomination. The maxim "I am free" thus extended beyond politics and became "the source of innumerable intellectual vagaries" enabling "the public preaching of the most extreme religious doctrines."[91] When political freedoms diffused into the spiritual world, the concept of freedom became incongruous.

Religious freedom not only created spiritual individualism but fostered a relativity of issues that, to Mazzuchelli and others, were absolute. The great number of sects in America, according to Father Wilhelm P. Bigot, existed because "the authorities have free access to the Holy Bible, but no one to explain it." As a result, religion in the United States "is like arriving at Babel, with a Babylonish confusion." Such "confusion" was due to a lack of authority and a paucity of leadership, which contradicted the true composition of the church.[92] "In North America," Bigot concluded, "every religious and irreligious have their own opinion of their representative, from superstition we are not free, from disbelief not far. . . . From year to year it is getting more variegated and more insane."[93]

Mazzuchelli also deprecated the spiritual repercussions of a Protestant relativism. Not only could all ministers interpret the faith, but also "all persons are imbued with a spirit of misunderstood religious independence, which leads them to consider themselves sole and absolute masters and competent judges of the truths to be believed and the morality to be practiced." It thus followed that "in America the opinion of the one who teaches is considered no more worthy of belief than that of his pupil; the interpretation of the hearer is considered of equal authority with that of the minister; and the meanings of Holy Scripture are such and so many that it is absolutely impossible to find any uniformity in them."[94] The sacred world thus had come to resemble the secular world. The fact that individuals belonged to a certain sect did not mean that they held a steadfast conviction in its teachings but rather that in a spiritual marketplace they preferred one preacher to another. The church, its leaders hoped, would "soften the manners of society" and "curb the spirit of pride which denies respect to superior authority, or tends to a belief that we were created to be independent of each other, — ideas unfortunately too common in the early stages of democracy."[95] Yet here again individuals could choose their own authority and foster their own pride. And the possibilities of religion were endless. "Any religious novelty whatsoever," Mazzuchelli judged, "when supported and promulgated by biblical fanaticism, by the secret financial or political interests of any shrewd hypocrites, will make proselytes." Americans, Mazzuchelli stressed, "like a flock without a shepherd, go here and there to listen to anyone who can offer them beautiful words." Perhaps such words were beautiful, but they were not necessarily "true."[96]

Protestant Europeans were also not at ease with what one Lutheran clergyman called "these blooming vagaries about freedom [*disse velsignede Frihedsgriller*]."[97] Although Protestant sects shared an animosity toward the Church of Rome, they often feared the consequences of freedoms of religion as well. European Protestant religious traditions, particularly the more liturgical branches of the Lutheran and Reformed Churches, also struggled with the many manifestations of what one Lutheran called a "churchly confusion . . . in this land harrowed by so many erring sects" that followed directly from religious freedom.[98] First, Protestant leaders grappled with a religious freedom that bred disarray among sects and congregations. The wife of a Norwegian Lutheran pastor believed that two congregations under the leadership of her husband "were insane." "They want to build churches," she wrote, "but they are to be open to any odd tramp who wants to come and preach to them, and of these there are a large number in this country. . . . This is a free country, they say, and everyone can do as he pleases."[99] Second, an infatuation with democracy within the church could taint religious truth. Some argued that if majority rule functioned in government, it should also be practiced in the church. Even Europeans enamored of the Republic and the separation of church and state expressed amazement that, as one put it, congregations were "given a formal right to act contrary to God's Word if [they] can merely summon a two-thirds majority for a decision."[100]

Despite these deeply held fears, it is remarkable that these same church leaders nonetheless remained optimistic about the future of their faiths in the United States. That optimism was based on yet another instance of complementary identity, a syncretism that applauded both American freedom and religious truth. The structures of religious freedom, argued immigrant clergymen, actually would strengthen the faith and result in a victory of religious belief. The perspective of Norwegian Lutheran pastor Herman Amberg Preus, therefore, who worried about "the modern rage for 'natural and inalienable human rights,'" treasured the separation of church and state. The church, he observed, was protected, if not supported, by the state. And precisely because that support was lacking, the state could not dictate church policy. Thus in America the church body was not sustained by "ordinances of human devising . . . or privileges under civil law, but only [by] God's Word." In the United States, a pure church could be maintained only if "every activity can be directed according to God's Word" and its leadership could "work for the salvation of souls" and act as "servants of the Word without being hemmed in by the prejudices, constraints, and burdens of the state church."[101]

Even a Catholic leader such as Mazzuchelli was hopeful that truth would emerge victorious despite, or perhaps because of, the tendencies of excess. "The press and free preaching," he argued, "carry religious innovations to extremes as soon as they are born." Yet Catholic writers "whose pens are never idle" could attack that fanaticism. Using superior logic and armed with spiritual truth, they could check "the innate tendency to non-Catholic principles." As the church combated error, it was certain that "the followers of error must eventually submit and profess the truth or else, rejecting every religious system whatsoever, abandon themselves to unbelief which is, in its effects, little different from paganism." Precisely because of the freedoms of religion and the press and political equality, Mazzuchelli argued, Catholics would be able to maintain their beliefs and eventually exert some influence in the governing of the nation. Thus he was able to praise the opportunity to preserve differing religious convictions and simultaneously maintain his absolutist faith in the validity of the church. Ironically, his optimism about the future of Roman Catholicism was based on an acknowledgment of American immoderation: the excesses of freedom of belief would ultimately create a path toward belief in absolute Catholic principles.[102] Whereas Preus perceived a church free from the dictates of the state, Mazzuchelli envisioned an untrammeled discourse that would lead to a stronger church.

As powerful and compelling as these formulations based on the complementary identity may have seemed to immigrant leaders, they often created intellectual quandaries. For one thing, they suffered from an underlying paradox that Peter Berger and others call "cognitive contamination."[103] By attempting to control the modernizing forces that swirled around nineteenth-century American life, the leadership was attempting to guide them. In striving to regulate these forces, they were accepting ideas—the possibilities of choice, the use of manipulation—that were "modern" in and of themselves. By making compromises, they were implicitly accepting terms with which they disagreed.

In a more immediate sense, their solutions begged the questions underlying spiritual confrontation. Perhaps American providence would result in a Catholic or Lutheran "victory." Perhaps one religion would "win" because it would naturally occur to the citizenry that it was better. But how should the leadership of one faith, or one ethnic predilection, confront "defeat" if its adversary won the war for the hearts and minds of the West? How would such leaders be able to accept the idea of majority rule when the majority might not necessarily be right? And how were they to stem the tide of freedoms in the family and community if they were celebrated in the region and the polity? These questions would endure among the immigrant families embedded in the rural communities that dotted the nineteenth-century Middle West.

Conclusion

The past two chapters have argued that for those of "foreign" and "Puritan" pasts alike, the West represented a locale of providential possibility. It was a place where material wealth predicted the potential for the fulfillment of human promise. Yet because people had different definitions of that potential, the cultural development of the West throughout the nineteenth century was expressed in large part by the countervailing forces of the minds of the West. Basic precepts of individualism and hierarchy, authority and relativism, materialism and piety, confronted one another in the West, a locale that by all accounts was to play a crucial role in the future of the United States, if not the world. And these contending principles, as contemporaries were well aware, were based on fundamental intellectual disputes of the "minds" moving westward.

Protestant republicans, as we observed in Chapter 1, forcefully outlined a scenario in which European immigrants, dupes of a regressive, authoritarian, and hierarchical leadership in the United States *and* Europe, were key players in a diabolical plot that could destroy the American Republic and its potential for progress nearly as efficiently as the curse of slavery that continued in the South. Nativists shuddered at the conundrum wherein the ideals of the Republic contained within themselves the possibility of their own subversion. Americans were uneasy about the troubling fact that the Republic provided people who were so inclined with the freedom to be authoritarian. American nativists hoped to solve the problem by stemming the immigrant tide. Others were convinced that the republican government, replete with its democratic political and educational structures, would transform the immigrant and create "Americans" who were able to make the "correct" decisions.

For European cultural leaders, the puzzle was turned on its head. They did not fear the freedoms to be authoritarian so much as the ominous prospects for structures of authority in a land that privileged "freedom." Immigrants and their leaders were often quite willing to venerate the American republican system, not least because its alleged freedoms permitted them to retain Old World beliefs. They often respected the voluntary church, in which "true" belief could be separated from state patronage. Yet they were forced to grapple with the inherent ambiguities of "freedom" and "authority." And in so doing, the spiritual leaders of European immigrants expressed concern about the long-term consequences of allowing the assumptions of liberal Protestantism to be played out. With its emphasis on individuality, the American system weakened basic corporate forms in society. From these perspectives, Europeans were challenged less by assaults from the outside than by insidious change from within.

Questions of cultural change and cultural retention thus became a central pivot on which immigrant communities in the rural Middle West (and elsewhere) turned. Much of the contention within immigrant communities pitted religious leaders who hewed to authoritarian structures against a laity who had breathed in the freedoms of American life. Chapter 4 will illustrate how immigrants—both Catholic and Protestant—argued vociferously about spiritual rights with their leaders and among themselves. Yet immigrants not only reconfigured authority in their communities, placing at risk the power invested in the clergy, but also contested patterns of authority in such basic institutions as the family, as we shall see in Chapter 7. Whereas husbands and fathers might argue with their spiritual leaders about rights, they often were less sympathetic to ideologies of "freedom" within the home. The complementary identity, in short, contained an intrinsic tension. American society permitted its residents freedoms of belief, and the West gave them the opportunity to found colonies where former cultural patterns could be replanted. Yet how could the freedoms be contained? How could their communities be buffered from the possibility that new freedoms would diffuse into their communities?

One strategy made possible by the vast amounts of available land in the West, a strategy that worried American nativists, was for immigrants to wall themselves off, to isolate themselves and cluster away from outside influences. As settlement unfolded, the planned colonizations aimed at the creation of ethnic "states" were never fulfilled. Yet the behavior of the families moving westward manifested the maintenance of bonds of kinship and ethnicity. The ties among migrants from the East and Europe were central to the reestablishment of communities in the West. The freedom to move unchecked ironically led not to the creation of atomized individuals but rather to the formation of ethnic enclaves that resembled in no small degree the earlier planned colonizations that often failed so miserably. The dread among American nativists in the antebellum era that cultural differentiation would socially partition the West came to pass, albeit in less severe form than they feared. And that segmentation persisted well after the war to save the Union.

The manifestations of this segmentation, of course, were not as boldly defined as that between the diabolical Catholic and the materialistic Yankee. Myriad ethnocultural traditions were reestablished in the West. Yet each subculture entered a region where its tradition was transplanted according to local conditions, opportunities, and constraints. Here the members of the various subcultures were forced to blend the traditions of family and community of their cultural past with their societal future. They were compelled to reweave their cultural fabric into a new milieu. Each subculture, moreover, was forced to interact with others, which fostered social diffusion and cultural change. The West—or the Middle West, as it came to be called as invasion and colonization of the North American continent continued—would become an ideal laboratory for the study of profoundly different cultural systems reestablished in a new environment.

Those who celebrated the potential "freedoms" in the nineteenth-century West anticipated many outcomes. For some, they promised the certainty that Europeans would become Americans, throw off their Old World habits, and become part of a Crèvecoeur-like melting pot. For others, they foretold a situation that provided immigrants with the opportunity to cluster in culturally segregated enclaves and maintain Old World patterns detrimental to American freedoms. Both outcomes occurred in some form, creating an intrinsic tension within immigrant communities. Immigrants were able to utilize a complementary identity to enable them to participate in the political process but not necessarily at the expense of cultural beliefs carried across the sea. And they tended to cluster together in settlements where common beliefs could be maintained. Within their settlements, the immigrants were able to maintain Old World hierarchies of family and community. Yet by accepting and celebrating "freedom"—even the freedom to remain unfree, as some nativist critics might have characterized it—they also unwittingly sanctioned the diffusion of other freedoms in their homes and communities, freedoms that were inimical to their cultural traditions.

PART TWO

THE COMMUNITY

CHAPTER 3

We'll Meet on Canaan's Land

Patterns of Migration

Come, all ye Yankee farmers who wish to change your lot," proclaimed a popular song among New Englanders migrating westward, "who've spunk enough to travel beyond your native spot / And leave behind the village where Pa and Ma do stay."[1] The bravado of such a pronouncement was a common thread in migration literature. It supported the notion that an enormous migration was laying the groundwork for an atomized, individualized society. During the mid-1850s, a period of massive land acquisition and westward migration, writers marveled again and again at the volume of westward movement, further compelling proof of the opportunity in the West. "Still they come," trumpeted the editor of the *Keokuk (Iowa) Whig*. "By railways and steamers, the flood of immigration continues pouring into the great West. . . . And still they come from Pennsylvania, from Ohio, Indiana, and other States, until, by the side of this exodus, that of the Israelites becomes an insignificant item, and the greater migrations of later times are scarcely to be mentioned." Perhaps, he suggested, the West was a Canaan. "We repeat again," the editor wrote, "let them come. . . . Let them flee from their tax-ridden and miserably governed Egypts of Ohio and Pennsylvania, to the Land of Promise, flowing with something better than milk and honey, and possessing capabilities such as they have hardly dreamed of."[2]

The centripetal pull of great opportunity purportedly was attenuating ties to family and links to home. Residents in the United States, Charles Augustus Murray reported, had for decades been an extremely mobile lot, and that mobility weakened their connections to state and region. "The American agriculturalists seem to have little local attachment," he wrote. "A New Englander or Virginian, though proud and vain of his state, will move off to Missouri or Illinois, and leave the home of his childhood without any visible effort or symptom of regret, if by so doing he can make ten dollars where he before made eight."[3] Basil Hall agreed. "Under such constant changes of place," he wrote, "there can be very little individual regard felt or professed for particular spots. I might almost say, that as far as I could see or learn, there is nothing in any part of America similar to what we call local attachments. There is a strong love of country," Hall concluded, "but this is quite a different affair, as it seems to be entirely unconnected with any permanent fondness for one spot more than another."[4]

European community ties were also seemingly weakened in the West. Hezekiah Niles, not without pleasure, observed the failure of planned German settlements to retain their membership. "The social ties which united these emigrants when in Europe," wrote Niles, "for the prosecution of a common object are, for the most part, dissolved as soon as the end of the journey is attained." Paul Follenius, who led a colonization project to found a New Germany "in the western parts of the United States, was abandoned soon after his arrival in America, and before he reached the intended seat of his new settlement, by far the greater part of his companions, who endeavored to provide for themselves, only 2 or 3 families remaining with him." This dispersion was especially apparent among servants who "left their masters even at the port in which they landed, because they found opportunities to better their condition, by obtaining higher wages, without regard to the engagement they had entered into in Europe and which the American laws afford no means of compelling them to fulfil."[5]

The West apparently made one free, free from former inequalities, free to undertake new endeavors, free of past beliefs and associations. The enormous migrations, one might surmise, had introduced a vast array of newcomers with few ties to the homes and kin they left behind. As a writer in the *Burlington (Iowa) Hawkeye* put it in 1839, "The whole territory is now full of strangers. Our city has become a perfect Gotham, as emigrants from every state, and, in fact, every civilized country on the globe, are flocking in clouds to our place."[6] With regard to American republican fears of the Scylla of foreign domination and the Charybdis of a chaotic devolution of society in the West, the latter appeared to many to be of greater relevance as immigration swelled in the decades prior to and following the Civil War.

Yet upon closer inspection, the migration was not as chaotic as contemporaries claimed. Ironically, because of the purported atomization of society, the advantages inherent in maintaining complex webs of kinship throughout the region increased. Hidden beneath the exaggerated aplomb expressed by the migrants and their sense of the immensity and chaos of the migration itself were individual uncertainties and fragilities underlying the decisions of the countless migrants. After all, migration separated loved ones and, in so doing, attenuated bonds between family and friends. The decision to move to distant places, moreover, was fraught with apprehension. Migrants, as a result, tended to rely less on "spunk" and more on tactics to temper separation from home and unfamiliarity with a new locale. A common solution was to encourage the additional migration of people migrants had left behind. Furnished with information often supplied by family, friends, and acquaintances who had already made the journey, new migrants were provided a balm both to ease the doubts of relocation and to enable reunion in a new setting.

These individual decisions writ large created a vast network of ties that tended to focus and direct patterns of migration in the Middle West. Besides kin who were reunited in new places, former neighbors joined one another as well. As migration intensified in specific neighborhoods to the east, and as the migration networks became increasingly intricate, settlements in the Middle West were based more and more on ties and affiliations carried westward. This pattern of movement had enormous significance not only for the individuals who migrated but also for the cultural development of the region. Despite the failures to colonize the region and create separate homogeneous territories, the multitude of individuals who participated in the polyglot migration nonetheless tended to settle in neighborhoods defined in large part by common cultural background (see figure I.1). Family, friends, and countrymen crossed hundreds, even thousands, of miles to return in a sense to webs of affiliation based on kinship and nationality in the rural settlements of the West.

Farewell, My Friend . . . : Individual Patterns of Migration

Farewell, my friend I'm bound for Canaan
I'm travelling through the wilderness
Your company has been delightful
I hope you do not feel distressed

I go away behind to leave you
Perhaps never to meet again

But if we ever have the pleasure
I hope we'll meet on Canaan's land
—Traditional ballad

The immense westward migration in the nineteenth century did not by itself lessen the sense of loss that accompanied departure. Forsaking family and friends was a decision of great meaning. When loved ones left, who could say that their farewell would not be the last meeting they would have on this earth with those they left behind? In spite of perceptions of opportunity in the western United States, moreover, the decision to migrate there was not simple. Even American migrants, who traveled shorter distances and had greater familiarity with the United States than their European counterparts, often perceived the western lands as distant and foreboding places. In short, for American-born as well as European migrants, migration was not a deed to be taken lightly. For those Americans and Europeans who made the fateful decision to leave their homes for the West, additional movement that reunited friends and kin was a common solution to a separation that was often distressing. The location of Canaan to nineteenth-century migrants was ambiguous. Whether it was situated in the West or in Heaven, however, reunion there was a commonly expressed hope.

Consider the ruminations of Newell W. Bixby. A Free Will Baptist minister from Vermont, he had by 1846 "for sometime felt it to be [his] duty to go to the West to blow the gospel trumpet." The decision whether to leave Vermont for the Middle West, however, was not easily made. Some of his brethren spoke words of encouragement, "while others have seemed rather unfavorable to the idea of my going there. But," he concluded, "I have tried to make a careful and candid conclusion as a matter of duty between God and my own soul, and feel that God's Spirit bids me go doubting nothing."[7]

Nonetheless, Bixby's doubts remained. As the time to leave approached, he wrote: "But oh! how friendship draws like cords around my heart."[8] After all, he and his wife were leaving a community they knew well in order to travel to a faraway land. Using the word "brethren" in contexts of both kinship and friendship, he observed that "a large circle of brethren & friends in various towns, parents and brethren & sisters, dear to our hearts, we must leave and go among *strangers in a distant land.* 'Yes *my native land* I love thee,'" he continued, "'all thy scenes I love them well.' Still for the sake of Christ and the Gospel I leave them and that with the hope of seeing the work of the Lord in the salvation of souls."[9] When the day of his departure on "the long journey" dawned, Bixby wrote:

The scene of parting was tender and impressive especially with our afflicted mother. I inquired of her if she felt any feelings or had any thoughts that we were not doing right in going away so far, and she said "no" and added that she had enjoyed a glorious time that morning. At dawn she arose, and prayed and felt to shout and praise God. She gave some advice and wished it remembered that we had left a friend. Several brethren and sisters wept as they said the last farewell. . . . My mind yesterday seemed awake to the reality that I had taken the last look on my dear relatives & brethren, that I had done for the cause of God in that region all that I should do for the present and that I had undertaken a great work. Often when I thought of it my eyes were suffused with tears and my soul seemed to cling to the promises of the Lord with some delight.

"Today," he concluded, "I do not feel so much of a devotional spirit as at sometimes." [10]

Similar sentiments of loss from separation were expressed by those who remained behind. Among the many who coupled departure and death with reunion and spiritual afterlife, Emma Seaton penned a letter to Allettie Battey upon hearing of her friend's imminent departure. "When I think of you going away it makes me feel so sad," she wrote. "To be sure we shall always write to one another, but O Let I am afraid that we shall never see each other again in this world but let me believe that there is a better world in store so let us try to live so that we may meet where parting is never known." [11] Young Emma's fears of earthly separation indicate the deep sense of loss from migration, no matter how short the distance: Allettie, unlike trans-Atlantic immigrants, was only moving from Michigan to Dakota.

Even more poignant examples of grief over separation were expressed by the elderly who were left behind. The diary of Sarah Browne Armstrong Adamson, who herself had emigrated from England in 1797, is particularly illuminating in connecting Christian consolation to anxieties of loss stemming from migration. Throughout the late 1830s and early 1840s, she observed with sadness the departure of her children from their Fayette County, Ohio, home. Habitually aware of anniversaries, Adamson noted in her diary on 2 June 1839 that on that day not only had she buried her first husband thirty years before but also her son William had set out for "Ioway," "another bereavement," she added, "for me to endure." Some four years later, when "my Benj'n" also departed for Iowa, she wrote, mixing references to kinship and abandonment, "May Israels God go with you and protect you, may you find in Jehovah a friend that sticketh closer than a brother, he has promised that when Father and mother forsake thee he will never leave thee." When Benjamin returned a few months later only to depart once again, she concluded, "And now my dear Benj'n is gone again Oh, when will my sorrow have an end never never till this fluttering heart ceaces [*sic*] to beat." [12]

For Adamson, departure, death, and hopes of salvation were intricately intertwined. After her daughter Charlotte moved away on 21 September 1841, Adamson attempted to place migration within a divine plan: "Could nothing save you my dear children Oh I wish to say it is the Lord. Let him do what seemeth good in his sight." Yet the frightful parallels between death and departure continued to haunt her. When a group of kin set out again for Iowa, she sighed, "Oh for fortitude to bear this heart-rending painfull dispensation May God of peace go with them. Oh may we meet where all this parting will be at an end." In a letter written to her children in 1844, she prayed that God might spare them until they could return to her. She then cited a verse that read in part:

> Peace, then my troubled heart,
> I'll leave them in thy care;
> Although like death to part
> Yet God is with them there.
>
> He will support you then,
> Amidst your present pain,
> And by His all supporting arm
> Will bring you back again.
>
> Yes! I believe He will
> Answer my warm request
> That I may see my children dear
> Before I sink to rest.

The verse concludes with an oft-repeated hope: "We'll join with those who've gone before / Where pleasures ever flow." [13]

Adamson's worst fears, however, were soon realized when her daughter and granddaughter died in the faraway land of Iowa. Again attentive to anniversaries, she expresses a palpable sorrow in a series of passages penned on 16 October 1841. "This day I am 59 years old," she began, "in tolerable Health for which I desire to be thankfull But oh none of my children at home. . . . Shall we all meet together again? This I can not answer but oh may we meet where parting will be no more." In her next passage, she wrote, "Little did I think when writing the above in less than two hours, I should know from painfull certainty. I never should meet my beloved Charlotte or Mary Catherine untill I meet them in Eternity Oh what a stroke Oh what a scene." In anguish, she concluded, "They are gone They are gone Mothers imagine my feeling if you can. My Charlotte my beloved Charlotte. Gone yes for ever gone far far beyond this gloomy vale of tears, what see her no more? Oh this heart this beating heart." [14]

From that time forward, Adamson's diary was peppered with disconsolate references to the loss of her daughter and granddaughter. In late 1842, for instance, Adamson remembered Charlotte's birthday: "But oh she is gone yes forever gone but your death will be my sorrow as long as I live Oh my Charlotte my Charlotte." And on the second anniversary of Charlotte's death, Adamson revealed that her grief remained fresh when she wrote, "Oh my beloved Charlotte the grave has closed on you and I shall never, never see you more, untill Gabriels Trumpet shall sound, 2 years, 2 painfull years has pass'd since that heart rending providence took place and I am yet alone oh could I say from the heart, 'Thy will be done.'" [15] Adamson eventually chose not to continue to passively accept "heartrending providence." In order to live among family members before more "graves were closed," she replicated the actions of countless Europeans and Americans: she moved to join her children, all of whom now lived in a rural settlement in Lee County, Iowa. The migration of her children had precipitated her own relocation.

Many of those who moved to strange new locales continued to muse about the distance between and separation of their forsaken kin and themselves and the possibility of heavenly reunion. Myranda Underwood, for example, who had migrated from Vermont to Wisconsin, wistfully reminisced to her "absent Brother and Sister" in a letter. "My health is now good and my spirits light," she wrote, "and with a thankful heart I would record my Heavenly Fathers goodness to the wanderer." "O what a satisfaction," she continued, "it would be to see our family all together once more and to hear each familiar voice. Dear brother and sister how does age affect you? Do grey hairs appear on your heads? I always think of you as the same youthful couple that I saw 17 years ago forgetting that time has been busy with you as well as with myself." As was typical in many letters to absent kin, her thoughts then turned toward death and the afterlife. "I shall be 34 years of age the 10 of Nov. and I feel that I am on the decline to the grave. Yes I feel that I have passed the meridian of my days and I do not wish it to be otherwise. Beautiful as these wide spread prairies look I feel that it is with sacred delight that I turn to contemplate those regions where the inhabitants shall no more say I am sick." Confident that she would never meet them again on earth, she concluded by admonishing her siblings. "Dear friends are you preparing for Heaven. Search well the foundation of your hope," she stressed, "and be sure to build on the Rock Christ Jesus and so live that we may meet in Heaven."[16]

Sentiments of loss from separation were especially acute in times of tragedy. Betraying contrition for his absence, Oliver Parsons set down his thoughts in his diary upon learning of his mother's death. "She devoted every energy of her mind and body to accomplish the happiness of her children," he wrote. "Oh the deep, sincere earnest and devout love of a Christian Mother's heart; how fond Memory transports me back to the days of my childhood and Youth." Then his thoughts, inspired again by Christian beliefs, shifted to his father, whom he had also abandoned: "My dear Father how lonely you must feel, but there is a Divine hand that will guide and protect you as you stand on the shore of the river."[17]

Like their American-born counterparts, European immigrants' thoughts often turned to reunions in the afterlife when discussing sickness and death with their absent loved ones. John and Mary Thomson responded to their brother in England with solemn reminiscence and dark foreboding after being informed of the death of their father. "It is with feelings of Deep regret When we hear the Death of any of our friends," they wrote from their Wingville, Wisconsin, home. "But when its the nues of the departure of our Parents it call furth recolections of past events of no ordinary kind. I wold to God that it would be santified [sic] to us all and mak us think more of our oun depertur."[18] Other English immigrants writing from Dubuque, Iowa, to their "dear brothers and sisters and mother" noted with sadness the sickness of their mother. "We should like to see her very mutch," they wrote. "But it cannot be now But we all hope to Meat in Heaven. . . . May we pass into a vast eternity and with our Servant happy be forever more. We are very glad to hear you say," they concluded, "that you are going to stop and take care of Mother. It is a very good thought of you I am shure." Immigration, in this case, had separated parents and children. Yet despite the sorrowful tone of their letter, the immigrants could not resist closing it by sharing information that ostensibly promoted the emigration of other kin: "About 15 pounds," they observed, "will bring you here very well."[19]

Immigrants were often torn between the prospect of opportunity in the West and their sense of responsibility at home. For most, the benefits of migration offset the guilt and heartache of separation, as a poignant letter from a Dutch immigrant to his father reveals. "Departing from you, dear father," wrote Sjoerd Aukes Sipma, "was very hard on me, much harder than I let on. But I think it must have been much harder on you when you as in a moment had to say good-by to your nearest of kin. But oh, dear father, we did not leave to get away from you, as you know very well. It was for the purpose of going to a country where we, by working hard, could expect a better way of life than in Vriesland. And we have not been disappointed in this." The prairies of Iowa had provided Sipma with land; "just to think," he marveled, "of living on one's own land!" Parting was difficult, but Sipma concluded that in the end "it must do you good, dear father, to receive news concerning us now and then, and to know that we are in a better country and that your children prosper."[20]

Even when material advantages outweighed kinship responsibilities, migrants—including American migrants from the eastern United States —often expressed fears about living in their new location. Upon the receipt of correspondence from friends in New York State, Charles A. Dean responded from his new Iowa home that he enjoyed getting "letters from our friends in *this strange land*."[21] Juxtaposed with images of a "strange land," however, were kernels of information about life in the West that often encouraged migration. One letter writer, for instance, chided his brother's ignorance as he informed him of the features of Iowa. "Able [apple] and Cherry Trees are in blume and every thing green [and] flourishing out here," he wrote, "in *this barren country* as you call it."[22] Another migrant outlined the emotional shifts she had experienced after moving from Vermont to Wisconsin in the 1840s. "I may venture to say there never was a person more prejudiced against coming to this region or more dissatisfied with the place than I was," she wrote, "but I have become very much attached to my prairie home and think I should prefer it to returning to Vt." She added, "The boys all wonder why all the Green Mountain folks do not come onto the Prairies to live."[23] The Morse family in Iowa also gave an evenhanded assessment of prospects in the West and offered subtle encouragement of migration. Henry Morse wrote his brother Francis from Iowa in 1856 that he hoped to give him information in order to "enable you to come to a decision." He also indicated the advantages of kinship. "If you are in want of a house on the Prairie," Henry wrote, "I will exchange work with you."[24] Francis and his family soon joined his brother.

Other correspondents made more flamboyant claims. "If the farmers of New England could but see this country once," exclaimed a letter writer to acquaintances in the East, "they would soon bid adieu to the rocks and hills of their old homestead, and with their wives and children would locate upon some of the broad prairies of the New England of the West."[25] A youth who wrote to his family in Maine was even more to the point. "Pour Souls how I pitty you," he wrote, "contented to drag out a miserable life in a land where grass hoppers can hardly live, where toads can be seen crying for a little sorrel, and even the poor *weevils* had to *emigrate* in order to get a little *wheat*, & I don't blame them. . . . It . . . should teach man an important lesson."[26]

Not everyone learned the "important lesson." Most remained at home and eventually severed family bonds so that reunification, if it was to occur, could happen only after death. Yet the information in migrants' letters about kin and opportunity did successfully encourage the additional migration of countless Americans and Europeans who were reunified with their loved ones in the West. The experiences of Sarah Adamson encapsulate the process. As she remained at home in Ohio and witnessed the departure of her children, Adamson kept track of the movement in her diary, noting at one time that her son had left to "seek a home in a *far distant country*" of Iowa.[27] Iowa at first was indeed a "far distant country" to her. After an almost constant back-and-forth migration between Ohio and Iowa, her children sent her information and letters "more valuable than gold."[28] In spite of her initial apprehension about the West, Adamson little by little became more familiar with the region. As her fears dissipated, her longing for her children intensified; her advancing age made her increasingly dependent, and Sarah finally joined her children in what she once had considered a "far distant country." Part of a massive movement, Adamson's migration was enclosed within a circle of kin.

The Way the West Was Then Settled: Migration and Settlement, 1830–1860

Our relatives and friends left behind in the East began loading their goods into
covered wagons and plodding out over the old Ridge Road with bulbs of
prairie homes. . . . This, as they used to say, tended to build up the country. It
was the way the West was then settled. — Herbert Quick, *One Man's Life* (1925)

Later, in the interests of both riches and religion, which the old man had
always shrewdly worked together, he had sent back to Prussia and got a dozen
families to come and settle on his land, promising them help in getting started
on the condition that they should all become German Methodists. He had
been afraid that the German Catholics, who had a settlement over in the hills
at Holy Cross, would "get a hold" in the Turkey timber. That was the way
that the large German Methodist community had first started.
— Ruth Suckow, *Country People* (1924)

Correspondence thus played a dual role in sustaining old cords of friendship and kinship. On the one hand, letters served as a balm to ease the distress caused by separation and to preserve attenuated ties of kinship and friendship. Communication, on the other hand, provided encouragement and information—oftentimes inadvertently—which in turn led to reunions in the new western settlements. Through written and spoken words, the possibilities of migration spread not only to kin and friends but also to others within the locality. The inextricable combination of a yearning for a reunion with family and friends and the prospect of living under more sanguine circumstances led many to follow the initial migrants to their new homes.

Certainly not everyone could undertake a journey of reunion. Migration did not occur without financial cost, and many without the means to move were forced to stay behind. The experiences of Sarah Adamson notwithstanding, moreover, the elderly were more likely than youth to endure a permanent separation from kin, at least on earth.[29] Others who made the trip found little satisfaction. Edmund Flagg, who observed eastern American migrants along the banks of the Ohio and Mississippi Rivers in 1836, worried, "Poor woman! . . . Little do you dream of the trial and privations to which your destiny conducts, and the hours of bitter retrospection which are to come over your spirit like a blight, as, from these cheerless solitudes, you cast back many a lingering thought to your dear distant home in New England."[30] For European immigrants who crossed the sea, the voyage was typically even more difficult. Accounts of the horrors of the nineteenth-century passage from Europe are legion. A wearisome journey of seven weeks was often punctuated by storms, during which travelers, old and young, were cramped in the dark underbelly of a wooden vessel.[31] A ship from Liverpool transporting an old man full of "all life and spirits" because "he is going to end his days with his children in America" also carried "a poor old Irish woman sitting in the hold and weeping bitterly."[32]

Although migration spawned separation, migrants developed strategies to bridge the divisions that initial moves created. Not only did reunions of kin and former neighbors in a new locale ease feelings of loneliness, but they also provided support and aid to those who could migrate to an ostensibly more abundant locale and supplied ready-made trade partners, farm laborers, and sources of knowledge about crops and markets. Those lacking the wherewithal to move thus often were given prepaid tickets or other forms of financial aid by family and friends. Herein lay the mechanisms of the "chain migration." Information and encouragement coupled with promises of emotional and material support were critical factors in precipitating additional decisions to migrate. Because reliable information often came from friends and family in the "strange land," the migration was directed toward them in a chainlike fashion.[33] As information about migration opportunities spread, chain migrations not only linked localities across space but also tended to increase the volume of migration from the sending communities. Researchers, using national and regional aggregates of migration flows, repeatedly have discovered the significance of family and friends in influencing migration intensity.[34] As webs of kinship and friendship reunited groups of individuals, the migrants were enmeshed in colonies defined by ties not only of kinship but also of regional background. Flows of information eastward, in short, were followed by flows of migrants to the West.

Significantly, chain migrations to the rural Middle West were common among Americans from the eastern United States as well as among Europeans.[35] "Every mail from the West," according to one Yankee, teemed "with the Macedonian cry, come over and help us."[36] Joseph V. Quarles's series of letters from Kenosha County, Wisconsin, to his former home in New Hampshire illustrates how westering folk informed their readers about the region while cajoling them to join the migration. In a letter written to the postmaster of his former hometown in 1837, Quarles noted that a man named Young "may come on I will guarantee that he shall do well—I will hire him if he can not do better." Quarles concluded, "I think that you had better come and see for your self." Later letters were replete with information. In 1838, Quarles wrote, "The soil is very rich and produces abundantly—The low prararas [prairies] are flat and wet but produce grass abundantly and will grow grain or corn vastly better than N. H. lands."

Besides the "abundant" economic opportunity, western society was splendid. "The state of the society here," he continued, "is good a large proportion of them are N Englanders—*Scarcely any foreigners*—very intelligent and polite." And then he offered help: "If any of our friends would like to have land here If they will send the money I will attend to it and make as [good a] selection as I possibly can. . . . I think you would double your money in a short time." Quarles finally coaxed through the use of riddle. "A large proportion of the emigrants & settlers here are from N. Y. but few from N. H.," in spite of the fact that the latter has poorer land. Why? "I can think of but one solution—the land is so poor & hard [in New Hampshire] that if a man could cease laboring long enough for an idea in relation to emigration to shoot across his brain his whole family would perish with hunger."[37]

The act of migration itself, once the decision to move was made, was often simplified by the presence of family and friends along the way. Newell Bixby's fears of moving to the West were eased somewhat by the fact that he and his wife stopped at the homes of New England acquaintances along their route to Iowa in 1847.[38] F. W. Bryant also knew of the comforts of kin during migration. He tarried with his family on his way west from New York to Iowa.[39] Although family ties were significant, a developing sense of regional affiliation also provided some comfort. A letter written from Galena, Illinois, in 1845 by a New England migrant illustrates the satisfaction of enjoying a common tradition in new circumstances. "Thus you see we meet New England people every where," the writer explained, "and I have seldom felt that we were among strangers."[40] Once again migrants to the West expressed a curious admixture of trepidation about entering a strange land and delight at being reunited with former friends. In spite of this apparent paradox, the relationship between "strangeness" and "companionship" was clearly inverse: the more friends who migrated, the less strange the new land might be.

Companionship on occasion was created by emigrant associations. Often founded on common religious ties, associations pooled capital and hired agents to judge and acquire land for the group. Since the migrants traveled together to ready-made settlements, the risks of migration were reduced. The ties of home were often maintained as well. The migrants who traveled in 1858 to their new home of Sand Springs in Jones County, Iowa, for example, all originated from Ware, Massachusetts.[41] Although the landscape was strange, the faces were familiar.

Many other chain migration patterns were less formalized than these planned ventures, yet the common bonds that knit them together were probably even stronger. Like that of Sarah Adamson, migration from New England that united kin in the Middle West characterized much of the movement. A particularly well documented case involves a Connecticut family that began to move to the Genesee country of New York in 1816. Within a decade, thirteen of fourteen siblings and their families had relocated to New York. In 1834, one of the siblings moved again to the Western Reserve of Ohio to join an uncle who was already there. By 1839, his parents and eight of his brothers and sisters and their families had moved to Ohio. Another migration commenced in 1850 to Michigan.[42] Members of the Kellog family also migrated westward from Connecticut and located in Racine County, Wisconsin, in 1836. Establishing a community soon known as Kellog's Corners, the kinspeople were able to gather for prayers in one another's homes each evening after the dishes were washed.[43]

Migrant streams among eastern Americans also extended beyond bonds of kinship so that sections of entire eastern communities were transplanted. William Salter, a Congregationalist missionary, noted in his 1844 diary the regional as well as religious background of the settlements he visited on his journeys. One neighborhood, "the best settlement in the county," was composed of families "nearly universally from N York and Maryland."[44] Despite his attempts at proselytization, his prejudice against non–New England settlers remained. After hearing a sermon by one of his coreligionists, Salter proclaimed to his diary, "Oh, it was delightful to hear the memories of our Puritan ancestors spoken of with veneration and love this side of the Mississippi."[45]

The veneration of common Puritan ancestors was fostered among those living in compact settlements because they were often able to nurture their group memories. The settlement of Crow Creek in Scott County, Iowa, formed in 1836, for example, was peopled entirely by New Englanders.[46] The first colonists west of Dubuque in 1836 consisted of two groups, one from Philadelphia, the other from Ohio.[47] Some years later, a group of twenty families from Washington, Vermont, left home destined for " 'that garden of Eden,' where the 'land flows with milk and honey.' "[48] Even more remarkable, 1,000 migrants from Richmond County, Ohio, were reportedly moving to Iowa in the fall of 1854.[49]

To the north, newspapers also recounted other chain migrations of American-born settlers in the 1850s. In 1853, for example, the *Minnesota Democratic Weekly* noted the plans for the village of Gormantown along the Cannon River, a region that "is as good as any in Minnesota, and is rapidly filling up with hardy farmers from New England."[50] The following year, the *Daily Minnesotan* reported that thirty-five families were bound for Minnesota to settle on the Cannon River.[51] Within months reports appeared in the same paper of a migrant group from "Ohier." This colony of ninety persons was moving from Marietta, Ohio—itself a New England colony some years back—to Hastings, Dakota County. "They," the editor concluded assuredly, "are the right kind of people."[52]

European migrants to the Middle West also relied on kinship, friendship, and common backgrounds for support.[53] As in the American migrations westward, the aggregate of the individual decisions created the larger pattern of chain migration, which is exemplified by a case from Somersetshire, England, in the 1840s. When economic opportunities began to worsen in the region, individuals such as James Plaister began to write to relations in the United States to inquire about the advisability of migration. In a letter addressed to James Dyer in Iowa in 1847, Plaister recounted the widespread shutdown of mills in north England and then noted that a relative was "very anxious to hear from you as he is entirely resting on your opinion of America to make up his mind about going out, for his trade is so bad that he is determined to get at something else [rather] than stay in it."[54] Dyer's father, who remained in England, also wrote to his son in the United States and mentioned that "the America Fever is raging horribly amongst us at present." The father expressed the hope that his other son would remain in England, perhaps out of fear of his own loneliness. Yet his daughter, who was planning her migration to Iowa, disagreed; she was "very desirous" that the son should join the emigrating party. "If you really think it would be advantageous for him to come out," the father concluded to his son, "let us know in your next letter."[55] As was typical of many new residents in the West, Dyer encouraged the migration of his siblings, and soon an English colony was established in northeastern Iowa. Following an initial wave of thirty-two families, the emigration diffused throughout Somersetshire and beyond.

English-language newspaper accounts repeatedly recognized the significance of European chain migrations in the settling of the Middle West. In 1851, the *Minnesota Democratic Weekly* recounted the visit of an "intelligent Swedish farmer" to the Minnesota Territory who selected a location for a Swedish colony. The settlement, according to the report, expected "the addition of thirty or forty more families to their number."[56] Twelve years later, the *St. Paul Daily Press* reported on a Dutch immigration to Minnesota. The Dutch immigrants "have come through direct, on the advice of their friends here. . . . Most of these Hollanders have gone to Carver County, where their friends live."[57] And the maintenance of ties continued. "Swedish settlers in one county in Minnesota," reported the *St. Anthony Falls (Minnesota) Democrat* in 1870, "have sent $5000 to Sweden during the past year, to aid friends and relatives in emigrating to this country."[58]

Foreign-language newspapers, not surprisingly, were even more familiar with the individual ties among Europeans that influenced the direction and volume of emigration. The *Dubuque National Demokrat*, for example, detailed the 1858 migration of a member the Lusch family, who bought land in Grundy County, Iowa. The next year, the paper concluded, "he will be followed by friends and acquaintances from Germany."[59] Magnus W. Sampson related his migration to a Dakota County settlement in *Emigranten* in 1859. Following his move from the Koshkonong settlement in Wisconsin in March 1854, other families migrated the next year. By the time of Sampson's account, sixty "well-to-do and satisfied settlers" resided in the settlement.[60]

Although abundant local narratives from all ethnocultural groups testify to a chain migration process, they fail to indicate the degree to which migrants moved within migration chains. How many of those with common regional backgrounds traveled to common settlements? An answer that encompasses the migration in the entire rural Middle West is, of course, unattainable. But we can obtain an overview of the entire migration by analyzing the example of migration from a single locale in Europe. The intricately detailed community history of Fortun, a parish on the western coast of Norway, provides a rare opportunity to chart the migration behavior of the 2,145 individuals in 842 migrant parties who left their home in the nineteenth and twentieth centuries.[61]

The migration and settlement patterns among immigrants from Fortun were characteristic of those among other migrating groups. Like other pioneer migrants, the first colonists from Fortun initially settled near others with common origin. To be sure, a minority of immigrants moved

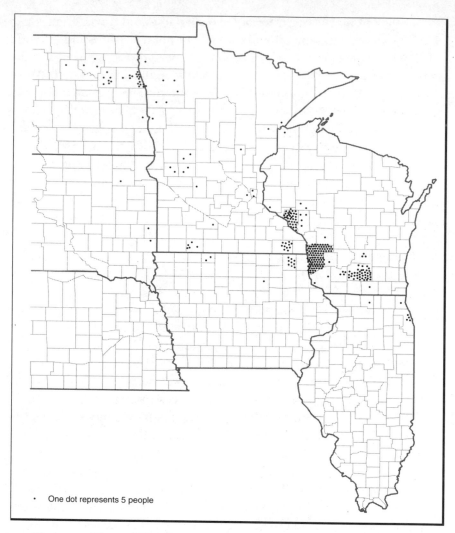

One dot represents 5 people

Figure 3.1. Place of First Residence in the United States for Immigrants from Fortun, Norway

independently to locales where no one else from their parish lived. The vast majority, however, clustered in areas with others of common Fortun background (see figure 3.1). Fortun immigrants first moved to settlements in Dane County, Wisconsin, peopled by prior immigrants who had been born near Fortun (see table 3.1). As the availability of land diminished in these settlements, the immigrants from Fortun began in 1853 to seize the open land to the west in the coulees of western Wisconsin. Within five years, a region on the border of Crawford and Vernon Counties became the focus of migration.[62]

The first immigrants to arrive in Vernon County were quickly followed

THE COMMUNITY

Table 3.1. First Place of Residence, Immigrants
from Fortun, by Date of Emigration

	Quintiles				
	1 (Before 1859)	2 (1860– 1869)	3 (1870– 1882)	4 (1883– 1894)	5 (After 1894)
Crawford and Vernon Counties, Wisconsin	41.3%	50.7%	40.0%	39.5%	39.9%
Buffalo County, Wisconsin	5.8	11.1	11.6	10.5	1.5
Dane County, Wisconsin	32.7	5.3	5.8	6.5	2.2

Source: Lars E. Øyane, *Gards- og Ættesoge for Luster Kommune* (Oslo: Norbok, 1984), vol. 1.

by a throng of migrants from Fortun. Within two years, immigrants had inhabited a four-township cluster in Vernon and Crawford Counties that eventually became the center of the Fortun settlement. By 1859, one-fifth of all immigrants who would depart from Fortun had emigrated, and 41.3 percent of them had settled in the two-county area. In the next decade, over one-half of the immigrants moved to the Crawford/Vernon County colony. In the later phases of immigration, open land to the west beckoned to the immigrants. Nevertheless, two-fifths of the immigrants from Fortun after 1883 made the Crawford/Vernon County settlement their first home in America. The region eventually was peopled by an estimated 4,000 immigrants from Luster, the county of which Fortun is a part, and Årdal, a county to the east of Luster. Together, immigrants from these two counties formed thirteen Norwegian church congregations in the region. "Nowhere in America," wrote an early observer, "can one hear the resounding Sogning dialect so pure and genuine as here."[63]

Despite the importance of the Crawford/Vernon County settlement, other smaller colonies were established by immigrants from Fortun parish throughout the Middle West. Part of a process recognized long ago by Marcus Lee Hansen, satellite communities originating from the mother settlement were formed as a response to population growth and narrowing opportunities in the original settlement.[64] Yet whether they moved to mother settlements in Wisconsin or satellite colonies in Iowa or Minnesota, the early immigrants from Fortun parish—like so many other migrants to the Middle West—traveled within the confines and under the "auspices" of people from their home community. Over four-fifths of the immigrants between 1848 and 1860 moved to one of the four major Wisconsin counties. Thereafter, migrant destinations tended to shift to the west, where land was cheaper and more available, to settlements first in southeast Minnesota and later in the Red River valley of Minnesota and North Dakota. Yet many migrants retained ties with the mother settlements, in large part because they had lived there for a time and had been enmeshed in migration webs that connected neighbors and relations who had known each other in Europe and had become reacquainted in the rural Middle West. Even with the westward drift of settlement, Fortun immigrants continued to consider these areas cultural centers in the United States. As late as the 1940s, descendants of immigrants from specific localities in Fortun held family reunions at which "the whole tribe"—including 200 members from South and North Dakota—gathered at their old Wisconsin homes.[65]

The Exodus Continued: Migration and Settlement after 1860

The movement of settlers toward Dakota had now become an exodus, a stampede. Hardly anything else was talked about as neighbors met one another on the road or at the Burr Oak [Iowa] school-house on Sundays. Every man who could sell out had gone west or was going. . . . "We are wheat raisers," they said, "and we intend to keep in the wheat belt."—Hamlin Garland,
A Son of the Middle Border (1917)

Following the Civil War and especially after the depression of 1873, the prairies of western Iowa, Minnesota, Nebraska, and the Dakotas, with their vast tracts of land available for sale, rather than the mixed woodland-prairies farther east, became the focal point of thousands of settlers.[66] Middle western newspaper editors made a springtime ritual of observing the many migrants who passed through town. "Iowa is winning notably," contended *Die Iowa* in 1881, "in this year's immigration." Two years later, after noting that immigrants, mainly of German, Swedish, Bohemian, and Norwegian background, "come through in great multitudes," the editor concluded in German-English, "*Da buhmt's* [there it's booming]."[67] Yet the middle western editors often mused wistfully about times gone by. "Westward, westward!" wrote the *Dubuque National Demokrat* in 1876. "Last week for sure many were reminded of the 'good, old times,' for Dubuque by the very extraordinarily large number of wagons passing through our streets westward,—of the times when these 'prairie schooners' found their goal within fifty miles of Dubuque and there cast their anchor, of the time when there was no talk of unemployment and trade blossomed, wholesale and retail. These times are past for Dubuque," the paper concluded, because "now the goal of the passing settlers is mostly west."[68] A drama that had played out decades before in the eastern United States was occurring among middle western immigrant groups in the late nineteenth century.

The maturing society of the Middle West offered new challenges and opportunities for its residents. The opening of land farther west simultaneously created additional possibilities to move west again and economic competition for farms that were already established. Like Hamlin Garland's family, many continued to pursue the prospects of large wheat harvests promised by the fertile lands on the frontier, which competed with the settled farms to the east. Still others moved west because land was cheaper and in greater quantity. As early as 1850, a journalist noted the sacrifice made by immigrants who moved to clustered ethnic settlements. "It too often happens," he wrote, "that new arrivals flock together in the old settlements, with the sad result that they either have to buy land at high prices or spend their savings while trying to locate the kind of land that they have heard that the government sells at 10 skilling per acre, or that becomes yours after living on it for one year."[69] A settler noticed the same thing nineteen years later. "We have settled too close to each other," he concluded. As a result, "the smaller farmers are forced to give way and are eagerly purchased by their neighbors, and thus, in time, there will be fewer farmers, but larger and more efficiently worked farms."[70]

Whether migrants moved out of disappointment over high land prices or in hopes of speculative gain, the centrifugal forces of migration posed challenges to stable ethnoculturally defined settlements. As the settlements were built by those with common pasts, land availability within them became more competitive. The opportunity to move west in one way reduced the potential for conflict within the ethnic settlements but also created the continual risk that the community would be weakened by a perpetual diaspora.

For these reasons, it is noteworthy that prairie migrants, like those who came before, often traveled under the auspices of kin, friends, and countrymen. It is true that immigration promotion became increasingly institutionalized after the formation of federal and state agencies in the 1860s.[71] Likewise, organized colonization schemes, which nonetheless were often based on common backgrounds, became more numerous.[72] Correspondence in newspapers continued to provide a ready source of information about potential places of settlement. Here boosters used cultural as well as economic factors to encourage migration. A correspondent to *Die Iowa*, for example, encouraged fellow German Catholics to consider relocating to the area around his home. "With so many Catholic families in Iowa and elsewhere looking for a new home, it's good to point out the advantages of our locality," which, for the German immigrant amid a political temperance battle, included not only cheap land, good timber, and good water but "beer too."[73]

As before, however, the most effective promotion of migration to rural areas continued to be the less formal and less institutional personal ties that encouraged and directed individual acts of migration. A subscriber to *Folkebladet*, a Norwegian-language paper, wrote in 1886 that "it's a common practice among the Scandinavian farmers to send tickets home [to Norway or Sweden] to young fellows who want to come here."[74] After the journey, many immigrants, such as a group from Germany that arrived in Delano, Minnesota, in 1880, were "received . . . at the depot" and were likely "to locate in [the] vicinity." Following a decades-old pattern, they were apt to report, as did a group of Westphalians who also arrived in Stearns County, Minnesota, in 1880, that "there are others from the same place who will follow shortly."[75] The result, of course, was the replication of earlier settlement patterns, creating colonies based on primary ties carried from another locale. For many observers, the human geography was often considered more significant than the physical characteristics of the region. A newspaper correspondent described one settlement, situated on the flat bluestem prairie of western Minnesota that was quite unlike the mountains and fjords of Norway, by stating that it "in many ways, resembles some part of Norway."[76]

The ethnic map of the prairie Middle West, like that of the expanses settled before the Civil War, was profoundly informed by these migration tendencies (see figure I.1).[77] Danish and Yankee, Luxemburger and Dutch settlements, among others, dotted the region.[78] Among the larger European groups that fanned out into the prairie regions, the Scandinavians—and especially the Norwegians—tended to take a northwesterly course into the Dakotas and western Minnesota. Moving to the rich wheat lands of the Red River valley, many of those who had previously lived in Wisconsin and southern Minnesota set out toward the west shortly after the Civil War to form yet another settlement, to find yet another home. "Seven long trains of Norwegians and Swedes from Eau Claire county, Wis., passed thru this city the early part of the week," reported the *St. Anthony Falls (Minnesota) Democrat* in 1871, "destined for the . . . Red River Valley." "They reported," concluded the journalist, "that 'lots more are coming' from the same locality."[79] Similar newspaper reports, which continued into the 1880s, tended to specify the origins and destinations of sizable colonies that moved increasingly to the Dakota prairies.[80]

THE COMMUNITY

Pioneer chronicles indicate a sense of Scandinavian and American provenance among western migrants. A settlement founded in 1869 in western Minnesota, for instance, initially consisted of forty families from "Fillmore and other southern counties," many of whom "come from [the Norwegian region of] Hedemarken."[81] Another group of settlers moved from Highland Prairie in the eastern part of Fillmore County, Minnesota, to what became known as the Buffalo settlement in Clay County, Minnesota. As migrant parties continued to arrive, the settlement grew, and, as an early settler remembered, "now, we had quite a settlement on the little Buffalo [River]." "And the funny part of it," he continued, "was that all of these settlers that had settled here so far had emigrated from the same district in Old Norway." Reflecting a common pattern, the township in which the Buffalo settlement was situated was named Moland, after the parish in Telemark, a "district in Old Norway," where the settlers had originated.[82]

The German migration tended to move both north and west. A large settlement region extending from central Minnesota was composed of Germans, many of whom had formerly lived in the Middle West.[83] Some of the migrants originally from Oldenberg, Hanover, and Westphalia, who would form the Meire Grove settlement in Stearns County, Minnesota, once lived in eastern Iowa.[84] Others, such as a group of over twenty German families who in 1879 settled on the prairies near the town of Pepperton in Stevens County, Minnesota, relocated from the woodlands of eastern Minnesota.[85] Yet another cluster of sixty Illinois farmers from DuPage County near Chicago had by 1883 acquired "big and little parcels of land" in Martin County, Minnesota.[86] Apparently, a migration tradition was established since three years later twenty German families from Elgin, Illinois, near DuPage County, relocated to St. James, a town just north of Martin County.[87]

Germans also moved westward and settled ethnic enclaves in the western prairies of Iowa and Nebraska.[88] The settlement in Carroll County, Iowa — largely German, largely Catholic — illustrates the pattern. Although the first white settlers arrived in the vicinity as early as 1854, migration to the county intensified in the late 1860s and 1870s. Migrants of German Catholic background came predominantly from eastern Iowa. "The number of immigrants who select this county for their home is extraordinarily great this year," wrote a former Dubuque County resident to a newspaper in 1876. "Every train brings new ones . . . coming mostly from the counties Dubuque, Tama, and Clinton, near Freeport, Ill., and from the east." The reason for the migration was simple: "Carroll land is about the best in Iowa."[89] Thereafter, towns and rural settlements around them sprouted up on the prairie. The settlement around the village of

Mount Carmel, six miles north of Carroll, contained over 200 German Catholic families in 1877, mostly from Dubuque County, and was known among Americans tellingly as "the Catholic settlement."[90] The town of Carroll in 1877 contained 80 German Catholic families; Hillsdale, eight miles south, had another 120 German Catholic families; and satellite settlements were forming throughout Carroll County and in neighboring regions. "Such," concluded a correspondent to *Die Iowa*, "is the increase in Catholicity in western Iowa."[91]

Although ties among the American-born were less noticeable on ethnic maps, old middle western ties remained a force that continued to link migrations toward the arid West. The migration from Clinton County, Iowa, in the extreme eastern part of the state to Sac County in the west was so large that a township in Sac County was named Clinton, after the migrants' old home.[92] A similar thread reached from Dubuque County, slightly north of Clinton County, to Ida County, just west of Sac County. After visiting the western Iowa residents, a friend and former neighbor reported in a local paper that they now owned 1,900 acres of improved land.[93] And even as migration moved into the semiarid reaches of Nebraska, some old ties remained intact and new ones were formed. Representing a new ethnic definition, the "Iowa colony" was formed in the Niobrara country of the Nebraska sandhills.[94]

Perhaps based at first on the yearning for reunion, then, chain migrations created a human matrix throughout the Middle West that linked people with common pasts and ultimately offered them social and economic benefits. Settlements that contained former acquaintances and family members often offered opportunities to work and accumulate capital for wages that were usually higher than those in Europe. Economic aid continued. One immigrant who arrived in 1892 at a destination common to many of his friends and kin remembered that he received all the supplies he needed on credit.[95] Economic betterment, in sum, was often more readily found under the auspices of kin than through the individual pursuit of wealth.

Conclusion

Various songs at mid-century proclaimed that the migration to the nineteenth-century rural Middle West was a decision individuals often made to improve their economic circumstances. Yet the personal calculus for the decision to migrate was not so simple. When contemplating the move west, potential migrants were forced to consider the world they would leave behind, including their familial responsibilities for parents and other kin. Once the decision was made and individuals left home, the webs of relationships within which they were enmeshed were altered. Many chose not to join those who moved first, and surviving letters and diaries illustrate the sense of loss that such migrants felt due to their separation from loved ones. Yet many chose to follow earlier migrants to an ostensibly more abundant Middle West, a decision that was often precipitated not only by the chance for reunion but also by promises of aid and support and glowing reports of opportunities offered in the West. Beneath the bravado of individual initiative to migrate was a complex network of kinship and acquaintance.

For our purposes, these patterns of migration were important because they tended to reunite those who shared common cultural pasts, which in turn profoundly informed the process of social interaction and community formation in the Middle West. These structures of migration and settlement did not in and of themselves create an ethnic community. The migrants found themselves in circumstances very different from those of their old homes. Although many, such as Sarah Adamson, moved to join their families, most of those who migrated within the confines of kith and kin based their moves at least in part on a desire for economic betterment, an improvement that was made possible in many ways by the support of former acquaintances. Rural settlements were formed out of these common backgrounds, and residence within them continued because community membership often promoted economic betterment. Yet economic improvement and material prosperity, as many community leaders quickly discovered, were fragile bases for communal solidarity. Even though this massive migration did not atomize society, the communities were nonetheless challenged, as we shall see in the next chapter, by competing social and economic objectives.

Not all migrants to the Middle West, of course, traveled under the auspices of kin or friends or among people of common nationhood. Not all settlers took root in neighborhoods replete with cultural ties that bridged the migration. All agricultural migrants, however, did settle in locations out of which extremely meaningful localized rural communities developed. And common pasts and cultural predilections carried from the cultural hearth were a powerful cement that bonded families in social and economic relationships in many such communities. To be sure, arrangements within settlements would change over time; some colonies grew while others dissipated. Yet the ethnic divisions that remained a vigorous societal force politically and socially well into the twentieth century can be traced to migration patterns that from the very beginning of white settlement divided the migrants into culturally distinct cells. A palpable fear of mid-nineteenth-century nativists was realized in the migration to the Middle West: settlers entered the region not simply as Americans but rather under the auspices of a multitude of ethnic and religious allegiances. The fact that the settlement patterns that ensued resembled an "ethnocultural patchwork quilt" is more than a colorful metaphor. A structurally segmented society was forged in the rural Middle West.

CHAPTER 4

You Can't Put All
Your Horses in One Corral

Conflict and Community

Migration patterns can be analyzed from varying points of reference. The previous chapter concentrated on the structures of migration and focused on the degree to which settlers moved to locales already peopled by kin and acquaintances. An alternative focus—the aim of this chapter—is on the consequences of these migration patterns on local configurations of colonization, community development, and cultural adjustment to the new milieu. From this perspective, we concentrate less on the chain migrations that linked migrants across space than on their impact on the "communities" that the migrants formed. Once they ceased moving, migrants often lived in neighborhoods that contained others who shared a common religion, language, culture, and kinship. "Kinship communities" formed out of chain migrations became a typical basis of rural settlement.[1] In these relatively isolated rural milieus, varying patterns of life were nurtured throughout the nineteenth century that fostered the creation of an ethnoculturally diverse Middle West.[2]

Rural enclaves, however, were not simply locales where former ethnocultural loyalties were rerooted. They were also settings where new ties were forged. Clearly, migration patterns resulted in the formation of neighborhoods that brought together people with common backgrounds; they buffered "ethnic" clusters from others who maintained different cultural traditions. Migrants to rural districts built "communities" ostensibly based on common backgrounds, beliefs, and cultural patterns carried from their places of origin. Yet "community" membership was based on a process of constant renegotiation and reevaluation as rural settlements matured. In the United States, the affiliations with institutions on which communities were centered were voluntary, a radical departure for Europeans, who for centuries had been born into a society and born into a church.[3] To complicate matters further, the definitions of affiliation were fluid and multilayered. Germans, for example, could adhere to local, regional, and national loyalties simultaneously; they could affiliate with various religious and political organizations. Within this matrix of voluntary affiliation, old antagonisms resurfaced while new ones were fashioned under the aegis of the newly created institutional structure of the community. Rural "communities," in short, were often punctuated by conflict, not least because of the ambiguities inherent in the character of community development itself.

The progression of settlement in one rural middle western district illustrates this process in microcosm. The first white migrants to a rural tract near the small city of Dubuque, Iowa, were American-born settlers who moved to the region as preempters in 1834, two years before the land survey began. They broke the land and planted corn before they departed, only to return later for the harvest. As their residences became permanent, they were joined by other Americans, and together they began to form community institutions.[4] Followers of differing sects from a variety of cultural backgrounds, the settlers had by 1845 established Baptist, Campbellite, Methodist, and Congregational churches.[5] Their numbers were soon augmented by English-born immigrants who, owing to common religious beliefs and language, joined the American-born in religious and political associations. By the 1840s, then, these four fledgling communities had formed around Protestant churches and English speech, if not common nationality.[6]

Meanwhile, Irish settlement of another rural tract had commenced. Beginning in 1838, immigrants from County Cork and, to a lesser extent, the neighboring County Limerick began to arrive in an area then known as Makokiti. By the summer of 1840, a Roman Catholic church had been formed to minister to the approximately 100 people in the settlement, now called Garryowen. Still the migration continued. The *Bloomington Herald* noted in 1842 that "about fifty Irish families, just over from Europe . . . selected points along the Maquoketa [River]."[7] Augmented by outlying settlers who walked up to fourteen miles to attend services, the congregation of the Garryowen church—not surprisingly christened as St. Patrick's—numbered some 600 souls by 1843.[8] In one sense, the community was resolutely Irish Catholic. A correspondent to the *Boston Pilot* in 1852 stressed the Catholicity of the settlement following his visit to the "backwoods" where the Garryowen community was situated. At a church service, the priest "delivered an eloquent discourse . . . on the firmness with which the Irish people have ever clung to and supported the religion of their fathers." And "in this rustic Irish congregation of Garry Owen" were many immigrants "direct from their demolished homes and bearing indelible marks of the Saxon whip."[9]

Despite its outward appearance as a "rustic Irish congregation," however, the settlement was internally divided and redefined by regional affinities carried from Ireland. Tension was rife from the outset. Although the settlers could agree on St. Patrick as the patron saint of their church, their decision to call their settlement Garryowen was made with less harmony. Garryowen, it seems, was a place in Limerick, and only after a great quarrel did Cork settlers agree with the Limerick minority to accept it.[10] As tension characterized relationships within the settlement, moreover, "Americans" observed the "Irish" with hostility and confusion. One exchange is particularly illuminating. A family recently arrived from Ireland in 1854 was advised by the priest at St. Patrick's that they might rent a certain farm. But there was some doubt that they would be permitted to lease the land, remembered a daughter in the family, because "Old Jake Brumbo, the owner, had it in for the Catholics. When Father . . . went out to see about renting the place the old man asked father, 'Are you from Cork?' and when father said he was not Old Brumbo let him have the place." The ambiguities of descent were revealed when "later on he said to my father, 'Jones, I thought you said you were not Catholic?' 'No,' father said, 'You didn't ask me that. You asked if I came from Cork.' 'Well,' said Old Brumbo, 'I thought all Catholics came from Cork.'"[11] In this case, the American conflated Catholic belief with County Cork and, by so doing, omitted Irish nationality entirely.

German Catholic migration began only a few years after American, English, and Irish migration. A group of five families, originally from Oldenburg, Hanover, and Westphalia, moved west after dwelling for ten years in Muenster, Ohio, near Cincinnati, in May 1843. Following a careful search for fertile soil, they purchased land in a precinct then known as Wilson's Grove in western Dubuque County, Iowa. In short order, they began to write letters that encouraged family and friends in Ohio and Germany to join them. Their entreaties were successful. When Mathias Loras became the first priest to visit the settlement three years later, he found seventeen families.[12] By 1848, the young community had built a church of hand-hewn logs on a stone foundation in what was now called the settlement of Neue Wien, honoring the Vienna-based Leopoldine Society, the Roman Catholic immigrant-aid organization so despised by American nativists.[13]

The New Vienna community, as it came to be known, flourished, and another group of forty-two Germans in ten families made its way to the vicinity in 1846, after a year's sojourn in St. Louis. The new immigrants' choice of western Dubuque County was perhaps influenced by the fact that a German colony already existed there. Nonetheless, in spite of their common German background and similar Catholic beliefs, the two settlements remained distinct. The later immigrants initially joined the New Vienna parish, but they immediately perceived themselves to be in a disadvantageous position in the community. Not only were they Bavarian rather than Low German, but they were recent arrivals, unlike the New Vienna settlers, who had resided in the United States for more than a decade.[14] After a growing population crowded New Vienna's St. Boniface church, the leadership of the Low German contingent in 1855 told the Bavarians not to expect accommodations in the church since the parish had problems providing enough seating even for its own membership. Thus, nearly ten years after the Bavarians arrived, they were still singled out as outsiders. They concluded that they had little choice but to establish a separate parish, whose church was situated six miles from St. Boniface. Ostensibly of similar faith and national background, the two settlements thenceforth lived in clearly demarcated rural communities defined by regional background carried from Germany and status grounded in the United States.[15]

The patterns of settlement of this district, singular only insofar as they are so well documented, were repeated over and over again as the Middle West was repopulated following the displacement of the Native American peoples. As such, this example illustrates the main points of argument in this chapter. To begin with, communities based on common pasts dotted the Middle West. They became places where former beliefs seemingly could be reconstituted. They were locales where social arrangements were reconfigured and where community membership provided social and economic advantages. Yet as in Dubuque County, the communities were voluntary organisms based on a variety of crosscutting attributes such as religion, regional background, and language. As a result, they were shaped and reshaped by a process of continual internal definition and redefinition. Seasoned Westphalians and newly arrived Bavarians both might have appeared to be German to outsiders, but within their Catholic parish, differences were magnified, which resulted in a division of the church community. The conflict that often erupted within ethnic communities, in short, was part and parcel of an underlying social tension that permeated rural settlements experiencing a perpetual process of redefinition.

The intellectual and theological underpinnings of such conflicts illustrate social divisions and the quandaries of churches transplanted to a sectarian landscape.[16] Since the church often served as a principal community organization, temporal battles based on differences in status and background were often contested in a spiritual setting. When theological debates entered the communities, they were often informed by social cleavages within the community not only between laity and clergy but among the laity as well. And whereas the church community members voluntarily reconstructed old social relationships in a new environment, the institutional structure—especially in European immigrant communities—was a reformulation of church patterns carried from the cultural hearth. Many immigrant communities attempted to reroot theological systems that privileged a corporative and authoritative structure. Congregational strife in these contexts was especially vexing and all the more likely to occur under conditions in the United States that separated church and state and led to the development of denominational differences. The terms of discussion in this new institutional environment illustrate how liberal, majority-based conceptions diffused into debates that once had not accepted such terms. As such, the church-centered confrontations within the community powerfully depict ways in which ethnic communities were intellectually permeable. They show how conflicts within European communities, which ostensibly were attempts to maintain pure and proper doctrine, led to and were framed by new conceptions of cultural and political forms of American life. Whereas rural communities based on common religious and ethnic traditions appeared impenetrable, the debate within them, often framed by expressions of new cultural forms, indicated that they were not.

Community and Conflict in the Settlements

> The Norwegians have managed to isolate and clump themselves together in colonies and maintain their Norwegian memories and customs. I often had to rub my eyes and ask if I really was in America. . . . Farmers' wives plodded down the road speaking dialect. They had a church [that was] like the churches at home with a pulpit . . . and with a pastor in gown and collar. They sang Norwegian psalms and listened to Norwegian sermons. Was this America?
> —Kristofer Janson, *Hvad jeg har oplevet* (1913)

The observations of Kristofer Janson concerning the isolation of Norwegian communities represent a common impression that segments of America contained tightly knit ethnic communities that preserved subcultural configurations and institutions at variance with the "American" patterns of life around them.[17] Nowhere was that impression more suitable than in the rural Middle West, where migrants from the eastern

United States and Europe, nestled in rural enclaves, were able not only to reestablish former ties but also to maintain patterns of language and custom. In these clustered settlements, insulated and isolated from the hostility of others, migrants were able to preserve linguistic traditions, reestablish former cultural and religious conventions, and beget new kinship ties.

These enclaves typically were institutionalized around voluntary organizations that served as cultural and social centers of the community. Occasionally, the community centers were secular associations such as the Free Mason's Lodge or the *Turnverein*. Most often, however, the church served as the principal vehicle through which cultural patterns were reestablished.[18] Indeed, as the ethnic settlements matured, no other symbol demonstrated more clearly the commitment to both cultural tradition and material success than the church edifice. Whether the edifice was a gothic wood structure built by Swedish Lutherans, a white frame chapel constructed by New England Congregationalists, or a large limestone or brick basilica erected by German Catholics, rural ethnic communities often expended considerable resources to witness to their faiths.[19] Consider, for example, the report of thirty families who had come together in the autumn of 1876 to dedicate the "wonderful" St. Joseph's church they had built at a cost of $9,000. As a hallmark and bulwark of the community, the "beautiful brick church," wrote a German-language paper, stood "in the middle of a lovely prairie [and declared] itself as Catholic afar by its cross."[20]

Ethnic clusters supported by institutions such as the St. Joseph's church remained defining features of the rural Middle West from the beginnings of white settlement well into the twentieth century. They created boundaries between social groups that in turn fostered cultural segregation.[21] As late as 1940, an Iowa farmer considered ethnic differentiation natural because, as he put it, "you can't put all your horses in one corral." The different "corrals" still contained, according to a rural anthropologist, "a marked variety of ways and values of life" that were defined not so much by social class as by "nationality background [and] religion." In short, after over a century of life punctuated by wars, depressions, and governmental centralization, the distinctiveness of different ethnocultural "corrals"—of American and European background alike—remained an essential ingredient in local cultural patterns.[22]

It was within this community context that faiths and languages were maintained. Many European immigrants, particularly women, lived their entire lives without learning English.[23] These tendencies, moreover, persisted across generations. Over forty years after migration into the region had commenced, "very few" of the second-generation Germans in a community in Dodge County, Wisconsin, in 1892, according to a local resident, understood "a word of English."[24] In Jefferson County, Wisconsin, German immigrants were "able to use the English language to some extent," but German was still the primary language, even between the generations.[25]

The home language was retained in part because it was treasured as an essential ingredient of culture. An aging immigrant argued, "I have nothing against the English language, I use it myself every day. But if we don't teach our children Norwegian, what will they do when they get to heaven?"[26] It is thus no surprise that language was a volatile issue in the church. Many German leaders insisted that faith and language were inextricably intertwined. If one was lost, the other would follow.[27] Elderly Danish Lutheran churchgoers labeled a transition to English within their congregations as "*den engelske syge*" — the English disease.[28]

Commonalities of language, kinship, religion, and nationality within settlements came to provide not only bonds of similarity but also means to determine the character of others. As late as the 1940s, when Peter A. Munch asked his Norwegian-born respondents how they compared Norwegians with others, he found that they considered their countrypeople harder workers, more reliable, more honest, friendlier, more religious, more law-abiding, and more ambitious and thought they had better-behaved children. Although a sizable minority found little difference between people, nearly two-thirds (66.2 percent; N=89) argued that Norwegians worked harder, and well over half felt that they were more neighborly (56.0 percent; N=75). Perhaps because of their perception of Norwegians' exemplary characteristics, fellow Norwegians generally attempted to find out if someone was Norwegian (77.0 percent; N=87), an effort made easier by the fact that nearly two-thirds (63.6 percent; N=88) claimed they could identify a Norwegian from his or her appearance.[29] Moreover, nearly two-thirds (63.7 percent; N=80) admitted that they would vote for a Norwegian candidate even if they considered both nominees equally able.[30]

These preferences based on collective community ties, which doubtless were common in other rural communities and which certainly had developed long before 1940, fostered economic as well as social alliances. Opportunities for credit and work, for example, were often centered on one's nationality background. In 1947, nearly half of Munch's respondents (47.7 percent; N=88) preferred hiring Norwegians.[31] These preferences were likely due in part to the common trust between worker and employer that usually benefited those within the community or with common backgrounds. Landed farmers preferred to employ "a local man or boy" over outsiders because they would be "taking a chance" hiring someone sight unseen.[32] But such preferences were certainly due as well to perceptions that the character of members of their nationality group was better.

Privileged information, channeled through social exchanges, proved advantageous not only in finding work but also in creating trade. Post–World War II Norwegians continued to favor trade with those of common background.[33] Moreover, community interaction in and of itself had additional benefits. Knowledge about economic opportunities, gained in informal meetings, carried no financial costs. Farmers might be apprised of land available for purchase or lease or of laborers who were free to work. This "free" information brought a high rate of return to those within the community who possessed it.[34] The benefits of membership in a community, in short, were not simply of a social nature; economic advantages were accumulated as well.

The metaphor of ethnic corrals, which deftly characterized a segmentation of minds in the region, nonetheless implies a sense of permanence that did not exist within the "community" for a number of reasons. First, the status of households within the community itself was not static. Families moved in and they moved out. Some households that stayed were able to outstrip others in wealth. The fluidity of settlement, in short, created a volatile environment; the connections were less stable in the rural Middle West than they had been at home.[35] Second, community fluidity was often exacerbated by reformulations of membership, which was never based on a concrete, objective understanding. Enclaves that coalesced under the aegis of a single congregation and thereby institutionalized the ethnic community, as the rural settlements around Dubuque illustrate, often contained a hierarchy of affinities. A community based on common Catholic or Protestant faith could be divided by language and national background; one formed around nationality—such as Irishness or Germanness—could be splintered by regional backgrounds. Not only did these differing attributes within the community create the basis for cleavages, but also their significance was often modified, in the context of the inherently voluntary and volatile disposition of community membership, which created the possibility for new rifts and subsequent conflict.

The ethnic diversity and its attendant conflict were also present in many settlements of American origin. Newell W. Bixby, for example, settled in what was known as the Yankee settlement in Clayton County, Iowa. Only one other family from Starksborough, Vermont, his former home, lived there, and most of his Yankee neighbors were "heretofore strangers to us."[36] When he preached at a neighboring settlement in 1849, other prejudices surfaced. "Southern notions and prejudices were so prevalent there," he wrote in his diary, "that they were not as willing to recieve [sic] the word from me on account of my Anti-Slavery & Missionary sentiments."[37] Here regional diversity overrode a sense of religious commonality. Just over two decades later, in a letter home to Massachusetts from Adair County, Iowa, a migrant observed that "the people around here do not trouble themselves much to get acquainted with the Yankees, as they call us."[38] As late as the twentieth century, the descendants of migrants from the poorer regions of Tennessee, North Carolina, and Missouri remained a distinct social group in Hardin County, Iowa. Their clustered residences along the riverbanks earned them the derogatory epithet of "timber rats."[39] Clearly, differentiated neighborhoods that came together to form a community around a church could later fragment over issues that divided the community.

Immigrant settlements based on common pasts and transplanted European traditions were also frequently racked by strife. The patterns of intracommunity discord were affected by the nature of European church organization. Roman Catholic parishes, formed around the unity of the Catholic faith, tended to include a laity whose members were more varied in background than their Protestant counterparts. Single-nationality parishes were typically composed of blocs of people whose differing regional backgrounds, as in Dubuque County, occasionally cleaved the community.[40] Philip Gleason reports that one quarrel between Alsatians and Hesse-Darmstadters in rural Ohio over whose traditional hymns would be used became so bitter that the disaffected burned their house of worship to the ground.[41] Roman Catholic church communities also knit together people of different linguistic and national pasts.[42] Whereas some accounts of multiethnic Catholic parishes underscored an amicability within the community, they more commonly provided examples of conflict. One Catholic parish in Iowa that included equal numbers of German and Irish families was punctuated by "quarrels and disorder"; another that also had equal numbers of German and Irish settlers was characterized by "feuds" that divided the parish.[43]

The contention within multinational Catholic communities often was further complicated by patterns of social class connected to time of arrival in the settlement. When the first priest arrived at St. Francis Xavier church in western Dubuque County in 1857, his flock contained poor, recently settled Irish families and wealthier German farm households. The inherent tensions in the maintenance of unity and hierarchy despite class and ethnic divisions erupted when the priest reputedly showed preference for the poor Irish families at the expense of the more powerful Germans. He was reportedly maligned and ultimately forced to leave the settlement, never to be heard of again. Yet the victory of ethnic division over Catholic unity for the Germans was not clear-cut. Tradition had it that "the ill-treated priest" predicted that the German community leaders who forced his departure would receive a punishment from God. After three of the four German leaders later died suddenly, parishioners wondered if this eerie realization of prophecy illustrated the authority of the church and its leaders. "Parents," concluded a local historian, pointing to the deaths of these men, "told their children repeatedly that they should never oppose God's ordained priests in their ministry as shepherds of souls."[44]

Opposition to "shepherds of souls" due to ethnic divisions remained common nonetheless. Consider the quandary of the priest of a church in Iowa City in 1865 who had arrived a year before. "Principally the Germans built the first Catholic church in Iowa City," he wrote to another priest. "The Irish, however, increased more rapidly in number and gradually the Germans formed the minority, until they became only an appendage to the parish." After one priest supposedly favored the Germans more than the Irish, his successor reversed the preference. Since the Germans "never did harmonize well with the English[-speakers]," they separated to form their own parish, which soon also included Bohemians. The first priest of the new parish was Bohemian in background, but he favored the Germans because the Bohemians did not contribute adequately to the upkeep of the church. The Bohemians then bolted from the church just as the new priest arrived in town. Asking the advice of his colleague about his predicament, the priest concluded: "After my arrival, I tried to win the Bohemians back to the church. But they replied, that the Germans had declared, that they would throw the Bohemians out. I assured them that I would not tolerate that, and that they might come without any fear. The Germans were not pleased; but I obliged them to give the Bohemians at least standing room. . . . An attempt to unite the Germans and Bohemians, I consider a mere illusion," he mused. "What shall I do?" His dilemma, clearly expressed in terms of nationality, seemed impossible to resolve.[45]

The intracongregational conflicts often bordered on the absurd. When Irish parishioners were displeased with their bishop in Dubuque in 1852, they threatened to stop making contributions to their church. Only after the bishop threatened to place an interdict on the entire congregation did the donations reappear.[46] When Irish and German parishioners could not even agree on a patron saint in a rural Jackson County, Iowa, parish, the bishop intervened and chose one for them. Nonetheless, the church still had two sets of trustees—German and Irish—and a divided cemetery to segregate deceased Germans from deceased Irish.[47] Divisions according to language and nationality that splintered the local community were often set in larger ethnic and linguistic contexts. One German, nestled in his ethnic enclave but struggling with Irish neighbors for control of the community institution, mused, with no sense of irony, "How sad . . . that many think that this country is English!"[48] In short, some Catholics went so far as to repudiate their leadership by seceding from their parishes to create separate church edifices and congregations without the consent of the church hierarchy. They often did this at a considerable emotional and financial price so as to be free to control their own destinies.[49] They did it because inclusiveness in a Catholic church in many instances was not catholic in the ethnically divided Middle West.

Protestant clergy also encountered frequent divisions within their congregrations and between laity and themselves during the early years of settlement, and they were less able to rely on a tradition of stability and hierarchy from an established church authority. The greater fluidity of church organization permitted the laity to fashion church communities based on more specific European backgrounds than those of the multi-national Catholic parishes. Yet as in Roman Catholic parishes, differences in class, status, and culture contributed to congregational divisions among European Protestants who were leaving countries dominated by a state church. When Ole Munch Ræder attended a rural Norwegian American church service in the late 1840s, for example, he was struck by its regional diversity. "One thing which distinguished this gathering from an average country congregation in Norway," he wrote, "was the fact that there were people here from all parts of Norway." Ræder argued that this regional pluralism was propitious since it "removed many of the local prejudices people brought with them from various parts of Norway," but he acknowledged that "such prejudices have not completely disappeared."[50] Although Ræder correctly identified the importance of these regional differences, he grievously erred on two counts: regional pluralism tended to heighten rather than remove local prejudice, and the prejudices lasted for decades.

Cultural antipathies among Protestants created many lines of cleavage. They often divided pastors from their parishioners. In the early years of settlement, for example, members of the European pastorate differed radically from the peasant immigrants they hoped to serve. In a fictional account, a pastor's wife visited the homes of her husband's parishioners. Many of these farmers "came from parts of Norway where they had slight knowledge of sanitation, and it was almost impossible to taste their well-meant offers of food, served in dirty or black wooden bowls."[51] The contrasts were as stark in real life. And the cultural conflicts, often perceived by parishioners as an indication of their freedom in America to oppose the clergy, were as pointed. In the mid-1840s, for example, a local clergyman faced the antipathy of a community member. "Since shortly after Christmas," the pastor wrote, "there has hardly been a week that this man has not either by day or by night used abusive language about the pastor, cursed and shouted, and sung the vilest and lewdest songs about the pastor, sometimes just outside and sometimes inside the fence at the pastorage. . . . Shameful abuse of my honor both as a man and as a pastor, coupled with threats against my life, have poured from the mouth of this man, drunk or sober."[52] In another settlement, a puppet adorned in clerical attire was displayed in a local window to the delight of those who passed by. The pastor, in wry understatement, wrote that "these constant chicaneries I got tired of."[53]

These clear expressions of tensions of class and status were also signified by conflicts within the laity over cultural symbols. Quarrels within a German Lutheran community in Dodge County, Wisconsin, for example, commenced in the late 1840s and caused such rancor that a new congregation was formed. One of the most potent issues in the conflict pertained to fiddle playing in the parochial school. The German schoolteacher, around which one faction coalesced, saw no threat in the use of the violin in school. The German pastor, who led the other group, seized upon a common European fear of the violin as an instrument of the devil and argued that a teacher of religion should not play the fiddle, especially in church school. As both parties remained intractable, the stakes increased. After the minister refused the teacher the sacrament of communion, a large section of the community withdrew from the church to form an independent body and named the fiddler as their pastor, a position he held for at least twelve years. These migrants, like many others throughout the Middle West, as a local historian phrased it, did not "long eat their bread in peace."[54]

The fact that many rural ethnic enclaves did not "long eat their bread in peace," then, was due in large part to the process of community institution building amid varied migration and settlement patterns. Countless chain migrations to rural middle western soil had enabled a transplantation of cultural traditions and predilections carried from home. Yet as voluntary members of a community and its institutions, parishioners also frequently observed differences in culture and status. Members who felt themselves aggrieved came together to form factions, and since they were in a milieu characterized by voluntary organizations, they were able to withdraw. When grievances within the community became irresolvable, the community often divided and the members redefined their allegiances to one another and to the community itself. The community was thus constantly undergoing a process of reformulation and redefinition. The basis of community was a basis for conflict as well.

Freedom and Authority in
European Ethnic Communities

Go . . . out in the congregations, and look on the schism where the scornful
laugh of Satan mixes with the death cries of the people as the billows of party
strife dash the people against the rock of salvation only to have them fall again
into the sea of their own agitation. . . . Go into the community, and see the
glances of Cain exchanged; see the people pass each other on their way to
church, and hear the church bells ring strife into the air. — Reverend Gjermund
Hoyme, 1887, quoted in J. A. Bergh, *Den Norske Kirke Historie i Amerika* (1914)

When observers would "look on the schism," in the words of the Norwegian Lutheran pastor Gjermund Hoyme, that periodically divided European religious communities, they often noted the tensions inherent in a
voluntary institution whose leaders attempted to maintain an authoritarian cast. American principles that separated church and state meant
that religious bodies obtained no financial aid from the government and
were thus dependent on their memberships for support. Participation in
a middle western ethnic settlement that was voluntary in nature thus involved the noncompulsory assistance of like-minded people in a religious
organization. The church body, which its members chose to join and to
support, typically was forced to incorporate some forms of lay representation into its mechanisms of governance.[55] Taken together, these factors
fostered a tendency toward a more democratic, voluntaristic, and individualized arrangement that contrasted with the patterns of religion that
some hoped could be refabricated in the West. European clerics of various religious traditions, however, repeatedly insisted that the doctrine of
the cultural center — despite its new voluntarist structure — was not subject to negotiation. In sum, American rights, which included the right to
choose and practice one's religious beliefs, often came into conflict with
certitudes of faith.[56]

These tensions were not without their incongruities. Whereas abstrac-
tions of freedom and democracy often compromised notions of authority
embedded within many European church structures, "freedom," as we
observed in Chapter 2, was a concept that was often valued as an American inheritance. The Roman Catholic church grappled with issues of the
authority of its clerical hierarchy as it tried to maintain the faith of its followers amid repeated condemnations by Protestant critics in the United
States for its alleged antidemocratic, anti-American composition. Many
Protestant church leaders from Europe also contended with tensions as
they defined their conception of authority and interpreted American beliefs.[57] Members of the Lutheran clergy, according to Gerhard Armauer

Hansen in 1888, who attempted to inhibit the "bad habits" resulting from freedoms, were the only Norwegians who "failed to understand that they were in a new country and a new environment." It was they who endeavored to perpetuate the authority they had been accorded at home.[58]

Amid the ambiguities of freedom and authority, European church leaders simultaneously praised religious freedom, a hallmark of American life, and warned about its diffusion into churchly matters. A Norwegian immigrant pastor framed the issue in gendered terms when speaking in Oslo in 1867. American Lutheranism, he assured his audience of Lutheran clergy, was "like a more vivacious daughter . . . not as demure and considerate as her mother." Although this daughter "has some bad habits because she feels so free and is not yet used to her freedom," he assured his listeners, "she is still the inwardly beautiful bride of Christ."[59] Many of the clergy, in short, embraced the outcomes of American liberty articulated in the nineteenth century. They were ever willing to attest to the benefits of a free church that created a vitality and vibrancy lacking in the churches of Europe.[60] As C. F. W. Walther, a leader of German Lutheranism in America, wrote, "We live here in a State in which the church enjoys a freedom unsurpassed since its origin, and at present to be found scarcely anywhere else in the world. . . . We have here full liberty to regulate everything according to God's Word and the model of the church in its best days and to give our church a truly Christian and apostolic form." Walther concluded, "if we take a glance at our old German Fatherland, how entirely different do we find it! There the church is bound in chains."[61]

The tensions between religious teachings and American church structures, between freedom and authority, however, were often the grist for profound contention within the community. Whereas the leadership frequently quarreled over the direction the church and the freedoms and rights of the membership in the new American milieu, those within the community often argued with their leaders and bickered among themselves. The contention oftentimes pitted the leader against his flock. In a fictional account, a pastor recently arrived from Europe chastised his congregation for the inadequate welcome he had received from the community. His brief lecture did little to quell dissent. "And now there is one thing I will tell you . . . priest," replied a lay leader in a speech that encapsulates common perceptions of freedom in America,

and that is you had better not be as unyielding and haughty as the priests in the old country, for here it is the common man that rules, you see. Here we are in a free country, you see, and the bondage we struggled under there, is at an end here in America, you see. And here we have no treasury that will pay you, so, nor any king or bishop to tell us we must do so and so. It is we farmers that steer the ship around here, you see. And if you don't want to bend to our liking, then it will be worse for yourself, for then you will find yourself starving on a rock pile. And then we would send you home again at your own expense. But if you are good and go on sensibly, as a proper pastor should, I know that folks are not a bit worse here than other places, and they will do what is right for all of you, big and small.[62]

Another Norwegian parishioner was more succinct after his pastor warned his flock that he had been called by the Almighty: "We are the ones who are paying him," he observed, "not the Almighty."[63] In both cases, the lesson was simple: if the congregation paid the pastor's salary, he was an employee who would face reprimands if he did not adequately perform his duties, a judgment paradoxically to be made by people who were at once his parishioners and his employers.[64]

If the congregation could determine its leadership, it followed that questions of church law and doctrine could also be resolved by majority rule. As one man, amid a religious controversy, argued simply in O. E. Rölvaag's novel *Peder Victorious*: "In all democratic organizations the majority ruled; it had to be so, or there would be anarchy."[65] Historical events mirrored historical fiction. During an intense debate over a theological issue in 1885, for example, a congregation called for a vote to settle the matter. The pastor objected, asking rhetorically, "How could a majority determine what was God's law?" The congregation considered his protest, but a vote was taken nonetheless. Its members contended that the ministry did not necessarily possess any greater insight than the congregation into the interpretation of God's law and that perhaps the wisdom of the majority would come as close to the truth as possible. One member was bold enough to suggest that the pastor, because he opposed the vote, was a "false teacher."[66]

Issues of voluntary membership and democratic representation in secular and spiritual matters that divided leadership and laity tended to cleave congregations as well. Importantly, theological divisions were often expressions of developing ethnic identification and changing religious prescription. Two remarkable examples of community strife—one Lutheran, the other Roman Catholic—illustrate the social tensions that were expressed spiritually. The result of a complex dynamic of voluntary alliances and religious doctrine transplanted and modified in the United States, they both underscore the ambiguities of freedom and authority in the American church and the ambiguities of conflict and community in the developing social setting.

The first conflict occurred in the Norwegian Synod, the "high church" alternative for Norwegian Lutheranism in the United States.[67] Doctrinal divisions, often centered on attempts to merge Lutheran interpretation with American society, had vexed the synod for decades. In the 1880s, a schism arising out of the question of election finally tore the Norwegian Synod apart. The orthodox view, associated with the German Lutheran Missouri Synod, argued that election or predestination was based solely on God's grace. The competing theory, based on the theology of the Lutheran Church in Norway, gave women and men a greater role in their salvation, a role that the Missouri Synod and its allies in the Norwegian Synod argued made faith the cause of election. This position ultimately repudiated the sovereign activity of divine grace in salvation. In short, the powers within the Norwegian Synod, by accepting the "objective" justification of faith, seemed to advocate a doctrine that affirmed Calvinistic determinism. The opposition group that developed, known as the Anti-Missourians, placed greater regenerative possibility in the individual, a "subjective" justification that was propounded by the Lutheran state church in Norway at the time.

The controversy began among the clergy but quickly spread to the laity. Church members passionately discussed the theological questions, according to one participant, "on the streets and in the alleys, in stores and in saloons, and through a continuous flow of agitating articles [in newspapers and periodicals]." Words occasionally led to fights. "They argued predestination in the saloons, with their tongues," said one, "and settled it in the alley with their fists."[68] Although fisticuffs were rare, certain Norwegian congregations suffered wrenching internal strife. "The ties of old friendships broke," remembered one man. "Neighbor did not speak to neighbor. The daughter who was married to a member of the other party became a stranger in her father's house. Man and wife turned into dog and cat. Brothers and sisters were sundered from one another. On the other hand, old enemies became friends and were reconciled only when they found themselves on the same side of the insurmountable fence which had been raised between the [Anti-Missouri] and [Norwegian] Synods."[69] Even the goodwill between strangers was contingent on intellectual purity. When requesting lodging for the night at a Norwegian household, one immigrant complained, a traveler was questioned whether he was "a 'Schmidts-man' or 'Missourian' a 'Synode-man' or a 'Konferents-man.' If all these questions were answered in a satisfactory manner," he continued, "the traveler was likely to receive great hospitality, perhaps even looked upon as a guest and extended all hospitality without any charge, if he was so fortunate as to meet people of the same political and religious opinion; but if his luck failed him and he met with people of opposite viewpoints he would soon become aware of its influence on the hospitality in the opposite direction."[70] Divisions between people and within congregations were not isolated instances. One-third of the pastors and congregations withdrew from the synod as a result of the conflict. In Minnesota alone, sixty-nine congregations left the synod. More tumultuous conflict occurred in twenty-three other Minnesota congregations that ultimately split apart, one faction remaining in the Norwegian Synod while the other joined the new Anti-Missourian brotherhood.[71]

The Crow River Lutheran Church in central Minnesota was one of the communities split by the predestination controversy. The emerging coalitions in the community were based on a varied combination of maturing theological divisions and sociocultural dissimilarities that had developed from a decades-old pattern of colonization and community development. The settlement of the Crow River community in Kandiyohi County, Minnesota, commenced in 1859 when a group of Norwegian immigrant families, in a classic case of chain migration, moved from the Scandinavia settlement in central Wisconsin. As colonization accelerated in the late 1860s, the Crow River community was increasingly spatially segregated into subcommunities defined by the regional origins in Norway of the immigrant families (see figure 4.1). The spatial segregation was fortified by ties of kinship as youths tended to marry within their own regional subcultures (see table 4.1). Immigrants and their children in the Stord subcommunity, for example, celebrated 55 marriages between 1862 and the turn of the century. Forty-six wed partners of Stord origin, while only 9 married outside of the subcommunity.

As these subcommunities evolved, they accented cultural variations carried from Norway as well as differences in wealth created in the United States. For example, strikingly different patterns of courtship that resulted in varying incidences of prenuptially conceived children were customary in the regions of origin. Fragmentary evidence indicates that these patterns were replicated in Crow River between the earliest settlement in 1859 and 1889. Because the earlier regional subgroups were able to choose from a greater expanse of land and generally paid a lower price for it, moreover, they were able to acquire more land than the regional groups that followed. In short, segmentation by regional background was often overlaid by divisions of social class, status, and wealth.[72]

The cleavages that existed in the community were not expressed in the earliest stages of settlement but emerged as the colony developed. The earliest immigrants came together to form a church as "Norwegians," but over time the Crow River settlement fragmented into regional subcommunities as immigration increased and more land was purchased. Settled

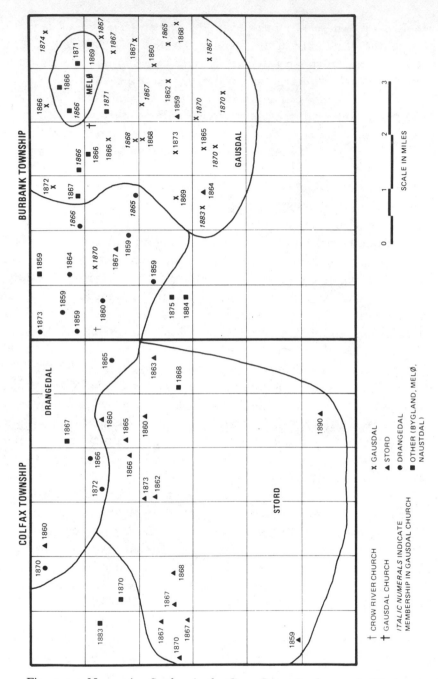

Figure 4.1. Norwegian Settlers in the Crow River Settlement by Region
of Origin and Time of Arrival. From Jon Gjerde, "Conflict and Community:
A Case Study of the Immigrant Church in the United States,"
Journal of Social History 19 (1986): 685.

Table 4.1. Patterns of Intermarriage within Crow River's
Regional Subcommunities, 1858–1899

Subcommunity	Actual Marriages		Expected Marriages	
	Endogamous	Exogamous	Endogamous	Exogamous
Early settlers	1	9	.3	9.7
Gausdal	16	18	5.5	28.5
Stord	23	9	6.9	25.1
Naustdal	11	7	1.9	16.1
Smaller subcommunities*	8	6	1.1	12.9

Sources: Crow River Lutheran Church Records, Luther Seminary, Dubuque, Iowa; Carl M. Gunderson, *Crow River Evangelical Lutheran Church, 1861–1961* (1961).

Note: Expected number of endogamous marriages is based on indifferent in/out marriage in relation to actual experience.

*Melø, Bygland, and Drangedal.

in a Norwegian Lutheran church community, immigrants were able to satisfy their spiritual needs under the aegis of a Norwegian Lutheran church while living in increasingly demarcated subcommunities.

The Crow River community avoided open spiritual conflict with respect to the election controversy until 1890. The theological question at that time provided the congregation with a vehicle through which to dispute correct doctrine and to express past grievances and indignities. The question was addressed democratically, and the majority of the 114 voting members decided to retain Norwegian Synod allegiance, thus implicitly supporting the synod's views on predestination. In response, the minority declared that they would withdraw to form their own church. Events moved quickly as the new church membership set out to construct a place of worship. Significantly, the new church edifice was situated within the subcommunity of immigrants from Gausdal, Norway. Christened the Gausdal Norwegian Lutheran Church, the church's very name echoed the fact that 29 of the 33 original households in the new church came from Gausdal. Although the vast majority of seceders originated in Gausdal, not every household of Gausdal origin seceded from the Crow River church. Gausdal immigrants who remained tended to be wealthier and to have married outside their regional group. Those in the Gausdal subcommunity who clustered in a spatially distinct enclave, who were poorer, and whose patterns of marriage had been endogamous in the past, on the other hand, were likely candidates for dissatisfaction within the community. As theological discord based on intellectual disputes swirled about the rural community, the lines of conflict paralleled social cleavages that had existed for decades and had come into the open when the theological issue concerning predestination was introduced.

At approximately the same time that debate over church authority divided the Norwegian Lutherans, dissension also split Roman Catholic parishes. Like the schism in the Crow River congregation, the conflict that developed within St. Dominic's Catholic Church in Sinsinawa Mound, Wisconsin, was a local instance of a larger conflict. Irish and German ecclesiastics within the church throughout much of the late nineteenth century quarreled over church policy, especially with regard to language, nationality, and Americanization of the church. In the case of the Sinsinawa church, the quarrel erupted when the Archdiocese of Milwaukee, which had already been accused of being controlled by a German priesthood, appointed a German priest in the predominantly Irish parish.[73] The struggle that ensued began as a reflection of ethnic divisions within the community but ultimately became a forum for and an illustration of the incongruities and paradoxical beliefs about freedom and authority, democracy and hierarchy among Roman Catholics in the American Republic.

St. Dominic's Church, first known as St. Augustine's, was built mainly by Irish immigrants in 1842 and enlarged in 1856.[74] As the settlement around it continued to grow, by 1871 the parish of about 100 families needed a new church to accommodate its members. The disagreement over the location of the new church building unveiled a growing geographical and ethnic breach in the congregation. Most of the more established Irish families and a few of the older German households favored the construction of a new church on the old site, which was situated on a wooded mound of exceeding beauty "around the sacred spot" where memories were clustered "which death alone can obliterate."[75] A growing faction, however, proposed a new site "in the prairie," less centrally located in the parish as a whole but centered in the heart of the growing German minority enclave.

Amid this uncertainty, Archbishop Michael Heiss assigned a new priest to the parish in the summer of 1880. An event of seemingly minor importance at the time, the appointment of Father Theodore Jacobs, a German priest in the predominantly Irish parish, would ultimately be the catalyst that would trigger a confrontation. During Jacobs's first year of leadership, the congregation failed to decide on the location of the new church. Finally, in the summer of 1881, the families agreed to defer the issue to Archbishop Heiss. A representative of the archbishop traveled to

St. Dominic's in June 1881 to ascertain the opinions of the congregation. Apparently impressed "by the beauty of the old church site" and aware of its central location, the representative recommended to the archbishop that a new church be built at the traditional place. The archbishop in turn reportedly sent a letter to Jacobs with a message to that effect.

Privately unmoved by the recommendation, Jacobs began a tour of his parishioners ostensibly to take up collections for the new church. Yet his visits were selective. Among the majority that favored the old site, he avoided the wealthiest households and called only on the poorer families, advising them not to contribute to the church due to their poverty. On the other hand, he called on all of those who favored the "prairie" site and cajoled the neutral households to join the minority. A few days later, he secretly visited the archbishop in Milwaukee and then returned to Sinsinawa in time to celebrate Mass the following Sunday. It was then, on 15 July 1881, that Jacobs read from the altar a letter from the archbishop. As the congregation listened in incredulity, Jacobs recited the letter, in which the archbishop announced his decision, "couched in terms of extreme severity and displeasure," that the new church should be constructed at the prairie site. Jacobs then spewed violent language and threats at his astonished parishioners.

Dissension worsened over the long, cold winter that followed. On a bitter day in January, the congregation assembled for Mass at the scheduled time only to find the church locked. To their chagrin, they soon discovered that Mass was being celebrated in a small schoolhouse near the site of the proposed church on the prairie. Only later did they find out that the archbishop had declared that services no longer be held in the old church.[76] Since it was too late in the day to travel to neighboring parishes, the majority of the congregation missed receiving the sacraments. Sister Theresa Marten poignantly inscribed in her diary the significance of the event. When the people came to Mass, she wrote, "their dear old Church was cold and empty. . . . The poor people who had for nearly 40 years come there to Mass were heart-broken and so were we [the Dominican sisters]."[77] Mass was not celebrated at the old site for weeks, and parishioners were even denied the sacraments on Ash Wednesday, the beginning of the Lenten season. Despite the gravity of the situation, however, leaders opposed to Jacobs nonetheless preached docility. The Mother Superior instructed the Dominican sisters: "For the first time in the history of our community, we are deprived of Mass. But you will not talk of it with others or among yourselves. I entreat you not to be uncharitable, even in your thoughts. Leave it all to God," she cautioned, "and He will bless us."[78]

Despite appeals for submissiveness, the conflict escalated rapidly by late winter. After the building of the prairie church commenced, Sister Theresa Marten lamented in her diary that "the Germans" were at work near the old church. "My heart ached," she concluded, "as I saw them pass here."[79] More remarkably, however, the dissidents began to build their own church on the traditional site. After the dissidents removed the altar and other furnishings, they began to tear down the old church, which had been vacant for six weeks. A structure filled with the memories of a community, it nevertheless legally did not belong to them. "I hear the hammering," wrote Sister Theresa with both joy and nostalgia in her diary. "They have commenced to break down the old St. Dominic Church. May God grant that they may have the pleasure to build a new one in his honor as it is at present their full intention." Day by day, Sister Theresa observed the progress of the church construction and appealed to God and St. Joseph for help.[80] Convinced that they had the archdiocese's permission to build, the congregation majority raised a church at a cost of $10,500—a church that ultimately would never be used.[81]

The parishioners' convictions notwithstanding, the construction of the new church was a flagrant defiance of church authority from the perspective of the archbishop. By building the church, the parishioners had raised the stakes in what was becoming an increasingly rancorous conflict. Jacobs broadened the range of the conflict when he published his version of the controversy in the *Galena (Illinois) Gazette*, a newspaper disparaged by his adversaries as a "secular Protestant" organ. In spite of a restraining order from the archbishop, he wrote, the parishioners had committed what in his mind was a sacrilege. "The manner in which the house of God was torn down," he wrote, "can be imagined from the fact that the altar with a sacred vessel (ciborium) enclosed in the tabernacle was taken out and thrown into an old barn, where it lies to this day."[82]

The conflict intensified yet again when Jacobs in June 1882 read from the pulpit a letter from the archbishop that excommunicated all those who had torn down the old church. There followed many years of antagonism exacerbated by Jacobs's increasingly bizarre behavior. When the dissidents traveled to neighboring parishes to give confession, Jacobs sent messengers who called the priests out of the confessionals and presented them with papers that prohibited their administration of the sacrament to the dissidents. To make matters worse, Jacobs then boasted to members of the congregation of his victories. The dissidents sent their children to Mass, but since the youths were compelled to listen to abuse of their parents and descriptions of their excommunication, their parents ultimately withdrew them.[83]

Reports of Jacobs's eccentric behavior often contained allusions to the

Irish-German split that underlay the conflict. At a Fourth of July picnic fund-raiser, for example, Jacobs "made himself conspicuous by assuming the responsible position of bartender." By the end of the day, many of his parishioners "went home at night in a drunken condition," to their great scandal. His obvious love of German customs inspired a fantastic rumor that he intended to convert the old church at Sinsinawa Mound into a beer saloon. The dissidents realized that this might sound "incredible," but they reasoned that given Jacobs's past behavior, "we cannot but fear some truth" to the rumor. "Should they interfere in any manner with this church," the dissidents wrote ominously, "our leaders will not be responsible for the consequence which may follow the rash act."[84] In retrospect, the majority argued that had they been German, they would have received redress from their German archbishop and priest. Instead, "national prejudice" divided the congregation.[85] Because their construction of a new church was ruled illegal in a court of law and they were excluded from their old church's community, the Irish majority argued as late as 1893 that the rift would never be healed.[86]

The misunderstandings leading to the conflict were profound on all sides, and the bitterness that resulted was venomous. But the attitudes of the contending parties gain greater clarity when examined in light of the fact that the authority of the church was being tested within a nation that preached the superiority of representative political systems. Archbishop Heiss was forced to adjudicate the controversy between the contending parties. He found it difficult to understand why those who lost would not follow his dictates. When representatives of the majority sent entreaties to him, he ignored them. In a letter to Jacobs a month before the old church was torn down, Archbishop Heiss returned "an unread letter" from the majority and informed Jacobs that he had been visited yet again by dissatisfied parishioners from St. Dominic's. "I could not bring it over myself to listen to them," he wrote. "That Sinsinawa Mound makes me more heart pain than the whole diocese," he concluded.[87] Yet to Archbishop Heiss's amazement, the majority repeatedly requested that a priest be appointed to serve a church built in direct defiance of his authority. In a letter written in 1883, he confessed that he was "astonished" by the supplication for a priest at "a church, built under such circumstances." "I pity you in your present position," he concluded, "but I cannot help you. May God give you light from above to make you understand what you are doing, and lead you to repentance before it will be too late. This is the prayer of your deeply grieved Archbishop, Michael Heiss."[88]

Seemingly nonplussed by their failures, the majority sent off a flurry of letters to church leaders throughout the United States, to Rome, and even to Pope Leo XIII himself. The communications repeatedly mourned the loss of religious attention, which, they asserted, was the direct result of an unfair use of ecclesiastical power. "Something must be done and soon for the Spiritual welfare of the vast majority favoring the old Site," they wrote Cardinal Simeoni in Rome in 1883, "or many will lose their faith entirely." The "many and aggravated" complaints against their pastor included his refusal "to Baptize our children," which forced them "to bring those tender infants miles away from home . . . to distant and neighboring Pastors to perform this Sacred rite which is denied us at home." They were compelled to "go miles and miles to make our Easter duty" but discovered that Jacobs had "strained every nerve, brought into requisition every exertion to influence neighboring Priests from performing any rites or granting us any privileges as Catholics." "He is no friend of our people," the letter concluded, and "we can place no confidence in his integrity as a christian man or gentleman to do us the least iota of Justice in this case."[89]

The majority continued to make their entreaties despite their lack of success. "A little band of your children in America," they beseeched Pope Leo in 1884, "[we] most humbly and respectfully implore your Holiness to listen to our appeal and to help us in our misery." Their misery was profound because "we are not allowed to hear Mass anywhere in this Arch-diocese for the neighboring Priests have been forbidden to attend us or to allow us in their Churches." Worse still, "our children are growing up in this Protestant land surrounded by the worst temptations, without any Religious instruction except what we ourselves give them." "Listen to us," they implored, "your oppressed children."[90] Yet another entreaty to the archbishop of Baltimore reiterated the "incredible" injuries that the congregation had been forced to bear. "We have written to Rome three times, once in Latin," the letter concluded, "but surely they could never have received them for how could Rome be indifferent to the loss of souls, or how could Rome be unjust[?]"[91]

The letters to ecclesiastical authorities were written with a tone of docility and submission. "We are simple farmers," they wrote to Cardinal Simeoni, "knowing little of such matters [of ecclesiastical administration], but we have been taught from earliest childhood to believe that in Rome lay the remedy for all ills and refuge from all injustice."[92] Yet their language—like their actions in repudiating the authority of the archbishop by building their own church—betrayed a changing conception of "proper" adjudication of disputes within the church. The injustice of rule by a minority was stated over and over again in their supplications. To the archbishop, they wrote that "it seemed only natural to us to expect the majority would rule."[93] They even stressed the relevance of representation in their letters to Pope Leo. In a draft of the letter to be sent to the Pope, they wrote that they "naturally supposed that the wishes of the majority would rule, as they do in other things." In a significant revision, the letter they sent to the Pope argued that they "expected that the majority would rule *as they do elsewhere in America.*" [94]

Not surprisingly, the contentions of the majority were even more pointed in their response to Father Jacobs in the secular press. Perhaps the ecclesiastical leadership thought the majority would obey and come "lamb-like to them without a murmur," they wrote. "We chose," they explained in harsh prose, "not to do so." Clearly, they argued, "we are prompted by no spirit of unreasonable opposition to recognized church authority." Nonetheless, they stressed that they "would not be forced away" from their church and launched a protest "against the *arbitrary exercise of power* that inflicts such needless suffering on so many hearts." [95] Relying on concepts of majority rule and using frames of reference reminiscent of the prose of republicans a half a century earlier, an Irish Catholic community nestled in the rural Middle West had apparently inculcated republican tenets and wielded them in an ecclesiastical combat.

These two church controversies encapsulate the ambiguities of tradition and change within the ethnic enclaves in the rural Middle West. They also illustrate the hazards of freedoms and authority in theological and, by implication, political battles. For the minority of the Crow River congregation, church doctrine in a supposedly more democratic environment had ironically shifted theologically toward a less egalitarian, less subjective position with regard to salvation. Structural inequalities in the community probably made this paradox especially objectionable to the poorer Gausdal subcommunity. Through a spiritual tyranny of the majority, a culturally distinct minority in the church were forced to accept an antidemocratic theological decision, a cruel twist of fate in the supposedly freer environment of the United States. The majority of the congregation illustrated the dangers of democracy and were in a sense worse than the authoritarian upper-class pastors in Norway who seemingly had held. their parishioners in contempt. The majority in America advocated an interpretation of election that not only contradicted Norwegian Lutheran doctrine but also was antidemocratic to believers in the most profound sense: it denied that all who believed had the opportunity to obtain eternal salvation. Voluntary membership and freedom of religion, however, provided those within the Crow River minority a means to redress their grievances. They seceded to form a church where *they* would be the majority. In so doing, they simultaneously righted theological errors and freed themselves from their subordinate status in the church community.

Similar actions were undertaken with less success by the Irish majority in the St. Dominic's community. The Irish parishioners seemingly fought to preserve their Catholicity, their hopes to catechize their children, and their desire to receive the sacraments that would insure God's grace. But in order to do so, they in effect seceded from their church and disobeyed its leadership. They were reprimanded by church leaders for this defiance, which altered the discourse in a vague but telling way. Although they claimed to remain true to the authority, hierarchy, and power of the church, the majority's concern about maintaining their faith encouraged them to accept concepts of representation that were at odds with premises on which the church was based. The flash point of the conflict was predicated on rights that members of the church had inculcated during their political education in the United States—rights that had been foreign to their leadership some years earlier.

The uproar in Crow River differed in some respects from that in Sinsinawa. Whereas the Norwegian secessionists in Crow River were a disgruntled minority of the community, the Irish dissenters in Sinsinawa composed a majority. Whereas the Crow River community was composed of a single nationality and linguistic group, the Sinsinawa community was multinational and multilingual. Whereas the Norwegians based their objections on the introduction of new theological positions in America, the Irish grappled with ecclesiastical authority and utilized new political perspectives in the United States to bolster their humble supplications. And whereas the Gausdal seceders in the congregationally based Lutheran Church succeeded, the Irish majority were unable to use freedoms of religion to ameliorate their situation in the more hierarchically arranged Roman Catholic Church.

Nonetheless, the schisms had basic social and intellectual similarities. The rudimentary causes were ethnic cleavages that evolved and matured within the communities as they grew and as their constituent households changed. An event or series of events catalyzed the underlying tension and brought conflict into the open. Importantly, the aggrieved subcommunities appealed to and often questioned ecclesiastical authority. Their appeals might have gone unheard, but they signified that the dissenters recognized their freedom to secede in order to redress their grievances, a freedom that paradoxically contradicted the very authority they hoped to reestablish in their new congregation. Perhaps after sailing across the Atlantic and traveling to the Middle West, they perceived the possibility of moving yet again, intellectually rather than geographically, if they felt aggrieved. Yet such perceptions of fluidity undermined any permanence of community since new aggrieved parties within their reformulated communities could continue to move again and again. Church bells, in sum, could "ring strife into the air" because of a complex transplantation and adaptation of an institution that defined not only orthodoxy but ethnicity. Such strife, of course, was not so severe in all communities, but it was made all the more probable by the fluid, dynamic nature of the society of which the citizens were now a part.

Conclusion

The migration and settlement in the rural Middle West of untold millions of people were often premised on the migrants' perception of a "freedom" to move and thereby improve their lives. Eastern Americans and Europeans alike trekked westward to a mythical garden that they hoped would recast their existence. Yet patterns of migration in practice connected old and new homes and in effect transplanted former cultural forms into the garden. In turn, they engendered segmented settlements that were based in vital ways on beliefs derived from their former homes. To be sure, the westering migrants carried with them outward behavior such as their language and dress. Still more important, they also brought cultural patterns and religious beliefs that were established under the auspices of the community and its leadership. Surely the West provided opportunity, but who would consciously forsake a chance for salvation simply to enjoy the material benefits the West offered? The fact that cultural underpinnings could be transplanted in the West was part and parcel of the migrants' perception that it was indeed a land of freedom.

The communities on which the intellectual systems were based, however, could only be reformulations of former patterns. In the dynamic society of the developing Middle West of the nineteenth century, individual households voluntarily joined others to create rural communities based on some semblance of a common past. Community identifications were constructed around common pasts and beliefs, and nowhere were these identifications more fluid than in the impressionable rural Middle West, a region only recently populated by Americans of European origin. Affinities of language, religion, and "nationality," as well as common kinship and regional backgrounds and differences in status and wealth, established a matrix of similarity and dissimilarity from which communities could be created and re-created.[96] Families thus often had the opportunity to join a community and also maintain their religious past. The "freedoms" that migrants celebrated in the Middle West, in short, promoted the expectations that they could build new communities that supported their sense of peoplehood and that transplanted their cultural institutions and beliefs. Yet for the very same reason, they also increased the likelihood of community division and conflict.

These tensions were particularly distressing to the leadership of the European "mind," especially those portrayed in this chapter who maintained Lutheran and Catholic traditions. Many hoped that the new environment, in which "freedoms" were accentuated, would produce a more responsive church since its parishioners would be inspired by religious truth without interference from the state. Yet they were also correct to fear freedom both as a cornerstone of schism and as a concept that spawned ambiguities among those who ought to maintain the absolute righteousness of their faith. Although they might be able to create a "pure" church in America, European church leaders also had to joust with parishioners who increasingly argued for majority rule and the right to secede from a faith that was ostensibly unequivocal.

Communities fixed around a faith were indeed repeatedly troubled by the recognition that their members asserted their right to secede, to re-create yet again their community. Embracing a rhetoric of freedom, even of individual rights, the church community faced bracing change. These innovations were particularly noticeable in communities, such as Crow River and St. Dominic's, shaken by ethnic schism. When segments of the community found themselves disadvantaged and saw themselves as victims of lower status, the theological meaning of the debate was heightened. At base, the church schisms indicated a struggle to regain or enlarge power in the congregation. Yet in the American context, they also were intellectual debates in which pointed discourse about "freedom" increasingly diffused inward. Indeed, in the case of St. Dominic's, the disputants maintained that their "freedom" to protest, to advance concepts of majority rule, and ultimately to contradict the wisdom of their leadership was based on their desire to remain Catholic. Even within a conservator of tradition such as the church, new intellectual conceptions diffused into and infused the community with "foreign" notions by the late nineteenth century.

The rural ethnic communities were thus animated by a curious amalgam of cultural retention and cultural change, tradition and modernity, authority and freedom. On the one hand, the rural ethnic enclaves remained insular. Conspicuous differences between ethnic settlements endured on many levels across generations in the rural Middle West well into the twentieth century. The following three chapters will illustrate how power, authority, and affect in the family varied in middle western ethnic settlements. Yet despite the "freedom" to transplant community and family, that transplantation remained imperfect. New societies were based on old ties and traditional beliefs, but these very re-creations established a possibility for cultural difference and structural inequality. Although the disputants in schisms, which arose out of this inequality, argued that they were maintaining a true faith, they also recognized that the disputes were based on a freedom to differ.

PART THREE

THE FAMILY

CHAPTER 5

Farming Is a Hard Life

Household and the
Agricultural Workplace

hen Sarah Morse sat down to pen a letter to her sisters in Massachusetts from her Iowa farm home in the autumn of 1862, she asked their indulgence for her short note. Since her time was "almost wholly occupied with my house work," she found occasion for "little or no leisure for any thing else." The situation was hardly different for her husband, who was "most worn out with hard work" and "gets little or no time rest [*sic*] of body and mind." "Hope he will not always have to work so hard," she concluded, "but farming is a hard life to lead."[1] Morse's message suggests central aspects of middle western rural life in the nineteenth century: farm work was relentlessly burdensome, and as a result, the burden was shouldered by members of a family who lived together and worked as a unit. As such, the institution of the family and its constituent members bore the responsibilities of reproduction and production on the farm, a complex system of relationships that rarely operated without conflict. Despite her never-ending "house work," Morse remarked to her sisters, she had to tolerate her floors being dirtied with newly threshed wheat recently harvested by her husband in the fields. The divisions between home and work, both literally and figuratively, were indistinct.

Morse's work-filled world is illustrative of what scholars have labeled the "household mode of production" that characterized early American farms.[2] Out of necessity or inclination, farm families early in the settlement process focused on production both for home use and for exchange. The labor that grew the crops for food or to generate cash, moreover, came in large part from the family itself. The knot of individual relationships within the home was structured on corporate familial concerns and on "lineality" rather than on individual self-interest.[3] Roles within the farm family as a result were multifaceted and often in tension. Social categories merged into economic ones. Children, from one perspective, were nurtured and cared for by their parents; youth was a period of socialization into a family, a kinship group, and society as a whole. Children's essential labor, from another viewpoint, recast them into employees. As "sons" and "daughters," they had little choice but to work for the family operation. Their social position in the household created an economic role for them that usually translated into subservience. Contemporaries who celebrated the egalitarian society of the rural Middle West usually overlooked the inequalities inherent within the household.

Rural patterns of life outside the home changed dramatically during the period from the days when Morse's floors were strewn with hand-threshed wheat until World War I. Over four generations, farm families encountered dizzying changes in agricultural implements, enlarged and improved markets, and shifting patterns of crop harvests and animal holdings. Despite this metamorphosis, meaningful continuities regarding the centrality of household labor endured. Although a frontier period when farmers relied on bountiful harvests of wheat gave way to diversified farms that grew a mixture of crops and animal products, the onerous labor that farm families performed continued. After some decades of farm building and family labor, a "corn belt" principally in Iowa and Illinois evolved to the south of the dairy regions of Minnesota and Wisconsin and to the east of the Great Plains, which remained characterized by a monoculture, principally of wheat.[4]

The transformation of cropping patterns and land use in the region was accompanied by and related to tremendous structural changes in the United States. A swelling rural population purchased and brought into production larger and larger amounts of land, which over time became increasingly expensive. The shortage of land, exacerbated by increased farm sizes, forced growing numbers of rural folk to move to the cities or to accept a status of landlessness. The burgeoning cities in turn created an immense market for agricultural products, which were now more efficiently and rapidly brought to market by enlarged transportational networks. The "household mode of production" was besieged by bewildering transformations just as household members profited from increasingly diverse opportunities.

The vast changes in farm markets and technology in the decades before World War I thus contrasted with continuities characteristic of the family farm. Indeed, the story of the rural community in the northern United

States, scholars have suggested, is centered on the struggle and inter-action between a conservative kin-structured community and a market agriculture that tended to restructure relationships on which the community was based.[5] This chapter grapples with the meaning of that struggle. It argues that a family morality was a central intellectual construct that worked to sustain the household-run farm. The family morality of middle western farms stressed the collective effort of the group in a setting that accorded some members, defined by age and gender, the right and opportunity to own and profit from land. In this context, then, customary kinship obligations were set in an environment where landownership not only was possible but also was a principal form of status and capital in an evolving marketplace. This ideology informed roles and relationships within the household and undergirded perceived rights and responsibilities within the home that remained strictly defined by an individual's place in the family distinguished by his or her gender, age, and household status.

Yet ideological and economic changes that continued to transform American society in the late nineteenth century modified the operation of this family morality. Great social and economic changes not only altered the way families farmed but also destabilized the relationships on which the household economy was based. Although these tensions had long challenged the household mode of production, moreover, the incongruities wrought by social and economic change intensified as the nineteenth century progressed.[6] Economic opportunities outside the home and constrained resources within it, for example, increasingly tended to undermine the authority of the household. Equally important, ideologies of individual rights continued to erode a corporate mentality. In short, although relationships between laborer and employer, between home and work, and between parent and child were thoroughly redefined in nineteenth-century cities, they remained knotted together much longer and in much more profound ways for the majority of Americans who continued to live on farms. As a locus where collective and individual interests converged and where household roles were played and obligations were performed, the farm family was rife with tension. Whereas agriculture changed dramatically throughout the period, one constant was that farming remained "a hard life to lead." Whereas the household remained central to farm life, another constant was the friction that existed within the home.

Agricultural Development from Earliest
European Settlement until World War I

When . . . turning the first furrows, with the smell of the fresh earth in the
nostrils and the freedom of the great outdoors all about him, there comes a
feeling of exhilaration and a sense of well being to the farmer that the indoor
worker can not know. The long term program of the farm is largely fixed and
unchangeable but there is more variety from season to season and day to day
or hourly. There is a broad languid sense of fulfillment at harvest time
which . . . brings a feeling of compensation that is unrelated to either economic
success or failure.—Frank T. Clampitt, *Some Incidents in My Life* (1936)

On my way westward, that summer day in 1887, rural life presented itself from
an entirely new angle. The ugliness, the endless drudgery and the loneliness of
the farmer's lot smote me with stern insistence.—Hamlin Garland,
Main-Travelled Roads (1891)

The farms created by westering migrants in the Middle West irrevocably
altered the region's landscape. Countless farms carved out of the wilderness transformed prairies and woodlands into neatly arranged fields of
grain. Forests were removed; swamps were drained; rivers were diverted.
Wild animals were supplanted by domesticated ones. In 1812, a company
of dragoons was forced to remain encamped along the Mississippi River
because the buffalo were so numerous that it could not travel safely to
its destination in what would become Iowa. When Iowans celebrated the
American Centennial sixty-odd years later, however, "every skinny prairie hen" in the vicinity had six hunters on its trail.[7]

The destruction of the wilderness in turn spawned contests concerning
how best to exploit available resources, competitions that were on occasion unintentionally resolved by environmental change itself. Among the
earliest settlers of the region were those who intended to utilize the power
provided by natural waterfalls to build local industrial concerns. As
farmers acquired land, however, they broke the fertile prairie and cleared
the timber, which despoiled many of the natural falls through sedimen-
tation. With no conscious planning, farmers environmentally preempted
the development of industries in many small mill towns.[8]

As farmsteads expanded, transportation lines were forged that linked
the once-isolated farm family with a regional and ultimately a national
economy. Amid these developments, farmers in the late nineteenth century grappled with capricious markets, natural hazards, and additional
agricultural competitors as settlement moved westward. Their successes
—and failures—in navigating through and around these challenges sketch
the agricultural narrative of the Middle West. Briefly stated, the abun-

dant grain harvests initially enjoyed by farmers on the cutting edge of white settlement placed eastern farmers, whose yields fell owing to soil depletion, at a competitive disadvantage. With smaller grain harvests but growing markets, farmers in settled regions diversified their operations. The golden fields of wheat that at first displaced the lush wilderness themselves gave way to variegated patterns of green corn and meadows and golden grain, herds of cattle, and droves of hogs as farmers moved into mixed-farming ventures.

Despite shifting patterns of agricultural production from earliest settlement until World War I, the structure of change was based on a series of continuities. The first continuities were the seasonal rhythms of farm production. Spring was the season for sowing; autumn was the period of harvest; the shortened days of winter were a time to perform tasks that did not demand attention in the busy summer season. A second constancy well beyond World War I was the heavy reliance on the toil of members of the farm family. Indeed, when one compares the work year of farm families across time and throughout the region, the seasonal rhythms of labor—whether they gave a "sense of fulfillment" or a feeling of "endless drudgery"—were surprisingly "fixed and unchangeable."[9]

The first phase of farm development—often described as the wheat period—was characterized by activities that enlarged the farm and sustained the family at home as well as providing wheat for the market. Wheat harvests that typically exceeded twenty bushels an acre created powerful incentives for farm families to invest heavily in market grain production.[10] Wheat production, however, required seasonally heavy work during sowing and especially during harvest, so available unattached workers were in great demand and could command high wages. The fertility of the soil at first enabled farmers to cut corners and thereby reduce their paid-labor costs. As Europeans unaccustomed to such rich land, both Frieslander Sjoerd Aukes Sipma and Norwegian Nils Sjurson Gilderhus noted that with heavy manual labor, one man by himself could do much of the work of planting and harvesting. Not only did the wheat not need to be harrowed, wrote Gilderhus from Wisconsin in 1842, but he had "even seen them sow without plowing."[11] Sipma concurred. Although maize required weeding, "the other grains are sown and then harvested; that is all there is done to them."[12]

Despite these laborsaving techniques, "shortages" of workers, an inconvenience most troublesome during the harvest, were offset by burdensome household toil. Consider the case of Rebecca Burlend. Soon after she and her husband immigrated to the Illinois frontier from England, her husband—"my dearest earthly friend"—became ill in 1831 just as their crop of wheat was ripe. With few alternatives, she was forced to take her oldest child to work with her in the fields while the next oldest tended to the father and cared for the youngest child, who was still unweaned. "The reader may probably suppose I am endeavoring to magnify my own labours," she concluded, "when I tell him I reaped, carried home, and stacked our whole crop of wheat, consisting . . . of three acres, with no other assistance than that of my little boy under ten years of age." But, like countless households forced to adapt its labor pool under unexpected exigencies, her descriptions were the "uncoloured facts."[13]

Amid shortages of hired labor and periodic crises among family workers, early farmers strove to reap large harvests. The fertile soil certainly was compliant. "At first," remembered Herbert Quick, "all we had to do was to tickle the new-broken prairie with a harrow and a few other things—a laborious tickle for us, of course—and it laughed with a harvest."[14] "We were all worshippers of wheat in those days," agreed a nostalgic Hamlin Garland. "We trembled when the storm lay hard upon the wheat, we exulted as the lilac shadows of noon-day drifted over it! We went out into it at noon when all was still—so still we could hear the pulse of the transforming sap as it crept from cool root to swaying plume. We stood before it at evening when the setting sun flooded it with crimson, the bearded heads lazily swirling under the wings of the wind, the mousing hawk dipping into its green depths like the eagle into the sea, and our hearts expanded with the beauty and mystery of it."[15] In spite of the toilsome periods of the wheat year, a bountiful harvest rewarded the cash-poor farmer with a considerable monetary return. Garland thus conceded that behind the romance of wheat was also "the knowledge that its abundance meant a new carriage, an addition to the house or a new suit of clothes."[16] The rewards stemming from wheat production encouraged farm families throughout the region to focus their labors on the glorious potential of the grain. As Quick remembered simply, "As soon as I was able to work, I became a bond servant to wheat."[17]

The yearly crop cycle during the wheat period began in the spring when the pace of farm life quickened in preparation for planting. "With the first honk of the wild geese in spring," wrote Quick of life in the 1860s, "our minds turned to the cleaning of seed wheat." After the chaff and light kernels had been removed from the seed, the family "went into the field," a ritual that Bess Streeter Aldrich observed was pregnant with meaning, a "great event on a farm" when tasks essential to the well-being of the farm operation were undertaken.[18] During the early years of farm development, the first journeys into the field in the spring occurred when wheat, that most important of grains, was planted. In that era, the seed was sown by hand. Quick remembered his father walking across the fields of black soil, "a two-bushel bag held open with his left hand and slung across his shoulder, while, as he stepped, his right swayed with perfect rhythm out to the end of his graceful gesture, back with a skilful twist of the wrist as the grain was scattered evenly, and with the same movement, went into the bag again for another handful."[19] A team of horses, often driven by a child, dragged a harrow behind the sower.

July typically was the month when the ripening grains were ready for harvest. At first, the wheat was cut by hand, but a series of innovations in mechanical reapers quickly supplanted manual labor. By the 1870s, farmers utilized a dropper that cut the grain and dumped it in untied bundles. Three men—hired laborers and family members alike—followed the machine, tying and moving the bundles. The dropper was soon replaced by a self-raking machine, which in turn was superseded around 1885 by the self-binder, eventually the principal harvesting implement.[20] When the grain had ripened, it demanded a rapid harvest and arduous work, which, on occasion, resulted in farm accidents. Local newspapers regularly reported the tragic accounts of harvest misfortunes, such as the case of an older son who lost control of a reaper that cut off his younger brother's leg in 1883.[21]

As in other tasks of wheat production, threshing at first was done by hand, a lonely, onerous task performed with the use of a flail.[22] But after it too was mechanized in the 1880s by steam-powered machines, threshing became a departure from family-oriented work since it required a reciprocal work exchange between neighbors.[23] Since threshing machines were expensive, adjacent farms typically pooled their capital to purchase a thresher and then pooled their labor to operate it. The onset of threshing machines thus ushered in the "threshing ring," a formalized social and economic arrangement among households. News, gossip, and new farming techniques were shared among farm families as they visited neighboring farms. Labor roles as always were demarcated by gender and age. Women were responsible for preparing the food for the large, hungry threshing crew. Young boys were not allowed to operate the threshing machine, but they were obliged to pitch heavy bundles of grain onto its conveyor belt. The end of threshing in September marked a dividing point. It ushered in the first period of leisure since the season had begun in March. As such, it signified a waning summer and reduced work in the months to follow. To celebrate the completion of grain work for the year, farmers in one community threw their old straw hats into the threshing machine after the last grain had been threshed. In a German community, farmers drank schnapps to toast the beginning of the end of the seasonal round.[24]

Although wheat was the principal market crop during the early phases of farm building, families raised other cereals, such as corn, barley, and oats, and animal goods, such as meat, dairy, and poultry products, for home use. As in crop production, farmers used the rich resource base of the region to reduce their work burdens in animal production. Farm families that tended livestock fenced off their relatively small cultivated fields, for example, so that adjacent ranges could serve as pasture. In one central Wisconsin settlement, farmers pastured their animals in common in surrounding woods and marshes. Distinctive cowbells led the owners to their herds in the evening. With marshy fields available for pasture and hay, farmers felt little need to plant clover or timothy.[25] Since animals demanded so little care and could fend for themselves, farmers in the Middle West butchered a smaller proportion of their herds than did farmers in regions of Europe.[26]

Throughout the seasonal routine of work raising crops and animals, early farm families labored to gain cash incomes and enlarge their operations. Following the harvest, farmers grappled with the critical tasks of marketing their products and capturing incomes as high as possible from them. As Quick observed about life on the agricultural frontier in Iowa, "There was no game to furnish skins for clothing . . . no maples for sugar . . . no salt licks for salt. In a thousand ways [pioneer farmers] were forced to resort to the production of a surplus to sell for money with which to buy supplies."[27] Wheat was a treasure not only because of its abundant harvests but also because it was a staple that often brought high prices and was relatively simple to market due to its compact, nonperishable attributes.

Early settlers' reliance on market exchange should not overshadow the inconveniences and adversities they often faced when they engaged in trade. The distance to market often created obstacles. A Wisconsin farmer in 1850 threshed and cleaned oats by hand for three days before he traveled twelve miles to market on foot, pulling a wagon that carried his eighteen bushels of grain. He received $2.90 for his products.[28] For those who lived in more remote settlements, the journeys were even longer. In an extreme case, an Iowa farmer recalled that in 1844 he spent two weeks traveling over 100 miles each way to market his wheat for 44 cents a bushel.[29] And as late as 1860, a man traveled forty miles round-trip to sell twenty bushels of potatoes for 15 cents a pound. After this burdensome effort, the *Dubuque Herald* argued, he took home not only some cash but also his dignity.[30]

The tyranny of distance was often compounded by the dishonesty of millers and merchants. Not only were markets and mills about sixty miles distant from Gottlieb Plisch and his neighbors in their north-central Wisconsin community in 1857, but the millers there could not be trusted alone with the grain. In order to mill their products, farmers in Plisch's settlement carried their corn and wheat on their backs and if the miller could not grind the grain the day they arrived, they carried it back home again rather than leave it with the miller. "The millers," recalled Plisch, "were very dishonest in those days and some times we were glad to get back the bags which contained the grain, if we left them over night."[31] Although merchants and millers provided a critical service to the farm community, they gained a reputation early on for cunning and dishonesty.[32] The market was a necessity for farmers, and merchants were a necessary evil.

During seasonal lulls, the farm family set out to increase its arable fields by clearing and grubbing the prairie and woodlands.[33] Such efforts not only enlarged the farm operation but also increased the value of the family's estate in what was typically an increasingly lucrative land market. It is a telling comment on the process of farm development in the United States that amid the uncertainties of labor and the caprice of the market, the most profitable endeavor in farm building was often land speculation.[34] During the land booms of the mid-1850s, Charles A. Dean, a former New Yorker, marveled in a letter home that up to $60,000 of land was sold daily in Dubuque alone. Offering the familiar suggestion of the advantages of migration, Dean contended to his friends that "you could make more in one year than you can in Fulton [New York] in Five."[35] A week later, he noted that people simply did not invest capital in houses because they could accrue greater profits from loans or land speculation.[36] Some years earlier, Sjoerd Aukes Sipma argued that speculation in land was the wisest course. In a letter encouraging immigration, he noted that land that sold for the government price of $1.25 per acre five years ago now garnered eight times as much. "That," Sipma concluded, "is better than putting your money on interest."[37]

Mastery of agricultural methods during the wheat period, of course, varied among farmers. Some mined the soil, but others were aware of the benefits of crop rotation even amid primitive markets.[38] Whereas some farmers were imprecise about market prices, others meticulously recorded their harvests and profits.[39] Competencies differed, but farm building remained an arduous task for all, a task made all the more difficult by the paucity of available labor. The conventional wisdom was that the lifespan of people in rural America was about 100 years too short. The reason was simple: it took a farm couple their entire lives to build a farm, after which they died without enjoying the fruits of their labor.[40]

As farm operations matured, rural families continued to face challenges. To be sure, labor demands per acre decreased for a number of reasons. First, grubbing woods or breaking prairie sod, which transformed uncleared acreage into cropland, was done only once. Second, the increased use and availability of farm implements decreased the amount of manual labor required in sowing and reaping, especially by the 1870s.[41]

Household and the Agricultural Workplace

143

Enlarged tracts of arable land, however, also demanded increased labor investments per farm simply because the planted fields were larger. Greater capital investments were made to augment labor productivity, but they often bred greater risk. *Die Iowa*, consistently wary of risky farming, argued that overspeculation in implements and land would result in financial difficulties. "Land problems," it argued, "are self-caused. Lured by cheap land many farmers have bought more than they can handle. To relieve this situation they buy expensive machinery on credit; come small harvests, which would have sufficed for keeping their family but are not big enough to reduce debt with high interest, and hard times are unavoidable."[42] Small harvests did indeed arrive as repeated crop failures and natural disasters—crises whose origins puzzled farmers—plagued the eastern sectors of the region in the 1870s.

The most significant point of concern was an increasing unreliability of wheat yields on farms in Iowa, Minnesota, Wisconsin, and Illinois that had once produced bountiful harvests. As late as 1869, for example, wheat harvests of twenty to thirty bushels per acre on newly cleared land in central Minnesota were common, a godsend to those cash-poor farmers who trekked westward.[43] Yet by the mid-1870s, eastern expanses of the Middle West entered into a period of steady decline in the performance of their wheat fields. Newspapers were punctuated by reports of poor wheat harvests in the late 1870s. In 1876, wheat suffered from chinch bugs and rust and in many regions "was not worth cutting." On some farms, pigs were sent into fields to devour the "wheat that the chinch bugs did not consume." The failure could be so extensive that local millers were forced to buy raw wheat from outside their vicinity to make flour.[44] Despite poor harvests, the farmers' response was tentative.[45] As the principal cash crop, wheat remained a grain of choice, even though its yields continued to disappoint. In 1877, farmers in eastern Iowa lost about a third of their crop, and harvests averaged eleven bushels per acre.[46] By 1881, farmers in western Iowa decided to burn off rather than cut their wheat since the yields were so small. One farmer estimated that a sixty-acre field would not even produce five bushels.[47] Fields that only years before had produced bountiful harvests were now for many financial disasters.

Wheat failures, it turned out, were caused by chinch bugs, Hessian flies, and rust often occasioned by overuse of the soil. When the land was broken, ecological changes in the soil encouraged the proliferation of these natural pests.[48] Farmers responded to the collapse of the wheat monoculture by making a slow, uncertain conversion to mixed farming. Rather than continuing to rely solely on a capricious harvest of wheat, they diversified their operations. In the northern zones of the region, they focused their operations on dairying. To the south, they transformed the region into the corn belt, a zone that would become synonymous with the Middle West.[49] Throughout the settled portions of the region, then, farmers devoted larger acreages to crops such as corn and to meadows, both of which they used to raise growing herds of cattle, hogs, and sheep.[50]

Cultivating an increased variety of animal and crop products tempered the risks of failure, but in turn it expanded the array of responsibilities demanded of the farm family throughout the work year. Dairying required the year-round care of cows, whereas corn was more burdensome to produce than wheat. The corn production cycle began with planting, which followed the sowing of small grains such as wheat or oats. Planting typically was done when "the oak leaves were as big as squirrels' ears" or "when the rippling in the wind of the small grain was easily observable," usually in early May.[51] After the soil had been prepared, the field was "checked," a procedure that had a striking sameness to it throughout the period. As Rebecca Burlend reported in 1848, the land was first plowed and harrowed, and then furrows about a yard apart were crossed at right angles by another set of furrows. "By this means, the field appears divided into numberless little square portions," she observed, "each somewhat less than a square yard as if hollowed at the centre." And into "each of these crossings," four seeds were thrown and covered with a hoe.[52] Although planting was no longer done by hand by the early twentieth century, checked cornfields were still common.[53]

As in the sowing of wheat, the male household head planted the corn, but its production remained a family responsibility. As the young corn grew, farm children went into the fields to plow with care between the mounds of small plants. Should a hill be covered, according to Carl Hamilton, the entire work team stopped to unearth the young shoots. "Farming was that kind of business," Hamilton concluded about life in the early twentieth century. "Each hill of corn was important to the point of stopping the whole procedure to uncover it—by hand."[54] After the fields had been plowed a few times in both directions, the corn was "laid by" around the Fourth of July, when, according to the traditional adage, it would be "knee-high."[55] By midsummer, the fields resembled a Grant Wood painting: the growing checkered cornfields were situated amid acreages of green grain that were fastidiously tended as they ripened into fields of blazing gold.

When the corn had ripened in the field, the farm family began the harvest, perhaps the most wearisome task in the seasonal round. Since corn matured later and could remain uncut longer without going to seed than small grains such as wheat, its harvest began in early autumn after the other grains had been harvested. As cornfields grew larger, the harvest season occasionally extended well into winter. The workday began at daybreak and lasted until late in the evening, when "it got so dark you could not see to quit."[56] The harvest began during the "warm and golden" days of September and often ended when snow lay on the ground. Farmers remembered days of sixteen degrees below zero and periods of sleety rains that coated the corn ears with ice, loaded the workers boots with partly frozen, muddy clods of clay and grass, and froze the workers' wet gloves on their hands. As Garland wrote simply, "Grim business this!"[57]

Not only were conditions often unfavorable, but the work itself was arduous. Before the advent of mechanical pickers after World War I, corn-picking was done entirely by hand. Workers trudged through the fields cutting the ears off the corn stalks. The most skilled could harvest up to 100 bushels a day.[58] The crew of workers, like the crew in the grain harvest, was composed of a combination of family members and hired laborers. The wage laborers were generally paid by the bushel, but children as family laborers received no pay for their toil.[59] The best they could expect was an improved status within the home and community since the corn harvest, according to an anthropologist, became "the medium through which rural youth could express its manhood in the tangible form of the number of bushels picked a day."[60]

Despite these burdensome responsibilities, mixed farming reduced the risks inherent in monoculture. One wonders, then, why the transition to mixed farming, which occurred only after successive years of poor wheat harvests, took so long. Quick argued that "we went on, as farmers nearly always do, sticking to a system which had become established."[61] Yet there were additional reasons apart from inherent rural conservatism. For one thing, wheat monoculture remained a gamble well into the 1880s and farmers could reap great profits when a wager paid off with a large harvest.[62] Moreover, a vicious circle of capital investment based on expected wheat profits in turn demanded cash returns to pay off debts. Despite diminishing harvests, wheat remained the most viable market crop. Unfortunately, although many farm families initially built their farms and lived off the profits of wheat, their operations later died because of their dependence on the fickle harvests of the crop. Those farmers who made the transition away from wheat, on the other hand, moved into a yearly cycle that included both crop production and animal husbandry, incorporated many tasks throughout the year, and reduced the risk that failure of one component of production would devastate the entire farm enterprise. This period of mixed farming encompassed, according to Quick, "the best years Iowa [and middle western] agriculture has seen."[63]

The transformation of agricultural patterns in the Middle West was accompanied, as it was informed, by profound shifts in the availability of labor and capital and in the sophistication and breadth of markets. The

THE FAMILY

rural response to access to these expanded options was ambiguous. Farm families hoped to remain reliant on themselves for labor and on their products for food. Yet they also had a greater latitude to utilize additional hired workers and increase their dependence on the trade of goods if they so desired. Paid laborers, of course, had commonly been hired, especially during periods of heavy work in the wheat period. The harvest of small grains and particularly wheat, which required a rapid harvest when it became ripe, was a time when labor was in demand and wages were higher as a result. Paul Hjelm-Hanson noted the varying fortunes of laborers in Norwegian American settlements in 1869. Consisting of those "who own no land, but depend on what work they can get for a living," the day workers received $2.50 a day during harvest, but "otherwise during the summer they are $1.00 and board."[64] Demand for labor was so great during the grain harvest that laborers were drawn from all quarters. Women worked in the fields if cultural traditions did not prohibit it. "Harvest work commenced in good earnest last week," reported the *Northfield (Minnesota) Recorder* in 1868, "as a number of persons who had Norwegian girls doing work for them found out, they having left for the harvest field where they can earn nearly the same wages as men."[65] A regularized male migrant labor stream soon developed that widened during periods of economic difficulty. During the depression in the late 1870s, middle-class observers deprecated the rude behavior of "tramps" who sought farm work, particularly during the harvest.[66] By the early twentieth century, the circle had widened so that men arrived from as far away as North Carolina to follow the reapers throughout the Middle West in good times as well as bad.[67]

The character of farm labor shifted in the late nineteenth and early twentieth centuries as higher land prices increasingly precluded the possibility that potential farmers would gain landholding status, as enlarged farm size demanded greater labor inputs per unit, and as mixed farming increased the necessary year-round farm chores. Since a system of mixed farming demanded the completion of repetitive daily tasks, especially with regard to animal care, laborers increasingly were hired throughout the agricultural work year. These "hired men" lived on the farm and were often seen "as part of the family"; they "ate with the family, slept in the house, sometimes sharing a room with the older boys."[68] Despite these changes, the wage cost for hired laborers increased slowly, in part because real wages were lower around the turn of the century than in the antebellum period.[69] Although output per acre and improved acreages increased in Iowa, for example, farm owners paid only slightly more in wages in 1899 than they had two to three decades earlier.[70] The fact that laborers were available did not necessarily mean they were hired. Rather, the more immediate labor source within the home remained central.

In short, the family continued to provide the indispensable source of labor on middle western farms, combined with an increased reliance on farm machinery. A common perception among rural folk well into the twentieth century was that farm families imposed an onerous workload upon themselves. The purchase of farm machinery was justified not to lighten labor but to increase production and profit.[71] With such a justification, machinery was used to obviate the need to hire labor from outside the home rather than to reduce the burdens on the family.[72] By the early twentieth century, the onset of spring meant that the family would begin to get up at five o'clock, a schedule that would last until Thanksgiving "if all went well."[73] "The kind of farming we do here," said a young farmer in western Iowa simply, "is a long hard job. We're never through."[74]

As farm families continued to rely mainly on labor within the home, their products, despite the increasingly sophisticated capitalist infrastructure, were not destined solely for market. The market for products widened during the mixed-farming period as transportation lines improved and processing firms grew in size. Thriving trade of an increasingly wide array of cereal and animal products developed. In addition to familiar grain exports, for example, farms in the mid-1880s exported about $2 million a month in eggs and butter from Iowa alone.[75] Yet the sale of farm products continued to be accompanied by home use. Animal goods, from eggs to beef to milk, brought in cash, but they also were used to feed the farm family. As late as 1940, about one-tenth of the output of farms in a western Iowa region was consumed at home.[76]

The fitful transition from household consumption to market agriculture is exemplified by the ambiguity that continued to define the relationship between humans and their stock. As the pork business that came to define the corn belt matured, farmers had access to an increasingly wide array of packinghouses to market their hogs. And market them they did, despite the horrific, almost surreal, conditions within the local slaughterhouses.[77] Animals were slaughtered on the farm as well. Butchering was timed to furnish the farm family with meat throughout the year. Hogs usually were butchered in early spring, part of the meat being eaten at once and part cured and made into sausage to be eaten in the summer until the spring-hatched chickens were ready for consumption.[78] The farm family's familiarity with the animals they ate explains the solemnity of the slaughter itself. Indeed, the curious relationship between humans and their animals illustrates as well as anything a rural world different from that which exists today. "Fanny has got so she is wild as a deer," wrote Mary C. Coffin in 1865 to her husband who was at war; "can run so fast as eny of them she is very fat. we had used up one half of Jack i have all of the round of the hind quarter salted to day."[79] Coffin was speaking not of her children or her pets but of her hogs, whose play she fancied and whose flesh she consumed.

The agricultural economy of the Middle West thus underwent a fundamental transformation between the beginning of settlement, when farmers relied on limited grain markets, and the mixed-farming economy of the late nineteenth century, when transportation and market networks crisscrossed the region. In spite of this metamorphosis, basic elements of life remained intact for individuals who stayed in their farm homes. Even as farming shifted from wheat monoculture to mixed farming and from a limited market to an extensive one, production continued to be the responsibility of rural families within a system of household labor. The transition occurred amid crisis, and those families that survived it continued to maintain the centrality of farm labor within the family. Within this "knot" of relationships and obligations, the farm household endured as a locus where the social and economic futures of parents and children were intertwined. Yet the next section illustrates that embedded within these continuities were powerful forces that increasingly challenged the logic of interrelationships on the family farm.

The Family and Farm Labor

Where land is free nobody will work for any one else for less than he can make working for himself; and land was pretty nearly free in Monterey County, [Iowa]. — Herbert Quick, *Vandemark's Folly* (1921)

Where a man is a man if he's willing to toil,
And the humblest may gather the fruits of the soil;
Where children are blessings, and he who has most
Has aid in his fortunes and riches to boast;
Where the young may enjoy and the aged may rest—
Away, far way to the land of the West!
—Herbert Quick, *The Fairview Idea* (1919)

The so-called family farm, a result of low ratios of labor to land, had for decades endured as a symbol of opportunity to Americans. Based on land owned or leased by the household head, it was worked by people, most of whom were kin, who lived in its symbolic and literal center: the farm home. In the earliest years of farm development, as Herbert Quick pointed out in his fictional accounts of rural Iowa, settlers would not work for a gentry for less than they could earn toiling for themselves. Since employers could not collect the surplus value of their workers' labor, their profits were nil.[80] As Quick and others argued, the region was a historical anomaly, a place where "poverty-stricken peasants succeeded, where the men with capital and aristocratic notions almost always failed."[81]

Subsequent research has pointed out the tendency to overstate the degree of equality and opportunity in the rural Middle West. To be sure, agricultural productivity per worker increased dramatically in the Middle West in the second half of the nineteenth century, as did the capital value of farmers' land. The costs of farm building in the early years of settlement, which included implements and livestock as well as land, however, were prohibitive for many migrants who were forced to work as landless laborers.[82] The constraints, moreover, increased over time as land prices escalated. Many families remained unlanded tenants for significant portions of their existence. Other individuals lived and worked as single, unattached, usually landless laborers who resided with a family fortunate enough to own or lease land. Still others moved to the city.[83]

If "poverty-stricken peasants" prospered, it was the result of family labor. Despite increasing tenancy and landlessness, the family continued to be the predominant source of labor on farms of every sort. The household mode of production prevailed on the northern farm well into the twentieth century, even as techniques of agricultural production were transformed. In regions of Illinois characterized by smaller farm operations, paid workers in the 1920s contributed only 15.5 percent of the labor in farm production,[84] a proportion slightly less than that in the entire United States in 1900, when 21.5 percent of the agricultural labor force was composed of hired workers.[85] Family workers continued to predominate not least because they remained the most reliable laborers. Adolescents, unlike hired laborers, did not have the option to leave home for higher wages. They were instead expected to remain with their parents in a cooperative effort to discharge the burdensome labor on which the family depended for survival.[86] Although Americans have tended to romanticize the equality made possible by the family farm, they have remained even less cognizant of the disparities within it. Ironically, whether or not free land made people free, it promoted a dependence and reliance within families that tended to trap certain members—such as children—in protracted subservient relationships.

The inequality within the farm family, which was a by-product of the household mode of production, was undergirded by a family morality that pervaded nineteenth-century rural American society. Built on a patriarchal and preindustrial foundation, this morality underscored the importance of what William I. Thomas and Florian Znaniecki, writing about the Polish peasant in the United States and at home, termed "familial solidarity," whereby the welfare of the household was privileged at the expense of individual gain and inherent inequalities within the home were common as a result.[87] Scholars studying the American-born have discerned a similar structure in western rural settlements, where a "corporate family economy" supported by state and community was a crucial institution. Here, too, was a form of familial solidarity that was justified by an organic subordination of its members to a common good.[88] Defined by a series of hierarchical arrangements and structured on the performance of reciprocal obligations, the family morality created both a corporatism and an inherent inequality within the home. Significantly, it could be adapted to the commercial agricultural world in the rural Middle West, where land was commodified. Landownership was one of the principal motives among American-born settlers who trekked west to improve the prospects of the entire family. Yet the augmented status of landholder was conferred on the male head who held title to the estate. It is no coincidence that immigration from Europe was occurring in an era when land commodification in the homelands was reinforcing the influence of a lineally oriented family and that motivations to move to America were often expressed as aspirations for improved status of the family through landholding.[89]

The family morality that was carried to the middle western farm not only emphasized authority and hierarchy within an organic ideal; it also tended to stress the power and influence of the older generation, particularly the adult male—the household head—in directing and benefiting from the operation of the family and household. It reflected the institutional and legal disadvantages of married women. Property in mid-nineteenth-century America commonly belonged to the household, which, following the conception of male leadership, meant the household head.[90] The family morality also contained an "intergenerational contract" between parents and children based on an "agreement" that placed the latter in a weak bargaining position. After all, the agreement was drawn up before the children were born. Parents nonetheless socialized their children to accept conditions guaranteeing that parents would profit from a flow of goods and services upward from the younger to the older generation, a situation from which the young would benefit only when they themselves ascended to parenthood.[91]

As a reflection of this socialization, obligations within the household—between husband and wife, son and daughter, parent and child—were clearly demarcated. In the farm home, the wife's work was explicitly differentiated yet intricately harmonized with that of her husband. Anglo-American women by the mid-nineteenth century, for example, were responsible for the productive and reproductive labor around the home, while men labored primarily in the fields. By the late nineteenth century, they continued to perform reproductive tasks such as sewing, cleaning,

Household and the Agricultural Workplace   151

and child care and also produced certain goods for home use and sale. Production of butter and cheese, the raising of eggs and poultry, and care of the family garden typically were the duties of Anglo-American women.[92] After dairy production became centralized in cooperatives in the twentieth century, women ceased producing butter and cheese at home, but they continued to bear the responsibility for the garden and poultry products. Work obligations, moreover, remained clearly defined even in chores that fused "male" and "female" tasks, as an example from a central Iowa county illustrates. In this community, the garden was deemed the wife's responsibility, but the husband tilled the plot in preparation for planting because plowing necessitated the use of a team of animals, which entered into the man's domain. On the other hand, the wife washed the milking equipment since that task involved heating water in the kitchen, which was controlled by women, even if care of the cattle had long since become men's work.[93]

These divisions of labor, built upon decades of custom, were reinforced by legal codes that defined work roles, and even the attire and behavior related to them, by gender. Two Swedish American women in Minnesota in the late nineteenth century were victims of such laws. In 1886, a Minneapolis paper reported the arrest of Anna Lindquist, a "poor Swede girl," for wearing men's clothing. As a farm laborer, she had been hired by a fellow Swede to "herd cattle and do a man's work." Since she found wearing a dress "inconvenient in the brush," she attired herself in men's clothing, which unbeknownst to her was illegal.[94] Seven years later, one Annie Hedström was arrested for donning "the habiliments of the sterner sex for over a year." Like Lindquist, she was a Swedish farm laborer, working under the alias Charles Parker, who claimed she was unaware that it was unlawful to "masquerade as a man." Clad in "rough laboring men's clothes"—"a dirty flannel shirt, open at the throat," and a "jumper, overalls, slouch hat and heavy shoes"—Hedström "said that she did not like woman's work around the kitchen, and, besides, she could earn more money as a man."[95]

The farm work of children was clearly defined by their maturity as well as by their gender once they reached a certain age. The chores of younger children were not strictly defined according to sex. Rather, parents found tasks, however small, for children to perform that benefited the family economy and lightened the load of the household. "Even quite small [children] can earn something to help support the family," advised a Norwegian immigrant guidebook in 1844.[96] One man recalled that his father "believed in keeping his children busy as soon as they were able to perform simple tasks." Accordingly, both boys and girls were sent into the cornfields to pull weeds. After the shift to mixed farming, the increased responsibilities for year-round care fell in large part on the farm family. The herding of grazing animals was a task small children could undertake. One settler recollected that it was so boring that grown men assigned it to boys "too small to rebel or resist"; it was, in short, "a boy's job that kills off a man." [97] In the winter, children were assigned duties of animal care, wrote Garland, "and one that I dreaded, was pumping water for our herd. This was not light job," he recalled, "especially on a stinging windy morning, for the cows, having only dry fodder, required an enormous amount of liquid." [98] The manure that the animals produced also provided work for the children since they were expected to participate in perhaps the least enjoyable task of all: moving the piles of dung from the barnyard to the fields in the late fall. [99]

As girls and boys matured, the value of their work increased while the divisions between it became increasingly rigid. By the time a boy was twelve, he took "a man's place" in the fields and on the threshing crew. [100] The idea of a boy performing housework was "deemed amusing" in a twentieth-century rural Iowa area. [101] Sons played a central role in activities such as the hay harvest. After the operation was mechanized through the use of a mower, an implement with a five-foot-long bar of slashing serrated teeth, farm children cut the hay. They then waited a day for it to dry before they trekked to the fields to begin yet another task: hand raking it into piles. [102] Girls, on the other hand, remained with their mothers in the house. One woman recalled her work "in the house" as a young girl and what she noted was "quite a division of labor at that time." Girls did not milk cows, but they did help their mothers care for the chickens since such a chore was "women's work." [103]

Since they provided needed labor, then, children were an asset within the home. Expected to work at home, each additional child enlarged the household's labor pool and thereby aided the operation of the farm. Unlike in Europe, a Norwegian-language guidebook concluded in 1844, "children [in America] may be counted as an asset rather than a burden for the poor father." [104] Here, the migrants who moved west prior to the Civil War were perceived as "fruitful tribes [that] make their home with us." [105] Some years later, a newspaper reporting on a man who had fathered nineteen children concluded, "He is the right man for the new land!" [106] He was the right man, another immigrant from Wisconsin implied, because "it is often said here that a numerous flock of children makes the man rich." [107]

Farm labor was not the only benefit that children conferred on their parents. Offspring tended to augment the status of families and kinship groups in local society. More tangibly, they served as a form of social security as their parents aged. In a society that institutionalized the care of the elderly within the family, the expectation that children would care for their elderly parents remained a central concern for the older generation.[108]

Whereas having many children was an obvious asset from the perspective that they provided labor, however, their prospective roles as caregivers of aging parents were more ambiguous. As children and their parents aged, the former became increasingly interested in their futures. Certainly children were socialized to be concerned about their parents' future well-being. But if socialization was the psychological stick, the farm's property was the economic carrot in rural households. Parents used their estate as a tangible resource to sustain them in their later years, whereas their children often saw it as a foundation of wealth that might enable them to sever their ties with the family of origin and create new families. Parents thus used the farm to provide for their attenuation as they grew old; children utilized it to establish their adult lives. An inherent conflict of interests often resulted between generations and among siblings, though it was muted by the very family morality that socialized parents and children into their respective roles.

Despite these tensions, there is no inherent reason why commercialization of agriculture should have undermined the performance of prescribed roles and assisted children in their efforts to escape the family morality. The household mode of production, which intricately tied the family to the land on which it produced goods for its sustenance and from which it accrued wealth to confer to subsequent generations, remained viable. Sexual divisions of labor were maintained after the market had become a central force on the farm. And intergenerational relationships actually became more meaningful as the farm became an increasingly valuable asset.[109] In this sense, the commercial capitalism that took root in the soil could actually have expanded the options available to farm families. Since community members together captured the benefits of the market, the defining characteristics of compact ethnic communities could have been strengthened and what Kathleen Neils Conzen calls the "cultural degrees of freedom" could have been increased. Capitalism, from this perspective, could have fortified community norms.[110]

Yet the effects of certain intellectual innovations that tended to accompany a capitalist, commercialized agriculture were difficult to avoid. Although the broadened "cultural degrees of freedom" could strengthen community norms, they could also widen the prospects of individuals living within farm families, which in turn could jeopardize the very premises on which the family morality was based. Changes in labor availability and farm mechanization, for example, magnified the options of farmers. Although the justification for increasing the use of hired labor or equipment might have been to strengthen the farm, these changes likely also engendered unintended changes that weakened it. The diffusion of technologies—which were readily accepted—probably also carried with it cultural clues and suggestions for social change that were in opposition to the family morality. Like the residents of Robert and Helen Lynd's Middletown, people accepted technological change in explicit terms much more readily than shifts in "moral" standards.[111] Yet by accepting the former, they implicitly introduced at least the possibility of the latter. And so it was with the rural community. The technological changes that were advanced to bolster community norms and strengthen the family farm could also undermine them.

It is in this context that shifting work responsibilities within the home are informative. Anglo-American women, for example, who tended to work in the fields early in the nineteenth century were absent from the fields a few generations later. The toil that Rebecca Burlend endured in the fields after bearing twins in 1831, which forced her "to rest on a sheaf several times during a day," was rarely experienced later in the century.[112] The views of a "stage Yankee" who commented that he preferred a farm girl to an urbane lady because she could "milk cows, set up the butter, make cheese, and darn me, if they ain't what I call raal downright feminine accomplishments" soon gave way to a new convention that divorced women from the care of cattle, if not production of the butter and cheese.[113]

Perhaps more important, the obligations of children to the family and the farm were altered as well. To be sure, children had often left their parents upon reaching adulthood early in the nineteenth century. Yet scholars have suggested that swelling outside opportunities, especially in the city, exacerbated the tendency of children to "default" on their implicit intergenerational contracts. These broadening parameters of the opportunity to default profoundly recast the family and its underpinnings. The balance between the division of labor, the intergenerational relationships, and the resources that supported them and could be transferred across generations was in flux.[114]

It is no coincidence that shifting material foundations coincided with an ideological transfiguration. As a capitalist market integrated farms more fully, liberal components of an American capitalist culture increasingly challenged farm families. The organic subordination within the household mode of production confronted liberal notions of individual equality and rights. In a variety of forms, an increased individuation of society and the household struck at the heart of the precepts of the family morality. Such influences included a tendency toward secularization; an increasingly active state that in many ways began to displace the func-

tions of the family; an educational system—an instrument of the state—
that also encouraged secularization; and a nascent feminism that advocated greater individual autonomy and power for women. These factors
contributed to ideological disputes about the conceptions of power and
authority as it had once been exercised within the household.[115]

The tensions between corporate responsibilities within the household
and individual rights and aspirations can be discerned, appropriately
enough, in frequent late-nineteenth-century reports of conflict involving
intergenerational property transfers. Since they were so ambiguous and
so important, bequests of real wealth, which coupled the concerns of the
older generation about care in their old age with those of youth about
resources on which to establish adulthood, had long been a point of friction. Late-nineteenth-century newspapers were peppered with examples
of intergenerational tensions pivoting on land. After a father disinherited
his daughter for marrying without his approval in 1876, his new son-in-
law retaliated by firing a shotgun at him through the window of his house
and mortally wounding him.[116] Some months later, the situation was reversed. An aging father transferred ownership of his farm to his daughter
when he was no longer able to work. His "heartless" daughter reciprocated by "disinheriting" the "modern King Lear" and pushing him "out
into the street."[117]

Other episodes were more complex. The extended diary of Emily
Hawley Gillespie paints a remarkable portrait of the strange twists and
turns in the overlapping intergenerational contracts and shifting relationships among herself and her father, husband, and children. In 1861, as a
young woman, Emily mused, "I cannot always have a home at Fathers,
why, because my Father will not live always." When she moved from her
parents' home a few months later, she wrote, "Alas 'tis hard to leave home
and friends, but the words 'we cannot always live at home' are too true."
Yet when her father, Hial Hawley, arrived unannounced and impover-
ished at her home in Iowa two decades later, she was less sentimental. "I
can scarcely believe that Father would have come here," she confided to
her diary in 1884. "I will do the best I can and see what we can do about
it." Despite her resolve, the relationship between father and daughter,
which was already strained, rapidly worsened. Within six months, the old
man moved out and began legal proceedings to regain from his daughter the few possessions he had brought with him. Gillespie, for her part,
determined that the only legal way to avoid supporting her father was to
return the deed to her farm, which she had held for eleven years, to her
mentally unstable husband whom she hated. In this way, she would in
effect be propertyless and thus would not legally be bound to support her
father, with whom she had once hoped to live forever. Her motivation for

making the deed transfer, however, went beyond simple spite of daughter toward father because in doing so she risked making it possible for her husband to carry out his earlier threat to prohibit their children from inheriting the farm. Gillespie found that in order to be rid of her father, she must risk disinheriting her beloved children. Her antipathy toward her father nonetheless compelled her to return the deed to her husband. It was a "*disgraceful affair*," she concluded. She maintained that her father, who subsequently went on poor relief, had "caused me too much trouble to make right."[118] A tangled tale of spite and malice, Gillespie's saga underscores the divisions within families and the tensions between generations concerning their prescribed responsibilities to one another.

These bloody and quarrelsome incidents in which concerns about old-age support went awry illustrate the pervasive tensions in what was clearly an extremely meaningful process. The timing and distribution of property transfers by their very nature were not equitable; one person's gain was another's loss. As "the modern King Lear" discovered to his chagrin, the relinquishment of property ownership indelibly altered the relationships of power and authority between parents and children. As Emily Gillespie's father found out, individual loyalties and affect could change throughout the life course. As most Americans were recognizing, the calculus of family moralities was in profound flux in the late nineteenth century.

Conclusion

A major theme in the narrative of rural communities in the late nineteenth century, then, is the diffusion of economic and ideological innovations into rural communities that challenged a family morality inherently conservative in its structures of kinship and family. Even though the family remained the principal source of labor throughout the period, perceptions of familial responsibility within the household seemed to be giving way to emphases on individual rights. Even if farm families produced much of their food for home consumption, the commodification of products and land altered the fortunes of individuals who increasingly wished to maximize their future prospects. It is likely that the uncertainties inherent in these tensions contributed to the conflict within homes in the late nineteenth century.

The fact that a family morality undergirded middle western farms, however, is complicated by the fact that the morality was created from dissimilar contexts. One variant was set in the American westward migration; the other was based on ideas of land and kinship evolving in

European communities and carried to the United States. Whereas the ethnic rural community endured as a central social arrangement that knit households together, moreover, it also mediated the degree to which households interacted with the larger society and the character of that interaction. The contours of change thus were modified by the intellectual content of the settlement communities and by the buffers created by segmented ethnic communities in the rural Middle West. Despite the presence of an overarching family morality in the middle western rural world, different minds in the West reestablished and reformulated varying prescriptions and expectations within the household that were informed by ethnocultural imperatives.

As a result, the region was characterized by a variation of patterns of household behavior in ethnic communities that tended to conform to political and theological premises. The community and its institutions, after all, nurtured cultural conceptions of authority and affect in the secular as well as the spiritual world. Stated boldly, the rural homes and communities of migrants with Yankee backgrounds were reacting to intellectual impulses that enabled a more developed individuation to sink deeper roots into the communities. Profoundly influenced by a republican and evangelical rhetoric that had contested an organic solidarity for decades, Yankee families found it simpler to discard a corporate family economy and accommodate to a contractual, liberal capitalist world. Yankee communities, moreover, were more permeable and susceptible to innovations from the outside, a process facilitated by the familiarity among Yankees with American currents of thought outside the community. European households, on the other hand, remained influenced by explicit attempts to reroot corporate systems of church and family in the Middle West. They were able to use an increasingly capitalist agriculture—at least temporarily—to foster a family morality that was more lineally oriented and less contractual and that continued to proclaim the merits of unequal and hierarchical power in the home. The implications of these differences, as we shall see in the next two chapters, were many. The varying household organizations begat noticeably dissimilar household interrelationships and different challenges for members of the family. Farming remained a hard life to lead as the individual difficulties faced by farm family members were informed by cultural patterns carried westward.

CHAPTER 6

A Tale of Two Households

Patterns of Family

When Horace Miner conducted anthropological fieldwork in Hardin County, Iowa, on the eve of World War II, he perceived distinct variations in household behavior among the different ethnocultural groups nestled in their rural neighborhoods. It was true, he wrote, that "the descendants of German immigrants [had] taken over the Yankee speech, dress, houses, manners of farming, and many of the values." Yet differences in intrafamily relationships had endured. After nearly a century of settlement in the county, the German neighborhoods remained "fully indoctrinated" in what Miner called a "dogmatic Lutheran and Evangelical tradition," which in turn spawned a corporate family organization that had become foreign to their Yankee neighbors.[1]

The foremost difference in Miner's eyes was a patriarchal tradition that was based upon the German Americans' religiocultural systems of belief and was expressed in relationships between husband and wife and father and child. "The Germans," Miner observed, writing of them as a group with common practices, "believe more in the subservience of the child and wife to the father, as the manager of the family farm." This behavior was considered " 'bad' by the Yankees," Miner concluded, "as cultural differences usually are." The German father, according to the Yankee critique, was no more than a "Tartar, working his family to the bone," whereas the American father, in his less corporate fashion, remunerated "his children and [gave] them independence of action." Yet independence, Yankee youths duly noted, could be costly. Subservience within the household, it seemed, was connected to accumulations of property "which are given the sons when they reach maturity." An arrangement within German households coupled the labor of children with land entitlements when they reached adulthood. Like a grasshopper observing an ant, the Yankee youth "resent[ed] the German boy being *given* a farm."[2]

Miner's remarks are noteworthy as a twentieth-century example of a pervasive and protracted series of observations of competing ethnoculturally defined family traditions that tied together patterns of household labor, affection and authority, and property.[3] A century earlier, Michel Chevalier perceived a similar pattern, though he focused less on parent-child relationships and more on the labor of women. "It is now a universal rule among the Anglo-Americans," he wrote, "that the woman is exempt from all heavy work, and she is never seen, for instance, taking part in the labours of the field, nor in carrying burdens." As a result, Anglo-American women had "escaped that hideous ugliness and repulsive coarseness of complexion which toil and privation every where else bring upon them." Others, however, were not as fortunate. Canadian French and Pennsylvania German women continued to toil in the fields "at least as much as the men" and as a result were "wretched objects, who are feminine only with the physiologist." "It is the glory of the *English* race," Chevalier concluded, "that they have every where, as much as possible, interpreted the superiority of the man to the woman, as reserving to the former the charge of the ruder and harder forms of toil. A country in which woman is treated according to this principle presents the aspect of a new and better world."[4]

Although women were objectified in both of his renderings, Chevalier nonetheless celebrated the Anglo-American "advance" in labor differentiation as part of a systematic shift in the distribution of power in the household, precisely the contrast that Miner would demonstrate a century later. In "the earlier times," Chevalier argued, "everything was swallowed up in the father." As time passed, "the individuality—the rights, privileges, and duties—of the wife and children was the successive growth of ages."[5] The United States was the locus of immense progress fueled by the religious and political systems under which the Yankee household existed. It was "under the influence of Protestantism and republicanism," Chevalier stressed, that "social progress had been effected by the medium of the spirit of individuality" since "protestantism, republicanism, and individuality are all one." Unlike the corporate German households that Miner would observe in 1940, "a farm" in Jacksonian America, Chevalier argued, "is an inviolable republic in the state; each individual is a republic by himself in the family."[6] Indeed, the American farmer spared his wife "all the hard work and employments unsuitable to the sex," according to Chevalier, in large part because he was "initiated" to "the series of that succession of progressive movements which have characterized our civilization ever since it quitted its cradle in the East."[7] For Chevalier, the corporate family morality that undergirded the household mode of production was already breaking down among Americans in the Jacksonian era.

Yet for Miner as well as Chevalier, cultural differences clearly influenced the resilience of traditional family forms. Although the migrants and their descendants confronted similar economic opportunities and legal constraints, their adaptations were based on differing cultural premises and institutional structures with regard to the household. Strict inequalities were characteristic of every household in the rural Middle West, but the extent and nature of those inequalities were arrayed dissimilarly according to different predispositions in customs of coresidence, property devolution, and intergenerational and intergender relationships —in short, customs of household power. Although rural migrants typically celebrated the promise of the West, their household systems—which themselves were expressions of cultural patterns of authority and hierarchy—demarcated the limits of that opportunity and set the parameters of behavior accorded individuals within the household. Just as they influenced developments within the ethnic community, the minds brought to the West colored the behavior of individuals within the home who confronted the rapid developments in the region.

The implications of these varying household systems were apparent on many levels. This chapter illustrates how household differences informed overarching structures of family and farm in the rural communities. Patterns of household, for example, influenced the degree to which farmers remained tied to the soil and to a household-centered pattern of production. Thus, they affected, as scholars have repeatedly noted in the past, rural community development. Yet the systems informed interpersonal relationships as well. Attachments within the home—affinities between husband and wife and between parents and children—were tempered by patterns of power intrinsic to the household organization. As commentators expressed satisfaction with their own patterns of family, they often chided the behavior of other cultural groups because it did not adequately conform to their norms.

Varying Patterns of Family and Farm

"No, Mother; and there ain't no excuse for me—not a bit," he said, dropping back into her colloquialisms. "I'm ashamed when I think of how long it's been since I saw you. I could have come."
"It don't matter now," she interrupted gently. "It's the way things go. Our boys grow up and leave us."—Hamlin Garland, *Main-Travelled Roads* (1891)

> The little old downstairs bedroom in the back now became "grandma's and grandpa's room," a small, dark, stuffy room with an uneven floor, one dingy, small-paned window. —Ruth Suckow, *Country People* (1924)

Prosaic patterns of life in the rural Middle West were inextricably intertwined with its large structures. The seemingly limitless wealth in the region, for example, altered the relationships between parents and children. As opportunity beckoned, children tended to "default" on the responsibilities their parents expected them to fulfill and the cement that held the household mode of production together tended to weaken.[8] As the ligaments of the family morality were compromised, the household as a mode of production was threatened. Yet as Middle West regionalist writers such as Ruth Suckow and Hamlin Garland repeatedly observed, the cultural systems in which individuals were enmeshed mediated the degree to which behavior was transformed. German parents in Suckow's fictional depiction enjoyed the presence of children in their old age, a circumstance denied Garland's mother in his semiautobiographical portrait.

American youths asserted their independence not only with regard to support for aged parents. They also tended to ignore their parents in making marriage choices. Courtship among Yankee youths was a private affair.[9] "We still maintain the custom in our part," wrote Herbert Quick in 1919, "of almost never speaking of engagements. Our parents never did. They kept it a profound secret, usually even from their parents." The decision by the prospective husband and wife to wed was made between themselves with little input from, and on occasion without the knowledge of, parents.[10] Marriage arrangements among immigrants were another matter entirely. "To us rather primitive Yankees," Quick remembered, "[German immigrant] courtships and marriages were matters of astonishment, not to say scandal," since Germans made few attempts to conceal what was essentially a community process.[11] Weddings, in turn, were celebrated with much ado within the European community. Adhering to a system that was patrilineal and often virilocal in residence, German immigrants attempted to integrate the wife into her new home and to mollify her parents for their loss. In a Missouri German community, for example, the *brautbitter* (the person who invited guests to the wedding) was a community spokesman who, when he arrived at the bride's parental home to fetch her for the wedding, made a speech in which he asked her parents to "be good to them from thy heart" so that the betrothed will enjoy the "married state without suffering" and "no discomfort will separate thee from peace."[12] Whereas Yankee mothers were resigned to the fact that "our boys grow up and leave us," German parents required reassurances from a community ritual that solemnized the loss of their daughters.

These dissimilarities in living arrangements among the aged and standards of courtship among the young are examples of profoundly different norms recast from familial customs of kinship and family carried from the cultural hearth. It must be stressed that the family systems embedded in the local and regional cultural fabrics of the eastern United States and especially in those of Europe were complex in their variety. The traditions of inheritance, coresidence, courtship, and work patterns often differed greatly from village to village, not to mention from region to region.[13] These traditions, moreover, were not timeless forms; they continued to undergo changes in the decades leading up to the migration that occurred in response to demographic, economic, and cultural shifts in the rural social fabric.[14] They would continue to be reformulated in the rural Middle West as residents there responded to changing opportunities and constraints.

Nonetheless, despite the widespread variation in behavior within specific households, we may posit the presence of two overarching cultural typologies transplanted to the region. By "typology," I mean a set of institutional and ideological structures that powerfully, if imperfectly, informed individual and interpersonal behavior. The structure of what I label the Yankee household typology stood in stark contrast to that of the other household form, embraced by communities originating in Continental Europe and the Celtic fringe, which I shall call the European American typology. It is significant that the typologies conform to the "Puritan" and "foreign" minds that had so captured the imagination of mid-nineteenth-century observers.[15]

The typological behavior was based on a succession of interlocking and reinforcing cultural patterns. First, different subcultures in the region possessed varying conceptualizations of authority and hierarchy. As Chevalier and Miner pointed out, household relationships reflected these differences. The European American household typology was distinguished by a more powerful and all-encompassing variant of patriarchy. Adults in the European immigrant household, derived from configurations of authority common in Roman Catholic and Lutheran traditions, tended to amass greater power than those in the American, particularly the Yankee, cultures. Such authority was often of spiritual as well as worldly importance. The *haustafel*, a table of duties in the home and society based on the Fourth Commandment, adorned church interiors for centuries and clearly authorized the power of parents in the ordering of the home.[16] Pastor Herman Preus advised his Norwegian Lutheran coreligionists that "wherever a Christian is, he shall show himself to be a spiritual priest to his spouse, his children, his own sisters and brothers, his household, his neighbors and friends." This spiritual responsibility, Preus affirmed elsewhere, had secular relevance reflected in the varying behavior of immigrants and the American-born. Unlike Norwegians, he wrote, Americans showed a "glaring lack of external discipline, obedience and order," which "inculcated in the children" the "principles of a false freedom and independence . . . that in time cannot but bear its tragic fruits in domestic relations with parents and masters and in civil relations with the authorities."[17] For their part, German Lutheran pastors in the early nineteenth century advised their flocks to scrutinize the anglicizing *Eirishdeutsch*, who spoke English and were integrating into American society and whose farms were not as well kept, families were not as happy, and children were not as loyal as their own. When children ceased "going to church—to the church where they are taught to honor mother and father" and "to esteem honest toil," they were transformed. "They won't get up in the morning, but will loll in bed like ladies and gentlemen," the argument continued. "Neither will they be ordered about; with their new self esteem they will be an independent, mincing set." Such children were enervated by materialism and shiftlessness; "what a tearful thing when wayward children do not honor father and mother but squander the fruit of their toil."[18]

The duty that children owed their parents, from the perspective of the flow of individual wealth within the home, succored the aged.[19] Yet many argued that the corporate family morality was a boon to all family members. A Czech American, for example, noted that those in his ethnic community, unlike the "Americans" about them, "were brought up to believe that the thing we were doing [like hard work] benefited our families as a whole, and that was reason enough for us to be proud of being different."[20] Familial success apparently advanced the constituents of the corporate whole.[21]

In contrast, corporate arrangements in Yankee households had eroded by the mid-nineteenth century. Responding to an increasingly powerful capitalist framework and vast opportunities for economic mobility, Yankee family patterns were altered by political and religious movements that privileged an individuation of the self.[22] Tempered first by liberal notions of the American Revolution and later by religious movements in the Second Great Awakening that gave individuals greater power to bring about their own salvation, family arrangements among Yankees trekking westward were in a profound period of change. As a result, conventions that had developed in the northeastern United States decades prior to the migration to the Middle West predisposed Yankee migrants more than Europeans to emphasize the rights of the individual and the contractual relationships between individuals—husbands and wives, parents and children—within the household.

Observers in Europe and America alike repeatedly recounted the perceived decline of patriarchy. Alexis de Tocqueville noted that "in our time . . . paternal authority, if not abolished, has at least changed form." These developments were even "more striking" in the United States, where "the father has long anticipated the moment when his authority must come to an end, and when the time does come near, he abdicates without fuss." "The son," on the other hand, "has known in advance exactly when he will be his own master and wins his liberty without haste or effort." [23] Tocqueville described how governmental structures informed family power. In aristocracies, the father was not only the civil head of the family but also the carrier of its traditions and customs, which were cemented by deference and "mingled with fear." To be sure, the members of families in an aristocratic age were closely bound together because their interests were connected. The democratic family, in contrast, hewed to a Lockean construction in which "the father scarcely exercises more power than that which is granted to the affection and the experience of age." Every word "a son addresses to his father has a tang of freedom, familiarity, and affection all at once." [24] For Tocqueville, "democracy loosens social ties, but it tightens natural ones." [25]

Other observers perceived this distinctiveness of American familial patterns. They continued to note the consequences of a unique American individualism. Writing about marriage in 1867, Auguste Carlier commented that "the predominant idea in America" was "that the individual was superior to the community." [26] Another Frenchman observed forty years later that "with us, one lives more for *the other*; in America each lives to advantage the *self*." [27] This tendency toward an individuation altered intergenerational relationships. The American family, wrote another French visitor, resembled "a nestful of sparrows" from which "the fledglings escape as soon as they have enough feathers to fly and claws to defend themselves. They forget the maternal nest and often the parents themselves no longer recognize their offspring." The reason for this was simple: "Parental authority has never been a rule that was strictly observed in the American family, nor has filial obedience been one of its greatest virtues." [28] In sum, the responsibility of parents toward their children was lessened as the responsibility of offspring toward their elders decreased. Thus, when Albert Barnes argued that "there is no class or order of men, except in the parental relation, who are entrusted by nature with any authority over any other," [29] he admitted implicitly that such authority dissipated as children aged. Without strong familial ties to the past and with little expectation of aid from children in the future, lateral intragenerational relationships increased in significance. Individuals, as a result, placed greater weight on conjugal ties.

An underlying critical difference between the typologies, then, was the structural importance of lineal ties among Europeans compared to the importance of lateral, and especially conjugal, ties within American homes. Following Francis L. K. Hsu's hypothesis, the prominence of one kinship dyad in the family influences other dyadic relationships. Thus, when particular bonds within the home are emphasized, the salience of other ties in the family is lessened.[30] The European American typology was dominated by the kinship dyad between father and son, often the first son. This lineal tie was strengthened when old patriarchal norms allied with contemporary legal shifts in Europe. The right to "own" land in the modern sense was a relatively recent phenomenon in many European states whereas it was the norm in the Middle West. And the possibility of bequeathing land to children, also a relatively recent prospect for most immigrants, confirmed that one was, in fact, a farmer.[31] This emphasis on land and lineage tended to reduce the prominence of the conjugal bond and of connections among siblings, while it augmented the patriarchal prerogative. Indeed, a perceived lack of affection between husband and wife, as we shall see, was a dominant theme in the Anglo-American critique of the European American family. At the time of settlement in the Middle West, on the other hand, the principal relationship in Anglo-American households connected husband and wife. Anglo-American families in the mobile Middle West—even in its rural regions—were thus characterized by arrangements that divided the generations. Anglo-American families tended to be laterally disposed, and they were more likely to exhibit discontinuities reflected both on the land and between the generations. The primacy of the conjugal bond among Anglo-Americans, in short, decreased the significance of the lineally disposed consanguineous relationship.[32]

Not all households with European roots, of course, conformed to the European American typology. Nor did all of those from the northeastern United States exhibit the Yankee pattern. As typologies, the two systems illustrate patterns of behavior in their most quintessential forms. Yet the fact that European Americans and Yankees clustered into identifiable types illustrates the power of the minds in the West to inform socioeconomic institutions such as the household in ways that essentially paralleled the diverse theological constructs of the region. Thus, social behavior stemming from these typologies became rooted in middle westerners' imaginations and critiques of each other.

The implications of household variation were sweeping; they influenced the large structures of community as they informed interpersonal relationships and individual opportunities. From a broad perspective, household imperatives merged with community growth or decline. Families in communities that valued lineality and authority tended to perceive the land as a resource to maintain that lineality. Those households characterized by intergenerational discontinuity, on the other hand, were less tied to the soil. Indeed, a pervasive theme in middle western fiction and scholarship alike—a theme best articulated by Marcus Lee Hansen— was the existence of a dichotomy in landholding that was culturally informed.[33] The ambition of the European farmer, epitomized by the German farmer, as Hansen put it, was "to see his sons on reaching manhood established with their families on farms clustered about his own." The American father, on the other hand, made no such effort on behalf of his offspring, for "to be a self made man was his ideal." Each new generation would create its place in society just as its predecessor had done.[34] Farmers of Continental European background, unlike their American counterparts, thus were likely not only to retain ownership of the family estate but also to engross lands around the estate.

Scholars have often suggested that the inherent conservatism of the immigrant explains this dichotomy between European and American behavior toward the soil. Land for the American became a saleable commodity that represented and created wealth. If Yankee families were dissatisfied with the land they bought or claimed, wrote Joseph Schafer, they "'sold out' with slight compunction and went elsewhere." Since Americans were "more speculative to the last, more imaginative and space-free," they were more likely to deplete their soil's fertility, confident that they could sell their land, gain a profit, and move to greener pastures. As farming proved less remunerative, Yankee farmers forsook their occupation, moved to the city, and entered other pursuits.[35]

Europeans, on the other hand, were resolved to create "a family estate."[36] Their concern for owning and sustaining property created a culture "less venturesome" or "more prudent, depending on the point of view." Profit, for Europeans, was a means of maintaining landownership; the causation was reversed for Yankees. As a result, Europeans' "caution and . . . phlegm were a protection." They were less likely to speculate on land; they were more likely to contribute to the development of a settled region; they were the "old world cultivators" whose social impact on settled rural regions increased as "the shadow of the Yankee" faded across the land.[37] Due to differing conceptions of land and its use and varying patterns of production and property devolution on the farm, the land itself took on a palpably different meaning for various cultural groups.

Embedded within this alleged economic "conservatism," however, were predilections within households expressed in interpersonal attitudes and dispositions that influenced the meaning of landholding. Domestic arrangements that emphasized lineality invested considerable power in the older generation, which in turn placed a greater importance on maintaining the ancestral land. Households that were conjugally oriented, on the other hand, tended to be created anew by each generation and were characterized by neolocal residence and an ethos of self-made adulthood. In these dissimilar situations, the meaning of the ancestral lands varied. In one system, they supported the lineage; in the other, they represented the resources to sustain the aged and perhaps to endow the children. In one system, keeping the land within the lineage was meaningful; in the other, land sales to finance new careers and new endeavors were often advantageous.

By the twentieth century, these systems had endured to the extent that Miner observed a "Yankee pattern" of land and wealth transfer in the Middle West that differed dramatically from the pattern that typified European households. Among Anglo-Americans, the farm owner envisioned retirement, which was financed by the sale of his estate. Property eventually devolved to children, but according to Miner, there was "no particular likelihood that the farm will pass on in the family." If it did, the farm was sold to a family member just as it would be to any other potential buyer.[38] Sentiments of kinship and coresidence among Yankees differed from those of Europeans as a result. Due to the capital derived from their farm, retired parents had little need to live with their children. More important, the father had little desire, as Miner phrased it, "to have his living given to him by his son." Conversely, children did not expect land to be bequeathed to them. A child might eventually take over his family's land, but the lease and sale were business arrangements in which the attitude that tied land to the family line was clearly absent.[39]

European Americans, on the other hand, retained a greater appreciation of the relation between land and lineage well into the twentieth century. A Norwegian American informant remembered that he had bought his maternal grandfather's farm because it "should not go out of the family."[40] As a result, an informant from another enclave noted, "most of the old farms are still in the family's ownership and named after the first settler."[41] This emphasis on lineality, which had deep legal and cultural roots, tended to temper the accessibility of resources for married women. In the 1840s, Norwegian immigrants in Wisconsin condemned what they called the *kjærringloven* (the old woman's law), which gave married women the right to own separate property within the family, in the new state constitution and vowed to oppose its ratification.[42] For them, the rights of the individual, especially the female individual, should not overshadow those of the household. The proclivity for lineal arrangements among residents of ethnic communities was also revealed when they clung to remnants of a juridical system that had inextricably tied landownership to lineage in Europe even though there was no such law in the United

States. The *odelsrett*, for example, which had operated in Norway for generations, enabled members of a kinship line that had held title to a tract of land for at least twenty years to repurchase it within five years it if had been sold outside the lineage. The logic was simple: the land belonged to the lineage rather than the individual who held its title and merely administered its operations; the individual did not have the right to sell what, strictly speaking, he did not possess. The degree to which this concept was transplanted by Europeans in the United States is difficult to determine. One Norwegian American farmer did suggest that the sentiment still existed in the twentieth century when he said simply that he would not sell his farm since it "belonged to the whole family." [43]

These patterns of family and farm had profound consequences for the resilience of household-centered production. Those families operating within the European typology were more likely than those following the Yankee pattern to retain land and continue farming. By retaining household power in the older generation and by stressing the significance of the intergenerational contract, European families tended to place greater emphasis on land as a familial resource than as a saleable commodity. Again, the work of Miner, who posited "two opposing life philosophies" of Yankee and European stocks, is useful. In the latter, the "German and Norwegian elements . . . were more inclined to value their own immediate possessions and ways of life over the speculative advantage of future 'advancement.' " The European "was more limited" than the Yankee, who had an "unbounded drive for profit"; Yankees in turn considered their European-stock neighbors "backward." [44] In short, as farm families were transformed by markets and machinery in the nineteenth and twentieth centuries, underlying cultural patterns informed the velocity of the evolution.

Families from cultural groups that tended to continue farming, moreover, were likely to live in thriving rural settlements. As historians have discovered variations in the desire to own and bequeath land, they have observed parallel, and related, patterns in the perseverance of settlement groups. [45] Ethnic groups, European farmers in particular, whose membership valued the preservation and engrossment of land maintained vital communities around their institutions. Those who tended to relinquish their land and move into other pursuits saw their ethnic communities shrink and their institutions wither. "No explanation needs to be given for the all but final dissolution of Protestantism" in one rural tract, wrote a local historian, "other than that these churches necessarily became empty as English and American settlers migrated to other districts when they sold their farms, homes, and stores to the Germans." [46]

Household arrangements that influenced the evolution of the community of which the families were a part also informed the individual relationships within the home. In their purest forms, they created dissimilar configurations of power and affect, hierarchy and authority, within the family. It is of great importance that contemporaries explicitly discerned the different relationships between family members that were created out of the matrices of power within American and immigrant homes. It is perhaps not surprising that they disparaged the "other" household system for the consequences it inflicted on individuals or on the family as a whole.

Relationships within the Household

Within the inherently unequal milieu of the rural household, varied arrangements of power and authority influenced the individual relationships within the home. Perhaps the clearest evidence of these variations was the negative reaction of those who expressed disdain for others who lived in arrangements different from their own. What is so important for our purposes is that by the mid- to late nineteenth century, relatively well developed critiques of the "immigrant" and "American" disparaged the respective family patterns of each. Contemporaries were quick to connect the problems of the overly individualistic or overly corporatist home with the cultural patterns that characterized the respective group. Although they did not use the same terminology, moreover, they noted the effects that these arrangements had on lateral relationships between husband and wife and lineal relationships between parent and child.

As American critics often made clear, the tendency within European American households to place greater value on the farm and lineage reinforced patriarchal and lineal kinship relationships. This household, which was predisposed agnatically as well as lineally, compromised the strength of the lateral conjugal tie. Put simply, European couples did not exhibit the "true love" that had long since become proper among Yankees. Their tendency to invest in women and children as laborers was criticized as well, especially when youths and wives were encouraged—or forced, if one believed the Yankee critics—to perform field work in order to extend the patrimony. The inclination among Yankees to emphasize individual contracts and to palliate the significance of lineal arrangements, on the other hand, created a more malleable system wherein family members were more inclined and able to express their self-interest. Less encumbered by lifetime household obligations, children were more likely to be self-centered, European critics noted, and to leave home. Placing greater emphasis on the conjugal tie, moreover, this system amplified the importance of "companionship" between husband and wife. These patterns had far-reaching consequences in defining work duties at home and in providing emotional resources, especially for married women. As wives found themselves isolated at home after their children departed, the significance of finding contentment within the conjugal relationship was magnified.[47]

Arrangements between Husbands and Wives

[Mary] tried to talk to Susette, to tell her that the first year of married life was
the hardest. After that people got accustomed to each other. She had heard
talk that the young American in Rushville gambled.
"You know what that means," Mary told her.
"Yes, and if I marry a foreigner, *you* know what that means," the girl retorted,
and Mary said no more. — Mari Sandoz, *Old Jules* (1935; emphasis in original)

The conjugal tie was for everyone a central bond in the family; the appropriate performance of husbandly and wifely duties and responsibilities was critical to the proper operation of the household. Importantly, however, expectations of work and the content of the conjugal bond differed across cultural groups. Anglo-American critics repeatedly pointed to the apparent absence of affect between husband and wife in the "foreign" household and the arduous conditions under which the women labored. Anglo-American patterns in turn were disdained by those of European immigrant background who marveled at the Anglo-American conjugal relationship, which apparently encouraged an idle and ornamental lifestyle among American women.

Herbert Quick, who grew up on an Iowa farm near German enclaves, was attentive to the various perceptions of arduous field work that women of different ethnocultural groups performed. The German housewife worked in the fields with her husband. "Nobody thought less of her for this field work," Quick observed, "that is, nobody in her circle of friends." Yet Quick connected labor differences to ethnic background and subtextually tied them to "progress." "Among us Yankees," he continued, "the German habit of working women in the fields was the sure mark of the 'Old Countryman.' We didn't even allow our women to milk the cows." In yet another instance in which he connected "progress," race and ethnicity, and women's work, Quick remembered that "Old Ebenezer McAllister used to say that among the Injuns the women did all the work, among the Hoosiers it was equally divided, and among the Yankees the men did it all."[48]

The fact that Yankee men "did it all" reinforced a domesticity that simultaneously freed and trapped American women. Emily Hawley Gillespie, as an American woman, despised farm work, which she felt was beneath her. After visiting her sister in 1883, Gillespie wrote in her diary that she resented the farm work her sister performed. "She looks more like a beggar than any thing else," Gillespie observed, "a perfect Slave to mans will & hard-work. indeed I am sorry. I do think woman [*sic*] ought to retain enough of their pride to keep themselves in a shape proper to their sex. no woman need to get so low as to do such filthy work." "I should despair," she concluded, "if my children, when I am gone, should remember me less than nobody in society."[49]

Contrary to Gillespie, most European men and some European women saw the absence of women in the fields as a sign not of enlightenment but of degeneracy. A correspondent to *Die Iowa* who had traveled throughout the Middle West described his delight when he finally reached a German settlement where he perceived proper arrangements between men and women. "To my joy," he wrote, "I found there the old good German custom of women and girls not avoiding work. . . . You see the healthy sturdy girls everywhere, binding sheaves, sitting on the machine or driving the corn plough. That's where the thousands of flitting about, gossiping, time-wasting dolls [*puppen*], should go and get the example: from those German daughters."[50] *Die Iowa* later even took issue with American women's domestic labors in its report on a lecture series for women on efficient food preparation. "We think the important feature will be dealing with *pie and sweetmeat*," the paper commented. "Then she will tell how to *get a dinner ready in fifteen minutes*."[51] Quick meal preparation was criticized because it provided women with expanded leisure time that made it possible for them to follow individual pursuits detached from family responsibilities.

A central feature of the European critique of American women was the condemnation of their indolence. To one Dutchman, "the women of the American people are terribly lazy."[52] A recently arrived Danish immigrant argued three decades later that "American wives are amazingly lazy. . . . It is quite appropriate to say that they sew not, they spin not, and they do not gather, but their menfolk feed them just the same."[53] A central image in the immigrant iconography of the American woman became the rocking chair, in which, according to one Norwegian woman, "the wife sits . . . and reads or usually just drones."[54] As a result, a correspondent to *Die Iowa* observed, German men in Beatrice, Nebraska, preferred "to stay unwedded rather than enter marriage with an American girl." The paper a few years earlier stated it even more succinctly. "In these times," contended the editor, "an 'American lady' is not a desirable housewife."[55]

European immigrant wives and their married daughters, in contrast, regularly labored in the fields. One German American community, according to a resident in 1892, could "hardly be considered progressive in adopting new methods or appliances in farming. Father[,] mother[,] sister & brother all turn out & put in their entire time to the cultivation of their farms, in most all cases in the good old fashioned way."[56] Wives in some European enclaves toiled regularly in the fields well into the twentieth century. Oscar Lewis, for example, noted the "important differences" in the division of labor and the position of women among European Americans and "old-line Americans" in rural Texas. Whereas Czech and German women and children customarily worked in the fields, it was considered "degrading" for white American women to do such work.[57] The conservative presence of women in the harvest fields, explained a female informant, reduced the incidence of "corn-pickers hands"—hands injured from corn-picking machinery—in a post–World War II Bohemian community.[58]

Clearly, when adult women rejected field work, added expenses to the farm operation were incurred. Especially during harvests, the employment of European women and children provided a method to decrease costs that was impossible, as Quick put it, "by the Yankee way."[59] On occasion, Americans objected to a sort of unfair competition made possible by what they considered immoral labor demands.[60] Its morality notwithstanding, female labor was strategically utilized in European households to reduce labor costs and thereby increase the income of the farm operation. Young wives typically worked with their husbands in the fields. In one case, according to Quick, a female domestic was hired to take care of the young children while the wife "kept on doing a man's work." The calculations of cost and benefit were explicit. If the mother had exclusively performed domestic duties, "they'd have had to hire a man, and hired girls were cheaper than hired men." As the family aged and the "children were big enough, they took their mother's place in the field and she took the hired girl's place in the house."[61] Such a life course for married women was fraught with arduous labor. A fictional German farmer whose mother and sister had worked with the men saw nothing wrong with the fact that his wife was so employed. "He expected it of his 'woman,'" wrote Ruth Suckow. And thus the wife settled quickly into a life of work and rapidly "'lost her giggles,' as the family said."[62]

The labor of European women in the fields, then, was perhaps a reflection of poverty, of the need to exploit all available labor within the household. That, at least, was the contention of a middle western foreign correspondent in 1884 who observed the toil of women in Europe. In Bavaria and Switzerland, barefooted women did half of the field work. Theirs was a life of "brutal work" in which they had become "beasts of burden"; the only liberty they enjoyed was the "liberty to work." "How I should like to have these poor over-worked women see an American farmer's wife in her sweet home," the journalist concluded, "beautifully carpeted, surrounded with books and papers and eating meat and cake and pies three times a day!"[63]

Yet many American critics contended that wealth made little difference in what they argued was the exploitation of female labor, which made the burdens imposed on European women in the United States all the more contemptible. Quick made a pointed comparison between the care of the cattle and the care of the wife in one German household. The husband "had built a concrete drinking tank for the cattle; all they had to do was to come and drink what they wanted." But "the woman who was his partner in life" was provided only "an iron pump handle and a gravel path" down which she carried buckets of water from the well to her kitchen. He had "money enough to build the finest farmhouse in the county," but he was too busy farming to do so.[64] Unlike these Germans, the narrator observed, "when I married my wife I told her that if the time should come when we couldn't make a living without her working in the field we'd starve together. . . . I believe in division of labor on the farm, and I'm just mossback enough to think that women's work is round the house."[65]

The creamery man in Hamlin Garland's short story of the same title made similar observations. The "Dutchmen," he said of German Americans, had fine houses and even bigger barns, but "their women were mostly homely and went around barefooted and barelegged, with ugly blue dresses hanging frayed and greasy round their lank ribs and big joints." Their houses looked like stables, and "their women work so much in the field they don't have any time to fix up." "I don't believe in women workin' in the fields," the creamery man concluded. "My wife needn't set her foot outdoors 'less she's a mind to."[66]

Another example of male patronization, this criticism of immigrant women's farm work was fused with deprecations of an exploitation resulting from the lack of affect, if not contempt, for the wife by the European male. Yankees were astounded by the lack of affection that seemed to characterize European patterns of courtship. In one case, an arranged marriage went awry when the wrong woman was sent from Germany to be married to a man in Iowa. The fact that the prospective husband married the woman anyway challenged the "sentiment of love" that Americans professed. The "acceptance of the substitute mate," Quick recalled, "and its failure to be regarded as anything but a good joke on [the husband] by his fellow-countrymen among us, had a tendency to set him and them off from us as a different order of beings."[67]

This purported lack of affection seemingly continued after marriage. One particularly unsettling incident encapsulates American condemnations of European work patterns and warrants an extended quotation. When the family went into the field to labor, Quick remembered,

> sometimes there would be a rattlesnake in a sheaf. One of our neighbors, a German settler fresh from the old country, took his wife into the harvest field to help with the binding. She took her baby along and parked it under a shock in the shade. One day the man came to the house of a neighbor just as they were sitting down to dinner. They invited him to join them and he accepted. After eating heartily, he confided to them that his wife was sick.
>
> "She vas vorkin' in te field," said he, "an' a snake stung her in de handt. Pretty soon she couldn't vork no more, ant so she vent to de house to git dinner; but ven I vent to dinner she didn't haf any got. I was hungry too."

The wife died later that night, exacerbating the "shocked contempt" the Americans felt. "A man who could stick to his work after his wife had been snakebit," concluded Quick, "send her to the house to get dinner after the virus in her veins had begun its deadly work, and then calmly sit down and eat a meal before mentioning it to a neighbor, stamped the entire class of immigrants in our rather narrow minds as being of a low order of intelligence."[68] Certainly, more work was done at a lower cost in these situations, but the absence of conjugal love created a household arrangement that, according to Quick's wife, "was a factory, not a family."[69] A "family" in Quick's world was composed of separate spheres in which husband and wife engaged in distinct but complementary undertakings.

This is not to suggest that marital bonds among Anglo-Americans were based on equality. Jane G. Swisshelm, for example, did not point to ethnic patterns in 1853 when she described the onerous combination of field labor and domestic work performed by women as part of the "masculine-superiority fever which has converted so many millions of men into ruffians."[70] Indeed, she argued that such a malady existed precisely because of the American church and state, both of which underscored the duties of the wife to obey her husband without giving her any rights. The "ignorant country bore" was not responsible for the inequalities because "he is only living up to the spirit of the age," a spirit articulated by a church that commanded her to keep silent and a government that placed her "half-way between the rational and irrational creature" and "deprives her of the right of self-government."[71]

By 1885, however, a Norwegian-born woman's rights advocate, in a remarkable melodramatic depiction of rural life, underscored behavior that reflected both the unyielding power of the immigrant church and the dissimilar paths of development that American and European cultural groups followed as a result. In "Kvinden skal være Manden underdannig" (The woman shall be subservient to the man), Kristofer Janson, a writer familiar with many of the rural Norwegian settlements in the Middle West, portrayed the conflict between an immigrant couple pulled in different directions by varying intellectual currents. Ola and Emma came to America for reasons common to many immigrants: it was "a land of freedom and adventure" where both Ola and Emma could enjoy "unbounded freedom" while they created a "material foundation" for their children's future.[72] But grinding toil and repeated childbirth took their toll on Emma, while Ola adhered to teachings within the church community that Janson presented as a source of oppression for womankind. Emma then encountered the possibilities promised by secular American society when an American lady (*Damen*) unexpectedly entered her life.[73]

As in American portrayals of immigrant rural households, Ola and Emma's home was a patriarchal setting in which the family endured relentless work to build a farm. Ola was depicted as the inflexible immigrant farmer whose "single passion," wrote Janson, "was to build up for himself and his family a well-being and respect." In his monomaniacal pursuit, "his brutality (*Raahed*) prohibited him from feeling his wife's privation." Emma found it increasingly difficult to perform the backbreaking labor both inside and outside the house. "[Ola] does not realize," she told the lady, "how grinding it is to keep the house in order especially when the children are screaming and crying and pulling from all directions."[74] Yet such conditions were normal in her community since, according to Emma, "the farmers' wives here are accustomed to such slave conditions (*Trællevilkaar*) from home that they don't believe life can be otherwise, that the earth indeed is a vale of tears."[75]

Ola's mastery of household power was thus consistent with community norms and, as such, was upheld by the community's pastor, who explicitly connected religious doctrine to family arrangements. When accused by the lady of upholding "a barbaric ideal that the wife must be man's servant," the pastor asserted the necessity of hierarchical arrangements in the home that vested power in the male. "There must nevertheless be a superior in the house," he argued, "a lord, and it has been established both in the order of society and through the witness of Scripture to be the husband. Would it be better, do you think," the pastor concluded, indicting American society, "if the circumstance were reversed, as I hear is the style now, that the husband shall be the wife's waiter? He comes in tired from his day's work while she sits on the sofa reading novels and then calls out: Tom! fetch water! Tom, warm up the oven! Tom, put a kettle on! Tom, shine my shoes! Tom, take care of the baby!"[76] As the pastor lectured Emma, he stressed that she must be her husband's subordinate in all things and that her subservience had deep cultural roots. "You were married," he reminded her, and in a marriage, the "husband is the woman's head just as Christ is the congregation's head."[77] Ola had clearly embraced this teaching. "I must insist that the womenfolk shall mind me," he told the lady. "There is to be only one ruler in my house."[78]

The American lady represented what Janson considered the more equitable possibilities inherent in American conjugal patterns. By stumbling into the strange immigrant world, the lady opened up new possibilities for Emma. She gave her money and feminist literature. After observing the inequalities in the household, she scolded Ola. "If I were *you*," the lady said, "I would be as ashamed as a dog and get down on my knees and beg for forgiveness. If I were *her*, I would not remain for a moment in your house, as, I can assure you, no American woman would." Ola's reply— "No, that I believe. . . . But we are, thank God, still Norwegians"—manifested the problem as the American lady, and Janson, saw it.[79] Norwegian immigrants perceived themselves as separate and culturally distinct from "Americans." Norwegian American settlements, moreover, attempted to restrict the diffusion of ideas into their communities through schools or literature. The pastor in the story argued that American periodicals contained ideas of freethinkers and thus should be forbidden. Schools that were not founded on religion, he contended, were "heathenist" and "an abhorrence to Christians," and thus he encouraged parents to keep their children out of the public schools.[80] In sum, not only were Norwegians distinct from Americans, but they also made concerted efforts to retain their distinctiveness.

Emma's life ended in tragedy. Enchanted by the new concepts to which she was introduced and disheartened by the continuing intractability of her husband, she severed her ties to the immigrant community and fled to her brother in Minneapolis. Greeted with little sympathy there, she was forced back to the prairie, where she was rejected by her former companions, including her husband and children. She ultimately ended her own life. For Janson, the insular immigrant community—represented in his story—paradoxically was free to set itself off from the freedoms of American society, which in turn inhibited cultural change. The authority of the community reinforced the hierarchy within the household. Individuals might rebel, but they found their options limited to conformity or exile. A well-defined cultural pattern, based on Scripture and "correct" behavior, that valued insularity informed the relationship between husband and wife, just as it informed the relationship, as we shall see, between parent and child.[81]

[Casper Kaetterhenry, a Pomeranian immigrant,] had always worked hard, and so had his wife. . . . Now he was going to make a landowner of himself. He brought up his children to know very little but work. The mother had little time for them. In the intervals of bearing them she had to work in the field. So did Lena, the oldest girl. . . . The older children had no chance for any schooling. . . . It seemed to Casper Kaetterhenry that his children were in clover. — Ruth Suckow, *Country People* (1924)

Contemporaries frequently argued that European patriarchal systems affected relationships between parents and children as well as those between spouses. One informant wrote in 1892 that the Germans combined a "frugality [that] almost amounts to niggardliness"[82] with the unremitting toil of adults and children alike. In order to build up estates, immigrant parents, Anglo-American critics contended, compelled their children to work long hours, oftentimes at the expense of their schooling. Since daughters performed the heavy work in the fields along with sons, Anglo-American observers found the toil of female children, like that of adult women, to be especially noteworthy and disgraceful.

The European perspective contradicted this representation. Children were expected to contribute to the family's labors and support their parents, but they also stood to benefit from their work, in spite of its drudgery. Through their hard work and frugality, continued the 1892 informant, the Germans "accumulated lands in very quick time & the size of their holdings is larger than other nationalities here."[83] The zeal to expand the farm increased the potential for an enlarged patrimony that benefited the family group. From a critical individualist perspective, however, children's exchange of labor for land and old-age support for inheritance remained ambiguous. The primary bond that knit property to lineage also tied patriarch to heir. Yet if only selected children — sons rather than daughters, the first-born instead of younger siblings — inherited the land, their siblings were disadvantaged, especially when all children, even daughters, were obliged to labor in the fields. Perhaps children hoped that their work would be rewarded with property when they came of age and the estate was bequeathed, but for many such a hope remained only a possibility.

The fact that child labor was common in the European home, then, did not mean that conflict between parents and children did not occur as a result of it. These moments of conflict enlarge our understanding of the often contradictory relationships between childhood roles and adolescent expectations. Consider Quick's portrayal of a fictional conflict within a German household. When the son wished to abandon his ties of residence and work with the family, "it meant that he wished to cut his family bond, go out into the world and work for himself, buy his own clothes, board himself, and be industrially a stranger." To his father, this seemed "a good deal like burying him, and he refused; but he was not able to refuse in such a way as to avoid making the breach wider." [84] "We are an old fashioned people," wrote Quick, underscoring the fluid interrelationship between kinship and class within the household, "and the father is his son's boss." When the father demanded that his son remain at home, the boy replied, "Then . . . I'm nothing more than a slave!" The father's response in turn revealed the older generation's assumption of regularity in overlapping intergenerational relationships: "You're no more a slave than I was at your age," cried the father. "Slave! The idea! As good a home as you've got! Don't let me hear any more of this, young man!" The exchange terminated in ambiguity. The son demanded, "'You let me have my way, or I'll have it anyway!,'" after which he went into the cornfield to labor, "for the habit of obedience," Quick concluded, "sometimes persists after obedience itself has ceased." [85]

This fictionalized exchange mirrored real-life events. Mary Woodward, a young American living in Dakota in the 1880s, deprecated in her diary the behavior of a German farm family that lived near her. A victimized son suffered many vicissitudes at the hands of his inflexible father. At last, he "ran away from home," she wrote, "thinking he had gotten too big to be whipped—he was six feet tall. He went off, out of the vicinity for awhile, and then returned to work at Green's, three miles from home, where he has been all the fall, plowing. His family have not found him yet. He works in sight of home, and can see his sister plowing, and she can see him, but she doesn't dream who he is." As a co-conspirator in the breakdown of what she considered a dour, brutal household, Woodward concluded: "I think that's fun." [86]

Characteristic of American comments on immigrant work patterns, Woodward's diary was also peppered with references to the labor of daughters. Americans, as in their assessment of field work by married women, deplored outdoor work among daughters not only because it was "backward" but also because daughters stood to gain less from enlarged landholdings. When writing of the German boy who ran away, Woodward also penned her observations about the labor of daughters in this well-to-do yet parsimonious household. "Elsie is plowing for her father, a stingy old German who makes women work out of doors," she wrote. "He thinks an hour long enough for them to prepare a meal, and affords them only the necessities of life, though he owns a half section [320 acres] of land with live stock and machinery." [87]

In a notation some years later, Woodward remained disturbed about the work responsibilities imposed on immigrant daughters while she simultaneously admired their forbearance. "Such young, slender German girls," she wrote in 1888, "how they can work like men is beyond my comprehension. They drive four-horse teams standing up like any teamster."[88] During the hay harvest a few months later, she again affirmed the varying patterns of labor, although she now expressed greater sympathy for the objective of the entire family's labor. "Our men are in the hay field," she wrote, distinguishing the field labor of men from her work responsibilities. In contrast, in the German family, "Elsie cut all forenoon, down in their big hay field alone. . . . Sometimes her sister, Lena, rakes. They have hauled home five loads apiece from the hay field, making thirty-five miles each. Elsie weighs 104 pounds. They have a man to pitch the hay on, and the girls build the load, haul it home, and pitch it off onto the stack which their father and mother build." The burdens imposed on children and adults alike benefited the family, she concluded, since "such people can make a living in Dakota." "[The parents] had only eighteen dollars in the world to start on. They took up land here, and now own two quarter-sections; have horses, cattle, sheep, trees, shrubs, a flower garden, and eight young ones."[89] The "eight young ones" were inextricably connected to the accumulation of "two quarter-sections."

Different treatment of children evoked comparisons, replete with value judgments of dissimilar and ethnically based household labor systems. The memoir of Mary Schaal Johns, a German American orphan who labored in a German household, pondered the differing prescriptions for work in the nineteenth-century Middle West. The conditions on the German farm were formidable. "In the summer," she wrote, "I went out and yoked the oxen. . . . Then while [her employer] plowed, I followed all day and whipped the oxen. I was too little to reach the off ox with my snake whip, so to strike him, I had to run around the plow. I was bare headed, bare-footed, and clad in only a little smock which I was sadly outgrowing."[90] She was only thirteen years old. After two years, a neighbor advised her to leave her employer. "'Mary, you leave [him],'" he recommended. "'You must get with some American family where you will learn English and American ways. . . . You can learn nothing following the plow!'"[91] When an opportune time came, she fled and ultimately entered the different world of "English and American ways."

The departure of children from European homes, represented by their flight to "American ways," occurred simultaneously with a slow cultural diffusion of those ways into immigrant homes, a process that immigrant parents often feared. Just as Americans disparaged the behavior of their European neighbors, criticism was aimed in the opposite direction. Work performed by children, like the labor of wives, was prized within the immigrant household. A daughter skilled at planting corn, for example, was a source of family pride.[92] The common European perception that American women were lazy was paralleled by similar views with regard to the behavior of children and especially of daughters. "American girls," wrote *Die Iowa* in 1878 bluntly, "do not want to work and even condemn servant's work."[93] The fact that children had free time and parents neglected their responsibilities and abdicated their power resulted in incidents that weakened the family and, by implication, society. When boys were arrested for breaking and entering in 1882, for example, *Die Iowa* argued that it was their parents who were at fault due to "their utter neglect."[94] Five years earlier, after a fifteen-year-old girl consumed rat poison because her parents had forbidden her to dance, the paper concluded with sarcastic disdain that here was "another beautiful little scamp [*Früchtchen*]!"[95]

Such behavior was summoned, many commentators observed, by the loosening of bonds that knit youths to their parents, an unraveling that seemingly was encouraged by an individualistic, secular society. As we shall observe in Chapters 9 and 10, leaders of many European American religious and cultural groups deplored the diffusion of ideas and behaviors that tended to undermine parental and community influences, especially those that competed with the family morality on which patriarchal sentiment and lineal orientation were built. They therefore worked diligently to preserve community controls that lessened the flow of destructive outside influences. With regard to youths, many—like the pastor in Emma's community—censured the public school as the principal institution through which innovations could diffuse into the community. Thus, the establishment of public schools became a charged political and cultural issue. The questions surrounding the schooling of youths, of course, were many. Almost everyone agreed that children should be socialized and educated. Yet public education instilled secular ideas in children as it taught academic skills; it also loosened parent-child ties as it competed with household labor for children's time. Public schools, in short, tended not only to fragment the family morality but also to produce a human capital that typically had to migrate from the community to be utilized, an out-migration that often was precisely the opposite of parents' intentions for their children's future.

European—and again particularly German—communities therefore saw less urgency in investing community or familial resources in public education. As a respondent wrote to Kate Everest about a German settlement in Wisconsin, "Their children as a rule attend the parochial school, many never enter the public school." "Education," he concluded, "is very largely neglected."[96] Field research undertaken in the 1940s indicated that similar patterns continued. A female interviewee in the Wild Rose community of Waushara County, Wisconsin, "confirmed the German reluctance for education" and contended that "it was only through the insistence of their mother that they were able to go to high school."[97] A German American man, on the other hand, justified that "reluctance." He could not see "much importance in education today" and argued that "no girl needs a high school education since she can get everything she needs in grade school to make her a good wife." Education for farm boys was equally meaningless, even detrimental, since "it does little to make better farmers out of them" and "if they do receive a higher education, they never return to farming."[98] "Too much schooling" was also opposed by Czech parents in Texas because they feared it "would make their children dissatisfied with farm life."[99] In the field notes of rural sociologists, Yankees expressed different sentiments even if they agreed with immigrants about the end results of education. Members of one of the "old original Yankee-English families" in the Wild Rose area were "firm believers in education." Indeed, the wife argued, "most people [in the region] who come from New York are." As a result of their interest in schooling, all of their children were college graduates. Their education had led all but one of their children to leave the community.[100] Due to kinship predilections, the Yankees seemed able to let go of their children; the European Americans could not.

In their starkest form, parent-child relationships within European homes were distinguished by fears of a cultural diffusion inward and a migration of children outward, a situation remarkably charged with conflict. Fictional characterizations again clarify the lines of conflict and affinity between parent and child in a European household. Whereas Janson's story described conflict arising from cultural diffusion, Hamlin Garland's "The Creamery Man," which also expresses a clear preference for a Yankee pattern, replicates the real-life drama of cultural variation, interaction, and change between parents and children. In this portrayal, the relationship between Nina, the daughter of a German farmer, and Claude, the American creamery man, demonstrates the complex intercouplings of ethnicity and class, household economies and individual propriety.[101] For the American, the blurred lines of gender in work roles within the German household decreased Nina's chances for intermarriage. She was "good enough—for a Dutchman," explained Claude, "but I hate to see a woman go around looking as if her clothes would drop off if it rained on her. And on Sundays, when she dresses up, she looks like a boy rigged out in some girl's cast-off duds."[102] Nina, on the other hand, performs her customary duties at home as she dreams of freedoms that might be provided by intermarriage and, by implication, status hypergamy. "She knew that the Yankee girls," wrote Garland, "did not work in the fields—even the Norwegian girls seldom did so now, they worked out in town—but she had been brought up to hoe and pull weeds from her childhood, and her father and mother considered it good for her, and being a gentle and obedient child, she still continued to do as she was told."[103] Despite her submission, Nina nonetheless "wanted to marry 'a Yankee,'" noted Garland, "not one of her own kind." It was true that "she had suitors among the Germans, plenty of them, but she had a disgust of them."

The encounter between Nina and Claude and the misperceptions that ensue reiterate the culturally dissimilar views of individual propriety and household roles. Claude, in his conversations with Nina on his milk route, represents to her the possibilities of the Yankee world. "'Say, Nina,'" Claude suggests, "'I wouldn't work outdoors on such a day as this if I was you. I'd tell the old man to go to thunder, and I'd go in and wash up and look decent. Yankee women don't do that kind of work, and your old dad's rich; no use of your sweatin' around a cornfield with a hoe in your hands. I don't like to see a woman goin' round without stockin's and her hands all chapped and calloused. It ain't according to Hoyle. No, sir! I wouldn't stand it. I'd serve an injunction on the old man right now.'" "'Yes sir!'" Claude counsels Nina. "'I'd brace up and go to Yankee meeting instead of Dutch; you'd pick up a Yankee beau like as not.'"[104] Unbeknownst to Claude, he becomes for her that Yankee beau.

As Nina falls increasingly under Claude's influence, she is pulled further away from the authority of her parents. When she greets Claude in her best dress, her mother confronts them both with invective. Impressed by Nina's appearance, Claude reiterates his male-centered prescriptions of proper female behavior. "'Now you're talkin'!'" he exclaims. "'I'd do a little reading of the newspaper myself, if I was you. A woman's business ain't to work out in the hot sun—it's to cook and fix up things round the house, and then put on her clean dress and set in the shade and read or sew or something. Stand up to 'em! Doggone me if I'd paddle round that hot cornfield with a mess o' Dutchmen—it ain't decent.'"[105] The mother not only laments the loss of labor and respect but also fears that after Nina and Claude marry, Claude will eventually inherit the farm. Importantly, it is Nina, the German daughter, rather than Claude, the American interloper, who dreams of a new world. The cultural adaptation that Garland portrays, moreover, in the life of Nina—an adaptation, as we shall see, which becomes increasingly common—involves more than changes in views on the propriety of labor. It also encompasses modification of the mixture of authority and autonomy in the household and shifts in the axis of the primary relationship therein: the primacy of the lineal relationship between parent and child in terms of property devolution and implicit care of the aged in the German household pivoted to a prominence of the conjugal tie between Nina and Claude.

Conclusion

The drama played out between Nina and Claude reiterates central features of farm life in the rural Middle West. It is yet another example of the clear perceptions of difference in family life and patterns of power and authority that existed between cultural groups in the region. Specifically, it illustrates the chasm that divided European immigrants from their Yankee neighbors with regard to the lines and degree of family authority, as expressed by each in their praise for their own customs and in their condemnation of those of the other group. Yet it shows as well that even if rural communities were insulated from the outside world, they were not impervious to cultural diffusion. The fictional portrayals of Nina and Emma together reveal how outside cultural influences provided alternatives and created internal tensions. Claude and the lady, each in their own way, challenged the fundamental structures of the household by pointing out what they saw as inequities to individuals living under the auspices of family systems different from their own. Whereas German daughters such as Nina lived under the purview of a household morality that preached obedience, they often were tempted by patterns of individualism and conjugal affect found elsewhere. Yet again we perceive a situation in which the retention of palpably different cultural systems transplanted to the Middle West occurred at the same time that powerful forces prompted their modification. Indeed, the expectations of different individuals were often contradictory. Mothers, for example, like Nina's mother, voiced fears of the diffusion of new patterns of conjugal affect and intergenerational discontinuity. Wives, on the other hand, often welcomed such new patterns. One Norwegian American woman, in an illuminating inversion of immigrant men's observations, complained that "the men like to sit with their feet on the stove and watch the women work." When she quarreled with her husband, her rejoinders were ethnically defined: "The next time she married," she told him, "it would not be with a Norwegian." [106]

Whereas these sentiments illustrate the structural incongruities that created long-term challenges for the European American household system, the Yankee system also encountered complications as the region developed. In the next chapter, we will focus on those challenges for individuals within the home and their impact on the community writ large.

Clearly, the special problems of individuals at particular stages of their life course were reflections of the weaknesses within the household systems. And the solutions to many individual dilemmas in the face of external social and economic opportunities in turn often led to a diffusion of new household roles.

CHAPTER 7

Mothers and Siblings among
the Corn Rows

The Individual Life Course and
Community Development

On 7 June 1846, G. Mellberg, a Swedish immigrant, penned a simple passage in his diary. "Sunday," he wrote, "Married to Miss Juli Etta Devoe by Pastor Unonius at 3 o'clock." About a month later, he noted, "Worked on my house. Set radishes. Juli Etta moved to my place." And four days after she arrived, Mellberg recorded that "Juli Ette washes and mends."[1] These prosaic notations belie the social significance of what were momentous events for Mellberg and his new wife. The marriage formed a conjugal link that would soon contribute to the reproduction of frontier society: Juli Etta bore her first child nine months to the day after she moved in with Mellberg. From a personal perspective, the marriage was a decision that would have profound implications for the individual life courses of both Mellberg and Juli Etta. Patterns of family reproduced those of society, yet they also informed the parameters of opportunity for the individuals who lived within them.

This is not to say, however, that individuals alone charted their own futures. On the contrary, they were enmeshed in households that represented social and economic arrangements replete with inherently unequal structures of power. Whereas intrafamilial relationships were played out in myriad ways, they typically were influenced by a family morality with customary conventions concerning household roles, rights, and responsibilities. As noted in the previous chapter, moreover, the varying ethnocultures in the rural Middle West defined and were defined by cultural patterns that structured power and authority differently in the home. "American" families were often depicted, especially by European observers, as environments of unusual equality between spouses and between generations. Throughout the nineteenth century, the individual freedoms celebrated in the American political tradition were considered to be features of the American household system as well.[2] A family system that emphasized the conjugal tie and valorized the individual freedoms of its constituent members, which I have identified as the "Yankee" typology, therefore tended to be less intergenerationally oriented. Other traditions placed a greater emphasis on patrimony and on the maintenance of the lineage. These ethnocultures, typically associated with relatively recent European immigrants, were simultaneously praised for their farming accomplishments and condemned for their rigorous regimes of labor. Broadly conceived, this "European American" typology also emphasized lineal relationships that in turn tempered the relationships between husbands and wives.[3] Within the Yankee typology, the principal dyad in the home was the lateral conjugal relationship; among families that corresponded to the European American type, lineal relationships between parents (usually fathers) and children (typically sons) were most prominent.[4]

This chapter explores not so much how relationships within the home revealed the household's operation as how incongruities within the home manifested its inner tension and conflict. From this perspective, we profit from focusing on relationships outside the central dyads. In the Yankee family, the relationship between mothers and children illustrates the quandaries that women faced in nineteenth-century rural America. In European American families, we observe the different life chances enjoyed by brothers and sisters and the drama of conflict among siblings in inherently unequal homes. When we examine these tensions in two detailed case studies, we can discern critical junctures in the life course of the household during which family members were at special risk.

Just as customary household practices determined the influence of individuals within the home, the resiliency of these customs was related to how the tensions between household members, in the context of increasing alternatives, were resolved. Incongruities became especially apparent in immigrant families. The children of immigrants came of age in an era of constricted opportunity near the turn of the century when their community leaders counseled obedience while American secular society increasingly advocated individual rights and freedoms. In sum, the predicaments within European American homes manifested inherent weaknesses that not only affected individuals but ultimately served as significant vehicles for communitywide cultural diffusion and change.

Incongruities within Household Systems

While out [taking the census in rural Minnesota], we were amused at some of the facts elicited from the Norsemen. One happy looking father gave the ages of his children as "one at nine, one at eight and two months, one at seven, two at six, one at five, and two at three." — *St. Paul Daily Press*, 2 August 1870

So God created man in his own image, in the image of God he created him; male and female he created them. And God blessed them, and God said to them, "Be fruitful and multiply, and fill the earth and subdue it." — Genesis 1:27–28

Each of the two household typologies that took root in the rural Middle West contained its own internal logic. The European American pattern tended to emphasize a lineality and parental authority that encouraged those who practiced it to place great emphasis on the maintenance of the land as more than a liquid commodity. It encouraged family members to work the soil and in the best of circumstances to etch a niche for the family's descendants. Yankee behavior was more fluid and more contractual, both in family relationships and in financial arrangements. With less incentive to maintain the homestead, families could liquidate the property to benefit their constituent members. Due to contractual, less lineally oriented intrahousehold relationships, children were less beneficial materially to their parents.

The dissimilar logic that summoned varying expressions of individual affect and authority within the home is also reflected in a series of demographic measures that we can reconstruct quantitatively. The American-born, less encumbered by obligations and structural ties to the home and patrimony, tended to live in smaller and less complicated households than the foreign-born. A tedious reorganization of the 1905 Wisconsin state manuscript census by George Hill and his colleagues in 1950 enables us to compute household size by age of head and parentage for the entire state.[5] The recalculation clearly indicates the degree to which foreign-born heads presided over larger households than native-born heads. In households whose heads were native-born or of native parentage and were aged between 45 and 54, for example, over two-thirds (68 percent; N=9,114) were comprised of five or fewer members. Conversely, over one-half of those domestic groups headed by the foreign-born (54 per-

Household Size	Foreign-born	Foreign-parentage	Native-born
Heads Aged 35–44			
1	7%	9%	7%
2–3	16	21	25
4–5	27	33	34
6–7	28	24	22
8+	23	14	11
N	(22,640)	(24,211)	(10,095)
Heads Aged 45–54			
1	5	8	7
2–3	16	18	29
4–5	25	28	32
6–7	26	24	20
8+	28	23	12
N	(25,249)	(15,253)	(9,114)
Heads Aged 55–64			
1	6	10	11
2–3	32	31	46
4–5	32	29	27
6–7	18	17	10
8+	12	13	5
N	(21,348)	(3,696)	(5,760)

Source: Data reformulated from tables in George Hill Papers, State Historical Society of Wisconsin Archives, Madison, Wisconsin.

cent; N=25,249) and nearly one-half of those headed by someone born in the United States with foreign parentage (47 percent; N=15,253) contained six or more coresidents. Indeed, the latter two categories were nearly twice as likely to contain eight or more members than households headed by "Americans" or third-generation Europeans (see table 7.1).[6]

Variations in household size unquestionably influenced the social context in which people lived. Larger domestic groups found more frequently among European Americans obviously involved greater domestic and kinship complexity. Sizable sibling sets increased the intricacy of sibling relationships. The presence of the aged, reflected in three-generation

Table 7.2. Children Ever Born by Parentage in 1900
to Married Women Born 1855 or Before

	Children Ever Born				
Parentage	1–2	3–4	5–7	8+	N
"American"	14.9%	21.4%	33.6%	29.9%	107
German	6.7	9.3	20.0	64.0	75
Norwegian	6.3	15.2	34.2	44.3	79
Irish	12.4	20.9	20.0	46.7	105

Source: Fourteen-township sample from 1900 federal manuscript censuses of Dubuque County, Iowa, and Crawford and Vernon Counties, Wisconsin.

Note: Married women are included only if they bore one or more children. Background is based on place of nativity of the women's parents.

households, expanded the possibilities of cooperation and conflict between the generations. More intricate networks of kin at home and in the community that were a direct result of household arrangements of lineality and inequality, on the other hand, likely also served to further reduce the relevance of the conjugal tie.

Large households, however, not only influenced the family context but also challenged the long-term feasibility of the household systems themselves. In order to understand this predicament, we begin by examining the first proximate cause of differences in household size: varying patterns of marital fertility. An oft-stated belief in the Middle West was that those who originated in Continental Europe and the Celtic fringe maintained patterns of frequent childbearing whereas the American-born—and especially Yankees—were much quicker to initiate a sustained fertility decline. An analysis of a sample of married women in fourteen rural townships in Iowa and Wisconsin taken from the 1900 manuscript census strikingly confirms this conventional wisdom (see table 7.2).[7] Among married women born before 1855 who bore at least one child, nearly two-thirds of the women of German parentage (64.0%; N=75) mothered at least eight children. In contrast, less than one-third of the women of American birth and parentage (29.9%; N=107) bore as many babies. Norwegian and Irish women had fewer children on average than their German counterparts. The mean number of children born to rural families in six middle western states that were included in the public-use samples of the 1900 and 1910 federal censuses shows a similar pattern. Households originating in the northeastern United States had fewer children than those from Europe, and especially Germany (see table 7.3). Ethno-

Table 7.3. Differential Fertility between Immigrants and the Native-Born, 1900 and 1910

Place of Wife's Birth	Children Ever Born		
	N	Mean	*sd*
1900 census			
Mid/North Atlantic	61	4.6	3.0
Middle West	104	5.6	3.5
South	13	6.5	3.4
England/Scotland	11	7.2	3.7
Ireland	6	7.0	4.4
Scandinavia	67	6.5	3.6
Germany	70	7.0	3.3
Eastern Europe	19	7.9	3.9
1910 Census			
Mid/North Atlantic	54	5.8	3.3
Middle West	332	5.6	3.3
South	7	6.3	3.5
England/Scotland	13	4.6	3.3
Ireland	10	6.9	2.6
Scandinavia	140	6.8	3.2
Germany	148	7.5	3.3
Eastern Europe	37	8.3	3.1

Source: Public-use samples from 1900 and 1910 manuscript censuses, distributed by the Interuniversity Consortium for Political and Social Research, Ann Arbor.

Note: Data includes rural women from Iowa, Minnesota, Nebraska, North Dakota, South Dakota, and Wisconsin whose marriages were still intact at the time of the census and who had attained at least the age of 45. For the 1900 data, rural status is determined by presence in a county with no city of more than 10,000 and not adjacent to such a county. For the 1910 data, rural status is determined by residence on a farm. (This latter measure is too restrictive but necessitated by the format of the census data.) For both 1900 and 1910, the differences in children ever born between groups defined by mother's place of birth are statistically significant with at least 99% confidence.

cultural differences in marital fertility, of course, were not confined to the rural Middle West. Indeed, scholars have repeatedly and consistently discovered that upon marriage, European immigrant women in the United States—in cities and in the countryside, in the East and in the West—bore more children than their American-born counterparts.[8] Daniel Scott Smith, in contrast, has observed the "Yankee peculiarity," his term for the tendency of women of Yankee origins to initiate a fertility decline much earlier than their neighbors in the rural Middle West.[9]

The work of historians and economists provides a theoretical framework for investigating why these differences might have occurred. If children accorded their parents greater advantage, argues John Caldwell, more were likely to be born. The greater authority vested in parental roles within immigrant homes was part of that advantage. European American parents, moreover, relied on their deferential children to continue to labor on the farm. As such, the children's pecuniary contribution to the household endured as well. Since Yankee parents, on the other hand, expected less deference and prepared their children to leave home, their anticipation of financial and emotional benefits from the labor and presence of children was lower than that of their immigrant counterparts. In short, differing "wealth flows" engendered varying expectations of the benefits and constraints of childbearing.[10]

Fertility was more likely to be controlled, moreover, in domestic arrangements in which the wife's influence was greater. Because the burdens of childbearing fell disproportionately on women, they would presumably seek to reduce the number of children born. As Daniel Scott Smith and Carl Degler have contended, greater affinities between husband and wife tended to broaden the lines of communication between the conjugal pair and thus increase the influence of the wife. The European American emphasis on lineal arrangements, on the other hand, which increased not only the financial but also the emotional value of children, tended to deemphasize affect between husband and wife.[11]

Nineteenth-century diarists rarely recorded their most private thoughts about childbearing and sexual relations. Yet they did comment on the varying birth experiences of middle western women and offered opinions that tended to corroborate these theories about the utility of children. James L. Broderick, a Yorkshireman who visited the Middle West in 1877, wrote that "the Yankee ladies do not look upon it as a great misfortune to have no children, and few of them, I am told, will have more than three or four."[12] Four years earlier, Emily Hawley Gillespie, a woman of Yankee background, mused in her diary about a woman with five young children. "How thankful I am that I am not in such circumstances," she concluded. "It seems I could not endure so much trouble, Aye, the old saying is but too true,—'those capable of enduring most have most to bear.'"[13] With only two children, Gillespie made sure she did not have to "endure so much trouble."

Recalling his childhood during the same period, Herbert Quick later reflected on changing rural childbearing strategies. "A swarm of children," he wrote, "was not looked upon as a blessing in the circle [of

Yankees] into which I was born. . . . The 'Yankee women' [by which he means women of New England and New York stock] had for decades before I was born been slowly gaining a reputation for parsimony in bestowing on the world the treasures of their progeny." Quick was aware of the costs and benefits of such a course. On the one hand, "to the farmer a family of boys is an economic advantage. The land employs them. They labor without hire." Nonetheless, Quick contended, in anticipation of Smith's "domestic feminism," that "the families of farmers fell off with those of the rest of the population" due to the increasing influence of women and a new concern for the welfare of offspring. "American women," Quick argued, "had come to regard the bearing of many children as a part of the primal curse which they were, in large numbers, resolved to avoid." As a result, "their conversation among themselves, their advice to their daughters, their whole mental attitude, was against the large family. They recognized no binding force in the command, 'Multiply and replenish the earth.' They were becoming intelligent." Not only were women progressing to "avoid the physical burdens of childbearing," he concluded, but fathers and mothers alike had "an ambition to give the children 'a better chance.' "[14]

It is striking that while some "Americans" celebrated a Yankee tendency toward conjugal and affinal affect, others from ethnocultural groups that continued to exhibit patterns of high fertility derided them for their behavior. From this perspective, reduced childbearing was not a reflection of "becoming intelligent" but a sign of moral decline. An article in *Die Iowa* entitled "The Blessing of Children," for example, reported on a couple who had been married nineteen years and were the parents of twenty-four children, all of whom had been born as twins. It concluded, somewhat cryptically, that "many American women can take an example here."[15] An article in the same paper written in 1884 was more to the point. "From the State Superintendent of Schools," wrote *Die Iowa*, "it seems to be clear that Dubuque County has more children of school age than Polk County, — with good reason. Dubuque has two-thirds German, Irish, and mostly Catholic. In Polk Co., the Yankee tradition [*Yankeethum*] is more at home, and there the *American evil pervades*."[16] An example of progress for some, reduced childbearing was for others a symptom of evil, a prophesy of decline.

German American correspondents repeatedly linked high marital fertility to the presence of "real families."[17] Quick recalled an English-born neighbor who made similar assessments. He "habitually sneered at the Yankees for [their small families]," wrote Quick. " 'Give me a good old-fashioned family of ten or twelve,' he would say, 'and not a "Yankee company" of two or three!' Thus he hinted," Quick concluded, "that

the Yankees were not really married in the good old-fashioned sense." [18]
Celebrations of "old-fashioned" families and lamentations of creeping
"American evils" came from women as well as men. A Polish woman
who had lived most of her life in Wisconsin, for example, expressed pride
to a rural sociologist in the twentieth century that she had borne fourteen children. She also voiced fears about what the future might bring.
Coupling together the importance of family ties, old cultures, and large
families, she was apprehensive about the indifference of the younger generation to these values. [19] Some years earlier, a Norwegian journalist noted
that Yankees in Dane County, Wisconsin, said "the Scandinavians in this
country distinguish themselves by great fertility," an observation corroborated by differences in birth rates. "But the Germans and certainly the
Irish," the journalist continued, "do not take a back seat to anyone in this
respect. Consequently, Americans of the older generation admit that 'the
future belongs to the European immigrants of the present century.'" [20]
The hierarchical household remained for European American farm folk
a central institution that not only defined individual opportunities but
also ordered and reinforced a proper organization of society. As long as
European American families remained immersed in a system that celebrated the authority that maintained the traditional flow of wealth from
children to parents, they would continue to bear large flocks of daughters
and sons. The parameters of authority and hierarchy in the household
system reinforced decisions to maintain that very system.

Despite the inner logic that operated within households, however,
European American families were often forced to wrestle with inherent
contradictions that became increasingly apparent across the generations.
European households were larger than American households in part because of their heightened marital fertility, but they were also larger because the family typically contained older children who were awaiting
the opportunity to marry. Perhaps because marriage was controlled to a
greater degree by parents in European immigrant families, age at first
marriage among immigrants' children tended to be higher than that
of either the immigrants themselves or later generations. Quantitative
evidence repeatedly indicates differences in marriage patterns between
ethnocultural groups. The two-county sample of fourteen townships derived from the 1900 federal manuscript census illustrates the common
pattern of higher age at first marriage among those of European background. The indirect mean age at marriage for American women was
21.4 years, a figure consistently lower than that of their German, Irish,
and Norwegian counterparts. The public-use sample of the 1900 federal
census indicates a generational pattern. Although those in the immigrant
generation were able to marry at relatively young ages, the age at mar-

Table 7.4. Indirect Mean Age at Marriage for Women by Background and Generation, Two Datasets Based on 1900 Federal Census

	Indirect Mean Age	N
Three Middle Western Counties		
American background*	21.4	336
German background	23.0	206
Irish background	24.0	169
Norwegian background	24.9	154
1900 Public-Use Sample		
White native-born, native-parentage	21.8	11,436
Second generation	23.9	5,183
Foreign-born	22.0	3,606

Sources: Fourteen township sample from 1900 federal manuscript censuses of Dubuque County, Iowa and Crawford and Vernon Counties, Wisconsin; Miriam King and Steven Ruggles, "American Immigration, Fertility, and Race Suicide at the Turn of the Century," *Journal of Interdisciplinary History* 20 (1990): 358.

*Background is based on place of nativity of the women's parents.

riage of their children in both and city and countryside departed significantly from the "American" norm (see table 7.4).[21]

More important, not only did European American women on average marry later than Yankees, but they were also less likely to marry at all. Miriam King and Steven Ruggles's analysis of the 1900 manuscript census public-use sample establishes that second-generation women in their late thirties and early forties were nearly twice as likely to remain unmarried as women whose parents had been born in the United States. The proportion of second-generation women aged 35–39 who had never married was nearly twice as large (19.2 percent; N=642) as that of native-born women of native parentage (10.9 percent; N=1,797).[22] This nationwide pattern of nonmarriage among children of immigrants was even more striking in rural middle western populations. A longitudinal dataset that charts the life chances of immigrants from Luster, Norway, and their children in the late nineteenth and early twentieth centuries indicates that only 85.4 percent of the women who survived to age twenty-five married at any time in their lives. More remarkable still were the nonmarriage rates of their brothers: over one-quarter (26.3 percent) of all men who came of age remained unmarried.[23] The high rates of nonmarriage thus were due not to the lack of unmarried youths of the other sex but apparently to familial demands and a paucity resources upon which to base marriage.[24]

The family, then, remained an arena of strict individual inequality, but cultural patterns informed the parameters of the inequality. Variations in status and social class undoubtedly influenced configurations of marriage and work. Yet those families that hewed to customs that were tied to land and lineage generally demanded more of their children. Not only did children labor in the fields, but they also tended to remain at home longer working with and caring for their parents. In one Norwegian American population, one or more children continued to coreside with their parents late into their lives. Among households in which the head was over eighty years old and childbearing had been concluded for about thirty-five years, 71.4 percent still contained adult children awaiting their ascension to independence through marriage.[25] In many cases, independence would never come. Although lineally disposed households theoretically provided for the whole family, they often failed in practice to do so. They may have provided parents with greater security in their old age, but children labored amid apprehensions that their marriages would be delayed or that they would not be able to marry at all. Our consideration of tensions within European American families, then, will focus on the relationships among siblings.

Yankee families in their purest form, on the other hand, experienced fewer of these tensions. As they stressed the relevance of the conjugal tie and the tendency for intergenerational discontinuity, they vested parents with less authority over and fewer responsibilities for their children. Yet in so doing, they created for their members different challenges played out at various stages in the life cycle. Among those living within the Yankee typology, nuptial decisions were critical for two reasons. First, the fact that the decision was more firmly vested in the individual tended to result in younger ages at marriage and the potential for ill-conceived marriage decisions. Second, the emphasis on the conjugal link within the Yankee household tended to distance parents from their children and place the aged at greater risk when children left home as the intergenerational contract was replayed later in life. In the life of Emily Hawley Gillespie, we observe the isolation one woman endured as her marriage deteriorated.

Individual Life Chances within the Yankee Typology: The Emily Hawley Gillespie Story

When . . . a man always chooses a wife for himself without any external coercion or even guidance, it is generally a conformity of tastes and opinions

that brings a man and a woman together, and this same conformity keeps and fixes them in close habits of intimacy. —Alexis de Tocqueville,
Democracy in America (1835)

The contradictions within the Yankee household created interlocking challenges to the system itself and its constituent members. Due to its varying "use" of children, the Yankee household was rife with contradiction, tension, and disappointment. By bearing fewer children, Yankee mothers allegedly gave their children "a better chance," but not without household costs. The smaller labor pool within Yankee households placed them at a competitive disadvantage to their European neighbors. Immigrant homes used their large flocks of children, not to mention married women, to reduce their labor costs. These "unfair labor practices" summoned occasional complaints from the native-born.[26] Perhaps not coincidentally, they also contributed to the fact that there came to be fewer American farmers.

More important for our present purposes, the individualism of the American home and the importance of the conjugal tie also created pressing challenges for women at specific points in their life course. Here in capsule was the encounter with courtship and marriage that lacked "external coercion or even guidance" observed by Alexis de Tocqueville already in the 1830s.[27] Yankee youths who were able to marry earlier and with greater frequency, according to Horace Miner, were "oriented toward economic independence and separation from the family." Yet freedoms accorded to children to separate from the family entailed risks if the love that cemented their marriages eroded.[28] A cultural pattern that enabled a greater proportion of Yankee women and men to marry made the decision concerning whom to marry all the more important.

It is true that Americans celebrated the companionship that fostered stable relationships, especially when compared with European wives, who reputedly suffered from a lack of marital affect. It is also true that life-long friendships developed between spouses. "I am just as happy as I can be," wrote a newlywed to his brother in New York in 1877. "I neaver [*sic*] thought there was half so much comfort in a wife. I tell you Charley, its nice to know that you have some one to help bear your troubles."[29] A young woman agreed. "O Aunt," wrote Maria Freeland from New York, "I wish you knew him he is one of the best men he is not pretty at all but homely people are always the best you know I did not know as there was so much goodness in him (or in a man) until after I had married him."[30]

Individual freedoms that could inspire true love could also place individuals at risk later in their lives. People who based their marriage on "romantic" love faced hazards when affection between husband and wife deteriorated or when their "conformity of tastes and opinions," as Tocqueville described them, began to fragment.[31] Nineteenth-century newspapers were replete with accounts of domestic violence that underscore the gravity of the marital decision.[32] The American response to these horrors varied. To counteract violence and inequality, Yankee feminists increasingly advocated state intervention in household affairs as a means of providing support and succor for the household's constituent elements. Women sought collective female "bonds" that lay outside the home. Couples also turned increasingly to divorce.[33] Within the home, mothers often redirected their love toward their children and away from their husbands, with whom their lives had gone awry.

Although it was logical that Yankee women would choose to focus on nurturing their children, by doing so they entered into relationships whose fluidity became apparent when their children began to leave home. Armed with a cultural prerogative to marry and depart, children could make individual decisions that could place their parents in jeopardy. When offspring married, not only did parents confront questions about the emotional and economic security of their children, but more immediately they were forced to consider their own old-age support. They encountered these uncertainties during a period when intellectual shifts among youth featured a decreased sense of responsibility for their parents.[34] Women, who often found greater support from their children than their husbands, simultaneously validated and feared their children's departure. It is no accident that the common characterizations of the West juxtaposed the promise of opportunity with the image of the forlorn farm mother.

For those whose marital and economic endeavors were successful, the attenuated years could be comfortable. Adult children often did not play central roles in aging parents' lives. Miner argued, for example, that not only were Yankee farm children oriented toward independence, but their parents did "not want many children and [were] looking toward eventual retirement."[35] Retired Yankees tended to dispose of their property and move out of farming. With the capital they gained from the sale of their increasingly valuable lands, they often moved to town. Since they typically had fewer children to endow, parents were better able to grant them the means to establish their future. As strong advocates of higher education in the rural milieu, many American parents hoped to equip their children with skills upon which to establish themselves. In so doing, they assured that their children would be likely to leave their parental homes, not to mention their communities. The process was circular and

reinforcing. Their transfer of real property into liquid capital and investments eased the move away from the farm. Their emphasis on education
encouraged their children to leave the home.[36]

Although it was an expected transition in the life course, the dissolution
of the estate could dishearten the aged. After Sarah Browne Adamson
and her husband settled their estate with their son in the mid-nineteenth
century, she wrote, "This day closes our living at my Benjn's Table and
we are now at the age of 71 and 60 and have to provide for ourselves. Oh
what a disappointment to me."[37] The separation could also be daunting.
An elderly woman in a fictional account by Hamlin Garland recalled
raising children, "though I am all alone now." Her afterthought, "It's
lucky we keep our health," betrays a fear that infirmity would worsen
her solitude.[38] The separation between aged parents and adult children
of course was not irrevocable. Adamson herself, like many other parents, moved in with her children, encouraging a pattern in which nuclear
families were augmented by a single aged co-occupant, which became
increasingly common in the late nineteenth century.[39] An apparent solution to the infirmities of the aged, the arrangement nonetheless reflected
the individualism of children and the lack of authority vested in the older
generation.[40] Unable or unwilling to keep children at home, Yankee parents' intergenerational contracts with their children were not as advantageous for them as they had been some generations before.

The quandaries that Yankee mothers faced with respect to their children are no better illustrated than in the life of Emily Hawley Gillespie,
whose remarkable diary we have encountered in past chapters.[41] Span-
ning over thirty years, Gillespie's notations recount an unhappy life replete with intergenerational tension and a sorrowful marriage. Although
it contains examples of intergenerational reciprocity, the diary also repeatedly portrays the lines of cleavage between parents and children.

Emily Hawley was married on 18 September 1862 to James Gillespie.
After spending the wedding night with his new bride, James returned to
his parents' home the next morning to begin the protracted process of
dividing his former family from his new one. The young couple were reunited two weeks later when Emily moved in with James's family. Emily
and her husband took pains to separate themselves literally and figuratively from his parents. Within a month of her arrival, they had parti-
tioned off a few rooms to create a private living space.[42] James's mother
showed a greater willingness than his father to recognize the young
couple's independence and aid in the separation. In December 1862, over
the objections of her husband, she gave her son the deed to a farm that
she had held by "right of dower" in payment for his wages since he had
come of age.[43] After Emily became pregnant the following year, she and

her husband stepped up their efforts to form an independent household, an effort that entailed heavy psychological costs. As a result of the unending conflict with his parents, James became ill. The older couple, Emily wrote in mid-1863, "have harped & bothered him ever since they gave him the Deed for his farm. they seem to think he ought to give it back or pay them something." Yet the father remained intransigent: he continued to expect the labor of his son as he attempted to block the young family's efforts to move out of the home. Tension within the household became so bitter that the old man showed no interest in seeing his newborn grandson. Finally, when the child was two months old, Emily wrote that "Ma [James's mother] came in got Baby and carried him in the other room. I guess to let James' father see him[.] would I live in a house with a grandchild for eight weeks and not go in to see him?" she asked rhetorically. "I think not!"[44]

The tension ultimately was resolved in typical Yankee fashion. The young couple soon irrevocably moved from the parental household to begin their new life.[45] But patterns had been set. Despite an early period of contentment, James remained emotionally unstable throughout his life, suffering bouts of depression and occasional fits of rage. More important for our purposes, he replicated the behavior of his father in intergenerational transactions between himself and his children. In many ways, moreover, Emily, in her greater solicitousness toward her children, came to resemble her mother-in-law. The emotional instability of both husband and wife diminished the intimacy of the important conjugal link. One telling example suffices. One dark night, after years of discord, Emily and James were "coming home through a brushy dismal place and talking . . . when to my very unpleasant surprise he said '*Emily* I believe you mean to kill me sometime. I want you to tell me if you do. I want to meet God prepared.'" Aghast, Emily attempted to assuage his fears. Her conclusion was not surprising: "I *was very thankful* when we arrived *safe* home," she wrote. "It seemed like riding with a maniac in a *dark dark* night alone."[46]

As the couple's relationship continued to deteriorate, James became increasingly isolated emotionally from his wife and children. Meanwhile, Emily chose to devote herself to her offspring. As early as 1872, she sublimated her own disappointments in concern about her children's well-being. Upset that James would not allow her to attend the fair, she mused in verse:

> When a man *wont*
> A woman can not
> We must try to not despair
> Our little children yet need care,

May God be with us every day,
To guide us safely through
And help us to endure
The trifles which crowd their way.[47]

The leitmotifs of beleaguered wife and loving mother were again expressed five years later. After noting that a woman from a nearby farm was taken to an insane asylum, she wrote, "I only wonder that more women do not have to be taken to that asylum, especially farmers wives." "Their only happiness," she concluded, "lies in their children. with fond hopes that *they* may rise higher, that *they* perhaps may be an ornament to society."[48] Again prevented from attending a public event—this time a speech by Susan B. Anthony—she felt "almost a hermit" and resented not "being any higher in society than merely to be always at home." But again, she concludes, "I must *not* give up *no, no*, my children are too noble. I must use every effort to help them to be, what I might have been, tis my only pleasure to see them happy."[49]

Emily encountered what must have been a relatively common dilemma for American mothers. Her ebbing conjugal love was supplanted by a concern for her children. But by attaching great hopes to the success of her children, she faced the likelihood that they would be forced to leave her to be successful. After one of her husband's tantrums, Emily penned an extended passage about her hopes for her children. "He does not want the Children to go to school," she began.

> Thinks there is no need of it—but wants them to stay at home & work—tis well for all to work—yet it seems to me we are placed here on this earth, for something higher than merely to use our hands, toil and toil—merely to eat, and die in debt to our brains—to hoard up money—he does not like me to raise turkeys because I use the money they bring to send the Children to school. I *do pray* that I may *know* and *do right*. they love to go to school—with God's help I will try to educate them that they may through life have the advantage of a good education, with their noble hearts, their virtue and industrious habits.[50]

But acquiring good educations was the first step in the process of leaving home, which would leave Emily lonely. Emily's ambivalence is palpable in a diary passage written on the eve of her only daughter's departure for normal school. "I do hope she will enjoy going to the Normal & that she will get a certificate," Emily wrote, "because she would be disappointed if not." Nonetheless, Emily observed, "I would so like for her to stay at home with me, yet if she wants to teach, I am willing & wish her the best success." Then, with greater resolve, she declared, "No no I would not keep my children at home away from doing what is right & best for them to do, though I am so lonely without them. yes I will help them all I can." [51]

The frequent absences of her children only underscored her ambivalent sense of loss and pride in the accomplishments of her offspring. "Henry and Sarah are gone," Emily wrote in 1885. "I am in thought with them each day and night." [52] Again, she noted, "*O how* lonesome when Henry and Sarah are both gone, it is all right however and when I know they are doing well it makes me happy." [53] A few months later, when her children were again absent, she wrote, "Were it not for my journal, I feel so lonely that I could not endure the quietude, no cheery words are spoken." [54]

Gillespie's tragic life was only one example among the millions lived in the rural Middle West, but her experience is an exception that proves the rule. Amid conjugal conflict, Emily took increasing pride in her children, whereas her husband found little joy in them. Yet Emily's attempts to foster lineal ties were frustrated by her expectations that her children had the right to leave and chart their own lives. It was her husband—less solicitous of his offspring—who demanded that the children remain at home to labor on the farm. [55] Clearly, not all American households were so rife with conflict, and few were so tragic. But in Emily's case, greater freedoms for her children created greater possible challenges for herself.

Individual Life Chances within the European American Typology: Two Norwegian Immigrant Communities

The country around the Monastery was settled by Irish immigrants. Most of them married young and had large families but the majority of the next generation did not marry or married too late in life to raise a family.
—Joseph Edwin McGovern, *As I Recall* (n.d.)

European American families also faced challenges that channeled individual life chances within the home. Since European American households were typically larger than those of Yankees, the internal dynamics within them were more complex, involving more people and thus more cleavages of power. Larger families broadened a crucial dilemma encountered by farm families in the rural Middle West: how could the present needs of the household be balanced with the future of the children? As part of a corporate endeavor, sons and daughters hoped to work and build up a family patrimony from which they would profit when they came of age. From this perspective, children were a boon to the home. High rates of marital fertility among European immigrants, when compared with those of Americans, must have been due to the perception that a large number of children accorded benefits to the family enterprise and the parents.

The social security provided to parents by children was reciprocated when children were bequeathed an abundant future. Recalling a particularly prolific German family, Quick noted that "if babies had been treated as are motor-cars now, [a German couple] would have been obliged to get one more set of license plates every year as long as I knew them. There was a new pupil in school every year from that family." At least in this case, Quick admitted, through hard work, the strategy had paid dividends. Sons were each given a quarter section of land upon coming of age; daughters received $1,000 as a wedding present. As the patriarch observed, he had "done pretty goot." [56]

Yet many children within the typically larger immigrant farm households were not so fortunate. In a sense, they were victims of a demographic disequilibrium stemming from economic abundance in the West. Western European societies traditionally had curbed population growth by limiting marriage opportunities. [57] When marriage was delayed—or if it did not occur at all—the period during which women were at risk to bear children was reduced. The custom also had a homeostatic function: better times resulted in younger brides, higher rates of marriage, and the birth of more children. When this system was transplanted to the Middle West, marital checks were drastically weakened and marital fertility reached high levels, particularly in the early years of settlement when land, the economic basis needed to form a family, was easily found. Large numbers of children were desirable because they increased the family labor pool. Each child in large sibling sets, however, was more likely to receive a limited inheritance, all other things being equal, when he or she grew to adulthood. Ironically, a system that granted primacy to lineal arrangements between generations created systematic hindrances to the future of children.

The European immigrant families used a group of strategies, which were often culturally informed, to address the trade-offs between children as labor and children as inheritors. One strategy that tempered the tensions arising from inequality simply was to engross land and provide for offspring so that parents and children could indeed do "pretty goot." Immigrant farmers, particularly those from regions of Europe where partible inheritance had been practiced, attempted to settle more than one child on farms surrounding the original homestead. This strategy, based on a lineal orientation of the family, was aimed at providing resources to all children under the aegis of the older generation. And communities based on this system, because all children were ideally under the control of a network of authority, were more successful in tempering outside influences. Dreams of extending the patrimony nonetheless inevitably confronted the realities of a finite land base. Families that divided the estate would bequeath small tracts of land unless the patrimony could be enlarged. This was the goal of farmers in a land-rich environment. And the engrossed land testified to their degree of success.[58]

A second strategy, inherently unequal in intent and outcome, was the stem-household pattern, in which all or most of the real property was bequeathed to a single heir who would in turn give his parents the necessary support as they aged and compensate his siblings with cash as they left home. This practice, which was common in broad regions of Europe, tied the family line to property so that the parental couple, the heir, and the heir's wife and children lived together under one roof when the heir came of age.[59] Much more than an informal arrangement, moreover, stem households in Europe had explicit institutional frameworks.[60] Formal legal contracts were written that transferred estates to heirs in exchange for precisely defined care and sustenance of the aged. Known as the *kår* and *undantag* in Scandinavia and the *Altenteil, Ausgedinge,* and *Auszug* in Germanic regions, this system symbolized lineality and exclusivity. The sole heir from birth was set apart from his siblings as he matured and married. To be sure, the heir typically paid for the estate, and his siblings were provided a share of the estate's value. Yet nonheirs were forced to find a mate who was landed if they hoped to remain propertied in land-poor societies. Not surprisingly, emigration to the United States and elsewhere was common from regions in which this system was practiced.

Communities that transplanted stem-household traditions in the Middle West provide exemplary contexts in which to explore relationships within homes and the life chances of individuals living within them. Stamped by their inequality, stem families offer a fascinating arena for viewing the diffusion of individualist ethics into the corporate home. In principle, the lineal orientation of this system gave prominence to the well-being of the corporate household group rather than the prospects of its individual members. Yet in practice, the household system institutionalized advantages for specific household members. Parents, and especially fathers as current holders of the patrimony, maintained power and demanded respect. And by maintaining their capital as property, they tied the future prospects of their children to the success of the farm. As a result, parents retained the upper hand in the intergenerational bargain even as they strove to amass resources that would provide for their children. The children, in turn, were forced to remain within the purview of the household and measure their future possibilities according to the property accumulations of the domestic group.[61] In this strictly unequal milieu, the heir's siblings were expected to work for the family as youths and fend for themselves as adults with the wealth given them by their parents. In this way, upward wealth flows continued in the form of labor and deference provided by all of the children, and old-age care was maintained by the heir. As long as children accepted this inherent inequality, the tension within lineal families and corporate arrangements was tempered. But tensions resulting from these norms were likely, especially in an American context that stressed individual rights.

A considerable body of evidence suggests that stem-household arrangements were transplanted from Europe to the rural Middle West. Farm families in communities that originated in European stem-household regions continued to be complex domestic arrangements in comparison with norms in the United States.[62] Farmsteads could contain two dwellings, one of which was outfitted for the grandmother — "a little home of her own," remembered a Wisconsin farmer, similar to the *kårstue*, or pensioner's cottage, in Norway.[63] In other cases, the retiree's living space was attached. An adult respondent in 1949 remembered that in his childhood his grandfather had a "room in the back of the house" where he would go "almost every evening" to hear tales about Norway.[64]

The existence of complex household structures, of course, did not mean that an explicit contractual framework binding the generations to each other existed as well. Clearly, common legal customs in the United States did not, as in regions of Europe, inextricably connect estate transfer to explicit intergenerational contracts. Nonetheless, legal and customary arrangements that resembled retirement contracts have been discovered in various European American communities. These systems relied on a series of *inter vivos* transfers of property and responsibility. The most remarkable arrangement was the "bond of maintenance" contract, which, like contracts in Europe, tied property transfer to the care of the aged.[65] One "bond of maintenance" cited by Carl F. Wehrwein in his study of German American inheritance patterns required the younger couple to furnish strictly enumerated goods and a clearly defined living space to the son's parents. The older couple, according to the contract, "reserve for themselves the south half of the dwelling house now situated on the said premises, the said south half including cellar room, two rooms on the first floor and two rooms on the second floor." If that portion of the house was destroyed, the contract required that it be replaced.[66] The incidence of "bonds of maintenance" contracts was widespread in European American communities. Wehrwein discovered 108 registered bonds of maintenance between 1870 and 1899 at the Register of Deeds in one Wisconsin township alone. Kenneth H. Parsons and Eliot O. Waples observed that about one-fifth of the farms in a section of eastern Wisconsin under study used bonds of maintenance.[67]

Bonds of maintenance contracts were complemented by other methods of tying together the farming generations. Kin tenancy, for example, was especially common in a European region of central Iowa by the early twentieth century. In this arrangement, parents rented their land to a child who farmed it on a share basis. The system provided the requisite financial security for the child as he proved his abilities to his parents, who in turn were concerned both about their own immediate well-being and the future prospects of the land and the lineage.[68] Although the actual legal transfer of property ultimately occurred later in the household life course in this system than in stem households, the understanding existed that the transfer would eventually occur.

It must be stressed that testacy remained the most common means of transferring property in the Middle West. Nonetheless, *inter vivos* transfers were frequent in European American communities typified by linearity. And although the incidence of bonds of maintenance contracts declined over time, they were still used in the twentieth century. As late as 1947, a respondent in a western Wisconsin Norwegian community recalled a system of inheritance that closely paralleled patterns of estate transfer in Norway. "When the son took over the farm," he said, "he managed to buy it and pay his co-inheritors. A contract was often set up with the parents in which they were permitted to live on the farm for their lifetime and get so much potatoes, corn, and other goods in addition to money." The system, he concluded, had become less common by the mid-twentieth century due to intermarriages, but it had been widely practiced earlier among Germans and Bohemians as well as Norwegians.[69]

The stem-household customs that were carried westward affected not only the destinies of families within the context of the community but also the life chances of individuals enmeshed within their household nets. I have reconstructed the demographic history of two settlement areas that originated from a stem-household region in Norway that clearly indicates the structural inequalities faced by children, defined by varying orders of birth and sex.[70] It should not be forgotten that the most critical stages in the life cycle of those living in stem households occurred during youth. A most crucial question was not whom to marry but whether marriage would occur at all. Recall that married life was a condition that was denied to a significant segment of European American society. The chance to marry, moreover, was of great importance because only individuals with children were to be able to benefit from advantageous intergenera-

Table 7.5. Marriage Prospects for Sons and Daughters by Birth Order, Children of Luster Immigrants

Birth Order	Ever Married	Mean Age	N	Age at Father's Death	Age of Father at Marriage	Father Alive at Marriage
Sons						
1	81.1%	29.4	201	40.2	61.2	77.5%
2	71.3	28.1	171	38.9	60.7	83.4
3	68.4	27.7	171	36.4	62.4	79.4
4	69.4	29.1	144	35.0	65.1	76.1
5	76.0	29.2	104	33.7	67.7	77.1
6	74.3	28.3	350	30.7	71.3	77.6
Daughters						
1	92.3	23.8	155	41.1	54.5	84.2
2	82.6	23.7	144	38.0	56.9	82.5
3	83.9	24.5	118	37.3	59.1	81.1
4	88.6	23.9	105	35.5	60.4	83.5
5	85.9	23.9	99	34.5	62.1	82.5
6	82.1	24.5	263	30.8	67.8	76.3

Source: Luster, Norway, genealogy dataset.

Note: The percentage of children ever married is based only on those who survived to the age of 25. The mean age of the child at his or her father's death and the mean age of the father at the date of the marriage are both based on what the ages would have been if all parties were still living at each of those events. Thus, the figure captures the real age spread that existed between children and their fathers without being distorted by cases of premature death. The percentage of fathers still alive at the time of their children's marriages is noted separately.

tional relationships later in their lives. In stem households, therefore, the relationship between the parents and the principal heir, although it was not without conflict, was focused primarily on the timing of the transfer. The point of transfer, in turn, was often connected to the point at which the marriage of the heir was to occur. Unlike the heir, the remaining siblings were forced to etch out their niches more independently. Whereas the parent-heir dyad was one of stability, then, the relationship between siblings was one of tension and flux.

The data reveal structural inequalities between siblings on many levels. Disparities were manifested in patterns of the timing of and possibilities for marriage among rural children according to birth order and gender (see table 7.5). In the first place, children of both sexes were more likely to marry if they were the first child born to a couple. Among first-born sons who survived to age twenty-five, 81.1 percent wed. In contrast, marriage percentages for males who survived to adulthood declined in the second through fourth birth orders to a low of 68.4 percent for the third-born boy. The likelihood of marriage then increased among sons in later birth orders. The daughters' pattern mirrored that of their brothers. More than nine out of ten first-born girls who survived to age twenty-five married. The proportion declined for daughters in the second and third birth orders and increased again among later-born girls. Although the trend lines of chances to marry by birth order were similar for both sexes, the absolute differences between them are noteworthy. Girls, who remained unmarried at greater rates than boys in Norway, were noticeably more likely to become married in rural America.

The analogous birth order trends for both sons and daughters were probably the result of differential opportunities inherent in the household when they came of age. The first-born were accorded advantages through the family patrimony that made marriage more likely. The fifth-born or beyond married in relatively large proportions because their contributions were less essential to the future of the household. Coming of age after many parental concerns had been resolved, they were accorded greater latitude. It was the children in the second, third, and fourth birth orders, babies delivered five to ten years after their parents' marriage, who faced the greatest risks. Lacking the cultural importance of the first-born and maturing when their family's future was challenged, they seemed to suffer the worst of both worlds.[71]

These patterns of inequality were further modulated by the level of economic opportunity imposed by conditions on and off the farm over the course of the late nineteenth century. Based on economic prospects, a three-phase evolution of family life and individual opportunity unfolded.[72] In the first phase, roughly encompassing the three decades after 1840, the availability of land challenged the household system and distorted former restrictions on marital fertility. Although the cultural system of family responsibilities transplanted to the West in principle demanded a sublimation of individual interests to the well-being of the corporate unit, economic opportunities outside the home during the first decades of settlement tended to undermine the system. Perceptions and celebrations of an open economic environment compromised the expected privileges within the family. In part because of these expectations and in part because the age structures of communities were truncated in their earliest stages of settlement, household structures in immigrant communities tended to be simpler than those left behind in Europe. Six-sevenths

(85.5 percent; N=179) of the families in the immigrant communities were nuclear in composition in 1860.[73] First-born children perhaps continued to enjoy an institutionally secure position on the farm, but they no longer were assured of an advantageous status in relation to their siblings.

Many children were born into these families. The total marital fertility rate (TMFR) of 11.8 for women in the two populations between 1840 and 1869 approached the biological maximum observed for human populations.[74] The women, who bore their last child on average at age 41.7, tended to marry earlier—and begin bearing children earlier—than in Europe. On average, 6.4 children were born to each family, a fertility that satisfied the needs for labor but would strain the resources accorded children when they came of age.

In the second phase, lasting roughly between 1870 and 1890, Norwegian cultural practices, such as stem-household structures, were rekindled in these immigrant communities. By 1880, one-seventh of all households (14.3 percent; N=294) in the Norway Grove/Spring Prairie, Wisconsin, dataset had at least two married couples from different generations co-residing. These stem households were augmented by an additional 8.2 percent of the sample households that were extended by single parents. The existence of this household complexity is made more significant by the fact that a larger percentage of the population lived in stem households in the immigrant settlements in 1880 than in the old country.[75]

Changing household structures reflected the tensions between opportunity outside the home and obligations within it. Children's decisions to remain in the parental home presumably were based on a resolution of conflict between household needs and responsibilities and perceptions of individual opportunities elsewhere. For many reasons, sons by 1880 were likely to remain at home for longer periods than their sisters. As European American women reduced their field labor in the late nineteenth century, their importance to the operation of the farm decreased. Given the patrilineal bias of property descent, boys typically had a greater proprietary interest in the farm than their sisters. Indeed, in the classic stem household, the heir never left. Available data indicate that sons did remain at home longer than daughters.[76] In 1880, for example, nearly half of the women aged 17 to 24 were away from home compared to slightly over one-third of the boys (see table 7.6). After age 25, boys were increasingly likely to begin the exodus from the home. Yet decisions concerning whether to remain or leave were also influenced by birth order. And again countervailing patterns are discernible. First-born girls were likely to leave home at an earlier age than sisters born after them. In contrast, later-born boys tended to move out of the home earlier. In 1880, at least,

Table 7.6. Proportions at Home by Age, Birth Order, and Sex,
Two Norwegian American Populations, 1880

	Men			Women		
Birth Order	At home	Not at home	N	At home	Not at home	N
Aged 17–24						
1	85.7%	14.3%	14	33.3%	66.7%	18
2	63.6	36.4	22	58.8	41.2	17
3	63.2	36.8	19	53.8	46.2	26
4 or higher	67.0	33.0	100	58.6	41.4	104
Total	67.7	32.3	155	55.2	44.8	165
Aged 25 or Higher						
1	21.3	78.7	47	13.1	86.7	38
2	23.5	76.5	34	16.7	83.3	36
3	21.9	78.1	32	19.0	88.0	21
4 or higher	18.4	81.6	38	28.9	71.1	45
Total	21.2	78.8	151	20.0	80.0	140

Sources: Luster, Norway, genealogy dataset; Norway Grove/Spring Prairie,
Wisconsin, family reconstitution dataset.

care for aging parents fell disproportionately on first-born boys and their
younger sisters.[77]

The formal structure of these Norwegian American families, in short,
implied prescribed expectations, rights, and obligations for youths who
lived within them. Yet despite the increased incidence of stem households, the patterning of life chances among children around 1880 seemed
to be undergoing a process of reformulation. First-born boys still accrued
advantages such as greater likelihood of marriage. Yet it appears that the
exclusive rights of the first-born as probable heirs was beginning to wane.
First-born sons over age 25 were slightly more likely in 1880 to reside in
their parents' homes than their younger brothers who were also 25 years
or older, but they were much less likely to do so than their counterparts
in Norway.[78] Their sisters, on the other hand, continued to follow the
centuries-old pattern of leaving home. Yet first-born daughters, leaving
home in a more abundant American environment, enjoyed more options
than girls in the past. Their life courses in many ways reflected these options.[79]

Table 7.7. Age at First Marriage over Time,
Two Middle Western Samples, 1830–1899

| | Two Norwegian Datasets | | | | Fourteen-Township Sample* | |
| | Men | | Women | | Women | |
Date of Marriage	Age	N	Age	N	Age	N
1830–39	24.9	2	21.6	2	—	—
1840–49	27.6	20	25.4	15	—	—
1850–59	27.1	181	25.3	192	—	—
1860–69	27.4	145	23.9	148	21.4	213
1870–79	26.8	193	23.9	193	22.3	233
1880–89	28.7	155	25.5	159	23.7	176
1890–99	28.5	178	24.7	177	23.7	345

Sources: Luster, Norway, geneology dataset; Norway Grove/Spring Prairie, Wisconsin, family reconstitution dataset; fourteen-township sample from 1900 federal manuscript censuses of Dubuque County, Iowa and Crawford and Vernon Counties, Wisconsin.

*Indirect mean age of marriage. The fourteen-township sample was designed to measure marriage age of women only.

The third moment in household development occurred in the two decades straddling the turn of the century. In this phase, clues of a quickening cultural diffusion were coupled with the reality of daunting economic challenges for youths. After 1890, the large numbers of children in immigrant families faced increasing difficulties in finding opportunities in rural society. The value of land spiraled upward, especially after 1890. After having remained stable for thirty years, land prices tripled in Vernon and Crawford Counties, the home of most Luster immigrant families, between 1890 and 1910 and increased by roughly 250 percent in the area around Norway Grove.[80] It was in this period that the intergenerational arrangements between parents and their heirs should have become more fixed while the obligations between parents and other children grew more difficult to fulfill. In reality, only the latter occurred: mounting land prices placed increasing burdens on children, as the incidence of stem households—as well as other household customs carried from Norway—began to wane.

The constraints faced by farm youths of European background in the late nineteenth century are repeatedly reflected in demographic measures. Age at first marriage, for example, increased, while frequency of marriage declined. In a sample of households in Dubuque County, Iowa, and Crawford and Vernon Counties, Wisconsin, the mean age at marriage for all women increased from 21.4 years among those married before 1871 to 23.7 years in the decade of the 1890s (see table 7.7). Youths in the Norway Grove settlement region also tended to marry later, especially after 1880. Age at first marriage for men rose on average to well over 28 years between 1880 and the turn of the century. Although the increase for women was less steady over time, women nonetheless were marrying on average well into their twenties between 1880 and 1900.[81]

More significantly than increased ages at marriage were decreased likelihoods that marriage would occur at all, at least for men. Among women in the Luster sample who survived to a marrying age, the percentages of women ever wed remained steady at around 85 percent (see table 7.8).[82] Boys typically were less likely to marry than their sisters in all time periods, but the prospect decreased especially among youths coming of age in the late nineteenth century. Only 71.6 percent of those born between 1861 and 1880, and thus reaching a marrying age between 1886 and 1905, ever married. Garrison Keillor's Norwegian bachelor farmers thus have a basis in fact.[83]

As fewer youths married, more remained in the parental homes for longer durations. In the two samples, for example, over two-fifths of all first-born sons over age 25 remained at home in 1900, nearly twice the percentage of their counterparts who were at home in 1880 (see table 7.9). These sons perhaps stood to inherit the farm, but their brothers did not, and they too were more likely to still be at home in 1900. Girls aged 17 to 24 in 1900, especially first-born girls, had moved from their parents' homes in strikingly fewer numbers than daughters of similar ages in 1880.[84] In sum, children's, and especially boys', ascensions to landholding, to marriage, and indeed to "adulthood" remained in doubt for longer periods of their lives at the turn of the century.

The personal challenges borne out of constrained external conditions certainly exacerbated tensions stemming from an inequality inherent in the European household. Because of their perception that fewer opportunities existed, children remained under the purview of their parents longer into their lives. As property at home increased in value, the meaning and timing of the property transfer grew and the prerogative of the heir to the property increased vis-à-vis his or her siblings. As agricultural resources were increasingly constrained and children's independence was delayed, conflict between parent and child and brother and sister was likely to increase. These individual inequalities ultimately created challenges for families and the community as a whole. The larger number of children who did not marry increased the likelihood that many would

Table 7.8. Marriage Prospects for Second-Generation Youth Based on Descendants of Immigrants from Luster, Norway

Proportion Ever Married by Birth Cohort
and Sex of Those Who Survived to Age 25

	Male		Female	
Birth Cohort	%	N	%	N
Before 1860	82.5	120	84.8	92
1861–1880	71.6	482	85.7	398[a]
1881–1900	74.4	395[b]	84.3	319
1901–1920	70.3	128	88.9	72
Total	73.7	1,141	85.4	884

Characteristics of Sample Data

	Male	Female
Total children in data	1,893	1,824
N who died before age 25	241	209
% of those who died before age 25 who married	2.5	6.2
N with unknown age at death	489	725
% of those with unknown age at death who married	58.9	73.9

Source: Luster, Norway, genealogy dataset.
a. Of these, the marital status of one observation was unknown.
b. Of these, the marital status of two observations was unknown.

leave the vicinity. Those who remained within the community and were forced to accommodate cultural patterns of family and worsening economic realities, on the other hand, faced increasing individual tensions.

Narrative and quantitative sources alike suggest that old structures of family underwent a process of profound change stemming from these challenges. As familial practices were transplanted imperfectly in a new milieu, they created pressures that fostered discontent, which in turn weakened traditional arrangements within the home. Quick was well aware of the difficulties that farm parents faced. From their point of view, a family strategy that utilized child labor to build up "a sheet anchor of property . . . to hold the family to the farm" ironically generated "a wind of discontent that would eventually sweep [children] from their moorings."[85] With less hope of independence near home, children fled when

THE FAMILY

Table 7.9. Proportions at Home by Age, Birth Order, and Sex,
Two Norwegian American Populations, 1900

Birth Order	Men			Women		
	At Home	Not at Home	N	At Home	Not at Home	N
Aged 17–24						
1	82.6%	17.4%	23	72.4%	27.6%	29
2	80.0	20.0	30	66.7	33.3	18
3	70.0	30.0	20	95.0	5.0	20
4 or higher	71.1	28.9	83	63.5	36.5	96
Total	74.4	25.6	156	69.3	30.7	163
Aged 25 or Higher						
1	42.8	57.2	56	17.5	82.5	57
2	32.7	67.3	55	32.6	67.4	43
3	28.9	71.1	38	9.7	90.3	41
4 or higher	27.8	72.2	158	24.6	75.4	130
Total	31.6	68.4	307	22.1	77.9	271

Sources: Luster, Norway, dataset; Norway Grove/Spring Prairie, Wisconsin, family reconstitution dataset.

opportunities presented themselves. Retired farmers, as a result, spent their time "talking about the ungratefulness of sons and the worthlessness of hobo help."[86]

In these Norwegian households, however, resentful sons and daughters were probably more common than disappointed parents. And resentment that resulted from a crystallization of old European patterns also engendered dissatisfactions that could foster change, even within those European homes. Those who felt disadvantaged by their position were encouraged to seek new avenues and to adopt new patterns of behavior. In earlier decades, youths had been more likely to leave home. Now the winds of discontent that swirled around households that operated under what Quick called "hardscrabble logic" were exacerbated by the diffusion of unfamiliar behavior among those who remained.

As life chances hardened in these communities, household structures as well as expectations of responsibility and rights within the home began to soften. Although children coresided longer with their parents, they lived as unmarried adults in families that increasingly failed to conform

Table 7.10. Households Augmented with Parents by Parent-Child Relationship of Male Household Head, Norwegian and Norwegian American Populations

Relationship	Norwegian		Norwegian American	
	N	%	N	%
Father	27	37.0	14	14.7
Father-in-law	5	6.8	9	9.5
Mother	34	46.6	29	30.5
Mother-in-law	7	9.6	43	45.3
Total	73	100.0	95	100.0

Source: Balestrand, Norway, 1865 manuscript census; federal manuscript censuses, Dane County, Wisconsin, 1860–1910.

to stem-household structures. Instead, households in the rural Norwegian communities in the sample tended to consist of nuclear families augmented by single kin. Only 7.2 percent of households in 1900 and 1910 consisted of two or more married couples of different generations.[87] Especially after the second generation came of age, the simple family system with the notable presence of extended families became increasingly common. Similar to a pattern that characterized the Anglo-American household, many parents now joined the young families of their children rather than remaining at home.[88]

This declining exclusivity was coupled with a greater malleability with regard to the performance of household responsibilities. Care for the aged, for example, took on both a matrilineal *and* a patrilineal orientation (see table 7.10). In Balestrand, Norway—the root parish of many of the Norwegian American households examined—44 percent (N=73) of parents living with their children in 1865 were fathers. In contrast, mothers in their children's home comprised 76 percent (N=95) of the parental extensions among Norwegian Americans in the United States between 1860 and 1910. Even more significantly, mothers-in-law of the household head became the dominant parental type in extended households in the United States. Parental care was a patrilineal responsibility in Norway, a responsibility clearly tied to the stem family, retirement contracts, and estate transfers. Among immigrants in the United States, care of aged parents eventually became the charge of either sons or daughters. And it is meaningful that daughters increasingly accepted the responsibility and that wives possessed the prerogative to bring their mothers into the household.[89]

Not only did daughters increasingly bring their mothers into their homes, but mothers, using once unfamiliar dictates of law, were increasingly able to control resources. Aging women, for example, tended to remain unmarried and retain power upon widowhood in the Norway Grove community. By 1910, 8.5 percent of all households in the population consisted of widows and their children compared to only 3.5 percent that comprised widowers with children.[90] This variance, due in part to differential mortality between men and women, reflected the fact that Norwegian American widows were increasingly likely to choose not to remarry, especially when compared to those who stayed behind in Europe.[91] More significantly, widows were increasingly considered heads of households: 3.3 percent of the households in the Norway Grove community were headed by a widowed mother with a married child and his or her family present.

In sum, the Norwegian American households, despite a weakened stem-household structure and a diminished orientation of exclusivity between male head and male heir, retained their lineal alignment. Indications of continued parental power were still apparent although power was shared more by fathers and mothers. Ironically, older married women in what was purportedly a patriarchal European American society tended to have etched out greater security than many of their American counterparts, such as Emily Gillespie, by the late nineteenth century.

Yet these same arrangements in their various forms continued to impose onerous burdens on youths. Another irony is unmasked when we compare rates of marriage among the children of immigrants to rates among those who remained behind in Norway. In a sample from late-nineteenth-century Luster in Norway, 87.6 percent of the men who did not emigrate married, a proportion considerably higher than that among Norwegians of the second generation in the United States.[92] Despite frequently voiced sentiments that emigration occurred for the sake of the children, it is meaningful that the second generation of immigrants was denied the state of marriage at rates higher than those who remained behind.

We thus encounter yet another amalgam of continuity and change in the rural communities of the Middle West. Norwegians reestablished the principles of the European pattern of marriage. They continued to adhere to stem-household arrangements carried from Europe as their communities matured. As their settlements faced increasing pressures in the late nineteenth century, they altered patterns of life, but they did not simply adopt "American" practices. Well into the twentieth century, distinctive patterns of work and responsibility within the home remained conspicuous. Yet failed expectations created tensions that opened up the possibility of a hastened sequence of cultural innovation.[93] Among the most unequal household environments, such as stem-household cultures carried from Europe to the Middle West, changes occurred within the home. Not surprisingly, it was those who were disappointed—who were also often youths—who fomented change. As we shall see in later chapters, their dissent was perceived not only as a protest against their predicament but also as a challenge to the family morality that undergirded the European American home.

Once again, the work of Hamlin Garland, who was cognizant of the tragedy of forsaken parents yet who maintained a clear sympathy for American ways, is useful in his depiction of an instance when cultural differences between youths effectively promoted a diffusion of innovative behavior into immigrant homes. In "Among the Corn Rows," first published in 1891, Julia Peterson, a Norwegian's daughter, had a "secret dream." She worked in the fields, "faint with fatigue," and toiled "back and forth between the corn rows, holding the handles of the double-shovel corn plow while her brother Otto rode the steaming horse. Her heart was full of bitterness, and her face flushed with heat, and her muscles aching with fatigue." Despite her bitterness, "the corn must be plowed, and so she toiled on, the tears dropping from the shadow of the ugly sunbonnet she wore. Her shoes, coarse and square-toed, chafed her feet; her hands, large and strong, were browned, or more properly *burned*, on the backs by the sun." And as the "horse's harness '*creak*-cracked' as she swung steadily and patiently forward," she took comfort in her "constant, tenderest, and most secret dream." "Someone," she mused, "would come to release her from such drudgery. . . . *He* would be a Yankee, not a Norwegian; the Yankees didn't ask their wives to work in the field. He would have a home. Perhaps he'd live in town." "Perhaps," she dreamed, he would be "a merchant!"[94]

The likelihood that Julia's dream would be fulfilled was diminished by the insularity and "backwardness" of her family. She had tried to convert her mother to "Yankee ways," but she promptly decided that it was futile. As a result, she "was all too well aware of the difference between her home and the home of her schoolmates and friends"; she "knew that it was not pleasant for her 'Yankee' friends to come to visit her." Despite living in an ingrown Norwegian world, then, Julia had foreign contacts. She knew non-Norwegians and she wanted change. "She didn't believe in keeping up the old-fashioned Norwegian customs," and "it was [the mother's] jealousy of the young 'Yankees' that widened the chasm between the girl and herself."[95] More specifically, Julia wished to perform duties and maintain hopes for a future that differed from the future she had been given to expect. "I c'd stand the churnin' and housework," she spoke to her Yankee beau in a dialect that unmasks Garland's blending of social class and ethnicity, "but when it come t' workin' outdoors in the dirt an' hot sun, gettin' all sunburned and chapped up, it's another thing. An' then it seems as if [her father] gets stingier 'n' stingier every year. I ain't had a new dress in—I d' know—how—long. He says it's all nonsense, an' Mother's just about as bad. *She* don't want a new dress, an' so she thinks I don't. . . . I've tried t' go out t' work, but they won't let me. They'd have t' pay a hand twenty dollars a month f'r the work I do, an' they like cheap help."[96]

When her dream was at hand, however, Julia faltered. After her suitor —himself a second-generation German American—asked her to leave her parents, she feared their reaction. "I don't care," he replied. "Do you? They'll jest keep y' plowin' corn and milkin' cows till the day of judgment." She continued to equivocate. "They'd never let me go," she argued. "I'm too cheap a hand. I do a man's work an' get no pay at all." It would be different with him, her sweetheart assured her. She would receive half the value of their production. Their conversation was interrupted when Julia's father shouted at her to continue working. Her fiancé then donned her sunbonnet and began to perform her work among the corn rows. When Farmer Peterson saw "the familiar sunbonnet above the corn rows," he "went back to work, with a sentence of Norwegian trailing after him like the tail of a kite—something about lazy girls who didn't earn the crust of their bread."[97] Among the corn rows, Garland portrays the strict divisions between the exploitative European patriarch and the purported opportunities for autonomy in American life. No longer under the dominion of "her stern father and sullen mother," Julia was attracted more and more to "the independence and the love promised." Among the corn rows, Julia's fiancé symbolically violated social proscriptions by donning women's clothing while performing men's work. Even among the corn rows of a farm distinguished for its insularity, cultural diffusions occurred that encouraged a pivoting of the axis from lineal to lateral orientations and resulted in Julia's flight from her family.

Conclusion

Private worlds—informed by structures of customary practice—created private challenges for individuals living in their rural middle western homes. Emily Gillespie fancied the success of her children as she feared their departure. Julia Peterson felt an obligation to her parents as she sensed the allure of Yankee ways. The sum total of decisions of individuals who grappled with similar quandaries informed the directions in which their rural settlements were headed.

The changes on middle western farms were especially significant for recent European immigrants. They moved to the rural Middle West because the soil abounded with promise and because the vast space enabled them to build communities that reestablished cultural patterns—such as relocated kinship networks, religious institutions, customary household relationships, and marital conventions—carried westward. Yet these inheritances, the immigrants discovered, could not simply be transplanted to the new land. The European system of marriage in which marriage and thus marital fertility levels were curbed by economic constraints was placed in a disequilibrium by the heightened fertility enabled by the opportunities of the West. In the long run, children faced declining opportunities when they came of age near the turn of the century.

The strains were more severe in European communities that had practiced impartible inheritance—such as the Norwegian populations analyzed in the preceding section—than in those that had attempted to settle multiple heirs around the family farm. Families that divided the patrimony were able to limit interaction with the outside world, whereas a single heir put his siblings at risk, which made them more likely to search further afield for options.[98] Every family system nonetheless had to cope with tensions when heightened fertility was combined with limits to land. In addition, the household within the European system, with its lineal, more corporate posture, whether or not it divided land among heirs, consistently was challenged by intellectual influences that privileged ideas of individual rights and lateral family orientations. These influences contributed to the diffusion of innovations into immigrant homes varying from changes in marital fertility to different relationships between fathers and sons. Not unexpectedly, these changes were championed most by youths, not coincidentally those within the home who faced the greatest risk.

In this way, shifts in household behavior within the ethnocultural community were not unlike those occurring simultaneously in spiritual life (see Chapter 4). Again we perceive the inward diffusion of behavior, this time on the household level. The aggrieved, whether the minority of the congregation or the disadvantaged within the home, were attracted to the purported freedoms promised by cultural forms outside the community or the home. They welcomed changes within the community or the home that ultimately challenged intracommunity conventions. In both cases, a selective cultural diffusion, a complex acceptance of some unfamiliar facets of life and a rejection of others, transfigured critical societal institutions.

Challenges both to the church and to the household, moreover, were based upon a diffusion of individualist and contractual configurations that questioned the authority and hierarchy of the church and the family. Whereas the church stood as a guardian of community mores, the family enforced a hierarchy and authority between individuals. Yet patterns of behavior within the household, as in the community, were shifting in important ways. Thus, even European communities that outwardly were clearly set apart culturally from American patterns around them seemed to succumb to aspects of American life. As such, furtive forces within ethnic communities encouraged change.

Of course, the models of innovation that filtered into rural ethnic communities derived from other cultural groups. Julia Peterson used the world of her Yankee friends as a model against which to judge her own family's ways. Whereas the insulated communities provided an environment in which to renew former patterns of life, the permeability of the region facilitated a diffusion of outside influences. The next section explores these interactions and the efforts by many within European ethnic communities to inhibit cultural diffusion. It illustrates how settlements in the variegated cultural landscape were set in conflict and how they changed. It notes not only that patterns of inheritance varied among European groups but also that larger community structures in society were instrumental in protecting and sequestering the family or in leaving it at risk. And it shows how larger political and social organizations were formed out of societal interactions in the public sphere. As they developed, these organizations among ethnic groups often encouraged further integration. Yet in surprising ways they also became vehicles for political opposition, particularly among specific European cultural traditions, to the diffusion of "American" behavior into immigrant communities.

PART FOUR

THE SOCIETY

CHAPTER 8

They Soon Abandoned Their Wooden Shoes

Ethnic Group Formation

When Herbert Quick wrote his autobiography in the 1920s, he considered at length his immigrant neighbors, principally of German birth, with whom he had socialized throughout his life. His musings highlight the local color that the immigrant peoples splashed across the Iowa countryside in the late nineteenth century. As a child, Quick's German friends enabled him "to step from the atmosphere of frontier Iowa to a land of wooden shoes and peasant simplicity"; he was able to travel spiritually "to a new moral world without leaving the farm." He observed a folklore, common in Germany, that took root in the middle western soil. He was told about the mystery of a butterfly that flew through a barn in Germany on a bitterly cold winter day as workers thrashed grain. When Quick ventured that the butterfly had survived the cold because it had been hatched in the warm barn, he was quickly corrected. "It vasn't a butterfly at all," his acquaintance contended. "De man ve vas vorkin' for vas a vitch" who had "made himself into a butterfly so he could fly in to see if ve vas vorkin' hart enough!" Images of witches had moved to the United States along with the immigrants themselves.[1]

Despite this cultural transplantation, Quick assumed that the "process of assimilation" of immigrants into American life had begun, "as is always true in such cases, with conflict of minds."[2] "The human elements" in Iowa, he argued, "were thrown together into a human hash" and "from it time has cooked a dish of perfectly good Americanism." The American character resulted, in Quick's mind, from two powerful forces. First, following his Turnerian instincts, he stressed that the environment fostered prosperity and in turn engendered a material diffusion. German farmers "rapidly grew prosperous," he observed, and they "soon abandoned their wooden shoes." Second, societal institutions encouraged interaction between the peoples of the region. The children of immigrants went to common schools, "mingled with the Yankee children, studied with them, played with them, fought with them." The immigrant farmer "traded with [the Yankee] and with him discussed . . . common problems." Intermarriage, which once was unknown, became routine. In short, "dress, language, circles of acquaintance, politics, lodges, the common interest in roads and schools, farm organizations—a thousand things gradually produced forgetfulness of those early differences."[3]

There is much in Quick's portrait of rural society—an assimilationist description shared by many of his contemporaries—that rings true. A cultural diffusion resulted in innovations in immigrant households and immigrant communities that worked to alter their character. Yet Quick's explanation of an inevitable cultural convergence needs further inspection. Indeed, his own prose betrays that the process of assimilation was more incomplete and more complex than he would have us believe. When he wrote that "the German neighborhoods in Iowa are now as American as the rest of the country," he inadvertently unveiled the complexity, the sense of multilayered identity, that existed in the rural Middle West. And when he asserted that "a conflict of minds" resulted in "a process of assimilation," he begged the question of why the conflict should necessarily end with assimilation of American patterns. Instead of asking how or why Germans quickly and almost effortlessly left a world of witches and wooden shoes to become American, we should ask how simultaneous identities were created, maintained, and disputed and why things American often emerged victorious.

To consider these issues, we once again return to the concept of the complementary identity in the Middle West. In the preceding chapters, we have observed how the settlement of the rural Middle West was powerfully influenced by the presence of communities formed from dense migration networks based on common ancestry, nation, or religion. The fact that people with similar pasts possessed the freedom to colonize vast tracts of farmland also enabled them to live in a new environment apart from others with differing worldviews. The fact that they were able to transplant traditions sanctioned the opportunity to reconfigure cultural practices carried from home in cultural communities in the United States. In a very real sense, these conditions promoted a renewal of localized traditional societies. Waldemar Ager wrote in 1905 that his Norwegian countrymen were in some ways "more Norwegian here [in the United

States] than they are in Norway." Nestled in their communities, oftentimes hewing to beliefs that clashed with the views of others around them, they preserved old faiths and continued to read devotional and religious tracts about predestination while their countrymen in Europe were reading Hamsum or Ibsen.[4] The West apparently provided its residents with the freedom to retain old beliefs in a new context. Archaic convictions evidently hardened in localized rural communities that simultaneously celebrated their American conversion. "German communities" indeed could be as "American as the rest of the country."

Yet for these very reasons, conditions in the West were decisively different than they had been in Europe. Not only did the region provide a basis of wealth unlike that most had enjoyed in Europe, but communities and the relationships within them were reconfigured according to their perceptions of American life. Although the religious community and household arrangements were ostensibly based on values carried from home, they were also reformulated around the experiences and conditions in the new environment. The voluntary nature of household participation in church communities, as seen in Chapter 4, profoundly influenced the way in which parishioners interacted on a theological plane. The opportunity to secede and redefine community introduced an instability that at once emphasized American freedoms and questioned the influence of religious leadership. Interrelationships within households likewise indicated the fragility of familial bonds. Whereas very different patterns of behavior were observed in the rural Middle West based on explicit ethnocultural constructs, those family systems, as we saw in the preceding chapter, were placed under increasing stress as the nineteenth century drew to a close. The expectations of those living under the purview of the family farm were restructured as notions of individual rights and possibilities diffused into their American prairie and coulee homes. Implanted in the chance to create very distinct ethnic communities in the United States were the seeds of their own transformation.

This chapter inverts the discussion: rather than focusing on the community and household within ethnic settlements, it explores the local communities' encounters with outside influences and the larger public sphere that these communities together created. It argues that whereas localized traditions powerfully informed patterns of life in the community, at the same time they competed with larger national and ethnic structures of which the communities were increasingly a part. Rural communities, in short, were triangulated by the interaction of forces of a local culture with assimilationist pressures and expressions of a more globally defined ethnicity. The latter two, set in conflict in many ways, nonetheless often worked in tandem to alter local society.

The first section of this chapter reinforces and further explains observations made earlier: local communities were not immune to an innovation and diffusion of outside practices. As a result, although the ethnic context of settlement communities in the rural Middle West remained vital to local life well into the twentieth century, the cultural contents of communities were simultaneously modified. Dress and household furnishings, for instance, were altered by immigrants and their children, who observed that their possessions were becoming at least outwardly more "American." The use of English increasingly invaded non-English-speaking settlements. And people of varying ethnic pasts interacted more frequently. Although Quick goes too far in stating that a diffusion of behavior and beliefs "cooked" society into "perfectly good Americanism," it is true that people from different communities did increasingly "mingle" with one another and that behavior, in part because of the privileged position given to "American" manners, was recast.

The obverse of the process of diffusion and innovation of outside practices in ethnic communities, outlined in the second section, was the construction of ethnically defined interest groups in larger society. Whereas Ager observed that the Norwegians in the United States were "more Norwegian" than those who remained in Europe, a Swedish immigrant argued that the immigration to the United States actually created a "Swedish-American nationality," separate from Swedes in Europe and other nationalities in the United States.[5] As ethnic settlements were evolving, then, collective identifications with particularistic groups emerged.[6] Residents of local communities were increasingly tied into broader collective identities that were classified according to national background, religious beliefs, economic class, or political persuasion. Yet in the Middle West, ascribed statuses of religion and nationality remained the primary axes of larger identities that formed the foundation for interest groups based on perceptions of common pasts. Workers and capitalists, Republicans and Democrats, not to mention farmers and merchants, were customarily viewed as members of particular ethnic groups as well. This process, labeled "ethnicization" by scholars, remade immigrants into ethnics who formed interest groups based on invented but easily identifiable ethnic pasts with common national, linguistic, or religious backgrounds.[7]

The symbolic expressions that gave testimony to American citizenship and ethnic membership, like the relationships between local and broader allegiances, were in constant tension. Clearly, as immigrants made themselves into ethnics, they created interest groups based on ideologies that were defined with reference to others as well as to themselves. Yet the instrumental uses of ethnic groups were at least implicitly based on membership in a larger economy and polity. Immigrants' enlistment in the broader "invented community" of American citizenship explicitly influenced the ethnic walls they were creating. Their complementary identities thus fostered ethnic traditions within the larger American context. Paradoxically, they valorized their allegiance to American citizenship as they reified their ethnic affiliations. Thus "German communities" could be "American."

Patterns of Diffusion in and Interaction among Ethnic Communities

[Norwegian immigrant] August Christensen was warming up his log school house on the bank of the Buffalo River, and the pupils, mostly of the primary grade, were well behaved and wanted to "learn Yankee." — Otto Augustus Christensen, *Man behind the Plow* (n.d.)

Local traditions, transplanted to the region by migrants from the East, often evolved in relative seclusion. In some cases, rural settlements remained so isolated that the contrasts between city and farm broadened over time as new values diffused more rapidly into the former.[8] The seclusion is exemplified by the experiences of a farm youth growing up in the early twentieth century who recalled that he was eighteen years old before he saw the principal trading center near his home, only about eight miles away.[9] Folkways in rural communities, as a result, were often remarkably persistent. Charivaris commonly disturbed newly married couples in rural districts at least until late into the nineteenth century.[10] Religious festivals such as Corpus Christi processions or Rogation festivals, when priests ceremonially blessed the fields and the seeds to be planted in the spring, engendered a colorful ritual life until well into the twentieth century.[11] Medicine remained based on home remedies and folk cures. A study made in the mid-twentieth century recounts the medical practices within an Iowa Czech rural community. The cure for a stomach ache consisted of burning a piece of bread, placing it under a glass of water, and then setting both on the stomach. To be rid of warts, one found an old bone, rubbed in on the warts, and threw it over the left shoulder.[12] Accidents, on the other hand, were a curse of fate. Someone who had not "done right" by a neighbor risked inevitable punishment.[13] A community-defined moral correctness thus enabled its members to escape the ever-present possibility of calamity.

Despite the ethnic segmentation that characterized the settlement of the rural Middle West, however, the communities that preserved ethnic practices and beliefs obviously were not hermetically sealed. New ideas and beliefs coursed through the region, entered rural settlements, and doubtless tended to challenge conventional wisdom. The diffusion of cultural and social innovations that continuously confronted localized folkways changed the context of local society. Members of rural communities, in the face of these challenges, did on occasion consciously attempt to hinder the intrusions of the outside world. They periodically sought to circumscribe or to control deliberately institutions—such as the public school—that served as the principal conduits of cultural change.[14] Most simply, they advocated that people continue to live in rural settlements, which were more resistant to cultural diffusion than urban environments.

Rarely, however, were rural ethnic communities so isolated and so consciously separate that they could avoid the influences of a quickening cultural evolution in the late nineteenth century. Significantly, Americans were not immune to European innovations. Ole Munch Ræder, on a visit to the United States in the 1840s, noted that Wisconsin had already acquired a strong "European flavor" due to its many immigrants from Germany, Ireland, and Norway.[15] Although Germans in Dubuque in 1877 were reportedly "not too enthusiastic about the Yankee holiday [*Feiertag*]" of Thanksgiving, Americans one year earlier had feasted at Thanksgiving on "sour Krout, a German dish made of fermented cabbages," in the town.[16] A British visitor some weeks later went to "a German saloon" and enjoyed "a glass of most excellent Lager Beer."[17] A group of Norwegians served portions of *flatbrød* and *fløtegrøt* to a Yankee, who declared them " 'first-rate' as he licked his lips."[18] As American Protestants adopted new foodways, they began to take additional vacation days around Christmas and New Year's Day, "a Catholic influence," according to *Die Iowa*, that the "Yankees follow without knowing it."[19] The use of languages other than English also diffused in some cases to English speakers. Schools, especially Roman Catholic schools, gave instruction in non-English languages; in one school, German Catholics found it "very touching" when Irish girls recited poems at school celebrations in German.[20]

These instances notwithstanding, the principal direction of change was toward "American" traditions and the English language. The cultural innovations that diffused into the relatively isolated rural ethnic settlements were propelled by two parallel forces that fostered modifications in local society. First, members of local communities tended to accept seemingly neutral innovations that lightened work loads or changed fashions, innovations commonly seen as elements of "American" life. Although these novelties were often eagerly embraced by the rural folk, they frequently begat inadvertent changes in local society. Because it was a common aspiration to "learn Yankee," the vectors of change among the descendants of European immigrants tended to move toward the assimilation that Quick witnessed.[21] These ostensibly innocuous diffusions worked in concert with a second less charitable process. Those in religious or linguistic minorities were often painfully aware that they held institutionally and culturally subordinate positions. The censure of immigrant behavior and culture, whether deliberate or inadvertent, placed minorities in positions that frequently forced them to accept new patterns of behavior. In sum, both benign and hostile forces powerfully encouraged cultural change in immigrant America.

As Quick stressed in his passages about "Americanization," a force that was instrumental in encouraging change was a material diffusion that gratified people of varying ethnocultural backgrounds as it created resemblances in appearance and patterns of behavior between them. "Modern" conveniences that lightened work loads and enhanced statuses became increasingly available to families that could afford them. Sewing machines, for example, began to appear in local communities in the Middle West in the 1860s. The first family to buy such a contraption in one German community was visited frequently by neighbors who used the machine and most likely showered admiration on the family.[22] Perhaps the Germans in his community "were not of a go-ahead class as in some other places," an informant admitted in English to historian Kate Everest, "but they have all the improvements in agricultural machinery etc. that is out."[23] These innovations in and of themselves did not betoken "Americanization." Yet even though German farmers were not "go-ahead," the fact that they purchased farm implements had inadvertent repercussions on community and household life.

Other material innovations, including changes in clothing styles and household furnishings, however, were seen explicitly as an adoption of American ways. Kate Everest's informants in rural Wisconsin in the 1890s repeatedly noted that people in German communities conformed to an "American" pattern of dress.[24] The new apparel was often tied directly to greater wealth. "As their property increased," wrote a resident of Dane County, the Germans "gradually changed their customs and followed those of the American people . . . so that their present customs and manner of dress is the same as that of their American neighbors." Echoing Quick, he contended that "American life has americanized them."[25] Another German who lived in Sheboygan County agreed, noting that his countrymen "dress well, American," and that they were "generally up to the latest 'Butterick' styles."[26] As their dress was being Americanized, new modes of fashion were occasionally conflated with language. The German people, affirmed a resident of Grant County, wear "English dress."[27] Changes in attire were matched with new household furnishings. When an elderly woman who had lived "under primitive conditions" in Norway and the Middle West visited her pastor's parlor, for example, she was amazed. According to the pastor's daughter, the woman surveyed "a light pleasant room with four windows covered with lace curtains. There was a carpet on the floor, a corner sofa, one round and one oblong table, a what-not filled with knickknacks, cane-seated chairs, and a rocker. The walls were covered with pretty paper and there were many pleasing pictures." The old woman "clasped her hands and said, 'This is beautiful. It's just like heaven.' "[28]

To be sure, the new styles in immigrant homes were not exact replicas of those of their American-born neighbors. Hamlin Garland's depiction of a German home indicates the differences. The room "used as the best room, and modeled after the best rooms of the neighboring Yankee homes . . . was emptier, without the cabinet organ and the red carpet and the chromoes."[29] Perhaps this austerity was due to the German penchant for farm improvement. One German informant wrote in 1893 that his neighbors kept their buildings in "good order," improving "first the barns, then the residences."[30] These tensions between farm work and household luxury, between the old ways and a new elegance, are remarkably embedded in the observations of a correspondent from Dodge County who in 1892 noted that some of his German acquaintances still wore wooden shoes and slippers. Farmers found this lingering custom "very useful" at work and at home since after wearing the wooden shoes "in the stable and on the yards, flipping them off, when they enter the house," they could "aid the mistress of the [house] in keeping the parlor and the setting room clean."[31] The juxtaposition of wooden shoes and parlors unveils the shifting patterns of taste and a selective diffusion wherein immigrant families filtered innovations according to changing proprieties of work and home.

Material diffusions welcomed in ethnic communities obviously did not in themselves suggest an "Americanization." Accepted by a community on its own terms, the innovations were perhaps integrated into the dominant beliefs and regulated by community leaders. But the remarks of farm families that adopted the innovations indicate that this diffusion was a sign of the acceptance of American life. More insidiously, the changes within the society most likely had unanticipated results in other areas in which innovations were not sanctioned. Perhaps sewing machines reduced work, but what impact did they have on the relationships between mothers and daughters? Perhaps a room with carpet and wallpaper was "like heaven," but what if it encouraged a longing for luxury that undermined the denouncement of materialism of community leaders? Material changes elicited less apprehension than explicitly moral ones, but they almost inescapably brought about the latter.[32]

Material changes that encouraged modifications within local societies worked in tandem with forces in institutional arenas that explicitly fostered the diffusion of American practices into immigrant society. The institution most instrumental in bringing about such diffusion was the public school. To be sure, the influence of the public school grew only to the degree that immigrant children attended it. Since cultural leaders have always been well aware of the power of the school in imparting knowledge, whether it be "good" or "bad," the public school has remained a cultural battleground from its inception. Ethnic leaders often attempted to encourage the formation of parochial schools for their descendants. They argued that their church schools succeeded in providing ethical and religious instruction without the secular education that was by definition nonsectarian and included students and teachers with varying religious beliefs. Yet despite the appeals for parochial schooling and the controversies surrounding the schools, pupils with different ethnic pasts were increasingly thrown together in public schoolrooms.[33]

In such environments, the teacher often served as a conduit through which nonsectarian—and not coincidentally nonethnic and nonrural—beliefs and behavior diffused. English was typically the explicit language of instruction.[34] Many youths attended schools in order to learn, as one student put it, to speak English "more readily."[35] English even dominated in some schools where it was not the home language of the majority of pupils. Quick, for example, taught a class composed entirely of German youths. English was the medium of communication in the classroom, but no English was spoken on the playground or elsewhere in the school. As a result, the German children learned to read, write, and speak English; as Quick put it, he "[made] them over into Americans."[36] Lessons implicit as well as explicit were weighted with cultural meaning. Civil War songs were frequently sung in schools in the late nineteenth century, one school building "[echoing] with 'Marching through Georgia,'" which united immigrants and the children of immigrants with northern Americans in celebration of the great victory over the South.[37] Some years later, rural schools, according to one anthropologist, focused on urban life, which tended to prepare youths for a life—and a set of beliefs—outside of their communities of birth.[38]

Besides these implicit and explicit lessons on American life, a cultural hierarchy tended to denigrate immigrant life among children. American children in one Iowa school "poked fun" at the Germans, whom they called "the 'dirty Dutch.'"[39] In another locale, the first day of public school for two Swedish girls around 1870 was marred when older students threatened to "set fire to [their] hair."[40] The meaning of these frequent humiliations, both large and small, extended long past childhood. A Bohemian woman who eventually became a teacher claimed that at first she did not want to join the education profession because of her earlier role models. After suffering with her classmates who "had been discriminated against because of their home life," she admitted that her "feeling about teaching, at first, was not positive."[41]

After young children were introduced to American life in the schools, their American education continued in the workplace. For young women, the locus of instruction was often in American homes, where they worked as domestic servants.[42] There they not only performed tasks that were different from those required of them by their parents but also observed household arrangements that varied from those in their own communities. They came "into possession," as Joseph Schafer observed, "of the manners and customs of the Yankees, acquired their speech, and gained some insight into their distinctive views of life."[43] Ethnic Americans differed in their assessments of the merit of these encounters. Clara Jacobson remembered that when she left Wisconsin for Chicago to perform housework, as did many immigrant children, her father was anxious that she would discard immigrant institutions and beliefs. His fears, she assured her readers, were ungrounded because she was like most other immigrants "trained in city ways," who "returned to their country homes and married thrifty farmers." "They were not," she concluded, "spoiled by life in the large city."[44] Perhaps Clara's experiences did not mirror those of Theodore Dreiser's Sister Carrie or Hamlin Garland's Rose of Dutcher's Coolly, fictional young women from Wisconsin who moved permanently to Chicago and experienced the hopes and fears of big city life, but her training in "city ways" probably did have an impact on her relationships with others in her community and with her "thrifty farmer" husband. As we have seen, many immigrant and ethnic men did not esteem the changes that were wrought in "their" women by such contact.[45]

Immigrant men also labored for strangers who were American-born and more well-to-do than themselves. Like women, male workers on farms were educated in various subjects of American life outside of work. As in the public schools, their "non-American" disabilities must have caused them frustration, which in turn most likely encouraged the desire at least to understand American ways. One comic incident is illustrative. A Yankee in the 1860s employed laborers of Irish, Norwegian, and Scottish descent on his farm. When they were working in the field one day, the Scottish worker called to the Norwegian to "go up on to that brae faer and bring doon that bag that lies by that muckle stane." The Norwegian, newly arrived from Europe, did not understand. "What tivel old fool him say Tim?" he asked the Irishman, who in turn repeated the Scot's request in nearly the same language. When the befuddled Norwegian returned with a jug rather than a bag, the workers erupted in an argument carried out in Scottish brogue and "a mixture of broken english and Norwegian" that would have been more spiteful "if anyone could have understood just what [the Norwegian] said." The Norwegian became a stock figure of humor on the farm; he was "always getting into trouble and making some blunders," his employer observed.[46] He also must have felt a shame that prompted him to accept American ways and the English language.

Whether it stemmed from shame or a desire to "learn Yankee," bilingualism became increasingly common in middle western communities. The most secluded and resolutely non-English-speaking settlements, to be sure, were more successful in retaining the home language.[47] Yet the pressures against doing so mounted. As early as 1858, a German-language newspaper counseled its readers to study English. Perhaps they could speak a "sad English," the editor noted, but many German immigrants could not compose "the simplest English letter." A solution to "this evil," he argued, "was the thorough study of English" during "a long winter evening"; after all, "many most distinguished Americans are self-taught by lamplight."[48] A Norwegian journalist writing in the 1840s noted that as soon as Norwegian young men mastered a few current English phrases, "they at once become strangers to their less fortunate countrymen and are very loath to admit their Norwegian origin."[49] As the years passed, more and more immigrants in the Middle West improved their English skills. Even though German was taught in school in the vicinity of Fountain City, Wisconsin, "the english language," according to a German American informant, "is spoken almost everywhere."[50] Proper etiquette demanded multilingualism. "Among Germans," reported a Luxemburger editor, "German should be their language of conversation [*Umgangssprache*]" since "nothing is more ludicrous than two Germans mangling [English] between them." But, he continued, "if an American is present, then, for courtesy, English is spoken."[51] In many cases, English eventually became the language of preference of immigrants and their children. In one twentieth-century case, a third-generation child, according to his bilingual father, did not understand Norwegian. The father explained that "there was no point in having the boy learn the language since practically all of his friends are non-Norwegian."[52] Here was the self-reinforcing dynamic wherein interaction at school and elsewhere created friends of other cultures—who in and of themselves encouraged diffusion and change—which led in turn to further shifts in language and culture.

Following their schooling and hired work, young men and women continued to encounter an American world when they set up their own farm households. They might interact with other cultures when they purchased goods, as did one Norwegian man who bought "castor oil, Rubiform,

Kick-a-poo Indian Oil, and Pain Killer" from an English merchant.[53] And when they marketed goods, they typically met in an American forum. Some marveled at the benefits of this interaction. On one particularly busy market day in Dubuque in 1860, a newspaper editor reported that the streets were crowded with "piles of merchandise . . . heaped on the sidewalks," through which "eager pedestrians wended their way along." Among them were the "sturdy American yeoman," "the pale faced occupant of the city store," "the honest German but recently from the Faderland," the "rollicking Irishman," "the quick and polite Frenchman," the "staid but solid Englishman," and "the canny Scotsman." At one time, the editor noted, "their ancestors regarded each other as hereditary foes," but under the auspices of the American nation and the American market, they lived together and enjoyed the goods that America could bestow.[54]

Despite this bucolic portrayal of ethnic tranquility in the market, however, pervasive inequalities persisted in larger American life. Although immigrant peoples could be considered "honest," "polite," and "canny," they were also often the victims of negative portrayals in the media. English-language newspapers were peppered with derogatory references to people with European backgrounds. Although sometimes deemed "rollicking," the Irish were more often depicted as simultaneously stupid and cunning in politics.[55] "All the Eastern papers say that the emigration from Ireland this year is very large," reported the *Daily Minnesotan* in 1857. "We hope to gracious none of these Paddies will hear where St. Paul is. We consider that those now here can poll a large enough vote provided they vote often enough apiece."[56] Germans, on the other hand, might be "honest," but they were also portrayed as commonly drunk, speaking with heavy accents, and reeking of "a villainous smell of raw onions and ancient malt." One man described as a typical German was an "irascible" bartender who kept his saloon open past the legal closing time because he "schawered he tidn't gare von tam vor te vellers vot make ter tam orderance." After he was hauled into court and fined, he discovered that he did in fact give "von tam" about "dem vellers."[57]

In short, broad institutions through which people interacted created structures that tended to seduce or cajole immigrants and their children to accept behavior and beliefs defined as American within and outside their communities. On the one hand, these institutions established a forum in which immigrants were at a structural disadvantage. Activities conducted in English and according to American customs tended to belittle the importance of immigrant traditions. Ethnic Americans found themselves encountering others with varying pasts who were pressured into attempting to behave like "Americans." On the other hand, the institutions provided alternatives that often were appealing to immigrants and their children.

These alternatives were made all the more enticing by the material diffusion that permeated American life in the late nineteenth century.

The liberty to establish an ethnic America in tightly knit settlements, therefore, remained in an uneasy tension with the freedom to embrace new cultural forms. In a very real sense, moreover, the conditions that enabled the formation of the immigrant community also promoted cultural change. Local ethnic leaders who feared the effects of outside influences were often proactive; many actively encouraged their flocks to reject consciously the siren calls of American life.[58] They preached that aspects of American life were deleterious to their followers' physical and moral well-being. At the very least, they encouraged their adherents to accept changes only on the cultural terms of the community.[59]

Kathleen Neils Conzen suggests that essentially this is what occurred, that "localized" rural cultures "responded to the transforming pressures of modern life on a parallel trajectory of their own." Localized cultures did not disintegrate; indeed, they "continued to evolve and became, in effect, locally hegemonic."[60] Evidence supports Conzen's contentions. Members of ethnic communities often did remain conscious of their collective identities. When those of other cultural traditions encroached on their enclaves, they ignored the outsiders. One man, who had been born in a different region of Norway than the dominant regional group of the neighborhood, admitted that he still considered himself a "foreigner" after living there for twenty-three years; in another place, Welsh farmers never entered their nearest neighbor's residence because the neighbor was German.[61] Some local communities remained more resolute than others in their zeal to isolate themselves. Rural sociologists often noted informants' observations concerning the relative "clannishness" of local ethnic communities and their purported imperviousness to change. Not surprisingly, English-speaking groups—Irish, Welsh, and English—typically were perceived to be less "clannish," whereas Continental immigrants—especially Germans—were seen to be more so.[62] As we shall observe in the next chapter, the intellectual postures of religious traditions powerfully influenced the propensities for change among various immigrant groups.

Encounters with new patterns of life, however, challenged conventional wisdom even among the most clannish. Local communities that rejected innovations were nevertheless forced to confront them. Simply by admitting the existence of new cultural patterns, communities faced the possibility that neighbors in their midst might begin to embrace them. The patterns of this diffusion among individuals was informed by their spatial position in the settlement and their age and generation. As both Quick and Schafer noted, the rate of change was greater at the margins of settlements, where interaction with "foreigners" was more common.[63]

Perhaps at the center of settlements, where suspicion of the intrusion of foreign ideas was often strongest and interaction least frequent, localized cultures could most successfully be "hegemonic."

Even here, however, social control remained difficult. Consider the experiences of Father Michael Flammung, the spiritual leader of the Luxemburger Catholic settlement of St. Donatus who resolutely attempted to create a rural idyll in the nineteenth century.[64] Although "rural people often appear dead to the beauty amid which they live," Welker Given, who chronicled the settlement, argued, such an indictment "of sordid or sodden materialism will not hold against the wakened and thrifty Luxemburgers" at St. Donatus. "Under a dual influence" of the loveliness of nature and the lowliness of man, the immigrants built "an island washed on many sides by the rough waves of the advancing pioneers" and their "American pioneer materialism."[65] Flammung fought migration from his settlement to the materialistic world, advising those who left "to throw their children into the river that their bodies and not their souls should be lost in the outside world." Yet despite these pleas, out-migration swelled as materialism diffused into the community. Young girls were charmed by "the feverish attractions of luxury and fashion," and when they found the opportunity to be typists or "telephone girls," they seized it.[66] Despite Flammung's best efforts, the experiment in anti-materialism was in many ways a failure.

The pace of cultural change in middle western rural communities quickened in the twentieth century. As societal innovations multiplied, they were still comprehended through the lens of local culture. Farm communities continued to be influenced by, though distrustful of, urban forces. Farmers in Horace Miner's rural Iowa wished to identify their occupation as an "industry," thereby linking it to an "urban" enterprise, at the same time that they questioned the virtues of urbanity.[67] And as urban influences—aided by the automobile, the telephone, the radio, and motion pictures—inexorably diffused into rural homes, they increasingly tied the farm to the city, with its attendant images of prosperity and decadence.

No encounter illustrated this ambivalence more clearly than the farm household's relationship to the cinema. In one rural community, movies were "approved of" at the same time that they were identified as the most important single factor influencing youths to forsake the farm.[68] Folks in Hardin County, Iowa, were even more dubious about Hollywood. Certainly, the time spent at the theater was important socially, but the content of the movies themselves was so foreign and antagonistic to local values that they were rarely a topic of conversation among local people. Only among youths, who were more acquainted with the themes of movies, did films have a direct influence on "dress styles, vocabulary, gestures, basic sex mores, and success values." And it was among youths that Hollywood themes encouraged an appreciation of and a migration to the bright city lights.[69] Again, people seemed able to accept explicitly the technological change of the cinema that created new social opportunities. Yet by and large, many did not tolerate, indeed did not even understand, the moral themes implicit within the social gatherings that were the movies. By suffering the presence of movies, however, they tacitly embraced the possibility of the cultural changes that Hollywood seemed to encourage.[70]

Conversion to an "American" language and a "modern" style was reflected in prosaic but meaningful modifications of demographic patterns and customs throughout the Middle West. Changing practices in child naming, for example, symbolized the diffusion of current fashion. In one fictional Norwegian community, "Eivind . . . very soon became Edwin, and later just plain Ed," and German immigrants in another fictional middle western settlement gave "elaborate names to their children, which sounded absurd with the old German surnames: Maxine, Velda, Delight, Gwendolyn, Eugene, Dwayne."[71] These changes indicate not only the diffusion of new cultural forms but also a rejection of meaningful traditions. Naming customs carried to the Middle West illustrated a symbolic commitment to lineage and community and a denial of individuality. Children named for ancestors were placed within the kinship net as they symbolically maintained the spirit of those who preceded them. Among Norwegians, for example, a child's name did not betoken a new individual so much as the continuance of an old line.[72] By the 1880s, the custom had nearly dissolved in Norwegian settlements.[73]

Perhaps of greater consequence was the increased potential for cross-ethnic marriage, an event of profound importance for the survival of the ethnic community. To be sure, intermarriage in rural communities occurred at notably low percentages into the twentieth century.[74] Yet when intermarriage did occur, it both resulted from and encouraged diffusions into ethnic neighborhoods as it broke down social barriers and fostered social change in the community. On the one hand, it was aided by the school and greater mobility, which increased the interaction between youths. On the other hand, it profoundly affected the preservation of Old World customs. When one Norwegian man married a German woman, according to sociologist Peter A. Munch's field notes, there were "no old country transitions in the home, neither German nor Norwegian."[75] Intermarriage itself, many observers noted, was often the result of other demographic changes that were also diffusions of behavior. Since farm fertility was decreasing, the pool of available spouses within one's own ethnic group was smaller. Youths had to look further afield for an appropriate marriage partner, which meant that they looked across ethnic lines. As one Wild Rose resident put it, "There aren't enough Norwegians to go around."[76] When no "Norwegians" were available, they were forced to marry "others."

"Local hegemony," although it might be sought by segments of the community, thus was often an unrealized ideal. Change in ethnic rural communities might be slow, but it did occur. As they encountered institutional contacts at school or at the market, as they faced cultural intolerance in English-language publications, as they accepted material innovations at home, ethnic Americans—even those nestled deep in secluded communities—did indeed begin to change their behavior, much to the chagrin of local leaders who sought to protect their communities from outside influences. When local hegemony was achieved, it evolved from a process of cultural negotiation that typically was contentious and replete with social tension. When explicit changes, sustained by the putative merit of American behavior, challenged orthodoxy, they contributed to a tension in the locality that was manifested in many forms. Conzen is correct to note that the ethnic communities that dotted the rural Middle West were not disappearing but changing—in part because segments of European communities "learned Yankee," in part because other segments explicitly sought to prohibit such diffusion. She is also accurate to argue that the complex amalgam of cultural innovation and preservation should not be characterized simply as assimilation. Indeed, as individuals were grappling with innovations that challenged their local community values, they coincidentally were encouraged to join, as the next section indicates, broad organizations outside of their localities that were based on a devised common "ethnicity."

Ethnic Group Definition in the Middle West

He was not interested in nationalities and wanted to forget about his nationality background. He was American. . . . In spite of his assertions he had stereotypic views about other nationalities. One could not converse long with an Irishman[, he asserted,] before he was told [by the Irishman] that he was Irish—in this manner, they were worse than Norwegians. He characterized Germans as "bull-headed."—Summary of interview with Alf Langhus, Peter A. Munch field notes, 1947, Peter A. Munch Papers, Norwegian-American Historical Association Archives, St. Olaf College, Northfield, Minnesota

Because complementary identities were multilayered, they could simultaneously foster allegiance to national traditions and encourage celebrations of immigrant inheritances. Citizenship enabled immigrants to maintain collective identities beneath the larger rubric of "American." For immigrants and their descendants, a principal symbolic expression of these local identities was a common ethnic or religious past. The rural landscape was segmented into communities that, though occasionally rife with conflict, were composed of people who hewed to symbols of a shared tradition.[77] Yet the lines drawn to encircle a community obviously also differentiated its members from those on the outside. Those outside the symbolic boundaries of a community might share a collective citizenship as Americans, but they also had different beliefs, customs, and practices. Layered allegiances to nation and subgroup thus were set in a continual tension. Seemingly, one could simultaneously be "American," with no interest in nationalities, and yet espouse firmly held stereotypes of others based on their national origins.

In the rural Middle West, ethnic segmentations were based on spatial divisions that often originated at the outset of white settlement. Despite innovations that were altering localized traditions as the nineteenth century progressed, rural neighborhhoods typically continued to be defined ethnically. And whereas the contacts between communities often encouraged diffusion, they also stimulated the development of stereotypes and ascriptions of others. Clashes based on nationality differences, in fact, often occurred among Europeans even before they landed in the United States. A Swedish immigrant, reminiscing about his journey to America around 1870, remembered that when his ship stopped in Ireland, Irish immigrants were placed on deck above the Swedes. "There soon developed quite a lot of animosity between the two nationalities," he recalled, still resentful of the disadvantageous position of the Swedes on the ship. "The Irish would throw some of their trash down on the Swedish people. We would retaliate in any way we could."[78]

Ethnic differences and animosities between nationality groups matured following the immigrants' arrival. Public displays and private prejudices continually revitalized antagonisms between ethnic groups. As late as the 1940s, a woman in rural Wisconsin perceived what she called the "fighting spirit" between those of Norwegian ancestry and those of Irish background, though she "could not explain it." "I guess the Norwegians have always regarded the Irish as nothing but dirt," she remarked, whereas the Irish still considered the Norwegians "newcomers." Moreover, she concluded significantly and somewhat circularly, "it is easier to classify people when you know their backgrounds."[79]

These classifications were expressed both privately and publicly throughout the nineteenth-century Middle West. A migrant from the East who worked for "Irish people" complained about the food in a letter to his brother but concluded that "we have to get used to such things in this country."[80] Another letter writer advised his friend not to go to Valley City, North Dakota, "for it is all filled with people from Norway." One woman characterized a German neighborhood in Sauk City, Wisconsin, some years later as a locale with "men fat, red-face, heavy cheeks, many saloons . . . hideous, loud talk, laughter without mirth."[81] Even in the mid-twentieth century, a Norwegian American illustrated his perception that the Irish were shiftless by noting that "if you want to see the unpainted houses, you would have to go into an Irish community." He undoubtedly would have been displeased by the statement from a Yankee neighbor that the Norwegians and the Irish had the "same temperament."[82]

Built broadly upon these local identifications, ethnic groups—encouraged by ethnic leaders in the press, politics, and business—were formed out of shared symbols within the group and negative references to those outside of it. Imagined common immigrant pasts, based on similar linguistic, national, or religious heritages, provided the foundation for the "creation" of ethnic groups in the United States. In a process labeled "ethnicization" by scholars, immigrants became ethnics.[83] Invented ethnic groups commonly served as vehicles for mobilization and cooperation that were useful, especially to an ethnic leadership, in undertakings ranging from politics to business. Ethnicization segmented American society in city and country alike since in order to maintain allegiance to a particular group, one needed to refer negatively to "others." But that segmentation was useful, Jonathan D. Sarna argues, because in addition to providing a mobilizable clientele for the leadership, the ethnic group became an easily identifiable group for leaders of nonethnic institutions such as political parties or the state.[84]

Privately shared prejudices often were solidified in the public sphere by an increasingly influential media. The immigrant press, for example, was crucial in defining and expressing ethnic differences symbolized by political orientation and definitions of appropriate behavior. One German American in a newspaper article differentiated a rural tract in Iowa dominated by German Catholics from Glidden, "this county's bulwark of *Americans and of Republicanism*," which lay only seven miles away.[85] After passing through the German Catholic settlement of St. Joseph's in north-central Iowa, a German American traveler noted that within six miles, the character of the country changed. "We think the rule of the Methodists starts here because from here on we found preachers of their sect as common as '*worthless money*' [*schlechtes Geld*] all the way to Sioux City."[86] Jasper County, Iowa, likewise, was a "paradise" where German farmers "try to win their daily bread honorably and worthily." But if they had to do business in the county seat of Newton, a Yankee fortress, "they have to go to one of the pumps on the corners of the Court House square [to slake their thirst]. Temperance," concluded the journalist scornfully, "holds sway there."[87]

The English-language press in turn disparaged the immigrant. The *Dubuque Times*, for example, perhaps in an attempt to curry the favor of its American readers, depicted "Germans as asses," which in turn incurred the wrath of German-language newspapers in the region. In Goodhue County, Minnesota, Norwegians' alleged efforts to avoid the draft during the Civil War by feigning maladies were "almost enough to make a horse laugh."[88] Some years later, an American Republican paper revealed its prejudices as well as its underlying fears. "Two [train] carloads of immigrants" from the countryside traveling to Dubuque to get their citizenship papers in order to be allowed to vote "resembled . . . cars of debris."[89]

It is not surprising that an uneasy peace was periodically broken when prejudices against cultural and behavioral differences, which underlay ethnic disharmony, exploded in violence. Riots stemmed from both personal enmities and political disputes. Yet rioters, as a series of clashes in Minnesota illustrates, were distinguished almost exclusively in the press by their nationality. A "shameful" and "desperate" row in a German beer garden in 1863 pitted offended Germans against Irishmen who had disrupted a quiet Sunday gathering of families.[90] Six years later, Swedes and Irishmen squared off in a railroad camp battle that lasted three hours and left three men dead and seven others badly wounded.[91] Americans, with the aid of the local police force, in an attempt to "clean out the d—d Swedes," attacked a group of Swedes in Brainard in 1872.[92] Angry Norwegians, who gathered to lynch an American who had robbed one of their countrypeople, were dispersed by the sheriff with the aid of nearby Americans in Steele County, Minnesota, two years later. "The way the 'Norsks' lit out," reported an English-language paper, "was amusing to behold."[93]

The boundaries that divided ethnic groups, then, evolved out of emerging local stereotypes, tensions, and sporadic violence. Yet they also proved useful to ethnic leaders and their followers as a means of creating and maintaining group unities that accorded benefits to those within the collectivities. In business, for example, common nationality created a perception of trust in an arena often characterized by fraud. Farmers, especially those with little knowledge of English or understanding of American law, repeatedly were victimized by swindlers and confidence men. "Farmers should keep their eyes open," advised Nicholas Gonner in *Die Iowa*. "The whole state is flooded with salesmen of every sort, most of whom intend only to fool the farmer." "Farmers should above all sign no papers," Gonner warned, "be they notes, orders, or innocent-looking contracts, — before talking it over with a knowledgeable neighbor."[94] The lesson was inescapable: because of the number of confidence men who operated in the region, "farmers cannot be sufficiently warned against trusting unknown peddlers" and instead should deal only with people they know and trust. Perhaps some predators might use common national and linguistic traditions to cheat their own "people," but cultural leaders nonetheless encouraged farmers to place their trust in common ties.[95]

Ethnic merchants thus often created for themselves a niche as distributors who served as intermediaries between the nationality communities and the market. Two merchants in the German Catholic settlement around Dyersville, Iowa, for example, opened a general merchandise store in 1858 based on their ties to the ethnic community. By 1870, their enterprise expanded into grain and stock buying. Since they enjoyed the trust and confidence of countrypeople within their community, they also acted as bankers.[96] In another ethnic settlement, a Norwegian immigrant utilized similar ties to the local Norwegian American farm community to develop a large tobacco brokerage firm. In these and many other examples throughout the region, merchants who positioned themselves "between the community and the outside" were able to earn the trust of local farmers by adeptly marketing their products.[97] Nationality thus performed not only a social function but also an economic one.

It was a short step from utilizing common local ethnic backgrounds to emphasizing "imagined" affinities based on similar national, linguistic, or religious pasts. Segmented ethnic identifications thus came to serve as familiar vehicles to bind together sellers and buyers, patrons and clients. The use of "Germanness" in the vicinity of Dubuque is illustrative. As early as 1859, the town already contained nationality-specific German and American hotels and restaurants.[98] Within a few years, many German merchants advertised in German and announced to their clients, like one German firm, that they were "the only German notion store in Dubuque." Others followed the example of J. J. L. Breitbach, which simply exclaimed, albeit in English, "Hurrah for the Dutch."[99] Public welfare, under the auspices of the German Poor Assistance Association, was administered within the confines of nationality.[100] German attorneys explicitly served a German clientele, while expert German cabbage choppers were indispensable to the German community, since cabbage for sauerkraut was in great demand.[101]

Nowhere, however, is ethnicization better illustrated than in local electoral politics. Nationality quickly became an integral symbol in elections and in patronage within American government.[102] The expanding American city was obviously the site where the influence of public works projects was most remarkable. Yet ethnicity and politics were connected to patronage in the country and the small town as well. The "City Government is so fundamentally Irish," complained a Dubuque German-language weekly prior to the Civil War, "that there is not one German who got a job from it." [103] Twenty years later, Germans who found themselves in positions of power "let [their] benevolence shine on a German rather than an Irishman." [104] The situation was scarcely different in countywide public works projects that affected the rural world. In 1881, "Uncle Sam" observed that "Americans" faced difficulties as members of the Democratic Party. "The wires are so arranged that the interests of the German and Irish candidates are to be subserved," he argued, "and the American Democrats are to be sent to the rear and be given some unimportant minor office." The ultimate question for him was whether Americans were to be recognized within their party or forced to become Republicans. [105] Importantly, their potential conversion to Republicanism was premised on the accessibility of more desirable political fruits.

Ethnic patronage in these instances was inextricably tied to electoral politics: in order to be able to dispense public work, ethnic candidates had to win elections. "Several Workers" writing to a local Iowa German paper in 1858 were explicit about the connection. In the previous year, before the Republican Party gained control of local politics, half of all city workers in Dubuque had been German, but now only seven of sixty-seven workmen were German. So much for "Republican reform," they sighed. [106] County-level positions were little different. The "principle trouble" for the "professional county [Democratic] politicians" in one Iowa county in the 1880s was "to satisfy the German voter and keep him in solid colum [sic] until election day." The only solution was to provide German voters with a German candidate. [107] A Swedish-language newspaper, for its part, was annoyed some years later when its countrymen were passed over for leadership roles within the Republican Party. "Are the Swedes going to vote for these Irish bums forever?" the paper wondered. The problem, it continued, was that "these bums openly and boastingly and everywhere refer to the Scandinavians as 'voting cattle' or ill-mannered ignoramuses." Yet the Republican Party depended on the Scandinavians for its very existence. It was time, the editor concluded, to "chastise the 'bullies' at the ballot box." [108] The implications were clear: votes ought to be cast or withheld in relation to the proportion of leadership positions accorded to ethnic leaders. In order for them to dispense patronage to their countrypeople, ethnic leaders needed to be nominated. In order to win elections, political parties had to get out the vote. Nationality remained central in both endeavors.

The association between nationality and party in some localities was so fixed that observers assumed that the fortunes of political parties rose or fell according to demographic shifts in the nationalities of citizens present. It was "a happy sign," wrote the *Carroll (Iowa) Demokrat* in 1876, "that we can mark up over 100 new Democratic votes because our German countrymen went to the Courthouse in troops to get their citizenship papers." Happy perhaps for the Democrats, the editor continued, but "the Republicans became quite uneasy [*schwulig zu Muthe*]"; "we heard several Republicans remark to the effect that the hopes of their county office candidates had disappeared."[109]

Single nationalities, however, rarely had the numerical clout to determine the outcome of elections, especially less localized ones. Electoral politics therefore were typically determined by coalitions of ethnocultural groups who tended to be allied with particular political parties. Party preferences were common knowledge to contemporaries. A derisive account about a group of small-town Iowa Lincoln Republicans in 1860 revealed their negative views of the Germans and the Irish. After the Republicans could not figure out how to fire a cannon, wrote a journalist, they "swore and raved; they *damned the Dutch, the Irish*, the locofoco and Seward men" and went home "to take some warm milk and retire."[110] A traveler who visited a Minnesota Swedish settlement observed that "being zealous Lutherans, they naturally tend to become republicans from opposition to the Irish Catholics, who in Minnesota, as elsewhere, are generally Democrats."[111]

These ethnicized structures, perhaps best exemplified by political alliances, created identifiable groups led by visible ethnic leaders and spokespersons. They served as interest groups that could work for the welfare of their memberships and channel fragmented discontent into more articulate expressions by the group. Yet because they operated within the larger American structure, the discontent and the possibilities expressed by the various segments of the membership tended to be muted and balanced by the leadership.[112] Ethnicized political institutions, for example, formed around cross-ethnic alliances and contained coalitions of ethnic leaders who might be on opposing sides in other battles. The German and Irish Catholics, who both tended to belong to the Democratic Party, for example, disagreed fiercely on the direction their church should take on issues of "Americanization" in the United States. German Protestant and Catholic leaders were worlds apart from German working-class leaders on the "labor question." Scandinavians might join the Republican Party, but they remained at odds over theological questions that racked their churches. Here again cross-cutting allegiances tended to direct ethnic expressions. As Amy Bridges has argued, competing identifications resulting from the formation of new allegiances and coalitions tended to mute the assessments of American life and its problems.[113] Like the cultural diffusion into ethnic communities discussed above, these ethnicized patterns did not illustrate an "Americanization" or assimilation. But they did contribute to a pluralist structure in American society that rationalized and organized it.

Conclusion

Political and economic structures that emerged in the Middle West, then, were based on a series of overlapping identities. At the most basic level, rural folk were members of localized communities defined by common religious, linguistic, or cultural backgrounds. Such fundamental units were then knit into "ethnic" groups—institutional creations that served a common political, social, or economic purpose—and other institutional organizations with political or economic objectives. These "imagined sub-communities" were opposed—and periodically sustained—by a loyalty to and sense of membership in the American Republic. The rural communities thus were not necessarily cooked into a "dish of perfectly good Americanism," as Quick would have had us believe. Rather, following the multilayered expressions of identification, immigrants and their children found it useful to reify, to reconstruct, and sometimes to reinvent multiple traditions and allegiances within the United States. The contours of American political and economic life, like the American landscape itself, remained segmented by culture.

This is not to say, however, that forces of centralization, to which Quick alluded, were insignificant in the late nineteenth century. Nor does it mean that some form of "assimilation," which Quick characterized as an acceptance of outward forms of language, dress, and political allegiance, did not occur. Indeed, this chapter has argued that local communities were increasingly tied into larger structures as the century wore on. A material and intellectual diffusion, in part imposed on and in part sanctioned by members of local communities, was abetted by more efficient and powerful intrusions into local society. Various media, from the newspaper to the motion picture, increasingly influenced local culture. And they fostered altered behavior, which set in motion a process that furthered cultural change.

The imposition of these forces of homogenization was paralleled by the expansion of ethnicized structures that also enveloped local communities and gave institutional expression to common background. Although these structures reified and, in so doing, strengthened ethnic definitions, however, they could also alter foci of identification, a process best exemplified in political behavior. When ethnics joined broad political organizations that demanded cooperation across subcultures in American society, they saw the peculiarity of their voices muted. When they entered political debate, they countenanced the validity of the debate itself.

These developments spawned other consequences, as we shall see in the next two chapters, that were not entirely unifying or harmonious in outcome. On the one hand, an accelerating cultural diffusion, the next chapter argues, was often not accepted passively, nor was it particularly desired by many members of local ethnic communities. Critics in the late nineteenth century increasingly regretted the embrace of "modern" and "American" patterns of life, which they linked to a decline in the family, a fundamental institution on which society and the local community were based. The tensions stemming from assimilationist pressures caused some leaders to make concerted attempts to solidify local hegemonies under the auspices of the institutions of community and family that were aimed at protecting their followers from this decline.

On the other hand, many leaders advocated political activism to counteract cultural changes, accelerated by assimilative pressures, which they considered deleterious to their group. They argued that societal decay, which boded ill for the future not only of their local community but also of the nation as a whole, ought to be abridged and that the political sphere was one arena in which to achieve this end. Ethnicized political structures, then, were undergirded by ideologies based on cultural issues distinctive to the religioethnic groups that were constituent elements of the coalitions comprising political bodies. As in social life, structures of family and community and their relationships to state and society were among the most significant political issues.

As these questions became more urgent in the late nineteenth century as the size and influence of American government expanded, they were particularly perplexing for those from European American traditions who privileged family and community rather than the state in their constructions of society. Here we can observe the "foreign mind" splintering according to intellectual and theological perspectives on family, community, and the state. As we shall see in the next two chapters, the intellectual perspectives of some ethnic and religious groups, despite their acknowledgment of the importance of local institutions, enabled them to be folded into liberal political discourse more quickly and less effortlessly than others. On the other hand, the leadership of religious groups that explicitly championed the roles of the family and community and remained skeptical of an emerging liberal world illustrated growing discomfort with American life by advocating the expansion of separatist and particularist strategies. Using the political arena and strengthened by an increasingly powerful media, they moved to politicize their followers. As male ethnic citizens of varying stripes were enmeshed in political coalitions, they expressed their concerns about society and their prescriptions for rectifying its problems and thereby influenced the programs of the political parties to which they belonged. In sum, local religious and cultural leaders attempted to protect their followers by sequestering and guiding them. But as they politicized cultural issues, these leaders increasingly fought their battles in a pluralist political arena that ironically became one of their principal bulwarks for championing family and community ideals.

CHAPTER 9

Teach the Children Domestic Economy

Conceptions of Family, Community, and State

Twenty years ago," wrote a Reverend Sassel in an 1882 German Catholic newspaper, "one seldom heard of a murder, now every daily paper has a half-dozen to tell of. . . . Formerly people hardly knew the meaning of the word divorce, now it's a child's game." Contemporary American society, moreover, was saturated with "bad novels and newspapers," " 'police news,'[and] 'dime novels,' " and "American saints are Guiteau [and] Jesse James."[1] For Sassel and many others, the cultural evolution of the late nineteenth century had created a societal crisis. Civil society was deteriorating; public scandal was common; morality was in decay. Americans of many stripes condemned this disintegration, but nowhere was the condemnation more shrill than among spokesmen such as Sassel who represented communities of European immigrants and their children. Their jeremiads rehearsed a litany of fears for an American nation victimized by its society's penchant for excessive and unsound individualism. Disorder, epitomized by increased murder and divorce, threatened the very core of American society.

For European American cultural leaders, and especially those like Sassel within the religious leadership, the moral decline was often explicitly related to what they considered the changing role of the community and especially the family in society. As we have observed in past chapters, conceptions of power and authority, individual rights and corporate configurations, varied across ethnic groups in the Middle West and elsewhere.[2] Yet we have also seen that European family arrangements on American farms came under increasing pressure as the century progressed. Demographic and economic realities, which often created predicaments for youths coming of age and their parents on European American farms,[3] worked in tandem with cultural pressures that diffused into rural communities and challenged conventional wisdom.[4] Together these forces acted like a vise to crush established arrangements in the home and the community. Such forces apparently were quickening in the late nineteenth century. The first section of this chapter illustrates that societal change, for Sassel and countless others, represented distortions of what they deemed to be proper patterns of behavior in the family and community. Women and children were forsaking traditional roles and responsibilities, which weakened the family and the authority inherent in it. Regrettably, they were being seduced by intellectual and social influences, often connected to the behavior of "Americans," that increasingly permeated local community life. It is not too much to suggest that their communities and families were under siege from foreign "American" values and conduct.

The fears of ethnic leaders such as Sassel, however, did not stem simply from perceptions of a family and a society weakened by the tendencies of modern society and the models of behavior of their "American" neighbors. They were also connected to varying models of the order and construction of society. Many European American groups tended to accept a corporatist ideology, explained in the second part of the chapter, that stressed the centrality of institutions of church, community, and family as intermediaries between the individual and the state. The webs of authority and hierarchy inherent in the community and the family were viewed by this leadership to be critical, "natural" structures that undergirded society. The family and the community protected the faith and acted as crucial strongholds against the encroachments of creeping changes in society. In contrast, the activist state invaded the family and the community and compromised the influences of the intermediary institutions. Thus Sassel would perceive efforts to enact temperance legislation, an instance of state activism, to be "a gross, brutal blow to the face of any man in whose breast still beats a freedom-loving heart."[5]

In addition to many Roman Catholics, a broad array of European leaderships, such as Scandinavian and German Lutherans and Dutch Calvinists, independently proclaimed the need to privilege the intermediary institutions of family and community and to limit the influence of the state. Yet the degree to which they succeeded in convincing their followers varied. The third section of the chapter argues that the communities most likely to hew to the teachings of their leaderships were those, exemplified by Roman Catholics and German Lutherans, that, for historical reasons, nurtured a less compromising sense of solidarity in the community and a greater suspicion of the liberal state. These conditions in turn enabled them to foster institutional structures, such as the parochial school, that further restricted the debate within the ethnic community. Other groups, in contrast, such as Scandinavian Lutherans, who arrived in the United States with a greater level of comfort with the state, were more responsive to the temptations of a secular society and more willing to participate in liberal political discourse.

Perceptions of Societal Crisis
in Family and Community

Our youth live in a world which has been almost completely seized by Materialism. American life today is characterized by a rush after material things. People want gold. They want goods. They want pleasure.
—S. Eldersveld, "Materialism," *Gereformeerde Amerikaan*, translated in
James D. Bratt, *Dutch Calvinism in Modern America* (1984)

In 1901, an article entitled "The Disorganization of the Family" appeared in the *Catholic Tribune*, a German Catholic newspaper that had made the transition to the English language. As its title suggests, the article outlined "the causes that are disorganizing family life *upon which the entire social structure rests*." Its conclusions, which assumed the centrality of the family in society, were not reassuring. The article's author discerned "an evil" of familial decline that was "spreading over all classes of society." And its consequences were frightful. "Statistics tell the woeful story," he wrote, "of the increase of crime against born and unborn children, the deeds of inhuman cruelty and especially the stupefying increase of crime among the younger generations."[6]

Roman Catholic households were the victims of a moral decay, the writer maintained, whose roots lay in three fundamental causes. The most basic cause was "the RUIN OF RELIGIOUS BELIEF which . . . brought on a weakening of the principles of morality." This "ruin" was caused by "the godless school" and "a bad press," both of which attacked the very basis of society; "by ruining the religious belief among the people, they have destroyed the very foundation of all social order." The second cause was a mindless yearning for social mobility, which was "the general desire to which many parents have sacrificed everything else, namely, to see their children raised to some position above their own." It was a sad fact, the paper argued, that "very few people know how to be contented with their position in life" and tend to "look higher only." The third cause was a "SPIRIT OF PLEASURE-SEEKING . . . that draws the parents from the home, separates them from the children, for whom they have no time." The remedies for these problems were a "return to religious belief" in schools and in society and an assurance that the marriage tie "be made sacred" so that "the legal destruction of family life, the odious divorce laws, must be considered what they are in fact: the official sanction of successive polygamy and prostitution."[7]

Whereas this commentary argued that German Catholic immigrants were endangered by American materialism and a secularized state, a remarkable tract penned in 1889 by Rev. Anton H. Walburg, a priest living in Cincinnati, contended that many of the native-born were already their victims. Walburg's gloomy pamphlet focused on the evil of "false Americanism," a "pharisaical, hypocritical spirit" that puts "on the garb of virtue when all is hollowness and rottenness within."[8] This "spirit" promoted "infidelity and materialism"; it was "mammon worship"; it "adores the golden calf and is directed to the accumulation of wealth with an ardor which is unquenchable and with an energy that never tires." The problem with these tendencies of false Americanism, he contended, was that the "eagerness for wealth" controlled "every other feeling" and money became the "ideal" for American youths. Walburg admitted that money was a power everywhere, but in the United States, it was the "supreme power." Indeed, Mammon was the "one god" that Americans acknowledged. These weaknesses were not trivial; they were "the curse of our society" and were "demoralizing us." "The hunger and the thirst after money," he continued, "consume like a raging fire all warmer sympathies, all better feelings of our nature. It dwarfs all higher aspirations. What are moral excellence, culture, character, manhood, when moneybags outweigh them all? How can better sentiments be impressed upon the children, when all about them teach them that these are of no value without money? Hence the startling dishonesty in the race for riches. Hence the bribery of officers, the purchase of office, the corruption and jobbery, the general demoralization, that threaten our institutions." The worship of Mammon, Walburg concluded apocalyptically, would most likely continue "to increase in strength and violence, till death put an end to the raging malady." "A republic that is not based upon morality and religion, where virtue is depressed," he noted, implying that such values were lacking among Americans, "is ripe for an ignoble grave."

The scourge of materialism, Walburg admitted, infected many residents of the United States. Whereas "a man enjoys his competence" in Europe, "no one has enough" in America. "No laborer," it seemed, "is satisfied with his wages; no millionaire, however colossal his fortune, ceases in his greed for more." Greed was most fully accepted by the "Anglo-American nationality." They were "the devotees at the shrine of mammon"; they composed "the syndicates, trusts, corporations, pools, and those huge monopolies that reach their tentacles over the nation, grinding down the poor and fattening in immense wealth." In short, "the educated villain, the expert burglar, the cool, calculating, deliberate criminal, generally belongs to the American nationality." "Foreigners" who were corrupt, on the other hand, "have in a great measure been corrupted by the example of Americans."

In addition to American materialism, Walburg listed other imperfections that, as we shall see, comprised a litany of Americans' failings sounded by immigrant leaders. The "American nationality" was "often the hot-bed of fanaticism, intolerance, and radical, ultra views on matters of politics and religion. All the vagaries of spiritualism, Mormonism, free-loveism, prohibition, infidelity, and materialism, generally breed in the American nationality." It was, Walburg asserted, "so puffed up with spiritual pride, so steeped in materialism, that it is callous, and impervious to the spirit and the doctrines of the Catholic religion." His inference was clear: although "whatever is honorable in our history and worthy of esteem in our institutions" was due to the Anglo-American forefathers, the future of the Republic would have to be safeguarded by those with German or Irish pasts. Paradoxically, it was they who would have to preserve what America's forefathers had created; they would have to maintain "America" without the aid of an irresolute "American" nationality.

These commentaries encapsulate a persistent critique evident not only among Catholic observers. Spokespersons for many ethnic groups on the social landscape of the late nineteenth century connected a growing materialism to a decline in the family and a purported weakening of society. At base, family structure and the traditional roles that supported it were being undermined; the individualism and materialism that ensued further jeopardized the family and its members; and, taking advantage of the family's vulnerable condition, outside institutions increasingly usurped the roles that the family had once performed for its members. Like Walburg's essay, the profoundly conservative critique also censured, both implicitly and explicitly, the family and society of the "American." It was the American, after all, who advocated the public schools as a forum for education; it was the American who celebrated material success; and it was American men who voted for changes in suffrage.

These interpretations, to be sure, did not speak for all recent immigrants from Europe. Many immigrants and their children, in fact, celebrated the public school, temperance, and women's rights. The progressive Norwegian-language newspaper *Fremad*, for example, advocated universal suffrage in 1868 for "men and women of all colors," including "Chinese ladies, Indian squaws, Negro matrons."[9] Influential liberal Roman Catholic leaders, such as Archbishop John Ireland, were prominent advocates of abstinence.[10] The *Catholic Tribune*'s denouncement of materialism, moreover, was counterpoised with other expressions by Catholic immigrants that unveiled an admiration of the Americans' material success. German men were urged in an 1879 issue of *Die Iowa* to "employ the good qualities of the Americans—their independent life, their self-confidence, their free conduct, their swift grasp and quick decision, their resourcefulness."[11] The *Davenport (Iowa) Demokrat* had made the same recommendation a few years earlier, noting that "the Yankees are the smartest nation in the whole world."[12] Decades before, Charles Wilson, a Norwegian who had Americanized his name, argued that immigrants should mingle freely with the Yankees so that they could learn English as well as "Yankee tricks" such as "how to shift and turn and take every advantage without much scruple." They would gain "the enterprising spirit necessary to stay on an equal footing with the Americans," who not only seemed to lack "scruples" but also were "far superior to the Norwegians in mental development."[13]

Yet much had changed between the time when Wilson expressed his admiration of the Yankee at mid-century and the time when the *Catholic Tribune* decried the evil of familial decline. Clearly, the United States was an increasingly urban, industrialized nation. And although writers occasionally marveled at the magnitude of societal change, immigrant leaders—and especially religious leaders—often stressed the perils that stemmed from it. When they focused on threats to family and community, writers and journalists conveyed the fears of their principally male readership. A series of accounts in German Catholic periodicals illustrates the perception of three interlocking challenges that the family and society encountered, challenges that taken together would be difficult for German families to withstand.[14] The first factor was the temptation of leisure and education, which seemed to destroy virtues of work and imperil loyalties to older, perhaps God-designed, duties. The obvious differences that we observed in work patterns on the middle western farms in Chapter 6 were expressed yet again by spokespersons who criticized American society. German men and women were counseled to continue to value work and to remain true to their "proper" places in the family and society. Consider the woman who could "pray 'Our Father' in seven different languages" but whose husband had "to sew buttons on his own shirts."[15] German Catholic editors repeatedly merged a condemnation of upper-class American women with an admonition to others not to abdicate their proper responsibilities. The "Ladies Literary Association," for example, was composed of "bluestockings" who "abused English, Latin, and, even Greek literature and art." Yet "can the ladies," the editor asked, "cook a competent soup or sew a button on their husbands' pants? We doubt it."[16] Elsewhere, one journalist commented that the "local bluestockings" would do better "to write something on patching stockings, on making shirts, or on peeling potatoes" than on Schiller, Goethe, or Boccaccio.[17] These literary societies were repeatedly reprimanded for abrogating conventional responsibilities; they were also chastised for compromising relationships within the household. Rather than learning to write creatively, "the young ladies," argued the editor, ought "to take a cooking ladle in hand instead of a quill, and to learn not how to ruin a *ready in five minutes* dinner, but rather how to make a good soup and prepare a juicy piece of meat so their husbands, if they ever catch on, would not have to rush to the liquor bottle and look like the black death."[18]

Leisure time, resulting in part from the neglect of "proper" duties and in part from "vacations from the Lord," bred excess, another failing of American society.[19] The theater was marred by "brazen, immoral shows," while "the ways in which the figures of women [were] used in advertising designs [were] simply appeals to the lower passions and . . . a degradation of womenhood."[20] Fashion made people—especially women—"odd fools" when they dressed, for example, in precisely the same material as that worn by prison inmates.[21] When "Americans" embraced a new pastime that involved shooting at glass balls, it illustrated their character: "An American has absolutely no sense for moderation in things. Everything, even the most harmless pleasure, is exaggerated."[22]

The behavior of modern children, which also epitomized leisure and excess, was equally disgraceful. "Young America" was condemned by the *Dubuque National Demokrat* in 1876 as composed of "corner loafers" who drifted about "cursing and swearing."[23] Still other Americans raised their children with "crazy ideas," such as holding masquerades. "Masked children!" shrieked *Die Iowa*. "Can these parents not see that by doting, they nurture and cultivate the sort of passions that are capable of making their children unhappy in later life[?]"[24] The so-called "Broom Brigade" in Fredericksburg, Iowa, in which young women did military exercises armed with brooms, was castigated not because of its militarism but because it would be "better if they mended stockings and patched trousers or petticoats."[25] "American girls [*Backfische*]" struggling with "sheer boredom," according to one report, took to riding horses with their beaus, a most unladylike pastime.[26] Catholic writers condemned the story of Santa Claus, but they found amusing the report of a girl who received a "simple darning needle and a ball of yarn" in her stocking on Christmas morning, a gift that reminded her of the responsibilities she had forsaken.[27] Scandinavians' beliefs certainly were not praised by German Catholics, but at least "everybody worked in a Scandinavian family," and "even the well-to-do farm people sent their daughters to the cities to perform domestic service."[28]

The modernizing, industrializing economy was a second factor that threatened the family and, by implication, society. Unlike Scandinavian daughters, young women increasingly were employed in occupations outside domestic labor. What was worse, they often preferred it.[29] As the *Milwaukee Seebote* noted, "It is a sad comment on the times that housemaids are in short supply while retailers and manufacturers always get more young women than they need."[30] "It was another sign of the times and women's emancipation," *Die Iowa* agreed sarcastically, that young women would "rather cripple themselves sewing for starvation wages in a factory than work at good pay in a decent home."[31] Why? Labor in manufacturing or as a clerk permitted women to "go about in the latest getup, their hair artfully arranged upon their foreheads, as though God had begrudged them the bare [*freie*] brow that distinguishes us from the beasts."[32] Women reportedly relinquished positions as domestic servants in favor of less remunerative jobs as clerks because they had "more free time for circulating and prettying up." The overall pattern was disheartening to these observers. As a clerk, it was simpler "to get a *fellow* and to look down their noses on serving girls even though they—as slaves to the sewing machine or playthings of the buying public—stand far beneath them." Once they got that "fellow," clerks were less prepared than domestic laborers to be wives and mothers: "[Servants] can run a house, [clerks] cannot. One knows children, the other does not. One helps to keep the man content and to raise a good family; the other not."[33]

Women with recent immigrant pasts were not as tainted by the world of commerce as their "American" counterparts. An exchange paper observed that Americans searching for domestics asked "in the first place for a good 'green' German girl," which meant "a girl upon whom the odor of the ship yet clings, who wears her hair combed down, without 'bangs' or 'Langtry waves' or artificial hairpieces, a girl whose hands are red and with calluses and who can, of course, do everything that transpires in a house." Yet the transformation even of "green" immigrants was rapid: "Soon the 'green' one is no longer 'green'" since "she imitates her friend, sloughs off the old-fashioned getup, stops parting her hair in the middle and letting her braids hang down the back."[34]

Concerns over modifications in work roles inside and outside the home were combined with a third misgiving: the growing materialism reflected at work and at home fostered a sensuality in American society that in turn further weakened parental power and the family. Perhaps the best illustration of this sensuality was the piano, that most well defined symbol of leisure. Its diffusion into middle-class society, argued a newspaper editorial, was both "a social disease [*Modekrankheit*]" and a "plague" that spread "horribly because fashion says so." "Educated girls now simply must play the piano" because for "the vapid mother [and] the near-sighted father . . . it is what's done." "No one cares" if "the child bleaches out white, grows nervous, [or] becomes a skinny stooping little creature." But it was a girl's mental metamorphosis rather than her physical health that served as the focus of the editorial. Playing the piano nurtured "feminine vanity and superficiality," and "fantasy is stirred along with erotic feelings." Girls "pound[ing] the keyboard for years, waste time and cost money," and in the end "they think they are too good to work." They "squandered" time that should "go into domestic crafts; because they believe themselves so grand, they neglect their filial duties." Indeed, girls began to believe that domestic skills and the duties of motherhood were "unworthy," and thus ultimately "they become useless housewives, hapless mothers and often to blame for all the grief deriving from an unfortunate marriage."[35]

Perhaps blaming piano playing for "all the grief" associated with bad marriages went too far, but the piano, these writers contended, begat an eroticism that became the basis for "true love." True love, in turn, was a force that excluded parents from courtship and became a precarious foundation upon which to establish a marriage. The indiscriminate mixing of the sexes in public prohibited proper supervision of youths by their elders, which often resulted in unfortunate marital choices.[36] One couple who wed at a young age exemplified the "downright immorality growing in America's young people." Perhaps people "call them a *romantic couple*," *Die Iowa* concluded rhetorically, but "where will that lead?"[37] Another case of misbegotten love, the paper concluded, "shows how lightly the most important act of life, matrimony, is undertaken here."[38] The chronic outcome of poorly planned marriages was divorce, a decision that further weakened the family and unfortunately was "an unmistakable sign of the times."[39]

In sum, the keys to the decay of society and the prescriptions for its renewal, for many European ethnic groups at this time, were discovered in the family.[40] The "disorganization" of family life, as the *Catholic Tribune* phrased it, resulted at root from a "weakening" of morality expressed in a widening individualism and hedonism. The solution to the problem was simple: a return to an organic family that presumably had once been the basis of rural society. Romanticized and idealized pictures of obedient and subservient children within corporate homes became stock-in-trade images that were opposed to the reality of moral decline throughout society.

Given these challenges, cultural leaders faced a dilemma. They could advocate the benefits of isolating the community from the evils of the American world and thereby risk that the world's problems would grow and eventually overwhelm them. Or they could go out into the world and attempt to reform it but perhaps be polluted in the attempt. In fact, they used both strategies. Exemplifying an isolated idyll, the middle western farm came to be portrayed as a paragon of morality by many immigrant leaders. The hazards of the city and the factory to the family and the community were juxtaposed with the stability of rural homes, where the virtues of patriarchal and clerical authority were less likely to be challenged. Liberal Catholic John L. Spaulding, writing about the Irish in America, argued that the farmer was the most moral, religious, and conservative member of the social body. The natural environment in which he worked—"a part of an infinitely mysterious Providence"—kept him close to God, whereas living in a man-made city led to "flippancy and rationalism."[41] Rural life not only kept farmers close to nature but also safeguarded religious attitudes and encouraged strong, unified, and large families.[42] If farm households were morally superior to families in the city, it was only one step further to argue that the cultures of peoples who tended to remain in farming were superior to the cultures of those who rejected it. Nicholas Gonner contended in a provocative 1887 pamphlet that the civilization of immigrant stock was preferable to that of consumptive Yankees. One of the central reasons, he maintained, was that Germans chose to live close to God as farmers whereas Anglo-Americans pursued commerce and manufacturing.[43]

As much as life on farms in rural enclaves was deemed preferable, however, it did not address the question about the direction of society and polity writ large. After all, as we have seen, people who were secluded from the world in rural communities were nonetheless affected and altered by it. European leaders were well aware that the failings they condemned in the homes of "Americans," though more noticeable there, were creeping into their own families.[44] Thus, while attempting to protect the integrity of their secluded immigrant communities by isolating them, they also participated in political debates that pondered the course of late-nineteenth-century American society. Prizing the rural home for what it did for religion and society, moreover, leaders maintained explicit intellectual traditions that posited the centrality of the household and community as the source of order in society. These intellectual traditions among many immigrant groups, more so than among the dominant American society in which they lived, stressed the importance of intermediary institutions between individual and state in the maintenance of order in society. The leaderships of diverse religious traditions were at odds on a variety of spiritual and secular issues. Yet in one arena the adult male leadership agreed: the family was an institution that was a central and "natural" brace sustaining society. If it was endangered, so was society itself.

Changing Institutional Structures in Family, Community, and State

Teach the children domestic economy, and political economy will follow naturally. — *Catholic Tribune*, 4 May 1899

Residents of the United States often affirmed that home and society were powerfully interrelated.[45] American-born Protestant Edward Norris Kirk stated explicitly at mid-century that families were "the nation in miniature; for as they are, the nation will be."[46] Although nearly everyone agreed that the family was a central institution, there was less consensus on how its influence should be weighted in relation to other institutions in society. To what degree should the individual be accorded latitude in the context of the home? How were the powers of the local community and the state to be configured in relation to the family and its members? The behavior of people living in diverse local ethnic communities, as we have observed throughout this book, suggests that they formulated different answers to these questions. As the litany of complaints cited in the foregoing section indicates, many immigrant leaders saw society as moving in a most unsalutary direction as a result of changing arrangements within the home that encouraged a decline in the power and influence of the family's natural authorities.

In part, these expressions of difference with regard to the family were reflections of the response of immigrants and their children to an advanced capitalist economy, one whose society differed fundamentally from the world they had been accustomed to in Europe in the past. Yet these differences were overlaid by another critical factor: the flowering of intellectual movements carried from Europe at mid-century built upon fears of familial and societal decline, which profoundly influenced European Americans in the United States. These movements were forged from corporatist foundations that tended to privilege "natural" institutional forms such as the family and the community rather than "mechanical" and "artificial" structures such as the state. They tended to fear the excesses rather than celebrate the possibilities of individualism in the context of a burgeoning capitalist, industrial, and "materialist" economy. In addition to liberal impulses that crossed the Atlantic, then, corporatist, antiliberal sentiments became increasingly instrumental to many ethnic religious leaders as the nineteenth century progressed. Thus when leaders of European cultural groups denounced the "liberal," "individualist," and "materialist" American character, which they believed increasingly dominated life in the United States, theirs was not merely a simpleminded, anti-intellectual protest against "American" life, as many of the misogynist barbs in the foregoing section might suggest. Rather, it was built on an intellectual and institutional framework that regretted the uncertainties wrought by an ideological revolution.

Corporatist thought flourished in German-speaking areas, where romantic notions of an organic society composed of people enveloped by groups took root over the course of the nineteenth century. As it developed, it emphasized the organic connections between people and their social agglomerations, such as the family, guild, and community, an emphasis that eventually found expression in Social Catholicism, which grappled with the meaning of the vast economic and social changes of late-nineteenth-century Europe.[47] Troubled by the "social problem" of an industrializing Europe and the tendencies toward socialism that ensued from it, Roman Catholics led a movement that denounced the abuses of liberal capitalism. They disdained the discrete compartmentalization of individual lives characteristic of modern "liberal" society.[48]

It is significant that the "failed encounter" between Catholicism and liberalism also occurred among European Protestant groups.[49] Non-Catholics such as Dutch Calvinist Abraham Kuyper, who was also profoundly influenced by German corporatist ideologies, explicitly professed an antiliberal perspective. His convictions, which excoriated modern liberalism, privileged the community over the individual; when implemented institutionally, they transformed the Netherlands. In criticizing Methodism, for example, he objected to its "individualism and subjectivity[, which] could not reach the social questions."[50] In his quest to confront "the question of poverty," he condemned "the artificial authority based on individual free will" and a materialism ("a kneeling before Mammon") created out of the French Revolution. In its stead, he envisioned "a God-willed *community*, a living, human organism. Not a mechanism put together from separate parts; . . . but a *body* with limbs, subject to the law of life."[51]

These traditions crossed the Atlantic and found fertile ground at mid-century in the religious convictions of ethnic intellectual leaders who molded corporatist ideas to conform to their own beliefs and the American context. German Catholics in the United States, well aware of intellectual and political developments in their homeland, were also cognizant of their place in the American church hierarchy. Less powerful than the Irish clerical leadership, they coupled a Social Catholicism, which in part was a protest against Bismarck's *Kulturkampf*, with an antiliberal, anti-Americanization posture in the United States. They were thus able to distance themselves from liberal Irish leaders in the church and society while they simultaneously elaborated a corporatist vision that mirrored German Social Catholicism.[52] Likewise, although segments of the Dutch American community continued to maintain a deeply held pietism, Kuyper's thought had great influence on Dutch Calvinist immigrant communities in the late nineteenth century, especially those in the Christian Reformed Church.[53] Diverse strains of corporatist thought also altered mid-nineteenth-century immigrant Lutheranism. Under the influential leadership of C. F. W. Walther, German Lutheranism in the Missouri Synod by mid-century was characterized by a structure that sanctioned the power of the congregation and family rather than the individual or the state.[54] The roots of corporatist ideologies did not sink deeply into Scandinavian Lutheran traditions in the United States.[55] Although many within the Scandinavian Lutheran leadership were less willing than the German Lutherans to embrace this Continental corporatism, considerable segments of the leadership nonetheless welcomed aspects of corporatist thought into their folds.[56]

Despite dissimilar intellectual and theological postures on many facets of life, immigrant religious leaders remarkably agreed quite self-consciously to oppose what they perceived to be the dominant currents of American thought, and many rejected the liberal drift in a modernizing world. In so doing, they built different models of the constituent elements of society—the individual, family, community, and state—they believed should be privileged. Eschewing liberal conceptions of society, they tended to stress the importance of the institutions of family and community, which mediated between individual and state. Simultaneously, they castigated the liberal tendency to emphasize the individual's compact with the state, which they felt exacerbated shortcomings apparent in the construction of American society and in the behavior of "Americans." In effect, the structural issues for them were threefold.

First, European immigrant cultural and religious leaders reasserted the power and influence of the family and the local community. Using their perception of the American family as the standard, they regretted that families in the United States were becoming increasingly porous and that society, as a result, was becoming increasingly weak. Mid-nineteenth-century European critics repeatedly disparaged the liberal, contractual American farm family that such celebrants as Michel Chevalier had characterized as "an inviolable republic in the state."[57] They ridiculed the free relationship between parents and children and the lack of authority that characterized American homes. For many, such as the critic in the *Catholic Tribune* who detailed the "disorganization of the family," the failings were becoming more and more disturbing as the nineteenth century drew to a close.

Despite its censure of patterns of behavior in American homes, however, this critique of the family was more than a simple deprecation of American ways. Rather, corporatist thought often explicitly reasserted the centrality of authority in the family and unequal arrangements of power among family members as critical features of the family itself. Utilizing varying traditions of natural law, these ideologies typically depicted the family as a "natural" institution that was central to societal order. A strong patriarchal household that harmonized relationships within the home was thus an indispensable building block of society. Conversely, a weak family engendered weakness throughout.

The local community, like the family, was a central construct. European corporatist theories consistently stressed a *Ständeorganisation* that privileged social organizations such as the guild or the religious community.[58] The theories of Social Catholicism that ensued also stressed the centrality of collective arrangements such as those found within occupational groups rather than those of the state. Although most admitted the necessity of the state, they emphasized that it should devote itself only to issues that could not be adequately administered by subsidiary groups such as the family and community.[59] In rural Middle West societies, the local community thus was central for Roman Catholics who followed this corporatist ideology. German Lutherans, under the leadership of Walther, who was also influenced by nineteenth-century German corporatist theory, empowered the congregation and the community so that the individual was connected organically to the group interest.[60]

A second point followed from the first: when the intermediary institutions of the family and the community were compromised, the individual was unduly advantaged, which was a root cause of the growing tendencies toward individualism. As children abrogated their responsibilities to their parents, the authority within the household diminished. And as domination of the household was diluted, individual freedoms were accentuated. The individualism that increasingly characterized household relationships was distinguishable in the larger society as well and was not healthy in the home or in society. Whereas many European groups expressed scorn for individualism, German Catholics were notable for their bluntness.[61] Individualism was "a cold-hearted principle," the *Catholic Tribune* argued in 1899, that "is always destructive, for it is based upon egotism, pure and simple." This "egotism excludes the spirit of sacrifice" from which Christian charity derives. Individualism, unlike Christian charity, "tears man from man" and "proclaims selfishness as the main spring of all human actions." Ultimately, individualism "is making humanity like a den of wild animals, where the more powerful devours the weaker, and only the most powerful trusts, monopolies, combines, etc., survive when the fight for existence is once acknowledged as a matter of fact."⁶² In this Social Darwinist world, members of "corporative organizations" must stem the tide. Indeed, "individualism, that basic principle of advanced democracy," argued the *Luxemburger Gazette*, was a great threat to the church; it would "inflict great wounds . . . if it [was] not checked in time." Thankfully, one of the most effective "means to check individualism" was the "corporate organization" such as the church itself.⁶³

Since the church did not control American life, however, it was continually threatened by individualism. This was especially true because of a third consideration: individuals were more and more tied into relationships with the state that were usurping duties performed at one time by the family and community. These developments were troubling because the state in and of itself was not necessarily a construct that was salutary for society. To be sure, religious traditions varied in the degree to which they were suspicious of state power. Dutch Americans who followed the thought of Kuyper saw the state as an "artificial" creation necessitated by human sin. Although it was ordained by God and mirrored the hierarchical family, it was both "mechanical" and "artificial." People were thus warned to fear a state that might meddle in institutions such as the family. When it did so, the state imposed "intolerable interference" on the "terrain of free society."⁶⁴ Lutherans, especially those of German ancestry, also stressed the dualism of the secular and spiritual worlds, which mitigated the importance of the state in daily activity, but simultaneously feared creeping state activism. Lutheran natural law admitted the necessity of the state at the same time that it argued that it was not so much a Christian institution as one based on irrational law necessitated by the state of sin.⁶⁵ Roman Catholics argued that the state performed central roles in society even if it was a relatively recent arrangement formed after the family and the church. Whether they saw the state as a necessary evil or an institution that must be humored, the leaderships of these religious groups agreed that it was not by itself an adequate foundation for society. In effect, the "positive" influences of the state interfered with the "natural" order of domestic and community groups. Those who advocated an activist state whose power would be enlarged at the expense of an authority inherent in the family and community were to be opposed.

These three theoretical distinctions found repeated expression in prescriptions for private and public life. Although the different ethnoreligious traditions varied in the rigor with which they maintained each proposition, they agreed about the importance of family to society. The biblical commandment to honor parents was frequently interpreted by Catholic and Lutheran theologians as an admonishment to obey all forms of authority. The leaders of the Roman Catholic Church were among the most resolute advocates of the idea that the family was a crucial, "natural" institution upon which society was founded. They argued openly that the individual pursuits within the home were subject to sacrifice to benefit the whole. Children in particular were prescribed to obedience. Father W. Cluse, in a speech to the *Katholikentag* in Germantown, Illinois, for example, noted the "constant and unfortunately justifiable complaint of our time and especially of our land that the principle of authority [*Autoritätsprincip*] is increasingly disappearing from human society." Young America (*Jung-Amerika*) acquired "each day a more dismal distinction since it would not tolerate submitting to the yoke of obedience and subservience." But hope existed in the maintenance of Catholic traditions, Cluse averred. Certainly the "American atmosphere of freedom" impeded one's ability to raise children "to maintain their obedience." But because life within the German Roman Catholic Church could nurture "obedient, well-brought-up children," it provided "proof that even in the land of freedom it is entirely possible to cultivate a real Christian spirit of obedience in the children."[66]

Cluse's imagery summoned a distant—perhaps mythical—past. He noted that German American parents voiced "common lamentations [*Klageleider*] and praised and prized the good old days in the German fatherland when the obedience of the children was generally ever so proper and was the joy and crown of the parents." Invoking images of the stem family, he honored those days when "adult married sons and daughters were under the command of their fathers . . . to greater comfort of the aged parents and to the rich blessing [*Segen*] for themselves and for their own children."[67] These ideals of a distant past were used by Cluse to maintain an abstract ideal for the present that repeatedly affirmed the importance of parental power in social situations, large and small.

Family authority was not only a "rich blessing" for parents but also a sustaining force in state and society. In 1888, another German Catholic essayist grappled with the concepts of authority and freedom in American society. Unfortunately, he argued, "in our times, the confusion of ideas has meant that authority is viewed as the antithesis, the negation, the death of freedom." Nothing was further from the truth, since "without authority, freedom for men would be a very pernicious [*verderbenbringend*] gift." The crisis of the liberal, capitalist, and individualist world in the late nineteenth century arose from its celebration of absolute freedoms and its denial of the necessary reinforcing structures of authority.[68] "The freedom of any person," the writer concluded, "is dependent upon the degree to which he makes his body subservient to his spirit [*Geist*] and his spirit subservient to God's domination."

Once again, the household took on an indisputable relevance in questions of authority and freedom. True freedom itself was defined by the obligation to serve God, and that freedom was defended and regulated by three authorities: "der kirchlichen, der häuslichen und der bürgerlichen." Therefore, the more one served God, the greater freedom one possessed; the more "[I] fulfill my obligations to the three authorities, Church, parents [*Eltern*], and state, the more I am free." Whereas children were freed through fulfilling their obligations to parents, the supreme deity "established clear authority in which the wife is subservient to the husband."[69] The liberal configuration of society, not to mention women's rights organizations, endangered these "freedoms." As another writer phrased it, the Catholic Church defended "Christian culture" through the preservation of "the most sacred institutions and foundations of a sound society: property, religion, and *the family*." And it was "precisely these qualities that [were] in danger" in the modern struggle.[70]

Since families performed essential roles in society, Catholic leaders remained suspicious of the function of the state with regard to family politics. Pope Leo XIII's 1891 encyclical, *Rerum novarum*, for example, argued that "the 'society' of a man's own household" was "a true 'society,' anterior to every kind of State or nation, with rights and duties of its own, totally independent of the commonwealth." Because the family preceded the state, the idea that "civil government should, at its own discretion, penetrate and pervade the family" was "a great and pernicious mistake." Likewise, "paternal authority," the Pope contended, "can neither be abolished by the State, nor absorbed; for it has the same source as human life itself." In the end, " 'the child belongs to the father' and is, as it were, the continuation of the father's personality." Because a child was biologically connected to his or her lineage and family, it followed that the child took "its place in civil society not in its own right, but in its quality as a member of the family in which it is begotten."[71]

European Protestants, also inspired by the mandate that children should honor their parents, agreed with their Roman Catholic adversaries that the family, because it stressed the duty of children, was a critical institution. Norwegian Lutherans were taught to revere both the reciprocal nature of parent-child relationships and the power of the parental generation. Consider the 1874 meeting of the congregation of Our Saviour's Lutheran Church, at which H. G. Stub, the church's pastor, who would later become president of the Norwegian Synod, led a discussion on the Fourth Commandment.[72] At the meeting, parents were advised of two central obligations toward their children: care for both their physical and spiritual welfare. The latter was particularly important because parents were "placed over their children in God's stead." When children erred, parents were instructed to teach them that their deed had grieved not only their parents but God as well. On the other hand, children, by honoring their parents, were also honoring God. It was thus clear that children "should not consider their parents as their own equals." Rather, parents were "far above" them since their authority was "given them by God."

Stub rehearsed the common refrain that parental authority was weakened on the American landscape. "It seems as though in America" the parent-child relationship "is more and more broken up," he concluded, "because as soon as the children become of age, they do not wish to accept the authority of the parents." But he stressed that parental authority "should continue until death." Even as adults, then, children remained children; they were prescribed to defer to the authority of their parents and to honor their wishes. In the event of a disagreement over a child's prospective marriage partner, for example, his or her father "as the head of the family should make the final decision." These structural inequalities within the family remained firmly held, at least in theory, in profound and prosaic ways. As late as the twentieth century, a Lutheran pastor disapproved of the child's game "Four in a Boat" simply because it contained the phrase, "We don't care what the old folks say!"[73]

Dutch immigrants, perhaps even more pointedly than Scandinavian Lutherans, also borrowed from a European corporatism to stress the centrality of the family. Kuyper maintained that the family was the basic unit of society because it was the only social institution that predated the Fall and had an express mandate from God. The family, because it patterned society and established its well-being, took precedence over other institutions just as its defense was fundamental to a healthy society.[74] The Dutch in America, who followed the teachings of Kuyper, thus argued like Klass Schoolland that "all of human society proceeds from family life." Others were more maudlin, such as B. K. Kuiper, who wrote: "The Home! Wonderful creation of God! Wonderful in its simplicity! Wonderful in the complicated relationships among its component parts, so simple in themselves! As for the individual the proceeds of life are from the heart, so for society are the proceeds of life from the Home."[75] If the state was at best a necessary evil, Kuiper concluded, "the Family is Society in germ."

German Lutherans also stressed the significance of family. The church organization of the Missouri Synod, for example, faithfully hewed to a corporate order based on societal estates. In essence, its leadership, reciting the three authorities invoked by German Catholics, argued that a well-ordered society was one that kept the state (*Wehrstand*), the family (*Nährstand*), and the community (*Lehrstand*) in balance.[76] Although they countenanced the state, however, German Lutheran leaders placed greater emphasis on the local arrangements of family and community. The church community crucially ordered relationships between social categories. The family orchestrated and controlled bonds between parents and children, between husbands and wives, and within the home itself.[77] As late as 1924, a German Lutheran wrote that family was "the foundation not only of the Church but also of the State."[78] The structures within the family, based on inherent inequalities and specific reciprocities, privileged those in power. Women and children were subsumed in the home and excluded, as a result, from the theological politics of the church. They were to be represented in church affairs by their male household head.[79]

These theoretical formulations provided a basis for many members of middle western immigrant faiths to oppose what they perceived to be the dangerous course of American society and to propose solutions to correct it. Although they often professed an enmity for one another, the varying religious traditions nonetheless retained similar constructions carried westward with regard to family. Clerical leaders thus worked diligently to warn their flocks of the dangers of the modern world. They plaintively preached against "American" behavior that increasingly placed their traditions in jeopardy. They noted the breakdown of the family; they cautioned against the decline of authority in society; they argued that a "cold-hearted" individualism separated people from their community and their obligations to others. With their traditions imperiled, leaders in fact attached increasing importance to sustaining the structures of family. Thus, the rhetoric of a family and community morality, already influential among clergy and laity alike, was energized in the face of a changing world.

Dissimilar Paths of Secular Change

[The German American Lutheran] has never quite become a modern
American because he has remained a Lutheran. —Heinrich Maurer,
"The Lutheran Community and American Society" (1928)

Despite broad agreement among clerical leaders that the family ought to be a privileged institution, church communities differed in their success at shielding the family from innovation. Certain traditions—such as Roman Catholicism, Mennonitism, and German Lutheranism—remained relatively steadfast to corporatist dogma and practice. Others—such as Scandinavian Lutherans—were increasingly attracted to liberal notions despite the best attempts of segments of their leadership to reroot corporatist traditions in the Middle West. An understanding of how these traditions played out in a changing world goes a long way toward explaining the political and social conflict that punctuated middle western society in the late nineteenth century as it illustrates the historical development of ethnic groups in the region.[80]

A principal factor explaining this variance was the way in which church leaderships balanced the family in relation to the two other primary institutional structures: the community and the state. Those that successfully convinced their followers to forge local institutional structures and to distrust intrusions from the outside were more able to shield customary beliefs concerning family propriety. Their levels of success were informed by two conditions. First, family authority was sustained in religious systems that more successfully professed a particularism in their church community. By particularism, I mean the pronouncement by church authorities that they represented the one true faith.[81] Second, intrusions into the local community were impeded by groups that maintained a suspicion of the role of the state and of governmental intervention in the United States. Typically, these factors worked in tandem: the greater the tendency toward particularist beliefs, the greater the skepticism about permitting an amoral state to hold power over the fold of believers.

The debate over particularist convictions was contested in churches, Catholic and Protestant alike, over the course of the nineteenth century. It cleaved Presbyterians and Baptists in the 1830s and divided Roman Catholics in the 1890s.[82] Despite widespread conflict within church bodies, however, it is significant that particularist beliefs tended to enjoy a recrudescence in the mid-nineteenth century in churches peopled by recent immigrants. Importantly, this revival was related to intellectual strains associated with corporatist ideologies situated in Europe. Social Catholicism, which encompassed corporatist ideologies and papal pronouncements—from the first Vatican Council's acceptance of papal infallibility in 1870 to Pope Leo XIII's condemnation of "Americanism" in 1899—reaffirmed the particularism of the Roman Catholic Church. A segment of the leadership in the United States attempted to oppose this trend. Liberal clerics, led typically by Irish Americans such as Cardinal James Gibbons, Archbishop John Ireland, and Archbishop John J. Keane, moved toward an "Americanist" outlook that valued the state and desired an Americanization of Roman Catholicism. American Roman Catholicism thus was buffeted by conflict in the late nineteenth century over questions of particularism versus pluralism. Yet it appears that the majority of the church laity, dominated principally by the German Catholic leadership and a conservative wing of the Irish hierarchy, embraced a conservative formulation of society that feared the materialism of capitalist America and posited the centrality of obedience to authority in church and society.[83]

Immigrant Protestants were also influenced to varying degrees by particularist ideas reflected in nineteenth-century theological developments. The evolution of Lutheranism in the United States affords the best example of an increased particularist presence in the mid-nineteenth century. When immigrants of Lutheran pasts entered the United States in increasingly large numbers at mid-century, they found a German American Lutheranism dominated by those who stressed rationalism and ecumenicalism.[84] Conservative leaders among both Scandinavian and German Lutheran immigrants rejected the ecumenical spirit. This reaction was particularly pronounced among German immigrants who founded the Missouri and Buffalo Synods. There evolved in these churches a confessional fundamentalism that embraced a biblical literalism and held that the sixteenth-century Lutheran confessions, like Scripture itself, were definitive expositions of truth. Equally important, they argued that the outward unity of Christians was possible only when there was complete agreement on doctrine. If such agreement was lacking, it followed that association with others was wrong, even though it might be aimed at converting those in error. Walls were thus to be built to separate those with true belief from others—Methodist, Catholic, and nonbeliever alike. When Walther asked if communities could "absorb others—Methodists, etc. or join with them?," he answered his own question: "No, when it is a question of morality, such association is sinful."[85] To be sure, the temptations to associate were rife in a nation that tolerated diverse beliefs and in a region both alien and fluid. Yet under clerical leadership, a church community was organized around this congregational polity that would work against unnecessary commingling.[86] Perhaps in no other place were the walls so effective as in the rural Middle West, where local communities could be most effectively isolated from outside influence.[87]

Intellectual and social structures among German Lutherans who belonged to the Missouri Synod thus were explicitly utilized to sustain its spiritual particularism. Here the corporate, organic arrangement in which members of the group were perceived to be part of a larger whole not only ordered local society but protected the faith. The power inherent in the *Lehrstand* (church community) gave it a prominent role and endowed its leadership, the ministry, with great power.[88] The interest of the community in turn helped maintain the faith and cemented the distrust of outside influences, especially those advocated by an activist state.[89]

The dissimilar experience of Scandinavian Lutherans, also of recent immigration, is instructive. It is true that some Swedish Lutheran leaders, such as L. P. Esbjörn and Eric Norelius, were inspired by a confessional theology and a particularism inherent within it.[90] Such influences were even greater among those in the Norwegian Synod who were swayed by Walther and the teachings of his synod.[91] But, significantly, neither they nor their Swedish coreligionists were able to command the authority of the leaders of German Lutheranism. Rather, Scandinavian Lutheranism remained stamped with a greater affinity for a pietism that focused more on individual conversion and influenced even those who hewed to more corporatist convictions. As a result, Scandinavian Lutherans were tutored by leaders who increasingly pushed them toward a more liberal "Americanizing" posture than that of German Lutheranism.

These theological differences within Lutheranism were amplified by varying attitudes toward a national state carried from Germany and Scandinavia. Previous chapters have noted the tendency among immigrants to celebrate the possibilities of American society in part because its government permitted freedoms of religion under the aegis of the state. However content immigrants and leaders were with this arrangement, it is also true that they carried varying understandings of and attitudes toward the state to America. The failure of a particularist theology to take root among Scandinavians was perhaps due in part to a greater level of comfort with the state than that felt by Lutherans emigrating from Germany. Lars Trägårdh has brilliantly probed the differences between Sweden and Germany. The "people [*folk*]" of Sweden, he contends, conceived themselves to be linked historically to the state, which was seen by the people as antielitist in its opposition to the gentry. The peasants' independence and self-rule were honored for centuries, and they and the King were the two pillars of the state. The nobles were the villains, duplicitous agents willing to trade Swedish independence for their own gain. In effect, Trägårdh argues, the peasants' antielitism was prostatist.[92] The German idea of "people [*volk*]," on the other hand, predated the nation-state and took on a significance independent of the state. Because they were denied a central role in governmental affairs, German peasants maintained both antielitist and antigovernment sentiments. Further, they evinced no particular loyalty to democracy or the state, although they were increasingly viewed by antimodern thinkers as anchors of society.[93]

For Trägårdh's purposes, these ideological differences of peoplehood help untangle the contrary historical paths taken by Sweden and Germany in recent times. Yet they also indicate different sympathies toward the state that Scandinavian and German immigrants carried to the United States.[94] Although Scandinavian clergy ministered to immigrants who were more willing than their German counterparts to transfer their allegiance to the state from Europe to the United States, they most likely were less able to instill a particularism in congregations whose membership willingly acceded to a pluralist United States.

In sum, groups that maintained particularist sentiments and feared the intrusions of the state resolutely attempted to keep external influences out of their domain. Toward that end, they strove to build institutional structures that would shelter their communities and, in so doing, would contribute to the maintenance of the authority of "natural" institutions such as the family. Thus it was true that the families of immigrant groups such as Scandinavian Lutherans were built on patriarchal practices similar to those of their German Lutheran and Catholic counterparts. But because they were less concerned about governmental intrusions and therefore failed to build a large intraethnic institutional structure to shield their believers, groups such as Scandinavian Lutherans were more influenced by outside perspectives—including views on changing family roles and proprieties—that increasingly intruded into their local communities.[95]

One of the best illustrations of the relative influences of particularism and the levels of comfort with state intervention is the battle over public and parochial schools that occurred within ethnic groups in the late nineteenth century. Inextricably connected to the appropriate socialization of youths, schools were institutions in which the influence of the family, the community, and the state were often in conflict. By focusing on the battle within Roman Catholicism and the dissimilar experiences of German and Norwegian Lutherans, we can observe the relationship between the degrees of success in building religious schools and the intellectual premises on which they were based.

By the late nineteenth century, the parochial school had for decades been an institution used by Roman Catholics to protect their faith from the perceived assaults of American society. Debates occurred among members of the church at this time, however, about the role of the school in modern American society.[96] Liberal factions within the church leadership increasingly wished to grant the state a larger role in education, as in other realms of society. Educational experiments in Minnesota and New York, with the approval of liberal clerics, unified local Catholic and public school systems. Bishop John Lancaster Spaulding acknowledged that the state, "to protect itself[,] . . . is forced to establish schools."[97]

Spaulding's contentions, however, were a minority view; few in the church leadership or the laity throughout the nineteenth century acknowledged the state's agency in education. That responsibility had for millennia belonged to the church and the home.[98] As James Conway would write in an 1890 essay that expressed the commonly held wisdom of the church leadership, "According to natural law, which is the basis of the moral order and of all positive legislation, education is the business of the parents, to the exclusion of all others." The state, "according to the same divinely-constituted order," was not the educator of children. To be sure, it could promote education, but "any further interference . . . is not only violent and unjust" but also "destructive to religion, to morality, to genuine culture, and to the social order of nations."[99]

Antagonisms multiplied in the last decade of the nineteenth century when Thomas J. Bouquillon, a liberal Catholic theologian, suggested that perhaps the state should play a role in education. In his pamphlet entitled *Education: To Whom Does It Belong?*, Bouquillon agreed that education was the province of the family and church. But the state, he suggested cautiously, had a function as well. In fact, he wrote, education "belongs to the individual, physical or moral, to the family, to the State, to the Church, to none of these solely and exclusively." Since "man is not an isolated social being," these three units should work together in education. Indeed, "in the divine plan," Bouquillon concluded, the state, church, and family "should combine their effort for the common good of humanity."[100]

Bouquillon's thesis elicited a flurry of responses that pointed out his errors in the context of Catholic natural law. Conway, in a pamphlet revealingly entitled *The State Last*, argued, following natural law, that "parents have the *indispensable duty* . . . to educate their offspring." Since "an indispensable duty corresponds to an *inalienable right*," parents' influence on their children's education was paramount.[101] Inalienable rights, after all, could not be forfeited, even by a popular majority. The state had "neither the right nor the mission, nor the authority" to usurp parental rights by instituting either compulsory education or prescribed programs. This restraint of state power, Conway argued, did not make Catholics less patriotic. After all, "our American freedom" consisted of personal rights "so that every one who comes to our shores from European states . . . feels that the heavy burden of paternalism and bureaucracy has been lifted from his shoulders; and that he breathes more freely." In fact, Conway concluded, "it would be highly unpatriotic, or, at best, mistaken patriotism, to swerve from the time-tested principle, that a man's home is his castle, and to make ourselves and our children wards of the state."[102] Allegiances to Catholic natural law and American ideals apparently were entwined in the maintenance of parental powers.

Whereas the "state was last" for Conway, Rev. R. I. Holaind argued that the "parent was first." In his pamphlet, Holaind agreed with Conway that no one "has the right to educate the children of anybody else unless the parents give him that power." Liberals such as Bouquillon, Holaind contended, "ignore natural law, and try to find in legality the fount of every right." But Holaind declared that "the family is the true society, anterior to every kind of State or nation, with rights and duties of its own totally independent of the commonwealth." Because the family preceded the nation, moreover, it "must have rights and duties which are prior to those of the [state]." [103]

Holaind found others besides Conway to support his claims. He cited the seventeenth-century Catholic moralist Cornelius Otto Jansen, who argued, "It is with perfect right that parents call their children *their own*, and hold them as such." The social order, Jansen argued, was based on webs of authority within the family, an institution that preceded the state. It "is so designed by its divine author," Jansen claimed, "that its very elements are drawn from the order of the household; for the family, considered in its *nature*, is prior in existence, and the same thing may be said of parental authority." Thus "parental authority should not depend on the State" but should be left "to the family itself, under the guidance of a natural impulse, so to perfect its members that they may become valuable social elements." A different principle would "utterly destroy civil society, because it would transfer to the government, not only parental but also conjugal authority." [104] In short, here again we are presented with a world in which the family—braced by parental and conjugal authority—is the support upon which civil society rests. And here again, Jansen concluded, "order within the household requires that children should be perfectly obedient to their parents." [105]

The school debate was represented in everyday events as well as in theoretical formulations. Those who condemned the public school illustrated how its systematic attacks on the natural authority of parents resulted in deleterious effects on the society of youths. Most simply, the public schools were notorious for their "lax moral [*leichte Moral*]" standards. [106] More specifically, they introduced issues in society that were better left at home. Teachers, for example, reportedly lectured their pupils on temperance, which German editors found to be not only inappropriate in and of itself but also threatening to the authority of the home. When "women teachers gave talks on temperance" in school, the *Marshalltown (Iowa) Beobachter* observed, they "put the craziest notions in the children's heads." [107] In short, the public school taught profane values to fill the void left by the absence of godly morality, as defined, of course, by Roman Catholic moralists. [108]

The state schools were also perceived to be dangerous because they emphasized knowledge for knowledge's sake, which did not necessarily improve the moral climate of society. Local crime statistics that revealed that everyone arrested could read and write proved, according to the editor of *Die Iowa*, that "idleness is the source of all vice and that *school-learning does not prevent crime*." [109] Indeed, Conway argued, the "unlettered" were not the perpetrators of the "catalog of crime which is daily and weekly chronicled in our newspapers." Rather, "young America," instructed by a "godless education" and well-read in dime novels, "are bursting the bonds of domestic society in this country." State education not only "subvert[ed] the natural order instituted by the Creator" but also entailed "the most serious *consequences for morality*."[110]

Once again, spokespersons who correlated institutional failures with the decline of society focused on youth, and especially on girls. In 1880, for example, two farm girls "caught Amazon fever," ran away from home, donned men's clothing, cut their hair, and began to search for work as jockeys at horse races. It was apparent to the editors of *Die Iowa* that "reading 'dime novels' turned these geese into Amazons."[111] Four years later, the editor reported three suicides within twenty-four hours by young women from the town of Council Bluffs. Although one of the girls took her life because of her brutal stepfather, the editor nonetheless argued that "if they had to work as they should, thoughts of suicide would not have crossed their mind. *Accomplished education* will not do that."[112]

As public schools fostered unruliness and unhappiness, critics argued, their influence broadened. Advocates of public schools demanded the compulsory attendance of students without their parents' consent, yet another incursion on parental authority that elicited yet another "humbug."[113] While all school-age children were mandated to attend classes, their younger siblings were also victimized by a "school-madness" exemplified by attempts to establish kindergartens. For German Catholics, "the best kindergarten is the family," where parents "should raise their own."[114] And when children left the home, the best school was under the aegis of the church.

German Lutherans, like Roman Catholics, were also successful in affirming the value of private schools, which protected their youth from the power of the state and the detrimental influences of society. That success was in large part due to leaders such as Walther, whose advocacy of a Lutheran organic notion of the community as incompatible with the individualized state continued to inform the German Lutheran judgments about the utility of education.[115] Among the three estates of society, the community was responsible for education. It was the community that insured proper instruction in a social order that preached obedience to parental, matrimonial, domestic, and civil governments.[116]

German Lutherans, more than their Scandinavian coreligionists, were more troubled by the inherent ambiguities of living in the world but not being of it. The secular world was a place characterized by sin and therefore was not to be trusted. Civil government, moreover, was a negative force that checked evil rather than secured justice. The church school worked to shield the community from the public schools, which were distinguished by "rationalism," "materialism," and "indifferentism." Without the church school, neither the community nor the family was safe since ultimately, "schools of the state are schools of heathens [*Staats-schulen sind Heidenschulen*]." [117] "Thanks especially to the public schools," wrote a German Lutheran theologian in 1919, the "unbelieving part" of the American people live "in an atmosphere of blasphemy as if it were its life element." [118] The German Lutheran leadership successfully contended for decades that the parochial school was central to protecting the community and the family from a secularization that would create godless citizens and willful children characterized by insubordination and unresponsiveness to traditional moral convictions.

The contrast between the experiences of the German Lutheran leadership with regard to parochial schools and those of the Norwegian Lutherans is informative. [119] Although both groups feared the secular world and the "false freedoms" it wrought, German Lutheran leaders were more tenacious and ultimately more successful than Norwegian Lutherans in their advocacy of the parochial school. That difference was in part due to the fact that the pietist wing of Norwegian Lutheranism from the outset neglected the formation of parochial schools. But the less pietistic members of the Norwegian Synod posited the centrality of parochial schools, and their churches successfully established them. [120] The synod's clerical leadership, inspired by a vigorous evangelical movement in nineteenth-century Norway and powerfully influenced by the Lutheran orthodoxy of Walther and the German Missouri Synod, sought to establish an active school system organized around language and faith. Parochial schools were desirable, the leadership argued, for practical reasons. Subjects in the common schools in the rural Middle West were typically poorly taught. Clerics feared, moreover, that their native language would be lost. A crucial underlying issue, however, was more deeply embedded in religious belief and considered the proper structure of society and citizenship.

The public school issue proved to be a weighty topic of debate among Norwegian Americans in the decade following the end of the Civil War. In 1866, a convention of the Norwegian Synod adopted an educational policy that mirrored that of the Missouri Synod. The convention agreed that "the fact that religion is not taught [in public schools] is a necessary result of the religious freedom which it is our good fortune to enjoy under the present constitution of the state." But because the public school by definition was devoid of religion, essential duties of religious instruction were necessary "both in the home and in the congregational schools." The synod ultimately commanded its members not to "abandon our children to the discipline of teachers who are Roman Catholics, Methodists, or atheists" and who would fail to provide the "blessings of Christian discipline." In a learning environment stamped with a "glaring lack of external discipline, obedience, and order," "the principles of a false freedom and independence" would be "inculcated in the children, a practice that in time cannot but bear its tragic fruits in domestic relations with parents and masters and in civil relations with the authorities." [121] One pastor's six-year-old daughter inadvertently illustrated the "false freedoms" of the public school when she returned home with a "curious observation." "Just think, Papa," she said, "the schoolma'am calls us 'Ladies and Gentlemen'!" "What wild pedagogical ideas," the pastor concluded equivocally, "lie in this one remark!" [122] Schools that failed to inculcate the hierarchy of family and society clearly were suspect.

Eight years after this convention, another synodical meeting was called to address yet again the common school issue. And yet again the question of the respective roles of state, family, and community was central. One segment of the clergy, led by Bernt J. Muus and H. A. Preus, argued that parental authority ought to be placed above that of the state and that parents had the right to disobey and even oppose the state. Their voices were silenced, however, when they failed to convince the majority of their colleagues who maintained that parents must obey the laws unless they were contrary to the word of God. Parents could not simply choose which laws they would obey. In this instance, the laws of the state were paramount. [123]

Despite its efforts to establish parochial schools, then, the leadership of the Norwegian Synod, unlike its Missouri Synod counterparts, had by 1874 already failed to create a vigorous religious school system. This failure stemmed in part from financial constraints exacerbated by the depression of the 1870s. But it was primarily due to an opposition, less particularist and ultimately more integrationist and pluralist, that evolved both inside and outside the synod. To be sure, voices continued to advocate church schools. As late as 1877, Rev. F. A. Schmidt caustically declared that "schools where the Word of God is not the authority are the 'Gates of Hell.'" For him, the solution was to establish either religious schools or no schools at all. Five years later, the *Decorah-Posten* contended that public schools placed too much emphasis on economic issues and not enough on teaching the veneration of parents. [124]

Critics of church schools, however, became increasingly strident. Knud Langeland, the editor of *Skandinaven*, connected religious and cultural issues when he argued that Norwegian leaders were misled by "the German Missouri strait jacket, tyranny, and hierarchical domineering." [125] Rather than believing that parochial schools taught the only truth, scholars such as Rasmus B. Anderson argued that Norwegians should work within public schools so that their voices and influence could find a place in them. Toward that end, he demonstrated an acceptance of other commonly held beliefs of the dominant culture and the state. Anderson noted repeatedly (in fact, it was inscribed on his letterhead) that "whosoever directly or indirectly opposes the American common school is an enemy of education, of liberty, of progress. Opposition to the American common school is treason to our country."[126] Anderson's cultural pluralism ultimately proved more palatable to his countrymen than the particularism of the clerical leaders. When the debate over the Bennett Law, which required the instruction of the English language and American history, unfolded in Wisconsin in the late 1880s, the school issue flared up again among Norwegians, but the intensity of their reaction to the law in no way compared to the response among German Lutherans or Roman Catholics. Most Norwegian Lutherans had accepted the common school, which in turn profoundly modified their relationship with civil society and with their faith.[127]

The German Lutheran leadership, on the other hand, persevered in its quest to protect the church from state interference. That effort was abetted, as it was among Roman Catholics, by an authoritarian church structure that placed great power in the hands of the pastoral leadership. A privileged pastoral leadership, moreover, was founded upon Lutheran beliefs that explicitly separated state and community and empowered the latter. As Heinrich Maurer argues, the group allegiance preserved the idea of a "religion of the whole," but that whole—which included the family, the parish, the neighborhood, and the church—tempered the role of the state.[128] For these Lutherans, a reformist Christianity such as a Social Gospel that seemingly toiled in league with the state was nothing more than "secularized sectarianism," which was also to be avoided.[129] Ultimately, the state was an inherently imperfect institution with strict powers to govern a society mired in a condition of sin: it was, Maurer wrote, "at once a divine institution and yet not a Christian affair." Immigration to the West, after all, had been motivated by the possibility of isolation from the state, even as the state simultaneously enabled freedoms of belief to be protected.[130] Once again, the freedom to be authoritarian, granted in part by private schools, characterized selected immigrant communities.

Conclusion

For significant segments of the European immigrant leadership, the parochial school was part of a strategy to protect community and family from an apparent decline that, as one newspaper put it, was simply "against nature."[131] In the porous society of the rural Middle West, it was a local remedy to reduce diffusion from an American society increasingly flawed by liberalism, materialism, and individualism. Because the church and household were major stabilizing influences on state and society, moreover, religious schools ultimately served to strengthen the latter. Secular institutions, exemplified by the public school, on the other hand, lacked the moral anchors of church and home. A "state monopoly," *Die Iowa* concluded, hurt the nation and raised "a godless generation" who ironically undermined "the foundations of the state" that fostered such schools.[132] The influence of the parochial school, which would teach not only community morality but the authority of the family, ought to be paramount.

Despite a willingness to protect family, community, and even state by nurturing parochial schools, however, ethnoreligious groups, in particular those from Lutheran and Catholic traditions, differed in their success toward that end. Because they carried a favorable attitude toward inclusion in the state from Europe and developed a less deeply rooted particularist ideal in the United States, Scandinavian Lutherans were better able to make the transformation to a liberal, pluralist political world. German Lutherans were less willing to do so; they "never quite [became] . . . modern American[s]," Maurer wrote, because they remained committed to a fundamentalist confessionalism. These theological differences were played out in myriad sectors of American society. Cultural diffusion was inhibited by groups such as German Lutherans and Roman Catholics that built intellectual walls guarding against intrusions fostered in turn by powerful institutional structures within the community. These factors perhaps explain in part the tendency toward higher marital fertility and more vigorous support for the maintenance of hierarchy within the family among Roman Catholics and German Lutherans.[133] On the other hand, the varying comfort levels with the state and its governmental apparatus help explain the relatively active role in politics played by Scandinavian immigrants. Whereas eleven out of fourteen Minnesota governors between 1893 and 1940 were of Scandinavian origin, for example, "remarkably few American politicians emerged" from the Missouri Synod, as Richard Jensen notes, whose German Lutheran members steadfastly distrusted political parties.[134]

Despite their best efforts to avoid interaction with the state, however, members of even the most particularist groups, as we shall see in the next chapter, were pulled into political debate. And it should come as no surprise that the intellectual foundations of the cultural groups to which they adhered informed their political outlooks. Those who belonged to groups with particularist traditions seethed at the prospects of the success of a political agenda that sanctioned the actions of an activist, liberal state. They resisted the advocates of these programs, often identified as "Americans," who championed the enactment of liberal legislation that tempered the atomistic weaknesses of society, a solution that for many of a particularist and corporatist bent merely compounded the problems of a liberal, individualistic society.

In contrast to those who posited local and particularist solutions to society's ills, however, others feared an increasing segmentation that might result from these very solutions. Indeed, many residents of the United States came to advocate a more complex integration of governmental agencies in the realms of family and community at the precise time that particularist groups championed the retrenchment of home and community. They supported the growth of public schools and state-run agencies for child protection to expand the roles of state and local governments in the undertaking of child raising. They favored the rulings of American courts that began to posit explicitly the sovereign authority of the state to intrude into family units when acting in the interests of children. And they feared the tendency of particularist groups to oppose these developments. At the end of the nineteenth century, then, questions of the roles of family, community, and state were decisive issues in political debate. And the imprint of the minds of the West on the region remained central. The majority of residents of the United States rued the crises that repeatedly racked their society, but their solutions to the crises varied. These different solutions unmasked many of the intellectual foundations of dissimilar ethnic groups that became the basis for profound disagreement in the political debate that punctuated middle western society in the decades straddling the turn of the century.

CHAPTER 10

So Great Is Now the Spirit of
Foreign Nationality

Late-Nineteenth-Century Political Conflict

In an essay written in 1887, Father Edward McGlynn argued that the Know Nothingism of the previous generation had been a tragedy. It had been "prompted by an insensate and vulgar theological hatred," he contended, "precisely of the kind that still makes Orangemen and Catholics beat and kill each other." More troubling, it had attacked a perceived problem that had in fact not threatened the nation. Immigrants, Catholic and non-Catholic alike, had not been disloyal, a premise on which Know Nothingism had been based. Rather, McGlynn stressed, they had convincingly demonstrated "their love of American institutions, and their pride in American citizenship." They had been, he assured his readers, "eager to assimilate themselves to the common American type."[1]

McGlynn sensed that, regrettably, the immigrants of modern America differed in outlook from those who had been subjected to the loathing of the Know Nothing Party at mid-century. Thus McGlynn's fears that Know Nothingism might recur in his contemporary society were not based on the behavior of American nativists. Rather, "what, most of all, might seem well adapted to revive and intensify the old hateful and bigoted spirited of Know-Nothingism, and justify its fears and predictions," he charged, was the prevailing behavior of the foreign-born. Instead of assimilating, immigrants and their leadership hoped to take control of the schools and perpetuate their native tongue. German American leaders wished to "pour hundreds of thousands of her people on our shores," an "insane hope . . . cherished chiefly in Wisconsin and in the Valley of the

Northern Mississippi." Foreign-born citizens made no attempt to conceal their "contempt of Americans, and of American manners and traditions." The most stinging reproach that a German American youth could receive from his teachers and parents was "*Du bist ein Amerikaner*," a censure that not only defamed "Americans" but also castigated the youth for his "manliness and independence."[2] For McGlynn, "so great is now the spirit of foreign nationality among foreign-born citizens that many among them make no concealment of their sense of superiority." The fragile interaction between the American nation and its cultural groups had been placed in a disequilibrium of separatism and particularism. It was now the foreign-born rather than American nativists who were intolerant.[3]

McGlynn, who pledged steadfast loyalty to both nation and church, feared the increased separatism and particularism among his coreligionists. He suggested that the mutually reinforcing allegiances to nation and ethnic group that balanced what we have called a complementary identity had been thrown into a disequilibrium for many ethnic Americans. Whereas immigrants once had celebrated the American environment because it offered the possibility of retaining religious, linguistic, and ethnic practices, he implied that many ethnic leaders rejected this cultural-pluralist model and increasingly aspired to privilege their particular beliefs. Unlike their republican adversaries who sought homogeneity at mid-century, moreover, these groups knew that they could not convert the diverse nation to their beliefs. Rather, by turning inward and affirming their community of belief over the national community, they hoped to temper the influence of outside forces, particularly that of the increasingly powerful state, on their families and communities. In short, because family and community institutions were instrumental in maintaining order and hierarchy in society, many European American leaders chastised those who would sacrifice them on the altar of a liberal state.

McGlynn's criticism of an immigrant particularism that distorted the complementary identity appeared at a time when other Americans who feared the immigrant presence in the United States proposed that American society more forcefully intrude into ethnic enclaves. One prong of this offensive was an effort to extend the influence of the American state into the homes of its citizens. Crusades, which were often sponsored by "Americans," continued to be aimed, as in the Know Nothing movement of past generations, at a conversion to American and Protestant ways that would contribute to the creation of a homogeneous United States. One of the most prominent examples in the Middle West was the American Protective Association (APA), a nativist anti-Catholic organization, which from its inception in Clinton, Iowa, in 1887 not only castigated Catholics but also stressed the importance of a national state that could influence and direct the behavior of its individual citizens. The strength of the organization, which rose to prominence in the early 1890s, was not trivial: at its height, the APA reportedly had nearly 2.5 million members concentrated in the middle western states.[4]

Josiah Strong's *Our Country: Its Possible Future and Its Present Crisis*, which appeared in 1885 and sold 167,000 copies in six years, also illustrated the concerns many Americans felt about ethnic and religious differences in the late nineteenth century.[5] Like the APA, Strong reiterated old complaints about immigrants in general and the Catholic church in particular. Echoing grievances voiced decades before, he contrasted the principles of the church with those "of our free institutions," which were grounded on "individuals . . . capable of self-government." Unlike absolutist regimes in which man existed for the state, the church and state existed for man in "republican and Protestant America."[6] Late nineteenth-century liberal "Americans" thus rekindled notions that "Americanization" was crucial, a foreshadowing of the "Americanist" and Progressive rhetoric that would come to full flower in the early decades of the twentieth century and would impugn the cultural pluralism that had characterized the complementary identity in earlier decades.

It is not surprising that the Middle West was the setting where these diametrically opposed postures found their most pointed political expression. Old canards were retold in the late nineteenth century. The Middle West again was perceived as an environment ripe for disruption. The Roman Catholic Church, Strong claimed, was "concentrating her strength in the western territories" because "as the West is to dominate the nation, she intends to dominate the West."[7] He stressed, moreover, that the Middle West remained both a landscape defined by ethnocultural difference and a center of European immigrant culture replete with powerful ethnic institutions. Strong anchored his suspicion of conspiracy on the reality that European immigrants and their children maintained "an unhappy tendency toward aggregation, which concentrates the strain upon portions of our social and political fabric." These people, who, Strong noted, lived in colonies that in some cases encompassed over 300 square miles, were "building up states within a state, having different languages, different antecedents, different religions, different ideas and habits, preparing mutual jealousies, and perpetrating race antipathies."[8] One-half century after Samuel F. B. Morse, then, Strong and McGlynn directed their gaze toward the Middle West, where they saw both a region of great importance to the nation and the site of schemes to segregate a foreign mind.

In addition to rehearsing time-worn outlooks that informed the problem, Americans advanced new strategies to address it. The late nineteenth century, the first section of this chapter argues, was an era increasingly punctuated by political movements seeking to merge local communities into a larger whole under the aegis of state and national governments. Whether these campaigns found expression in movements to regularize schools across larger political boundaries or in endeavors to control behavior such as the consumption of alcohol, they were consistent attempts to enlarge the power of the state and to protect individuals within its sphere. These efforts, by considering the prerogatives of the family and the community in relation to the rights of its constituent members, raised critical questions in a region stamped by its ethnic diversity. When they entered the political arena, these questions were not merely symbolic issues but crucial matters of power and influence. The political debate of the late nineteenth century thus divided Americans as they grappled not only with attitudes regarding separatism and assimilation in American society but also with questions of the relative influence of family, community, and an increasingly powerful state.

The coalitions that formed to grapple with these issues were not *defined* by ethnic and cultural background. Liberal efforts to expand the role of the state, for example, were promoted by a coalition that included segments of voters with recent immigrant pasts. But coalitions were *informed* by the intellectual programs of the religious and ethnic groups of which their memberships were a part. Those cultural groups that tended to question individual contracts with the state and to distrust the benevolence of state intrusion were less comfortable with efforts to enlarge the state's role in everyday life. Because the concern about divided loyalties often focused on Roman Catholicism, it betrayed an undercurrent of anti-Catholicism in tone and substance. Middle western politicians built coalitions based on ethnic coalitions that in turn were shaped by conceptions of the proper institutional structures of society.

The second section of the chapter illustrates how the more particularist segments of ethnic America perceived this program of governmental expansion to be a violation of their structures of family and community and thus the order of society itself. Specific ethnic traditions that had successfully continued to posit organic societal structures comprehended issues surrounding the public school, women's rights, and temperance to be explicit attempts to weaken the influence of the family and community in their relationship with state and society. Leaders in these groups, as I argued in the preceding chapter, saw society as an array of institutional structures that supported one another. Weakening the family and the community would indelibly weaken society. Apparently, their arguments convinced the male electorate. In a series of referenda on the specific issues, voting returns clearly indicate not only that the electorate was interested in these issues but also that religious and cultural groups divided as we would expect. The more corporatist and particularist European groups voted against temperance and women's suffrage, while their liberal counterparts were more likely to join predominantly "American" agglomerations in favoring legal change.

Although single issues most effectively exposed political cleavages, underlying questions about the nature of the state and family, individual and community, were influential in other political contexts. They informed electoral politics as they affected the political programs of discrete ethnic and religious organizations. Political historians, as we shall see in the final section of the chapter, have for some time argued correctly that cultural and religious groups tended to cluster in political parties with whose platforms they were most comfortable. Thus, as immigrant groups were "ethnicized," they not only brought their inclinations into the political debate but also demanded that political parties, which depended upon them for support, take their considerations seriously. Meanwhile, others among them maintained positions, exemplified by the remarkable commentary of the German Catholic leadership, that lay outside the scope of mainstream politics and that contested core principles of liberalism in modern American society. Influenced by corporatist ideologies emanating from Europe and facing perceived political threats in the United States, they foresaw the decline of the United States and stressed that it was only through the maintenance of "Catholic" principles that the United States could continue as a nation. Particularist in construction, their program concluded that perhaps the Republic should cast off its republican heritage.

The Family, the Community, and the State in Late-Nineteenth-Century Political Debate

The Pope denies the right of the state to cross the domestic threshold and includes within the pale of domesticity the education of the young. . . . Let the State concede this right and the rising generation will be Americans only in name, but in reality subjects of a foreign paparchy. —W. J. H. Traynor, "The Menace of Romanism," *North American Review* (1895)

The manner in which the family, the community, and the state were defined legally and politically went a long way toward explaining the construction of political power in society. Many Americans, although they treasured local institutions like the family, felt increasingly comfortable with political movements that attempted to insure an equity for family members that was not forthcoming from the family itself. This activist outlook expanded to address myriad contemporary problems, including perceptions that ethnic separation was dividing society and that families and society were racked by social problems. It appealed especially to those in the Middle West with backgrounds in the eastern United States who, not coincidentally, tended to be bourgeois residents of small towns who were members of the Republican Party. It was they who kept questions regarding the roles of family, community, and state at the center of the public discussion in the decades surrounding the turn of the century.[9] And it was they who demanded a centralization of government that would assure an "assimilation" of immigrants by the state.

The activist perspective was informed by at least three overlapping convictions. First, nativist sentiments, particularly those anti-Catholic in expression, feared that the private sphere of family and community indoctrinated children and laity in behaviors and beliefs detrimental to the nation. The APA and Strong were extreme examples to be sure, but their popularity resulted in part from the articulation of a deep-seated distrust of immigrants, especially those who confessed their obedience to the church. Time and again, anti-Catholic tracts expressed concern that the loyalty of Roman Catholics to the state was ambiguous. Repeatedly, they pointed to the growing conservatism of the Holy See with regard to its demands for obedience. The church allegedly criticized basic American freedoms of belief and conscience and cautioned its adherents to obey religious authority in all of its forms.[10] For Strong, an "irreconcilable difference" existed between what he called "Papal principles" and the "fundamental principles of our free institutions," which included the freedoms of speech and religion and the liberty of conscience.[11] W. J. H. Traynor, president of the APA, agreed, writing that "the State requires most perfect and complete fidelity and obedience to the Republic." On the other hand, "the voice of the Papacy is no less uncertain; it demands the unqualified obedience of its adherents to the Pontiff."[12] Elsewhere, he argued that the American Constitution and the encyclicals of the church were "utterly irreconcilable one with the other, unless the United States be regarded merely as a province of the papal church." Traynor, Strong, and many others contended that loyalty was a zero-sum game: one's loyalty to church detracted from one's allegiance to nation. "Where the people are strong, where the state is powerful," Traynor argued, "the papacy is weak."[13] It followed that where the papacy was strong, the state and people were weak, a situation that Traynor assured his readers was fraught with danger.

Anti-Catholicism was thus underlaid by a second viewpoint that looked with increasing favor on state intervention as it reiterated the dangers of the structure of Roman Catholicism to American society. As we observed in Chapter 1, the West—the region that would become the Middle West—was already a setting where institutions were formed explicitly to instruct the citizenry in its civic duties. The fears that either an untutored populace or one that hewed to regressive faiths would lead the region to ruin compelled gatherings of citizens to consider the advantage of institutions, such as schools, that would inform the behavior of residents. Their reasoning was based on the belief that schools would educate impartially and that individuals would gain from that edification the intelligence and judgment to make correct choices. If children, on the other hand, were indoctrinated in group goals, as was the case in parochial schools, their opinions obviously would be skewed. It followed that government could play a role in issues such as education and enact laws that interacted not only with the rights of parents but also with the certainties of faith. These beliefs were easily integrated into expressions that appeared to favor an "assimilation" of "American principles."

Spokespersons espousing this perspective suggested that the state had the right to intrude into matters of home and community. Youths nurtured entirely within families that accepted the authority of religious leaders would not be brought up with an independence of mind and would not develop adequate loyalty to nation. "Let the State concede this right [that is, the right to enter the household]," Traynor warned, "and the rising generation will be Americans only in name, but in reality the subjects of a foreign paparchy." It would only be a matter of time before "the Republic as established by the signers of the Declaration of Independence be merely a memory." [14] "Individual culture and responsibility," which were sustained by a "public school system, where education is provided by the State and is free from sectarian control," were thus essential. [15]

A third factor that defined this worldview, a factor embodied in the public school system, was the perception that government institutions should play an active role in improving society. Significantly, many who expressed liberal beliefs were becoming decidedly comfortable with the positive role of the state in the decades after the Civil War. [16] Contained within this perspective was a progressive impulse, reformist in intent, aimed at uncovering social ills and working to improve them, often through state influence in institutional or legal contexts. It was defined in particular by the growing political influence of women's groups that eventually blossomed in the early decades of the twentieth century into what historians have characterized as a welfare-state "maternalism" resulting from women's "domestication of politics." [17] Welfare maternalism was represented by metaphors of women bringing their roles as housekeepers within the family to governmentwide duties, of the state as a large family, and of the boundaries between the public world and the private family being dissolved as a result. The logical conclusion was that a national family—composed of individuals living under its auspices—could influence and occasionally supersede the purpose and functions of other local institutions.

Not everyone who advocated increased state activism subscribed with equal enthusiasm to these convictions. But the constellation of these perspectives did contribute to a centering of political debate on ethical issues in the late nineteenth century principally because many perceived state intervention to be a satisfactory way to address social ills. Because it was activist, this movement brought questions of social reform into the political realm either through electoral politics, referenda, or legal efforts to alter the institutional structures of government. "Blue laws," the abolishment of capital punishment, questions of criminal rights, the sale of tobacco to minors, and the restriction of first-cousin marriages were only some of the moral questions taken up in middle western state legislatures.[18]

More significant, however, were three movements that were powerfully informed, each in their own way, by a combination of nativism and anti-Catholicism, notions of liberal arrangements between state and individual, and a progressive, reformist impulse that valued public, and often governmental, intervention into the private world of home and community.[19] Debates surrounding the public school, temperance, and women's rights, which preoccupied politicians and the citizenry in the late nineteenth century, afford us a view of how their advocates linked individuals and families to broad government structures.

Advocacy of the public school was based on the fear that its parochial counterpart taught ignorance and sectarian beliefs inappropriate for an increasingly complex, increasingly pluralist society. The school debate, of course, was not new. Critics had argued for decades that parochial schools denied individuals the freedom to mature and to act as citizens under the auspices of the state. They had contended, moreover, that parochial schools not only limited individual growth but also created an ignorant society. But by the final quarter of the century, the debate was renewed with increasing vigor. In 1875, no less a figure than President Ulysses S. Grant explicitly correlated freedom with the public school. In a remarkable speech at the ninth annual meeting of the Society of the Army of the Tennessee on 29 September 1875, Grant warned, in a veiled attack on the immigrant—and especially the Catholic—population, of an "enemy who tries to hinder the progress of our free institutions." He cautioned that "if we are to have another contest in the near future of our national existence, I predict that the dividing line will not be the Mason and Dixons but between patriotism and intelligence on the one side and superstitions, ambition, and ignorance on the other." His Manichaean perspective thus made it imperative that public schools remain state-run institutions wherein children were provided with a "good elementary education . . . free both of sectarianism and atheism" and that religion be left to "the family, the altar and the church."[20]

Grant did not stop there. Some months later, he submitted an amendment to the Constitution that would make public schools mandatory in all states and prohibit the use of public school monies for any religious purposes.[21] The debate that ensued tied together myriad questions of states' rights and the future of Reconstruction, but the place of the Catholic Church in the United States was central to it. Disturbed by the pronouncements of the Holy See, observers in the United States promoted public schools with increasing urgency as institutions that fostered American beliefs.[22] Whereas the Roman Catholic Church was a hierarchy that advanced the notion that people were incapable of thinking for themselves, the *Davenport (Iowa) Gazette* argued in 1875, "the Bible teaches individual responsibility for sin, and republicanism teaches that every citizen must be capable of judging of public affairs." In the end, it concluded, a "Christianity that thinks, and Republicanism that thinks, is the normal condition in America, and free schools are necessary to both."[23]

Grant's proposal framed the debate over the public school for years to come. Although the impetus for a constitutional amendment faded, the perception developed as the public school system expanded that it should be coordinated and systematized to meet a single standard in each state. The legislatures of Wisconsin and Illinois, among others, enacted bills requiring that the schools in their respective states be inspected regularly. The Bennett Law, passed by the Wisconsin legislature in the spring of 1889, compelled parents and guardians to send children aged seven to fourteen to school at least twelve weeks out of the year. The major point of controversy was the definition of a school. "No school shall be regarded as a school," section 5 of the law stated, unless "part of the elementary education of children" included "reading, writing, arithmetic, and United States history in the English language." Perhaps most important of all, boards of education, rather than parents, were given final authority over the education of children.[24] The Edwards Law, also enacted in 1889, required English-language instruction of children in Illinois schools. It also obliged children between the ages of seven and fourteen to attend public school at least sixteen weeks a year.[25] Ostensibly dispassionate mandates to regulate the tutelage of youths, these laws cut to the heart of the question of the rights of parents and community in relation to those of the state. As a result, they became burning political issues throughout the region.

The temperance question was a second issue that illustrated deep cultural rifts in the late nineteenth-century Middle West and stemmed from differing ideas of how the state should adjudicate social issues. As in the case of the public school problem, temperance had long inspired social and political activism and often wedded a reformist perspective to governmental activism and anti-immigrant nativism. Proponents of temperance, like public school advocates, were particularly active in pushing through measures in the late nineteenth century. The symbolism of temperance often focused on the family, and the saloon was frequently juxtaposed with the family to warn that the former would ultimately wipe out the latter if it was not eliminated.[26] In order to protect families, laws had to be enacted not only to restrict access to the saloon but also to define proper behavior within domestic groups.[27]

The temperance movement gained momentum throughout the nineteenth century and periodically flared up as a pivotal political issue. By 1893, fifteen states had passed legislation prohibiting the sale of alcohol.[28] Temperance proponents were especially active in middle western states, where efforts to add temperance regulations to state constitutions resulted in referenda in Iowa, Ohio, and Michigan in the 1880s.[29] These legal initiatives were periodically supplemented by extralegal violence of citizens, many of them women, who led raids on saloons in attempts to destroy liquor.

The temperance crusade was commonly identified with people of American birth, Protestant (and especially Methodist) faiths, and small-town virtues. Influential Protestant churches—including the Methodist, Congregational, Baptist, Presbyterian, United Brethren, and Christian Churches—passed resolutions to support the restriction of alcohol. The crusade was also an entrée for women into political activism. The Women's Christian Temperance Union (WCTU), as its name suggests, connected women and their churches to the temperance cause. Often meeting in the buildings of religious groups, the members of the WCTU denounced the evils of alcohol and ultimately expanded their concerns to other issues that they feared compromised the American family, such as gambling and prostitution.[30]

Temperance advocates also frequently betrayed a nativist prejudice. As *Die Iowa* wrote simply during a referendum campaign to revise Iowa's constitution by adding a prohibition amendment: "The foundation of the temperance question is xenophobia [*Fremdenhass*]."[31] The *Dubuque Herald* lamented that debate had stimulated "a war of races."[32] The *Des Moines Register*, an influential advocate of the amendment, illustrated its nativism by applauding those who answered German opponents to prohibition by saying, " 'If you do not like this country and its people, the world is full of other countries to which you can go.'" "American ideas are going to rule in the American republic," it concluded, "and it is time for all the world to understand it, and for everybody who comes here to live from abroad to come here with this one fact understood."[33] The issue also clearly demarcated cultural groups. When a prohibition law was passed in Iowa, the prognosis for its successful implementation was culture-coded. In central and western Iowa, wrote a disheartened *Die Iowa*, where a "high proportion of Yankees from the east" lived, enforcement was vigorous. On the borders of the state, "where Germans and Irish predominate, less effort has been invested to enforce the 'majesty' of this tyrannical law."[34]

Embedded in the divisions over the temperance movement, as in the public school issue, were questions of family and community rights and state intervention. Temperance proponents often argued that the evil of drink infiltrated the family and endangered its weakest members. They thus sought to encourage and ultimately to legislate limitations on the use of alcohol in order to protect those within the domestic group. Temperance legislation, argued a paper published in the protemperance town of Cresco, Iowa, made men "better husbands and better fathers." And laws prohibiting strong drink were essential. "A pledge not to *use* intoxicating liquors is good," it argued, "but it is not enough. A man ought also to pledge himself not to permit the *sale* of liquor of any kind as a beverage."[35]

The third in the trio of crucial political questions in the late nineteenth century—women's rights and, more specifically, women's suffrage—was also wrapped in cultural codes of family and community. As a nascent political movement, women's suffrage received less political attention than either temperance or the public schools in the late nineteenth century. When women were first granted the ballot, they were allowed to vote in only local or school elections. The movement became increasingly meaningful, however, not only because activists wed it explicitly to other issues such as temperance but also because women gained additional rights over time. Women suffragists, who portrayed the government and its citizenry as one large family, were able to illustrate dramatically the place of mothers and wives within it. Thus women, like men before them, would become individuals separate from the family and community structures of a private sphere that historically had restricted their political rights.[36]

The political coalitions that formed around these cultural issues were based on a number of factors. Certainly negative reference and contemporary political currents, exemplified by anti-Catholic movements, influenced voters. But intellectual formulations based on the relationships between individual and state, family and community, most likely were even more pivotal in predicting voters' political postures. Significant proportions of those who advocated temperance and women's rights, then, sprang from American traditions carried westward, such as American Methodism, which sought the perfection of the individual and increasingly countenanced the role of the state in working toward that end. Yet many leaders of European traditions also championed liberal political programs. Consider the liberal Roman Catholic leadership. Ceaselessly wary of an anti-Catholicism that was laced throughout "Americanizing" movements, the liberal wing of the Catholic Church, including such leaders as Archbishop John Ireland and Cardinal James Gibbons, grappled with ways in which the church could be integrated into American society. Mindful of the centrality of Roman Catholicism in the lives of their parishioners, they also sought avenues to mold Catholics into what they considered loyal Americans. The more radical clerical wing, embodied by McGlynn, concurred. His condemnation of conservatives in the clergy was also a liberal paean to American nationality. The remedy for the crisis in the late nineteenth century, he argued, was "securing to all men the largest liberty compatible with the liberties and rights of others, and therefore granting absolute equal justice to all, and never the slightest privilege or favor to any." Only then could "one magnificent American nationality, covering a whole continent, speaking one language, enjoying equal laws . . . and accomplishing for humanity greater wonders of civilization than the world had yet ventured to hope for," be perpetuated.[37]

This outlook was visible in many contexts. The school question profoundly divided members of the church. Liberal Catholics supported public schools—Ireland called them "our pride and our glory"—and developed a plan for state-supported sectarian schools.[38] Liberals also promoted the increased integration—indeed, they called it "Americanization"—of their laity into American society and chafed at attempts to bolster old structures of language and European nationality. When the leadership of the church was divided at the turn of the century over the "Cahensly movement," which promoted an ecclesiastical structure composed of dioceses based on nationalities, leaders such as Ireland and John L. Spaulding attempted to foster an "American Catholicity" that was characterized by a liberalism and Americanism feared by their adversaries.[39]

Although these sentiments were shared by a minority in the Catholic Church, they found more common expression among Protestant immigrants who were stung less often by ugly religious nativism, who were more familiar with reformist movements such as temperance, and whose religious foundations tended to be less corporatist and particularist. A growing apprehension among the Protestant foreign-born concerning the alleged political machinations of Catholicism in the United States in fact actually propelled many toward sympathy with anti-Catholic organizations. *Norden*, a Norwegian-language paper, agreed with *Svenska Amerikanaren* that Catholicism tended to slow intellectual growth and weaken patriotism in lands where it held sway. Scandinavian, British, and Canadian immigrants, moved by such anti-Catholic sentiments, swelled the membership rolls of the APA as a result.[40]

A centuries-old hatred of Catholicism, moreover, was fortified by pro-state and liberal postures with which some ethnic intellectual traditions were becoming increasingly comfortable. Ethnic and religious traditions that had not developed parochial school systems were less moved by the school issue. A host of immigrants would have agreed with *Sändebudet*, a Swedish American paper, that a free public school secured American liberty as it formed "our safest protection against Catholic intrusions."[41] Other immigrant subgroups carried traditions of temperance across the Atlantic.[42] Many among Scandinavian and Dutch Protestant faiths pursued prohibitionist activities in their new land, and the more liberal among them were willing to support governmental efforts to restrict access to alcohol.

Most of the foreign-born, however, realized that they should use liberal "Americanizing" principles, especially those espoused by nativist organizations such as the APA, with some caution. One Norwegian newspaper warned its readers that if they countenanced the attacks by the APA on one type of immigrant, they might be jeopardizing their own place in society in the long run.[43] Despite their early support of the APA, Swedish Americans eventually argued that the organization smacked of "know-nothingism" and "Yankeeism"; immigrants, claimed one Swedish American, were not ready to recognize the intellectual superiority of the "anaemic, pale, tea-drinking natives."[44] By championing the public schools in order to attack Catholic parochial institutions, moreover, they were empowering the state to be the instructor of religion. By assaulting Catholicism, they ultimately might be endangering their own Lutheranism.[45]

Although political postures with regard to cultural issues were not neatly arranged according to ethnic and religious groups, the intellectual underpinnings expressed by their leaderships were nevertheless significant in predicting political behavior. Whereas those from some ethnic intellectual traditions showed increasingly less concern about governmental incursions into their home and community, others became more and more troubled by the growing power of a liberal state. The predicament for the latter was represented by the growing concern over both "American" and secular intrusions into their communities. The conflict swirling around the schools, restrictions on alcoholic drink, and women's rights illustrated for them these quandaries and reveals the ways in which similar political issues could be used to symbolize varying conceptions of the relative place of the family, the community, and the state in society.

Cultural Symbolism in Political Debate:
The Common School, Temperance,
and Women's Rights

> The RUIN OF RELIGIOUS BELIEF . . . has brought on a weakening of the principles of morality. This is essentially the work of the godless school; it is also the result of the spreading of a bad press and the license given all attacks against religion and its dogmas. . . . To-day some are beginning to see that their blows . . . , by ruining the religious belief among the people, . . . have destroyed the very foundation of all social order. —"The Disorganization of the Family," *Catholic Tribune* (1901)

Despite the drift of many in ethnic America toward liberal conceptions of society, others, such as the editors of the *Catholic Tribune* at the dawn of the new century, were more hesitant. They reflected the view that the social and economic changes in the late nineteenth century challenged family and community. They reacted against a liberal solution that they felt only compounded these misfortunes, in large part because it destroyed the intermediate ligaments of family and community that served as a brace against untrammeled individual interests within civil society. These weaknesses, the argument continued, were further complicated by the role played by the state. A liberal civil society that privileged relationships between individuals and the state diminished the influence of the intermediary institutions that fortified society. Importantly, those who embraced these positions built large private institutional structures—such as parochial schools—that checked deviations from the path laid out by the community and religious leadership.

By revisiting the issues of the public school, temperance, and women's suffrage from these perspectives, we can observe how significant segments among European Americans used each to illustrate their sense of the proper structure of society. The debate around each issue thus divided people—liberals and corporatists, women and men—within European ethnic and religious traditions. Yet those European ethnic traditions that were most steadfast in retaining (and elaborating upon) a view of inviolable family and community structures were also most troubled by what they perceived to be incorrect incursions of the state represented by these issues. They connected the movements to the increased power of the government, which would allow an "artificial" state in effect to regulate "natural" institutions such as the family and community. Symbolically, moreover, each issue illustrated their contentions from different angles of vision. The school controversies considered the place of children and the degree to which they were members of family and community or young citizens of the state. The debate over women's suffrage specifically focused on the power of women within home and society and illustrated the viewpoint that women's suffrage would place the "natural" order of the family in disarray. Temperance was viewed by many of its opponents not only as yet another invasion of home and community but also as an illustration of the logical conclusion of state intervention. Many of the foreign-born argued that excessive behavior of individuals within the society—abuse of alcohol, for example—was addressed by excessive invasions by the state, which enacted laws that destructively constrained the proper authority of families and communities. Ultimately, they saw their theory confirmed in observed behavior: state intrusions created mayhem among people living in weakened families and communities.

The school question remained especially meaningful to ethnic and religious groups that had fostered successful parochial school systems. Roman Catholics by the late nineteenth century had developed a school system aimed at protecting family and faith. German Catholics, stung by the consequences of intemperate nationalism in their homeland stemming from Bismarck's *Kulturkampf*, were especially intent on shielding their believers from public schools. Thus, when Grant began his concerted attack on parochial schools in the United States, the parallels with Germany seemed clear. As one newspaper editor wrote sarcastically in response to Grant's 1875 Des Moines speech that defended the public school, "The *Kulturkampf* has officially begun in our free United States."[46] Some months later, when Grant introduced his constitutional amendment to Congress, the *Luxemburger Gazette* reminded its readers that Grant "has inaugurated the *Kulturkampf* officially and formally."[47]

When the political controversies over public schooling erupted around the Bennett and Edwards Laws thirteen years later, Roman Catholics joined German Lutherans in defending their system of education, which sustained the authority of the local community and family.[48] They disparaged the encroachments of the state into these crucial structures of power and influence. The Roman Catholic bishops of Wisconsin, Richard Jensen notes, intensified the political conflict by issuing a manifesto that officially opposed the Bennett Law because it obstructed "the rights of the Church and of the parent." Seeking to promote the influence of community and family, they argued further that the law was aimed at placing "parochial and private schools under the control of the state."[49] German

Lutherans, who administered a complex parochial school system, also defended their schools from a perspective of community rights.[50] The Wisconsin Synod argued that the Bennett Law permitted "unjustifiable encroachments upon parental rights and family life." The Wisconsin District of the Missouri Synod contended that the law was "a violation of the natural rights of parents and the Constitution."[51]

The degree to which this official rhetoric was endorsed by male voters is illustrated by electoral results. Indeed, the fallout stemming from educational reform shook the political structure of Wisconsin in 1890.[52] Following the passage of the Bennett Law, Roman Catholics and German Lutherans coalesced to rescind it and punish the Republican Party, which they held responsible for the law. As Jensen has shown, this opposition emphasized the rights of parents and the church, on the one hand, and assailed a law that they considered an attack on non-Yankee culture, on the other. The Democratic Party, in a masterful 1890 campaign, was able to profit from the support of ethnic voters—German Lutherans, Roman Catholics, and even Norwegians—who were irritated by the nativist character of the pro–Bennett Law camp and wished to condemn what the Wisconsin Democratic platform called the "needless interference with parental rights and liberty of conscience." Roger Wyman has noted that between 1888 and 1890 "Yankee Protestants" increased their support for the Republican Party, German voters shifted to the Democratic Party, and Scandinavians decided not to vote at all.[53] The Republicans lost every major political office except one in what was termed "the Lutheran land-slide."[54]

As in the school debate, many European American leaders perceived the advocacy of women's rights to be a flagrant attack on family and community. Whereas the public school was portrayed as a governmental invasion of the community that corrupted children, women's rights efforts were seen by many among the principally male commentators as bald attempts to alter the natural role of women and thereby disrupt the natural order of family. These perceptions were situated in the seeming obsession with the ambiguities of sex roles that were in turn connected to the declining influence of the family.[55] Whereas public schools allegedly created unruly and unhappy children, manlike women and womenlike men resulted from political rights for women. When *Fædrelandet og Emigranten*, a Norwegian-language paper, reported on the convention of the American Equal Rights Society in 1869, it argued that "the American ladies [*Damer*] no longer want to be women and wear skirts. They want to exchange family life for public life, skirts for trousers, and roam around the country playing political intrigue and giving public speeches."[56] Jörgen Jensen, the editor of *Budstikken*, another Norwegian-language paper, linked social class and "Americanness" to women's rights movements when he condemned the delegates at an international women's convention as "bluestockings and cranks, with which America is so richly endowed." Overdressed women, symbolizing luxury and extravagance, threatened the Republic, just as "masculine" voting women endangered electoral politics.[57] When a woman was nominated to be county recorder in Dubuque County, the *Dyersville (Iowa) Demokrat*, a German-language paper, coupled changes in political rights in the public sphere with shifts in power at home. Following women's suffrage, it predicted, a man will "sit in his house singing *Bye, rocker bye, baby* while his better half goes though the county making stump *speeches.*"[58]

The dangers of women in politics were thus intrinsically related to fears that women might forsake their homes. The *Lutheran Witness*, the Missouri Synod's official English-language paper, wrote of the "new women" who "cast the church aside, because it teaches subordination of the wife to the husband." She "enjoins domestic duties from which the 'taste' of the new woman revolts. The new woman hates children, and is madly exerting her ingenuity in frustrating the ends of matrimony."[59] Two years earlier, a family journal of the same church maintained that "woman's ambition in the past decade has tended more or less manward. That is, having grown discontented with her divinely ordained sphere, she has been endeavoring to overstep her bounds and pose as that she is not, nor ever can be."[60] As late as 1920, the *Lutheran Witness* prophesied that female suffrage would cause many women to "be so busy about voting and political office that the home and children will have no attraction for them, and American mothers and children, like Christian charity, will be a rarity."[61] As Alan Graebner points out, German Lutherans condemned the feminist movement as *Zeitkrankheit* and female suffrage an *Unordnung.*[62]

The growing influence of women in other realms of the public sphere such as the school also spawned a storm of criticism. When *Die Iowa* observed in 1883 that nearly three-quarters of the teachers in Iowa were women, it commented that it was "no wonder so few men of Iowa have character" since "education by women is an evil full of ominous, pernicious consequences."[63] The misogyny was even more shrill when aimed at women who served as elected school officials. Because school administration politics, a nexus of education and politics, was an arena where women were able to garner their most visible political power in the late nineteenth century, the attacks against them were among the most malicious.[64] The election of a female school superintendent in one case led to musings that "as time goes on perhaps men will get to feed the babies, wash the dishes and do other domestic duties so the lord ladies have opportunities to take on tasks of the so-called stronger sex."[65]

Enmeshed in regrets that women's increased influence in the public sphere distorted sex roles was the fear that the family—a natural institution in which men and women played complementary roles—was endangered. Women's role, the argument went, was focused on procreation and the family; men's role involved theological and political duties in the world. The innovations associated with the women's rights movement were essentially unnatural, even inhumane.[66] As Pope Leo XIII wrote in *Rerum novarum* in 1891, "A woman is by nature fitted for home-work, and it is that which is best adapted at once to preserve her modesty, and to promote the good bringing-up of children and the well-being of the family." Eight years later, the *Catholic Tribune* agreed when it wrote that "every demand or every desire to increase woman's influence is to be condemned when it goes beyond the sphere of her activity as traced out by the laws of nature."[67]

The public debate in the political and religious sphere about the private roles of mother and wife was defined principally by male commentators. After all, women were not invited to enter the sphere of public discourse, and the degree to which various voices were heard obviously informed what was spoken.[68] But in the few cases when they were able to offer public opinions within the context of Lutheran or Catholic Church traditions, women often couched their criticisms of society in expressions similar to those of the male leadership.[69] The National Catholic Women's Union, for example, opposed what it called "False and Perverted Feminism" and revered "first and foremost . . . the mother, the homemaker, the guardian of the fireside at which children are reared for the glory of God and the honor of the Christian name."[70] These opinions appeared late in the period under discussion. As Philip Gleason observes, women's auxiliaries grew precipitously in the 1920s as men became increasingly active in arenas that were less ethnically defined whereas women moved from a strictly domestic sphere into an organizational life that was demarcated by ethnic and religious group. Ironically, an "Americanization" that gave women a more active public voice permitted them to voice conservative sentiments.

These "laws of nature" had by the late nineteenth century come to conform in striking ways to the notion of separate spheres, which held that women were central to the home and their activity outside that sphere was unnatural. The "influence of good women" on the history of the world had been great, the *Catholic Tribune* contended, but it had been indirect. "The woman who encourages her husband in his struggle and in his undertakings for the best aims in life," it asserted, "is sufficiently co-operating in the best manner possible to better humanity." Likewise, "the mother who raises sons that rise to distinction" is "a benefactor of humanity." These women, the editor concluded, are "more praiseworthy than any of the modern mannish, short haired convention goers."[71] Again, an ideology of natural family law was conflated with bourgeois conventions of women's role in American society.

Political campaigns underscore the ethnic dimension in the male electorate's perception of women's rights. The suffrage debate had been raging for decades when Iowa voters in 1916 barely rejected an amendment to sanction women's suffrage in the state constitution.[72] The electorate was nearly evenly divided on the issue—48.5 percent voted in favor of the amendment—but there were broad regional variations within the state. Whereas just over one-quarter of the voters in Dubuque County voted for female suffrage, nearly two-thirds in Page County endorsed the amendment. Not surprisingly, the regional dissimilarities were rooted in ethnic variations.[73] The average prosuffrage share of the vote in townships dominated by German Americans was 18.7 percent; for Czechs, 24.3 percent; and for the Dutch, 25.8 percent. Among Germans, Lutherans were only slightly more likely than Catholics to support suffrage. In contrast, men in townships where British Americans predominated voted in favor of women's suffrage at a rate of 51.1 percent. Nearly one-half of the voters (49.0 percent) in Swedish American townships favored the amendment. County-level correlation coefficients corroborate these percentages (see table 10.1). Iowa counties that tended to be German American, foreign-born, Roman Catholic, and Democratic strongly opposed the amendment. Those that were Protestant, Republican, and would vote the next year in favor of prohibition correlated with support for the amendment. Ida Husted Harper's complaint about the defeat of a women's suffrage referendum in South Dakota seemingly was valid in Iowa as well: it was "the same old story[;] principally the foreigners, especially the Germans," had "once more denied to American women the privilege which they, themselves, had acquired so easily."[74]

Temperance, the third and perhaps most contested issue, also divided cultural groups in the Middle West. European ethnic groups varied in their views on the consumption of alcohol and the degree to which laws should be passed to regulate it. The fact that temperance represented yet another intervention by the state into the community and family, however, was not lost on many of them.[75] The question, then, was how community and family authority and the perceived need to control alcoholic drink should be balanced.[76] Dutch Calvinists found the problem especially perplexing because they both dreaded the effects of alcohol and feared an activist state. In the Netherlands and the United States, members of these communities, as James D. Bratt illustrates, distrusted alcohol because it weakened the conscience and thus connected temperance

Table 10.1. Simple County-Level Correlations of Selected Variables in Relation to 1916 Iowa Suffrage Referendum

Variable*	Correlation Coefficient
1917 prohibition vote	.72
German foreign stock	−.55
Non-German foreign stock	−.11
Roman Catholic population	−.51
Republican primary vote	.51
Republican general election vote	.25
Amendment:primary ratio	−.56
Farm population	−.02

Source: Thomas G. Ryan, "Male Opponents and Supporters of Woman Suffrage: Iowa in 1916," *Annals of Iowa* 45 (1981); 541.

*The variables are specifically prosuffrage percentage in 1916 referendum vote; pro-prohibition percentage in 1917 referendum vote; German foreign stock percentage according to 1930 federal census; non-German foreign stock percentage according to 1930 federal census; Roman Catholic percentage of 1916 church membership; percentage voting Republican in 1916 gubernatorial primary; percentage voting Republican in 1916 general election for state auditor; total votes cast in suffrage referendum as a percentage of total votes cast in gubernatorial primary; and farm population as percentage of total 1930 population.

with faith. Their leaders in America detailed additional evils of alcohol, arguing that it damaged the family, destroyed people's minds and bodies, and led to damnation.[77] But these same Dutch communities were also ambivalent about the role of the state. How could they balance the fact that laws that occasioned positive results were enacted and enforced by the state whose increased power they questioned? The Dutch community ultimately was divided. Whereas some argued that the evil of alcohol was so complete that laws should be passed to restrict it, others saw prohibition as an ominous encroachment of the state into "the free life of home and society."[78]

Other Europeans—including many German Lutherans and Roman Catholics—were less troubled by these ambiguities. Indeed, their discussion of the temperance movement represents yet another instance of the denouncement of the unrighteousness of state interference in community and family. Significantly, they often focused on the results of temperance enactments rather than the reasons for temperance advocacy. Whereas temperance proponents depicted instances of abusive families that resulted from drink, their opponents commonly noted the disorganized families of temperance supporters. Again, women—in part because they were powerful temperance advocates—were often portrayed as domineering or manlike usurpers of established male roles, whereas male temperance advocates in contrast were depicted as emasculated and browbeaten. One newspaper, for example, reported that "hordes of Temperance females with their male (?) consorts" crossed the border into Missouri in 1884 and that these "temperance witches from Iowa" wrecked the saloonkeeper's property and burned his house down.[79] In another Iowa locale, a newly opened saloon faced opposition in 1875 from "the 'ladies' and 'ladies' men'" who appeared at the saloon and "sang some pious songs."[80]

As in the women's rights movement, blurred gender boundaries among temperance advocates were connected to tendencies to forsake appropriate family duties. Following the Iowa constitutional referendum on temperance in 1882, the *Des Moines Anzeiger* wrote that the temperance "crusade" had been aided by "an army of women the majority of whom abhor housework and the surroundings of quiet homes whose sole ambition is to mingle among the sterner sex." Election day, the editor concluded, ended ominously with "the severest storm of the year lighting the heaven with continued flashes of dazzling, piercing lightning and shaking the earth with the most appalling peals of heaven's artillery, quaking the deluded women who had forgotten their homes and firesides."[81]

But the symbolism of women's role in the temperance movement went beyond the threats to conservative prescriptions of family; it also portended a future when government would be even more powerful and intrusive. Contemporary state-run institutions such as the public school weakened society by circumscribing the authority of the family and community and breeding ill-mannered children. Regrettably, the individual flaws that resulted did not cause its advocates to consider the ill effects of an expanded civil code and a weakened home and community. Rather, they prompted further state intervention, in the form of such enactments as temperance laws, to constrain individuals legally who could not restrain themselves. As C. F. W. Walther, leader of the German Lutheran Missouri Synod, had long argued, this strategy was wrongheaded. One might encourage "abstinence as a thing out of love," he contended, but it was a violation of "Christian freedom" to make it compulsory. "It is indeed easier," he concluded, "to stand hypocritically on external facts [that is, to observe prohibition]—with which man's law, the Devil and the flesh are satisfied, and which serves only to strengthen one's own self-righteousness—than it is to become a different person."[82] In sum, although laws were needed to restrict individual excess, it was the tendency toward excess that unmasked a weakness in the configuration of

American society and the behavior of its citizens. And although temperance crusades attacked individual excess, they ironically were movements that in and of themselves illustrated immoderation.

It is in this context that the temperance movement and its leaders were incessantly denounced by their foes for their "fanaticism." Paradoxically, a movement that was focused on abstinence, an excess of denial, was led by fanatics. How else to explain the "female hyenas" who led a mob that "knocked in the bottoms of beer kegs"? Or the distributor of "temperance Bibles" who omitted passages that mentioned wine or spirits? Or the temperance advocate who warned "that the children of parents who drink beer are most susceptible [*ausgesetzt*] to [diphtheria]"?[83]

Accusations of fanaticism were particularly common in heated political campaigns aimed at extending temperance laws. When voters in Iowa ratified a referendum for a constitutional amendment on temperance in 1882, for example, the *Des Moines Anzeiger* called it "an unmistakable victory for the fanatics."[84] Commentators often went one step further and associated fanaticism with the American-born supporters of temperance.[85] The *Des Moines Register*, a temperance partisan, in 1882 charged that "the people here are growing tired of this rising cry of men of foreign birth about 'American fanaticism.' "[86] For ethnic foes of temperance, the "American fanaticism" was symptomatic of a culture that seemingly required excessive movements and legislation to constrain immoderation among society's members. Because Americans lacked moderation in all things, they were forced to rely on legal structures, constructed with their typical fanaticism, to outlaw excessive behavior. An article reprinted in *Die Iowa* described the American need for temperance succinctly. "When an American gets schnapps in him," it maintained, "he's a beast. He shows it with insults and brutal [*rohe*] attacks on people who are unlucky enough to get in his way."[87] An account some years later in an English-language paper reiterated the same theme in greater detail. In the wake of a referendum on temperance in Iowa in 1882, a reporter noted the common sentiment that had been voiced in the American press in the past few years: "If the Dutch [meaning the Germans] don't like it they can go." Yet the Germans were not, the reporter argued, "as an occasional *fanatic* is wont to picture them"; "aside from the single fault of liking their beer, their good citizenship would hardly be questioned by even the most extreme temperance man." Germans clearly were not a "law-despising and law-defying class." Rather, they were, by their own admission, moderate. One German noted, for example, that "I drink but little" and "I have never been drunk in my life. . . . I know [my beer] hasn't been as injurious as ice-water or lemonade, gulped down as you Americans gulp your drinks on a hot day." Yet now, he continued, "a few *fanatics* who indicate that they themselves haven't the moral backbone to look at a glass of beer, or pass a saloon without getting drunk, come along and tell me that I am incapable of behaving myself or keeping sober, and so they propose to take care of me by law. That is what I resent." Germans apparently were different from Americans. "If you will become acquainted with the German people you'll find that they have a sense of honor that is strangely lacking in many people educated up to this theory of *making people temperate by law*. Your American will readily and carelessly sign a false certificate to the end of obtaining his beverage; he counts it as nothing. The German," he concluded, "recognizes that as perjury."[88]

In sum, prohibition laws were inspired, wrote a German American, by the need for "instilling morals into people by iron-clad laws." Following the ratification of a referendum to illegalize liquor by the drink in Iowa, a German editor asked, "Why aren't the drunks punished and the *people of moderation* left alone?"[89] The usual response was that Americans were not people of moderation, that their fanaticism and their tendency toward excess were embodied in the individualist American society. Significantly, this individualism was nurtured in an environment that systematically weakened the family as an arbiter of morality while it expanded the power of the state. Thus, when Germans criticized the temperance movement, they placed the relationship between household and the state into the political equation. As the German man cited above noted, "I've always been a law-abiding citizen. I've accumulated property, taken care of and have been kind to my family. In a word, I have been a man."[90] It was his sense of diminished status as a man stemming from temperance laws to which he objected.

Political contests over temperance again illustrate that the male electorate tended to hew to the arguments of their leaderships. Whereas the school issue dominated Wisconsin politics, Iowa politics focused on the question of temperance.[91] As early as 1855, the Iowa legislature enacted a temperance statute modeled on the prohibitory Maine law. Within three years, the law was weakened, but temperance agitation was rekindled some twenty years later in large part because of the activities of the WCTU. The state legislature approved in 1880 and 1882 a temperance amendment to the state constitution. In 1882, a special election was held to determine if the voters approved the amendment, which gives us a window through which to view electoral behavior from the perspectives of nationality, religion, and social class. In the election, 55.3 percent of the voters favored the amendment, but the levels of support, as in the case of the 1916 women's suffrage referendum, varied widely across the state. Again, the political contours conformed to the ethnic landscape; thus, German Americans in western Iowa proudly claimed that no one

Table 10.2. Simple County-Level Correlations of Selected Variables
in Relation to 1882 Iowa Prohibition Referendum

Variable*	Correlation Coefficient
Democratic presidential vote	−.75
Republican presidential vote	.59
German foreign-born	−.57
Roman Catholic	−.48
Methodist	.35

Source: Thomas G. Ryan, "Supporters and Opponents of Prohibition: Iowa in 1917," *Annals of Iowa* 46 (1983): 520.

*The variables are specifically pro-prohibition percentage in 1882 referendum vote; Democratic percentage of 1880 presidential vote; Republican percentage of 1880 presidential vote; German foreign-born percentage according to 1885 state census; Roman Catholic percentage of 1890 church membership; and Methodist percentage of 1890 church membership.

in their township voted for the amendment.[92] Simple county-level correlations indicate more broadly the strong relationships between political party affiliation and ethnic and religious background (see table 10.2). Whereas the correlation coefficient for the percentage voting for the Republican candidate for president in 1880 and for the amendment was strongly positive, that for the percentage voting Democratic and favoring the amendment was even more notably negative. County-level correlations between support of the amendment and membership in German-born and Roman Catholic groups were also negative. In contrast, positive correlations in counties with large Methodist memberships suggest that Methodists tended to support the amendment. One speaker reportedly proclaimed that "the Amendment was not so much a matter of the drinking problem as the supremacy of the Methodist sect in Iowa and in the nation."[93] Whether or not he was right, Methodists clearly voted for the amendment.

The amendment was a smashing victory for temperance forces, but the battle in Iowa was far from over. Violence and contentious polemics ensued after the referendum.[94] When the Iowa Supreme Court later ruled that the amendment was technically invalid, temperance campaigns focused once again on the legislature, which passed a series of strict temperance laws in the 1880s. A backlash against the zeal with which the Republican Party had pursued temperance enactments resulted in a hiatus of rigorous temperance legislation until 1908, when temperance advocates again renewed their offensive. Legislation that by 1913 effectively reduced

Table 10.3. Simple County-Level Correlations of Selected Variables
in Relation to 1917 Iowa Prohibition Referendum

Variable*	Correlation Coefficient
German foreign stock	−.76
Foreign stock	−.66
Non-German foreign stock	−.19
Roman Catholic	−.74
1916 women's suffrage	.72
Methodist	.71
Lutheran	−.26
Farm population	.17
Urbanism score	−.23
Republican auditor vote	.19

Source: Thomas G. Ryan, "Supporters and Opponents of Prohibition: Iowa in 1917," *Annals of Iowa* 46 (1983): 516.

*The variables are specifically pro-prohibition percentage in 1917 referendum vote; German foreign stock percentage according to 1930 federal census; foreign stock percentage according to 1930 federal census; non-German foreign stock percentage according to 1930 federal census; Roman Catholic percentage of 1916 church membership; prosuffrage percentage in 1916 referendum vote; Methodist percentage of 1916 church membership; Lutheran percentage of 1916 church membership; farm population as percentage of total 1930 population; urbanism score, 1920; and percentage voting Republican in 1916 election for state auditor.

sales of alcoholic drinks by half was followed by yet another effort to add a prohibition amendment to the state constitution. The state legislature approved the proposed amendment in 1915 and 1917, and the Iowa voters were summoned to the polls in 1917 for yet another referendum.

To the chagrin of temperance advocates, the nearly half a million men who went to the polls in October 1917 this time did not approve the amendment. Simple county-level correlations indicate that members of those groups most responsible for the defeat in 1882 again opposed the amendment thirty-five years later (see table 10.3). Negative correlation coefficients between the level of support for the amendment and the proportion of voters who were German foreign stock, were foreign stock, or confessed to Roman Catholicism were strong. In contrast, the correlation between the percentage who were Methodist and the degree of amendment support was strongly positive. Well into the twentieth century, the temperance debate was defined by a clash of cultures.

In sum, the political battles concerning the public school, women's suffrage, and the consumption of alcohol that swirled across the Middle

West were issues that animated the electorate. Voter turnout in a prohibition referendum in Iowa in 1917, for example, was higher than in gubernatorial and senate elections in the following year.[95] These matters were meaningful because they involved more than simply whether Catholic children would be forced to read a Protestant Bible or whether a German immigrant could enjoy a Sunday beer as had been his custom at home. From the perspective of proponents of temperance legislation and the public school, these campaigns were increasingly urgent efforts to regulate behavior and socialize children to common values. Their opponents, on the other hand, often perceived them to be graphic illustrations of "American" assaults on the essence of family and community. This onslaught assailed not only customs of everyday life but also the very nature of social organization; it cut to the heart of questions of power and entitlements within the household. Women's suffrage not only expanded the electorate but also violated the "natural" prescriptions for women as it potentially weakened the family. The school not only acculturated children but also questioned beliefs and cultural patterns at home. It not only introduced "Protestant" and "American" subjects but also challenged the very authority of the patriarchal household that many ethnic authorities wished to maintain.

What was perhaps even more frightening from this perspective was the apparent inadequacy of the Yankee mind. Both the school and temperance movements exemplified the fanaticism and excess that seemed to have gripped the American. And if Americans in their excess, in their inability to moderate their behavior, in their paranoid fanaticism, were unable to control themselves, it did not mean that they had to attack the cultural constructs of those who could. Through legislation to modify legally excessive behavior, many ethnic leaders feared that unsalutary modifications would be forced on the households of their followers. Not only would the authority of mothers and especially fathers be weakened, but individualist behavior would diffuse into the family so that instability and immoderation would soon characterize the homes of Americans and immigrants alike. Until that happened, it was a small leap from these views to the opinions of Walburg and others—expressions that so troubled McGlynn—that ethnic families rather than those of Americans were becoming the moral backbone of the American Republic.

Ethnic Politics in the Context
of a Pluralist Framework

That's progress. It has two sides, shadow and light. —*Die Iowa*, 19 July 1877

The politicization of the family and community in the Middle West was linked to the ethnicization of politics. Political party platforms gave expression to cultural predispositions maintained by ethnic and religious groups, especially in regions like the Middle West, where the landscape was segmented into deeply professed and profoundly diverse worldviews. The discovery of this fact is not new: it was forcefully set forth two decades ago by historians such as Paul Kleppner and Richard Jensen, who compellingly illustrated how ethnocultural worldviews were connected to political party allegiance in the late-nineteenth-century Middle West. They demonstrated quantitatively that voters of various nationality and religious groups tended to affiliate disproportionately with one of the two major political parties according to the cultural premises they carried with them to the political debate. One bloc of ethnocultural groups in the late nineteenth century, because of their "liturgical" or "ritualist" perspectives, emphasized "right belief." These voters were prone to support the Democratic Party, which tended not to promote interventions by the state to control behavior. Others, due to their "pietism" and concern for demanding "right" behavior, tended to adhere to the Republican Party, which exhibited an inclination to be more activist.[96] Both "pietists" and "liturgicals" might have feared the future prospects of an increasingly urban and industrial nation, but their programs to address such challenges varied according to their intellectual constructions of a stable society.

The pietist-ritualist dichotomy is a foundation upon which broader questions concerning the proper construction of society can be built. The pietist perspective was connected to the possibility of religious and political conversion and to a pluralist vision that operated under the auspices of an expanding American government that pietists themselves increasingly championed. It was built on a "subjective piety" wherein emotion, conversion, and right behavior were central and in which subjective experience was pivotal.[97] This perspective had long been expressed in sectors of middle western society, particularly among those identified with the "Puritan mind" at mid-century. By the end of the century, it appealed to a broader spectrum of Americans—from liberal and radical Catholics to APA supporters—who, for various reasons, expressed increasing comfort with the tendencies toward centralization and more uncompromising allegiance to an American nation. The competing perspective, based on an "objective piety" of ritualism and right belief, was oriented to the power of God; it was built on structures of power in family and community and thus was more likely to be separatist and particularist. It suspected enlarged governmental programs both because it distrusted state activism and because it posited the role of local institutions in strengthening and ordering society. From the ritualist viewpoint, not only were families and communities weakened by centralizing powers of the state, but state and society were weakened when the authority of the family and community was undermined. These visions, then, were not simply symbolic religious outlooks: they addressed core questions about American society and polity. And they were politicized when subgroups, based on religious or ethnic identification, were identified and mobilized under the aegis of larger political party structures.

The ethnocultural perspectives brought to electoral organizations were reflected in the parties' political programs. Put simply, the Republican Party relied on an activist state to tie together an increasingly diverse nation. Its members tended to favor centralized schools and to enforce strictures against the use of alcohol. They affirmed the middle-class values held by the native-born who swelled the party's ranks. Their tendencies toward liberalism and state interventionism, moreover, appealed to immigrants and ethnics such as pietistic Scandinavians who had increasingly come to appreciate liberal and activist constructions of a national community. The Democratic Party, whose program tended to be less centralist, was usually the political home of those of European ethnic traditions who hoped to stem the tide of American decline by repositioning the family and community as central components of order and stability in society.

Since middle western politics remained deeply colored by ethnic concerns, political leaders learned to their chagrin that they paid a high price when they miscalculated the magnitude of issues around which ethnic groups coalesced. The prohibition issue, for example, not only energized the Iowa countryside in political contests over referenda and laws but also weakened the Republican Party's political control of the state.[98] When Joseph Hutchison was named Republican gubernatorial candidate in 1889, he transformed the election into a referendum on prohibition. By connecting prohibition to "Americanization," he alienated many ethnic voters who moved into the ranks of the Democratic Party. Hutchison's loss tempered later prohibition initiatives and caused the Republican Party to move away from temperance as an electoral issue. At precisely the same time, Wisconsin Republicans blundered when they supported the Bennett Law and suffered devastating defeats in the 1890 elections.[99]

Whereas political debate was influenced by the predilections of ethnocultural groups, however, it set them in a larger societal context. Political leaders were forced to chart a path between the contradictory goals of creating a coalition of voters based on meaningful party principles and broadening the party's appeal to attract the largest possible membership. Unlike debate over single issues such as the school question or temperance, electoral politics linked ethnocultural considerations, political platforms, and electoral success. Although political parties were vehicles that gave expression to different ethnocultural worldviews, they tended to bring a consistency to political debate because their principal objective was to build coalitions in order to win elections.

The ramifications of this fact were many. First, political parties tended to accentuate collective points of reference among their members. Ethnicized subgroups were useful creations for political parties because they could be managed.[100] In addition to ethnicity, Andrew R. L. Cayton and Peter S. Onuf illustrate how other clusters of voters defined by attributes of social class, region of birth, and race were used by political parties to create coalitions of voters distinguished by their political attitudes. The Republican Party, for example, favored not only a cultural centralization but also a centralized economic program. It thus became a leading voice in the recommendation of high tariffs that appealed to particular economic interests. Democrats, on the other hand, appealed to states' rights advocates, economic interests that favored a low tariff, and others who stood for more localistic solutions to economic problems.[101]

The second ramification, which is related to the first, was that political parties muted the more uncommon, peripheral, or radical critiques of American society. Electoral politics thus tended to homogenize issues and to blunt the expression of radical solutions for America's ills. They were less likely to welcome ideas that strayed outside of the pluralist and liberal political structures of which they were a part, and they expressed decided suspicion of particularist concepts that called into question those very structures. As members of ethnic groups brought their perspectives on issues to political contests, then, the structure of political debate informed, truncated, and transformed many of their convictions. Whereas the issues of family and community, of state and society, were open questions, the debate was often bounded when political parties marginalized the more radical programs.

This is not to say that radical programs were not advanced. Indeed, historians have chronicled the intellectual currents of labor activism, socialism, and populism that challenged the state of the Union in the decades straddling the century but did not enjoy electoral success. Historians have shown less interest in the programs of those who posited conservative—indeed, reactionary—proposals to solve America's ills that lay outside the discourse of mainstream parties. By returning again to a segment of the German Catholic leadership, we can observe a remarkable program that illustrates not only an agenda beyond the ken of electoral politics, but also one that was corporatist and particularist, certainly was opposed by most Americans, and could not have been sustained in pluralist political debate. Clearly, most German Catholics at this time were loyal members of the Democratic Party. German American leaders profited from political patronage derived mainly from Democratic Party allegiance, and Catholic ideas about public schools and temperance found expression in party platforms. But other German Catholic perspectives were presented outside the bounds of Democracy.

Given the frightful prospects of families and communities weakened by the centralizing powers of the state, this German Catholic program merged a continued faith in corporate Social Catholicism with a grim view of contemporary society. It contended that American behavior not only lacked proper Christian morality but also created an unjust political economy. In such a situation and amid the upheaval of the late nineteenth century, German Catholic corporatists eschewed any sympathy for socialist solutions, which in and of themselves were atheistic, and instead flirted with ultramontane and antirepublican concepts. Perhaps, they suggested, a monarchy was the best solution to the ills that had beset the United States.

The path to ultramontane ideas was cleared both by antipluralist and by antiliberal perspectives. To begin with, writers insisted that individualism and liberalism were inherently "irreligious [*ungläubige*]." [102] The connections between liberalism and irreligion, moreover, were insidious, for wherever liberalism ruled, reforms were sought wherein "the unbelievers are victorious over Christendom." [103] "C.S.R.," writing in 1887, indicted liberalism, Free Masonry, and Judaism as "the archenemies of Christ's church" because they were ideologies that could destroy Christian values and morals and replace them with a liberal state. [104]

The liberal state, however, not only fostered irreligion but also nourished capitalism's proclivity for economic centralization and the state's appetite for political centralization. In so doing, it nurtured a "dangerous [*gefährliche*]" capitalist system that threatened the people. [105] Capitalism, the *Luxemburger Gazette* contended in 1887, was a menace of relatively recent origin; it did not grow out of worthy activities such as farming or artisanal trades which people had been engaged in for the last several centuries. Rather, modern capitalism in this "menacing time of troubles" evolved from new economic structures exemplified by big business (*Gross-Geschäftsbetriebe*) and large governmental structures that not only amassed huge federal debts but were intricately and insidiously connected to corporate America. In sum, money ruled the contemporary world, and the ruinous (*verderbliche*) power of capital crushed the worker. The end result was a frightful society characterized by division among social classes and declining civic virtue, in which "the transaction of money flourished while farming, handwork, and small business declined." It was an environment where "renters, capitalists, millionaires sprang up like mushrooms out of the earth while the hardworking men from every class grew weak under taxes." Working together, expansive capitalism and the growing state encouraged technological changes and innovations that aided the capitalist class but did not benefit the common man.

Twelve years later, the *Catholic Tribune* reiterated a similar lament. Capitalism, which continued to work in league with "liberalism" and "individualism," remained injurious both materially and spiritually to the "common man." Liberals, even liberal Catholics, it argued, "are enemies of the laboring classes" because they promulgated principles that "are today prevalent in our naturally rich country, and that make the wealthy all-powerful in the state and that increase the poverty and burdens of the poorer classes." [106] "Individualism[,] free and unlimited[,] and disorderly competition," the paper continued, were "the causes of the concentration of wealth in the hands of a few rich, and the poverty of the many." Liberalism and individualism, moreover, were intricately intertwined because the latter was a principle that was fostered by the "liberal system of political economy which now governs *our* country." [107] Perhaps worse, liberalism had not only "robbed the laboring men of their bread but also of the hope for an eternal reward." Because liberalism was "essentially atheistic," "every true Christian" was impelled to be its "enemy . . . in religion and in economics." [108] In large part because liberalism excluded "the supernatural order" in religion and in the economy, it failed the poor and weak on both a sacred and a secular plane.

What forces existed to abridge this modern, liberal, capitalist world fraught with growing inequality and increasing immorality? One possibility was the national state, whose laws could "break this concentrated power of capital." [109] But most German Catholic observers distrusted an American government that not only had consistently advantaged capital but was in and of itself liberal and thus amoral. The liberal state, from this perspective, enabled freedoms that were not anchored in "true" belief. As the *Katholische Volkszeitung* put it, there existed "no real freedom outside the Catholic Church because there is no certainty other than the Catholic belief." One who was guided only by opinions rather than by the "certainty" of belief was "a true slave [*Sklave*]." [110] Whereas certainty of belief enabled true freedom, "untrue" freedom created licentiousness (*Zügellosighet*). And it was the abuses stemming from licentiousness and ultimately from individual, liberal premises that led Catholic spokespersons to reevaluate fundamentally the American system of government.

By 1901, the *Catholic Tribune* noted the dangers of electoral politics in this liberal world of corporate capitalism by calling attention to the "disadvantages of our liberties." Echoing the argument submitted earlier by the *Katholische Volkszeitung*, the paper observed that "thoughtless people only boast of our liberties, while the wise man considers both sides, their advantages and disadvantages." If "liberty for good" was laudable, "liberty for evil and the wicked is a curse. We," the paper concluded ominously, "possess both liberties." [111]

Even worse, in a society premised on "equal rights," "error has the same right as truth," and although right and wrong were expected to "live together harmoniously," such a circumstance was impossible. After all, "the wicked will always strive to oppose the good, and the good will always be obliged to fight for their endangered rights." "*Our* American liberties" thus were "fraught with great disadvantages because good must continually be on the alert and fight so as not to be oppressed." And the "dangerous weapon at the disposal" of both was "the sovereignty of the people and universal suffrage." It was true that "if the good have a majority all will be well." On the other hand, "if the wicked gain the ascendancy then woe to the good!" As history showed, the wicked triumphed more often than not because "the wicked are more active, unscrupulous and more daring than the good." [112]

A knot of seeming contradictions, the argument set in the context of "our American liberties" betrayed a particularist perspective that was willing to proscribe long-standing political liberties in an attempt to safeguard "good." Ultimately, the *Catholic Tribune* questioned the utility of the republic itself. Put simply, the political system failed to perform its duties. Based on an individualized electoral system, it formed unstable coalitions as it vied for the citizens' votes. "Each [political] party lives in the hope of having a majority at the next election," and when it succeeds, "the dominant party again does not seek the welfare of the people at large, but rather the strengthening and power of its own party." Then, as a part of this quest, "it squanders the national revenue, favors its adherents and seeks to deprive the adherents of the other party of their influence and power." As they strove to win elections, parties had no responsibility to the whole when they succeeded: "No tyranny is harder than that of a republican majority" because "whatever the dominant party desires . . . is considered right" and "the rights and wishes of the minority are not respected." This tyranny of the majority was aggravated by the fact that it was orchestrated by a privileged minority. In the United States, "our government is simply helpless against the trusts and the money power. It is too unwieldy to undertake legislation to protect the laborer." Marred by self-serving politicians and manipulative financiers, the American government, the author suggested, would be better run by a sovereign who "stands above all parties, is a member of no party, but wishes to do justice because it is his interest."[113]

After decades of political development, then, this spokesperson, by proposing a monarchy, ultimately challenged the very basis of the American experiment itself. The American Republic, increasingly controlled by "the wicked," was proving unable to protect its citizens. The *Luxemburger Gazette* had given similar warnings in 1888. "The destruction and plundering of the nation can only be successfully concluded," it argued, "when its masters and defenders are eliminated. Only a beguiled people is capable of executing the work of self-destruction. Only through coarse democracy [*rohen Demokrati*] can the last blow against Christian culture be engineered." Increasingly characterized by class warfare and moral unrighteousness, secular society had only "throne and altar" to conquer as it careened toward the precipice.[114] Amid continuing turmoil, the *Catholic Tribune* reiterated the complaint at the dawn of a new century: the American Republic perhaps had been a mistake after all. Because "the frame of a monarchy is stronger than a republic," it contended, "a monarch can more easily oppose mighty corporations and capitalists and groups of capitalists than the powers of a republic."[115] Amid perceptions of increasing chaos, the demise of the Republic ultimately might be fortuitous for American citizens or, perhaps now put differently, its subjects.[116]

These expressions clearly invoked conceptualizations of a distribution of power that varied from those that sustained the liberal political arena. With their greater emphasis on institutions of authority that were to maintain freedoms—as they understood them—and enable justice, they highlighted the utility of the household, the community, and ultimately the state, personified in a benevolent monarch. The ironies of this perspective abound. Its proponents saw themselves as defenders of a tradition that protected their country against the evils of individualism, liberalism, and materialism that characterized "Americans." By invoking the good of the whole, they were using frames of reference reminiscent of those of an earlier classical republicanism to argue for the destruction of the American Republic.

This German Catholic critique endured beyond the turn of the century.[117] In 1905, *Was wollen wir* (What we want), a pamphlet that described the objectives of Volksverein für Amerika, continued to question liberal capitalism and to reflect forthrightly the influences of European corporatist thought. "All Christian sociologists" were called upon to remove the "present social evils in the state": "The overlordship of capital must be replaced by the dominion of the natural corporative order [*Ständeordnung*] and the reign of justice."[118] Ten years later, Father William J. Engelen wrote, using an obvious metaphor of the household, that "the divinely ordained purpose of the state is that it should be the final assistance and support of all its children in the great national family."[119] Yet these spokespersons rejected the liberal individualism that currently characterized American society and posited instead a nation built on classes and estates so that "the state would again become an organism." Because the American Constitution embraced individualism and rejected the principle that "every society should be structured according to *estates*," a German Catholic convention agreed, the United States would continue to be characterized by class conflict and social antagonism. Only Catholics appreciated the importance of immutable estates; only they realized the importance of *Lehrstand, Wehrstand und Nährstand*; only they understood that modern society was "sick because it is *wrongly organized*."[120] Even if these criticisms endured, they would never be the basis, due to their radical—and particularist—premises, of any major political party platform.

Conclusion

On the eve of World War I, intellectual quandaries similar to those that perplexed the first white settlers who wandered into the Upper Middle West persisted. Whereas many continued to fear the threat of separate cultures detached from mainstream national concerns, others distrusted what appeared to be expanding concerted efforts to alter their culture and religion to the detriment both of local communities and of larger society. Both of these perspectives found political expression.

Political debate from these varied perspectives was informed by postures regarding the relative roles of family, community, and state in American society. In so doing, it cut to the heart of conceptions of authority in worldly society and beyond. It contended with questions of where power lay and how the society in which people lived ought to be organized. Members of communities that were uncertain about a powerful state and about the advisability of liberal political traditions arrived at different conclusions than those who based their worldview on a liberal tradition that was increasingly interventionist and statist. As each local community was changing and even the most isolated environments were confronting a diffusion of behavior, the political sphere became a final battleground on which differing outlooks clashed.

Indeed, the battleground became increasingly contentious because the disputants feared that their adversaries were ratcheting up their rhetoric and advancing even more extremist programs. Ever more strident particularist positions unnerved those, such as McGlynn, who envisioned a pluralist American landscape. They encouraged others, such as Strong and Traynor, to believe that Catholicism and Americanism were incompatible. Particularistic voices, for their part, starkly portrayed a crisis of liberal capitalism in the late nineteenth century. They condemned the peccadilloes of "Americans," which they contended illustrated an inability to cope with the challenges of modern life. And some suggested that a single public good ought to be reaffirmed, even to the point of reaffirming it in the person of a sovereign—a recommendation that would certainly have unnerved observers such as McGlynn and Strong.

As it turned out, however, the fears of McGlynn, Strong, and Traynor were misplaced. Although the Middle West continued to be a place where communities could be sequestered and even where antirepublican voices could be heard, the particularists' programs—in part because they were particularistic—were unable to articulate their beliefs beyond their membership. They found it difficult to compete with political programs of the mainstream parties that sought to guide their followers into political coalitions in order to gain electoral success. Likewise, because political parties forged ethnic coalitions, they forced members of ethnic communities to join alliances that diluted the force of their complaints and truncated the range of debate. Ethnic segmentation remained a remarkable fact of the rural Middle West into the twentieth century, as well as a cultural diffusion that was challenging arrangements in European immigrant communities and families. The acids of modernity, despite the best attempts of the ethnic leaders, were inexorably corroding the institutional structures on which ethnic communities were based. Political activity perhaps was a viable recourse to abridge social change by illustrating cultural difference and protecting cultural forms. As it pulled citizens into a liberal, if pluralist, discourse, however, politics only contributed to the challenge.

EPILOGUE

Iowa Governor William Harding showed a lack of political vision when he visited the Danish settlements of Audubon County on Independence Day in 1918. In a speech to the largely Danish American audience, he voiced regret that the children who grew up in the vicinity were not really American. Amid the white-hot patriotism of the World War I era, he argued that youths in the locality, even after their schooling, "are full grown 100 per cent Dane." If this were not impolitic enough, Harding proceeded to observe that what the Danes had done to develop the farms and fields of Audubon County did not compare with what had been bestowed upon them in the United States. "Now, think of a man who was brought from the filth of Denmark," he remarked, "and placed on a farm, for which he paid perhaps $3 an acre. Ye gods and fishes, what Iowa has done for him he never can repay!"[1]

Harding's speech summoned a storm of protest. Danish Americans, who must have stood incredulous as they listened to his tirade, quickly took up their pens to admonish him.[2] Karl Rasmussen admitted in a letter to the *Des Moines Register* that Danish Americans "have in some measure taken advantage of the great opportunities offered us in this great state and nation." But these very opportunities, he continued, in yet another expression of a complementary identity, encouraged them to be "Americans in spirit, heart, and actions." Yet now they were being condemned by Harding's "misinformed" statements, he concluded, simply "because we are also able to use our mother tongue," a condemnation to which they, "as American citizens," objected.[3] A *Des Moines Register* editorial added another layer of rhetoric to the controversy. It suggested that Independence Day—a holiday to celebrate "the birth of a nation set apart by its founders for the oppressed of all lands under the blessings of a free flag on a free soil"—perhaps was not the time for Harding to voice these opinions. It concluded, moreover, that the Danes were "Americans not so much because they have bought cheap land in this new world, as because they have found freedom."[4] Once again, tropes of "freedom" and "Americanization," of immigrants and "free" land, were central images in the public discourse nearly a century after the first white migrants journeyed to the West.

The debate in the rural Middle West during World War I, illustrated by Harding's comments, serves as an appropriate ending point to our discussion. The war, of course, did not end the debate over how ethnic groups ought to be integrated into American society, nor did it transform the social boundaries that continued to demarcate ethnic communities throughout the region. Rural communities still were defined by ethnic and religious background well after World War I. As they continued to be buffeted by internal change and external pressure, ethnic neighborhoods that maintained institutional and ideological structures to temper outside influences remained the most successful at fostering a localized ethnic culture.[5] Culture wars, moreover, continued to course across the middle western landscape as well. Prohibition of alcohol was written into the Constitution, and public and parochial school debate was considered by the electorate, the courts, and the state and national legislatures in the 1920s.[6] Church communities, increasingly besieged by the mores and ideas of modern America, were again forced to fold their beliefs into a secularized, liberal, and pluralist American society.[7] And varied models of the proper institutional design of society would continue to be posited. Ideologues, using intellectual foundations already in place prior to the war, would continue to prescribe solutions to America's ills well after the next world war.[8] Debate regarding family breakdown and "family values," the role of the state and religion in society, and questions of cultural diversity in relation to the cohesion of the nation would endure. Indeed, they remain with us in their varied forms to the present day.

Although World War I did not resolve questions that had engaged middle westerners for decades, it was an urgent context that fostered arguments for an increasingly powerful state at the same time that it encouraged portrayals of ethnic groups as suspicious, even subversive, elements in American society. Amid the exceptional circumstances of war mobilization, middle westerners grappled in extraordinary ways with questions of loyalty to nation and ethnic group that had been present for some time. Many, certain that their region's iron and foodstuffs were crucial to the war effort, questioned the loyalty of their neighbors. Rehearsing fears that had been articulated for decades, they expressed concerns that those sheltered in European ethnic communities, as Harding's speech illustrates, were not "American." Amid the rare predicament of war, they suspected that these communities were part of a fifth column secretly supporting America's enemies.

Local battles were fought at home as well as "over there." Because the

United States declared war on Germany, German neighborhoods became principal focal points of suspicion and later of attack.[9] Time and again, they were invaded by neighbors who maligned them for their lack of patriotism and their failure to be American. In Lowden, Iowa, for example, a German pastor was forced to leave town within forty-eight hours in late 1918 while other "pro-Germans" were rounded up, paraded through town, and forced to salute the American flag and make cash contributions to the Red Cross.[10] Some weeks later, an Iowa farmer was nearly lynched when he compared the Kaiser to a local deputy marshal.[11] A German Evangelical minister, who reputedly contended from the pulpit that the war was "for capitalists only" and that the Liberty Bond was "a great humbug," was convicted of violating the 1917 Espionage Act, and his church was burned under suspicious circumstances.[12]

Dutch communities, perhaps because they were commonly confused with German settlements, also faced intemperate hostility. Homes in one southwestern Minnesota Dutch community were painted yellow by vigilantes because of "disloyal" statements made by their owners.[13] Examples of enmity toward Dutch settlements in central Iowa were even more pointed. Near the town of Peoria, the pastor of a Dutch Calvinist church fled, never to return, after county authorities warned him that his life was in danger. Arson followed. The Dutch Reformed Church in New Sharon was the first to be torched, followed by the Christian Reformed School in Sully. Citizens in nearby Peoria, alerted to the threat of arson, began to stand guard at night to protect their church. Only when the dangers appeared to be subsiding did they discontinue their watch. They were mistaken: their church was set afire days thereafter. Religious services were subsequently held in a horse barn, and children attended the public schools until the Christian school was rebuilt.[14]

Local tensions also illustrated how groups that had been suspicious of an increased role of the state with respect to the family, community, and religion maintained their beliefs even though they were powerfully challenged during the war years to grapple with the governmental infringement on their local communities. Although many among them softened their rhetoric, they continued to question the role of the state at a time when legal and extralegal pressures took on extraordinary dimensions. Germans, because the United States was at war with their ancestral homeland, endured exceptional scrutiny when they failed to contribute enough money to the coffers of the government or enough sons to the army. And other communities that remained dubious of state power also faced difficulties in the face of war. When a Dutch community in southwestern Minnesota placed an American flag in its church sanctuary, it was an Americanist gesture that produced heated debate since many members of the church felt it betokened a step toward the establishment of a state church.[15]

Those who posited the enduring relevance of the complementary identity or who questioned an increasing role of government, however, faced unprecedented challenges in the charged circumstances of a nation at war. And it was these exceptional conditions that empowered Americanizers to use state agencies to attempt to transform the region. The need to mobilize armies and war matériel obviously increased the influence of the state and national government in local affairs. And remarkably powerful societal forces were able to connect these centralizing tendencies to notions of "Americanism" that often questioned the loyalty of many American citizens. Whereas "Americanist" movements forcefully strove to eliminate such "un-American" elements in society as those who held objectionable political views, they also wished to blot out the influence of immigrant and ethnic institutions and the use of non-English languages.[16] As the *Minneapolis Tribune* wrote in 1918, anticipating the thoughts of Governor Harding, "There is absolutely no need of perpetuating a Germany, or a Norway, or any other country in America. People have left there," it continued, "because this land of opportunity will enable them to gain a position they never could have attained in their European home, and why, then, should that European country be held up to the detriment of America through the medium of the public school?" "Pass a law prohibiting every language but American in our schools," the newspaper concluded, "and then enforce it."[17] Many state legislatures followed this advice: some twenty-one states enacted English-only language laws during World War I or shortly thereafter.[18]

The vigorous centralizing and Americanizing undertakings during war therefore remarkably challenged and altered ethnic cultures in the Middle West. At few points in the history of the region were attempts to eradicate ethnic, linguistic, and religious traditions so strident. Because these efforts were championed by arms of the state and federal government, moreover, they not only weakened local culture but also legitimized state intervention. In sum, policies that many government leaders perceived to be necessary to win the war powerfully shifted the balance in the debate over the propriety of state intervention in local societies. Consider the Minnesota Commission of Public Safety (MCPS), an agency created in April 1917 by the state legislature. Formed a few days prior to the American entry into World War I, the commission set up a statewide web of speakers, information agents, and informers. The "Assistant Publicity Director in Charge of the Foreign Press" monitored all non-English-language papers at the same time that he supplied "general matter" that could be disseminated in foreign-language papers. Some months later, all foreign-language newspapers were required to provide full English translations of all non-English articles dealing with government policy or the war to their local postmasters in order to be permitted to use the federal mail system.[19]

In early 1918, the MCPS required all noncitizens to register with local officials. The registration forms stipulated a full inventory of real and personal property, citizenship status, and length of residence. They also required aliens to explain why they had not taken steps to become citizens. Refusal to register could result in confiscation of property, and in order to insure a full registration, special agents were granted the power to compel anyone with information about evasion of the process to testify under oath. Aliens were also prohibited from teaching in any school, private, public, or parochial.[20] The alien registration effort allegedly was a great success. One MCPS report argued that it had done more than any other law or edict "to bring foreign-born civic slackers—to the number of 225,000—within the full sway of our laws and the American spirit."[21]

Consider Governor Harding's language proclamation issued on 23 May 1918, two months prior to his address in Audubon County. The directive contained four extraordinary rules regarding the use of language that were to remain in force as long as Iowa was at war. First, English was to be the sole language of instruction in every school, public and parochial. Second, public conversation—including on trains or over the telephone—was to be conducted in English. Third, all public lectures were to be spoken in English. Finally, those who could not speak or understand English were ordered to conduct religious services in their homes instead of in public houses of worship.[22]

These remarkable mandates struck at the heart of constitutional guarantees that had been a magnet for immigrating peoples for decades. In defending his actions, Governor Harding acknowledged that freedom of speech was protected in the United States but asserted that the medium of discourse was not. No one had the right, he decided, to use "a language other than the language of the country—the English language." Freedom of religion was also protected, but such a guarantee did not "protect the person in the use of a foreign language." People had the right to practice their religion, but it did not necessarily extend to understanding what was said in the worship services.[23]

These changes during World War I suggested an unquestionable victory for those who had advocated a state-induced "Americanization" and assimilation. The governmental agencies formed explicitly to promote allegiance to the English language and to "American" virtues had little patience with particularist expressions that privileged ethnic or religious subgroups. To be sure, various subgroups remained resolute and continued to voice views that were increasingly unpopular. German Lutheran spokespersons observed that nationalism had always been pronounced in the United States and that now a nationalism had "grown out of all bounds with the war," in part because it was "a nation which has been drowned in a service to Mammon as no other nation has."[24] Yet the immense pressure—both legal and extralegal—forced even the most resolute to reassess their perspectives. Many fell into line. The Missouri Synod leadership commissioned a treatise proving the church's loyalty to the United States rather than to the German Kaiser.[25] Nicholas Gonner, a Luxemburger Catholic who for years had disparaged the direction in which American society was headed, urged loyalty after the U.S. declaration of war, albeit still from a Roman Catholic natural law perspective. "War," he wrote, "was declared not by a man, but by Congress. It is the authority of our country and hence according to God's order we as American citizens must obey; and that thus united in the spirit of sacrifice and obedience we may save our Fatherland."[26] Catholic natural law remained Gonner's basis of belief, but the Fatherland had become the United States.

Violations of civil rights and the fervor for forceful Americanization, however, abated in the decade that followed the war. Attempts to legislate a program of Americanism and English language in the schools that gained momentum during the war were only partially successful thereafter. The state legislature of Minnesota enacted a measure in 1919 that demanded that English be the medium of instruction in public schools, whereas its counterparts in Iowa and Nebraska banned non-English instruction in all elementary schools, private and public alike.[27] A 1920 referendum in Michigan to eliminate private schools failed to pass.[28] Judicial rulings, moreover, rescinded some of the more excessive violations of civil rights inherent in the English-only laws. By 1923, the U.S. Supreme Court struck down the Nebraska measure and, by implication, others similar to it.[29]

Yet the war was a transfigurative event because, as an intellectual watershed, it tipped the balance in an ongoing debate both regarding the relevance of the complementary identity and the relative importance of an activist state. In future decades, an Americanist ideology would continue to dominate. European immigration as a result would be drastically curtailed by federal laws in 1921 and 1924. Likewise, the war foretold an increasingly powerful national state in the decades of depression and war that marked the twentieth century. Those who advocated a cultural pluralism or who advanced an institutional structure of society that privileged the local community found the parameters of the debate to be redefined. The rural middle western ethnic communities, following World

War I, would never be the same. Neither would the region segmented by them.

As such, Harding's speech to his Danish listeners and the rejoinders stemming from it encapsulate the condition of the minds of the West in 1918. For Harding, America's land had freed the Danish peasants who moved to Audubon County and the countless millions of immigrants to the Middle West; they should have made themselves into Americans out of gratitude. For the editors of the *Des Moines Register*, freedom was a condition exceptional to the United States that encouraged the Danish settlers, who enjoyed material advantages unavailable to them at home, to become American. For Karl Rasmussen and his neighbors, the latitude that American freedoms sanctioned, including freedoms of speech and religion, were why they were American. Amid war with Germany's Kaiser, Americans such as Rasmussen could still give expression to a complementary identity in which an immigrant past and an American citizenship mutually reinforced one another. But they asserted them in a dutiful fashion and under the panoply of an American pluralist vision. Ethnic communities would endure, but strident particularist and separatist proclamations were muted and would never again provoke the range of fear in the Middle West that they had prompted earlier. Samuel F. B. Morse, Lyman Beecher, and Josiah Strong, not to mention Albert Barnes, would have been content to know that the heterogeneous minds of the Middle West, although they continued to exist, were being forcefully merged in a world at war into an Americanist whole.

NOTES

Abbreviations

The following abbreviations are used throughout the notes.

CDH	Center for Dubuque History Archives, Loras College, Dubuque, Iowa
CFHS	Cedar Falls Historical Society Archives, Cedar Falls, Iowa
DSSM	Dominican Sisters Archives, Sinsinawa Mound, Wisconsin
ISHDDM	Iowa State Historical Division Archives, Des Moines, Iowa
ISHDIC	Iowa State Historical Division Archives, Iowa City, Iowa
MHS	Minnesota Historical Society Archives, St. Paul, Minnesota
NAHA	Norwegian-American Historical Association Archives, St. Olaf College, Northfield, Minnesota
SHSW	State Historical Society of Wisconsin Archives, Madison, Wisconsin
UILSC	University of Iowa Library Special Collections, Iowa City, Iowa
WPA Papers	Works Progress Administration Papers

Introduction

1. Albert Barnes, *Home Missions: A Sermon in Behalf of the American Home Missionary Society* (New York: William Osborn, 1849), 11, 12 (emphasis added). For a similar argument, see Albert Barnes, *Plea in Behalf of Western Colleges* (Philadelphia: William Sloanaker, 1846). Barnes (1798–1870) was a New School Presbyterian who, in league with Lyman Beecher and Charles G. Finney, promoted a Protestant revival in the middle decades of the nineteenth century.

2. Barnes, *Home Missions*, 12–14.

3. See Reginald Horsman, "Origins of Racial Anglo-Saxonism in Great Britain before 1850," *Journal of the History of Ideas* 37 (1976): 387–410, and Barbara Miller Solomon, *Ancestors and Immigrants: A Changing New England Tradition* (Cambridge: Harvard University Press, 1956).

4. See Susan E. Gray, *The Yankee West: Community Life on the Michigan Frontier* (Chapel Hill: University of North Carolina Press, 1996); Lois Kimball Mathews, *The Expansion of New England: The Spread of New England Settlement and Institutions to the Mississippi River, 1620–1865* (Boston: Houghton Mifflin, 1909); and Richard Lyle Power, *Planting Corn Belt Culture: The Impress of the Upland Southerner and Yankee in the Old Northwest* (Indianapolis: Indiana Historical Society Publications, 1953).

5. See Kathleen Neils Conzen, *Making Their Own America: Assimilation Theory and the German Peasant Pioneer* (New York: Berg, 1990); Jon Gjerde, *From Peasants to Farmers: The Migration from Balestrand, Norway, to the Upper Middle West* (New York: Cambridge University

Press, 1985); Robert C. Ostergren, *A Community Transplanted: The Trans-Atlantic Experience of a Swedish Immigrant Settlement in the Upper Middle West, 1835–1915* (Madison: University of Wisconsin Press, 1988); Walter D. Kamphoefner, *Transplanted Westfalians: Chain Migration from Germany to a Rural Midwestern Community* (Princeton: Princeton University Press, 1987); and Royden K. Loewen, *Family, Church, and Market: A Mennonite Community in the Old and the New Worlds, 1850–1930* (Urbana: University of Illinois Press, 1993). On new and old spaces, see Benedict Anderson, "Memory and Forgetting," in *Imagined Communities: Reflections on the Origins and Spread of Nationalism*, rev. ed. (London: Verso, 1991), 187–206.

6. J. Hector St. John de Crèvecoeur, "Letter III: What Is an American?," in *Letters from an American Farmer*, ed. Albert E. Stone (New York: Penguin, 1963), 66–105.

7. Frederick Jackson Turner, "The Significance of the Frontier in American History," in *The Frontier in American History* (New York: Holt, Rinehart and Winston, 1920), 1–38. See also Rowland Berthoff, "Peasants and Artisans, Puritans and Republicans: Personal Liberty and Communal Equality in American History," *Journal of American History* 69 (1982): 579–98.

8. Barnes, *Home Missions*, 19–20.

9. The Middle West was settled by American-born migrants traveling westward from the cultural hearths of New England and New York, the mid-Atlantic states, and the Upland South. See John Fraser Hart, "The Middle West," in *Regions of the United States*, ed. John Fraser Hart (New York: Harper and Row, 1972), 258–82, and John C. Hudson, "North American Origins of Middlewestern Frontier Populations," *Annals of the Association of American Geographers* 78 (1988): 395–413.

10. Frederick Jackson Turner, "The Middle West," in *Frontier in American History*, 138.

11. Richard K. Vedder and Lowell E. Gallaway note that the foreign-born accounted for 79 percent of the net migration into the Old Northwest in the 1840s and 88 percent in the 1850s. About 16 percent of the in-migrants in the 1830s were foreign-born. See Richard K. Vedder and Lowell E. Gallaway, "Migration and the Old Northwest," in *Essays in Nineteenth-Century Economic History: The Old Northwest*, ed. David C. Klingaman and Richard K. Vedder (Athens: Ohio University Press, 1975), 165–66.

12. The proportion of residents who were foreign-born in the east north-central and west north-central states roughly paralleled the proportions of foreign-born residents in the mid-Atlantic and New England states until the 1890 census. Only the mountain and Pacific Coast states had a significantly higher percentage of foreign-born residents.

13. Kathleen Neils Conzen, "Immigrants in Nineteenth-Century Agricultural History," in *Agriculture and National Development: Views on the Nineteenth Century*, ed. Lou Ferleger (Ames: Iowa State University Press, 1990), 304.

14. Ibid.

15. I am indebted to Robert C. Ostergren and the University of Wisconsin Cartographical Laboratory for their help in constructing the figures. The influence of the foreign-born and their children in the Upper Middle West in comparison with their influence in other American regions is illustrated by a county-level map of the United States based on the 1910 census in Martin Ridge, *Atlas of American Frontiers* (Chicago: Rand McNally, 1993), 90.

16. Colman J. Barry, *The Catholic Church and German Americans* (Washington, D.C.: Catholic University of America Press, 1953), 6.

17. Richard Jensen, *The Winning of the Midwest: Social and Political Conflict, 1888–1896* (Chicago: University of Chicago Press, 1971), 85–87.

18. Ibid., 62.

19. Robert C. Ostergren, "The Immigrant Church as a Symbol of Community and Place in the Upper Midwest," *Great Plains Quarterly* 1 (1981): 225–26. Ostergren's work complements Jensen's since he has mapped the "church population" in 1890 to demonstrate the high degree of church membership at that date in the region.

20. For a good overview, see Andrew R. L. Cayton and Peter S. Onuf, *The Midwest and the Nation: Rethinking the History of an American Region* (Bloomington: Indiana University Press, 1990).

21. It is telling that the American exceptionalist tropes of "freedom" and "liberty" were emphasized more frequently than "equality." See Berthoff, "Peasants and Artisans."

22. Bruce Levine also notes the acceptance as well as the rejection of the rhetoric of "freedom" by German Americans. See Bruce Levine, *The Migration of Ideology and the Contested Meaning of Freedom: German Americans in the Mid-Nineteenth Century* (Washington, D.C.: German Historical Institute, 1992). See also Kathleen Neils Conzen et al., "The Invention of Ethnicity: A Perspective from the U.S.A.," *Journal of American Ethnic History* 12 (1992): 10–11.

23. Crèvecoeur, "Letter III," 69. On these points, see Conzen, "Immigrants in Nineteenth-Century Agricultural History," and Jeremy Atack and Fred Bateman, *To Their Own Soil: Agriculture in the Antebellum North* (Ames: Iowa State University Press, 1987).

24. In this setting, Werner Sollors's distinction between "consent" and "descent" is useful particularly in the context of the writings of Randolph Bourne. Bourne, Sollors's exemplar of "wholesome provincialism," wrote that "assimilation . . . instead of washing out the memories of Europe, made them more intensely real. Just as . . . clusters [of immigrants] became more and more objectively American, did they become more and more German or Scandinavian or Bohemian or Polish" (Randolph Bourne, *The Radical Will* [New York: Urizen, 1977], 248, cited in Werner Sollors, *Beyond Ethnicity: Consent and Descent in American Culture* [New York: Oxford University Press, 1986], 184).

25. Jean-Jacques Rousseau, "Discourse on the Sciences and Arts (First Discourse)," in *The First and Second Discourses*, ed. Roger D. Masters, trans. Roger D. Masters and Judith R. Masters (New York: St. Martin's Press, 1964), 59.

26. Henry Eyster Jacobs, *A History of the Evangelical Lutheran Church in the United States* (New York: Christian Literature Company, 1893), 404.

27. Laurence Oliphant, *Minnesota and the Far West* (Edinburgh: William Blackwood and Sons, 1855), 104.

28. Geographers and historians have detailed for decades the social and cultural "ways" that originated in the eastern "cultural hearths." See, for example, David Hackett Fischer, *Albion's Seed: Four British Folkways in America* (New York: Oxford University Press, 1989).

29. See, for example, Conzen, *Making Their Own America*; Gjerde, *From Peasants to Farmers*; Kamphoefner, *Transplanted Westfalians*; Ostergren, *A Community Transplanted*; and Loewen, *Family, Church, and Market*.

30. Immigration to the United States from Europe was enumerated at 98,797 between 1821 and 1830. It was roughly at that level in the previous decade and certainly less than that between 1801 and 1810. In comparison, nearly 500,000 Europeans arrived between 1831 and 1840, and over three times that number arrived in the next decade. See Stephan Thernstrom, ed., *Harvard Encyclopedia of American Ethnic Groups* (Cambridge: Harvard University Press, 1980), 1047.

31. See, for example, Peter Steinfels, "The Failed Encounter: The Catholic Church and Liberalism in the Nineteenth Century," and Philip Gleason, "American Catholics and Liberalism, 1789–1960," both in *Catholicism and Liberalism: Contributions to American Public Philosophy*, ed. R. Bruce Douglass and David Hollenbach (Cambridge: Cambridge University Press, 1994), 19–75, and Theodore G. Tappert, ed., *Lutheran Confessional Theology in America, 1840–1880* (New York: Oxford University Press, 1972), 3–37.

32. See, for example, Edwin G. Burrows and Michael Wallace, "The American Revolution: The Ideology and Psychology of National Liberation," *Perspectives in American History* 6 (1972): 167–306, and Jay Fliegelman, *Prodigals and Pilgrims: The American Revolution against Patriarchal Authority, 1750–1800* (Cambridge: Cambridge University Press, 1982). On

women, see Linda K. Kerber, *Women of the Republic: Intellect and Ideology in Revolutionary America* (Chapel Hill: University of North Carolina Press, 1980).

33. Burrows and Wallace, "American Revolution."

34. Gordon S. Wood, *The Radicalism of the American Revolution* (New York: Alfred A. Knopf, 1992).

35. See, for example, Helena Wall, *Fierce Communion: Family and Community in Early America* (Cambridge: Harvard University Press, 1990); Burrows and Wallace, "American Revolution," 262–67; and Daniel Scott Smith, "Parental Power and Marriage Patterns: An Analysis of Historical Trends in Hingham, Massachusetts," *Journal of Marriage and the Family* 35 (1973): 419–28.

36. See Michael Grossberg, *Governing the Hearth: Law and the Family in Nineteenth-Century America* (Chapel Hill: University of North Carolina Press, 1985).

37. Wood, *Radicalism of the American Revolution*, 185.

38. Martin E. Marty, *Pilgrims in Their Own Land: 500 Years of Religion in America* (Boston: Little, Brown, 1984), 169; Nathan O. Hatch, *The Democratization of American Christianity* (New Haven: Yale University Press, 1989).

39. See, for example, Joyce Appleby, *Capitalism and a New Social Order: The Republican Vision of the 1790s* (New York: New York University Press, 1984), and James T. Kloppenberg, "The Virtues of Liberalism: Christianity, Republicanism, and Ethics in Early American Political Discourse," *Journal of American History* 74 (1987): 9–33.

40. Edward Norris Kirk, *The Church Essential to the Republic: A Sermon in Behalf of the American Home Missionary Society* (New York: Leavitt, Trow, 1848), 6. The Catholic Church was commonly the central focus of objections concerning hierarchy and authoritarianism. Note, however, that here Kirk is also indicting European "state churches."

41. Ibid.

42. Ibid., 12.

43. Michel Chevalier, *Society, Manners, and Politics in the United States: Being a Series of Letters on North America* (Boston: Weeks, Jordan, 1839), 368, 428–31 (emphasis in original).

44. William I. Thomas and Florian Znaniecki, *The Polish Peasant in Europe and America*, 5 vols. (New York: Alfred A. Knopf, 1927), 1:89.

45. Vilhelm Moberg, *Den Okända Släkten* (Stockholm: Albert Bonniers Förlag, 1950), 34. Unless otherwise noted, all translations are my own.

46. Thomas and Znaniecki, *Polish Peasant*, 104.

47. Nils Wohlin, *Faran af Bondeklassens Undergräfvande i Sammanhang med de Gamla Arfvejordåskådningarnas Upplösning, Emigrationen och Bondjordens Mobilisering* (Stockholm: Kungl. Boktryckeriet, 1910), 1.

48. See C. F. W. Walther to Otto Herman Walther, 4 May 1840, *Letters of C. F. W. Walther: A Selection*, ed. and trans. Carl S. Meyer (Philadelphia: Fortress Press, 1969), 31–37.

49. For Thomas and Znaniecki's view of this process, see *Polish Peasant*, 87–128.

50. In Scandinavia, a pietist flame that had flared in the early eighteenth century but had been tempered by clerical rationalism during the Enlightenment was rekindled by leaders such as Hans Nielsen Hauge in the early nineteenth century and Carl Olof Rosenius at midcentury. Divisions within the National Reformed Church led to the secession in the Netherlands of over 100 churches by pietists who objected to the "cold formal orthodoxy" of theological rationalism. A pietist revival, wrapped up in German romanticism and nationalism, also occurred in Germany simultaneously with rancorous efforts to unite the Reformed and Lutheran Churches. On developments in Sweden, see George M. Stephenson, *The Religious Aspects of Swedish Immigration: A Study of Immigrant Churches* (Minneapolis: University of Minnesota Press, 1932), 1–48, and G. Everett Arden, *Augustana Heritage: A History of the Augustana Lutheran Church* (Rock Island, Ill.: Augustana Press, 1963), 4–12. On Norway, see John T. Flint, *Historical Role Analysis in the Study of Religious*

Change: Mass Educational Development in Norway, 1740–1891 (Cambridge: Cambridge University Press, 1990), 12–33, and E. Clifford Nelson and Eugene L. Fevold, *The Lutheran Church among Norwegian Americans: A History of the Evangelical Lutheran Church*, 2 vols. (Minneapolis: Augsburg Publishing House, 1960), 1:3–45. On German Lutherans, see J. L. Neve, *A History of Christian Thought*, 2 vols. (Philadelphia: Muhlenburg Press, 1946), 2:128–41, and Heinrich H. Maurer, "The Problems of a National Church before 1860," *American Journal of Sociology* 30 (1925): 534–50, and "The Problems of Group-Consensus: Founding the Missouri Synod," *American Journal of Sociology* 30 (1925): 665–82. On Holland, see Henry S. Lucas, *Netherlanders in America: Dutch Immigration to the United States and Canada, 1789–1950* (Ann Arbor: University of Michigan Press, 1955), 471–528, and James D. Bratt, *Dutch Calvinism in Modern America: A History of a Conservative Subculture* (Grand Rapids: William B. Eerdmans, 1984), 3–13.

51. Timothy L. Smith, "Religion and Ethnicity in America," *American Historical Review* 83 (1978): 1165–68.

52. On this confessional revival among Lutherans, see E. Clifford Nelson, ed., *The Lutherans in North America* (Philadelphia: Fortress Press, 1975), 150–51, and Tappert, *Lutheran Confessional Theology*.

53. For a brief overview, see Steinfels, "Failed Encounter," 19–44.

54. H. Richard Niebuhr, *The Social Sources of Denominationalism* (New York: Henry Holt, 1929), is still useful on this topic.

55. On Continental corporatist thought, see Ralph H. Bowen, *German Theories of the Corporative State, with Special Reference to the Period 1870–1919* (New York: McGraw-Hill, 1947), and Matthew H. Elbow, *French Corporative Theory, 1789–1948: A Chapter in the History of Ideas* (New York: Columbia University Press, 1953). Corporatist theory was organicist first because it was based on the belief that the demands of the whole, in society as well as in a body, took precedence over the demands of its single parts since the survival of a part (or individual member) depended on the continuation of the whole whereas the whole could survive without certain constituent parts. Moreover, just as some parts of the body were more important to the whole than others, people were unequal in social—but, importantly, not in divine—worth. Hence an inherent social inequality in society and a corporatist and hierarchical organization of authority were natural. Organicist thought also concluded that a social body—like a living organism—must resolve internal conflicts peacefully and gradually and must maintain peace between its constituent parts. This theory thus regretted the perceived chaos of the nineteenth century and rejected the inheritance of the individualism of the Enlightenment, the egalitarianism of the French Revolution, and the atomism of liberalism and Marxism.

56. Otto von Gierke, *Political Theories of the Middle Ages*, trans. William Maitland (Cambridge, 1938), 22.

57. On the many permutations of these principles, see Melvin J. Williams, *Catholic Social Thought: Its Approach to Contemporary Problems* (New York: Ronald Press, 1950), 263–308.

58. For Lutherans, wrote Heinrich H. Maurer, society was "organized on the order of the patriarchal family; economically it was a natural economy, usufructuary manor, or a guildshop, held together by traditionalism and the fear of the Lord" (Heinrich H. Maurer, "The Sociology of Protestantism," *American Journal of Sociology* 30 [1924]: 268).

59. Ibid., 269–70.

60. See Wilhelm H. Riehl, *Die Familie*, 12th ed. (Berlin: J. G. Cotta, 1904), and Frédéric Le Play, *Les Ouvriers européens: Études sur les travaux, la vie domestique et la condition morale des populations ouvrières de l'Europe, et leur relations avec les autres classes, précédé d'un exposé de la méthode d'observation* (Paris: Imprimerie Impériale, 1855), and *L'Organization de la famille, selon le vrai modèle signalé par l'histoire de toutes les races et de tous les temps* (Tours: Mame, 1871). English translations of Riehl and Le Play are found in Carle C. Zimmerman and

Merle E. Frampton, eds. and trans., *Family and Society: A Study of the Sociology of Reconstruction* (London: Williams & Norgate, 1935); Catherine Bodard Silver, ed. and trans., *On Family, Work, and Social Change* (Chicago: University of Chicago Press, 1982); and Pitirim A. Sorokin, Carle C. Zimmerman, and Charles J. Galpin, eds., *A Systematic Source Book in Rural Sociology*, 3 vols. (Minneapolis: University of Minnesota Press, 1931), 1:350–53, 2:76–84, 94–100. A valuable overview of Riehl and Le Play and their intellectual influence is found in David Warren Sabean, *Property, Production, and Family in Neckarhausen, 1700–1870* (New York: Cambridge University Press, 1990), 88–94.

61. The best description of this ideology is found in Philip Gleason, *The Conservative Reformers: German-American Catholics and the Social Order* (Notre Dame: University of Notre Dame Press, 1968). See also Barry, *The Catholic Church and German Americans*. French Canadian Catholics, who lived mainly in the eastern United States, also advocated Social Catholicism. See Gary Gerstle, *Working-Class Americanism: The Politics of Labor in a Textile City, 1914–1960* (New York: Cambridge University Press, 1989), 247–50.

62. See Kerby A. Miller, *Emigrants and Exiles: Ireland and the Irish Exodus to North America* (New York: Oxford University Press, 1985), 528–33, for an unsympathetic portrayal of the "conservatives," and Jay P. Dolan, *The American Catholic Experience: A History from Colonial Times to the Present* (Garden City, N.Y.: Doubleday, 1985), 311–20, which notes that the conservative position was "the majority viewpoint among the rank-and-file clergy and laity."

63. A. R. Wentz, *A Basic History of Lutheranism* (Philadelphia: Fortress Press, 1955), 116.

64. See Jacobs, *History of the Evangelical Lutheran Church*; J. L. Neve, *A Brief History of the Lutheran Church in America* (Burlington, Iowa: German Literary Board, 1916); and Maurer, "Problems of a National Church," 534–50, and "Problems of Group-Consensus," 665–82.

65. Swedish immigrants gravitated toward pietistic expressions that led them to forsake Lutheranism in significant numbers, whereas Danish Americans were divided between pietists and adherents of N. F. S. Grundtvig, the great Danish nationalist theologian. Within Norwegian Lutheranism, a corporatist formulation was advanced by the clergy and major battles were fought between the leadership and followers who questioned them. See Arden, *Augustana Heritage*; Jette Mackintosh, *Danskere i midtvesten: Elk Horn-Kimballton bosættelsen, 1870–1925* (Copenhagen: Akademisk Forlag, 1993), 102–29; Nelson and Fevold, *Lutheran Church*; and Theodore C. Blegen, *Norwegian Migration to America: The American Transition* (Northfield, Minn.: Norwegian-American Historical Association, 1940), 100–174, 241–76, 418–53.

66. See Lucas, *Netherlanders in America*, and Bratt, *Dutch Calvinism in Modern America*.

67. For Kuyper, the French Revolution attempted to "build up an artificial authority based on the free will of the individual" that "destroyed that organic tissue, broke those social bonds, and finally, in its work of atomistic trifling, had nothing left but the monotonous self-seeking individual, asserting his own self-sufficiency" (Abraham Kuyper, *Christianity and the Class Struggle*, trans. Dirk Jellema [Grand Rapids: Piet Hein Publishers, 1950], cited in Bratt, *Dutch Calvinism in Modern America*, 23).

68. See Turner, "Significance of the Frontier"; Thomas and Znaniecki, *Polish Peasant*; and Oscar Handlin, *The Uprooted: The Epic Story of the Great Migrations That Made the American People* (New York: Little, Brown, 1951).

69. The Upper Middle West is outlined in figure I.1. Cultural differences between the American-born (particularly those from the New England migration stream) and the European immigrant stand in clearest relief in this region. On the other hand, this focus makes comparisons between different American-born migrant streams more difficult because those who migrated from the Upland South typically occupied tracts in more southerly latitudes. See J. F. Rooney, W. Zelinsky, and D. R. Louder, eds., *This Remarkable Continent: An Atlas of United States and Canadian Society and Cultures* (College Station: Texas

A&M University Press, 1982), 10, which maps the traditional rural culture regions of the eastern and central United States.

70. See, for example, John Mack Faragher, *Sugar Creek: Life on the Illinois Prairie* (New Haven: Yale University Press, 1986); Hal Barron, *Those Who Stayed Behind: Rural Society in Nineteenth-Century New England* (New York: Cambridge University Press, 1984); Conzen, *Making Their Own America*; and Ostergren, *A Community Transplanted*.

Chapter One

1. Richard K. Vedder and Lowell E. Gallaway, "Migration and the Old Northwest," in *Essays in Nineteenth-Century Economic History: The Old Northwest*, ed. David C. Klingaman and Richard K. Vedder (Athens: Ohio University Press, 1975), 161. To be precise, the population of the Old Northwest grew from 272,324 in 1810 to 1,470,018 in 1830.

2. Ibid.; William J. Petersen, "Population Advance to the Upper Mississippi Valley, 1830–1860," *Iowa Journal of History and Politics* 32 (1934): 313. In 1860, 6,926,884 people lived in the Old Northwest.

3. Paul W. Gates, *Landlords and Tenants on the Prairie Frontier: Studies in American Land Policy* (Ithaca: Cornell University Press, 1973), 56, 63.

4. Counting the number of wagons and their occupants was an oft-used method to illustrate the volume of migration. *Niles' National Register* reported in 1834 that a "gentleman who lately travelled from Paoli, Indiana, to Vincennes, a distance of 65 miles, counted, in that distance, no less than four hundred wagons moving emigrant families to Illinois and Missouri" (15 November 1834, 163). A correspondent to the *Des Moines Valley Whig* from Indiana wrote in 1851, "We think it reasonable to say that an average of three hundred wagons per week have passed thro' for the past three or four weeks. At an average of four persons to the wagon, we judge 5000 persons will have passed through Indianapolis by the close of the season" (*Des Moines Valley Whig* [Keokuk], 6 November 1851, cited in Petersen, "Population Advance," 325).

5. *Cincinnati Chronicle*, cited in *Niles' National Register*, 15 June 1843, 311.

6. *Philadelphia Sentinel*, 1 June 1836, cited in *Iowa News* (Dubuque), 24 June 1837, 3 (emphasis added).

7. *Dubuque Reporter*, cited in Stewart H. Holbrook, *The Yankee Exodus: An Account of Migration from New England* (New York: Macmillan, 1950), 136.

8. *Niles' National Register*, 9 August 1834, 398–99.

9. Captain Marryat, *Diary in America, with Remarks on Its Institutions*, 2 vols. (London: Longman, Orme, Brown, Green & Longmans, 1839), 2:207.

10. *Niles' National Register*, 15 June 1843, 312.

11. Fredrika Bremer, *The Homes of the New World: Impressions of America*, trans. Mary Howitt, 2 vols. (New York: Harper and Brothers, 1853), 1:554–55.

12. J. Leavitt's memorial to Congress, cited in "The Missionary Field in the Mississippi Valley," *Home Missionary* 14 (1841): 177.

13. U.S. Congress, *Congressional Globe*, 28th Cong., 2d sess., 1844, 51–52.

14. Ibid., 29th Cong., 1st sess., 1846, 1059–62, cited in Mary E. Young, "Congress Looks West: Liberal Ideology and Public Land Policy in the Nineteenth Century," in *The Frontier in American Development: Essays in Honor of Paul Wallace Gates*, ed. David M. Ellis (Ithaca: Cornell University Press, 1968), 92.

15. Ibid.

16. U.S. Congress, *Congressional Globe*, 24th Cong., 2d sess., 1837, 420–21.

17. *Iowa News* (Dubuque), 26 August 1837, 3, cited in Arthur A. Halbach, *Dyersville: Its History and Its People* (Milwaukee: St. Joseph's Press, 1939), 20.

18. *Iowa News* (Dubuque), 3 June 1837, cited in Halbach, *Dyersville*, 21.

19. *Dubuque Herald*, 24 October 1860, 3.

20. A Pioneer, *Northern Iowa: Containing Hints and Information of Value to Emigrants* (Dubuque: Nonpareil Publishing House, 1858), 14. This free-labor ideology endured. Yet another immigration-promotion pamphlet published in 1870 was offered "to all Working Men, who live by honest toil, and would thereby contribute their part toward the development of a free and prosperous State; To all Land Men and Women, of both the Old World and the New, who desire beautiful homes in the fairest portion of the green earth; To all Good Men and Women, who aspire to independence, either for themselves or their children after them, and who will contribute, either of mind or muscle, to carry Iowa forward to her grand and glorious destiny" (Iowa Board of Immigration, *Iowa: The Home for Immigrants, Being a Treatise on the Resources of Iowa* [Des Moines: Mills, 1870], 72).

21. Charles Augustus Murray, *Travels in North America during the Years 1834, 1835, 1836, Including a Summer Residence with the Pawnee Tribe of Indians and a Visit to Cuba and the Azore Islands*, 2 vols. (London: Richard Bentley, 1839; reprint, New York: DaCapo Press, 1974), 1:218. Murray went so far as to argue that it was not necessarily the political institutions of the United States that created prosperity. Rather, for Murray, the "possession of a territory boundless in extent, unequalled in variety and fertility of soil, and watered by lakes and navigable rivers, such as are known in no other part of the world," better explained American greatness (ibid., 2:300–301).

22. Myranda Underwood to Absent Brother and Sister, September 1847, SHSW.

23. Sjoerd Aukes Sipma to My Relatives, to All the Farmers, and to the Director of Youth at Bornwerd, [Friesland,] 26 September 1848, trans. Edward E. Fikse, ISHDDM. In another letter written in March 1848 to a schoolteacher in Bornwerd, Sipma wrote, "Here is land and work. Oh how often I think of the poor in Friesland as we sit to eat. Pork and beef we have three times a day, that is the American custom. . . . A farmer can also do well here because he has no expenses other than labor. What more he has to pay is small indeed. Oh I'm so glad I'm in America" (Sjoerd Aukes Sipma to Dear Friends, March 1848, trans. G. A. Sipma, ISHDDM).

24. John and Mary Thomson to Dear Brother, 24 January 1850, SHSW.

25. C. J. A. Ericson, "Memories of a Swedish Immigrant of 1852," *Annals of Iowa* 8 (1907): 2.

26. Ole Munch Ræder, *America in the Forties: The Letters of Ole Munch Ræder*, ed. and trans. Gunnar J. Malmin (Minneapolis: Norwegian-American Historical Association, 1929), 63–64. Elsewhere in Ræder's letters was the simple yet profound observation of a Norwegian immigrant: "Here even a tramp can enjoy a chicken dinner once in a while" (ibid., 69).

27. Sjur Tøgersen Aasen to Dear Parents and Siblings, 16 August 1849, in Gunnar Urtegaard, "'Og Huen tages ikke av Hovedet for noget Menneske': Amerikabrev frå 1848–1850," *Tidsskrift utgjeve av historielaget for Sogn* 27 (1981): 74. Ræder noted that one of "the glorious privileges of life in America" was that "one need not take his hat off in the presence of an official" (Ræder, *America in the Forties*, 79–80).

28. Over forty years later, for example, a German immigrant writing from Minnesota to his brother restated the theme. "This is a free land," he wrote, "No one can give orders to anybody here, one is as good as another, no one takes off his hat to another as you have to do in Germany" (Johann Peter Schmitz to his brother, 4 July 1891, in Merle Curti and Kendall Birr, "The Immigrant and the American Image in Europe, 1860–1914," *Mississippi Valley Historical Review* 37 [1950]: 221).

29. Edward Norris Kirk, *The Church Essential to the Republic: A Sermon in Behalf of the American Home Missionary Society* (New York: Leavitt, Trow, 1848), 16.

30. "Our Country," *Home Missionary* 21 (1849): 221.

31. *Niles' National Register*, 29 September 1832, 68.

32. *Niles' National Register*, 21 June 1845, 247–48.

33. Michel Chevalier, *Society, Manners, and Politics in the United States: Being a Series of Letters on North America* (Boston: Weeks, Jordan, 1839), 113–14.

34. *Richmond Comp.*, cited in *Niles' National Register*, 23 November 1839, 195.

35. Lyman Beecher, *Plea for the West* (Cincinnati: Truman and Smith, 1835), 34–35.

36. Albert Barnes, *Home Missions: A Sermon in Behalf of the American Home Missionary Society* (New York: William Osborn, 1849), 8–9 (emphasis in original).

37. "The Missionary Field in the Mississippi Valley," *Home Missionary* 14 (1841): 177.

38. *Muscatine Democratic Enquirer*, 19 July 1851, cited in Petersen, "Population Advances," 333.

39. Dwight, for example, feared the western settlements, but after considering the relative dangers of the restless elements moving west or staying in New England, he concluded in 1797 that migration was "of very serious utility to the ancient settlements." "Providence has opened in the vast wilderness," he asserted, "a retreat sufficiently alluring to draw [restless inhabitants] away from the land of their nativity. We have many troubles even now, but we should have many more if this body of foresters had remained at home" (Timothy Dwight, *Travels in New England and New York*, ed. Barbara Miller Solomon, 4 vols. [Cambridge: Belknap Press, 1969], 2:323–24).

40. "Reaction of the East upon the West," *Home Missionary* 14 (1841): 182 (emphasis in original). See also "The Refluent Wave," *Home Missionary* 11 (1839): 209.

41. Frederick Saunders and T. B. Thorpe, *The Progress and Prospects of America* (New York: Edward Walker, 1855), 264.

42. Thomas R. Whitney, *A Defence of the American Policy* (New York: DeWitt & Davenport, 1856), 179.

43. Saunders and Thorpe, *Progress and Prospects of America*, 264.

44. See, for example, Ray A. Billington, *The Protestant Crusade: A Study of the Origins of American Nativism* (New York: Macmillan, 1938), and David H. Bennett, *The Party of Fear: From Nativist Movements to the New Right in American History* (Chapel Hill: University of North Carolina Press, 1988), 68–155.

45. Whitney, *Defence of the American Policy*, 325.

46. Saunders and Thorpe, *Progress and Prospects of America*, 377.

47. Stephen E. Maizlich, "The Meaning of Nativism and the Crisis of the Union: The Know-Nothing Movement in the Antebellum North," in *Essays on Antebellum Politics, 1840–1860*, ed. Stephen E. Maizlich and John J. Kushma (College Station: Texas A & M University Press, 1982), 166–98; Tyler Anbinder, *Nativism and Slavery: The Northern Know Nothings and the Politics of the 1850s* (New York: Oxford University Press, 1992), 44–47. Maizlich has noted that Eric Foner argues that the so-called free-labor ideology inherently rejected nativism. See Eric Foner, *Free Soil, Free Labor, Free Men: The Ideology of the Republican Party before the Civil War* (New York: Oxford University Press, 1970), 237. Yet Maizlich points out, I think correctly, that nativism particularly in an anti-Catholic form could be used as a central component of an ideology that celebrated American liberty as opposed to the slaveries in the less-developed world.

48. Whitney, *Defence of the American Policy*, 94–96 (emphasis in original).

49. Ibid., 99–101. Although Whitney's examination of the implications of slavery among the "Romanists" and freedom among the "American Republicans" was one of the more explicitly defined analyses, he was not alone in perceiving the presence of slavery and freedom in the respective systems. C. B. Boynton, in fact, was even more explicit in connecting the slaveholder to the priest. The central belief of the nation, he argued, was that the government "was designed for the overthrow of slavery." Protestantism, more-

over, was central to liberty, and it was not destined to be "led in chains by a priesthood, nor betrayed by a jesuit." Rather, it was a Protestantism "with the right will, and power to defend itself, and Liberty seeking deliverance for all." Boynton concluded that "there are two dangers which threaten our noble Republic": "the Papacy and Slavery." With God's help, however, "the American eagle [will] never dwell in peace with [the] coiling serpent of slavery." With God's help, America would be "Protestant and Free!" See C. B. Boynton, *Address before the Citizens of Cincinnati, July 4, 1855* (Cincinnati, 1855), cited in Maizlich, "Meaning of Nativism," 177–78.

50. The literature on "classical republicanism" is vast. See J. G. A. Pocock, *The Machiavellian Moment: Florentine Political Thought and the Atlantic Republican Tradition* (Princeton: Princeton University Press, 1975), and Gordon S. Wood, *The Creation of the American Republic, 1776–1787* (Chapel Hill: University of North Carolina Press, 1969). For observations on its development and modification in the nineteenth century, see Sean Wilentz, *Chants Democratic: New York City and the Rise of the American Working Class, 1788–1850* (New York: Oxford University Press, 1984), and Rowland Berthoff, "Conventional Mentality: Free Blacks, Women, and Business Corporations as Unequal Persons, 1820–1870," *Journal of American History* 76 (1989): 753–84. For critical assessments of the school, see Thomas L. Pangle, *The Spirit of Modern Republicanism: The Moral Vision of the American Founders and the Philosophy of Locke* (Chicago: University of Chicago Press, 1988), and Joyce Appleby, *Liberalism and Republicanism in the Historical Imagination* (Cambridge: Harvard University Press, 1992).

51. See, for example, Anbinder, *Nativism and Slavery*; Daniel Walker Howe, *The Political Culture of the American Whigs* (Chicago: University of Chicago Press, 1979), 161–79; and Kathryn Kish Sklar, *Catherine Beecher: A Study of American Domesticity* (New Haven: Yale University Press, 1973), 107–21.

52. The more notable nativism tracts of the 1830s, for example, were written by Samuel F. B. Morse, an advocate of labor and the Democratic Party, and Lyman Beecher, staid minister of the Congregational Church, a Whig, and later a Republican. See Ray A. Billington, "Anti-Catholic Propaganda and the Home Missionary Movement, 1800–1860," *Mississippi Valley Historical Review* 22 (1935): 361–84, for a discussion of Morse and Beecher and early experiences that provoked their vicious anti-Catholicism. On the political importance of nativism in the 1850s, see Anbinder, *Slavery and Nativism*, and William E. Gienapp, *The Origins of the Republican Party, 1852–1856* (New York: Oxford University Press, 1987).

53. Samuel C. Busey, *Immigration: Its Evils and Consequences* (New York: DeWitt & Davenport, 1856), 132, 134.

54. Saunders and Thorpe, *Progress and Prospects of America*, 288.

55. Ibid., 283; Busey, *Immigration*, 131–32.

56. Busey, *Immigration*, 131–32, 134, 139–40.

57. Whitney, *Defence of the American Policy*, 156–62.

58. Beecher, *Plea for the West*, 40–41, 9–12 (emphasis added).

59. "Our Country," *Home Missionary* 21 (1849): 222.

60. Observe the assimilationism of liberal William Seward in Howe, *Political Culture of the American Whigs*, 200–203.

61. Judge James Hall in *Illinois Monthly Magazine*, 1831, cited in Beecher, *Plea for the West*, 19n.

62. Whitney, *Defence of the American Policy*, 166 (emphasis in original). Whitney concluded not surprisingly that "European immigration is unquestionably the 'Grecian horse' of the American Republic."

63. Samuel F. B. Morse, *Foreign Conspiracy against the Liberties of the United States* (New York: Leavitt, Lord, 1835), 58–59.

64. Beecher, *Plea for the West*, 116–18.

65. *Stuttgard Universal Gazette*, cited in *Niles' National Register*, 3 November 1832, 148; *Niles' National Register*, 24 November 1832, 197 (emphasis in original). Another account was much more succinct in its criticism of the plan. "We shall bid them 'welcome,'" it wrote, "when they arrive—but the idea of forming a state is chimerical and would be injurious on many accounts" (*Niles' National Register*, 3 November 1832, 148). See also Kate Asaphine Everest, "How Wisconsin Came By Its Large German Element," *Wisconsin Historical Collections* 12 (1896): 304.

66. Franz Löher, *Geschichte und Zustande der Deutschen in Amerika*, 2d ed. (Göttingen: Georg H. Wigand, 1855), 502, cited in Everest, "How Wisconsin Came By Its Large German Element," 306. Texas was also a favored site for German colonization, much to the chagrin of the Americans there. "I dread European influence more than all the world besides," wrote G. W. Bennett. "The emigrations from the United States are comparatively few, while those from the European governments will be by multipled thousands! There is one association here styled the 'German Emigrating Company,' consisting of thirty-one princes and counts! . . . [Prince Victor] says he will settle 250 families on that land this spring, and 300 families higher up on the Guadaloupe river at the same time. . . . Should the annexation [of Texas to the United States] question be long delayed, may not the government pass out of our hands?" (G. W. Bennett in *Niles' National Register*, 1 February 1845, 337). "By the last news from Europe," Niles concluded, "we learn that the tide of emigration from Swabia, &c. for Texas, was pouring by hundreds towards the seaports, the determination seeming to be to make a new European colony of Texas, to be composed of people, in sentiment, feeling, and country, foreign to the United States." Everest notes that although plans for German colonization waned as time passed, Germans as late as 1857 advocated intervention by German states to enable German colonization in the United States. Proponents of colonization in Germany stressed that the American central government was too weak to prohibit German governmental intervention and that its weakness might hasten a catastrophe feared by many: the breaking up of the Union into two or more groups of states—divided not between North and South but between those under Anglo-American and those under German rule. See Everest, "How Wisconsin Came By Its Large German Element," 305–9.

67. *Freeman's Journal and Catholic Register* (New York), 22 April 1843, cited in Sister Mary Gilbert Kelly, *Catholic Immigrant Colonization Projects in the United States, 1815–1860* (New York: United States Catholic Historical Society, 1939), 174.

68. "Grand Scheme for Planting Irish Catholic Colonies in the Western States," *Home Missionary* 15 (1842): 145–58 (emphasis added).

69. See David Brion Davis, "Some Themes of Countersubversion: An Analysis of Anti-Masonic, Anti-Catholic, and Anti-Mormon Literature," *Mississippi Valley Historical Review* 47 (1960): 205–24.

70. Beecher, *Plea for the West*, 59, 68–70.

71. "How the Potentates of Europe Regard Us," *Home Missionary* 14 (1841): 180–81 (emphasis in original).

72. "The Missionary Field in the Mississippi Valley," *Home Missionary* 14 (1841): 181; "Romanism in Iowa," *Home Missionary* 15 (1842): 170.

73. The Know Nothing Party, for example, was more successful in the urban environments of the northeastern United States than in the Middle West. See Anbinder, *Nativism and Slavery*.

74. Busey, *Immigration*, 88, 39.

75. Beecher, *Plea for the West*, 43–44.

76. "Grand Scheme for Planting Irish Catholic Colonies in the Western States," *Home Missionary* 15 (1842): 154.

77. "The Refluent Wave," *Home Missionary* 11 (1839): 209.

78. Albert Barnes, *Plea in Behalf of Western Colleges* (Philadelphia: William Sloanaker, 1846), 13. On this confidence, see also J. C. Holbrook, "Romanism Not to Be Underrated," *Home Missionary* 19 (1846): 171.

79. Thomas Jefferson, *Notes on the State of Virginia* (Paris, 1785), in *The Life and Selected Writings of Thomas Jefferson*, ed. Adrienne Koch and William Peden (New York: Modern Library, 1944), 217–18. Jefferson thus suggested that a slower natural growth of the American-born was preferable to immigration. In this way, the government would be "more homogeneous, more peaceable, more durable."

80. *Newark Daily Advertiser*, cited in *Niles' National Register*, 9 November 1839, 165. The commentary ended with a pronouncement that continues to be voiced today, in varying forms: "While the descendants of thousands of Americans who fought, and bled and died in our cause, would not go west to get an acre, the descendants of thousands of Englishmen and Hessians who came to *oppress and enslave us*, would come to our shores, go out west, and inherit this land without paying a dollar" (emphasis added).

81. A good overview of the proposed anti-immigration legislation is found in Bennett, *Party of Fear*.

82. Busey, *Immigration*, 127–29 (emphasis in original). Some racialists attached their Anglo-Saxon past to the American Republic. Saunders and Thorpe, for example, noted that "the Republic of the United States is Anglo-Saxon in all its bearings." The conversion of non-Anglo-Saxons to republicanism, from this perspective, would be extremely difficult, if not impossible. See Saunders and Thorpe, *Progress and Prospects of America*, 252.

83. This program was fostered in particular by evangelical Christians such as Beecher. See Howe, *Political Culture of the American Whigs*, 150–80, and Sklar, *Catherine Beecher*, 107–21.

84. Cited in Richard Lyle Power, *Planting Corn Belt Culture: The Impress of the Upland Southerner and Yankee in the Old Northwest* (Indianapolis: Indiana Historical Society Publications, 1953), 6.

85. Note that these institutions would also address the issue that Timothy Dwight and others had voiced earlier: the concern that an uncivilized and uninstitutionalized West would foster a society marred by license rather than blessed with liberty. See Lois Kimbell Mathews, *The Expansion of New England: The Spread of New England Settlement and Institutions to the Mississippi River, 1620–1865* (Boston: Houghton Mifflin, 1909); Holbrook, *Yankee Exodus*; Power, *Planting Corn Belt Culture*, 172; and Joseph Schafer, "The Yankee and the Teuton in Wisconsin: III. Some Social Traits of Yankees," *Wisconsin Magazine of History* 6 (1922): 393–94.

86. Beecher, *Plea for the West*, 37, 29–30, 15–16, 23 (emphasis added).

87. The Yale Band, which moved to Illinois in 1830, attempted to assist in the creation of churches and schools in Jacksonville, Illinois. The Iowa Band, which worked originally in Denmark, Iowa, consisted of graduates of Andover Theological Seminary who thirteen years later dedicated themselves to the transplantation of Congregationalism in the West. Indeed, individual Protestant clergy throughout the region wrote copious reports of their efforts in eastern periodicals in part to gain additional contributions to their cause. See Don Harrison Doyle, *The Social Order of a Frontier Community: Jacksonville, Illinois, 1825–1870* (Urbana: University of Illinois Press, 1978), 23–38; Holbrook, *Yankee Exodus*, 133; and F. I. Herriott, *Did Emigrants from New England First Settle Iowa?* (Des Moines: Bishard Brothers, 1906), 6.

88. Salter in his diary thus found it simple to deprecate a Catholic bishop who allegedly offered to heal a child "idiotic in mind and helpless in body" if he would join the church. "How disgraceful," he concluded, "[is] the attempt to promote superstition in this 19th century." See William Salter diary, 11 November 1843, 27 February 1845, in Philip D. Jor-

dan, ed., "William Salter's 'My Ministry in Iowa,'" 1843–1846," *Annals of Iowa* 19 (1935): 547, 20 (1935): 44.

89. Ephraim Adams, *The Iowa Band* (Boston: Congregational Publishing Society, 1870), 11. Like their Roman Catholic counterparts, American Protestant missionaries played a central role in the formation of culturally distinct colonies in the West. During the early years of settlement, when the uncertainties of life in the region were great, numerous New England colonization companies pooled capital, purchased large tracts of land, and organized migration and settlement. According to Lois Kimball Mathews, twenty-two colonies that had originated in New England or New York were established in Illinois alone between 1830 and 1840. New England colonies also arose farther west in Iowa, Wisconsin, and Minnesota, though they were more scattered there than in Ohio and Illinois. By mid-century, small towns established as a result of a planned New England colonization—including Oberlin, Ohio; Beloit, Wisconsin; Grinnell, Iowa; and Northfield, Minnesota—dotted the landscape. See Mathews, *Expansion of New England*, and Holbrook, *Yankee Exodus*, for descriptions of Yankee colonization schemes.

90. Beecher, *Plea for the West*, 73.

Chapter Two

1. Cited in "Rt. Rev. Mathias Loras, D.D., First Bishop of Dubuque," *Annals of Iowa* 3 (1899): 591.

2. For a good overview of Catholic colonization, see Sister Mary Gilbert Kelly, *Catholic Immigrant Colonization Projects in the United States, 1815–1860* (New York: United States Catholic Historical Society, 1939).

3. Rev. Francis X. Pierz, *Die Indianer in Nord-America, ihre Lebenweise, Sitten, Gebräusche, u.s.w.* (St. Louis: Franz Saler, 1855), appendix, translated in *Acta et Dicta* 7 (1935): 121–30.

4. Mathias Loras memoirs, cited in Sister Mary Cleo Tritz, "St. Donatus: A Settlement of Luxemburgers in Northeastern Iowa" (M.A. thesis, Catholic University of America, 1954), 14–15.

5. Samuel Mazzuchelli, *The Memoirs of Father Samuel Mazzuchelli, O.P.* (1844; Chicago: Priory Press, 1967), 300. Here is a good example of the variations in the invented meanings of historical events. The American-born often posed the American Revolution as a successful overthrow of the papists of England.

6. Pierz, *Die Indianer in Nord-America*, 121–30. Germans would lead the settlement, according to Pierz, since they were the first Europeans in the vicinity and had beheld the apparition of the cross.

7. *Freeman's Journal and Catholic Register* (New York), 2 September 1854, cited in Kelly, *Catholic Immigrant Colonization Projects*, 155.

8. See, for example, "Letters and Documents," *Iowa Catholic Historical Review* 6 (1933): 40–42. See also M. M. Hoffmann, *The Church Founders of the Northwest* (Milwaukee: Bruce Publishing, 1937), and Kelly, *Catholic Immigrant Colonization Projects*.

9. The Propagation of the Faith Society of Lyons, the Leopoldine Society of Vienna, and the Ludwig Missions-Verein of Munich sent millions of francs and thousands of florins to the Catholic hierarchy in the West. See, for example, A. J. Rezek, "The Leopoldine Society (Leopoldinen Stiftung)," *Acta et Dicta* 3 (1914): 305–20, and M. M. Hoffmann, "Europe's Pennies and Iowa's Missions," *Iowa Catholic Historical Review* 5 (1932): 39–48.

10. Catholic leaders were often explicit about their attempts to sequester their flocks from contact with incorrect beliefs. Pierz, for example, challenged potential migrants to Catholic settlements to "prove yourselves good Catholics [by not bringing] with you any

free-thinkers, red republicans, atheists, or agitators" (Pierz, *Die Indianer in Nord-America*, 121–30).

11. Hans Kohn, *American Nationalism: An Interpretative Essay* (New York: Macmillan, 1957). See also Yehoshua Arieli, *Individualism and Nationalism in American Ideology* (Cambridge: Harvard University Press, 1964); Paul Nagle, *This Sacred Trust: American Nationality, 1798–1898* (New York: Oxford University Press, 1971); and Samuel P. Huntington, *American Politics: The Promise of Disharmony* (Cambridge: Harvard University Press, 1981).

12. Alexis de Tocqueville, *Democracy in America*, ed. J. P. Mayer, trans. George Lawrence (New York: Anchor Books, 1969), 396–97.

13. Benedict Anderson, *Imagined Communities: Reflections on the Origins and Spread of Nationalism*, rev. ed. (London: Verso, 1991); Herbert David Croly, *Promise of American Life* (Cambridge: Harvard University Press, 1965), 3. On nationalism, see also Ernest Gellner, *Nations and Nationalism* (Ithaca: Cornell University Press, 1983), and Eric J. Hobsbawm, *Nations and Nationalism since 1870: Programme, Myth, Reality*, 2d ed. (New York: Cambridge University Press, 1992).

14. It must be underscored that these paragraphs speak of the overwhelming majority of immigrants to the West who were of European background and therefore defined as "white." The naturalization acts of the United States from 1790 until the aftermath of the Civil War defined access to citizenship according to "whiteness." The relatively simple passage to citizenship was restricted to "white" immigrants, whose encounters with the American nation, it goes without saying, contrasted starkly with those who were defined as "nonwhite." On citizenship, see James H. Kettner, *The Development of American Citizenship, 1608–1870* (Chapel Hill: University of North Carolina Press, 1978). On the construction of whiteness, see David R. Roediger, *Wages of Whiteness: Race and the Making of the American Working Class* (New York: Verso, 1991).

15. Carl J. Friedrich et al., *Problems of the American Public Service* (New York: McGraw Hill, 1935), 12, cited in Huntington, *American Politics*, 30.

16. See Philip Gleason, "American Identity and Americanization," in *Harvard Encyclopedia of American Ethnic Groups*, ed. Stephan Thernstrom (Cambridge: Harvard University Press, 1980), 31–34; Kathleen Neils Conzen et al., "The Invention of Ethnicity: A Perspective from the U.S.A.," *Journal of American Ethnic History* 12 (1992): 6–9; and John Higham, "Integrating America: The Problem of Assimilation in the Nineteenth Century," *Journal of American Ethnic History* 1 (1981): 7–16.

17. Thomas R. Whitney, *A Defence of the American Policy* (New York: DeWitt & Davenport, 1856), 29 (emphasis in original).

18. Ibid., 129–30.

19. Samuel F. B. Morse, *Foreign Conspiracy against the Liberties of the United States* (New York: Leavitt, Lord, 1835), 167–71.

20. Ole Rynning, *Ole Rynning's True Account of America*, ed. and trans. Theodore C. Blegen (Minneapolis: Norwegian-American Historical Association, 1926), 22–23 (emphasis added).

21. Ole Munch Ræder, *America in the Forties: The Letters of Ole Munch Ræder*, ed. and trans. Gunnar J. Malmin (Minneapolis: Norwegian-American Historical Association, 1929), 22.

22. *Emigranten*, 17 September 1852, cited in Harold M. Tolo, "The Political Position of *Emigranten* in the Election of 1852," *Norwegian-American Studies and Records* 8 (1934): 105–6.

23. *Dubuque National Demokrat*, 1 February 1859, 1, trans. J. K. Downing, CDH.

24. G. Unthank letter, 16 February 1826, MHS.

25. Mary Kevin Gallagher, ed., *Seed/Harvest* (Dubuque: Archdiocese of Dubuque Press, 1987), 13.

26. Karl Mathie, Marathon, Marathon County, 1893, Kate Levi field notes, Kate Levi Papers, SHSW.

27. Cited in Joseph Schafer, "The Yankee and the Teuton in Wisconsin: V. Social Harmonies and Discords," *Wisconsin Magazine of History* 7 (1923): 158–59. Ræder observed a similar misidentification of Democrat with democracy among German, Irish, and Norwegian immigrants. On the other hand, "Englishmen, who have a constitutional education and have learned to think for themselves, or, as the Locofocos would say, have been corrupted by the aristocracy which infests Great Britain, willingly take sides with the Whigs" (Ræder, *America in the Forties*, 22–23).

28. Michel Chevalier, *Society, Manners, and Politics in the United States: Being a Series of Letters on North America* (Boston: Weeks, Jordan, 1839), 187.

29. *Nordlyset,* cited in Ræder, *America in the Forties,* 180.

30. *Folkets Røst,* 24 July 1858, 2.

31. Johan Reinert Reiersen, *Pathfinder for Norwegian Emigrants by Johan Reinert Reiersen,* ed. and trans. Frank G. Nelson (Northfield, Minn.: Norwegian-American Historical Association, 1981), 176, 182–83.

32. Lars Fletre, "The Vossing Correspondence Society of 1848 and the Report of Adam Lövenskjold," *Norwegian-American Studies* 28 (1979): 267.

33. August Blümner to his relatives, 3 April 1838, in *News from the Land of Freedom: German Immigrants Write Home,* ed. Walter D. Kamphoefner, Wolfgang Helbich, and Ulrike Sommer (Ithaca: Cornell University Press, 1991), 103 (emphasis in original). See also letters in ibid., 164–65, 307, 393, 427, 478, 481–82, 494, 585, 602.

34. Fletre, "Vossing Correspondence Society," 267.

35. R. Puchner to Kate Everest, New Holstein, Calumet County, 1890, Kate Levi Papers, SHSW.

36. Ludwig Dilger to parents and brothers and sisters, 5 November 1886, cited in Kamphoefner, Helbich, and Sommer, *News from the Land of Freedom,* 494 (emphasis in original). Despite his disparagement of American freedom, it is noteworthy that later in his letter Dilger wrote that "the worker will soon realize what his freedom is all about," as evidenced by the recent electoral victories among socialists.

37. Grigorij Machtet, "The Prairie and the Pioneers," *The Week,* nos. 47 and 48 (November 1874), in *America through Russian Eyes, 1874–1926,* ed. and trans. Olga Peters Hasty and Susanne Fusso (New Haven: Yale University Press, 1988), 21–22. Machtet was a member of the "American circle" of Russian populists, who attempted to form settlements in the United States in the 1870s.

38. Ibid. On the importance of myths of mobility and the influence of electoral politics in muting criticism of U.S. society, see, for example, Ira Katznelson, *City Trenches: Urban Politics and the Patterning of Class in the United States* (Chicago: University of Chicago Press, 1981); Stephan Thernstrom, *Poverty and Progress: Social Mobility in a Nineteenth Century City* (Cambridge: Harvard University Press, 1964); and Alan Dawley, *Class and Community: The Industrial Revolution and Lynn* (Cambridge: Harvard University Press, 1976).

39. Jonathan D. Sarna notes that larger collectivities were configured out of previously divisive groups in "From Immigrants to Ethnics: Toward a New Theory of 'Ethnicization,'" *Ethnicity* 5 (1978): 370–78. On "boundaries," see Fredrik Barth, *Ethnic Groups and Boundaries: The Social Organization of Cultural Difference* (Boston: Little, Brown, 1969), 9–38. See also William L. Yancey et al., "Emergent Ethnicity: A Review and Reformulation," *American Sociological Review* 41 (1976): 391–403, and Nathan Glazer and Daniel P. Moynihan, *Beyond the Melting Pot: The Negroes, Puerto Ricans, Jews, Italians, and Irish of New York City* (Cambridge: Massachusetts Institute of Technology Press, 1963).

40. The subgroup within the complementary identity, as I shall outline it, could be based on class and status identification. It is very important to keep in mind, however, that divisions at mid-century tended to be based on racial, religious, and ethnic concerns. See Conzen et al., "The Invention of Ethnicity," 8.

41. On the concept of a "complementary identity," see Peter A. Munch, "In Search of Identity: Ethnic Awareness and Ethnic Attitudes among Scandinavian Immigrants, 1840–1860," in *Scandinavians in America: Literary Life*, ed. J. R. Christianson (Decorah, Iowa: Symra Literary Society, 1985), 1–24. See also David M. Potter, "The Historian's Use of Nationalism and Vice Versa," in *History and American Society* (New York: Oxford University Press, 1973), 74–75, and Morton Grodzins, *The Loyal and the Disloyal: Social Boundaries of Patriotism and Treason* (Chicago: University of Chicago Press, 1956).

42. Huntington, *American Politics*, 27.

43. Indeed, immigrants saw "Americans" as those with Anglo-Saxon backgrounds. "Americanization," from this perspective, was impossible.

44. *Den Swenske Republikanen*, 21 August 1857, cited in Munch, "In Search of Identity," 7.

45. Ræder, *America in the Forties*, 19.

46. Cited in Joseph Schröder, *Verhandlungen der vierten allgemeinen Versammlung der Katholiken deutscher Zunge der Vereinigten Staaten von Nord-Amerika in Pittsburgh, Pa., Am 22, 23, 24 und 25 September, 1890* (Pittsburgh, 1890), 69–70, cited in Colman J. Barry, *The Catholic Church and German Americans* (Washington, D.C.: Catholic University of America Press, 1953), 124. Father Goller extended the metaphor when he noted that immigrants "may still treasure in their hearts the sweet memories of childhood; for only the renegade can forget the mother that bore him." But "far more dearer to them than the memories of childhood is the strong and beautiful bride, Columbia, who taught them to walk erect on God's earth in the proud consciousness of manhood" (ibid., 173).

47. See, for example, *Die Iowa*, 12 July 1883, 8.

48. *Dubuque National Demokrat*, 16 March 1876, 3, trans. J. K. Downing, CDH.

49. *Die Iowa*, 13 July 1882, 5.

50. Whitney, *Defence of the American Policy*, 71. This quotation was intended to indict Hughes for substituting "the mitre for our liberty cap" and blending "the crozier with the stars and stripes." Yet it also clearly indicates the attempts to fuse the symbols of America with those of Catholicism in order to augment loyalties to both.

51. Cited in Dorothy Dohen, *Nationalism and American Catholicism* (New York: Sheed and Ward, 1967), 114.

52. See Sister Mary De Paul Faber, "*The Luxemburger Gazette*: A Catholic German Language Paper of the Middle West, 1872–1918" (M.A. thesis, Catholic University of America, 1948), 31.

53. Letter reproduced in *St. Raphaels Blatt* 1 (January 1886): 7, cited in Barry, *The Catholic Church and German Americans*, 7.

54. German Catholic immigrants during the *Kulturkampf* were especially sensitive to American religious freedom. A German immigrant, wrote a countryman who sustained his Catholic faith along with his uncritical acceptance of an American creed, becomes "as good an American citizen as those of any other nationality. He has as much love for free American institutions; there is certainly no danger that the German Catholics will prefer the hegemony of Prussia and of Bismarckism to the greatest and freest republic in the world, with its flag of stars and stripes and its glorious constitution" (Father Farber and Reverend Innocent Wapelhorst, *The Future of Foreign Born Catholics; and Fear and Hopes for the Catholic Church and Schools in the United States* [St. Louis, 1884], 12–14, cited in Barry, *The Catholic Church and German Americans*, 53–54).

55. Ernest Mayerhoff to Kate Everest, Wanewoc, Juneau County, 1893, Kate Levi Papers, SHSW.

56. Unnamed correspondent to Kate Everest, Centerville Township, Sheboygan County, 1892, Kate Levi Papers, SHSW. Other, more concise respondents made similar points. A correspondent from Jefferson County wrote that nearly all residents of his com-

munity were "proud to be *German*-Americans" (unnamed correspondent to Kate Everest, Jefferson, Jefferson County, 1892, Kate Levi Papers, SHSW).

57. Joh. Kilian to Kate Everest, Theresa, Dodge County, 1892, Kate Levi Papers, SHSW.

58. Fr. Farber, *Church Progress*, 13 June 1891, cited in Barry, *The Catholic Church and German Americans*, 147. The contention that "Americans" were "un-American," or somehow less American than their immigrant counterparts, was raised in the context of public celebrations as well as private beliefs. Protestant ministers, reported a German Catholic paper, refused to participate in Decoration Day ceremonies in 1880 because the holiday fell on a Sunday. "Curious people, these puritans!" the editor concluded (*Die Iowa*, 10 June 1880, 8). Following President Garfield's assassination, the Catholic Benevolent Association float in yet another parade contained thirty-eight girls representing the states of the Union. "It shows that Protestants and Unbelievers," argued a German Catholic, "do not have a corner on patriotism" (*Die Iowa*, 29 August 1881, 8).

59. Traditions invented in the United States by ethnic groups were often the reformulations of conventions developed in specific European homelands. As Kathleen Conzen points out, for example, nationalist rituals enacted in the German states were a basis of German American institutions and ritual traditions that affirmed dual loyalties in the United States. Dorothy Dohen argues that Irish nationalism in the United States was powerfully informed by Irish nationalism in Ireland. See Kathleen Neils Conzen, "Ethnicity as Festive Culture: Nineteenth-Century German America on Parade," in *The Invention of Ethnicity*, ed. Werner Sollors (New York: Oxford University Press, 1989), 44–76, and Dohen, *Nationalism and American Catholicism*, 59–63.

60. *Die Iowa*, 7 July 1881, 8. The scriptural allusion illustrates immigrants' belief that true faith could be cultivated in the United States away from meddling European states. But it also suggests the division between true believers and those outside the faith. See Matthew 10:14, Mark 6:7–13, and Luke 9:1–6.

61. *Die Iowa*, 30 May 1878, 8. These expressions of distaste for Germany were made amid the anti-Catholic *Kulturkampf*.

62. "X," *Die Iowa*, 4 May 1882, 5.

63. *Dubuque National Demokrat*, 5 July 1858, 3, trans. J. K. Downing, CDH.

64. Since varying sets of people were theoretically bound together depending on which level of identity was expressed, the boundaries that separated them differed according to the level of identity. It therefore seems problematic to conceptualize ethnic relationships, as Barth does, in terms of one set of boundaries that separated reified groups. Since multiple boundaries built on different levels existed, shared cultural constructions could conceivably divide and unite people simultaneously. See Barth, *Ethnic Groups and Boundaries*.

65. Kerby A. Miller, *Emigrants and Exiles: Ireland and the Irish Exodus to North America* (New York: Oxford University Press, 1985). See Kerby A. Miller, "Class, Culture, and Immigrant Group Identity in the United States: The Case of Irish-American Ethnicity," in *Immigration Reconsidered: History, Sociology, and Politics*, ed. Virginia Yans-McLaughlin (New York: Oxford University Press, 1990), for an abbreviated statement of the argument. See also Katznelson, *City Trenches*.

66. John Lancaster Spaulding, *St. Raphaels Blatt* 6 (1891): 63, cited in Barry, *The Catholic Church and German Americans*, 167.

67. *Emigranten*, 23 January 1852, cited in Tolo, "Political Position of *Emigranten*," 95–96.

68. *Emigranten*, 20 April 1857, 3. The editor of *Emigranten* was now less sanguine about the benefits of acculturation. Writing in English, he agreed that "our countrymen . . . benefitted by the intercourse with American-born fellow-citizens" and that they "generally appropriate for themselves as quickly as possible the *desirable* qualities and customs of the Americans." But, he concluded, "it cannot however be wondered at if some of the

nobler traits in the Norwegian Character is somewhat injured by the materialism insepa-rable from the life and pursuits in a country like this" (emphasis in original).

69. "Clement Smyth, Second Bishop of Iowa," *Iowa Catholic Historical Review* 9 (1936): 17.

70. James Cardinal Gibbons, *A Retrospect of Fifty Years*, 2 vols. (New York, 1916), 2:148–55, cited in Barry, *The Catholic Church and German Americans*, 163.

71. Bruce Levine hints at this problem in *The Migration of Ideology and the Contested Mean-ing of Freedom: German Americans in the Mid-Nineteenth Century* (Washington, D.C.: German Historical Institute, 1992).

72. See Amy Bridges, "Becoming American: The Working Classes in the United States before the Civil War," in *Working-Class Formation: Nineteenth-Century Patterns in Western Europe and the United States*, ed. Ira Katznelson and Aristide R. Zolberg (Princeton: Princeton University Press, 1986), 157–96.

73. Chevalier, *Society, Manners, and Politics*, 369.

74. Often these competing structures are not adequately addressed by scholars. Samuel Huntington, for example, argues correctly that the "American" ties within ethnic com-munities were "political and ideological" whereas the ethnic ties were "organic." Yet he is less willing to consider the consequences of a conflict between organic ideals nurtured in ethnic communities and political conceptions of individual freedom. Werner Sollors like-wise has portrayed the contention between consent and descent as a fundamental means of understanding the possibilities of surpassing ethnicity. Yet the conflict between consent and descent, which is metaphorically a tension between two axes, is complicated if the cultures of descent relied on communal control that obviated pure individual consent. See Huntington, *American Politics*, 27, and Werner Sollors, *Beyond Ethnicity: Consent and De-scent in American Culture* (New York: Oxford University Press, 1986).

75. See "Tidsaanden: Vi boe i et frit land," *Emigranten*, 18 August 1855, and P. L. Mosstu, "Frihedens sande væsen og betydning," *Emigranten*, 2 May 1856, both cited in Peter A. Munch, "Authority and Freedom: Controversy in Norwegian-American Congre-gations," *Norwegian-American Studies* 28 (1979): 28.

76. Ernst Troeltsch, *Religion in History*, trans. and ed. James Luther Adams and Wal-ter F. Bense (Minneapolis: Fortress Press, 1991), 210–34, 324–26.

77. See, for example, Patrick W. Carey, *People, Priests, and Prelates: Ecclesiastical Democracy and the Tensions of Trusteeism* (Notre Dame: University of Notre Dame Press, 1987).

78. These ideas emanated from a broad array of church leaders. As we saw in the Introduction, groups within Scandinavian and German Lutheranism, Dutch Calvinism, and Irish and German Catholicism evinced a suspicion of the rationalism and liberalism that were hallmarks of the Enlightenment. As the nineteenth century unfolded, Euro-pean church leaders in the United States voiced increasingly powerful reactions. Among the vast literature, see George M. Stephenson, *The Religious Aspects of Swedish Immigration: A Study of Immigrant Churches* (Minneapolis: University of Minnesota Press, 1932), 1–48; E. Clifford Nelson and Eugene L. Fevold, *The Lutheran Church among Norwegian Ameri-cans: A History of the Evangelical Lutheran Church*, 2 vols. (Minneapolis: Augsburg Publishing House, 1960), 1:3–45; Heinrich H. Maurer, "The Problems of a National Church be-fore 1860," *American Journal of Sociology* 30 (1925): 534–50, and "The Problems of Group-Consensus: Founding the Missouri Synod," *American Journal of Sociology* 30 (1925): 665–82; Miller, *Emigrants and Exiles*, 492–568; Philip Gleason, *The Conservative Reformers: German-American Catholics and the Social Order* (Notre Dame: University of Notre Dame Press, 1968); and James D. Bratt, *Dutch Calvinism in Modern America: A History of a Conservative Subculture* (Grand Rapids: William B. Eerdmans, 1984), 3–13.

79. Walter Lippmann, *A Preface to Morals* (New York: Macmillan, 1929), 8.

80. Ephraim Adams expressed this image in *The Iowa Band* (Boston: Congregational Publishing Society, 1870), 11. See Chapter 1. European immigrants, of course, were not the

only Americans who feared the excesses of individualism. George M. Fredrickson cites examples of American-born conservatives such as Horace Bushnell and Orestes Brownson who dreaded the ideas of the so-called anti-institutionalists. Yet he also dismisses the extent of the influence of "the church-centered, organic view of society, with its stress on tradition and authority," as "clearly out of tune with the dominant trends of American thought" (George M. Fredrickson, *The Inner Civil War: Northern Intellectuals and the Crisis of the Union* [New York: Harper and Row, 1965], 28). One wonders if he would have arrived at the same conclusions if he had been mindful that some one-quarter of adults in the northern United States in 1860 were foreign-born. See ibid., chap. 2.

81. Tocqueville, *Democracy in America*, 1:45, 47. Orestes Brownson, on the contrary, noted the tension between American Protestantism and American "civility." See, for example, Orestes Brownson, "Mission of America," *Brownson's Quarterly Review* 1 (1856): 409–44.

82. Herman Amberg Preus, *Syv Foredrag over de kirkelige Forholde blandt de Norske i Amerika* (Christiania, Norway: Jac. Dybwad, 1867), translated in *Vivacious Daughter: Seven Lectures on the Religious Situation among Norwegians in America by Herman Amberg Preus*, ed. and trans. Todd W. Nichol (Northfield, Minn.: Norwegian-American Historical Association, 1990), 166 (emphasis in original).

83. Ræder, *America in the Forties*, 69. Ræder also tried to convince Americans, without much success, that "a monarchical form of government can be combined with any liberty." After all, he wrote, a limited monarchy "must yield to the wishes of the majority" and "protect the minority against oppression so that everyone may enjoy a certain amount of liberty or, at any rate, freedom from arbitrariness on the part of anyone" (ibid., 84).

84. Jacob A. Ottesen to friends, 20 November 1852, in *Den Norske Tilskuer* (The Norwegian spectator), cited in Theodore Blegen, *Land of Their Choice: The Immigrants Write Home* (Minneapolis: University of Minnesota Press, 1955), 287.

85. *Emigranten*, 27 May 1857, cited in Munch, "In Search of Identity," 8. See also *Democraten*, 21, 28 September 1850; *Den Swenska Republikanen*, 31 July 1857; and *Hemlandet*, 4 April 1859, for similar appraisals. Some years later, Dr. Guy Hinsdale argued that the extraordinarily high rates of insanity among Scandinavians were due to "the restlessness and competition which characterize the social and industrial life in America," which "surpassed their limited strength" (*Svenska Amerikanska Posten*, 9 August 1892, 1).

86. O. F. Duus to Dear Ones at Home, 3 February 1856, in *Frontier Parsonage: The Letters of Olaus Fredrik Duus, Norwegian Pastor in Wisconsin, 1855–1858*, ed. Theodore C. Blegen (Northfield, Minn.: Norwegian-American Historical Association, 1947), 17. Duus's letters unconsciously underscore the challenges the leadership faced, for as he inveighs against materialism, he meticulously reports his speculative gains in land purchases. Blegen observes that "he seems to discern the will of God, and not a crass materialism," in his transactions (ibid., vi).

87. Anton H. Walburg, *The Question of Nationality in Its Relations to the Catholic Church in the United States* (Cincinnati, 1889), 44–45.

88. Preus, *Syv Foredrag*, in Nichol, *Vivacious Daughter*, 106.

89. See Jay P. Dolan, *The American Catholic Experience: A History from Colonial Times to the Present* (Garden City, N.Y.: Doubleday, 1985), for an overview of the Catholic Enlightenment and questions of authority raised by church leaders in the nineteenth century. See also Carey, *People, Priests, and Prelates*, for an optimistic portrayal of the Catholic Church's facility to balance "republicanism" and Catholic belief.

90. Mazzuchelli, *Memoirs*, 283–84 (emphasis added).

91. Ibid., 284.

92. Wilhelm P. Bigot, "Report to Germany about My First Work," in *Annalen der St. Michaelsgemeinde in Loramie [Berlin], Shelby County, Ohio, in der Erzdiözese Cincinnati von 1838 bis 1903* (Sidney, Ohio: Shelby County Anzeiger, 1907), 75, translated in *Annals of St.*

Michael's Parish in Loramie [Berlin], Shelby County, Ohio, in the Archdiocese of Cincinnati from 1838 to 1903, 65. After all, Bigot stressed, "not in vain did the Lord pray to his heavenly Father: 'I pray that all who believe in me, be one, and entirely one.' We Catholics know, acknowledge, and respect such a teacher, in the follower for whom the Lord prayed."

93. Ibid., 64.

94. Mazzuchelli, *Memoirs*, 284.

95. Cited in "Grand Scheme for Planting Irish Catholic Colonies in the Western States," *Home Missionary* 15 (1842): 154.

96. Mazzuchelli, *Memoirs*, 284, 290.

97. E. Clifford Nelson, ed., *A Pioneer Churchman: J. W. C. Dietrichson in Wisconsin, 1844–1850* (New York: Twayne Publishers, 1973), 143.

98. J. W. C. Dietrichson, in Munch, "Authority and Freedom," 15.

99. Caja Munch to her parents, 31 May–1 June 1857, in *The Strange American Way: Letters of Caja Munch from Wiota, Wisconsin, 1855–1859, with "An American Adventure" by Johan Storm Munch*, ed. and trans. Helene Munch and Peter A. Munch (Carbondale: Southern Illinois University Press, 1970), 97.

100. Preus, *Syv Foredrag*, in Nichol, *Vivacious Daughter*, 150. In this context, Preus was criticizing the Swedish Augustana Synod. Some church bodies, such as the Norwegian Synod, made distinctions between spiritual and temporal authority rooted in the Augsburg Confession so that the former was held solely by the clergy. These questions are addressed more fully in Chapter 4.

101. Ibid., 53, 178. See also J. St. Munch to Andreas Munch, 16 November 1857, in Munch and Munch, *Strange American Way*, 111. C. F. W. Walther, a leader of the German Missouri Synod, concurred with Preus and Munch. Reminding us again of a complementary identity, he wrote that "we live here in a State in which the church enjoys a freedom unsurpassed since its origin, and at present to be found scarcely anywhere else in the world. Our rulers, instead of allowing attacks to be made upon the rights of the church, exert all their power for the protection of these rights. We have here full liberty to regulate everything according to God's word." It was different in Germany, where "the church is bound in chains" and where a true follower who appealed "to Christian liberty" was "regarded a rebel." "How happy," Walther concluded, "are we, compared with our brethren in our old Fatherland!" See Henry Eyster Jacobs, *A History of the Evangelical Lutheran Church in the United States* (New York: Christian Literature Company, 1893), 404–5.

102. Mazzuchelli, *Memoirs*, esp. 185–86, 283–86, 296, 300–302. Some decades later, another Roman Catholic leader professed essentially the same belief. The American was a pragmatist, Martin Marty argued, "reasonable in his judgments," "not intolerant," one who "willingly listens and accepts things from others." He also had "freedom" and was "a lover of order, a friend of law." It thus followed that the American would appreciate the "universal worth" of Catholic principles, and "if he realizes that the Catholic Church really makes men better, he will also be a Catholic." See Martin Marty, *Verhandlungen der 32 General-Versammlung der katholischen Vereine Deutschlands in Munster i. W., 9–12 September 1885* (Munster i. W., 1885), 249, cited and trans. in Barry, *The Catholic Church and German Americans*, 39.

103. Peter Berger, Brigitte Berger, and Hansfried Kellner, *The Homeless Mind: Modernization and Consciousness* (New York: Random House, 1973), 176–77.

Chapter Three

1. "Michigania," cited in Lois Kimbell Mathews, *The Expansion of New England: The Spread of New England Settlement and Institutions to the Mississippi River, 1620–1865* (Boston: Houghton Mifflin, 1909), 227.

2. "The editor of the *Keokuk Whig*," in N. Howe Parker, *Iowa As It Is in 1855: A Gazetteer for Citizens and Hand-Book for Emigrants* (Chicago: Keen and Lee, 1855), 59–60.

3. Charles Augustus Murray, *Travels in North America during the Years 1834, 1835, 1836, Including a Summer Residence with the Pawnee Tribe of Indians and a Visit to Cuba and the Azore Islands*, 2 vols. (London: Richard Bentley, 1839; reprint, New York: DaCapo Press, 1974), 1:148.

4. Basil Hall, *Travels in North America, in the Years 1827 and 1828*, 2 vols. (Edinburgh: Cadell, 1829; reprint, Graz, Austria: Akademsiche Druck- und Verlagsanstalt, 1965), 1:146–47.

5. *Niles' National Register*, 15 November 1834, 164.

6. *Burlington (Iowa) Hawkeye*, cited in *Niles' National Register*, 9 November 1839, 168.

7. Newell W. Bixby diary, May 1846, UILSC.

8. Ibid.

9. Ibid. (emphasis added).

10. Ibid. See also Glenda Riley, "The Frontier in Process: Iowa's Trail Women as a Paradigm," *Annals of Iowa* 46 (1982): 178. Riley quotes the diary of young Mary Alice Shutes, who observes the behavior of her elders amid preparations for departure. Around a predawn fire, many family members and friends gathered to prepare a final breakfast and, as a "final display and effort of friendship," to see the family off. The perspective of departure through a youngster's eyes is informative: "The younger kids," she wrote, "know something unusual is going on but don't understand it like the older folks do. . . . Some of the older ones seem to welcome the solitude away from the fire. . . . They have said their goodbyes and are just waiting."

11. Emma Seaton to Allettie Battey, 5 September 1880, in Elizabeth Hampsten, *Read This Only to Yourself: The Private Writings of Midwestern Women, 1880–1910* (Bloomington: Indiana University Press, 1982), 115.

12. Sarah Browne Adamson diary, transcribed by Carol Benning, 11 May, 2 June 1839, 6 July, 12 September 1843, CFHS.

13. Ibid., 21 September 1841; Sarah Browne Adamson to her children, 1844, CFHS.

14. Sarah Browne Adamson diary, 16 October 1841, CFHS.

15. Ibid., 15 December 1842, 12 September 1843.

16. Myranda Underwood to Absent Brother and Sister, Fountain Prairie, Wisconsin, September 1847, SHSW.

17. Oliver Parsons diary, 17 June 1872, MHS.

18. John and Mary Thomson to Dear Brother, 24 January 1850, SHSW.

19. John and D. Thompson to Dear Brothers and Sisters and Mother, 17 December 1850, CDH.

20. Sjoerd Aukes Sipma to My Relatives, to All the Farmers, and to the Director of Youth at Bornwerd, [Friesland,] 26 September 1848, trans. Edward E. Fikse, ISHDDM.

21. Charles A. Dean to Dear Friends, Dubuque, Iowa, 4 November 1855, UILSC (emphasis added).

22. F. W. Bryant to Dear Brother, Epworth, Iowa, May 1877, UILSC (emphasis added).

23. Myranda Underwood to Absent Brother and Sister, September 1847, SHSW.

24. Henry A. Morse to Francis Morse, Genoa Bluffs, Iowa, 20 April 1856, in Glenda Riley, ed., "The Morse Family Letters: A New Home in Iowa, 1856–1862," *Annals of Iowa* 45 (1980): 216–17.

25. *Williamantic (Connecticut) Medium,* 10 May 1854, cited in *Daily Minnesotan,* 13 June 1854, 2.

26. Joseph V. Quarles to Isaac Thurston, 11 March 1839, in "Document: Letters of Joseph V. Quarles," *Wisconsin Magazine of History* 16 (1933): 311 (emphasis in original).

27. Sarah Browne Adamson diary, 28 June 1843, CFHS (emphasis added).

28. Ibid., 13 July 1840.

29. A Norwegian, for example, wrote to her son in 1909: "You mention that you would like to send a ticket for me and my daughter this spring. But she says she does not dare to travel with me alone, so that is quite impossible. Perhaps you do not remember how old I am now. I am 68 years old" (in Øyvind T. Gulliksen, "Letters to Immigrants in the Midwest from the Telemark Region of Norway," *Norwegian-American Studies* 32 [1989]: 164).

30. Edmund Flagg, *The Far West, or, a Tour beyond the Mountains,* 2 vols. (New York: Harper and Brothers, 1838), 1:54–55.

31. Interview of Mrs. Schindler by Peter A. Munch, Wisconsin, 1949, Peter A. Munch Papers, NAHA. In this interview, Schindler recalled the stories told her by her grandfather.

32. Benjamin Millward diary, Liverpool, England, 5 March 1854, in Timothy Walch, "The Voyage of an Iowa Immigrant," *Annals of Iowa* 44 (Fall 1977): 138–39. Travelers who migrated in order to reunite with loved ones risked death during their journey. A seventy-year-old man left Germany to spend his last days with his son in the interior of Iowa. After traveling across the Atlantic Ocean, through New Orleans, and up the Mississippi River to Dubuque, he died about twenty-five miles from his goal, succumbing to what the coroner called weakness of age. See *Dubuque National Demokrat,* 4 December 1858, trans. J. K. Downing, CDH. Other reunions were achieved only symbolically. An Englishman named Rawling came to Galena, Illinois, in 1882 to visit the grave of his brother, who had died in 1855. "The man sat on the hill for hours," wrote a local newspaper, "and cried for the deceased" (*Die Iowa,* 1 June 1882, 8).

33. See Charles Tilly and C. Harold Brown, "On Uprooting, Kinship, and the Auspices of Migration," *International Journal of Comparative Sociology* 8 (1967): 139–64; Harvey M. Choldin, "Kinship Networks in the Migration Process," *International Migration Review* 7 (1973): 163–75; John S. MacDonald and Leatrice D. MacDonald, "Chain Migration, Ethnic Neighborhood Formation, and Social Networks," *Milbank Memorial Fund Quarterly* 42 (1964): 82–97; Rudolph J. Vecoli, "The Formation of Chicago's Little Italies," *Journal of American Ethnic History* 2 (1983): 5–20; Robert C. Ostergren, "Cultural Homogeneity and Population Stability among Swedish Immigrants in Chisago County," *Minnesota History* 37 (1973): 255–69; and Hans Norman, "Swedes in North America," in *From Sweden to America: A History of the Migration* (Minneapolis: University of Minnesota Press, 1976), 256–61.

34. James A. Dunlevy and Henry A. Gemery, "Some Additional Evidence on Settlement Patterns of Scandinavian Migrants to the United States: Dynamics and the Role of Family and Friends," *Scandinavian Economic History Review* 24 (1976): 143–52; Michael Greenwood, "The Influence of Family and Friends on German Internal Migration, 1880–1885," *Journal of Social History* 13 (1979): 277–88; Mildred B. Levy and Walter J. Wadycki, "The Influence of Family and Friends on Geographic Labor Mobility: An International Comparison," *Review of Economics and Statistics* 55 (1973): 198–203; B. Lindsay Lowell, *Scandinavian Exodus: Demography and Social Development of Nineteenth-Century Rural Communities* (Boulder, Colo.: Westview Press, 1987).

35. Paul Wallace Gates noted that "western fever" engendered chain migrations among the American-born and the foreign-born alike (Paul Wallace Gates, *The Illinois Central Railroad and Its Colonization Work* [Cambridge: Harvard University Press, 1934], 231–35). For a more detailed account of chain migrations amid the settlement patterns of eastern Americans in the Middle West, see Mathews, *Expansion of New England.* See also Richard Lyle Power, *Planting Corn Belt Culture: The Impress of the Upland Southerner and Yankee in the*

Old Northwest (Indianapolis: Indiana Historical Society Publications, 1953); Stewart H. Holbrook, *The Yankee Exodus: An Account of Migration from New England* (New York: Macmillan, 1950); John Rice, "The Old-Stock Americans," in *They Chose Minnesota: A Survey of the State's Ethnic Groups*, ed. June Drenning Holmquist (St. Paul: Minnesota Historical Society Press, 1981), 55–72; and Susan E. Gray, *The Yankee West: Community Life on the Michigan Frontier* (Chapel Hill: University of North Carolina Press, 1996).

36. Power, *Planting Corn Belt Culture*, 46.

37. Joseph V. Quarles to Isaac Thurston, South Port, Wisconsin, 7 November 1837, 28 August, 29 September 1838, 19 May 1839, in "Document: Letters of Joseph V. Quarles," 299, 300–302, 303 (emphasis added). See also Riley, "Morse Family Letters," 212–27, for additional examples of offers of aid to entice New Englanders to relocate to the Middle West.

38. Newell W. Bixby diary, June 1847, UILSC.

39. F. W. Bryant to Brother Charley and Folks, 28 April 1856, UILSC. Absence of kin, on the other hand, often prevented potential migrants from migrating. When Bryant informed his brother in New York of the "Kansas fever" sweeping Iowa, he expressed his hesitance to join the migration. "But if I had somebody that was steady to go with me," he observed, "I would like it. To think of going off into a new country alone is not very pleasant" (F. W. Bryant to Dear Brother, 19 November 1876, UILSC).

40. Stephen H. Hayes to Friends, 17 June 1845, in "Letters from the West in 1845," *Iowa Journal of History and Politics* 20 (1922): 46. This sense of a common tie with other New Englanders and perception that they were encountered often are common threads running through Hayes's letters. Thus he writes on 29 May 1845 from Cincinnati that "we find everywhere people from New England" (Stephen H. Hayes to Friends, in ibid., 10).

41. *Dubuque National Demokrat*, 10 May 1858, 4, trans. J. K. Downing, CDH. See also Holbrook, *Yankee Exodus*, 174.

42. Robert M. Taylor Jr., "The Olin Trek: Migration, Mutual Aid, and Solidarity of a Nineteenth Century Rural American Kin Group" (Ph.D. dissertation, Kent State University, 1979).

43. Holbrook, *Yankee Exodus*, 119. See also Ada Mae Brown Brinton, "Eighty-Six Years in Iowa: The Memoir of Ada Mae Brown Brinton," *Annals of Iowa* 45 (1981): 552, which recounts another chain migration among Maine Staters.

44. William Salter diary, 25 March 1844, in Philip D. Jordan, ed., "William Salter's 'My Ministry in Iowa,' 1843–1846," *Annals of Iowa* 19 (1935): 603.

45. Ibid., 29. In view of its cultural salience, religion, as Salter indicated, was often a key determinant of common migration and settlement. When Henry A. Morse wrote to his "dear Brother" from his new Iowa home, for example, he noted that "all that are anything are Methodists here excepting our three families, several more families are coming in, also Methodists" (Henry A. Morse to Francis Morse, 20 April 1856, in Riley, "Morse Family Letters," 214). Glenda Riley illustrates that the Iowa settlement that would later become Grinnell had a similar religious, albeit Congregational, orientation. See Glenda Riley, ed., "Letter from Grinnell: Emery S. Bartlett to His Children and Grandchildren," *Annals of Iowa* 44 (1978): 419.

46. F. I. Herriott, *Did Emigrants from New England First Settle Iowa?* (Des Moines: Bishard Brothers, 1906), 6.

47. Arthur A. Halbach, *Dyersville: Its History and Its People* (Milwaukee: St. Joseph's Press, 1939), 20.

48. *State Banner* (Bennington, Vt.), cited in Nathan H. Parker, *The Minnesota Handbook for 1856-7, with a New and Accurate Map* (Boston: John P. Jewett, 1857), 9–10.

49. *Keokuk (Iowa) Dispatch*, cited in Parker, *Iowa As It Is in 1855*, 60.

50. *Minnesota Democratic Weekly*, 1 July 1853, 2.

51. *Daily Minnesotan*, 17 June 1854, 2.

52. *Daily Minnesotan*, 25 October 1854, 2. Migrants from southern states also enjoyed the comforts of kin and friends. For examples, see Power, *Planting Corn Belt Culture*, 14, and Herriott, *Did Emigrants from New England First Settle Iowa?*, 37–38.

53. Studies of European migration repeatedly underscore the salience of a common past in influencing the intensity of migration and location of settlement. See, for example, John Hudson, "Migration to an American Frontier," *Annals of the Association of American Geographers* 66 (1976): 242–65; Jon Gjerde, *From Peasants to Farmers: The Migration from Balestrand, Norway, to the Upper Middle West* (New York: Cambridge University Press, 1985); Walter D. Kamphoefner, *The Westfalians: From Germany to Missouri* (Princeton: Princeton University Press, 1987); Robert C. Ostergren, *A Community Transplanted: The Trans-Atlantic Experience of a Swedish Immigrant Settlement in the Upper Middle West, 1835–1915* (Madison: University of Wisconsin Press, 1988); and Royden K. Loewen, *Family, Church, and Market: A Mennonite Community in the Old and the New Worlds, 1850–1930* (Urbana: University of Illinois Press, 1993).

54. James Plaister to James Dyer Jr., 4 December 1847, in Halbach, *Dyersville*, 68–72.

55. James Dyer Sr. to James Dyer Jr., in ibid., 72–73.

56. *Minnesota Democratic Weekly*, 22 April 1851, 2.

57. *St. Paul Daily Press*, 12 May 1863, 4.

58. *St. Anthony Falls (Minnesota) Democrat*, 25 February 1870, 2.

59. *Dubuque National Demokrat*, 9 November 1858, 3, trans. J. K. Downing, CDH.

60. *Emigranten*, 14 March 1859, 3.

61. Lars E. Øyane, *Gards- og Ættesoge for Luster Kommune* (Oslo: Norbok, 1984), vol. 1. This work gives migration information on individuals who moved within and away from Norway that permits an analysis and comparison of patterns of internal migration and emigration. The information on each individual includes social background, demographic characteristics, timing of migration, and places of residence following migration. The data also include material on secondary migrations, thus providing a relatively complete picture of the patterns of migration not only to the initial destination but also beyond it. For a fuller discussion of this and another individual-level dataset, see Jon Gjerde, "Chain Migration: A Case Study from Western Norway," in *A Century of European Migrations, 1830–1930*, ed. Rudolph J. Vecoli and Suzanne M. Sinke (Champaign: University of Illinois Press, 1991), 158–81.

62. See Hjalmar R. Holand, *De Norske Settlementers Historie: En Oversigt over den Norske Indvandring til or Bebyggelse af Amerikas Nordvesten fra Amerikas Opdagelse til Indiankrigen i Nordvesten* (Eprhaim, Wis., 1908), 268.

63. Ibid.

64. Marcus Lee Hansen, "Immigration and Expansion," in *The Immigrant in American History*, ed. Arthur M. Schlesinger (Cambridge: Harvard University Press, 1940), 60–61.

65. Peter A. Munch field notes, 1947, Peter A. Munch Papers, NAHA.

66. See Ostergren, *A Community Transplanted*, 12–13, and John Fraser Hart, "The Middle West," *Annals of the Association of American Geographers* 62 (1972): x, for maps of settlement advance in the region.

67. *Die Iowa*, 23 June 1881, 8; 29 March 1883, 8.

68. *Dubuque National Demokrat*, 16 March 1876, 3, trans. J. K. Downing, CDH.

69. *Nordlyset*, 11 May 1850, trans. WPA, WPA Papers, MHS.

70. *Nordisk Folkeblad*, 17 March 1869, 3, trans. WPA, WPA Papers, MHS.

71. The U.S. government formed a Commission of Immigration in 1864, an action later imitated by many states also forming immigrant agencies. Iowa, for example, created the Board of Immigration in 1869, which, among other things, wrote and published literature extolling the virtues of migration to the state. A pamphlet entitled *Iowa: The Home for*

Immigrants was published not only in English but also in German, Dutch, Swedish, and Danish and was circulated widely. See Iowa Board of Immigration, *Iowa: The Home for Immigrants* (Des Moines: Mills, 1870; reprint, Iowa City: State Historical Society of Iowa, 1970), i–ii. On Minnesota, see Lars Ljungmark, *For Sale—Minnesota: Organized Promotion of Scandinavian Immigration, 1866-1873* (Göteborg, Sweden: Läromedelsförlag, 1971).

72. A colonization company, for example, purchased land that had been granted to the railroad companies in over fifteen townships on the prairies of Nobles County, Minnesota, and Oceola County, Iowa, in 1871 and laid out the town of Worthington on a portion of the land. In the spring of 1872, between 500 and 700 families from Ohio and Pennsylvania moved to the Protestant colonization company, which prohibited the sale of alcoholic beverages within its limits. See *St. Paul Daily Pioneer*, 22 November 1871, 4; 30 August 1871, 2; Arthur P. Rose, *An Illustrated History of Nobles County, Minnesota* (Worthington, Minn.: Northern History Publishing Company, 1908), 61–63; and Al Goff, ed., *Nobles County History* (St. Paul: Webb Publishing Company, 1958), 10. Whereas Protestant colonization schemes were notable among Yankees, Roman Catholic clergy played pivotal roles in Irish colonization activities. See James P. Shannon, *Catholic Colonization on the Western Frontier* (New Haven: Yale University Press, 1957).

73. *Die Iowa*, 17 March 1881, 5. Another correspondent to the paper noted that "the best land for the farmer is in western Iowa and still is generally to be had cheaply,—but that will not go on long," in part because "Catholic churches and schools and priests are just about all over [western Iowa]" (N. Keitges, in *Die Iowa*, 31 January 1884, 5). For examples of Norwegian boosterism, see Carlton C. Qualey, *Norwegian Settlement in the United States* (Northfield, Minn.: Norwegian-American Historical Association, 1938).

74. *Folkebladet*, 16 June 1886, 8, trans. WPA, WPA Papers, MHS. Immigrants also sent capital home to be converted into tickets for passage to the United States. Postal money orders worth an estimated $100,000,000 were sent to Sweden from the United States between 1885 and 1937; between 1848 and 1900, the remittances to Great Britain are estimated at $240,000,000. See Franklin D. Scott, "The Study of the Effects of Emigration," *Scandinavian Economic History Review* 8 (1960): 164, and Arnold Schrier, *Ireland and the American Emigration, 1850-1900* (Minneapolis: University of Minnesota Press, 1958), 105.

75. *St. Paul Daily Globe*, 14 June 1880, 2; *Minneapolis Tribune*, 14 September 1880, 8.

76. *Folkebladet*, 24 February 1885, 2, trans. WPA, WPA Papers, MHS. The polyglot nature of middle western settlement can be readily discerned by simply perusing the reports of settlement in newspapers. Many Russian Germans fleeing their former home in groups for "Dakota's glorious prairies" in 1876 were joined by Swedes who arrived in the eastern United States and traveled "directly from Philadelphia to their destination [Yankton, Dakota Territory] without changing cars." These groups were followed by Danes headed for Minnesota and by Welsh, Austrians, and Scots bound for colonies in western Iowa. "Little by little," an Iowa editor concluded, "the state fills up." See *Die Iowa*, 11 May 1876, 5.

77. See Ostergren, *A Community Transplanted*, 16–18; Holmquist, *They Chose Minnesota*; "The People of Wisconsin According to Ethnic Stocks," *Milwaukee Journal*, 21 September 1944; and William C. Sherman, *Prairie Mosaic: An Ethnic Atlas of Rural North Dakota* (Fargo: North Dakota Institute for Regional Studies, 1983), for maps that define ethnic settlement in the Upper Middle West, Minnesota, Wisconsin, and North Dakota, respectively. On Wisconsin, see also Guy-Harold Smith, "Notes on the Distribution of the German-Born in Wisconsin in 1905," *Wisconsin Magazine of History* 13 (1929): 107–20, and "Notes on the Distribution of the Foreign-Born Scandinavians in Wisconsin in 1905," *Wisconsin Magazine of History* 14 (1931): 419–36.

78. On Luxemburgers, see Nicholas Gonner, *Die Luxemburger in der neuen Welt* (Dubuque: Luxemburger Gazette, 1889); on the Dutch, see Henry S. Lucas, *Netherlanders in America: Dutch Immigration to the United States and Canada, 1789-1950* (Ann Arbor: University of

Michigan Press, 1955); on Danes, see Jette Mackintosh, *Danskere i midtvesten: Elk Horn-Kimballton bosættelsen, 1870-1925* (Copenhagen: Akademisk Forlag, 1993); and on Yankees, see Holbrook, *Yankee Exodus*.

79. *St. Anthony Falls (Minnesota) Democrat*, 25 May 1871, 3. Planned group migrations had occurred before the 1870s. Prior to the Civil War, groups of Norwegians living in Wisconsin settlements had moved on to southern Minnesota and northern Iowa. The *Daily Minnesotan*, for example, reported as early as 1854, only three years after Minnesota had been opened to white settlement, that 300 Norwegian parties from the vicinity of Madison, Wisconsin, had sold their farms and were bound for the territory (17 June 1854, 2). Just after the onset of the Civil War, the *Stillwater (Minnesota) Messenger* declared that the "flow of emigration to Minnesota, and other portions of the West, continues undiminished," citing another company of Norwegians who had left Norway Grove near Madison and were bound for Minnesota (12 June 1860, 3). On this pattern in a Norwegian context, see Gjerde, *From Peasants to Farmers*, 137–67.

80. See, for example, *St. Paul Daily Globe*, 24 June 1881, 1, which reported that twenty Scandinavians from Nicollet County had located in Kittson County, Minnesota, and *Minneapolis Tribune*, 15 April 1885, 1, which indicated that a colony of 250 Swedes from Goodhue County, Minnesota, was bound for Glenullin, Dakota Territory—a location in modern-day western North Dakota.

81. *Nordisk Folkeblad*, 1 September 1869, 1.

82. Levi Thortvedt memoirs, 35–36, Levi Thortvedt Papers, MHS. See also Torkel Oftelie, "Recollections of Clay County Folks from Norway," *Telesoga* 1 (1909): 1–13. The migration began before the Civil War and continued into the twentieth century. John Saterlie left his western Minnesota home in 1905 to visit his children in extreme western North Dakota and eight former neighbors who also lived in his children's settlement (John Saterlie diary, 7 June 1905, in author's personal possession).

83. The best work on this significant settlement region is Kathleen Neils Conzen, *Making Their Own America: Assimilation Theory and the German Peasant Pioneer* (New York: Berg, 1990).

84. Paulin Blecker, O.S.B., *Deep Roots: One Hundred Years of Catholic Life in Meire Grove* (St. Cloud, Minn.: Sentinel Publishing Company, 1958), 17, 19, 21, 36.

85. *St. Paul Daily Globe*, 8 February 1879, 1. The largest settlement area of Germans was in the vicinity of Stearns County in north-central Minnesota.

86. *Der Westliche Farmer*, cited in *Die Iowa*, 26 July 1883, 8.

87. *Minneapolis Tribune*, 16 March 1886, 1.

88. On Nebraska Germans, see Frederick C. Luebke, *Immigrants and Politics: The Germans of Nebraska, 1880-1900* (Lincoln: University of Nebraska Press, 1969), 16–32.

89. *Dubuque National Demokrat*, 6 April 1876, 3, trans. J. K. Downing, CDH.

90. A. N., in *Die Iowa*, 28 June 1877, 5; A. N. S., in *Die Iowa*, 11 October 1877, 5.

91. A. N. S., in *Die Iowa*, 18 October 1877, 5; A. N., in *Die Iowa*, 28 June 1877, 5. On the settlement of Breda, see Otto Weber, in *Die Iowa*, 27 December 1883, 5; on Carroll, see *Die Iowa*, 20 January 1876, 5; 28 April 1881, 8; and on neighboring Sac and Ida Counties, see A. N., in *Die Iowa*, 12 July 1877, 8; 27 April 1882, 5.

92. Clifford Merrill Drury, "Growing Up on an Iowa Farm, 1897–1915," *Annals of Iowa* 42 (1974): 161.

93. *Cascade (Iowa) Pioneer*, 10 August 1888.

94. Mari Sandoz, *Old Jules* (New York: Hastings House, 1935), 148.

95. Ragnar Standal, *Mot Nye Heimland: Utvandringa frå Hjøringfjord, Vartdal, and Ørsta* (Volda, 1986), 268.

Chapter Four

1. The term "kinship colony" was first used in Helge Nelson, *The Swedes and the Swedish Settlements in North America* (Lund, Sweden: C. W. K. Gleerup, 1943), 64. For two examples of local studies of such colonies, see Robert C. Ostergren, *A Community Transplanted: The Trans-Atlantic Experience of a Swedish Immigrant Settlement in the Upper Middle West, 1835–1915* (Madison: University of Wisconsin Press, 1988), on Swedish Americans; and John Mack Faragher, *Sugar Creek: Life on the Illinois Prairie* (New Haven: Yale University Press, 1986), on native-born Americans.

2. See Charles Tilly and C. Harold Brown, "On Uprooting, Kinship, and the Auspices of Migration," *International Journal of Comparative Sociology* 8 (1967): 146, which hypothesizes that "migration under the auspices of kinship" tends to delay "assimilation."

3. Mack Walker notes that in communities founded under these conditions, "commonality was developed in the place of settlement, not in the places of origin," and that the curious result was "that the *Gemeinschaft* here was a product and not an antecedent of *Gesellschaft*" (Mack Walker, "Sombart and the Sauk River Settlements," in Kathleen Neils Conzen, *Making Their Own America: Assimilation Theory and the German Peasant Pioneer* [New York: Berg, 1990], 36). On the significance of religious denominations as institutions that influenced religion and society in America, see Sidney E. Mead, "Denominationalism: The Shape of Protestantism in America," in *The Lively Experiment: The Shaping of Christianity in America* (New York: Harper and Row, 1963).

4. *History of Dubuque County, Iowa* (Chicago: Western Historical Company, 1880), 742–46.

5. Ibid., 743; Arthur A. Halbach, *Dyersville: Its History and Its People* (Milwaukee: St. Joseph's Press, 1939), 40–41.

6. See Halbach, *Dyersville*, 122; M. M. Hoffmann, *Centennial History of the Archdiocese of Dubuque* (Dubuque: Columbia College Press, 1937), 82–85; and Loren N. Horton, ed., *The Character of the Country: The Iowa Diary of James L. Broderick, 1876–1877* (Iowa City: Iowa State Historical Department, 1976). Broderick's diary is illuminative because, although he interacts with many American-born people, many of his visits are aimed specifically at people who, like himself, were born in the region of Swaledale in England.

7. Cited in Weston Arthur Goodspeed, *History of Dubuque County, Iowa* (Chicago: Goodspeed Historical Association, 1911), 480.

8. The early Irish settlers in the small town of Farley near Garryowen, for example, were forced to travel long distances to celebrate mass. After several years, visiting priests and monks performed mass in settlers' homes. Soon thereafter, a church edifice was constructed. See Hoffmann, *Centennial History*, 163.

9. K., in *Boston Pilot*, 1 November 1852.

10. "Irish Faces and Places in Eastern Iowa," *Monastery Seasons*, 1987, 4.

11. Catherine Jones Twohig, "An Epic of Early Iowa: Father Trecy's Colonization Scheme," *Iowa Catholic Historical Review* 3 (1931): 10. On the settlement, see also Samuel Mazzuchelli, *The Memoirs of Father Samuel Mazzuchelli, O.P.* (1844; Chicago: Priory Press, 1967), 224–26.

12. Although Loras could not speak German when he visited the Catholics in the settlement, he administered confession by permitting his new parishioners to point to the commandment in the German prayer book and hold up the appropriate number of fingers to indicate the number of times they had transgressed the teaching.

13. For background on the New Vienna colony, see Halbach, *Dyersville*, 55–58. Useful evidence can be found as well in the John Rauch Papers, CDH; "The Old Pioneer," in *Die Iowa*, 16 September 1875, 8; A. N., in *Die Iowa*, 25 October 1877, 8; and *Die Iowa*, 21 June 1883, 8.

14. See Halbach, *Dyersville*, 58–61.

15. Ibid., 61–64.

16. Ernst Troeltsch distinguished between sect-type and church-type forms of Christian churches. The latter was structured on an "objective piety" that privileged hierarchical structures of society and liturgical forms of worship. Although leaders of religious bodies that fit the description of a church-type such as the Roman Catholic and the national Lutheran and Reformed churches of Europe typically celebrated the freedoms of religion in the United States, they faced quandaries when attempting to transplant their churches to a religious environment of voluntary membership and sectarianism. See Ernst Troeltsch, *Religion in History*, trans. and ed. James Luther Adams and Walter F. Bense (Minneapolis: Fortress Press, 1991), 321–27, and H. Richard Niebuhr, *The Social Sources of Denominationalism* (New York: Henry Holt and Company, 1929), 17–21.

17. Janson's experiences were not unique. Gerhard Armauer Hansen, the Norwegian physician who identified the bacillus responsible for leprosy, wrote in 1888 that his "sentimental feeling" for his homeland in the Middle West was "particularly strong one day when I drove through a deep valley leading to the Mississippi. . . . The illusion was the more powerful since I went from sunrise to sundown hearing nothing but the Norwegian [Sogning] dialect" (Gerhard Armauer Hansen, *The Memories and Reflections of Dr. Gerhard Armauer Hansen*, trans. G. A. Hansen [Wurzburg: German Leprosy Relief Foundation, 1976], 114).

18. Rural sociologists in the twentieth century repeatedly stressed the institutional importance of the rural church. Horace Miner argued, for example, in 1949 that churches were community centers that continued to play "an important integrating role" in a rural Iowa county. See Horace Miner, *Culture and Agriculture: An Anthropological Study of a Corn Belt County* (Ann Arbor: University of Michigan Press, 1949), 14–15, 42, 56.

19. For a charming portrayal of rural Roman Catholic churches, see Loras C. Otting, "Gothic Splendor in Northeast Iowa," *The Palimpsest* 66 (1985): 146–73.

20. *Die Iowa*, 30 November 1876, 5. The paper contained frequent reports about the dedication of church edifices that represented considerable sacrifices on the part of parishioners. See A. N., in *Die Iowa*, 24 May 1877, 5, and *Die Iowa*, 15 July 1875, 5; 6 July 1876, 5.

21. Many studies have charted the tendency of nationality groups to congregate in rural neighborhoods throughout the region. Representative examples of works mapping European ethnic settlements in the rural Middle West are Ostergren, *A Community Transplanted*; Jon Gjerde, *From Peasants to Farmers: The Migration from Balestrand, Norway, to the Upper Middle West* (New York: Cambridge University Press, 1985); John G. Rice, *Patterns of Ethnicity in a Minnesota County* (Umeå, Sweden: Geographical Reports, 1973); and Peter A. Munch, "Segregation and Assimilation of Norwegian Settlements in Wisconsin," *Norwegian-American Studies and Records* 18 (1954): 102–40. For American migrant examples, see Douglas K. Meyer, "Native-Born Immigrant Clusters on the Illinois Frontier," *Proceedings of the Association of American Geographers* 8 (1976): 41–44, and Gregory S. Rose, "Upland Southerners: The County Origins of Southern Migrants to Indiana by 1850," *Indiana Magazine of History* 82 (1986): 242–63. See also June Drenning Holmquist, ed., *They Chose Minnesota: A Survey of the State's Ethnic Groups* (St. Paul: Minnesota Historical Society Press, 1981); "The People of Wisconsin According to Ethnic Stocks, 1940," *Milwaukee Journal*, 21 September 1944; and William C. Sherman, *Prairie Mosaic: An Ethnic Atlas of Rural North Dakota* (Fargo: North Dakota Institute for Regional Studies, 1983), for a systematic mapping of European and American ethnic groups in Minnesota, Wisconsin, and North Dakota, respectively.

22. Miner, *Culture and Agriculture*, 14–15, 42, 56. See also George W. Hill field notes, 1940, George W. Hill Papers, SHSW. This is not to say that social class had no bearing on

local cultural patterns. As the following examples show, it remained important within the context of the ethnic community.

23. Louis Falge observed that in Manitowoc County, Wisconsin, in 1891 "men as a rule speak English, not the women." I found, for example, that 6.3 percent of all women in a rural Minnesota community did not know English. See Louis Falge to Kate Everest, Reedsville, Manitowoc County, 1891, Kate Everest field notes, Kate Levi Papers, SHSW, and Gjerde, *From Peasants to Farmers*, 227.

24. E. J. Henning to Kate Everest, Herman, Dodge County, 1892, Kate Everest field notes, Kate Levi Papers, SHSW.

25. Unnamed correspondent to Kate Everest, Jefferson, Jefferson County, 1892, Kate Everest field notes, Kate Levi Papers, SHSW.

26. Peter A. Munch, *The Scandinavian Presence in North America*, ed. Erik Friis (New York: Harper's Magazine Press, 1976), 64. See also Peter L. Petersen, "Language and Loyalty: Governor Harding and Iowa's Danish-Americans during World War I," *Annals of Iowa* 42 (1974): 408–9.

27. Language was a divisive issue between German Americans and Irish Americans within late-nineteenth-century Roman Catholicism. See John Rauch diary, John Rauch Papers, CDH, and Colman J. Barry, *The Catholic Church and German Americans* (Washington, D.C.: Catholic University of America Press, 1953).

28. Petersen, "Language and Loyalty," 409. This transition to English exemplifies a cultural change that will be explored in Chapter 8.

29. Peter A. Munch field notes, 1947, Peter A. Munch Papers, NAHA. These preferences resulted at least initially in patterns of marriage that fortified bonds of kinship. Historians have long debated the degree and rapidity with which people of varying groups married one another. Among a sample from the area where Munch conducted his fieldwork, the transition was slow: only 7.3 percent of the Norwegian immigrants between 1845 and 1920 married non-Norwegians. What is perhaps more striking is that over three-quarters of those immigrants chose spouses who were born in their region of birth in Norway. Over time and over the generations, intermarriage increased. Yet even when Munch conducted his fieldwork, 73.2 percent of those surveyed (N=82) (and 68.3 percent of the "young" surveyed) objected to a Norwegian marrying a Catholic. Intermarriage *is* a pivotal process. If or when it occurs on a large scale, it thoroughly alters community relationships. Yet its absence reinforces kinship links within the community and therefore the solidarity of the community itself. See Chapter 8. On patterns of intermarriage in the rural Middle West, see Joseph Schafer, *The Wisconsin Lead Region* (Madison: State Historical Society of Wisconsin, 1932), 245–46, and "The Yankee and the Teuton in Wisconsin: V. Social Harmonies and Discords," *Wisconsin Magazine of History* 7 (1923): 157; and Richard M. Bernard, *The Melting Pot and the Altar: Marital Assimilation in Early Twentieth-Century Wisconsin* (Minneapolis: University of Minnesota Press, 1980).

30. Peter A. Munch field notes, 1947, Peter A. Munch Papers, NAHA.

31. Ibid. None preferred to hire Yankees; one (1.1 percent) preferred non-Norwegians and non-Yankees; the remainder said ethnic background made no difference in their hiring practices.

32. Edward O. Moe and Carl C. Taylor, *Culture of a Contemporary Rural Community: Irwin, Iowa*, Bureau of Agricultural Economics Rural Life Studies no. 5 (Washington, D.C.: U.S. Department of Agriculture, 1942), 45.

33. Of the respondents, 46.1 percent preferred trading with Norwegians; 2.2 percent with Yankees; 2.2 percent with others; and 49.4 percent said ethnic background made no difference in their trading practices. See Peter A. Munch field notes, 1947, Peter A. Munch Papers, NAHA.

34. See Robert T. Aubey, John Kyle, and Arnold Strickon, "Investment Behavior and Elite Social Structure in Latin America," *Journal of Interamerican Studies and World Affairs* 16 (1974): 71–95.

35. Frontier community fluidity, communities' attempts at consensus, and their tendency toward conflict are long-acknowledged historical issues. See, for example, Stanley Elkin and Eric McKitrick, "A Meaning for Turner's Frontier," *Political Science Quarterly* 69 (1954): 321–53, 565–602; Allan Bogue, "Social Theory and the Pioneer," *Agricultural History* 34 (1960): 21–34; and Don Harrison Doyle, *The Social Order of a Frontier Community: Jacksonville, Illinois, 1825–1870* (Urbana: University of Illinois Press, 1978).

36. N. W. Bixby to My Dear Brother Claflin, 28 April 1856, UILSC.

37. Newell W. Bixby diary, Delhi, Iowa, 1 July 1849, UILSC.

38. Ada Mae Brown Brinton, "Eighty-Six Years in Iowa: The Memoir of Ada Mae Brown Brinton," *Annals of Iowa* 45 (1981): 553.

39. Miner, *Culture and Agriculture*, 32.

40. *Die Iowa*, a German Catholic paper that published correspondence from and reports on rural German neighborhoods, repeatedly stressed the composition of the Catholic settlements in regional terms. The Luxemburg settlement in Dubuque County, Iowa, for example, not surprisingly was composed "mostly of Luxemburgers, who are, with a few Rhine Prussians and Low Germans mixed in," editor Nicholas Gonner observed in 1875, "mostly well off." All were "warm Catholics" (15 July 1875, 5). See also A. N., in *Die Iowa*, 22 November 1877, 8, and Nicholas Gonner, *Die Luxemburger in der neuen Welt* (Dubuque: Luxemburger Gazette, 1889), 294. Gonner's community-by-community description of Luxemburg settlement clearly shows the regional diversity that characterized "German" and Luxemburger settlements.

41. Philip Gleason, *The Conservative Reformers: German-American Catholics and the Social Order* (Notre Dame: University of Notre Dame Press, 1968), 21.

42. German leaders typically deplored multinational parishes within the church. They consistently argued for national parishes. See Barry, *The Catholic Church and German Americans*. See also *Die Iowa*, 24 February 1876, 6. Multinational Catholic churches were nonetheless quite common among Roman Catholic settlers. For examples, see P. B., in *Die Iowa*, 14 January 1875, 5; A. N., in *Die Iowa*, 20 December 1877, 8; and *Die Iowa*, 22 April 1875, 5; 20 May 1875, 5; 10 February 1876, 5; 31 May 1877, 5.

43. A. N., in *Die Iowa*, 11 October 1877, 8; 4 April 1878, 5. Correspondence in *Die Iowa* was laden with descriptions of internationality conflict. See M. M., in *Die Iowa*, 14 January 1875, 4; J. H., in *Die Iowa*, 12 October 1876, 4; A. N., in *Die Iowa*, 11 October 1877, 8; 21 March 1878, 8; 4 April 1878, 5; "German Catholic," in *Die Iowa*, 21 March 1878, 8; and *Die Iowa*, 31 January 1878, 5; 3 October 1878, 5.

44. See Halbach, *Dyersville*, 150–54. See also A. N., in *Die Iowa*, 18 October 1877, 8.

45. For better or worse, this priest's quandaries were solved when he was relieved of his position two weeks later. For an extended discussion of the dissension in the Iowa City church, see M. M. H[offmann], "Letters and Documents," *Iowa Catholic Historical Review* 9 (1936): 42–45, and Theodosius Plassmeyer, "The Church in Early Iowa City," *Iowa Catholic Historical Review* 9 (1936): 21–37.

46. Mary Kevin Gallagher, ed., *Seed/Harvest* (Dubuque: Archdiocese of Dubuque Press, 1987), 13–14.

47. Suzanne Dockal Rogers, "Settlement Patterns in the Tete des Morts Valley of Iowa, 1833–1860" (M.A. thesis, New York College at Oneonta, 1976), 92–93.

48. "A Catholic," *Die Iowa*, 13 March 1884, 5.

49. See J. S., in *Die Iowa*, 27 December 1877, 8. On divisions between Germans and Irish parishioners and priests, see *Die Iowa*, 3 January 1878, 8. Hoffmann, *Centennial History*, recounts numerous instances of division between ethnic groups within Catholic parishes.

50. Ole Munch Ræder, *America in the Forties: The Letters of Ole Munch Ræder*, ed. and trans. Gunnar J. Malmin (Minneapolis: Norwegian-American Historical Association, 1929), 135.

51. Kristofer Janson, "A Buggy Priest," originally published in *Præriens Saga: Fortællinger fra Amerika* (Chicago: Skandinaven's Bogtrykkeri, 1885), unpublished manuscript, trans. Oscar A. Christensen, 7, Oscar A. Christensen Papers, MHS.

52. Johannes Dietrichson, in *Parish Journal* (Koshkonong, Wis.), cited in *A Pioneer Churchman: J. W. C. Dietrichson in Wisconsin, 1844–1850*, ed. E. Clifford Nelson (New York: Twayne Publishers, 1973), 179.

53. Cited in *The Strange American Way: Letters of Caja Munch from Wiota, Wisconsin, 1855–1859, with "An American Adventure" by Johan Storm Munch*, ed. and trans. Helene Munch and Peter A. Munch (Carbondale: Southern Illinois University Press, 1970), 184.

54. William Foote Whyte, "History of the Settlement of the Town of Lebanon, Dodge County," unpublished manuscript, 6–8, William Foote Whyte Papers, SHSW.

55. The conversation between David A. Gerber and Patrick W. Carey is especially illuminating on lay trusteeism in the nineteenth-century Catholic Church. See David A. Gerber, "Modernity in the Service of Tradition: Catholic Lay Trustees at Buffalo's St. Louis Church and the Transformation of European Communal Traditions, 1829–1855," *Journal of Social History* 15 (1982): 655–84, and Patrick W. Carey, *People, Priests, and Prelates: Ecclesiastical Democracy and the Tensions of Trusteeism* (Notre Dame: University of Notre Dame Press, 1987).

56. See the discussion of the complementary identity in Chapter 2. See also Mead, "Denominationalism," which illustrates the problems denominational pluralism created for particularist churches.

57. Various belief systems carried over from Europe differed in the difficulties of incorporating their beliefs and structures into the American system. It is true that those who were members of more pietistic sects and who had not lived in countries with a state church in Europe had less difficulty than their more liturgically oriented Lutheran and Catholic counterparts. It is also true that the bulk of immigrants in the nineteenth century were historically affiliated with the latter churches.

58. Hansen, *Memories and Reflections*, 115. It was they, Hansen continued, who feared the ill effects of the public school and insisted that their religious teaching "was something above the law." The fact that the clergy's attempts to maintain their authority, biblical literalism, and a Lutheran natural law created political problems for them among their parishioners is no more clearly depicted than in their failure to condemn chattel slavery in 1861. See Theodore C. Blegen, *Norwegian Migration to America: The American Transition*, 2 vols. (Northfield, Minn.: Norwegian-American Historical Association, 1940), 2:418–53. See also Heinrich H. Maurer, "Studies in the Sociology of Religion: The Sociology of Protestantism," *American Journal of Sociology* 30 (1924): 257–86, for a discussion of the Lutheran natural law.

59. Herman Amberg Preus, *Syv Foredrag over de kirkelige Forholde blandt de Norske i Amerika* (Christiania, Norway: Jac. Dybwad, 1867), translated in *Vivacious Daughter: Seven Lectures on the Religious Situation among Norwegians in America by Herman Amberg Preus*, ed. and trans. Todd W. Nichol (Northfield, Minn.: Norwegian-American Historical Association, 1990), 34.

60. Preus stressed the benefits of the separation of church and state. See ibid., 178. See also Peter A. Munch, "Authority and Freedom: Controversy in Norwegian-American Congregations," *Norwegian-American Studies* 28 (1979): 3–34.

61. Henry Eyster Jacobs, *A History of the Evangelical Lutheran Church in the United States* (New York: Christian Literature Company, 1893), 404.

62. Janson, "Buggy Priest," 4–5.

63. Hansen, *Memories and Reflections*, 115.

64. Disputes between clergy and parishioners took their toll on the Lutheran clergy. Ræder noted in the 1840s, when writing about two Norwegian Lutheran pastors, that "in spite of their continued success in introducing Christian order among the motley crowd of people who had come here, full of earthly desires and often with the *strangest ideas as to the meaning of religious liberty*, nevertheless their position and their circumstances are such that one certainly cannot blame them for longing to return to their homes in Norway" (Ræder, *America in the Forties*, 51 [emphasis added]).

65. O. E. Rölvaag, *Peder Victorious* (New York: Harper and Brothers, 1929), 59–60. This was especially true in the United States, Rölvaag continued, where "full freedom in all matters of faith, that's the inalienable right of a free people! Oh, ho—so that was the idea: [The leader and majority of a church] intended to set up a state church and coerce people by force? . . . Did not the constitution of the land grant them full liberty? Did they not pay taxes to the government in order to have protection? Ought they consent to being shackled like slaves, out here in the kingdom which they themselves had wrested from the wilderness."

66. Fort Ridgely and Dale Lutheran Church records, 1885, Luther Seminary Archives, Dubuque, Iowa. The ballot ultimately failed since the congregation, located in Renville County, Minnesota, split into three congregations in 1885. See Munch, "Authority and Freedom," for an insightful discussion that stresses the class divisions between clergy and laity that served as a basis for conflict.

67. A more detailed discussion of the following case is found in Jon Gjerde, "Conflict and Community: A Case Study of the Immigrant Church in the United States," *Journal of Social History* 19 (1986): 681–97. A good description of conflict within the Norwegian Lutheran Church on which this and the following paragraph are based is E. Clifford Nelson and Eugene L. Fevold, *The Lutheran Church among Norwegian Americans: A History of the Evangelical Lutheran Church*, 2 vols. (Minneapolis: Augsburg Publishing House, 1960). For an earlier description, see Th. Eggen, "Oversigt over den Norsk-Lutherske Kirkes Historie i Amerika," *Norske-Amerikanernes Festskrift 1914*, ed. Johs. B. Wist (Decorah, Iowa: Symra, 1914).

68. U. V. Koren, "Hvad den Norske Synods har villet og fremdeles vil," *Samlede Skrifter* 3 (1890): 444.

69. J. A. Erikson, "Større end det Storste," in *Ved Arnen* (1939), cited and translated in Dorothy Burton Skårdal, *The Divided Heart: Scandinavian Immigrant Experience through Literary Sources* (Lincoln: University of Nebraska Press, 1974), 180.

70. *Folkebladet*, 3 June 1884, 2.

71. Nelson and Fevold, *Lutheran Church*, 1:254. Minnesota figures are based on congregational histories in O. M. Norlie, *Den Norske Lutherske Menigheter i Amerika, 1843–1916* (Minneapolis: Augsburg Publishing House, 1918), 436–80.

72. For greater detail with regard to these social divisions, see Gjerde, "Conflict and Community," 682–87.

73. On the German control of the Milwaukee Archdiocese, see Barry, *The Catholic Church and German Americans*, 45–50.

74. This discussion of the events of the Sinsinawa conflict is based on "History of St. Dominic's Church, Sinsinawa, Wisconsin," unpublished manuscript, ca. 1890, DSSM, and Sister Mary Paschala O'Connor, O.P., *Five Decades: History of the Congregation of the Most Holy Rosary, Sinsinawa, Wisconsin, 1849–1899* (Sinsinawa, Wis.: Sinsinawa Press, 1954). Not only was the series of events that unfolded in the conflict remarkable, but the documentation of the events was extraordinarily thorough, due in large part to the presence of St. Clara's Academy, a Dominican teaching institution in the locality.

75. "The Church Difficulty at Sinsinawa Mound: A Letter from Some Prominent

Members of the Congregation," *Galena (Illinois) Daily Gazette*, 7 July 1882, 2. This account provides a touching description of the settlers' sense of place.

76. Information from court documents, 2 March 1883, in "Description of St. Dominic Church," unpublished manuscript, n.d., DSSM.

77. Sister Theresa Marten diary, 23 January–19 February 1882, DSSM.

78. O'Connor, *Five Decades*, 233.

79. Sister Theresa Marten diary, 12 March 1882, DSSM.

80. Ibid., 13–25 March 1882.

81. "History of St. Dominic's Church," 4, DSSM.

82. Rev. T. Jacobs, "The Sinsinawa Mound Church Difficulty," *Galena (Illinois) Daily Gazette*, 28 June 1882, 3. The propriety of Jacobs's allegations was questioned, especially because they were broadcast in a secular forum. The dissenters initially refrained from replying "for very shame that Protestants should know such scandals." And secular papers played the conflict to the hilt. A Chicago paper, for example, picked up the story and reported that the altar was "thrown into an old field where it lies to this day." As a result, Father James M. Cleary, the previous priest of St. Dominic's, published rebuttals of many of Jacobs's contentions a week later, as did leading members of the congregation. The congregation leaders stressed that they had carefully placed the altar in a well-protected barn and covered it with canvas because "that was the best place we knew of to shelter it." See "Sinsinawa Mound Church Matters," *Galena (Illinois) Daily Gazette*, 5 July 1882, 2, and "The Church Difficulty at Sinsinawa Mound: A Letter from Some Prominent Members of the Congregation," *Galena (Illinois) Daily Gazette*, 7 July 1882, 2.

83. The sacrament of extreme unction was occasionally denied to the dissidents as well. One letter complained about the priest's behavior after being summoned to an elderly woman's home. "This old feeble creature," it reported, "lay at the threshold which separates time from Eternity, any moment may be her last on earth, her family expecting the Summons to call her to her final Judge. A member of the family is despatched for Father Jacobs to prepare this aged, infirm woman for this last Solemn hour. Father Jacobs refuses to go, a messenger is sent again and again [and] finally he makes a money compact with the aged husband at the fourth call, to Sign a note payable in Six months for the consideration of Fifty Dollars." "This fifty Dollars," the letter concluded sarcastically, "no doubt was a passport to the realms of never-ending joy." See draft of letter from St. Dominic's Parish to Cardinal Simeoni, ca. 1883, DSSM. Sums of up to $300 were demanded by the priest—apparently to fund his despised prairie church—in return for the performance of last rites. If the money was not forthcoming, the priest refused to perform the rites, oftentimes with tragic results. In the winter of 1884, a fourteen-year-old boy who worked as a farm laborer in a household in the community fell ill. When Jacobs refused to attend him, the boy—terrified at the thought of dying without a priest after the threats of excommunication he had heard every Sunday—rose from his sickbed and ran toward his home parish some miles away. He survived for three miles before he fell on the frozen road and perished. See letter from St. Dominic's Congregation to the Most Rev. Archbishop of Baltimore, 27 October 1884, and "History of St. Dominic's Church," 5, both in DSSM.

84. Draft of letter from St. Dominic's Congregation to the Most Eminent Prince Cardinal Simeoni, ca. 1884, and draft of letter from St. Dominic's Congregation to Cardinal Simeoni, ca. 1883, both in DSSM.

85. Account of the Sinsinawa Church conflict, ca. 1893, DSSM.

86. The issue of whether the Irish majority were excommunicated from their old church is not totally clear from surviving documents. But see Jacobs, "Sinsinawa Mound Church Difficulty," 3. *Die Iowa*, the German-language Catholic paper that condemned the behavior of the Irish majority, contended that Jacobs read from the pulpit a letter from the

archbishop excommunicating everyone who participated in tearing down the old church. See *Die Iowa*, 28 June 1882, 8. See also "Troubles in Sinsinawa Mound," *Die Iowa*, 6 July 1882, 8, and *Die Iowa*, 30 November 1882, 5; 15 February 1883, 8; 8 March 1883, 8; 28 February 1884, 5. A circuit court judgment in favor of the archbishop in February 1883 was upheld by the Wisconsin Supreme Court on 19 February 1884. See Patrick J. Dignan, *A History of the Legal Incorporation of Catholic Property in the United States, 1874-1932* (New York: Kenedy & Sons, 1935), 232, and "Heiss, Archbishop, etc. vs. Vosburg and others," in *Supreme Court of Wisconsin, January Term, 1884*, 59:532–39. The church structure that was built at great cost to the predominantly Irish majority stood unused until 1912, when it was razed. The complaints among the Irish notwithstanding, the congregation eventually was reunited and presently meets at the prairie church.

87. Michael Heiss to Theo. Jacobs, 13 February 1882, DSSM.

88. Michael Heiss to Joseph Murray, 4 January 1883, DSSM.

89. St. Dominic's Church to the Most Eminent Prince Cardinal Simeoni, 1883, DSSM.

90. St. Dominic's Parish to His Holiness Pope Leo XIII, 28 November 1884, DSSM.

91. Sinsinawa Mound, Wisconsin, parish to Most Rev. Archbishop of Baltimore, 27 October 1884, DSSM.

92. St. Dominic's Parish to Cardinal Simeoni, ca. 1882, DSSM.

93. St. Dominic's Church to Archbishop of Baltimore, 27 October 1884, DSSM.

94. Draft of letter from St. Dominic's Congregation to His Holiness Pope Leo XIII, ca. 1884, and St. Dominic's Parish to His Holiness Pope Leo XIII, 28 November 1884, both in DSSM (emphasis added).

95. "The Church Difficulty at Sinsinawa Mound: A Letter from Some Prominent Members of the Congregation," *Galena (Illinois) Daily Gazette*, 7 July 1882, 2 (emphasis added).

96. Although the church remained the principal ethnic institution well into the twentieth century, competing "communities," to complicate matters still further, were formed around other institutions as well. To be sure, the church community remained central, both socially and intellectually. Nonetheless, it increasingly competed with secular institutions ranging from secret societies to political parties to market cooperatives, all of which developed their own ideologies as the nineteenth century progressed. These organizations created further crosscutting allegiances that could sunder or reinforce ties to the central church community.

Chapter Five

1. Sarah Morse to My Very Dear Sisters, 20 September 1862, in Glenda Riley, ed., "The Morse Family Letters: A New Home in Iowa, 1856–1862," *Annals of Iowa* 45 (1980): 227.

2. For a good overview of the literature, see Hal S. Barron, "Listening to the Silent Majority: Change and Continuity in the Nineteenth-Century Rural North," in *Agriculture and National Development: Views on the Nineteenth Century*, ed. Lou Ferleger (Ames: Iowa State University Press, 1990), 4–8. See also James A. Henretta, "Families and Farms: *Mentalité* in Pre-Industrial America," *William and Mary Quarterly* 35 (1978): 3–32.

3. Henretta, "Families and Farms."

4. For an excellent overview of the developments discussed in this and the following paragraph, see William Cronon, *Nature's Metropolis: Chicago and the Great West* (New York: W. W. Norton, 1991), 97–259.

5. See, for example, John Mack Faragher, *Sugar Creek: Life on the Illinois Prairie* (New Haven: Yale University Press, 1986), and Jeremy Atack and Fred Bateman, *To Their Own Soil: Agriculture in the Antebellum North* (Ames: Iowa State University Press, 1987).

6. Scholars have tended to create a narrative where the relationship between the household mode of production and capitalism concludes with the inevitable triumph of the

latter. The principal point of debate among historians is when the transition to commercial capitalism occurs.

7. *Die Iowa*, 1 June 1876, 5. Whereas reports of attacks on stagecoaches by packs of gray wolves in central Iowa were common as late as 1858, twenty years later the bounty for wolves had been reduced from $5 to $1 in eastern Iowa. The sighting of two buffaloes near Glasgow, Iowa, resulted in a general hunt, a nostalgic incident that harkened back to the days of white contact with the wilderness. See *Dubuque National Demokrat*, 26 March 1858, 2, trans. J. K. Downing, CDH, and *Die Iowa*, 4 July 1878, 5; 25 September 1879, 5. See also Cronon, *Nature's Metropolis*, for an environmental perspective of the process.

8. A good description of the process is found in Howard C. Baldwin, *Cascade Centennial, 1834-1934* (Cascade, Iowa: H. C. Baldwin, 1934). This assessment had an ethnic component as well. The enterprises of the original Yankee and Irish protoindustrialists from the industrial centers of the East were unintentionally thwarted by the "German and Irish farming class" that came later and eventually created an almost exclusively agricultural economy.

9. I have examined available diaries and published schema of the agricultural work year from throughout the region to compare the seasonal round and have found them strikingly similar, governed in effect by the climatic needs of the crops and animals. The diaries themselves provide a glimpse of the farmers' work patterns, their exacting accounts of quantities planted, and their expectations of yields. See G. Mellberg diary, Koshkonong, Wisconsin, 20 May 1846–10 May 1849, SHSW; Mary St. John diary, Saratoga, Iowa, 29 April–28 September 1858, in Glenda Riley, ed., "A Prairie Diary," *Annals of Iowa* 44 (1977): 103–17; John W. Slemmons diary, Scott Township, Johnson County, Iowa, 11 April–30 December 1892, in H. Roger Grant, ed., "Terrace Mound Farm: The 1892 Diary of John W. Slemmons," *Annals of Iowa* 45 (1981): 620–44; John Saterlie diary, Fergus Falls, Minnesota, 17 September 1883–1 May 1908, in author's possession; Horace Miner, *Culture and Agriculture: An Anthropological Study of a Corn Belt County* (Ann Arbor: University of Michigan Press, 1949), 66; and "Labor Calendar for the Corn Belt," in H. C. M. Case, R. H. Wilcox, and H. A. Berg, *Organizing the Corn-Belt Farm for Profitable Production*, Bulletin no. 329 (Champaign: University of Illinois Agricultural Experiment Station, 1934), 297–98.

10. See, for example, John Giffin Thompson, *The Rise and Fall of Wheat Growing in Wisconsin*, Bulletin no. 292 (Madison: University of Wisconsin, 1909).

11. Nils Sjurson Gilderhus to Sjur Anderson Gilderhus [his father], 24 April 1842, SHSW. See also WPA interview with Peder T. Veum, SHSW, which discusses the grains grown and the manual labor required to produce them.

12. Sjoerd Aukes Sipma to My Relatives, to All the Farmers, and to the Director of Youth at Bornwerd, [Friesland,] 26 September 1848, trans. Edward E. Fikse, ISHDDM.

13. Rebecca Burlend [and Edward Burlend], *A True Picture of Emigration: Or Fourteen Years in the Interior of North America* (1848; reprint, Secaucus, N.J.: Citadel Press, 1968), 91.

14. Herbert Quick, *One Man's Life* (Indianapolis: Bobbs-Merrill, 1925), 191.

15. Hamlin Garland, *A Son of the Middle Border* (New York: Grosset and Dunlap, 1917), 147.

16. Ibid.

17. Quick, *One Man's Life*, 190.

18. Ibid.; Bess Streeter Aldrich, *The Rim of the Prairie* (New York: A. L. Burt, 1930), 162.

19. Quick, *One Man's Life*, 190.

20. Paul W. Gates, *The Farmer's Age: Agriculture, 1815-1860* (New York: Holt, Rinehart and Winston, 1960); Miner, *Culture and Agriculture*, 19–20.

21. *Die Iowa*, 8 August 1883, 8. See also *Dubuque National Demokrat*, 17 August 1876, 3, trans. J. K. Downing, CDH.

22. See Mac Ames, "An Old Settler's Story: Lime Springs, Iowa," unpublished manuscript, 1923, 2, ISHDIC, and Burlend, *True Picture of Emigration*, 106.

23. See J. Sanford Rikoon, *Threshing in the Midwest, 1820-1940: A Study of Traditional Culture and Technological Change* (Bloomington: University of Indiana Press, 1988).

24. See Carl Hamilton, *In No Time at All* (Ames: Iowa State University Press, 1974), 84–87; Clifford Merrill Drury, "Growing Up on an Iowa Farm, 1897–1915," *Annals of Iowa* 42 (1974): 182; Ada Mae Brown Brinton, "Eighty-Six Years in Iowa: The Memoir of Ada Mae Brown Brinton," *Annals of Iowa* 45 (1981): 564; Sjoerd Aukes Sipma to My Relatives, to All the Farmers, and to the Director of Youth at Bornwerd, [Friesland,] 26 September 1848, ISHDDM; and Sever Anderson and Rubin Anderson interview and Mr. and Mrs. Justine Gunderson interview by Douglas G. Marshall, 1946, Douglas G. Marshall field notes, Peter A. Munch Papers, NAHA.

25. William Henry Messerschmidt, "Autobiographical Notes," unpublished manuscript, 1926, 12–13, SHSW. G. Mellberg noted simply in his diary the risks inherent in such a practice when he wrote, "Our cow gone" (20 May 1849, SHSW).

26. Even calves were not slaughtered as in Norway, wrote Gilderhus, because the cost of their care was negligible (Nils Sjurson Gilderhus to Sjur Anderson Gilderhus, 24 April 1842, SHSW). Such minimal care often resulted in profound torment for the animals because they were forced to fend for themselves not only in the warm months but throughout the winter as well. Since livestock were not stabled as in Holland, wrote Sipma, they endured "terrible suffering" during the winter (Sjoerd Aukes Sipma to My Relatives, to All the Farmers, and to the Director of Youth at Bornwerd, [Friesland,] 26 September 1848, ISHDDM). Cats and roosters also suffered from the cold. Most of the cats on the Iowa farms one diarist visited had no ears because they had been frozen off, "which disfigures them very much." It was "usual" as well for cocks to have their combs and wattles and sometimes one of their feet frozen off. See James L. Broderick diary, 5 April 1877, in *The Character of the Country: The Iowa Diary of James L. Broderick, 1876–1877*, ed. Loren N. Horton (Iowa City: Iowa State Historical Department, 1976), 98. On animal suffering, see also Garland, *Son of the Middle Border*, 116.

27. Quick, *One Man's Life*, 189–90.

28. Carl O. Basinger, "Luxembourgers in Wisconsin," unpublished manuscript, 4, MHS.

29. *Die Iowa*, 12 December 1878, 5.

30. *Dubuque Herald*, 10 October 1860, 3.

31. Gottlieb Plisch to Kate Everest, Berlin Township, Marathon County, 1892, Kate Everest Papers, SHSW.

32. Observe the incredulity of merchant behavior described in Burlend, *True Picture of Emigration*, 107–8.

33. Ibid., 86.

34. Historians have long noted the irony of the fact that the greatest profits were realized in the "antisocial" speculation on land rather than in the "productive" production of food. To Quick, "two types of mind" existed "among the pioneer farmers. One looked on a farm as a means of making money from the rise in values. The other regarded it merely as a piece of soil out of which to produce a living for the family." A farmer following the former "antisocial" strategy had "the better chance to get rich" due to the "maladjustments of society by which he profits." See Quick, *One Man's Life*, 131. On questions of land speculation, see Paul W. Gates, *Landlords and Tenants on the Prairie Frontier: Studies in American Land Policy* (Ithaca: Cornell University Press, 1973).

35. Charles A. Dean to Dear Friends, 28 October 1855, UILSC.

36. Charles A. Dean to Dear Friends, 4 November 1855, UILSC.

37. Sjoerd Aukes Sipma to My Relatives, to All the Farmers, and to the Director of Youth at Bornwerd, [Friesland,] 26 September 1848, ISHDDM. Commodity speculation

was also common among early settlers. A letter from an Illinois farmer to a friend in Connecticut as early as 1818, for example, read like a shopping list of seed types to bring West, from squash varieties to fruit types to clovers. The writer concluded, in typical Yankee fashion, with an admonition not to "be satisfied with bringing enough for your own use, but bring some to speculate upon, and some for your humble servant." See George Churchill to Swift Eldred, 9 September 1818, in Richard Lyle Power, *Planting Corn Belt Culture: The Impress of the Upland Southerner and Yankee in the Old Northwest* (Indianapolis: Indiana Historical Society Publications, 1953), 31.

38. G. Mellberg's journal, for example, contains a sketch of the fields in which a crop rotation was planned. "Field II," for example, shows a rotation of winter wheat (1851), corn (1853), spring wheat (1854), pasture (1854–55), and winter wheat (1856), followed by oats, corn, and spring wheat in unspecified years. Fallowing moved from field to field so that even though most parcels of land were cropped in a particular year, each field enjoyed an uncultivated period at some point. See G. Mellberg diary, 1851–59, SHSW.

39. In an 1856 letter, a farmer noted his acreage, his wheat harvest of nearly twenty-seven bushels per acre, and the price of eighty bushels of Canada Club wheat sold for seed. Moreover, after G. Mellberg had planted six bushels of potatoes on 8 June 1847, he was already anticipating a yield of seventy bushels. See N. W. Bixby to My Dear Brother Claflin, 28 April 1856, UILSC, and G. Mellberg diary, 16 June 1847, trans. Albert O. Barton, SHSW.

40. James L. Broderick diary, 27 March 1877, in Horton, *Character of the Country*, 93.

41. Miner, *Culture and Agriculture*, 19–20.

42. A. N., in *Die Iowa*, 21 June 1877, 5.

43. Paul Hjelm-Hanson, in *Nordisk Folkeblad*, 5 January 1870, 2. See Quick, *One Man's Life*, 207–16, for an astute analysis of the transition from wheat to mixed farming.

44. *Die Iowa*, 6 July 1876, 5; 24 August 1876, 5; 15 March 1877, 8. The *Deutsch-Amerikaner* reported harvests of four to six bushels per acre the year of the Centennial (cited in *Die Iowa*, 10 August 1876, 5). See also James L. Broderick diary, 12 November 1876, in Horton, *Character of the Country*, 37, and *Die Iowa*, 17 August 1876, 5.

45. In the region around Waterloo, Iowa, for example, newspapers reported in 1877 that farmers planted 25 percent less wheat following the series of bad harvests in the preceding year (*Die Iowa*, 19 April 1877, 6).

46. *Die Iowa*, 2 August 1877, 5.

47. *Die Iowa*, 11 August 1881, 5. See also F. W. Bryant to Dear Brother, 2 October 1878, UILSC; *Die Iowa*, 8 August 1878, 5; 19 June 1879, 5; 25 September 1879, 8; 17 July 1881, 8; and Thompson, *Rise and Fall of Wheat Growing*.

48. To the west, farmers in the Dakotas, western Iowa and Minnesota, and Nebraska encountered the grasshopper, an even more daunting and mysterious pest, in the late 1870s. Settlers who expected large yields from their recently broken soil endured a singular natural disaster, an almost apocalyptic destruction of their livelihoods. Consider the horrible wonder of the description of the disaster by a Mr. Schleich: "The Spring up to August 17," he wrote to *Die Iowa*, "we had no grasshoppers. On the 18th, they came in such numbers that the sun was hardly visible through them. They came down like snowflakes and damaged corn and tobacco. Their flight is said to stretch over a strip of one hundred miles long and three hundred miles wide" (24 August 1876, 8). See also J. H., in *Die Iowa*, 12 October 1876, 4, and *Die Iowa*, 5 July 1877, 5. For an overview of grasshopper plagues, see Annette Atkins, *Harvest of Grief: Grasshopper Plagues and Public Assistance in Minnesota, 1873–1878* (St. Paul: Minnesota Historical Society Press, 1984).

49. See Allan Bogue, *From Prairie to Corn Belt: Farming on the Illinois and Iowa Prairies in the Nineteenth Century* (Chicago: University of Chicago Press, 1963).

50. See, for example, *Die Iowa*, 18 December 1884, 5. Even farmers in areas to the west

that remained within a wheat belt began to grow a wider range of cash crops to mitigate the impact of the wheat failure. Such advice is offered in a letter from a resident of Hallock, Minnesota, to *Svenska Amerikanska Posten*, 15 May 1895, 9.

51. Hamilton, *In No Time at All*, 70; Edward O. Moe and Carl C. Taylor, *Culture of a Contemporary Rural Community: Irwin, Iowa*, Bureau of Agricultural Economics Rural Life Studies no. 5 (Washington, D.C.: U.S. Department of Agriculture, 1942), 21. Moe and Taylor also report other pioneer practices that they attribute to "superstition." Root crops, for example, were generally planted "[in] the dark of the moon," whereas crops harvested above ground were to be sown "in the light of the moon."

52. Burlend, *True Picture of Emigration*, 61. In order to maximize production on the land that was cleared, squash and beans were planted among the corn, one of the few deviations from the pattern of corn planting practiced later in the century.

53. See Miner, *Culture and Agriculture*, 20, and Hamilton, *In No Time at All*, 70.

54. Hamilton, *In No Time at All*, 72.

55. Ibid., 71.

56. Miner, *Culture and Agriculture*, 20.

57. Ibid.; Garland, *Son of the Middle Border*, 162. See also Brinton, "Eighty-Six Years in Iowa," 563; Hamilton, *In No Time at All*, 78; and Burlend, *True Picture of Emigration*, 61.

58. See Drury, "Growing Up on an Iowa Farm," 182, and Brinton, "Eighty-Six Years in Iowa," 563.

59. Hamilton, *In No Time at All*, 78.

60. Miner, *Culture and Agriculture*, 20.

61. Quick, *One Man's Life*, 209.

62. The harvests in one Iowa vicinity, for example, were twenty-three bushels per acre in 1882. Amid years of failure, the paper reported, in this area, at least, "the farmers are all happy." See *Die Iowa*, 14 September 1882, 5.

63. Quick, *One Man's Life*, 216.

64. Paul Hjelm-Hanson, in *Nordisk Folkeblad*, 5 January 1870, 2. Six years later, the *Deutsch-Amerikaner* reported wages of $1.75 to $2.25 per day during the Iowa harvest, pay "quite below earlier years" (cited in *Die Iowa*, 10 August 1876, 5).

65. *Northfield Recorder*, cited in *St. Paul Pioneer Press*, 1 August 1868, 2. One year later, "the ladies of St. Paul" complained "considerably about the difficulty of securing and keeping hired girls. At Northfield, a large number of the hired girls (Norwegian and German) have gone out into the harvest fields to work, and are getting *three dollars per day*" (*St. Paul Daily Press*, 21 August 1869, 4 [emphasis in original]).

66. See, for example, *Die Iowa*, 3 August 1876, 3; 10 August 1876, 8; 17 August 1876, 3; 3 July 1879, 8; 10 July 1879, 5. Some journalists were careful to distinguish the seasonal workers from the "tramps." "With work available," *Die Iowa* argued, tramps "should disappear. But no! There are young fellows who look for work all week and thank God on Sunday that they haven't found any" (9 June 1881, 8). Others, however, correlated the arrival of the laborers with disorder. "As harvest work advances," wrote the *Dubuque National Demokrat* in 1876, "this scourge of the land, numbering in the thousands, comes to the northern towns of Iowa and with them robberies, break-ins, thieving come on the calendar" (13 July 1876, 3, trans. J. K. Downing, CDH). See also F. W. Bryant to Dear Brother, 16 June 1876, UILSC, for views about itinerant labor.

67. Miner, *Culture and Agriculture*, 19–20; Hamilton, *In No Time at All*, 68.

68. Hamilton, *In No Time at All*, 66; Moe and Taylor, *Culture of a Contemporary Rural Community: Irwin, Iowa*, 45.

69. Bogue, *From Prairie to Cornbelt*, 182–87. By this time, the custom of "hired women" performing the work with animals, typical in western European societies, had become uncommon among immigrants.

70. See Donald L. Winters, *Farmers without Farms: Agricultural Tenancy in Nineteenth-Century Iowa* (Westport, Conn.: Greenwood Press, 1978), 99–103. Using a sample drawn from twelve Iowa counties, Winters found that farm owners paid an average of $74 in wages in 1879. A statewide report in 1899 set the figure at $79.

71. As one farmer observed in the late 1930s, "since the introduction of farm machinery men work harder today than they used to. Seems they're always pressed for time" (Miner, *Culture and Agriculture*, 66).

72. Ibid., 19–20, 67.

73. Hamilton, *In No Time at All*, 3.

74. Cited in Moe and Taylor, *Culture of a Contemporary Rural Community: Irwin, Iowa*, 42.

75. *Die Iowa*, 1 May 1884, 5.

76. Moe and Taylor, *Culture of a Contemporary Rural Community: Irwin, Iowa*, 42–43. The precise figure is 9.7 percent.

77. See *Dubuque National Demokrat*, 23 November 1876, 3, trans. J. K. Downing, CDH, and *Die Iowa*, 27 January 1881, 8. Immense herds of hogs were driven to local slaughterhouses. At Ryan's Slaughterhouse in Dubuque, for example, sixty men were employed to slaughter and salt down the daily kill of 700 hogs in the summer. In the winter, the firm increased its labor force to 140 men, who slaughtered at least 1,600 hogs each day. This concern competed with six other slaughterhouses in the town. James L. Broderick, who visited "Ryan's pig-killing and Pork-packing Establishment" in 1876, was profoundly disturbed by the experience. "It is not easy to describe the horrors of such a place," he wrote. "The floor was very dirty. . . . We passed a host of butchers cutting up, next gutting, then about 15 scrapers, arranged on each side of a long bench upon which the pigs were rolled from one to another. We had some difficulty passing them as there was barely room to walk behind them on account of an opening between the flooring and the wall through which the scrapings fell. The vapor arising from the scalding-vat filled all the room with such a dense fog that it was impossible to see anything more than 1 yard off. We would hear the pigs screaming, the hot water splashing, see next to nothing, and the stench from the cleaners below was dreadful. Pushing forward we next came to the vat in which 5 or 6 newly killed pigs were being scalded. . . . It is very interesting and instructive to see such things done on a large scale," Broderick concluded, "but I must say that I have not the slightest desire to go there again." See James L. Broderick diary, 30 November 1876, in Horton, *Character of the Country*, 43–44.

78. Hamilton, *In No Time at All*, 147.

79. Mary C. Coffin to Alexander N. Coffin, 30 January 1865, in author's possession. See also Ruth Suckow, "The Little Girl from Town," *A Ruth Suckow Omnibus* (Iowa City: University of Iowa Press, 1988), 271–92, for a portrayal of urban sensibilities about the prospect of slaughtering animals.

80. See Evsey D. Domar, "The Causes of Slavery and Serfdom: A Hypothesis," *Journal of Economic History* 30 (1970): 18–32, and Gavin Wright, *The Political Economy of the Cotton South: Households, Markets, and Wealth in the Nineteenth Century* (New York: W. W. Norton, 1978), which stress the interrelationships between "free" land and labor systems.

81. Herbert Quick, *The Fairview Idea: The Story of the New Rural Life* (Indianapolis: Bobbs-Merrill, 1919), 92. Jeremy Atack and Fred Bateman argue that the small independent farms of this region constitute the "peculiar institution" of the northern United States, an "institution" that was rarer on the world stage than the "peculiar institution" of the South. See Jeremy Atack and Fred Bateman, "Yeoman Farming: Antebellum America's Other 'Peculiar Institution,'" in Ferleger, *Agriculture and National Development*, 25–51.

82. On changing conditions for farmers, see Bogue, *From Prairie to Cornbelt*, and Robert William Fogel and Jack L. Rutner, "The Efficiency Effects of Federal Land Policy, 1850–1900: A Report of Some Provisional Findings," in *The Dimensions of Quantitative Research in*

History, ed. William O. Aydelotte, Allan G. Bogue, and Robert William Fogel (Princeton: Princeton University Press, 1972). On the "safety valve," see Clarence H. Danhof, "Farm-Making Costs and the 'Safety Valve,' 1850–1860," *Journal of Political Economy* 49 (1941): 317–59.

83. For a narrative overview of farm labor early in the period, see David E. Schob, *Hired Hands and Plowboys: Farm Labor in the Midwest, 1815–1860* (Urbana: University of Illinois Press, 1975).

84. The reliance on family labor varied significantly in the Middle West, however, according to the size of the operation and the concentration of production. The importance of hired labor, for example, was much greater on corn-producing farms than on dairy farms. Since the contributions of parents and children remained largely fixed, moreover, the relative importance of hired labor increased in those regions distinguished by large farms. There, on average, hired laborers contributed 40.9 percent of the labor on each farm. See Sigmund von Frauendorfer, "American Farmers and European Peasantry," *Journal of Farm Economics* (1929), reprinted in *A Systematic Source Book in Rural Sociology*, ed. Pitirim A. Sorokin, Carle C. Zimmerman, and Charles J. Galpin, 3 vols. (Minneapolis: University of Minnesota Press, 1931), 2:167.

85. Harriet Friedmann, "Simple Commodity Production and Wage Labour in the American Plains," *Journal of Peasant Studies* 6 (1978): 73–74. Significantly, family members still composed 67.4 percent of the agricultural labor force in 1960. See also Harriet Friedmann, "World Market, State, and Family Farm: Social Bases of Household Production in the Era of Wage Labor," *Comparative Studies in Society and History* 4 (1978): 545–86.

86. Consider the plight of Micajah Shutt, an eighteen-year-old boy who fled his father's home in 1853. His father retaliated by placing an advertisement in the local newspaper warning against "harboring or trusting him." See Faragher, *Sugar Creek*, 99. Although the rights of children increased as the century progressed, children still felt that they were expected to labor within the home.

87. See, for example, William I. Thomas and Florian Znaniecki, *The Polish Peasant in Europe and America*, ed. Eli Zaretsky (Urbana: University of Illinois Press, 1984), 67, and Henretta, "Families and Farms."

88. See, for example, Mary P. Ryan, *Cradle of the Middle Class: The Family in Oneida County, New York, 1790–1865* (New York: Cambridge University Press, 1981), 21–43.

89. On the shift in the perception of land as "God's earth" to the perception of land as an exchange commodity, see Ulla Rosén, *Himlajord och handelsvara: Ägobyten av egendom i Kumla socken, 1780–1880* (Lund, Sweden: Lund University Press, 1994). On the importance of land in maintaining the "corporate family economy," see Ryan, *Cradle of the Middle Class*, 18–31.

90. As the century progressed, women within the household were accorded greater rights in inheriting and bequeathing property. See Carole Shammas, Marylynn Salmon, and Michel Dahlin, *Inheritance in America from Colonial Times to the Present* (New Brunswick, N.J.: Rutgers University Press, 1987), 81–122. These changes, of course, had an impact on the "family morality" of the household. See Chapter 6.

91. As long as members of the older generation were successful in fulfilling their expectations, as long as the "wealth flows" moved upward, the benefits of childbearing and high fertility would continue. For further discussion of the relationships between fertility and household power and structure, see Norman B. Ryder, "Fertility and Family Structure," *Population Bulletin of the United Nations* 15 (1983): 15–34, and John C. Caldwell, *The Theory of Fertility Decline* (New York: Academic Press, 1982).

92. The issue of the gendered division of labor on the farm and its implications for shifts in power and for changes in farm life has generated considerable attention. See, for example, Nancy Grey Osterud, "Gender and the Transition to Capitalism in Rural

America," *Agricultural History* 67 (1993): 14–29; Mary Neth, "Gender and the Family Labor System: Defining Work in the Rural Midwest," *Journal of Social History* 27 (1994): 563–77; Joan M. Jensen, *Loosening the Bonds: Mid-Atlantic Farm Women, 1750–1850* (New Haven: Yale University Press, 1986); Nancy Grey Osterud, *Bonds of Community: The Lives of Farm Women in Nineteenth-Century New York* (Ithaca: Cornell University Press, 1991); and Jane Marie Pederson, *Between Memory and Reality: Family and Community in Rural Wisconsin, 1870–1970* (Madison: University of Wisconsin Press, 1992). More specifically, see Mary St. John diary, Saratoga, Iowa, 29 April 1858, in Riley, "A Prairie Diary," 106; Sylvia Hill to My Dear Mrs. Herod, Cascade, Iowa, 23 May 1863, James Hill Collection, CDH; Emily Hawley Gillespie diary, Coffin's Grove, Iowa, ISHDIC, in Judy Nolte Lensink, Christine M. Kirkham, and Karen Paula Witzke, " 'My Only Confidant': The Life and Diary of Emily Hawley Gillespie," *Annals of Iowa* 45 (1980): 288–312, and Judy Nolte Lensink, *"A Secret to Be Burried": The Diary and Life of Emily Hawley Gillespie, 1858–1888* (Iowa City: University of Iowa Press, 1989); Drury, "Growing Up on an Iowa Farm," 181; and Quick, *One Man's Life*, 215.

93. Miner, *Culture and Agriculture*, 63. Miner stressed that labor shortages on occasion altered these arrangements. Women periodically helped men with the milking or picking corn if the family was poor, but "there is a definite loss of status thereby." See also Earl H. Bell, *Culture of a Contemporary Rural Community: Sublette, Kansas* (Washington, D.C.: U.S. Department of Agriculture, Bureau of Agricultural Economics Rural Life Studies, 1942), 58–62, and Moe and Taylor, *Culture of a Contemporary Rural Community: Irwin, Iowa*, 56.

94. *Minneapolis Tribune*, 11 June 1886, 5. The paper later portrayed Lindquist as less naive than first reported. Clearly, the paper stressed, she had donned "the sterner garments" before. See *Minneapolis Tribune*, 12 June 1886, 5.

95. *St. Paul Pioneer Press*, 12 October 1893, 5; *Svenska Amerikanska Posten*, 17 October 1893, 1. Known as "Cowboy Pete," Hedström was an "expert horsewoman" who had had run-ins with the law because of her "daredevil riding through the streets." Circumstances on occasion were reversed. A servant who had worked at a Dubuque hotel for four months disguised as a girl was discovered to be a boy. He lived at home with his mother, who had suggested that he take on the disguise "for the purpose of enabling him to obtain employment, which he could not get as a boy." See "An Amusing Discovery," *Dubuque Daily Times*, 12 November 1858, 3, and "Interesting Discovery," *Dubuque National Demokrat*, 13 November 1858, 3, trans. J. K. Downing, CDH.

96. Johan Reinart Reiersen, *Pathfinder for Norwegian Emigrants*, ed. and trans. Frank G. Nelson (Northfield, Minn.: Norwegian-American Historical Association, 1981), 72.

97. Hamilton, *In No Time at All*, 96–97.

98. Garland, *Son of the Middle Border*, 116.

99. Hamilton, *In No Time at All*, 162.

100. Drury, "Growing Up on an Iowa Farm," 181.

101. Miner, *Culture and Agriculture*, 63. Miner illustrated the strict division of labor between men and women, young and old, by describing the following incident. An eighteen-year-old son, after completing his morning milking, asked his mother to telephone a neighbor to request employment for him as a farmhand for a day. The mother refused, citing her busy schedule and implying that it was not her job to line up outside work for her son. The boy replied, "If I empty the ashes and feed the chickens [a woman's job], you should do that [for me]." The mother countered, "You aren't doing those things for me but for your sister."

102. See Hamilton, *In No Time at All*, 91–94; James L. Broderick diary, 30 November 1876, in Horton, *Character of the Country*, 43; and Mary Woodward letter, 14 July 1888, cited in *Read This Only to Yourself: The Private Writings of Midwestern Women, 1880–1910*, ed. Elizabeth Hampsten (Bloomington: Indiana University Press, 1982), 7.

103. Walter T. Henderson and Emma L. Henderson interview, 17–18, ISHDIC.

104. Reiersen, *Pathfinder for Norwegian Emigrants*, 120.

105. *Dubuque National Demokrat*, 7 June 1858, 3, trans. J. K. Downing, CDH.

106. *Die Iowa*, 6 May 1880, 5.

107. *Billed-Magazin*, 6 February 1869. On the economic roles of children and women, see Lee A. Craig, *To Sow One Acre More: Childbearing and Farm Productivity in the Antebellum North* (Baltimore: Johns Hopkins University Press, 1993).

108. An urban Irish immigrant was perhaps more pointed than most when she introduced her newborn twins to a settlement worker with the aside, "More insurance for me old age, you see!" Importantly, she equated additional children with increased security: the twins were her thirteenth and fourteenth children. See Esther G. Barrows, *Neighbors All: A Settlement Notebook* (Boston: Houghton Mifflin, 1929), 16–17, cited in Hasia R. Diner, *Erin's Daughters in America: Irish Immigrant Women in the Nineteenth Century* (Baltimore: Johns Hopkins University Press, 1983), 62.

109. See Marty Strange, *Family Farming: A New Economic Vision* (Lincoln: University of Nebraska Press, 1988).

110. See Kathleen Neils Conzen, "Immigrants in Nineteenth-Century Agricultural History," in Ferleger, *Agriculture and National Development*, 326. See also Kathleen Neils Conzen, "Peasant Pioneers: Generational Succession among German Farmers in Frontier Minnesota," in *The Countryside in the Age of Capitalist Transformation: Essays in the Social History of Rural America*, ed. Stephen Hahn and Jonathan Prude (Chapel Hill: University of North Carolina Press, 1985), 259–92.

111. Robert S. Lynd and Helen Merrell Lynd, *Middletown: A Study in American Culture* (New York: Harcourt, Brace, and World, 1929), 178.

112. Burlend, *True Picture of Emigration*, 124.

113. Cited in Power, *Planting Corn Belt Culture*, 99.

114. See William A. Sundstrom and Paul A. David, "Old-Age Security Motives, Labor Markets, and Farm Family Fertility in Antebellum America," *Explorations in Economic History* 25 (1988): 164–97, and Nancy Folbre, "Of Patriarchy Born: The Political Economy of Fertility Decisions," *Feminist Studies* 9 (1983): 261–84.

115. See Ron Lesthaeghe and Chris Wilson, "Modes of Production, Secularization, and the Pace of the Fertility Decline in Western Europe, 1870–1930," in *The Decline of Fertility in Europe*, ed. Ansley J. Coale and Susan Cotts Watkins (Princeton: Princeton University Press, 1986), 261–92; Ron Lesthaeghe, "A Century of Demographic and Cultural Change in Western Europe: An Exploration of Underlying Dimensions," *Population and Development Review* 9 (1983): 411–36; Caldwell, *Theory of Fertility Decline*; and Ryder, "Fertility and Family Structure."

116. *Dubuque National Demokrat*, 23 November 1876, 3, trans. J. K. Downing, CDH.

117. *Die Iowa*, 22 March 1877, 5.

118. Emily Hawley Gillespie diary, Morensi, Michigan, 12 May, 27 June 1861, and Coffin's Grove, Iowa, 15 May, 13 December 1884, 12 March, 6 June 1885, ISHDIC, in Lensink, *"A Secret to Be Burried,"* 46, 282, 291, 294–95, 300 (emphasis in original).

Chapter Six

1. Horace Miner, *Culture and Agriculture: An Anthropological Study of a Corn Belt County* (Ann Arbor: University of Michigan Press, 1949), 43.

2. Ibid. (emphasis added).

3. Oscar Lewis, for example, would write about a Texas rural community that "the Czech and German families are organized along patriarchal lines, with the wife in a sub-

ordinate position in the family and taking little or no part in affairs outside of the home. Czech women are not community leaders" (Oscar Lewis, *On the Edge of the Black Waxy: A Cultural Survey of Bell County, Texas* [St. Louis: Washington University Studies, 1948], 100). And Miner's observations in this vein were certainly not the last. See Sonya Salamon, *Prairie Patrimony: Family, Farming, and Community in the Midwest* (Chapel Hill: University of North Carolina Press, 1992), which has powerfully informed my interpretations in this and the next chapter.

4. Michel Chevalier, *Society, Manners, and Politics in the United States: Being a Series of Letters on North America* (Boston: Weeks, Jordan, 1839), 342–43 (emphasis added). The fact that Chevalier understood the labor differences as at least in part related to ethnic differences is underscored in his observation that the variations could be traced to England and Europe. "In England," he wrote, "a woman is never seen, as with us [in France], bearing a hamper of dung on her back, or labouring at the forge" (ibid., 342n).

5. Ibid., 414–15.

6. Ibid., 368–69.

7. Ibid., 430, 428. Writing about Native Americans, Thomas Jefferson observed in 1781 that women "are submitted to unjust drudgery," which was "the case with every barbarous people." He concluded, foreshadowing Chevalier, that "it is civilization alone which replaces the women in the enjoyment of their equality." See Thomas Jefferson, *Notes on the State of Virginia*, ed. William Peden (Chapel Hill: University of North Carolina Press, 1951), 60, cited in John Mack Faragher, *Sugar Creek: Life on the Illinois Prairie* (New Haven: Yale University Press, 1986), 114.

8. See William A. Sundstrom and Paul A. David, "Old-Age Security Motives, Labor Markets, and Farm Family Fertility in Antebellum America," *Explorations in Economic History* 25 (1988): 164–97, and Nancy Folbre, "Of Patriarchy Born: The Political Economy of Fertility Decisions," *Feminist Studies* 9 (1983): 261–84.

9. See Ellen Rothman, *Hands and Hearts: A History of Courtship in America* (New York: Basic Books, 1984), which notes the importance of self-determination in the choice of marriage partners among "Americans."

10. Herbert Quick, *The Fairview Idea: The Story of the New Rural Life* (Indianapolis: Bobbs-Merrill, 1919), 222. For nineteenth-century accounts of private courtship, see Auguste Carlier, *Marriage in the United States* (Boston: De Vries, Ibarra, 1867), 32–34. For twentieth-century accounts of private rural courtship, see Edward O. Moe and Carl C. Taylor, *Culture of a Contemporary Rural Community: Irwin, Iowa*, Bureau of Agricultural Economics Rural Life Studies no. 5 (Washington, D.C.: U.S. Department of Agriculture, 1942), 56; Earl H. Bell, *Culture of a Contemporary Rural Community: Sublette, Kansas* (Washington, D.C.: U.S. Department of Agriculture, Bureau of Agricultural Economics Rural Life Studies, 1942), 75, 80; and Miner, *Culture and Agriculture*, 60–61.

11. Herbert Quick, *One Man's Life* (Indianapolis: Bobbs-Merrill, 1925), 118–19. Joseph Schafer, writing at the same time as Quick, agreed. Among the differences from their German neighbors that concerned Yankees, Schafer argued, were the different "standards of decorum in the relations of the sexes." "No wonder that, when German families settled in groups near our own people," Schafer observed, "Yankee fathers and mothers often shook their heads doubtfully in contemplating the influence upon their children of these unfamiliar social customs." See Joseph Schafer, "The Yankee and the Teuton in Wisconsin: IV. Some Social Traits of Teutons," *Wisconsin Magazine of History* 7 (1923): 10.

12. William G. Bek, "Survivals of Old Marriage-Customs among the Low Germans of West Missouri," *Journal of American Folk-Lore* 21 (1908): 67–68.

13. See, for example, Michael Mitterauer, *Familie und Arbeitsteilung* (Vienna: Böhlau Verlag, 1992); Mack Walker, *Germany and the Emigration, 1816–1885* (Cambridge: Harvard University Press, 1964); Kathleen Neils Conzen, "Peasant Pioneers: Generational Suc-

cession among German Farmers in Frontier Minnesota," in *The Countryside in the Age of Capitalist Transformation: Essays in the Social History of Rural America*, ed. Stephen Hahn and Jonathan Prude (Chapel Hill: University of North Carolina Press, 1985), 259–92; Conrad M. Arensberg and Solon T. Kimball, *Family and Community in Ireland*, 2d ed. (Cambridge: Harvard University Press, 1968); Robert C. Ostergren, *A Community Transplanted: The Trans-Atlantic Experience of a Swedish Immigrant Settlement in the Upper Middle West, 1835–1915* (Madison: University of Wisconsin Press, 1988); Eilert Sundt, *Om sædeligheds-tilstanden i Norge*, ed. H. O. Christophersen (Oslo: Gyldendal, 1976); and Hal Barron, *Those Who Stayed Behind: Rural Society in Nineteenth-Century New England* (New York: Cambridge University Press, 1984).

14. See, for example, David Warren Sabean, *Property, Production, and Family in Neckarhausen, 1700–1870* (New York: Cambridge University Press, 1990); A. G. Roeber, *Palatines, Liberty, and Property: German Lutherans in Colonial British America* (Baltimore: Johns Hopkins University Press, 1993); and Ulla Rosén, *Himlajord och handelsvara: Ägobyten av egendom i Kumla socken, 1780–1880* (Lund, Sweden: Lund University Press, 1994), which suggests nineteenth-century shifts in social patterns of property holding in a Swedish locality.

15. See the Introduction. It is difficult to create a fitting nomenclature for these typologies. I distinguish the "Yankee" pattern from that of the upland southerner and therefore do not label it "Anglo-American," which would be too inclusive, or "northern American," which would be somewhat unwieldy.

16. The table of duties was called a *hustavl* in Scandinavia. See Theodore Tappert, ed., *Book of Concord* (Philadelphia: Fortress Press, 1959), 354–56.

17. Herman Amberg Preus, *Syv Foredrag over de kirkelige Forholde blandt de Norske i Amerika* (Christiania, Norway: Jac. Dybwad, 1867), translated in *Vivacious Daughter: Seven Lectures on the Religious Situation among Norwegians in America by Herman Amberg Preus*, ed. and trans. Todd W. Nichol (Northfield, Minn.: Norwegian-American Historical Association, 1990), 127–28, 64.

18. Summarized from *Evangelisches Magazin* in Heinrich H. Maurer, "Studies in the Sociology of Religion: II. Religion and American Sectionalism—The Pennsylvania German," *American Journal of Sociology* 30 (1924): 425. Note that this summary indicates that Eirishdeutsch—literally, Irish Germans—were associated with sloth and materialism.

19. See John C. Caldwell, *The Theory of Fertility Decline* (New York: Academic Press, 1982).

20. Robert L. Skrabanek, *We're Czechs* (College Station: Texas A & M University Press, 1988), 42.

21. These notions are difficult for us to understand today. Indeed, rural sociologists early in this century argued that the "psychosocial characteristics" of these household arrangements were so fundamentally different from modern arrangements that they were almost incomprehensible to the modern mind. Pitirim A. Sorokin contended that the rural family was characterized by a "greater mutual fusion of the personalities of its individual members into one collective family personality." Modern researchers, applying their own standards in the study of rural families, were mistaken in finding them "more autocratic, more despotic, and more tyrannical." Rather, Sorokin believed, "many forms of relationship that may appear as despotism to a very individualistic person are but manifestations of this great fusion [into a collective 'we']. By the members of the family they are not felt, interpreted, or thought of as exploitation or suppression." See Pitirim A. Sorokin, Carle C. Zimmerman, and Charles J. Galpin, eds., *A Systematic Source Book in Rural Sociology*, 3 vols. (Minneapolis: University of Minnesota Press, 1931), 2:13–14.

22. The shifts in family morality among northern Anglo-American farmers in the early nineteenth century are remarkable. Preindustrial farm families in New England, scholars argue, had been concerned about "traditional notions of family identity" that focused on

the lineage rather than the individuality of a family's constituent parts. Historians have pointed to various movements that besieged this morality. Some focus on the era of the American Revolution; see, for example, Edwin G. Burrows and Michael Wallace, "The American Revolution: The Ideology and Psychology of National Liberation," *Perspectives in American History* 6 (1972): 167–306, and Jay Fliegelman, *Prodigals and Pilgrims: The American Revolution against Patriarchal Authority, 1750–1800* (Cambridge: Cambridge University Press, 1982). Others stress the fallout from the Second Great Awakening in the early nineteenth century; see, for example, Mary P. Ryan, *Cradle of the Middle Class: The Family in Oneida County, New York, 1790–1865* (New York: Cambridge University Press, 1981). See also Daniel Scott Smith, "Parental Power and Marriage Patterns: An Analysis of Historical Trends in Hingham, Massachusetts," *Journal of Marriage and the Family* 35 (1973): 419–28, and James A. Henretta, "Families and Farms: *Mentalité* in Pre-Industrial America," *William and Mary Quarterly* 35 (1978): 3–32.

23. Alexis de Tocqueville, *Democracy in America*, ed. J. P. Mayer, trans. George Lawrence (New York: Anchor Books, 1969), 585.

24. Ibid., 587–88.

25. Ibid., 589.

26. Carlier, *Marriage in the United States*, 36.

27. Urbain Gohier, *Le Peuple du XXe Siècle aux États-Unis* (Paris: Bibliothèque-Charpentier, 1903), 34 (emphasis in original).

28. Ernest Duvergier de Hauranne, *A Frenchman in Lincoln's America: Huit Mois en Amerique — Lettres et notes de voyage, 1864–1865*, ed. and trans. Ralph H. Bowen (Chicago: R. R. Donnelley & Sons, 1975), 266–67.

29. Albert Barnes, *The Casting Down of Thrones: A Discourse on the Present State of Europe* (Philadelphia: William Sloanaker, 1848), 6.

30. See Francis L. K. Hsu, "The Effect of Dominant Kinship Relationships on Kin and Non-Kin Behavior: A Hypothesis," *American Anthropologist* 67 (1965): 638–61.

31. Consider the example of Sweden. The 1789 Skatteköpsförordningen (Act on Associations and Security), which gave Swedish peasants rights of landownership similar to those enjoyed by the nobility, formalized "owning" in a liberal sense. After this time, peasants were able to bequeath land to their children in an attempt to retain their lineage's status in land-poor districts. Even though they often transferred their land to nonkin, the possibility of transferring land conferred status as a farmer. See Rosén, *Himlajord och handelsvara*.

32. For historical narratives that address the origins of these developments, albeit with different focuses on timing, see Lawrence Stone, *The Family, Sex, and Marriage in England, 1500–1800* (New York: Harper and Row, 1977), and Carl N. Degler, *At Odds: Women and the Family in America from the Revolution to the Present* (Oxford: Oxford University Press, 1980). It should be noted that associations and voluntary organizations, which knit individuals together and also tended to have lateral rather than lineal organizational structures, were on the rise.

33. In addition to Hansen, Willa Cather, Herbert Quick, Hamlin Garland, and Ruth Suckow provide perceptive fictional portrayals of cultural differences in attitudes toward and tenure on the land. Cather's depictions of rural Nebraska, for example, distinguish the more mobile "Americans" from the settled "Europeans," who were more closely tied to land and to kin. See Willa Cather, *My Ántonia* (Boston: Houghton Mifflin, 1918), and *O Pioneers!* (Boston: Houghton Mifflin, 1913). Herbert Quick's insights on cultural differences permeate his fiction, his memoir, and his social criticism. See, for example, Quick, *One Man's Life* and *Fairview Idea*. See also Hamlin Garland, "Up the Coulee," in *Main-Travelled Roads: Six Mississippi Valley Stories* (1891; reprint, New York: Macmillan, 1962), 52, and Ruth Suckow, *Country People* (New York: Alfred A. Knopf, 1924). Twentieth-century

Americans who were disenchanted with farming due to the misfortunes of landlessness and tenancy stemming from agricultural capitalism tended to romanticize the European American farmer, who ironically seemed better able to maintain Jeffersonian yeoman convictions than his or her Anglo-American counterpart.

34. Marcus Lee Hansen, "Immigration and Expansion," in *The Immigrant in American History*, ed. Arthur M. Schlesinger (Cambridge: Harvard University Press, 1940), 60, 61.

35. Joseph Schafer, "The Yankee and the Teuton in Wisconsin: I. Characteristic Attitudes toward the Land," *Wisconsin Magazine of History* 6 (1922): 142–45. Schafer, for example, wrote that "whereas, in the course of four or five generations marked by material accumulations, the Yankee had grown somewhat selective in his choice of work, preferring the lighter forms, the foreigner gave him an example of willingness to take hold of anything however 'menial' or grinding" (Joseph Schafer, *The Wisconsin Lead Region* [Madison: State Historical Society of Wisconsin, 1932], 235). See also Joseph Schafer, "The Yankee and the Teuton in Wisconsin: II. Distinctive Traits as Farmers," *Wisconsin Magazine of History* 6 (1922): 277.

36. Schafer, "The Yankee and the Teuton in Wisconsin: II," 277. To Schafer, Germans represented Europeans. He focused on Germans because they constituted an especially large nationality group in Wisconsin. Yet he noted that although "other foreigners" remained in rural areas, "above all, the Germans persisted as farmers."

37. Ibid., 277–78, 271; Schafer, "The Yankee and the Teuton in Wisconsin: I," 134, 133, 142–45.

38. Miner, *Culture and Agriculture*, 64–65.

39. Ibid., 58.

40. Alfred Sordahl and mother interview, Viroqua, Wisconsin, 1947, Peter A. Munch field notes, Peter A. Munch Papers, NAHA.

41. M. N. Daffinrud interview, Viroqua, Wisconsin, 1947, Peter A. Munch field notes, Peter A. Munch Papers, NAHA.

42. Ole Munch Ræder, *America in the Forties: The Letters of Ole Munch Ræder*, ed. and trans. Gunnar J. Malmin (Minneapolis: Norwegian-American Historical Association, 1929), 25.

43. Karl Neprud interview, Soldiers Grove, Wisconsin, 1947, Peter A. Munch field notes, Peter A. Munch Papers, NAHA. The continuation of the same lineage on the land tended to increase people's valuation of a farm. As people at a café commented about a local farm, "It's a very good farm. Has been in the same family for three generations." See interview, Blanchardville, Wisconsin, 1947, Peter A. Munch field notes, Peter A. Munch Papers, NAHA. Likewise, the length of time a farm remained in the family was a source of pride among family members, as it was among freehold peasants in Europe. See Genevieve Erickson Bussian, "Tired Oxen Located Ericksons' Homestead," unpublished manuscript, 1–3, SHSW.

44. Miner, *Culture and Agriculture*, 26–27. To underscore his point, Miner noted the strong relationship between the frequency of land transactions in each township during a land boom and the proportion of the township's residents who were of Yankee background. When he correlated the percentages of farms sold with the percentages of Yankee rural population, the coefficient of correlation was +.57. One exception to the pattern occurred in a township whose residents had a Quaker background. When that township was removed from the equation, the coefficient increased to +.71. A rural sociological study in Shelby County, Iowa, moreover, noted that people with "European backgrounds" who hedged their speculation during World War I ironically were more likely to escape the ill effects of the postwar crash. Schafer himself pointed out that the "nation's lowest farm mortgage interest rates" were found in the regions of eastern Wisconsin peopled by German farmers. See Moe and Taylor, *Culture of a Contemporary Rural Community: Irwin, Iowa*, 75, and Schafer, "The Yankee and the Teuton in Wisconsin: II," 277–78.

45. For the most complete exploration of these related patterns, see Salamon, *Prairie Patrimony*.

46. Arthur A. Halbach, *Dyersville: Its History and Its People* (Milwaukee: St. Joseph's Press, 1939), 124. A Norwegian writer connected the disappearance of Yankees on the land to their profligate ways. "In general," Svein Nilsson wrote, "the Germans and Scandinavians who have come here from Europe seem to have achieved economic independence more easily than the Yankee from the eastern states. The hard work and thrift of the former lead to progress; unless some misfortune strikes them, their hopes for wealth and independence are realized. The latter, on the contrary, make many demands on life: the wife wants to live in style, while the husband's ideas of a decent existence often lead to expenses which do not correspond to their income" (Svein Nilsson, *Billed-Magazin*, 30 July 1878, in *A Chronicler of Immigrant Life: Svein Nilsson's Articles in Billed-Magazin, 1868-1870*, trans. and ed. C. A. Clausen [Northfield, Minn.: Norwegian-American Historical Association, 1982], 151). See Jon Gjerde, "The 'Would-be Patriarch' and the 'Self-Made Man': Marcus Lee Hansen on Native and Immigrant Farmers in the American Middle West," in *On Distant Shores*, ed. Birgit Flemming Larsen, Henning Bender, and Karen Veien (Aalborg, Denmark: Danish Worldwide Archives, 1993), 35–55, for an extended discussion of the work of Hansen and for contemporary references that reveal an understanding of the immigrant tendency to engross land at the expense of American-born settlements.

47. See Daniel Scott Smith, "Family Limitation, Sexual Control, and Domestic Feminism in Victorian America," *Feminist Studies* 1 (1973): 40–57, and Degler, *At Odds*.

48. Quick, *Fairview Idea*, 6.

49. Emily Hawley Gillespie diary, 15 August 1883, ISHDIC, in Judy Nolte Lensink, *"A Secret to Be Burried": The Diary and Life of Emily Hawley Gillespie, 1858-1888* (Iowa City: University of Iowa Press, 1989), 270.

50. *Die Iowa*, 26 July 1877, 5.

51. *Die Iowa*, 8 February 1882, 5 (italics written in English in original).

52. Sjoerd Aukes Sipma to My Relatives, to All the Farmers, and to the Director of Youth at Bornwerd, [Friesland,] 26 September 1848, ISHDDM.

53. Barbara Haukenberry, ed. and trans., "The Diary of a Danish Immigrant: Karl Pedersen in 1880," *Soundings: Collections of the University [of California at Santa Barbara] Library* 17 (1986): 29.

54. Helene Munch and Peter A. Munch, eds. and trans., *The Strange American Way: Letters of Caja Munch from Wiota, Wisconsin, 1855-1859, with "An American Adventure" by Johan Storm Munch* (Carbondale: Southern Illinois University Press, 1970), 73. See Jon Gjerde, *From Peasants to Farmers: The Migration from Balestrand, Norway, to the Upper Middle West* (New York: Cambridge University Press, 1985), 228–29, for other examples of Scandinavian critiques of the lifestyle of American women.

55. *Die Iowa*, 22 April 1880, 6; 7 November 1878, 8.

56. August Kickbusch, Wausau, Marathon County, Wisconsin, 1892, Kate Everest field notes, Kate Everest Papers, SHSW. Others argued that the use of implements increased even if labor responsibilities did not. The *Milwaukee Seebote* in 1876 noted that German workers in the field—"the farmer . . . with wife and child"—used the new labor-saving implements (cited in *Dubuque National Demokrat*, 20 July 1876, 3, trans. J. K. Downing, CDH).

57. Oscar Lewis did note that there was a difference between theory and practice since American women occasionally worked in the field although they did not like to admit it (Lewis, *On the Edge of the Black Waxy*, 24–25).

58. Edward Kibbe and Thomas McGorkle, "Culture and Medical Behavior in a Bohemian Speech Community in Iowa," unpublished paper, University of Iowa, 1957, 22–23, Peter A. Munch Papers, NAHA. Kibbe and McGorkle noted as well that after having

babies, women did not postpone going back to work, including field work. Few sources with European female voices are available to comment on the labor obligations of European women. Interviews of first-generation Mennonite women reveal that they were not forced to work in the fields but wanted to help in the operation of the farm. See Emerick K. Francis, *In Search of Utopia: The Mennonites in Manitoba* (Glencoe, Ill.: Free Press, 1955), 77.

59. Quick, *One Man's Life*, 196. Lewis noted that the failure to rely on the field labor of women and children caused Americans to hire more nonfamily labor. As a result, Americans took "a chance between high costs and high farm prices." See Lewis, *On the Edge of the Black Waxy*, 103.

60. Manitoban Anglo-Canadians went so far as to take their concerns to the Canadian House of Commons in 1878 and force the deputy minister of agriculture to promise to make sure that their Mennonite neighbors would "conform to the superior moral standards of Canadian society" (Francis, *In Search of Utopia*, 77).

61. Quick, *Fairview Idea*, 6. Another less conventional form of labor exchange was reported in 1878. An Anglo-American hunter shooting at a prairie chicken missed and instead hit a "good natured German woman who was toiling in a harvest field." Refusing to accept his apologies, "the practical farmer and his shot-bespattered wife" set him to work in the field "in place of the disabled female, who retired to her rural castle . . . to pick the shot out of her." See *St. Paul Pioneer Press*, 23 August 1878, 6.

62. Suckow, *Country People*, 56–58.

63. *Minneapolis Tribune*, cited in *Dubuque Daily Times*, 18 September 1884, 7.

64. Quick, *Fairview Idea*, 11–12.

65. Ibid., 7. The existence of separate spheres of labor on the farm for men and women, some Americans admitted, was not without its problems. Quick's narrative continued: "My wife picked up that last sheet and read it. 'Much you know about it,' says she. 'Many a day when I've been nearly crazy with loneliness and monotony of housework it would have been a real kindness to me if I could have gone out and raked hay or driven the binder— out where the men were. That's what women want and need—to work with men.'"

66. Hamlin Garland, "The Creamery Man," in *Main-Travelled Roads*, 157–58. Quick also linked women's field labor to the condition of the home. A German woman, he wrote, "said she'd rather do that than the housework, and, considering the home, I really can't blame her" (Quick, *Fairview Idea*, 6).

67. Quick, *One Man's Life*, 118–19.

68. Ibid., 196–97.

69. Quick, *Fairview Idea*, 7.

70. Jane G. Swisshelm, "Woman's Work and Man's Supremacy," in *Letters to Country Girls* (New York: J. C. Riker, 1853), 75. She did, however, write in what appears to be a southern dialect when she characterized the "ignorant country bore."

71. Ibid., 75–81. See also Ryan, *Cradle of the Middle Class*, 65–75.

72. Kristofer Janson, "Kvinden skal være Manden underdannig," in *Præriens Saga: Fortællinger fra Amerika* (Chicago: Skandinaven's Bogtrykkeri, 1885), 6–7.

73. The use of the term *Damen*—a title of status and respect—indicates an element of social class in the drama as well.

74. Janson, "Kvinden skal være Manden underdannig," 19.

75. Ibid., 20.

76. Ibid., 29.

77. Ibid., 32–33.

78. Ibid., 23–24.

79. Ibid., 23 (emphasis in original).

80. Ibid., 20–21, 28.

81. Janson wrote this story shortly after a controversy occurred within the church when Oline Muus, a Norwegian Synod pastor's wife, filed for divorce. In her statement to the church, Muus noted her "stand against the Synod's teaching of wife's blind and absolute obedience and subjection." She averred that "if God had created woman to be in all things a blind tool and slave, he certainly would not have given her independent intellectual and spiritual abilities and powers." Ultimately, her divorce became final, and her husband was allowed to continue to serve his church. Her champions saw the members of the Norwegian Synod as "a flock of subdued beings" who possessed "no principle, no will, excepting those of their master." See *Argus*, 18 March 1880, *Goodhue County Republican* (Red Wing, Minn.), 3 June 1880, and *Budstikken*, 23 March 1880, all cited in Kathryn Ericson, "Triple Jeopardy: The Muus vs. Muus Case in Three Forums," *Minnesota History* 50 (1987): 304–5. One wonders if this case, which became a cause célèbre among Norwegian American intellectuals, influenced Janson in the writing of this story. Years later, he complained about the "spiritual [*aandelige*] tyranny" and the "meaningless dogma" of the Lutheran Church. See Kristofer Janson, *Hvad jag har oplevet* (Kristiania, Norway: Gyldendalske Boghandel, 1913), 181.

82. August Kickbusch, Wausau, Marathon County, Wisconsin, 1892, Kate Everest field notes, Kate Levi Papers, SHSW.

83. Ibid.

84. Quick, *Fairview Idea*, 67–68.

85. Ibid., 68.

86. Mary Woodward diary, 25 October 1885, cited in Elizabeth Hampsten, *Read This Only to Yourself: The Private Writings of Midwestern Women, 1880–1910* (Bloomington: Indiana University Press, 1982), 229.

87. Ibid.

88. Ibid., 16 February 1888.

89. Ibid., 14 July 1888.

90. Mary Schaal Johns, "Home Mission Sermon and Schaal Family Reminiscence," unpublished manuscript, 1915, 4, SHSW.

91. Ibid., 5–6.

92. Quick, *Fairview Idea*, 7. I have found few sources in which children defend child labor. One fictional account that supports the practice couples class with household labor systems. "The whole family had worked in the beet fields together," wrote Ruth Suckow, "except the baby, and he almost did—the mother had to take him along because she was nursing him." When the mother's "American" suitor criticizes the practice, she contends that her lifestyle "was American too!" When she tells him about "the way [her father] used to lick the kids to make them work" and he becomes "indignant," she "defended her father. 'He had to make us earn our bread.'" See Ruth Suckow, *The Folks* (New York: Farrar and Rinehart, 1934), 546.

93. *Die Iowa*, 15 August 1878, 5. *Die Iowa* claimed that "the maids here are almost all immigrant Europeans." Yet due to European work patterns, Americans found even young European women in short supply during harvest time. A newspaper reported in 1869 that "the ladies of St. Paul complain considerably about the difficulty of securing and keeping hired girls" since the "hired girls (Norwegian and German) have gone out into the harvest fields to work" (*St. Paul Daily Press*, 21 August 1869, 4). See also *St. Paul Daily Press*, 1 August 1868, 2. Cather, *My Ántonia*, clearly depicts the differences between European and American daughters.

94. *Die Iowa*, 11 May 1882, 8.

95. *Die Iowa*, 12 July 1877, 5.

96. Louis Falge, Reedsville, Manitowoc County, 1891, Kate Everest field notes, Kate Levi Papers, SHSW.

97. Mrs. Alfred Attoe interview, Douglas G. Marshall field notes, 1946, Peter A. Munch Papers, NAHA.

98. Mr. and Mrs. Albert Feitz interview, 1946, Douglas G. Marshall field notes, Peter A. Munch Papers, NAHA. There were exceptions to this pattern among European Americans. A German respondent, "contrary to the prevalent belief," asserted the importance of education. Unlike the sentiment expressed among Germans, moreover, "education is a very important factor in [Norwegian American] culture." See Mrs. Hansel and her son and daughter interview and Sever Anderson and Rubin Anderson interview, 1946, Douglas G. Marshall field notes, Peter A. Munch Papers, NAHA.

99. Lewis, *On the Edge of the Black Waxy*, 55.

100. Mr. and Mrs. Isaac Smith interview, 1946, Douglas G. Marshall field notes, Peter A. Munch Papers, NAHA.

101. Garland, "Creamery Man."

102. Ibid., 158.

103. Ibid., 159.

104. Ibid., 161.

105. Ibid., 161–62.

106. Everson sisters interview, Viroqua, Wisconsin, 1947, Peter A. Munch field notes, Peter A. Munch Papers, NAHA.

Chapter Seven

1. G. Mellberg diary, Koshkonong, Jefferson County, Wisconsin Territory, 7 June, 6, 10 July 1846, trans. Albert O. Barton, SHSW.

2. See Introduction and Chapters 2 and 6.

3. Sonya Salamon utilizes a similar broad division between "entrepreneur" and "yeoman" typologies. See Sonya Salamon, *Prairie Patrimony: Family, Farming, and Community in the Midwest* (Chapel Hill: University of North Carolina Press, 1992).

4. See Francis L. K. Hsu, "The Effect of Dominant Kinship Relationships on Kin and Non-Kin Behavior: A Hypothesis," *American Anthropologist* 67 (1965): 638–61.

5. George Hill Papers, SHSW.

6. These figures are based on parentage rather than place of nativity. Therefore, household heads who were American-born and whose parents were American-born were subsumed in the "native-born" category. American-born heads whose parents were foreign-born were placed in the "foreign-parentage" category.

7. The populations included a sample of households from a cluster of seven townships in Dubuque County, Iowa, and seven townships in the contiguous counties of Crawford and Vernon, Wisconsin. The counties were characterized by both economic diversity and ethnic complexity. Considerable blocs of people of Scandinavian, Irish, German, and "American" backgrounds inhabited the townships.

8. See, for example, Wendell H. Bash, "Differential Fertility in Madison County, New York, 1865," *Milbank Memorial Fund Quarterly* 33 (1956): 161–68; Avery Guest, "Fertility Variation among the U.S. Foreign Stock Population in 1900," *International Migration Review* 16 (1982): 577–94; Michael Haines, "Fertility and Marriage in a Nineteenth Century American City: Philadelphia, 1850–1900," *Journal of Economic History* 40 (1980): 151–58; Tamara K. Hareven and Maris A. Vinovskis, "Patterns of Childbearing in Late Nineteenth Century America: The Determinants of Marital Fertility in Five Massachusetts Towns in 1880," in *Family and Population in Nineteenth Century America*, ed. Tamara K. Hareven and Maris A. Vinovskis (Princeton: Princeton University Press, 1978), 85–125, and "Marital Fertility, Ethnicity, and Occupation in Urban Families: An Analysis of South

Boston and the South End in 1880," *Journal of Social History* 9 (1975): 69–83; Olivier Zunz, *The Changing Face of Inequality: Urbanization, Industrial Development, and Immigrants in Detroit, 1880–1920* (Chicago: University of Chicago Press, 1982), 67–79; Mark J. Stern, *Society and Family Strategy: Erie County, New York, 1850–1920* (Albany: State University of New York Press, 1987); Joseph J. Spengler, *The Fecundity of Native and Foreign Born Women in New England* (Washington, D.C.: Brookings Institution, 1930); and Jerry Wilcox and Hilda J. Golden, "Prolific Immigrants and Dwindling Natives?: Fertility Patterns in Western Massachusetts, 1850 and 1880," *Journal of Family History* 7 (1982): 265–89.

9. See Daniel Scott Smith, "The Peculiarities of the Yankees: The Vanguard of the Fertility Transition in the United States," unpublished paper, IUSSP Committee on Comparative Analysis of Fertility, Sion, Switzerland, 1994, and "Culture and Family Limitation in Early Twentieth Century Iowa: Identity and Association," unpublished manuscript, 1992.

10. John C. Caldwell, *The Theory of Fertility Decline* (New York: Academic Press, 1982). See also William A. Sundstrom and Paul A. David, "Old-Age Security Motives, Labor Markets, and Farm Family Fertility in Antebellum America," *Explorations in Economic History* 25 (1988): 164–97.

11. See Daniel Scott Smith, "Family Limitation, Sexual Control, and Domestic Feminism in Victorian America," *Feminist Studies* 1 (1973): 40–57; Carl N. Degler, *At Odds: Women and the Family in America from the Revolution to the Present* (Oxford: Oxford University Press, 1980); and Hsu, "Effect of Dominant Kinship Relationships."

12. James L. Broderick diary, 28 March 1877, in *The Character of the Country: The Iowa Diary of James L. Broderick, 1876–1877*, ed. Loren N. Horton (Iowa City: Iowa State Historical Department, 1976), 93.

13. Emily Hawley Gillespie diary, 2 October 1873, ISHDIC, in Judy Nolte Lensink, *"A Secret to Be Burried": The Diary and Life of Emily Hawley Gillespie, 1858–1888* (Iowa City: University of Iowa Press, 1989), 174.

14. Herbert Quick, *One Man's Life* (Indianapolis: Bobbs-Merrill, 1925), 3–6.

15. *Die Iowa*, 19 December 1878, 6.

16. *Die Iowa*, 28 February 1884, 8 (emphasis added).

17. A. N. S., in *Die Iowa*, 11 October 1877, 5.

18. Quick, *One Man's Life*, 3–5.

19. Mr. and Mrs. Clint Hudriak interview, Wild Rose, Waushara County, Wisconsin, 1946, Douglas G. Marshall field notes, Peter A. Munch Papers, NAHA.

20. Svein Nilsson, *Billed-Magazin*, 3 September 1870, in *A Chronicler of Immigrant Life: Svein Nilsson's Articles in Billed-Magazin, 1868–1870*, trans. and ed. C. A. Clausen (Northfield, Minn.: Norwegian-American Historical Association, 1982), 155.

21. The 1900 manuscript census contained questions on age and the number of years married. From the responses to these queries, an indirect measure of age of marriage can be calculated. See Miriam King and Steven Ruggles, "Immigration, American Fertility Differentials, and the Ideology of Race Suicide in 1900," unpublished paper, 27, and "American Immigration, Fertility, and Race Suicide at the Turn of the Century," *Journal of Interdisciplinary History* 20 (1990): 347–69. The singulate mean age of marriage for white women was 21.9 in 1890. See Jon Gjerde, "Patterns of Migration to and Demographic Adaptation within Rural Ethnic American Communities," *Annales de demographie historique* (1988–89): 292.

22. King and Ruggles, "Immigration, American Fertility Differentials, and the Ideology of Race Suicide," 27. The proportions among the 45–49 age group are similar: 13.6 percent and 8.4 percent, respectively. See King and Ruggles, "American Immigration, Fertility, and Race Suicide," 358.

23. See table 7.8. The source of this data is discussed in note 70 below.

24. These patterns continued into the twentieth century. As early as 1920, Niles Car-

penter discovered that second-generation men and women were less likely to marry than either first-generation immigrants or native whites. The fact that the gap narrowed in later age categories led Carpenter to theorize that children were postponing marriage. David M. Heer found a similar circumstance using data from the 1950 census. See Niles Carpenter, *Immigrants and Their Children: 1920*, Census Monograph no. 7 (Washington, D.C.: Government Printing Office, 1927), and David M. Heer, "The Marital Status of Second-Generation Americans," *American Sociological Review* 26 (1961): 233–41. See also Stanley Lieberson and Mary C. Waters, *From Many Strands: Ethnic and Racial Groups in Contemporary America* (New York: Russell Sage Foundation, 1988), 103–5.

25. I examined information from the 1860–1910 federal censuses on the Norway Grove population described below to determine whether children were or were not present in households according to the age of the household head. The results indicate that children were present in an overwhelming proportion of cases. In families whose household head was aged 40–49, for example, 95.5 percent (N=375) had at least one child present. In families with household heads aged 60–69, the percentage was 85.2 (N=149). In households with heads 80 years or older, the proportion was 71.4 percent (N=63).

26. Recall from the previous chapter that Anglo-Canadians in the House of Commons complained about the failure of their Mennonite neighbors to conform to "the superior moral standards of Canadian society" because Mennonite women worked in the fields and created a form of unfair competition. See Emerick K. Francis, *In Search of Utopia: The Mennonites in Manitoba* (Glencoe, Ill.: Free Press, 1955), 77.

27. The significance of the so-called companionate marriage, as we have seen, is a central component of the domestic feminism argument with regard to the history of the "American family." See, for example, Smith, "Family Limitation"; Degler, *At Odds*; and Nancy Grey Osterud, *Bonds of Community: The Lives of Farm Women in Nineteenth-Century New York* (Ithaca: Cornell University Press, 1991).

28. Horace Miner, *Culture and Agriculture: An Anthropological Study of a Corn Belt County* (Ann Arbor: University of Michigan Press, 1949), 64.

29. F. W. Bryant to Dear Brother, Epworth, Iowa, 6 August 1877, UILSC.

30. Maria Freeland to Eliza Keyes, 6 June 1864, cited in Elizabeth Hampsten, *Read This Only to Yourself: The Private Writings of Midwestern Women, 1880–1910* (Bloomington: Indiana University Press, 1982), 112. For other examples of affection, see Sylvia Hill to Mr. Herod, Cascade, Iowa, 1862, James Hill Collection, CDH, and James A. Ramsey diary, Jefferson County, Indiana, 21 October 1868, ISHDIC.

31. European Americans often disparaged the use of "romantic" expressions in American society. When an eighteen-year-old boy wed a twelve-year-old girl, for example, the editor of *Die Iowa* condemned the marriage as "another case of downright immorality growing in America's young people." Americans "call them *romantic couple*," he complained, "and—where does that get you?"—certainly not to the "moral side" of the issue. See *Die Iowa*, 1 November 1883, 5 (italics written in English in original).

32. On domestic violence, see Linda Gordon, *Heroes of Their Own Lives: The Politics and History of Family Violence* (New York: Viking, 1988).

33. See Carroll Smith-Rosenberg, "The Female World of Love and Ritual: Relations between Women in Nineteenth-Century America," in *Disorderly Conduct: Visions of Gender in Victorian America* (New York: Knopf, 1985), 53–76, and E. T. May, *Great Expectations* (Chicago: University of Chicago Press, 1980), on divorce in the late nineteenth century.

34. Robert M. Dinkel, who explored parent-child conflicts in the mid-twentieth-century Middle West, discovered different senses of responsibility of children toward their parents according to religious group and place of residence. In a test of attitudes about the obligations of children toward their parents, he found that male and female rural Catholics were the most committed to their parents; urban, Protestant daughters were the least

committed. Whereas nearly half of the rural Catholic youth affirmed the statement that "children should give a home even to aged parents who interfere a lot in family affairs," only one-fifth of urban Protestants agreed. See Robert M. Dinkel, "Parent-Child Conflict in Minnesota Families," *American Sociological Review* 8 (1943): 412–19, and "Attitudes of Children toward Supporting Aged Parents," *American Sociological Review* 9 (1944): 370–79.

35. Miner, *Culture and Agriculture*, 64.

36. See ibid., 73, and Roy E. Wakeley, *Differential Mobility within the Rural Population in Eighteen Iowa Townships, 1928–1935* (Ames: Iowa State College, 1938). Because its inhabitants were advocates of higher education, Mrs. John Evans intimated, a rural Welsh community in Wisconsin experienced a heavy out-migration. See Mrs. John Evans interview, Wild Rose, Waushara County, Wisconsin, 1946, Douglas G. Marshall field notes, Peter A. Munch Papers, NAHA.

37. Sarah Browne Adamson diary, Bloomington, Fayette County, Ohio, 10 February 1843, transcribed by Carol Benning, CFHS.

38. Hamlin Garland, "Under the Lion's Paw," in *Main-Travelled Roads: Six Mississippi Valley Stories* (1891; reprint, New York: Macmillan, 1962), 144.

39. See Steven Ruggles, *Prolonged Connections: The Rise of the Extended Family in Nineteenth-Century England and America* (Madison: University of Wisconsin Press, 1986). A common pattern among rural families was for parents to follow their children who preceded them in moving west. For an example among English settlers, see Arthur A. Halbach, *Dyersville: Its History and Its People* (Milwaukee: St. Joseph's Press, 1939), 93. Adamson's behavior is outlined in Chapter 3.

40. Ruggles has argued that the stem-household pattern dominated American society throughout most of the nineteenth century and that aging parents did not join their children so much as selected children never left. Whereas Ruggles has clearly demonstrated that the stem-household pattern would cease in the twentieth century, his evidence supporting his contention that the multigenerational coresidence in the nineteenth century was largely the result of children staying with parents rather than aging parents joining their children's households is less convincing. See Steven Ruggles, "The Transformation of American Family Structure," *American Historical Review* 99 (1994): 103–28.

41. Emily Hawley Gillespie diary, ISHDIC, also available in Lensink, *"A Secret to Be Buried."*

42. Emily Hawley Gillespie diary, 31 October, 6 November 1862, ISHDIC.

43. Ibid., 29 December 1862.

44. Ibid., 9, 18 August, 25 October 1863.

45. Recall that Gillespie herself was perplexed when her own father later arrived unexpectedly at her door to live with her in his old age. See Chapter 5.

46. Emily Hawley Gillespie diary, 19 April 1884, ISHDIC (emphasis in original).

47. Ibid., 24 September 1872 (emphasis in original).

48. Ibid., 29 July 1877 (emphasis in original).

49. Ibid., 16 January 1878 (emphasis in original).

50. Ibid., 8 October 1881 (emphasis in original). One of the most interesting aspects of Gillespie's diary is its account of her efforts to distinguish herself from her husband with regard to education and "progress." She encourages her children to aspire to "something higher," whereas her husband remains first and foremost a farmer who is increasingly offered less and less help in his farmwork by his children and wife. His resentment undoubtedly smolders as he labors in the farmyard.

51. Ibid., 11 July 1883.

52. Ibid., 1 December 1885.

53. Ibid., 27 December 1885 (emphasis in original).

54. Ibid., 24 February 1886. Despite Gillespie's fears, her children did return to care

for her in the last years before her death in 1888, which is more than she did for her own parents.

55. Gillespie's comments in her diary provide only one angle of vision of the dynamic that operated within her home. Another view, transcribed in the diary, was offered by Emily's sister, with whom Emily also quarreled. The sister did not "blame James at all. he has always been a perfect slave to the children and you. . . . he is a perfect slave, worse than the niggers in the south." See ibid., 15 March 1885.

56. Quick, *One Man's Life*, 120.

57. See John Hajnal, "European Marriage Patterns in Perspective," in *Population in History: Essays in Historical Demography*, ed. D. V. Glass and D. E. C. Eversley (Chicago: Aldine, 1965), 101–43.

58. Kathleen Neils Conzen provides a map of Europe that clearly divides the regions of impartibility and partibility. See Kathleen Neils Conzen, "Peasant Pioneers: Generational Succession among German Farmers in Frontier Minnesota," in *The Countryside in the Age of Capitalist Transformation: Essays in the Social History of Rural America*, ed. Stephen Hahn and Jonathan Prude (Chapel Hill: University of North Carolina Press, 1985), 263. In addition, see Kathleen Neils Conzen, *Making Their Own America: Assimilation Theory and the German Peasant Pioneer* (New York: Berg, 1990), an exemplary study of a German Catholic cultural area that practiced impartible inheritance. Significantly, land used to provide for offspring could be obtained by forming settlements based on chain migrations to the west, where land was less expensive and more plentiful. See, for example, Royden K. Loewen, *Family, Church, and Market: A Mennonite Community in the Old and the New Worlds, 1850–1930* (Urbana: University of Illinois Press, 1993), 195–217.

59. This household pattern was particularly common in Scandinavia, central Europe (Germany, Czechoslovakia, Austria, and Switzerland), and the Celtic fringe of Europe. The literature on European household structures in general and the stem household in particular is large. The originator of the debate was Frédéric Le Play, who argued that household systems were divided into "patriarchal," "stem," and "unstable" systems. See Frédéric Le Play, *La Réforme sociale* (Tours: Mame, 1872), 352–58, and *Les Ouvriers européens: Etudes sur les travaux, la vie domestique et la condition morale des populations ouvrières de l'Europe, et leur relations avec les autres classes, précédé d'un exposé de la méthode d'observation* (Paris: Imprimerie Impériale, 1855). Much debate has centered on how pervasive the stem household was in Europe. See, for example, Peter Laslett and Richard Wall, *Household and Family in Past Time* (Cambridge: Cambridge University Press, 1972); Kenneth W. Wachter, E. A. Hammel, and Peter Laslett, *Statistical Studies of Historical Social Structure* (New York: Academic Press, 1978); and Emmanuel Todd, *The Explanation of Ideology: Family Structures and Social Systems*, trans. David Garrioch (London: Basil Blackwell, 1985). Yet the stem-household system certainly existed in areas where contracts that institutionalized it were common.

60. See David Gaunt, "The Property and Kin Relations of Retired Farmers in Northern and Central Europe," in *Family Forms in Historic Europe*, ed. Richard Wall (Cambridge: Cambridge University Press, 1983); Eli Fure, "Gamle i flergenerasjonsfamilier — en seiglivet myte?" *Historisk tidsskrift* 65 (1986): 16–35; Ulla Rosén, *Himlajord och handelsvara: Ägobyten av egendom i Kumla socken, 1780–1880* (Lund, Sweden: Lund University Press, 1994); Lutz K. Berkner, "The Stem Family and the Development Cycle of the Peasant Household: An Eighteenth-Century Austrian Example," *American Historical Review* 77 (1972): 398–418; Hans Christian Johansen, "The Position of the Old in the Rural Household in a Traditional Society," *Scandinavian Economic History Review* 24 (1976): 129–42; Thomas Held, "Rural Retirement Arrangements in Seventeenth- to Nineteenth-Century Austria: A Cross-Community Analysis," *Journal of Family History* 7 (1982): 227–55; Hermann Rebel, "Peasant Stem Families in Early Modern Austria: Life Plans, Status Tactics, and the Grid of Inheritance," *Social Science History* 2 (1978): 255–91, and *Peasant Classes: The Bureaucrati-*

zation of Property and Family Relations under Early Habsburg Absolutism, 1511–1636 (Princeton: Princeton University Press, 1983); and H. W. Spiegel, "The Altenteil: German Farmers' Old Age Security," *Rural Sociology* 4 (1939): 203–18.

61. The constraints that youths experienced might explain a relatively common observation that members of the second generation were "inferior in social character" when compared to their parents. See Joseph Schafer, "The Yankee and the Teuton in Wisconsin: IV. Some Social Traits of Teutons," *Wisconsin Magazine of History* 7 (1923): 15.

62. Over one-fifth (22 percent; N=109) of the immigrant households in Minnesota in 1885 that had originated in Rättvik, Sweden, for example, were extended. About one-seventh (14.3 percent; N=294) of the households in a Norwegian American community in central Wisconsin in 1880 had two or more married couples coresiding in a stem-family-like arrangement. These figures are noteworthy because they are considerably higher than figures for the United States as a whole, where from 4 to 7 percent of the population lived in "three-generation" households. Moreover, the incidence of stem households in the Norwegian American community slightly exceeded the proportion of such households in the sending community in western Norway in the mid-nineteenth century. See Robert C. Ostergren, *A Community Transplanted: The Trans-Atlantic Experience of a Swedish Immigrant Settlement in the Upper Middle West, 1835–1915* (Madison: University of Wisconsin Press, 1988), 257–58, and Steven Ruggles, "Prolonged Connections: Demographic Change and the Rise of the Extended Family in Nineteenth Century America" (Ph.D. dissertation, University of Pennsylvania, 1983), 10. Using the 1900 federal census public-use sample, D. S. Smith found that immigrants in the United States over age fifty-five (with the exception of the British-born) were more likely to live with their children than the New England-born, who typically lived alone, with their spouses, or with other kin. See D. S. Smith, "Modernization and the Family Structure of the Elderly in the United States," *Zeitschrift für Gerontologie* 17 (1984): table 3.

63. Olaf Walby family interview, Viroqua, Wisconsin, 1947, Peter A. Munch field notes, Peter A. Munch Papers, NAHA.

64. Knudt Rundhaug interview, Blanchardville, Wisconsin, 1949, Peter A. Munch field notes, Peter A. Munch Papers, NAHA.

65. See Mark W. Friedberger, "Handing Down the Home Place: Farm Inheritance Strategies in Iowa, 1870–1945," *Annals of Iowa* 47 (1984): 518–36, and *Farm Families and Change in Twentieth-Century America* (Lexington: University Press of Kentucky, 1988), chap. 4; Kenneth H. Parsons and Eliot O. Waples, *Keeping the Farm in the Family*, Research Bulletin no. 157 (Madison: Wisconsin Agricultural Extension Service, 1945); and Robert C. Ostergren, "Land and Family in Rural Immigrant Communities," *Annals of the Association of American Geographers* 71 (1981): 400–411.

66. Carl F. Wehrwein, "Bonds of Maintenance as Aids in Acquiring Farm Ownership," *Journal of Land and Public Utility Economics* 8 (1932): 396–403. Friedberger, *Farm Families and Change*, also provides examples of written agreements culled from the probate dockets of Benton County, Iowa.

67. Wehrwein, "Bonds of Maintenance"; Parsons and Waples, *Keeping the Farm in the Family*, 6. *Inter vivos* transfers, Friedberger stresses, were not undertaken exclusively by European Americans. Most contemporary analyses of the practice note that it was a European tradition brought into the Middle West. See Friedberger, "Handing Down the Home Place," 6.

68. Miner, *Culture and Agriculture*, 33.

69. M. N. Daffinrud interview, Viroqua, Wisconsin, 1947, Peter A. Munch field notes, Peter A. Munch Papers, NAHA. In another mid-twentieth-century neighborhood, neither the Bohemians nor the "Generalized Iowans" had a stem-family system replete with a second house for the retired couple. In this area, only the Amish continued their Old

World ways. See Edward Kibbe and Thomas McGorkle, "Culture and Medical Behavior in a Bohemian Speech Community in Iowa," unpublished paper, University of Iowa, 1957, 3, Peter A. Munch Papers, NAHA. Partible and impartible inheritance strategies, of course, could blend into one another according to the exigencies of individual households. Families that hoped to divide their real wealth could face situations in which equal bequests would provide land parcels too small to sustain heirs, therefore making unequal divisions necessary. Families that customarily practiced impartible inheritance of land, on the other hand, might deviate from impartibility to set up more than one child if the primary heir could sustain the parents adequately.

70. The following discussion is based on two datasets involving families of Norwegian-immigrant origin. The first population, originating in the Fortun and Dale parishes of Luster, Norway, has been assembled from a complete genealogical study (Lars E. Øyane, *Gards- og Ættesoge for Luster Kommune* [Oslo: Norbok, 1984], vols. 1–3) that includes not only the immigrants but also their children. This dataset comprises 706 immigrant couples married in the United States, of which slightly over one-half settled in the vicinity of Crawford and Vernon Counties, Wisconsin. These families had 3,783 children. The coding of the data has enabled me to determine the position of individuals within their households of origination in relation to future life chances such as schooling and marriage. The second population is from a group of church parishes in the Norway Grove and Spring Prairie settlements in Wisconsin. This dataset, consisting of 1,402 families (of which 261 couples or 18.6 percent were married in Norway) and 4,055 children, was compiled from information recorded in the Lutheran church books. Additional details on these families taken from the federal manuscript censuses of 1860, 1870, 1880, 1900, and 1910 were integrated into the dataset.

71. Although birth order influenced the chances to marry, it was less significant in affecting patterns of age at marriage. The first-born male, more secure in his likelihood to marry, nonetheless wed on average at an older age than sons born after him. The mean age at first marriage decreased from 29.4 years for first-born males to 27.7 years for third-born males (see table 7.5). In the later birth orders, age at marriage, like the proportion married, increased and again tended to mirror the patterns for the first-born male. Daughters, on the other hand, not only married at earlier ages than their brothers, but first-born daughters—in contrast to their male counterparts—wed on average at ages younger than any other group. The age of marriage for girls, in contrast to their brothers, tended to ascend in the middle birth orders. First-born boys married an average 5.7 years older than first-born girls, but the interval lessened as birth order increased.

72. For greater detail, see Jon Gjerde and Anne McCants, "Fertility, Marriage, and Culture: Demographic Processes among Immigrants to the Rural Middle West," *Journal of Economic History* 55 (1995): 860–87.

73. In the home community of Balestrand, 71.4 percent of the families were nuclear in 1801 and 1865 (N=913) and 66.4 percent in 1875 and 1900 (N=413). The mean age in the immigrant communities was only 18.7 years, which underscores the youth of the settlement. For a fuller discussion, see Gjerde, "Patterns of Migration," 277–97.

74. The TMFR measures the average number of children that would have been born to a woman in a marriage that lasted throughout a woman's period of fertility based on observed incidences of births in the population at risk. See Gjerde and McCants, "Fertility, Marriage, and Culture."

75. For further documentation, see Gjerde, "Patterns of Migration."

76. These and the following figures are derived from the two datasets described in note 69 above. I have integrated information from the decennial federal census manuscripts into each dataset. I am therefore able to portray tendencies of schooling and remaining within the household by age and birth order. Since the family reconstitution charts the

incidence of death among people within the population, no mortality bias exists within the data. The numbers of risk, however, are lower than those introduced above.

77. These patterns contrast with another study that found first-born boys in a national sample *more* likely to leave their home counties than their younger brothers and sisters. See Francesca A. Florey and Avery M. Guest, "Coming of Age among U.S. Farm Boys in the Late 1800s: Occupational and Residential Choices," *Journal of Family History* 13 (1988): 233–49.

78. The proportion of first-born sons who inherited estates in Norway from 1700 to 1780 was 83.7 percent (N=130); between 1781 and 1835, 81.1 percent (N=136); and between 1836 and 1900, 77.1 percent (N=140). See Øyane, *Gards- og Ættesoge.*

79. It is of interest, then, that life expectancy followed a similar pattern according to birth order and sex. Whereas first-born boys who survived to age five could expect to live 61.3 years, first-born girls who survived to age five lived an average of 68.8 years. And whereas the length of life increased for boys in the second and third birth-order positions, it decreased for girls in similar positions. Thus boys born third in a family lived on average 1.2 years longer than third-born girls, a clear deviation from the general trend of longer female life expectancy.

80. Thomas J. Pressly and William H. Scofield, *Farm Real Estate Values in the United States by Counties, 1850–1959* (Seattle: University of Washington Press, 1965), 32. Specifically, land values increased from $14 an acre in Vernon County and $10 an acre in Crawford County in 1890 to $43 and $29 an acre in 1910, respectively. Land prices in Dane County, where Norway Grove is situated, increased from $26 an acre in 1890 to $92 an acre in 1910.

81. It is noteworthy that marriage age was high in the immigrants' home regions of Norway. In the nineteenth century, the average age at marriage of men who inherited their parents' farms was 29.4. See Øyane, *Gards- og Ættesoge.* In Norway as a whole, the mean age at first marriage was 28.6 years between 1840 and 1865. See Michael Drake, *Population and Society in Norway, 1735–1865* (Cambridge: Cambridge University Press, 1969), 78.

82. Survival to marrying age is defined as living to at least age twenty-five.

83. See Garrison Keillor, *Lake Wobegon Days* (New York: Viking, 1985), 151.

84. The percentages for women twenty-five years and older, on the other hand, remained similar in 1880 and 1900. By 1900, girls' attendance at school had increased to the point that there was little difference between schooling for boys or girls by age, perhaps a sign of the improved status of women.

85. Quick, *Fairview Idea,* 8–10.

86. Ibid., 11–12.

87. In part, this reduction was the result of the reversion of multiple-family households to extended households upon the death of an older member. The simplification of household structure was also due somewhat to an altered age structure: the mean age in the population decreased from 27.9 to 24.6 years between 1880 and 1900. Yet longitudinal data, which chart household structure over time, reveal that the increase in extended households was more likely the result of family members—most notably elderly parents— joining simple households. The household structure prior to the creation of a household extended upward had been a simple family household over half of the time (51 percent; N=61). Only 15 percent had been multiple-family households with secondary units older than the head.

88. The augmentation of parents in Anglo-American households became increasingly prevalent in the late nineteenth century. Ruggles found that 21 percent of the households in a large sample from Erie County, New York, were "extended." See Ruggles, "Prolonged Connections," and Daniel Scott Smith, "Life Course, Norms, and Family Systems of Old Americans in 1900," *Journal of Family History* 4 (1979): 285–98.

89. Sweetser also notes the shift from patrilineal to matrilineal extensions in households

cross-culturally. The explanation given is structural, that is, the changing nature of work within the household resulted in different preferences for kin. See Dorrian Apple Sweetser, "Love and Work: Intergenerational Household Composition in the U.S. in 1900," *Journal of Marriage and the Family* 46 (1984): 289–93. See also Dorrian Apple Sweetser, "Asymmetry in Intergenerational Family Relationships," *Social Forces* 41 (1963): 346–52, and Smith, "Life Course," 285–98.

90. Aside from families composed of parents and children, households composed of widows and children remained stable for the longest duration.

91. That choice, in fact, was probably due to widows' ability to use land as a powerful tool in their relationships with their children. Sonya Salamon and Ann Mackey Keim argue with regard to a present-day German American community that women who controlled the patrimony after the deaths of their husbands augmented their authority in the household during their old age. See Sonya Salamon and Ann Mackey Keim, "Land Ownership and Women's Power in a Midwestern Farming Community," *Journal of Marriage and the Family* 41 (1979): 109–19.

92. The sample size derived from Øyane, *Gards- og Ættesoge*, was 461.

93. For a detailed analysis of cultural innovation with particular reference to changes in marital fertility, see Gjerde and McCants, "Fertility, Marriage, and Culture."

94. Hamlin Garland, "Among the Corn Rows," in *Main-Travelled Roads*, 108–9 (emphasis in original).

95. Ibid., 113–14.

96. Ibid., 114–15 (emphasis in original).

97. Ibid., 116–20.

98. It is perhaps not a coincidence that cultural groups that practiced partible inheritance tended to be those whose communities made great efforts to restrict outside interference from the state and society, efforts that will be considered in greater depth in the next section of the book.

Chapter Eight

1. Herbert Quick, *One Man's Life* (Indianapolis: Bobbs-Merrill, 1925), 115, 117–18.

2. Ibid., 115.

3. Ibid., 123–25.

4. Waldemar Ager, "Vore Kulturelle Muligheter," in *Cultural Pluralism vs. Assimilation*, ed. Odd S. Lovoll (Northfield, Minn.: Norwegian-American Historical Association, 1981), 49, 47.

5. Joh. A. Enander, *Valda skrifter af Joh. A. Enander* (Chicago, 1892), 1:64, cited in H. Arnold Barton, *A Folk Divided: Homeland Swedes and Swedish Americans, 1840–1940* (Carbondale: University of Southern Illinois Press, 1994), 67.

6. William L. Yancey, Eugene P. Ericksen, and Richard N. Juliani, "Emergent Ethnicity: A Review and Reformulation," *American Sociological Review* 41 (1976): 391–403.

7. Jonathan D. Sarna, "From Immigrants to Ethnics: Toward a New Theory of 'Ethnicization,'" *Ethnicity* 5 (1978): 370–78.

8. See John Useem and Ruth Useem, "Minority-Group Patterns in Prairie Society," *American Journal of Sociology* 50 (1945): 377–85, and Horace Miner, *Culture and Agriculture: An Anthropological Study of a Corn Belt County* (Ann Arbor: University of Michigan Press, 1949), 16.

9. Interview with Mr. Daffinrud, 1947, Peter A. Munch field notes, Peter A. Munch Papers, NAHA. In a fictional account by Ruth Suckow, a German couple who travel from their Iowa farm to the Mayo Clinic in Rochester, Minnesota, for medical treatment for

the husband just after World War I are amazed by the geographical and cultural variation. "They had never gone farther on the train together than to Dubuque, about thirty
miles away," wrote Suckow. "The trip up to Minnesota . . . had interest for them. It was
almost the first time that they had been in any other State than Iowa. . . . [The hus-
band] kept watching to see how the country looked. . . . He saw some nice farms, he
said. But the land was flatter than around home, and a fellow to whom he had been talking told him that they had more wind up here. [He] said he didn't think he'd like to live
where they were all Swedes and Norwegians. He hadn't seen any farms yet that looked
better than his own in Richland Township." See Ruth Suckow, *Country People* (New York:
Alfred A. Knopf, 1924), 117–19.

10. See *Dubuque Herald*, 28 March 1860, 3; *Dubuque National Demokrat*, 10 February 1876,
3, trans. J. K. Downing, CDH; and *Die Iowa*, 31 January 1878, 5.

11. See *Die Iowa*, 27 June 1878, 8; 19 June 1879, 5.

12. Edward Kibbe and Thomas McGorkle, "Culture and Medical Behavior in a Bohemian Speech Community in Iowa," unpublished paper, University of Iowa, 1957, 13–16,
Peter A. Munch Papers, NAHA.

13. Ibid., 20–21.

14. The best scholarship on these explicit efforts by the community leadership to control diffusion is Kathleen Neils Conzen, *Making Their Own America: Assimilation Theory and
the German Peasant Pioneer* (New York: Berg, 1990). In meticulous detail, Conzen describes
the German Catholic attempt to maintain a landed patrimony and to control the political and social institutions in order to preserve their "German peasant" world.

15. Ole Munch Ræder, *America in the Forties: The Letters of Ole Munch Ræder*, ed. and
trans. Gunnar J. Malmin (Minneapolis: University of Minnesota Press, 1929), 151.

16. *Die Iowa*, 29 November 1877, 8; James L. Broderick diary, 30 November 1876, in
The Character of the Country: The Iowa Diary of James L. Broderick, 1876-1877, ed. Loren N.
Horton (Iowa City: Iowa State Historical Department, 1976), 42.

17. James L. Broderick diary, 15 December 1876, in Horton, *Character of the Country*, 52.

18. Ræder, *America in the Forties*, 16.

19. *Die Iowa*, 29 December 1881, 8.

20. *Die Iowa*, 16 September 1880, 8; 7 July 1881, 5.

21. Differences between generations were commonly expressed as fault lines in the
conscious maintenance of cultural isolation. See, for example, Miner, *Culture and Agriculture*, 15.

22. See Clara Jacobson, untitled memoir, 27, SHSW.

23. Unnamed informant to Kate Everest, Herman, Dodge County, Wisconsin, 1892,
Kate Levi Papers, SHSW.

24. See John J. Senn to Kate Everest, Fountain City, Buffalo County, 1892, and unnamed correspondent to Kate Everest, Jefferson, Jefferson County, 1892, both in Kate
Levi Papers, SHSW.

25. Unnamed correspondent to Kate Everest, Burke and Windsor Townships, Dane
County, 1892, Kate Levi Papers, SHSW.

26. Unnamed correspondent to Kate Everest, Centerville Township, Sheboygan
County, 1892, Kate Levi Papers, SHSW.

27. Unnamed correspondent to Kate Everest, Marion Township, Grant County, 1892,
Kate Levi Papers, SHSW.

28. Clara Jacobson, untitled memoir, 31–32, SHSW.

29. Hamlin Garland, "Up the Coulee," in *Main-Travelled Roads: Six Mississippi Valley
Stories* (1891; reprint, New York: Macmillan, 1962), 74.

30. Ernest Mayerhoff to Kate Everest, Wanewoc, Juneau County, Wisconsin, 1893,
Kate Levi Papers, SHSW.

31. Unnamed correspondent to Kate Everest, Lebanon, Dodge County, Wisconsin, 1892, Kate Levi Papers, SHSW.

32. Robert S. Lynd and Helen Merrell Lynd, *Middletown: A Study in American Culture* (New York: Harcourt, Brace, and World, 1929), 178. See also Chapter 5.

33. See Chapters 9 and 10. On immigrants and the rural school, see Daniel F. Reilly, *The School Controversy, 1891–1893* (Washington, D.C.: Catholic University of America Press, 1943); Frank C. Nelsen, "The School Controversy among Norwegian Immigrants," *Norwegian-American Studies* 26 (1974): 206–19; and Theodore C. Blegen, "The Immigrant and the Common School," in *Norwegian Migration to America: The American Transition*, 2 vols. (Northfield, Minn.: Norwegian-American Historical Association, 1940), 2:241–76. For a local example, see Arne Anderson, "The History of School District Number Four, Town of Windsor, Dane County, Wisc.," unpublished manuscript, 1955, SHSW. In fact, if they did not go to school together, children were unlikely, according to an Iowa informant, to mix together. See Walter T. Henderson and Emma L. Henderson oral history, 7, ISHDIC.

34. The language of instruction was not exclusively English in school districts dominated by specific linguistic groups. Importantly, however, schools with heterogeneous student populations were usually taught in English.

35. Anderson, "History of School District Number Four."

36. Quick, *One Man's Life*, 249.

37. Anderson, "History of School District Number Four."

38. Miner, *Culture and Agriculture*, 73–74.

39. Children's essay competition, essay by a girl named Gellhorn, 1923, 2, ISHDIC.

40. John M. Stromsten, "Memoirs of My Life," 18, ISHDIC.

41. Anna Johnson, "Recollections of a Country School Teacher," *Annals of Iowa* 42 (1975): 486.

42. Young immigrant women were marked for domestic service to such a degree that the *St. Paul Daily Pioneer* commented that the arrival of a group of immigrants who were mainly young women "foreshadows a good supply of domestics in years to come." Odd S. Lovoll estimates that four-fifths of Norwegian women working outside of their homes served as domestics. See *St. Paul Daily Pioneer*, 3 July 1866, 2, and Odd S. Lovoll, *The Promise of America: A History of the Norwegian-American People* (Minneapolis: University of Minnesota Press, 1984), 167.

43. Joseph Schafer, "The Yankee and the Teuton in Wisconsin: V. Social Harmonies and Discords," *Wisconsin Magazine of History* 7 (1923): 154.

44. Clara Jacobson, untitled memoir, 31, SHSW.

45. Theodore Dreiser, *Sister Carrie* (New York: Doubleday, Page, 1900); Hamlin Garland, *Rose of Dutcher's Coolly* (New York: Macmillan, 1899). See Chapters 6 and 9.

46. William Foote Whyte memoirs, 17, 19, William Foote Whyte Papers, SHSW.

47. See the discussion of the differences between men and women, young and old, in resisting English in Chapter 4.

48. *Dubuque National Demokrat*, 23 November 1858, 3, trans. J. K. Downing, CDH.

49. Ræder, *America in the Forties*, 151, 40.

50. John J. Senn to Kate Everest, Fountain City, Buffalo County, Wisconsin, 1892, Kate Levi Papers, SHSW.

51. *Die Iowa*, 9 September 1880, 8. The virtues of bilingualism were made more evident by newspaper reports about the difficulties of monolingual people. In one case, a true "Babel" reigned when a woman who could speak only German had to hire an interpreter to speak to her son who had lived in New England for fourteen years. Another case was more complicated. A well-heeled American woman hired a Luxemburger coachman and a Hessian gardener. The woman and the Hessian were monolingual. In order for them to communicate, the woman gave instructions in English to her daughter, who translated

them into French, which the Luxemburger could manage to translate into German. See *Minneapolis Tribune*, 16 September 1871, 2, and *Die Iowa*, 4 May 1882, 8.

52. Sever Anderson and Rubin Anderson interview, Wild Rose, Waushara County, Wisconsin, 1946, Douglas G. Marshall field notes, Peter A. Munch Papers, NAHA. Diffusion in the opposite direction was so remarkable that it was reported in papers. One paper reported that Fred W. Lemmers, an American who had married a Swede, "was completely at home with the Swedish language" and that "many considered [him] to be almost a Swede." See *Svenska Amerikanska Posten*, 11 January 1887, 1.

53. Martha Reishus, *The Rag Rug* (New York: Vantage Press, 1955), 244.

54. *Dubuque Herald*, 23 May 1860, 2. The "town" continued to be a magnet. By the twentieth century, when the automobile had made it possible for rural people to pursue nonfarm activities, going to town on Saturday night was a summer "ritual" as well as a "family affair." See Carl Hamilton, *In No Time at All* (Ames: Iowa State University Press, 1974), 10–12.

55. On Irish stereotypes, see Dale T. Knobel, *Paddy and the Republic: Ethnicity and Nationality in Antebellum America* (Middletown, Conn.: Wesleyan University Press, 1986).

56. *Daily Minnesotan*, 5 June 1857, 3.

57. *St. Paul Pioneer*, 9 June 1866, 4; *Dubuque Herald*, 14 March 1860, 5.

58. Among the most successful groups in these efforts were Mennonite communities in the western United States. See, for example, Lee E. Deets, *The Hutterites: A Study in Social Cohesion* (1939; reprint, Philadelphia: Porcupine Press, 1975), and Royden K. Loewen, *Family, Church, and Market: A Mennonite Community in the Old and the New Worlds, 1850–1930* (Urbana: University of Illinois Press, 1993).

59. As we shall see in the next chapter, leaders of ethnic and religious organizations developed a parallel critique of the dangers of American life that they broadcast in print form throughout the region.

60. See Conzen, *Making Their Own America*, 9, 8.

61. Ferryville, Wisconsin, 1947, Peter A. Munch field notes, and Mrs. John Evans interview, Wild Rose, Waushara County, Wisconsin, 1946, Douglas G. Marshall field notes, both in Peter A. Munch Papers, NAHA.

62. August Kickbusch to Kate Everest, Wausau, Marathon County, 1892, and unnamed correspondent to Kate Everest, Herman, Dodge County, 1892, both in Kate Everest field notes, Kate Levi Papers, SHSW. In some neighborhoods, Norwegians were singled out for retaining their own language; in fact, they spoke their native tongue longer than more recent arrivals from Poland. See Mr. and Mrs. Torge L. Thompson interview, Wild Rose, Waushara County, Wisconsin, 1946, Douglas G. Marshall field notes, Peter A. Munch Papers, NAHA. Beneath these broad categories, however, local conditions decisively influenced the vectors of change, as interviews by rural sociologists clearly show.

63. Quick, *One Man's Life*, 249; Joseph Schafer, "The Yankee and the Teuton in Wisconsin: IV. Some Social Traits of Teutons," *Wisconsin Magazine of History* 7 (1923): 17–18.

64. Welker Given, *A Luxemburg Idyll in Early Iowa* (1922). See also Sister Mary De Paul Faber, "*The Luxemburger Gazette*: A Catholic German Language Paper of the Middle West, 1872–1918" (M.A. thesis, Catholic University of America, 1948), 20–21.

65. Given, *Luxemburg Idyll*, 5–6.

66. Ibid., 9–10. For boys, "the serpent that crept into their Eden carried a base ball and bat" (ibid., 11). "The American game," to Given, promoted a spirit of "efficiency, punch, teamwork, drive" that ruled sport and business and inhibited a European Catholic pattern of corporative equality.

67. Miner, *Culture and Agriculture*, 41.

68. Edward O. Moe and Carl C. Taylor, *Culture of a Contemporary Rural Community: Irwin, Iowa*, Bureau of Agricultural Economics Rural Life Studies no. 5 (Washington, D.C.: U.S.

Department of Agriculture, 1942), 53–54. After movies, radio was considered the next most influential force encouraging emigration of youth. Dancing was dangerous as well since it led folk down a slippery slope: "Once people get started, they want to do nothing but dance; then smoking and drinking follow, and then even more serious moral breakdown."

69. Miner, *Culture and Agriculture*, 50–51. As late as World War II, only 52 percent of rural Norwegian immigrants in a western Iowa community regarded attendance at movies as "proper." Only 16 percent approved of Sunday movies. See Useem and Useem, "Minority-Group Patterns," 383.

70. The episodes in both St. Donatus and Hardin County suggest that age was another crucial variable in determining the rates of cultural change in local ethnic communities. Youths repeatedly seemed more willing to use English; they were more influenced by the secular values prescribed by the commercial media. Importantly, these outside influences were not only more "modern" but also more focused on individualized behavior that challenged the conventions of family and community upon which immigrant settlements in the Middle West often relied.

71. Reishus, *The Rag Rug*, 152; Suckow, *Country People*, 194. On shifts in naming patterns, see Jon Gjerde, *From Peasants to Farmers: The Migration from Balestrand, Norway, to the Upper Middle West* (New York: Cambridge University Press, 1985), 202–31, and Einar Haugen, *The Norwegian Language in America: A Study in Bilingual Behavior* (Philadelphia: University of Pennsylvania Press, 1953). Haugen was one of the first scholars to note what he called "symbolic alliterative repetition," which modified the patronymic pattern so that names with an alliterative resemblance could substitute for old names (for example, Ed could substitute for Eivind).

72. The Scandinavian naming pattern followed clear rules. First sons were named after paternal grandfathers and second sons after maternal grandfathers. Daughters too were named after their grandparents, the first daughter often carrying the name of her mother's mother. If death occurred, the naming pattern was disrupted. If an infant who had been named after a grandparent died, the next child of the same sex took the same name, thus symbolically maintaining the souls of both sibling and grandparent. Likewise, if a spouse died, the first child born of the same sex to the survivor in his or her next marriage took the name of the deceased.

73. The custom had dissolved, that is, if the experiences of the Norway Grove settlement in Dane County, Wisconsin, are any indication. A dataset taken from the Norway Grove population tested the maintenance of traditional naming patterns within the population. I determined what percentage of families that contained two or more boys named their first two sons after their grandparents. The breakdown in naming customs in Norway Grove occurred in a stepwise fashion. About two-thirds of families between 1830 and 1849 maintained the pattern (65.9 percent; N=41); about one-half from 1850 to 1869 (47.7 percent; N=151); about one-quarter in the 1870s (24.4 percent; N=78); and almost none thereafter (4.8 percent; N=145).

74. See Chapter 4. See also Joseph Schafer, *The Wisconsin Lead Region* (Madison: State Historical Society of Wisconsin, 1932), 245–46, and Richard M. Bernard, *The Melting Pot and the Altar: Marital Assimilation in Early Twentieth-Century Wisconsin* (Minneapolis: University of Minnesota Press, 1980). Bernard discovered "out-group marriage rates" of 13.7 percent and 11.3 percent for first-generation Germans and Norwegians, respectively, in 1880; the respective percentages were 19.8 percent and 14.5 percent for the second generation. By 1910, the rates were significantly higher. See ibid., 66.

75. Mrs. Birkelo interview, Viroqua, Wisconsin, 1947, Peter A. Munch field notes, Peter A. Munch Papers, NAHA.

76. Mr. and Mrs. William Graydon interview, 24 July 1946, Douglas G. Marshall field notes, Peter A. Munch Papers, NAHA. Other interviewees also noted the connection between declining fertility and increased intermarriage. See Mr. and Mrs. Justine Gunderson interview and Mrs. Alfred Attoe interview, both on 23 July 1946, Douglas G. Marshall field notes, Peter A. Munch Papers, NAHA.

77. Kathleen Neils Conzen argues that these shared traditions were the basis for "pluralisms of place"—localized identifications that evolved out of core ethnic traditions that diffused outward into local society. See Kathleen Neils Conzen, "Mainstreams and Side Channels: The Localization of Immigrant Cultures," *Journal of American Ethnic History* 11 (1991): 13.

78. Stromsten, "Memoirs of My Life," 13.

79. Mrs. Philipson interview, Blanchardville, Wisconsin, 1949, Peter A. Munch field notes, Peter A. Munch Papers, NAHA. Public displays often reinforced for residents the salience of differing ethnic pasts. Dano-German conflict, for example, erupted in the town of Davenport, Iowa, when Danes annually commemorated a previous victory over the Germans in Schleswig-Holstein by staging a parade through town. Not surprisingly, German Americans lined the streets during the procession and disrupted the ceremony by shouting jeers and insults. See C. Carnahan Goetsch, "The Immigrant and America: Assimilation of a German Family, Part I," *Annals of Iowa* 42 (1973): 20.

80. F. W. Bryant to Brother Charley, Farley, Iowa, 1 October 1876, UILSC.

81. Hubbel Pierce letter, North Dakota, 4 June 1879, in Elizabeth Hampsten, *Read This Only to Yourself: The Private Writings of Midwestern Women, 1880-1910* (Bloomington: Indiana University Press, 1982), 176; May Morse Short diary, 16 July 1900, ISHDIC.

82. Phil Poulson interview and "salesman" interview, Blanchardville, Wisconsin, 1949, Peter A. Munch field notes, Peter A. Munch Papers, NAHA.

83. See Sarna, "From Immigrants to Ethnics," 370–78; Yancey, Ericksen, and Juliani, "Emergent Ethnicity," 391–403; and Nathan Glazer and Daniel P. Moynihan, *Beyond the Melting Pot* (Cambridge: Massachusetts Institute of Technology Press, 1963).

84. Sarna, "From Immigrants to Ethnics," 375.

85. Hortus Florum, in *Die Iowa*, 13 December 1877, 5 (emphasis added).

86. *Die Iowa*, 26 February 1880, 5 (emphasis added). Religion, as well as national background, as this quotation indicates, was often a basis of "otherness." "The Americans around here are most all Methodist," wrote a Dutchman, "but I believe there are very many good people among them" (Sjoerd Aukes Sipma letter, Pella, Iowa, March 1848, ISHDDM).

87. *Die Iowa*, 26 August 1875, 5. Newspaper correspondence noted not only the salutary effects of common ethnicity in encouraging settlement but also the problems that occurred when people with less desirable backgrounds lived nearby. As we observed in Chapter 7, because possession of land accorded both cultural and economic resources to the community and its membership and because it was finite, it was a resource coveted by ethnic groups. In one extreme case, members of a German community in central Iowa County would not permit a Yankee to purchase land in their midst even though he had married a German woman (Miner, *Culture and Agriculture*, 15n).

88. *Dubuque National Demokrat*, 9 November 1858, 3, trans. J. K. Downing, CDH; *Goodhue County (Minnesota) Republican*, 5 June 1863, 3.

89. *Dubuque Times*, 6 November 1876, cited in *Dubuque National Demokrat*, 9 November 1876, 3, trans. J. K. Downing, CDH.

90. See "A Shameful Riot," *St. Paul Daily Press*, 7 July 1863, 4; "Desperate Riot at Union Park Gardens," *St. Paul Pioneer*, 7 July 1863, 4; *St. Paul Pioneer*, 8 July 1863, 4; and "The Riot on Sunday," *St. Paul Pioneer*, 9 July 1863, 4.

91. See *Minneapolis Daily Tribune*, 25 December 1869, 3; *Duluth Minnesotan*, 1 January 1870, 3; *St. Anthony Falls (Minnesota) Democrat*, 7 January 1870, 2; and "The Bloody Affray at Moose Lake," *Duluth Minnesotan*, 8 January 1870, 3.

92. "Bloody Row at Brainard . . . Railroad Men vs. Swedes," *St. Paul Daily Press*, 31 July 1872, 4.

93. "Attempted Lynching in Steele County," *St. Paul Dispatch*, 4 February 1874, 4; "Robbery and Attempted Lynching," *Owatonna (Minnesota) Journal*, 5 February 1874, 3.

94. *Die Iowa*, 25 December 1879, 5. Different methods of fraud abounded. In one ruse, two apparent strangers on the road asked to spend the night at a farmhouse. They began to talk to one another, struck a deal, and asked the farmer to sign as a witness. Later, the farmer discovered that the document he had signed was a note. See *Die Iowa*, 15 November 1883, 5. Another swindle occurred when a cattle dealer purchased $100,000 worth of cattle, shipped the animals out of state, transferred their ownership to his brother, and then declared bankruptcy. Although the dealer was ultimately prosecuted, "business [was] crippled in the whole area" and "so great was the bitterness" that had the swindler been caught, he surely would have been hanged. See *Die Iowa*, 21 February 1878, 8.

95. *Die Iowa*, 14 August 1879, 8.

96. See Arthur A. Halbach, *Dyersville: Its History and Its People* (Milwaukee: St. Joseph's Press, 1939), 125–27.

97. See Arnold Strickon, "Ethnicity and Investment Behavior in a Wisconsin Rural Community," in *Entrepreneurship in Cultural Context*, ed. S. M. Greenfield, Arnold Strickon, and R. Aubey (Albuquerque: University of New Mexico Press, 1979), 173–77.

98. *Dubuque National Demokrat*, 5 February 1859, 3, trans. J. K. Downing, CDH.

99. *Dubuque National Demokrat*, 13 April 1876, 3, trans. J. K. Downing, CDH; *Cascade (Iowa) Pioneer*, 1 October 1880. See also Schafer, "The Yankee and the Teuton in Wisconsin: V," 156. Although business was often transacted within nationality channels, non-German merchants who hoped to increase their business share hired German employees and advertised in German newspapers to appeal to a German clientele. See *Dubuque National Demokrat*, 13 July 1876, 3, trans. J. K. Downing, CDH.

100. See *Dubuque National Demokrat*, 5 February 1859, 3; 7 December 1858, 3, trans. J. K. Downing, CDH, and *Die Iowa*, 27 November 1879, 8.

101. On attorneys, see *Dubuque National Demokrat*, 13 August 1858, 3, trans. J. K. Downing, CDH, and *Die Iowa*, 9 August 1877, 5. On cabbage choppers, see *Dubuque National Demokrat*, 8 October 1858, 3, trans. J. K. Downing, CDH.

102. See Richard Oestreicher, "Urban Working-Class Political Behavior and Theories of American Electoral Politics, 1870–1940," *Journal of American History* 74 (1988): 1257–86, which notes the centrality of ethnic groups in political mobilization.

103. *Dubuque National Demokrat*, 21 April 1858, 2, trans. J. K. Downing, CDH.

104. *Die Iowa*, 10 February 1881, 8. See also *Die Iowa*, 25 July 1878, 8.

105. "Uncle Sam," in *Cascade (Iowa) Pioneer*, 2 September 1881.

106. "Several Workers," in *Dubuque National Demokrat*, 21 June 1858, 3, trans. J. K. Downing, CDH.

107. *Cascade (Iowa) Pioneer*, 7 September 1883.

108. *Svenska Amerikanska Posten*, 10 May 1892, 4, trans. WPA, WPA Papers, MHS. The Irish were not known for their power within the Republican Party, but many other nationalities jealously assumed that they possessed an uncanny political acumen. "Germans in general have not much talent for politics," wrote a newspaper editor, and "Yankees only practice high politics and fish for such offices only where no office hours and tedious work is attached to the salary," but the "Irish are politicians by birth, and it is remarkable that none of them ever leave the old sod before some friends here have promised him an office" (*Cascade [Iowa] Pioneer*, 5 February 1892).

109. *Carroll (Iowa) Demokrat*, cited in *Die Iowa*, 9 November 1876, 5. *Die Iowa* also noted that the naturalization of Germans in Carroll County one year before made "it pretty sour for the Republican Party" (30 September 1875, 5). Republican partisans of German descent were reportedly so rare that it was news when the *Des Moines Register* discovered that someone thought to be German championed Rutherford B. Hayes's presidential campaign. When it came to light that the supporter was Polish rather than German, a German Democratic paper observed that "now the Poles are wrought up and say this Hayes flower did not grow in a Polish garden either" (*Dubuque National Demokrat*, 27 July 1876, 3, trans. J. K. Downing, CDH).

110. *Dubuque Herald*, 6 June 1860, 2 (emphasis added).

111. *St. Paul Daily Pioneer*, 30 August 1871, 2. When William Jennings Bryan spoke in a German and Irish area in the late nineteenth century, he assumed his audience was Democratic. He contended that he could tell Democrats from Republicans because the former were "better looking." After he pointed to a man "with an Irish face" and another "who looked like a German" and correctly predicted their allegiance to Democracy, "he saw a man with a Swedish face looking at him with a hostile eye." Bryan "thought he would have a little fun with him," so he asked, " 'You're a Democrat, aren't you, my good man?' " The man answered, " 'Naw, I ban no Democrat. I ban sick 'bout six weeks, makes me look like one.' " See Joseph Edwin McGovern, *As I Recall* (n.p., n.d.), CDH.

112. See Kerby A. Miller, *Emigrants and Exiles: Ireland and the Irish Exodus to North America* (New York: Oxford University Press, 1985), for a particularly convincing expression of this view.

113. Amy Bridges, "Becoming American: The Working Classes in the United States before the Civil War," in *Working-Class Formation: Nineteenth-Century Patterns in Western Europe and the United States*, ed. Ira Katznelson and Aristide R. Zolberg (Princeton: Princeton University Press, 1986), 157–96.

Chapter Nine

1. Reverend Sassel, in *Die Iowa*, 20 April 1882, 5.

2. See Introduction and Chapter 6.

3. See Chapter 7.

4. See Chapter 8.

5. Reverend Sassel, in *Die Iowa*, 20 April 1882, 5. Sassel's article was written during the heated debate in Iowa over a prohibition amendment to the state constitution that ultimately passed. See Chapter 10. Note that Sassel used the concept of "freedom" to critique societal developments involving behavior that seemingly resulted from excessive freedoms.

6. "The Disorganization of the Family," *Catholic Tribune*, 13 June 1901, 4 (emphasis added).

7. Ibid. Another 1901 article used statistics to show that divorce rates in the United States "surpass the entire REMAINING WORLD," indicating the "realities" that "we have polygamy legalized and flourishing more than in Turkey or other Mohammedan countries" ("Nothing to Boast Of," *Catholic Tribune*, 18 July 1901, 4).

8. Anton H. Walburg, *The Question of Nationality in Its Relations to the Catholic Church in the United States* (Cincinnati, 1889). Walburg distinguishes between "true" and "false" Americanism within the "American nationality." "True" Americanism promotes "the public good and the general welfare of the country" and thus desires the "growth and spread of the Catholic church" (ibid., 39–40). Yet it was "false" Americanism that Walburg analyzed in greatest depth. The following discussion is based on ibid., 40–62.

9. *Fremad*, 16 November 1868, 1.

10. Kerby A. Miller, *Emigrants and Exiles: Ireland and the Irish Exodus to North America* (New York: Oxford University Press, 1985), 534–35.

11. *Die Iowa*, 7 August 1879, 8.

12. *Davenport (Iowa) Demokrat*, 22 March 1877, 5, trans. J. K. Downing, CDH. In fact, the editor concluded, the old saying that "it takes six Turks to fool a Jew and six Jews to fool a single Armenian" could be expanded to maintain that "it takes six Armenians to clap a Yankee on the ear."

13. Charles Wilson (Wilhelm Bedø), in *Frihets-Banneret*, 25 December 1852, cited in Peter A. Munch, "In Search of Identity: Ethnic Awareness and Ethnic Attitudes among Scandinavian Immigrants, 1840–1860," in *Scandinavians in America: Literary Life*, ed. J. R. Christianson (Decorah, Iowa: Symra Literary Society, 1985), 7–8.

14. This analysis relies heavily on papers published in Dubuque such as the *Dubuque National Demokrat*, the *Luxemburger Gazette*, and *Die Iowa*. These papers, according to the *American Newspaper Directory*, as reported by *Die Iowa* in 1875, had by far the largest subscription lists of all German-language journals in Iowa. See *Die Iowa*, 17 June 1875, 6.

15. *Die Iowa*, 12 October 1876, 8.

16. *Die Iowa*, 15 January 1880, 8.

17. *Die Iowa*, 27 November 1884, 8. Yet another reference to the "Dubuque Bluestockings" asked: "How many of these women could cook a soup, do you think, or darn a sock?" (*Die Iowa*, 25 October 1883, 8).

18. *Die Iowa*, 10 February 1876, 8 (italics written in English in original).

19. Even American churches were seen as encouraging leisure. A Baptist tabernacle, for example, was converted into an ice-skating rink; an Episcopal church, which taught "the Gospel of Henry VIII of England," held no church services at all in July and August, indicating that its members apparently "do not require the Lord in summer." "Certain people," *Die Iowa* concluded, simply "have a very lowly conception of God's House" (21 September 1882, 8; 20 July 1882, 8).

20. *Die Iowa*, 23 October 1879, 8; *Catholic Tribune*, 28 September 1899, 4. Although the *Catholic Tribune* noted that it "may not agree with the ideas that actuate Women's clubs," it did agree with a resolution of the Federated Women's Clubs of Illinois that denounced the use of "the figure of woman for advertising purposes in either a suggestive or an immodest and immoral manner."

21. *Die Iowa*, 12 October 1882, 8.

22. *Die Iowa*, 8 August 1878, 8.

23. *Dubuque National Demokrat*, 24 February 1876, 3, trans. J. K. Downing, CDH. Children were not solely responsible for this disgrace because it was up to parents to be "severe enough and alert enough to keep their children from these hothouses of bad morals and vice."

24. *Die Iowa*, 19 May 1881, 5.

25. *Die Iowa*, 17 January 1884, 5.

26. *Die Iowa*, 24 August 1876, 8.

27. *Hampton (Iowa) Freie Presse*, cited in *Die Iowa*, 17 January 1884, 5. *Die Iowa* argued that the tradition of Santa Claus illustrated how "Catholic feasts" were "mishandled and degraded." "Americans," it declared, "have lost the meaning" of Christmas since "gift-giving Saint Nicholas" had replaced Christ. See *Die Iowa*, 18 December 1884, 8.

28. "Scandinavier in Amerika," *Luxemburger Gazette*, 29 June 1886, 4. Whereas women were castigated for their tendencies toward leisure, men were commended when they continued their labors. *Die Iowa* reported that a performance of Barnum's circus was attended mainly by American and Irish farmers. "There were few Germans visible," it noted, since "they do not abandon the harvest for the sake of a circus." See *Die Iowa*, 22 July 1880, 8.

29. On the moral implications of women working in factories in mid-nineteenth-century New York City, see Christine Stansell, *City of Women: Sex and Class in New York, 1789–1860* (New York: Alfred A. Knopf, 1982), 125–29.

30. *Milwaukee Seebote*, cited in *Die Iowa*, 16 August 1883, 8.

31. *Die Iowa*, 2 August 1883, 8.

32. *Die Iowa*, 16 August 1883, 8.

33. *Die Iowa*, 3 May 1883, 8 (italics written in English in original). The paper also pointed to the "perils to which girls in the factory are exposed, to the vile language often used there; or to the calumnies against God and man, especially when the factory owner is of lax morals."

34. German-language exchange paper, cited in *Die Iowa*, 24 January 1884, 5.

35. *Die Iowa*, 25 August 1881, 4.

36. The mixing occurred in many venues, including the skating rink, which was yet another example of the "corruption [*verderbnis*] incubating there." Thankfully, the newspaper reported, "a zealous priest . . . went in and dismissed the erring lambs," later delivering "a carefully wrought sermon on punishment." See *Die Iowa*, 24 April 1884, 8; 18 December 1884, 8.

37. *Die Iowa*, 1 November 1883, 5 (italics written in English in original).

38. *Die Iowa*, 28 June 1882, 5.

39. *Die Iowa*, 19 May 1881, 8.

40. It is crucial to note that these sentiments were held widely by immigrant groups. James D. Bratt's excellent study illustrates the laments of Dutch immigrant leaders about the materialism and licentiousness that seemed to be overtaking society. Norwegians, too, feared a growing generation gap. See James D. Bratt, *Dutch Calvinism in Modern America: A History of a Conservative Subculture* (Grand Rapids: William B. Eerdmans, 1984), 57–66, and Waldemar Ager, *Cultural Pluralism versus Assimilation: The Views of Waldemar Ager*, ed. Odd S. Lovoll (Northfield, Minn.: Norwegian-American Historical Association, 1977), 55–63.

41. J. L. Spaulding, *The Religious Mission of the Irish People and Catholic Colonization* (New York: Catholic Publication Society, 1880), 74–77.

42. Interest in fostering rural life based on the belief that it provided a better environment for religious and family life continued well into the twentieth century. The National Catholic Rural Life Conference founded in 1923 was committed to reducing migration to the city. See Philip Gleason, *The Conservative Reformers: German-American Catholics and the Social Order* (Notre Dame: University of Notre Dame Press, 1968), 187–90, and Douglas Fitzgerald Dowd, "The Theory of a Corporative Order: A Study in Social Catholic Thought, with Particular Reference to the United States" (Ph.D. dissertation, University of California at Berkeley, 1952), 30–35.

43. Nicholas Gonner, *Goliath, der Bastardphilister und David, der ehrliche Israelite, oder der Kampf des "katholischen" Anglo-Amerika mit dem katholischen Deutschtum* (Dubuque, 1887), cited in Colman J. Barry, *The Catholic Church and German Americans* (Washington, D.C.: Catholic University of America Press, 1953), 81. To be sure, much of the romantic nostalgia about the superiority of rural life descended from European thinkers. Wilhelm Heinrich Riehl, for example, romanticized the peasant as a source of virtue and obedience. The work of Catholic reformer Frédéric Le Play compared the natural virtue of rural families with the fragmented homes of families in European cities.

44. The small family, observed the German *Lutheran Witness* in 1908, was "no longer confined to the 'Yankees'; it has already invaded every class of the population, and also the Lutheran portion, German and otherwise, is no longer exempt" (cited in Alan Graebner, "Birth Control and the Lutherans: The Missouri Synod as a Case Study," in *Women in American Religion*, ed. Janet Wilson James [Philadelphia: University of Pennsylvania Press, 1980], 235).

45. Among the vast literature on the relationship between family and society, see Edmund S. Morgan, *The Puritan Family: Religion and Domestic Relations in Seventeenth-Century New England* (Boston: Boston Public Library, 1944); Jay Fliegelman, *Prodigals and Pilgrims: The American Revolution against Patriarchal Authority, 1750-1800* (Cambridge: Cambridge University Press, 1982); Edwin G. Burrows and Michael Wallace, "The American Revolution: The Ideology and Psychology of National Liberation," *Perspectives in American History* 6 (1972): 167-306; Linda K. Kerber, *Women of the Republic: Intellect and Ideology in Revolutionary America* (Chapel Hill: University of North Carolina Press, 1980); Mary P. Ryan, *Cradle of the Middle Class: The Family in Oneida County, New York, 1790-1865* (New York: Cambridge University Press, 1981); and Michael Grossberg, *Governing the Hearth: Law and the Family in Nineteenth-Century America* (Chapel Hill: University of North Carolina Press, 1985).

46. Edward Norris Kirk, *The Church Essential to the Republic* (New York: Leavitt, Trow, 1848), 8. French Catholic conservative Frédéric Le Play would most likely have disagreed with Kirk on many issues, but he concurred on the importance of the family: "Private life imprints its character upon public life; the family is the principle of the state." Conversely, he argued that "the family is the image of a society." See Frédéric Le Play, *Les Ouvriers européens* (Paris, 1855), 6 vols., in *Family and Society: A Study of the Sociology of Reconstruction*, ed. and trans. Carle C. Zimmerman and Merle E. Frampton (London: Williams & Norgate, 1935), 454, 468.

47. For a fuller description, see Matthew H. Elbow, *French Corporative Theory, 1789-1948: A Chapter in the History of Ideas* (New York: Columbia University Press, 1953), and Ralph H. Bowen, *German Theories of the Corporative State, with Special Reference to the Period 1870-1919* (New York: McGraw-Hill, 1947).

48. See Introduction.

49. On the "failed encounter," see Peter Steinfels, "The Failed Encounter: The Catholic Church and Liberalism in the Nineteenth Century," in *Catholicism and Liberalism: Contributions to American Public Philosophy*, ed. R. Bruce Douglass and David Hollenbach (Cambridge: Cambridge University Press, 1994), 19-44.

50. Abraham Kuyper, *The Work of the Holy Spirit*, trans. Henri de Vries (Grand Rapids: William B. Eerdmans, 1900), xiii.

51. Abraham Kuyper, *The Problem of Poverty*, ed. James W. Skillen (Grand Rapids: Baker Book House, 1991), 43-44, 52 (emphasis in original). This publication is a translation of a speech, first published in Dutch in 1891, entitled *Het Sociale Vraagstuk en de Christelijke Religie* (The social problem and the Christian religion).

52. See Gleason, *Conservative Reformers*.

53. See Bratt, *Dutch Calvinism in Modern America*, 37-54.

54. See Frederick C. Luebke, "The Immigrant Condition as a Factor Contributing to the Conservatism of the Lutheran Church—Missouri Synod," in *Germans in the New World: Essays in the History of Immigration*, ed. Frederick C. Luebke (Urbana: University of Illinois Press, 1990), 3-13.

55. On the corporatist formulations among Scandinavians in the United States, see Peter A. Munch, "Authority and Freedom: Controversy in Norwegian-American Congregations," *Norwegian-American Studies* 28 (1979): 29-30. On familism among Scandinavians, see Agnes M. Larson, "The Editorial Policy of *Skandinaven*, 1900-1903," *Norwegian-American Studies and Records* 8 (1934): 115.

56. Useful sources on society and religion in Scandinavia include G. Everett Arden, *Augustana Heritage: A History of the Augustana Lutheran Church* (Rock Island, Ill.: Augustana Press, 1963); Einar Molland, *Church Life in Norway, 1880-1950*, trans. Harris Kaasa (Westport, Conn.: Greenwood Press, 1957); and Lars Trägårdh, "The Concept of the People and the Construction of Popular Political Culture in Germany and Sweden, 1848-1933" (Ph.D. dissertation, University of California at Berkeley, 1993), 99-116. Significantly, many

Scandinavian and German Protestants confessed to non-Lutheran churches. Swedish American religious structure was especially characterized by church movements that rejected Lutheranism.

57. See the discussion in Chapter 6 that enlarges upon Michel Chevalier, *Society, Manners, and Politics in the United States: Being a Series of Letters on North America* (Boston: Weeks, Jordan, 1839), 342–43.

58. Bowen, *German Theories*, 1–38; Gleason, *Conservative Reformers*, 85–87.

59. See Dowd, "Theory of a Corporative Order," 73–93. A set of principles were later set down by Pope Pius XI (1922–39) for the regulation of responsibility in a corporative order. The principle of subsidiarity argued explicitly that all corporate groups of society should devote themselves only to those tasks that subsidiary groups could not administer effectively.

60. See Luebke, *Germans in the New World*, 3–12; Heinrich H. Maurer, "The Problems of Group-Consensus: Founding the Missouri Synod," *American Journal of Sociology* 30 (1925): 665–82, and "The Fellowship Law of a Fundamentalist Group: The Missouri Synod," *American Journal of Sociology* 31 (1925): 39–57; and Alan Graebner, *Uncertain Saints: The Laity in the Lutheran Church—Missouri Synod, 1900-1970* (Westport, Conn.: Greenwood Press, 1975).

61. Bratt cites a Dutch commentary that depicts "America's mind" as "superficial," "individualistic," and materialistic. See Bratt, *Dutch Calvinism in Modern America*, 58–66.

62. *Catholic Tribune*, 9 May 1899, 4.

63. *Luxemburger Gazette*, 27 September 1898, 4.

64. Bratt, *Dutch Calvinism in Modern America*, 26–27, 71.

65. To German Lutherans, Heinrich H. Maurer writes, the state curiously was "at once a divine institution and yet not a Christian affair" (Heinrich H. Maurer, "The Political Attitudes of the Lutheran Parish in America: A Study in Religious Sectionalism," *American Journal of Sociology* 33 [1928]: 582).

66. Father W. Cluse, "Das Christliche Familienleben," *Luxemburger Gazette*, 2 October 1888, 2–3.

67. Ibid.

68. "Autorität und Freiheit," *Luxemburger Gazette*, 7 August 1888, 4. This analysis tied original sin to authority since man's tendency toward evil had to be constrained by the authority sent by God.

69. Ibid. "Authority maintained by God," the author continued, "is a twofold power: the legislative [*Gesetzgebende*], 'your inclinations should be subject to the husband'; the power of discipline [*Disciplinargewalt*], 'he should be the leader.'"

70. "Bedeutung des Kulturkampfes," *Luxemburger Gazette*, 28 February 1888, 4 (emphasis added).

71. Pope Leo XIII, *Rerum Novarum*, in *Five Great Encyclicals: Labor, Education, Marriage, Reconstructing the Social Order, Atheistic Communism*, ed. Gerald C. Treacy (New York: Paulist Press, 1939), 4–7.

72. "Meeting of Our Saviour's Church Congregation, Monday, 25 March 1874," Luther Seminary Archives, St. Paul, Minn. I am indebted to Todd Nichol for this reference.

73. Martina Stoen and Gennie Kroshus, in Nancy North, "Sharing Good Times and Bad," *Annals of Iowa* 43 (1975): 204.

74. It is illuminating to juxtapose the roles and order of the family with those of the state. The former were organic; the latter were "artificial" and "mechanical." The former were essential to a properly functioning society; the latter were negative in purpose, a consequence only of the Fall. From this perspective, it was obvious that the family and not state-mandated laws ought to take precedence in society. See Bratt, *Dutch Calvinism in Modern America*, 26–27.

75. B. K. Kuiper, *Ons Opmaken en Bouwen* (Grand Rapids, 1918), cited in ibid., 71.

76. These three estates correspond to the authorities of "der kirchlichen, der häuslichen und der bürgerlichen," cited by German Catholics.

77. See Maurer, "Political Attitudes of the Lutheran Parish," "Problems of Group-Consensus," and especially "Fellowship Law," 39–57.

78. Jul. A. Friedrich, "The Family: The Foundation of the State," *Lutheran Witness* 43 (1924): 225.

79. Women were excluded from theological politics, wrote one late-nineteenth-century observer, "*because they are women*, not because they are always and necessarily inferior to men in mental capacity" (George Luecke, in *Lutheran Witness* 16 [1898]: 150, cited in Graebner, *Uncertain Saints*, 17 [emphasis in original]). As another put it, "If [women] will learn anything, let them ask their husbands at home." Yet "if any man be ignorant, let him be ignorant," and presumably his wife as well (cited in Maurer, "Fellowship Law," 46).

80. Ethnocultural political historians, for example, have stressed the broad cultural variations that informed worldview and political belief. Some time ago, Richard Jensen and Paul Kleppner perceptively connected the structures of religion with political expressions. See Richard Jensen, *The Winning of the Midwest: Social and Political Conflict, 1888-1896* (Chicago: University of Chicago Press, 1971), and Paul Kleppner, *The Cross of Culture: A Social Analysis of Midwestern Politics, 1850-1900* (New York: Free Press, 1970). These issues, however, touch on more than U.S. history. Cultural patterns and religious structures were central in informing policy toward family, community, and state in Europe. See, for example, Göran Therborn, "The Politics of Childhood: The Rights of Children in Modern Times," in *Families of Nations*, ed. Francis G. Castles (Aldershot, England: Dartmouth, 1993), 241–91.

81. Jensen stresses this characteristic as well, which, he argues correctly, is a central element in what he calls the liturgical worldview and an important influence on membership in the Democratic Party. See Jensen, *Winning of the Midwest*, 64–65.

82. Ibid., 64.

83. Kerby A. Miller argues that the conservative position was more popular than liberal and radical variants among the Irish American laity. See Miller, *Emigrants and Exiles*, 528–34. On French Canadians, who were more numerous in the eastern United States, see Gary Gerstle, *Working-Class Americanism: The Politics of Labor in a Textile City, 1914-1960* (New York: Cambridge University Press, 1989), 19–60.

84. The principal leader was Samuel Simon Schmucker, a professor of theology at the Gettysburg Seminary. Significantly, his beliefs, which were liberal and pietistic in tone, were known as "American Lutheranism." See Abdel Ross Wentz, *Pioneer in Church Unity: Samuel Simon Schmucker* (Philadelphia: Fortress Press, 1967), and Vergilius Ferm, *The Crisis in American Lutheran Theology: A Study of the Issues between American Lutheranism and Old Lutheranism* (New York: Century, 1927).

85. C. F. W. Walther, "Letter to Pastor Ottesen," *Norwegian Congregation* 2 (1866): 7–10, cited in German in Maurer, "Fellowship Law," 48. Elsewhere Walther wrote that "whosoever has comprehended Luther's famous Marburg dictum—'You have a spirit different from ours'—will comprehend that Yankees can tolerate it no better than did Zwingli and Okolampad. He will find himself filled with hostility toward the American spirit and its manifestations. . . . The fate of the European daughter-churches . . . is to sink gradually into the Calvinist pap" (C. F. W. Walther, *Lehre und Wehre* 3 [1853], cited in German in Maurer, "Fellowship Law," 49).

86. See Graebner, *Uncertain Saints*; Luebke, "Immigrant Condition"; and Arden, *Augustana Heritage*, 44–58.

87. Maurer's works are particularly useful in exploring these developments and their

connection to life in the Middle West. See, for example, Maurer, "Problems of Group-Consensus," 680–81.

88. See ibid., 673–74, and Maurer, "Fellowship Law," 40–57.

89. See Luebke, "Immigrant Condition," and Graebner, *Uncertain Saints*.

90. Theodore G. Tappert, ed., *Lutheran Confessional Theology in America, 1840–1880* (New York: Oxford University Press, 1972), 3–37; Arden, *Augustana Heritage*, 57–58.

91. Recall that the election controversy that divided the Norwegian Synod in the 1880s was based on competing theories of election. The Norwegian Synod, influenced by the ideas of the Missouri Synod, argued that election was based solely on God's grace. See the discussion in Chapter 4.

92. See Trägårdh, "Concept of the People," 151. See also Lars Trägårdh, "Varieties of Volkish Ideologies," in *Language and the Construction of Class Identities*, ed. Bo Stråth (Gothenburg, Sweden, 1990); Therborn, "Politics of Childhood"; and Eva Österberg, "Folklig mentalitet och statlig makt: Perspektiv pa 1500- och 1600-talens Sverige," *Scandia* 58 (1992): 81–102.

93. Since German society was purportedly corporate in structure, Riehl argued that "in the so-called educated world the human exists and functions far more as an individual; the peasant, on the other hand, exists and functions as group, as the totality of the *Stand*." See W. H. Riehl, *Die bürgerliche Gesellschaft* (Stuttgart, 1930), 55, cited in Trägårdh, "Concept of the People," 174.

94. Although Trägårdh's work does not explicitly consider Norway and Denmark, both were sites of nationalist movements that included the folk as central actors in the development of the state.

95. See Therborn, "Politics of Childhood."

96. For a good overview of education and the Catholic Church in America, see Jay P. Dolan, *The American Catholic Experience: A History from Colonial Times to the Present* (Garden City, N.Y.: Doubleday, 1985), 262–93. For the specific school controversy, see Daniel F. Reilly, *The School Controversy, 1891–1893* (New York: Arno Press, 1969).

97. Bishop John Lancaster Spaulding, "Religious Education in State Schools," *Educational Review* 2 (1891): 114, cited in Reilly, *School Controversy*, 73.

98. Reilly notes that only one statement from the pastoral letters of the American hierarchy between 1792 and 1884 might be interpreted as an admission of the state's right to educate. See Reilly, *School Controversy*, 106.

99. Rev. James Conway, *The Respective Rights and Duties of Family, State, and Church in Regard to Education*, 2d ed. (New York: Pustet, 1890), 32.

100. See Thomas J. Bouquillon, *Education: To Whom Does It Belong?* (Baltimore: John Murphy, 1891). See also Thomas J. Bouquillon, *Education: To Whom Does It Belong?—A Rejoinder to Critics* (Baltimore: John Murphy, 1892). For an overview of Bouquillon and his critics, see Reilly, *School Controversy*, 106–33.

101. James Conway, *The State Last: A Study of Doctor Bouquillon's Pamphlet, "Education: To Whom Does It Belong?"* (New York: Pustet, 1892), 10 (emphasis in original).

102. Ibid., 77.

103. Rev. R. I. Holaind, *The Parent First: An Answer to Dr. Bouquillon's Query, "Education: To Whom Does It Belong?"* (New York: Benziger Brothers, 1891).

104. "Three Theses of Jansen on the School Question," cited in ibid., 22–27 (emphasis in original).

105. Holaind could also summon no less an authority than Pope Leo XIII, who in his encyclical *Rerum novarum* defended *patria potestas* (the power of the father) when he cited Aquinas: "Children are something of the father." He wrote that "parental authority can neither be absorbed by the State nor abolished by it, for it has the same origin as human

life itself." In sum, Leo in *Rerum novarum* stressed that the "idea that the civil government should, at its own discretion, penetrate and pervade the family and the household, is a great and pernicious mistake." See Holaind, *The Parent First*, 11.

106. See, for example, *Iowa City Volksfreund*, cited in *Die Iowa*, 23 June 1881, 8.

107. *Marshalltown (Iowa) Beobachter*, cited in *Die Iowa*, 18 May 1882, 5. An essay contest on temperance in one school led *Die Iowa* to contend that the "public schools are considered hotbeds for all crazy ideas." It reported, moreover, that the state normal school offered a new course in "scientific temperance," to which *Die Iowa* responded "humbug." See *Die Iowa*, 17 May 1883, 8; 15 December 1881, 5.

108. See, for example, *Die Iowa*, 18 May 1882, 5.

109. *Die Iowa*, 10 November 1881, 8 (emphasis added).

110. Conway, *Respective Rights and Duties of Family, State, and Church*, 22 (emphasis in original). The library, another public institution, also contributed to the corrupt influences on youth. Libraries contained "not so much scientific and useful works," *Die Iowa* argued, as romances and novels: "Trash is bought and trash is read." In fact, "public libraries only contribute to unhealthy reading" since 73 percent of their holdings were "romances and novels, trashy ones [*Schund*] at that." The public insisted that they wanted to "be educated," but that was really a sham. "The libraries have the effect of deforming [*Verbildung*] youth," *Die Iowa* concluded, "especially the ladies' room." See *Die Iowa*, 29 December 1881, 5; 5 May 1881, 8. See also *Die Iowa*, 29 March 1877, 5. Fiction was not the only medium that corrupted readers. "Sensation at any price," contended the *Dubuque National Demokrat* in 1875, "is the word with many Anglo-American papers." "English papers," like dime novels, agreed *Die Iowa* two years later, "wallow in a puddle of sensationalism" so that whole columns were devoted "with real gusto" to "dirt for the readers." "Garbage," such as that printed in a local English-language paper that competed with *Die Iowa*, "is the most dangerous reading for a family that we can imagine." It was politically and socially corrupt, "without principles, without sensitivity." See *Dubuque National Demokrat*, 23 December 1875, 3, trans. J. K. Downing, CDH, and *Die Iowa*, 30 August 1877, 8; 10 October 1878, 8.

111. *Die Iowa*, 14 October 1880, 5.

112. *Die Iowa*, 3 April 1884, 5 (italics written in English in original).

113. *Die Iowa*, 9 March 1882, 8.

114. *Die Iowa*, 23 June 1881, 8. If that order was restored, *Die Iowa* contended, "we would not have so many *loafers* standing on the street corners" (italics written in English in original).

115. See Maurer, "Fellowship Law," 39–57, and "Political Attitudes of the Lutheran Parish," 568–85; Heinrich H. Maurer, "The Lutheran Community and American Society: A Study in Religion as a Condition of Social Accommodation," *American Journal of Sociology* 34 (1928): 282–95; and Carol K. Coburn, *Life at Four Corners: Religion, Gender, and Education in a German-Lutheran Community, 1868–1945* (Lawrence: University of Kansas Press, 1992). On the question of the school generally, see Walter H. Beck, *Lutheran Elementary Schools in the United States: A History of the Development of Parochial Schools and Synodical Educational Policies and Programs* (St. Louis: Concordia Publishing House, 1939).

116. See Maurer, "Fellowship Law," 50.

117. Ibid., 52. On the particularist and dualist Lutheran worldview, see Maurer, "Problems of Group Consensus," "Fellowship Law," and "Political Attitudes of the Lutheran Parish"; and Graebner, *Uncertain Saints*, 107–17.

118. *Theolog. Quartalsschrift* (Wisconsin, 1919), 272, cited in Maurer, "Political Attitudes of the Lutheran Parish," 571.

119. Swedish Lutherans abandoned parochial school projects even more quickly than segments of the Norwegian Lutheran population. But they too were troubled about the roles of church and state in the context of schools. In 1884, Carl Swensson, an Augus-

tana Synod pastor, marveled at "how God had blessed our settlements in this beautiful, flourishing, and liberty-loving state." The question of how youths "should obtain the necessary Christian education" was not easily answered. "Without the elevating influence exerted by a good school to mould the character of students and people, we would clearly be in danger of sinking into worship of the almighty dollar and materialism." Swensson concluded that a school should be founded in his Kansas settlement. See Carl Swensson, *Kansas-Konferensens Protokoll* (1884), 35–36, cited in Emory Lindquist, *Bethany in Kansas: A History of a College* (Lindsborg, Kans.: Bethany College, 1975), 2.

120. Recall that the Norwegian Synod was the most orthodox religious body among Norwegians. Especially good discussions of this debate are found in Theodore C. Blegen, *Norwegian Migration to America: The American Transition*, 2 vols. (Northfield, Minn.: Norwegian-American Historical Association, 1940), 2:241–76; Laurence M. Larson, "*Skandinaven*, Professor Anderson, and the Yankee School," in *The Changing West and Other Essays* (Northfield, Minn.: Norwegian-American Historical Association, 1937), 116–46; Arthur C. Paulson and Kenneth Bjørk, "A School and Language Controversy in 1858: A Documentary Study," *Norwegian-American Studies and Records* 10 (1938): 76–106; Frank C. Nelsen, "The School Controversy among Norwegian Immigrants," *Norwegian-American Studies* 26 (1974): 206–19; James S. Hamre, "Norwegian Immigrants Respond to the Common School: A Case Study of American Values and the Lutheran Tradition," *Church History* 50 (1981): 302–15; and Todd W. Nichol, ed. and trans., *Vivacious Daughter: Seven Lectures on the Religious Situation among Norwegians in America by Herman Amberg Preus* (Northfield, Minn.: Norwegian-American Historical Association, 1990).

121. Blegen, *Norwegian Migration to America*, 2:254–56; Nichol, *Vivacious Daughter*; Larson, *The Changing West*, 116–46.

122. A. C. Preus, in *Emigranten*, 29 November 1858, cited in Paulson and Bjørk, "A School and Language Controversy," 95.

123. Blegen, *Norwegian Migration to America*, 2:270–72. See also Larson, *The Changing West*, 116–46.

124. *Decorah-Posten*, 22 January 1882, cited in Arlow W. Andersen, *Rough Road to Glory: The Norwegian-American Press Speaks Out on Public Affairs, 1875–1925* (Philadelphia: Balch Institute Press, 1990), 35.

125. Schmidt was quoted to this effect in English in the *Madison Democrat*, 1877, in ibid., 125. See also Nelsen, "School Controversy," 215.

126. Blegen, *Norwegian Migration to America*, 2:269–70. This support of the common school occurred in tandem with an opposition to Catholicism. Thus Anderson would argue that parochial schools moved toward the road of Rome. See ibid., 2:272, and Larson, "*Skandinaven*," 116–46.

127. Despite losing the battle over the school, church leaders continued to calculate the costs. As late as 1925, O. M. Norlie wrote that "the secular schools by their very secular nature, not to speak of their anti-Christian spirit in many places, are de-Christianizing the land, no matter how much some of them try not to do so." See O. M. Norlie, *History of the Norwegian People in America* (Minneapolis, 1925), 377, cited in Nelsen, "School Controversy," 219. On Norwegians and the Bennett Law, see Andersen, *Rough Road to Glory*, 33–44; Jensen, *Winning of the Midwest*, 135–37; and Kleppner, *Cross of Culture*, 161–78.

128. Maurer, "The Lutheran Community and American Society," 287.

129. Ibid., 293.

130. Maurer, "Problems of Group-Consensus," 680; Heinrich H. Maurer, "The Religious Attitudes of the Lutheran Parish in America," *American Journal of Sociology* 33 (1928): 582–83. Similarly, a Mennonite wrote to potential immigrants in Russia that "we would like to see you here in free America," where they could enjoy "this noble and God-given gift[:] . . . complete freedom of conscience" to practice their beliefs (cited in Royden K.

Loewen, *Family, Church, and Market: A Mennonite Community in the Old and the New Worlds, 1850–1930* [Urbana: University of Illinois Press, 1993], 64).

131. *Council Bluffs (Iowa) Freie Presse,* cited in *Die Iowa,* 27 October 1881, 5.

132. *Die Iowa,* 25 August 1881, 5. So willing were these spokespersons to check the power of the schools that they opposed the teaching of foreign languages, such as German, in the public schools. Instruction in German, *Die Iowa* contended, should be offered in German Catholic parochial schools. See *Die Iowa,* 29 February 1880, 5. Some years earlier, those opposed to the schools denounced Bible reading in the "Republican" schools, arguing that children should "meet on a platform of equality and keep religion to the family and the church." See *Dubuque National Demokrat,* 17 September 1858, 2, trans. J. K. Downing, CDH.

133. See Daniel Scott Smith, "Culture and Family Limitation in Early Twentieth Century Iowa: Identity and Association," unpublished manuscript, 1992.

134. Jensen, *Winning of the Midwest,* 84. After all, "party loyalty," Jensen notes, "to the extent that it signified loyalty to forces that were in league with the devil, would never be palatable to these Lutherans." On Scandinavian political behavior, see Blegen, *Norwegian Migration to America,* 2:556.

Chapter Ten

1. Edward McGlynn, "The New Know-Nothingism and the Old," *North American Review* 144 (1887): 192–94. McGlynn was not a typical priest. An outspoken critic of economic inequality, he organized the Anti-Poverty Society and supported the candidacy of Henry George for mayor of New York City in 1886. He was excommunicated shortly thereafter.

2. Ibid., 195–96.

3. Although McGlynn did not cite examples of these expressions, I suggest the following: Anton H. Walburg, *The Question of Nationality in Its Relations to the Catholic Church in the United States* (Cincinnati, 1889); Father K. Algerwissen, "Knownothingthum," *Luxemburger Gazette,* 14 June 1887, 4; and Nicholas Gonner, *Goliath, der Bastardphilister und David, der ehrliche Israelite, oder der Kampf des "katholischen" Anglo-Amerika mit dem katholischen Deutschtum* (Dubuque, 1887).

4. Donald L. Kinzer, *An Episode in Anti-Catholicism: The American Protective Association* (Seattle: University of Washington Press, 1964), 177–80.

5. Ibid., 18.

6. Josiah Strong, *Our Country: Its Possible Future and Its Present Crisis* (New York: Baker & Taylor, 1885), 53–54.

7. The population figures that Strong cited illustrated the "concentration of strength": "In the United States a little more than one-eighth of the population is Catholic; in the territories taken together, more than one-third" (ibid., 57–58).

8. Ibid., 44–45.

9. On this issue, see Andrew R. L. Cayton and Peter S. Onuf, *The Midwest and the Nation: Rethinking the History of an American Region* (Bloomington: Indiana University Press, 1990), 103–23.

10. See, for example, Richard W. Thompson, *The Papacy and the Civil Power* (New York: Harper and Brothers, 1876).

11. Strong, *Our Country,* 47–59.

12. W. J. H. Traynor, "The Aims and Methods of the A.P.A.," *North American Review* 159 (1894): 68.

13. W. J. H. Traynor, "The Menace of Romanism," *North American Review* 161 (1895): 132, 139.

14. Ibid., 139.

15. J. L. Fairley, "Our Country's Danger from Romanism," *A.P.A. Magazine* 1 (1895): 62.

16. This development was related to a critical transformation in which dominant liberal antistate perspectives came into conflict with and ultimately gave way to the view that a welfare state was a necessity in the United States. See, for example, Sidney Fine, *Laissez Faire and the General-Welfare State: A Study of Conflict in American Thought, 1865–1901* (Ann Arbor: University of Michigan Press, 1956).

17. See Paula Baker, "The Domestication of Politics: Women and American Political Society, 1780–1920," *American Historical Review* 89 (1984): 620–47.

18. Ballard C. Campbell, *Representative Democracy: Public Policy and Midwestern Legislatures in the Late Nineteenth Century* (Cambridge: Harvard University Press, 1980), 60–65. See also Daniel J. Elasar, *Cities of the Prairie: The Metropolitan Frontier and American Politics* (New York: Basic Books, 1970).

19. For varying perspectives on these questions, see Michael Grossberg, *Governing the Hearth: Law and the Family in Nineteenth-Century America* (Chapel Hill: University of North Carolina Press, 1985), and Laura Gellott, "The Family, Liberalism, and Catholic Social Teaching," in *Catholicism and Liberalism: Contributions to American Public Philosophy*, ed. R. Bruce Douglass and David Hollenbach (Cambridge: Cambridge University Press, 1994), 269–95.

20. The references to the common school in Grant's speech caused a great stir in large part because they were so unexpected. See L. F. Parker, "President Grant's Des Moines Address," *Annals of Iowa* 3 (1897): 179–92, which contains a reproduction of Grant's handwritten speech. Grant was not alone in his observations. "Wherever Catholicism is dominant—wherever the power of Rome reaches and influences those who govern," wrote the *Davenport (Iowa) Gazette* in 1875, "there education is confined to comparatively few, and society stagnates." Loyalty to the nation continued to be an issue as well. Loyalties to the church and to the state were in tension and ultimately could be in conflict. One who confessed Catholicism "must obey Rome [in such areas as the public school], though the act required was contrary to his own view of the public interest, and the stability of free institutions." See "Catholic Supremacy," *Davenport (Iowa) Gazette*, 2 May 1875, 2. For further connections between the school and late-nineteenth-century anti-immigrant sentiments, see Kinzer, *Episode in Anti-Catholicism*.

21. Debate on the amendment introduced by Congressman James G. Blaine a few weeks after Grant's recommendation was critical throughout 1876, the year of a presidential election and the nation's centennial. Anti-Catholicism briefly waned after the election of 1876 but was renewed in the 1880s as a response to the Third Plenary Council in 1884. See Kinzer, *Episode in Anti-Catholicism*, 7–13.

22. According to the *Davenport (Iowa) Gazette*, Pope Pius IX wrote in his 1866 encyclical letter "that education and freedom were devices of the devil for the destruction of souls." See "The Catholics and the Schools," *Davenport (Iowa) Gazette*, 25 April 1875, 2.

23. "The Catholic Controversy," *Davenport (Iowa) Gazette*, 18 April 1875, 2.

24. The Bennett Law passed on the heels of the failure of the Pond Bill, which required all private schools to open their records and their doors to the state so that it could ascertain if adequate English-language instruction was provided. See Walter H. Beck, *Lutheran Elementary Schools in the United States: A History of the Development of Parochial Schools and Synodical Educational Policies and Programs* (St. Louis: Concordia Publishing House, 1030), 226–56. Beck provides the text of the Bennett Law in ibid., 227–29. See also Richard Jensen, *The Winning of the Midwest: Social and Political Conflict, 1888–1896* (Chicago: University of Chicago Press, 1971), 122–53, and Campbell, *Representative Democracy*, 114–18.

25. Beck, *Lutheran Elementary Schools*, 245–57.

26. Campbell, *Representative Democracy*, 105.

27. See Norman H. Clark, *Deliver Us from Evil: An Interpretation of American Prohibition* (New York: W. W. Norton, 1976), 40–44.

28. Joseph R. Gusfield, *Symbolic Crusade: Status Politics and the American Temperance Movement* (Urbana: University of Illinois Press, 1963), 100.

29. Jensen, *Winning of the Midwest*, 69–70, 89–121.

30. See, for example, ibid.; Baker, "Domestication of Politics," 637–38; Gusfield, *Symbolic Crusade*; Campbell, *Representative Democracy*, 98–114; and Clark, *Deliver Us from Evil*, 92–117.

31. *Die Iowa*, 22 June 1882, 8.

32. *Dubuque Herald*, 14 May 1882, 2.

33. *Des Moines Register*, cited in *Dubuque Herald*, 7 July 1882, 2. The paper continued, "We wonder that such oppressed people stay in such a country of oppression—and we wonder, if they are so abused and outraged here, and their freedom is taken away from them, that they do not go back to the country they came from. They have little spirit and less manhood, if they are oppressed and tyrannized over here as they say they are, for staying here and enduring it."

34. *Die Iowa*, 17 July 1884, 8.

35. *Howard County Times* (Cresco, Iowa), 15 February 1877, 1; 1 March 1877, 1 (emphasis in original).

36. See Campbell, *Representative Democracy*, 63–64, 118–20.

37. McGlynn, "The New Know-Nothingism," 203.

38. See, for example, Jay P. Dolan, *The American Catholic Experience: A History from Colonial Times to the Present* (Garden City, N.Y.: Doubleday, 1985), 271–75, and Daniel F. Reilly, *The School Controversy, 1891–1893* (Washington, D.C.: Catholic University Press of America, 1943).

39. See Dolan, *American Catholic Experience*, 294–320, and Colman J. Berry, *The Catholic Church and German Americans* (Washington, D.C.: Catholic University of America Press, 1953).

40. *Norden*, 1 July 1893, cited in Arlow W. Andersen, *Rough Road to Glory: The Norwegian-American Press Speaks Out on Public Affairs, 1875–1925* (Philadelphia: Balch Institute Press, 1990), 191; *Svenska Amerikanaren*, 28 April 1896, cited in Fritiof Ander, "The Swedish American Press and the American Protective Association," *Church History* 6 (1937): 168. On foreign-born activity within the APA, see John Higham, *Strangers in the Land: Patterns of American Nativism, 1860–1925*, 2d ed. (New York: Atheneum, 1978), 80–87; Kinzer, *Episode in Anti-Catholicism*, 113–16; and Ander, "Swedish American Press," 165–79.

41. *Sändebudet*, 29 March 1894, cited in Ander, "Swedish American Press," 174.

42. Temperance movements formed in Scandinavia beginning in the early nineteenth century, for example, were rerooted by immigrants in the United States. See Ross Evans Paulson, *Women's Suffrage and Prohibition: A Comparative Study of Equality and Social Control* (Glenview, Ill.: Scott, Foresman, 1973), 73–84.

43. *Syd Dakota Echo*, 29 November 1893, 25 April 1894, and *Reform*, 24 June 1894, all cited in Andersen, *Rough Road to Glory*, 190.

44. *Svenska Kuriren*, 18 March 1893, and *Rockford-Posten* (Illinois), 15 August 1896, both cited in Ander, "Swedish American Press," 175, 177.

45. *Amerika*, 11 October 1893, 9 May 1894, cited in Andersen, *Rough Road to Glory*, 189, 192.

46. *Luxemburger Gazette*, 5 October 1875, 4.

47. *Luxemburger Gazette*, 21 December 1875, 4. Some years later, the German Catholic antipathy toward Grant continued. After "*Kulturkampfer* Grant" gave speeches in Burling-

ton and Des Moines, *Die Iowa* asked rhetorically, "Aren't the eyes of the German Catholics about to open for this 'reptile'[?]" (4 December 1879, 8).

48. See Roger E. Wyman, "Wisconsin Ethnic Groups and the Election of 1890," *Wisconsin Magazine of History* 51 (1968): 269–93, and William F. Whyte, "The Bennett Law Campaign in Wisconsin," *Wisconsin Magazine of History* 10 (1927): 313–90.

49. *Milwaukee Journal*, 12 March 1890, cited in Jensen, *Winning of the Midwest*, 126. Significantly, all three of Wisconsin's bishops were German American.

50. The German Lutheran parochial school system was much stronger than the school systems of other nationality groups and religious denominations. Parochial schools among German Lutherans in the Missouri Synod taught 89,202 students in 1895. There was roughly one school for each congregation. In comparison, many churches in the Swedish Augustana Synod and the United Norwegian Synod lacked schools, and those with schools had predominantly summer schools that supplemented the public schools. See Beck, *Lutheran Elementary Schools*, 224.

51. Ibid., 231–32.

52. See Jensen, *Winning of the Midwest*, 122–53; Paul Kleppner, *The Cross of Culture: A Social Analysis of Midwestern Politics, 1850–1900* (New York: Free Press, 1970), 158–70; and Wyman, "Wisconsin Ethnic Groups."

53. Wyman, "Wisconsin Ethnic Groups," 281–85.

54. Kleppner, *Cross of Culture*, 166, 167.

55. See Orestes Brownson, "The Woman Question," *Catholic World* 9 (1869): 145–57. See also James J. Kenneally, "Catholicism and Woman Suffrage in Massachusetts," *Catholic Historical Review* 53 (1967): 43–57, "Eve, Mary, and the Historians: American Catholicism and Women," in *Women in American Religion*, ed. Janet Wilson James (Philadelphia: University of Pennsylvania Press, 1980), 191–206, and "Women Divided: The Catholic Struggle for an Equal Rights Amendment, 1923–1945," *Catholic Historical Review* 75 (1989): 249–63; Richard L. Camp, "From Passive Subordination to Complementary Partnership: The Papal Conception of a Woman's Place in Church and Society since 1878," *Catholic Historical Review* 76 (1990): 506–25; and Alan Graebner, "Birth Control and the Lutherans: The Missouri Synod as a Case Study," in James, *Women in American Religion*, 229–52, and *Uncertain Saints: The Laity in the Lutheran Church—Missouri Synod, 1900–1970* (Westport, Conn.: Greenwood Press, 1975).

56. *Fædrelandet og Emigranten*, 3 June 1869, 2.

57. Andersen, *Rough Road to Glory*, 92.

58. *Dyersville (Iowa) Demokrat*, reprinted in *Cascade (Iowa) Pioneer*, 26 October 1888 (italics written in English in original).

59. *Lutheran Witness* 17 (1898): 55, cited in Graebner, "Birth Control," 231.

60. *Concordia Magazine* 1 (1896): 33, cited in Graebner, *Uncertain Saints*, 18.

61. J. Frederic Wenkel, in *Lutheran Witness* 39 (1920): 330, cited in Graebner, "Birth Control," 231.

62. Graebner, "Birth Control," 231, and *Uncertain Saints*, 18. *Zeitkrankheit* means roughly a "sickness of the time" and *Unordnung* means "disorder."

63. *Die Iowa*, 19 July 1883, 5. See also *Die Iowa*, 8 September 1881, 5. In another issue, a female educator was described as "the school-teaching Amazon" (*Die Iowa*, 9 January 1879, 5).

64. Half of the candidates for school superintendent, *Die Iowa* observed sourly, were "ladies, young and old, especially old" (21 October 1875, 5). See also *Die Iowa*, 21 August 1879, 6.

65. *Council Bluffs (Iowa) Freie Presse*, cited in *Die Iowa*, 27 October 1881, 5. "X.Y.Z." whimsically argued in an editorial that a bill should be passed requiring that men "pre-

pare soup, tend the children and that only women would show at the ballot box" because then "we'd get no more laws from the women in the halls of the legislature" since "they would all talk each other to death" (*Die Iowa*, 29 January 1880, 5). The broadening of the authority of women in other areas of society typically provoked similar laments. "Insane matters [*verrückte Dinge*]," as one paper put it, were even creeping into churches. Commenting on a Unitarian church in Ann Arbor, Michigan, in which the minister and his wife took turns preaching from the same pulpit, *Lutheranische Kirchen=Zeitung* advised its readers that the "less the pastor's wife meddles with his affairs the better." See "Wie Er und Sie eine Gemeinde bedienen," *Lutheranische Kirchen=Zeitung*, reprinted in *Luxemburger Gazette*, 19 April 1887, 4. Given these pointed remarks, it is important to remember that most electoral contests engaged only male voters. In one school election in Boston in 1910 that included female voters, Philip Ethington has illustrated the salience of gender. Women voters in this case—irregardless of ethnic background—supported a progressive reformer over an Irish American woman backed by the Irish community leadership. See Philip J. Ethington, "Recasting Urban Political History: Gender, the Public, the Household, and Political Participation in Boston and San Francisco during the Progressive Era," *Social Science History* 16 (1992): 321–25.

66. As late as 1976, Pope Paul VI argued that "equalization of rights must not be allowed to degenerate into an egalitarian and impersonal elimination of differences. The egalitarianism blindly sought by our materialistic society has but little care for the specific good of persons; contrary to appearances it is unconcerned with what is suitable or unsuitable to women. There is, thus, a danger of unduly masculinizing women or else simply depersonalizing them" (cited in Camp, "From Passive Subordination to Complementary Partnership," 522).

67. Pope Leo XIII, *Rerum Novarum*, in *Five Great Encyclicals: Labor, Education, Marriage, Reconstructing the Social Order, Atheistic Communism*, ed. Gerald C. Treacy (New York: Paulist Press, 1939), 20; *Catholic Tribune*, 31 August 1899, 4.

68. Philip Gleason notes that one of the "old guard's watchwords" was "Die Frau gehört in's Haus [the wife belongs in the home]" (Philip Gleason, *The Conservative Reformers: German-American Catholics and the Social Order* [Notre Dame: University of Notre Dame Press, 1968], 251–52).

69. Ibid., 183.

70. *73rd General Convention . . . 1929*, 129–33, cited in ibid., 184. Gleason notes that this organization also rejected birth control, immodest dress, beauty contests, corrupting literature, and the fashion of eliminating religious images from the home. Yet he notes that it also advocated "new privileges in the age of democracy" for women and opposed anything that "cripples the unfolding of [a woman's] personality." See also Camp, "From Passive Subordination to Complementary Partnership," and Kenneally, "Eve, Mary, and the Historians."

71. *Catholic Tribune*, 31 August 1899, 4. The paper also cited approvingly Kaiser Wilhelm's argument that women "should not meddle with things that are outside the four 'K's' ": "Kinder, Kirche, Kueche, und Kleider [children, church, cooking, and clothes]."

72. See Thomas G. Ryan, "Male Opponents and Supporters of Woman Suffrage: Iowa in 1916," *Annals of Iowa* 45 (1981): 537–50, on which this paragraph is based.

73. The size of the community in which the voter lived and the percentage living in cities showed little effect on voting tendencies.

74. Ida Husted Harper, ed., *The History of Woman Suffrage*, 6 vols. (New York: National American Woman Suffrage Association, 1922), 6:591, cited in Ryan, "Male Opponents and Supporters of Woman Suffrage," 540.

75. Temperance advocates were correct to note that the state, one way or another, played a role in the distribution of alcohol. *The Prohibitionist* (Dubuque), for example, im-

plicitly connected Roman Catholicism to drink and sin and the state to alcohol regulation when it wrote, "It was Martin Luther who pronounced the sale of indulgencies [*sic*] by the Catholic church the price current of sin; but such sale is a small offense compared to a government licensing such hot-houses of sin and crime as saloons. . . . What crimes," it concluded, "are committed in the name of the republic! Where are her protecting wings? Is it possible that the rum power has clipped them so closely that thou can'st no longer protect thy young from the vultures?" (8 July 1886, 1).

76. The ways in which foreign nationalities differed in their views on this dilemma are illustrated by Scandinavians in the United States. In particularly pietist communities, the strength of temperance sentiment tended to overwhelm regard for community authority. The leadership of the Norwegian Synod, which stressed the importance of the community, on the other hand, was relatively silent on the temperance issue. See Lowell J. Soike, *Norwegian Americans and the Politics of Dissent, 1880–1924* (Northfield, Minn.: Norwegian-American Historical Association, 1991), 62–68; Andersen, *Rough Road to Glory*, 162–73; and Theodore C. Blegen, *Norwegian Migration to America: The American Transition*, 2 vols. (Northfield, Minn.: Norwegian-American Historical Association, 1940), 2:221–23.

77. See James D. Bratt, *Dutch Calvinism in Modern America: A History of a Conservative Subculture* (Grand Rapids: William B. Eerdmans, 1984), 4, 71–73.

78. Ibid., 71–74. Bratt is particularly insightful in illustrating how differing Dutch intellectual subcommunities arrived at different conclusions with regard to alcohol. The tensions between these subgroups is, in microcosm, representative of divisions between the liberal "Americanizers" and the "foreign" corporatists discussed below.

79. *Iowa Tribune* (Burlington), cited in *Die Iowa*, 3 July 1884, 5. The question mark suggests that the men were not *really* men.

80. *Die Iowa*, 26 August 1875, 5.

81. *Des Moines Anzeiger*, 30 June 1882, cited in *Dubuque Herald*, 4 July 1882, 2.

82. C. F. W. Walther, "Letter to Pastor Ottesen," *Norwegian Congregation* 2 (1866): 7–10, cited in Heinrich H. Maurer, "The Fellowship Law of a Fundamentalist Group: The Missouri Synod," *American Journal of Sociology* 31 (1925): 48.

83. *Die Iowa*, 27 July 1882, 5; 20 September 1883, 8; 25 September 1879, 5.

84. *Des Moines Anzeiger*, 30 June 1882, cited in *Dubuque Herald*, 4 July 1882, 2. According to this report, ethnic blocs were significant factors in the breakdown of voting on the referendum. "We could not believe," it commented, "that . . . any considerable number of the Irish, the Swedes, aye, even the German Methodists could be induced to betray their rights and liberties."

85. Yankee extremism was apparent not only in temperance activities. Even in mundane matters such as the eradication of sparrows from towns, *Die Iowa* argued simply, "the Yankee is quite extreme." At first, the editor wrote, "they could not praise the bird highly enough; today, it is worse than the worst of its feathered friends" (3 May 1883, 8). Individual excesses within the family were illustrated by phenomena such as the "suicide-mania" that befell young women in particular. See *Die Iowa*, 31 August 1882, 5. When a woman fasted to death, *Die Iowa* remarked that she should be "mounted in gold and shown for money as a splendid example of abstinence" (7 April 1881, 5). Here again both excess and abstinence, the obverse of excess but an "excessive" behavior, were tied to the Yankee.

86. *Des Moines Register*, cited in *Dubuque Herald*, 7 July 1882, 2.

87. Article in "*J. VZtg. [Joliet Volkszeitung?]*," reprinted in *Die Iowa*, 7 April 1881, 5.

88. *Cascade (Iowa) Pioneer*, 26 August 1887, 1 (emphasis added).

89. *Die Iowa*, 6 August 1882, 8 (emphasis added).

90. *Cascade (Iowa) Pioneer*, 26 August 1887, 1.

91. On temperance in Iowa, see Jensen, *Winning of the Midwest*, 89–121; Dan Elbert Clark, "The History of Liquor Legislation in Iowa, 1846–1861," *Iowa Journal of History*

and Politics 6 (1908): 55–87, "The History of Liquor Legislation in Iowa, 1861–1878," *Iowa Journal of History and Politics* 6 (1908): 339–74, "The History of Liquor Legislation in Iowa, 1878–1908," *Iowa Journal of History and Politics* 6 (1908): 503–604, and "Recent Liquor Legislation in Iowa," *Iowa Journal of History and Politics* 15 (1917): 42–69; Jerry Harrington, "Bottled Conflict: Keokuk and the Prohibition Question, 1888–1889," *Annals of Iowa* 46 (1983): 593–617; George W. McDaniel, "Prohibition Debate in Washington County, 1890–1894: Smith Wildman Brookhart's Introduction to Politics," *Annals of Iowa* 45 (1981): 519–36; Thomas G. Ryan, "Supporters and Opponents of Prohibition: Iowa in 1917," *Annals of Iowa* 46 (1983): 510–22; and Ballard Campbell, "Did Democracy Work?: Prohibition in Late-Nineteenth Century Iowa—A Test Case," *Journal of Interdisciplinary History* 8 (1977): 87–116.

92. *Die Iowa*, 13 July 1882, 5.

93. *Die Iowa*, 28 June 1882, 8.

94. The mayor of Carroll reportedly was kidnapped and threatened with lynching in August 1882 for his opposition to the amendment. See *Die Iowa*, 31 August 1882, 5.

95. Ryan, "Supporters and Opponents of Prohibition," 513.

96. See Kleppner, *Cross of Culture*; Jensen, *Winning of the Midwest*; and Paul Kleppner, *The Third Electoral System, 1853–1892* (Chapel Hill: University of North Carolina Press, 1978). The pietists, reflecting a common-core Protestantism of American northerners and European Protestants alike, tended to embrace the Republican Party, which sought state supervision and regulation of private behavior. Those who hewed to liturgical faiths such as Catholicism and German Lutheranism or whose background was southern, on the other hand, tended to join the Democratic Party. See also Elazar, *Cities of the Prairie*, 256–81, which delineates three types of political culture—individualistic, moralistic, and traditional—and illustrates how each influenced local politics in "prairie cities."

97. On the subjectivist-objectivist dichotomy, see Ernst Troeltsch, *Religion in History*, trans. and ed. James Luther Adams and Walter F. Bense (Minneapolis: Fortress Press, 1991), 210–34, 321–42; Robert Wuthnow, *Rediscovering the Sacred: Perspectives on Religion in Contemporary Society* (Grand Rapids: William B. Eerdmans, 1992); Timothy L. Smith, *Revivalism and Social Reform in Mid-Nineteenth-Century America* (New York: Abingdon Press, 1954), 15–33, 148–62; Michael J. Taylor, *The Protestant Liturgical Renewal: A Catholic Viewpoint* (Westminster, Md.: Newman Press, 1963), 11–15, 227–33; F. Ernest Stoeffler, *The Rise of Evangelical Pietism* (Leiden, Netherlands: E. J. Brill, 1971), 9–23; and Claude Welch, *Protestant Thought in the Nineteenth Century*, vol. 1, *1799–1870* (New Haven: Yale University Press, 1972), 190–99. I am indebted to Richard Johnson for discussing this matter with me.

98. See Jensen, *Winning of the Midwest*, 89–121.

99. Kleppner, *Cross of Culture*, 158–72; Wyman, "Wisconsin Ethnic Groups."

100. See Richard Oestreicher, "Urban Working-Class Political Behavior and Theories of American Electoral Politics, 1870–1940," *Journal of American History* 74 (1988): 1257–86, and Amy Bridges, "Becoming American: The Working Classes in the United States before the Civil War," in *Working-Class Formation: Nineteenth-Century Patterns in Western Europe and the United States*, ed. Ira Katznelson and Aristide R. Zolberg (Princeton: Princeton University Press, 1986), 157–96.

101. Cayton and Onuf, *The Midwest and the Nation*, 109–18.

102. This perception of conflict between the church and liberalism had deep historical roots. Indeed, "two cultures"—the Christian and the freethinking atheist—wrote the *Luxemburger Gazette* in 1888, had struggled with alternating success for leadership of the world since the Reformation. Utilizing notions of "freedom" and "reform" under the guise of the Enlightenment, the "heathen forces" eventually had been victorious in half of Europe. Within the heathens' domain, philosophers developed "heathenist systems of pantheism, materialism, rationalism, and fatalism." Some years later, the French Revolu-

tion was yet another victory in the movement to replace Christian ideals and values with heathen ones. And today the battle continued. Christians, and here the author meant Catholics, were in the middle of a momentous struggle. If the heathens won, the result would be "decay of the state, ruin, barbarism," for "what else can be left remaining when the torch, the petroleum, and the dynamite have completed their frightful work?" Their victory, moreover, was not unimaginable. As a result of the course of contemporary society, humans were moving "with giant strides" toward a "precipice." See "Bedeutung des Kulturkampfes," *Luxemburger Gazette*, 28 February 1888, 4.

103. "Woher der gefährliche Capitalismus," *Luxemburger Gazette*, 16 August 1887, 4.

104. "C.S.R.," "Freimaurerthum, Judenthum, Liberalismum," *Luxemburger Gazette*, 22 March 1887, 4.

105. "Woher der gefährliche Capitalismus," 4.

106. *Catholic Tribune*, 28 September 1899, 4.

107. Ibid. (emphasis added). Note the sense of allegiance to country despite regrets concerning its governing principles.

108. Ibid.

109. "Woher der gefährliche Capitalismus," 4.

110. "Die Freiheit der Katholiken," *Katholische Volkszeitung*, cited in *Luxemburger Gazette*, 3 April 1888, 4. He was "a slave of doubts, a victim of ignorance. He wanders about influenced by the winds of each new idea and he cannot be reassured or comforted. Only in the belief and with the certainty to possess the right [*wahren*] belief can one find freedom of mind and heart. The knowledge of truth is the only way to freedom." Only a "correct truth" freed the "spirit from the most evil tyranny, that of doubt and ignorance," whereas a false sense of freedom created licentiousness and "deplorable souls" existing in the "darkness of their spirit."

111. "The Disadvantages of Our Liberties," *Catholic Tribune*, 18 July 1901, 4.

112. Ibid. (emphasis added).

113. Ibid. The United States was not the only troubled republic. "Broad strata of society in France," the author continued, "are recognizing the superiority of monarchical institutions and are attributing the downfall of France to the fall of the monarchy." He asked rhetorically, "Are the facts more encouraging in the United States?"

114. "Bedeutung des Kulturkampfes," 4.

115. "The Disadvantages of Our Liberties," 4. According to the article, history taught us, moreover, that "republics—and especially large republics with democratic constitutions—could never last long." Most republics, in fact, were ultimately transformed into monarchies.

116. Ibid.

117. The best treatment of this movement is Gleason, *Conservative Reformers*, on which much of this paragraph relies.

118. Ibid., 85–87.

119. William J. Engelen, *Was wollen wir*, in *60. General Versammlung . . . 1915*, 130–37, cited in ibid., 131–32.

120. Engelen, *Was wollen wir*, and Frederick P. Kenkel, *61. General Versammlung . . . 1916*, 95–96, both cited in ibid., 137 (emphasis added).

Epilogue

1. *Des Moines Register*, 19 July 1918, 6. See Peter L. Petersen, "Language and Loyalty: Governor Harding and Iowa's Danish-Americans during World War I," *Annals of Iowa* 42 (1974): 411–12, and Jette Mackintosh, *Danskere i midtvesten: Elk Horn-Kimballton bosættelsen, 1870–1925* (Copenhagen: Academisk Forlag, 1993), 117–20.

2. See, for example, *Des Moines Register*, 18 July 1918, 4; 22 July 1918, 4; 27 July 1918, 4.

3. Karl Rasmussen, "The Danes in Audubon," *Des Moines Register*, 27 July 1918, 4.

4. *Des Moines Register*, 19 July 1918, 6.

5. See, for example, Kathleen Neils Conzen, *Making Their Own America: Assimilation Theory and the German Peasant Pioneer* (New York: Berg, 1990), 1–9; Jane Marie Peterson, *Between Memory and Reality: Family and Community in Rural Wisconsin, 1870–1970* (Madison: University of Wisconsin Press, 1992); and Sonya Salamon, *Prairie Patrimony: Family, Farming, and Community in the Midwest* (Chapel Hill: University of North Carolina Press, 1992).

6. On school debate, see Lynn Dumenil, " 'The Insatiable Maw of Bureaucracy': Antistatism and Education Reform in the 1920s," *Journal of American History* 77 (1990): 499–524.

7. See, for example, James D. Bratt, *Dutch Calvinism in Modern America: A History of a Conservative Subculture* (Grand Rapids: William B. Eerdmans, 1984); Alan Graebner, *Uncertain Saints: The Laity in the Lutheran Church—Missouri Synod, 1900–1970* (Westport, Conn.: Greenwood Press, 1975); and Gary Gerstle, *Working-Class Americanism: The Politics of Labor in a Textile City, 1914–1960* (New York: Cambridge University Press, 1989).

8. See, for example, Patrick Allitt, *Catholic Intellectuals and Conservative Politics in America, 1950–1985* (Ithaca: Cornell University Press, 1993).

9. See Frederick Luebke, *Bonds of Loyalty: German Americans and World War I* (DeKalb: Northern Illinois University Press, 1974), and Carol K. Coburn, *Life at Four Corners: Religion, Gender, and Education in a German-Lutheran Community, 1868–1945* (Lawrence: University of Kansas Press, 1992). For an example of ethnic settlements in relation to prowar mobilization, see Walter T. Henderson and Emma L. Henderson oral history, 9, ISHDIC. For a fictional account based on fact, see Ruth Suckow, *Country People* (New York: Alfred A. Knopf, 1924), 100–107.

10. *Des Moines Register*, 12 November 1918, 10, cited in Leola Allen, "Anti-German Sentiment in Iowa during World War I," *Annals of Iowa* 42 (1974): 427–28.

11. *Des Moines Register*, 24 November 1918, cited in ibid., 428.

12. Ibid., 426–27. See also Steven Wrede, "The Americanization of Scott County, 1914–1918," *Annals of Iowa* 44 (1979): 627–38.

13. Robert Schoone-Jongen, "The Dutch Experience in Southwest Minnesota during World War I," *Origins* 7 (1989): 6.

14. Garret Pothoven, "Peoria, Iowa: The War Years, 1917–1918," *Origins* 7 (1989): 9–12.

15. Schoone-Jongen, "Dutch Experience," 4–5. The Dutch community's church school soon became the center of intense debate. John S. Randolph, a local newspaper editor, charged that any institution that "decreases the respect or veneration of any number of children for the public school, is UN-AMERICAN." He was taken to task by A. S. De Jong, principal of the local Dutch Christian school, who responded that his community claimed "as citizens of FREE AMERICA the right to educate our children in schools controlled neither by the state nor by the church but by the parents themselves." He concluded that this right existed "provided that we are also in our teaching loyal and true to the Stars and Stripes." Randolph had the last word. "Too long have people of foreign birth and instincts," he concluded, "been allowed to go to dangerous limits in demanding their 'rights' in 'Free America.' In too many cases have there been small replicas of foreign communities allowed to spring up here. All this has appeared innocent and harmless, until sometimes the pet lion has grown into a devouring beast." See exchange in *Edgerton (Minnesota)*

Enterprise, 10 May–21 June 1918, cited in Schoone-Jongen, "Dutch Experience," 6–7. Veneration of the flag was the basis of another incident, this time including Mennonites who refused to salute the flag in Nebraska and faced the threats and depredations of their neighbors. See Royden K. Loewen, *Family, Church, and Market: A Mennonite Community in the Old and the New Worlds, 1850–1930* (Urbana: University of Illinois Press, 1993), 257–58.

16. Socialist and labor movements and political movements such as the Non-Partisan League faced particular scrutiny during the war.

17. Carl H. Chrislock, *Ethnicity Challenged: The Upper Midwest Norwegian-American Experience in World War I* (Northfield, Minn.: Norwegian-American Historical Association, 1981), 65.

18. Walter H. Beck, *Lutheran Elementary Schools in the United States: A History of the Development of Parochial Schools and Synodical Educational Policies and Programs* (St. Louis: Concordia Publishing House, 1939), 326.

19. A particularly good source on the MCPS is Chrislock, *Ethnicity Challenged*, 58–88.

20. This prohibition was already in effect in many local public school districts. On the MCPS, see ibid., 68–81; Schoone-Jongen, "Dutch Experience," 5; and June Drenning Holmquist, ed., *They Chose Minnesota: A Survey of the State's Ethnic Groups* (St. Paul: Minnesota Historical Society Press, 1981), 10.

21. *Report of the Minnesota Commission of Public Safety* (St. Paul, 1919), 22–23, cited in Chrislock, *Ethnicity Challenged*, 80.

22. Chrislock, *Ethnicity Challenged*, 81.

23. Ibid., 81–82.

24. *Theolog. Quartalsschrift* (Wisconsin, 1920), 125–28, cited in Heinrich H. Maurer, "The Political Attitudes of the Lutheran Parish in America: A Study in Religious Sectionalism," *American Journal of Sociology* 33 (1928): 571.

25. Theodore Graebner, *Testimony and Proof Bearing on the Relation of the American Lutheran Church to the German Emperor*, cited in Coburn, *Life at Four Corners*, 139.

26. *Luxemburger Gazette*, 17 March 1917, cited in Sister Mary De Paul Faber, "*The Luxemburger Gazette*: A Catholic German Language Paper of the Middle West, 1872–1918" (M.A. thesis, Catholic University of America, 1948), 47.

27. Chrislock, *Ethnicity Challenged*, 124–26. Iowa's law excepted religious instruction. Wisconsin, North Dakota, and South Dakota failed to enact English-only legislation.

28. Dumenil, "Insatiable Maw of Bureaucracy," 512.

29. Beck, *Lutheran Elementary Schools*, 324–38; Chrislock, *Ethnicity Challenged*, 126. Beck also outlined the issue in Michigan and Oregon in *Lutheran Elementary Schools*, 338–43.

INDEX

Note: Non-English-language terms used in the index are alphabetized according to rules of the language.

Abortion, 253

Adair County, Iowa, 111

Adamson, Sarah Browne Armstrong, 83–85, 88, 89, 101, 200

Ager, Waldemar, 226, 228

Agricultural markets, 146, 148; distance to, 142; dishonesty of merchants in, 142–43

Agriculture: continuities of, 136; on the Great Plains, 136; Illinois, 136; Iowa, 136; in Minnesota, 136; in Wisconsin, 136; changes in, 136, 137; technological change in, 141, 146, 155; commercialization of, 154

Aldrich, Bess Streeter, 140

Alsace: migrants from, 111

Altenteil, 205

American Equal Rights Society, 298

Americanism, 285, 317; during World War I, 322, 324

Americanization, 64–65, 225–26, 230–31, 232, 246–47, 285, 289, 300, 310, 319; dangers of, 164, 181, 248, 252, 294, 295; during World War I, 322–24. *See also* Assimilation; Cultural innovation and diffusion

"American Lutheranism," 16, 271, 396 (n. 84)

American Protective Association, 284–85, 288; and importance of national state, 284, 288; and foreign born members, 295; associated with Republican Party, 309

American Protestantism: associated with liberty, 12–13, 36–37, 47–48, 73–74, 160, 285, 291, 335 (n. 49)

American Revolution, 11, 164

Anderson, Rasmus B., 278

Andover Band, 47–48

Animal care, 362 (n. 26)

Animal production, 141–42

Anthony, Susan B., 202

Anti-Americanization, 263

Anti-Catholicism, 36–37, 284–86, 288, 290, 293, 294; among Protestant immigrants, 294–95. *See also* Nativism

Anti-liberalism, 262–63

Anti-Missourians, 118, 119

Assimilation: process of, 225–26, 240, 247; promoted by cultural diffusion, 226; promoted by social interaction, 226; pressures of, 227; desired by immigrants, 283; promoted by state agencies, 286, 288, 289

Audubon County, Iowa, 319, 323, 325

Augustana Synod, 346 (n. 100); parochial school system of, 403 (n. 50)

Ausgedinge, 205

Auszug, 205

Automobiles, 238

Bailey, Allettie, 83

Balestrand, Norway, 216

Baptists: in Middle West, 5, 82, 104; and particularism, 270; and temperance, 292

Barley, 141

Barnes, Albert, 1–4, 7, 10, 12–13, 18, 34, 45, 165, 325

Bavaria: emigrants from, 106; work in, 173

Beatrice, Nebraska, 172

Beecher, Lyman, 33, 37, 39, 40–41, 43, 45, 46–47, 48, 325

Bennett Law (Wisconsin): 279, 291, 310; as

restricting rights of parents and community, 297; voting behavior stemming from, 298

Berger, Peter, 73

Biblical literalism, 271

Bigot, Wilhelm P., 70

Bismarck, Otto von, 262, 297

Bixby, Newell W., 82–83, 90, 110

Bloomington (Iowa) Herald, 104

"Blue laws," 290

Boston Pilot, 104

Bouquillon, Thomas J., 274

Bourne, Randolph, 329 (n. 24)

Bowlin, James B., 28

Brainard, Minnesota, 243

Bratt, James D., 301

Breitbach, J. J. L, 244

Bremer, Fredrika, 27

Bridges, Amy, 65, 246

Broderick, James L., 193

Bryan, William Jennings, 391 (n. 111)

Bryant, F. W., 90

Budstikken, 298

Buffalo Synod, 17, 271

Burlend, Rebecca, 66, 68, 139–40, 145, 155

Burlington (Iowa) Hawkeye, 80

Burrows, Edwin G., 11

Busey, Samuel, 37, 38, 45, 46

Butchering: on the farm, 148; in slaughterhouses, 148, 365 (n. 77)

Cahensly movement, 294

Caldwell, John, 193

Calvinism, 16

Canadian Americans: membership in American Protective Association, 295

Capital punishment: abolishment of, 290

Carlier, Auguste, 165

Carroll County, Iowa, 99, 100

Carroll (Iowa) Demokrat, 246

Catholic Tribune, 253, 256, 259, 261, 263, 264, 296, 300, 313, 314, 315

Cattle, 139, 145; care of, 152, 155, 174; herding of, 153

Cayton, Andrew R. L., 311

Chain migration: from Europe, 8; defined, 89–90; patterns of, 91–96, 100; and economic aid, 100

Charivaris, 229

Chevalier, Michel, 13, 32, 57, 66, 160–61, 263

Chicago, 234

Child abuse, 276

"Child default," 155, 162, 199

Child naming customs, 239; among Scandinavian Americans, 388 (nn. 72, 73)

Child protection agencies, 281

Children: as farm laborers, 136, 152–53; as caregivers to aging parents, 153–54, 155

Christensen, Otto Augustus, 229

Christian Church: and temperance, 292

Christian Reformed Church, 263, 321

Church and state: relationship between, 68; separation of, 72, 107, 115

"Church-types": defined, 67, 354 (n. 16)

Cincinnati, 105

Cincinnati Chronicle, 26

Citizenship: immigrants' access to, 53–54; and ethnic group formation, 241; during World War I, 323; and naturalization according to race, 340 (n. 14)

Civil War, 233, 243, 245

Clampitt, Frank T., 138

Clannishness: among Europeans, 40; among Yankees, 40

Clausen, C. L., 56, 64

Clay County, Minnesota, 99

Clayton County, Iowa, 110

Clinton, Iowa, 284

Clinton County, Iowa, 99, 100

Clothing fashion, 232; and excess, 257; and sex roles, 298

Cluse, W. (father), 266

Coffin, Mary C., 148

Commission of Immigration, 350 (n. 71)

"Complementary identity," 8, 59–66, 72, 74, 75, 226, 229, 240, 284, 322, 324, 325, 346 (n. 101)

Confessional fundamentalism, 271–72

Conflict: between ethnic groups, 241–43

Congregationalists: in Middle West, 104; and temperance, 292

Connecticut: migrants from, 91

Contractualism, 11, 263

Conway, James, 273, 274, 275

Conzen, Kathleen Neils, 154, 237, 240, 343 (n. 59)

Coresidence: cultural differences in, 163

Cork, Ireland: emigrants from, 104–5

Corn, 139, 141, 145; harvest of, 145; planting of, 145; care for, 145, 152

Corn Belt, 136, 145

"Corporate family economy," 151, 158

Corporatism: among immigrants, 10, 15–16, 67, 74, 107, 151, 158, 294, 316, 331 (n. 55); in family and community, 21, 261–69, 271, 286–87; and German origins, 262; and Social Catholicism, 262; and political movements, 286–87

Corpus Christi processions, 229

Correspondence: as advancing migration, 88; in newspapers, 97

Courtship: cultural differences in, 162, 163; and "true love," 259

Crawford County, Wisconsin, 94, 95, 212, 213

Cresco, Iowa, 293

Cretin, Joseph, 57

Crèvecoeur, J. Hector St. John de, 2, 7, 32, 61

Criminal rights, 290

Croly, Herbert, 55

Crop failure, 144

Crow River community, 119–22, 128, 130

Cultural innovation and diffusion, 188; into households, 206, 212, 215, 218–19, 220–21; into local communities, 228; of European traditions among American born, 230; of American traditions among foreign born, 230, 236–37; causes of, 230–31; promoted by material diffusion, 231, 237, 238–39, 240, 247; promoted by institutions, 232–33; in public schools, 233–34, 240; in the workplace, 234–35; and market exchange, 235–36, 240; in relation to localized traditions, 237–38; associated with urbanness, 238; opposition to, 248

Cultural pluralism, 284, 285, 324

Czech Americans (Bohemians), 96, 112, 164, 173, 182; and transfer of estates, 207; and folk medicine, 229; and public education, 233; and levels of support for women's suffrage referendum, 301

Daily Minnesotan, 92, 236

Dairying, 136, 141, 144, 145; butter production from, 148, 152, 155, and cheese production, 152, 155

Dakota: immigrants in, 5, 83; migration to, 96, 98

Dakota County, Minnesota, 92, 93

Dane County, Wisconsin, 94, 195, 231

Danish Americans, 98; language maintenance among, 109; and their views of Americans, 172; during World War I, 319, 325; Lutheranism among, 332 (n. 65)

Davenport (Iowa) Demokrat, 256

Davenport (Iowa) Gazette, 291

Dean, Charles A., 87, 143

Decorah-Posten, 278

Degler, Carl, 193

Democratic Party: and political patronage, 245; associated with specific ethnic groups, 245–46, 309; and educational reform movements, 298; and its membership's level of support for women's suffrage referendum, 301; and its membership's level of support for temperance referendum, 306; associated with "liturgical" belief, 309; emphasizing "right belief," 309; associated with "right belief," 309, 310; associated with "ritualist" belief, 309, 310; associated with "objective piety," 310; associated with particularism, 310; electoral successes, 310; associated with localism, 310, 311; associated with states' rights, 311

Denominationalism: in American churches, 107

Den Swenske Republikanen, 60

Departure from parental home: according to sex and birth order, 210–11, 213, 215–16, 219

Des Moines, Iowa, 297

Des Moines Anzeiger, 303, 304

Des Moines Register, 292, 304, 319, 325

Devoe, Juli Etta, 187

Die Iowa, 96, 98, 100, 144, 172, 181, 194, 230, 243, 256, 257, 258, 259, 275, 276, 280, 292, 293, 299, 304, 309

Dime novels, 276

Divorces: rates of, 199; and family, 259

Dodge County, Wisconsin, 62, 109, 114, 232

Dohen, Dorothy, 343 (n. 59)

Domestic labor, 234, 258; immigrants preferred for, 258

Dominican Sisters, 123

Dreiser, Theodore, 234

Dress: patterns of, 231

Dubuque, Iowa, 86, 92, 96–97, 104–6, 112, 143, 230, 236, 243, 244, 245

Dubuque County, Iowa, 99, 100, 104–6, 111, 194, 299; age at marriage in, 213; and women's suffrage referendum, 301

Dubuque Herald, 142, 292

Dubuque National Demokrat, 56, 93, 96, 257

Dubuque Times, 243

DuPage County, Illinois, 99

Dutch Americans, 98, 172; and support of temperance, 295; and levels of support for women's suffrage referendum, 301; during World War I, 321, 408 (n. 15)

Dutch Calvinism, 17; and family, 252, 268; and corporatism, 262–63, 268; and pietism, 263; and state, 265, 301–2; and temperance, 301–2, 405 (n. 78)

Dutch Reformed Church, 321

Dwight, Timothy, 34

Dyer, James, 92

Dyersville, Iowa, 244

Dyersville (Iowa) Demokrat, 299

Eau Claire County, Wisconsin, 98

Edwards Law (Illinois), 291, 297

Eldersveld, S., 253

Election (predestination) controversy (Norwegian Synod), 119, 121, 127, 227

Emigrant associations, 91. *See also* Planned colonization

Emigranten, 56, 64, 67, 69, 93

Engelen, William J., 316

England: immigrants from, 83, 86, 169, 193

English Americans, 237; stereotypes of, 236; membership in American Protective Association, 295; and levels of support for women's suffrage referendum, 301

English-only language: laws, 322; proclamations, 323; in Iowa, 323, 324; in Michigan, 324; in Minnesota, 324; in Nebraska, 324

Enlightenment, 10, 14, 67, 70, 331 (n. 55), 406 (n. 102)

Environmental change, 138

Esbjörn, L. P., 271

Espionage Act (1917), 321

Ethington, Philip, 404 (n. 65)

Ethnic churches: authority of clergy in, 112, 123, 125; tensions between clergy and parishioners within, 113–14, 116; as voluntary institutions, 115, 127; au-thority of clergy questioned in, 116–17, 118, 125–27, 128; conflict within, 116–29 passim; lay leadership within, 117; conflict among clergy within, 118; democratic representation within, 121, 122, 130; division of, 121–22; as conservators of tradition, 130; and female authority, 404 (n. 65)

Ethnic communities, 19, 21, 241, 248, 315; resulting from patterns of migration, 103, 129, 226; as voluntary organizations, 104, 106, 110, 127, 227; multilayered loyalties within, 104–6, 226; and church institution, 108; and preservation of language, 108; and social alliances, 109; and economic alliances, 109–10; economic advantages resulting from, 110; and fluidity of settlement, 110; among American-born, 110–11; and social class, 111, 119, 121, 130; among immigrants, 111–14; social divisions within, 111–14, 119–22, 128; cultural variation within, 119; marriage patterns within, 119, 121; regional divisions within, 119–21; nationality divisions within, 122–25; enabled by available land, 129, 226; cultural variation between, 130, 167; insularity of, 130, 177, 218–19, 226, 229, 237, 260, 271, 316, 317; cultural diffusion into, 180, 218–19, 227, 229–30, 236–37, 260, 316, 317, 320, 388 (n. 70); and creation of localized societies, 226–29, 237, 320; conflict between, 241–43; as intermediary institution, 260, 263, 267, 269, 279, 296; as institution to temper power of state, 284, 286; and state, 284, 286, 289, 296; challenged by social and economic change, 296; challenged during World War I, 320–24

Ethnic groups: formation of based on common nationality, 228, 240–41, 242, 247; as interest groups, 228, 242, 244, 246; promoting economic exchange among their members, 243–44; and local politics, 244–46; and political patronage, 245; and political party allegiance, 245–47; and cross-ethnic group alliances, 246; divisions between, 288

"Ethnicization," 21, 59, 228, 242, 244, 246, 247, 248, 287, 309

European American household: and hierarchy, 163, 170, 176–77, 195, 197, 252, 263; typology defined, 163–66; and critique of Americans, 164, 171, 172, 180–81, 194, 248, 251, 252, 255, 259, 263; and importance of lineal ties, 166, 168–69, 170, 183–84, 188, 189, 197, 204–5, 207, 217, 220, 378 (n. 34); and intergenerational continuity, 167, 197, 205, 378 (n. 34); and thriving rural communities, 169; and tendency to remain in farming, 169, 178, 189, 197; and family labor, 170, 171, 172, 197; and female labor, 171, 172–74, 179–80, 182–83, 218–19; and advantages of family labor, 173, 203–4; and child labor, 178–80, 204; challenges encountered by, 183–84, 188, 204–5, 213–15; and cultural diffusion, 188, 206, 212, 215, 218–19, 220–21; size of, 189–90, 195; marital fertility rates in, 191–95, 204; age at marriage among, 195–97; tension among siblings within, 197, 205–6, 208, 213; and land engrossment, 204–5; and inheritance patterns, 204–8; parental power in, 206, 209; burdens placed on children in, 212, 214–15, 217; coresidence of children, 215; and care of aged parents, 216–17; increasing power of adult women in, 216–17; and corporatist ideologies, 252, 259, 263, 264, 265; associated with farming, 260; and subservience of wives, 267

European Americans: and family patterns, 158, 160, 163–66, 170–74, 178–81, 188, 190–91, 195–97, 203–19, 259

Everest, Kate, 61, 181, 231

Excess in American society: political, 68; economic, 69; in fashion, 257; in theater, 257; among youths, 257

Factory labor: preferred by women, 258; as moral hazard, 260

"Familial solidarity," 13–14, 150–51

Family, 20, 21, 248; and society, 66, 251, 253, 255, 260, 261, 263, 266, 279, 315; and family morality, 137, 150–51; and relationships between parents and children, 151, 154, 155, 159, 164, 165, 178–84, 199, 216–17, 252, 259; and relationships between husband and wife, 159, 166, 170–77, 267, 300; distribution of power in, 160, 176–77; and state, 165,

175, 199, 252, 261, 263, 266, 270, 274, 275, 278, 279, 286, 289, 291, 296; and parental authority, 165, 252, 259, 263–64, 266–67, 270, 273, 274, 275, 278, 291; and religious influences, 175–77; cultural change in, 180, 182–84, 213, 215, 218, 248, 252, 253, 256–59, 273; and inequality within, 197, 264; and domestic violence, 199; as intermediary institution, 252, 260, 263, 296; purported disorganization of, 253, 259; as "natural" institution, 260–61, 264, 265, 273, 275, 300, 301, 395 (n. 74); as antecedent to state, 275; and temperance movement, 292; challenged by social and economic change, 296; and separate spheres, 300

Family farms: and farm labor, 135, 148, 149, 150; and market agriculture, 137, 144; and family morality, 137, 150–51; and mechanization, 148; and hired labor, 148, 150; as symbol of economic opportunity, 149–50; capital values of, 150; and inequality among its members, 150, 151, 159, 197; and commodification of land, 151; garden on, 152; as resource for children's futures, 154, 161, 197

"Family morality," 137, 150, 154, 158, 187, 269; and hierarchy, 151; and individual prospects, 154; challenged, 157, 161, 181, 218, 370 (n. 22)

Fanaticism: associated with Americans, 255, 405 (n. 85)

Farmer: status of, 166; and landownership, 371 (n. 31)

Farm family: as symbol of stability, 260; as symbol of natural virtue, 393 (n. 43)

Farm labor: arduousness of, 135, 136, 139–40; performed by family members, 135–36, 139–40, 146, 148, 149, 150, 151–54, 159, 170, 178; seasonal rhythms of, 139; divided by gender, 141, 145, 147, 151, 153, 154, 155, 160, 171–74, 178, 182–83, 300, 367 (n. 101), 374 (n. 65); divided by age, 141, 145, 152–53, 178–79; and farm implements, 143, 146; availability of, 146; performed by hired workers, 146, 147, 366 (n. 84); real wages for, 147; productivity of, 150; cultural differences in, 163, 170–74, 178–81, 182–84, 392 (n. 28)

Farm production: for home use, 142, 148–49
Fayette County, Ohio, 83
Feminism, 156, 177, 199, 299, 300
Ficklin, Orlando B., 28
Fillmore County, Minnesota, 99
Filmer, Robert, 11
First-cousin marriages: restriction of, 290
Flagg, Edmund, 89
Flammung, Michael, 238
Folkebladet, 98
Folkets Røst, 57
Folklore, 225
Folk medicine, 229
Follenius, Paul, 80
Foodways, 148, 230, 244
Fortun, Norway: emigration from, 93–96
Fountain City, Wisconsin, 235
Fourth Commandment, 163, 265–66, 267–68
Fredericksburg, Iowa, 257
Fredrickson, George, 345 (n. 80)
"Freedom": as perceived by immigrants in United States, 57–58, 59–60, 66, 74, 115–17, 127, 176, 227, 274, 319, 334 (n. 28); and authority, 266–67, 279; and "false freedom," 278; abuses of, 314
Freedom of speech, 323, 325
Freeland, Maria, 198
Freeman's Journal and Catholic Register (New York City), 42
Fremad, 255
French Americans: stereotypes of, 236
French Canadians, 160
Friedrich, Carl, 55
Friesland (Vriesland), Netherlands, 86, 139
Fædrelandet og Emigranten, 298

Galena, Illinois, 90
Galena (Illinois) Gazette, 124
Garland, Hamlin, 27, 96, 97, 138, 140, 146, 153, 161–62, 174, 182–83, 200, 218–19, 232, 234
Gausdal, Norway: emigrants from, 121–22, 127
Gausdal Lutheran Church, 121
German Americans, 27, 52, 61, 80, 124, 141, 230, 254; religious beliefs among, 16; and political party allegiance, 56, 57, 246; political behavior of, 58, 59; and qualms about acculturation, 62–63, 69,

108; promoting group settlement, 98; in ethnic communities, 105–6, 108–9, 111, 112, 114, 122, 169, 225, 244, 321; in conflict with Irish Americans, 122–25; acculturation of, 159; as proponents of corporate family, 159, 164, 253; as able farmers, 167, 178, 232; labor patterns among, 171, 172, 173, 174, 178–81; and public education, 181–82, 233; rates of marital fertility among, 191, 194, 195, 220; age at first marriage among, 195; and transfer of estates, 206–7; folklore among, 225; and cultural innovation, 231; conditions of life among, 232; and English language, 235; stereotypes of, 236, 242; clannishness of, 237; prejudice against, 242, 243; as participants in ethnic riots, 243; and political patronage, 245; as safeguarders of United States' future, 255, 308; as admirers of Yankees, 256; as admirers of Scandinavian Americans, 257; and domestic labor, 258; and attitudes toward a national state, 272–73; identified as opponents to temperance, 292–93; and levels of support for women's suffrage referendum, 301; portrayed as steady, 302, 304–5; during World War I, 320–21
German Catholics: views of family and society among, 256–59, 266–67, 316; as proponents of corporatism, 262–63, 270, 312, 315–16; and public education, 276; and parochial education, 297; and levels of support for women's suffrage referendum, 301; attraction to ultramontanism, 312; fear of centralization, 312; opposition to Free Masonry, 312; opposition to socialism, 312; opposition to liberalism, 312, 313, 316; attraction to antirepublicanism, 312, 315; anxiety about modern capitalism, 312–13, 315; and national state, 313; opposition to liberalism, 313; and freedom, 313, 314; and justice, 316
German Lutheranism: and corporatism, 16, 263, 264, 269, 272, 276, 312; and freedom of religion, 116, 159; and cultural diffusion, 164, 280; and family, 252, 268–69, 277; and state, 265, 268–69, 271, 276; and community, 269, 271, 276, 277; and justice, 276; and public

education, 276, 279, 280, 297; and secular world, 276–77, 280; and politics, 280, 312; and public school political debate, 297–98; voting as opponents of educational reform, 298; and feminism, 299, 300; and levels of support for women's suffrage referendum, 301; and temperance, 303; and level of support for temperance referenda, 305–6, 307; as members of Democratic Party, 312; as particularist, 312; and pietism, 330 (n. 50); and parochial school system, 403 (n. 50). *See also* Buffalo Synod; Missouri Synod; Wisconsin Synod

German Poor Assistance Assocation, 244

Germantown, Illinois, 266

Germany, 322; emigrants from, 93, 96, 98, 99

Gibbons, James (cardinal), 61, 65, 270, 294

Gilderhus, Nils Sjurson, 139

Gillespie, Emily Hawley, 156, 171–72, 193, 197, 200–203, 217, 219

Gillespie, James, 200–202

Given, Welker, 238

Gleason, Philip, 16, 111, 300

Glidden, Iowa, 242

Gonner, Nicholas, 243, 260, 324

Goodhue County, Minnesota, 243

Graebner, Alan, 299

Grant, Ulysses S., 290, 291

Grant County, Wisconsin, 231

Grasshopper plagues, 363 (n. 48)

Grundtvig, N. F. S., 332

Grundy County, Iowa, 93

Guiteau, Charles, 251

Hair style, 258

Hall, Basil, 80

Hall, James, 40

Hamilton, Carl, 145

Hamsum, Knut, 227

Handlin, Oscar, 18

Hanover, Germany: emigrants from, 99, 105

Hanson, Gerhard Armauer, 115–16

Hansen, Marcus Lee, 95, 167

Hardin County, Iowa, 111, 159, 238

Harding, William, 319, 320, 322, 323, 325

Harper, Ida Husted, 301

Hatch, Nathan O., 12

Hauge, Hans Nielsen, 330 (n. 50)

Haustafel, 163

Hawley, Hial, 156

Hay, 153

Hedemark, Norway, 99

Hedström, Annie, 152

Heiss, Michael (archbishop), 122, 125

Hesse-Darmstadt: migrants from, 111

Hill, George, 189

Hjelm-Hanson, Paul, 147

Hogs, 139, 145; slaughter of, 148, 365 (n. 77)

Holaind, R. I., 274, 275

Home furnishings, 231–32

Home Missionary, 31, 33–34

"Hoosiers" (residents of Indiana), 171

Horseriding: and women, 257

"Household mode of production," 135, 136, 137, 150, 154, 161, 162

Households: average size of, 189–91; complexity of, 190–91; varying structures of, 200, 204–6, 209–10, 215–16; and European marriage pattern, 204, 217, 220; and partible inheritance, 204–5; and impartible inheritance, 205–6, 220. *See also* European American household; Family; Stem households; Yankee household

Hoyme, Gjermund, 115

Hsu, Francis L. K., 166

Hughes, John, 61

Huntington, Samuel P., 60, 344 (n. 74)

Hutcheson, Francis, 11

Hutchinson, Joseph, 310

Ibsen, Henrik, 227

Ida County, Iowa, 100

Illinois, 38, 40, 80, 291; farming in, 136, 144, 150

Immigrant press: disparaging Americans, 242

Immigrants: in Middle West, 3; and their acculturation to American political system, 53–54, 56–58, 59, 64; as culturally intolerant, 283–84; contempt for Americans, 284

Immigration: to Middle West, 5, 38; nineteenth-century volume of, 10, 37–38, 329 (n. 30); promotion of, 31, 350 (n. 71); restriction of, 46, 324; state and federal promotion of, 97, 350 (n. 71)

Indiana: migrants from, 79
Individualism: in American society, 11–12, 74, 158, 251, 266, 269, 280, 315; condemned, 67, 68, 69–70, 251, 264–65, 269, 345 (n. 80); and individual rights, 137, 157, 227; in the family, 160, 178, 181, 200, 206, 255, 259, 261, 264; and social justice, 262, 313; and individual freedoms, 264; and its relationship with state, 265, 294, 305; and excess, 305
Inheritance patterns: partible, 204–5, 382 (n. 69); and contracts, 205–6; and impartible, 205–6, 220, 382 (n. 69); and *inter vivos* land transfer, 206–7; and kin tenancy, 207
Intergenerational relationships, 151, 154, 155, 161, 164, 165, 178–79, 197; and transfer of property, 156, 163, 199; conflict in, 179, 200, 205–6
Intermarriage, 183; rates of, 239, 355 (n. 29); in relation to cultural diffusion, 239–40; attitudes regarding, 355 (n. 29)
Iowa, 25, 108, 156, 191; immigrants in, 5, 63, 174, 229; economic opportunity in, 29; migration to, 83–85, 87, 88, 92, 96; ethnic settlements in, 111; farming in, 135, 136, 142, 144, 152, 171; wages in, 147; schools in, 233; politics in, 246, 301; and temperance, 292, 293, 303, 304; 1916 women's suffrage referendum in, 301; 1882 temperance referendum in, 305–6; 1917 temperance referendum in, 307–8; during World War I, 321, 322, 324
Iowa Band, 338 (n. 87)
Iowa City, Iowa, 112
Iowa News (Dubuque), 29
Iowa Synod, 17
Ireland: immigrants from, 89, 241
Ireland, John (archbishop), 255, 270, 294
Irish Americans, 27, 32, 56–57, 59, 61, 63–64, 104, 234, 237; in ethnic communities, 111, 112, 122, 128; Roman Catholic clergy of, 16; in conflict with German Americans, 122–25; age at first marriage among, 195; speaking German, 230; stereotypes of, 236; conflict with Norwegian Americans, 241; prejudice against, 242; as participants in riots, 243; and political patronage, 245; and political party allegiance, 246;

as safeguarders of United States' future, 255, 308; identified as opponents to temperance, 293; and political acumen, 390 (n. 108)
Irish Catholics, 270
Irish National Land League, 61

Jackson County, Iowa, 112
Jacobs, Theodore, 122–25, 127
Jacobson, Clara, 234
James, Jesse, 251
James, John Angell, 44
Jansen, Cornelius Otto, 275
Janson, Kristofer, 107, 176–77, 182
Jasper County, Iowa, 242
Jefferson, Thomas, 34, 45, 369 (n. 7)
Jefferson County, Wisconsin, 109
Jensen, Jörgen, 298
Jensen, Richard, 5, 280, 297, 298, 309
Johns Mary Schaal, 180
Jones County, Iowa, 91
Juneau County, Wisconsin, 62

Kandiyohi County, Minnesota, 119
Kansas, 59
Katholische Volkszeitung, 313, 314
Keane, John J. (archbishop), 270
Keillor, Garrison, 213
Kenosha County, Wisconsin, 90
Keokuk (Iowa) Whig, 79
Killian, Joh., 62
Kindergartens, 276
King, Miriam, 196
"Kinship comunities," 103. *See also* Ethnic communities
Kirk, Edward Norris, 12, 31, 261
Kjærringloven, 168
Kleppner, Paul, 309
Know Nothing (American) Party, 37, 283, 284
Know Nothingism, 283, 295
Kohn, Hans, 55
Kuiper, B. K., 268
Kulturkampf, 16, 262, 297
Kuyper, Abraham, 17, 262, 265
Kår, 205
Kårstue, 206

Labor activism, 311
Land: and landlessness, 136, 150; and land ownership, 137; increased arable fields of, 143; speculation in, 143, 144, 167–

68, 169, 363 (n. 34), 372 (n. 44); prices of, 143, 150, 212; and corporate family economy, 151; transfer of between generations, 206–7

Langeland, Knud, 278

Language: maintenance among immigrants, 108–9; and transition to English among non-English speaking immigrants, 228, 388 (n. 70); and miscommunication, 234–35; and acquisition of English among non-English speaking immigrants, 235, 386 (n. 51)

Leavitt, J., 28

Lee County, Iowa, 85

Leisure: as evidence of moral weakness, 253, 256–58; resulting from factory labor, 258

Leo XIII (pope), 126, 127, 267, 300, 397 (n. 105); and condemnation of "Americanism," 270

Lewis, Oscar, 173

Liberalism, 21, 67, 155, 158, 248, 262, 266, 280, 287, 290, 311, 313, 315

Library: as agent of moral decay, 398 (n. 110)

Limerick, Ireland: emigrants from, 104–5

Lindquist, Anna, 152

Lippmann, Walter, 68

Localized traditions, 226–29, 237, 240, 247, 248; examples of, 229

Locke, John, 11, 165

Löher, Franz, 42

Loras, Mathias, 51, 52, 105

Lowden, Iowa, 321

Luster, Norway, 95, 196, 217; immigrants from, 212, 213

Lutherans, 16, 68, 71, 72; in Middle West, 5, 118–22, 130, 159, 163; and political party allegiance, 246; and family, 266. *See also* German Lutheranism; Norwegian Lutheranism; Scandinavian Lutheranism; Swedish Lutheranism

Lutheran Witness, 299

Luxemburger Americans, 98, 324; and language acquisition, 235; settlements of, 238

Luxemburger Gazette, 265, 297, 315

Lynd, Robert and Helen, 155

McGlynn, Edward, 283, 284, 285, 294, 308, 317

McGovern, Joseph Edwin, 203

Machtet, Grigorij, 59, 64

Maine: migrants from, 87

Maine Law, 305

Majority rule: in churches, 71–72, 107, 121, 126–27, 130

Marital fertility: of German Americans, 191, 194, 195; of Irish Americans, 191, 194, 195; decline in, 191, 194, 239; of Norwegian Americans, 191, 195, 210; variations of by ethnocultural group, 191–95; of Yankees, 191–95; and benefits of children, 193, 194; and female power, 193, 194; increases in on frontier, 204, 210, 220; and average age at last birth, 210

Marriage: cultural differences of, 162, 166, 170–77, 195–97, 259; age at according to nationality, 195–96; age at according to parentage, 196; age at according to sex, 208–9, 211, 212–13; age at according to birth order, 208–9, 212–13; rates of according to birth order, 208–9, 212–13; rates of according to sex, 208–9, 212–13; rates of according to residence in Norway or United States, 217; and courtship, 259

Marryat, Frederick, 26

Marshalltown (Iowa) Beobachter, 275

Martin, Theresa, 123–24

Martin County, Minnesota, 99

Marty, Martin, 12

Maryland: migrants from, 91

Masquerades, 257

Massachusettts: migrants from, 91, 111, 135

Materialism: in American society, 67, 68, 69, 280, 315; associated with Americans, 164, 238, 254, 255; associated with decline of family, 255, 261–62; associated with sensuality, 258–59; associated with public education, 277

Maurer, Heinrich, 269, 279

Mayerhoff, Ernest, 62

Mazzuchelli, Samuel, 52, 70–71, 72

Mellberg, G., 187

Mennonites, 399 (n. 130); and corporatism, 269

Methodists: in Middle West, 5, 104, 242, 271, 277; associated with individualism, 262, 294; and temperance, 292; and state activism, 294; and level of support for temperance referenda, 306, 307

Michigan: immigrants in, 5; migrants from, 83; and temperance, 292; World War I in, 324

Middle West: ethnocultural diversity in, 2, 4; as locale of "freedom," 6, 220, 227, 325; as site of acculturation, 18; as site of ethnocultural separation, 18, 220, 283, 285, 309, 316, 317; land purchases in, 25; population growth in, 25, 33–34; migration to, 80–81, 129, 328 (n. 9); as distant destination, 82; economic opportunity in, 90, 220, 227, 319; as site of ethnic communities, 106, 107, 129, 285, 316, 317, 320; environmental change in, 138; and ethnic groups, 247; as region of importance to United States, 285

Miller, Kerby A., 63

Milwaukee, Wisconsin, 123

Milwaukee Seebote, 258

Miner, Horace, 159–61, 168, 169, 198, 199, 238

Minneapolis, Minnesota, 177

Minneapolis Tribune, 322

Minnesota, 25, 273; immigrants in, 5, 51–52; migration to, 96, 98; farming in, 136, 144; ethnic riots in, 243; politics in, 246, 280; during World War I, 321–22, 324

Minnesota Commission of Public Safety (MCPS), 322–23

Minnesota Democratic Weekly, 92, 93

Missouri, 80; migrants from, 111; Germans in, 162; temperance in, 303

Missouri Synod, 17, 118, 263, 271, 277, 278, 298, 299, 303; criticized, 278; during World War I, 324; parochial school system, 403 (n. 50)

Mixed farming, 136, 139, 149; conversion to, 144; advantages of, 145, 146

Monarchism, 315, 317

Mormonism, 255

Morse, Henry, 87

Morse, Samuel F. B., 33, 37, 40, 56, 285, 325

Morse, Sarah, 135

Motion pictures: as an agent of cultural diffusion, 238–39, 247

Munch, Peter A., 109, 239

Murray, Charles Augustus, 30, 79

Muus, Bernt J., 278

Muus, Oline, 375 (n. 81)

National Catholic Women's Union, 300

Nationalism: in United States, 54–55

National Reformed Church, 17

Native Americans, 171

Nativism: in antebellum U.S., 35, 37, 42–44, 48, 55–56, 74; in eastern United States, 52–53; in late nineteenth century U.S., 236, 283, 284, 290, 294; in English language press, 243; and loyalty to state, 288. *See also* Americanization

Naturalization law, 38

Natural law, 15, 273, 274

Nebraska: immigrants in, 5; migration to, 96, 100; World War I in, 324

Netherlands, 301; immigrants from, 86–87, 93; National Reformed Church in, 330 (n. 50)

Newark Daily Advertiser, 46

New England: migrants from, 80, 87, 89, 90–91, 92

New Hampshire: migrants from, 90

New Sharon, Iowa, 321

Newspapers: as agents of moral decay, 253, 398 (n. 110)

Newton, Iowa, 242

New Vienna, Iowa, settlement, 105–6

New York, 273; migrants from, 90, 91, 182, 198

Niles Hezekiah, 26, 31–32, 41

Non-marriage: by parentage, 196

Norden, 295

Nordlyset, 57

Norelius, Eric, 271

North Carolina: migrants from, 27, 111, 147

North Dakota: migration to, 96

Northfield (Minnesota) Recorder, 147

Northwest Ordinance, 6

Norway, 322; emigrants from, 93, 96, 98, 99

Norway Grove, Wisconsin, settlement, 210, 212, 217

Norwegian Americans, 27, 128, 139, 228, 230, 234, 235, 244; political behavior of, 56, 57, 58; and views of acculturation, 64, 68, 69; language maintenance among, 109; and their evaluation of others, 109–10, 164; regional differences among, 113, 119–21, 237; differences in social class among, 116; conflict among, 118–22; patterns of labor among, 147, 152, 153; and family patterns, 163, 168–69, 175–77, 184, 195, 207–19; age at first marriage among, 195, 208–9, 212–13; and household arrangements, 206; and transfer of estates, 206–7; cultural diffusion into households of, 212, 215; conditions of life among, 231; and language acquisition, 235; and child naming customs, 239; conflict with Irish Americans, 241; prejudice against, 242, 243; as participants in riots, 243; as advocates of women's suffrage, 255; as admirers of Yankees, 256; and parental authority, 267–68

Norwegian Lutheranism, 118–22; and pietism, 272, 277; and parochial education, 278–79

Norwegian Synod (Norwegian Evangelical Lutheran Church of America), 118, 119, 121, 267, 272, 277, 278

Nuclear household: augmented by single kin, 200, 216

Oats, 141

"Objective piety," 118, 354 (n. 16)

Odelsrett, 169

Ohio, 111; migrants from, 79, 88, 92, 105; immigrants to, 91; and temperance, 292

Oldenberg, Germany: emigrants from, 99, 105

Oliphant, Laurence, 9

Onuf, Peter S., 311

Ostergren, Robert C., 5

Our Saviour's Lutheran Church (Minneapolis), 267

Page County, Iowa: and women's suffrage referendum, 301

Papal infallibility, 15

Parochial education, 253, 273; as fostering religious belief, 254, 280; among Roman Catholics, 273–76, 297; as protecting family and community, 280, 296; as threatening instruction in civic duties, 289; as creating ignorant society, 290; as denying individual freedoms, 290

Parsons, Kenneth H., 207

Parsons, Oliver, 86

Particularism, 248, 270; and Baptists, 270; and Presbyterians, 270; and Roman Catholics, 270; and national state, 270, 272, 284; and German Lutherans, 271; and Scandinavian Lutherans, 271–72, 278; and politics, 280, 281, 286, 311, 317; among immigrants, 284, 314, 325; among German Catholics, 314, 316; during World War I, 323–24

Patriarchalism, 11

Paul VI (pope), 404 (n. 66)

Pennsylvania: migrants from, 79

Pennsylvania Germans, 160

Peoria, Iowa, 321

Petersen, William, 25

Philadelphia: migrants from, 92

Philadelphia Sentinel, 26

Piano: associated with sensuality, 258–59

Pierz, Francis, 51, 52, 339 (n. 10)

Pietism, 10, 14, 67, 357 (n. 57)

Pius X (pope), 61

Plaister, James, 92

Planned colonization: among Germans, 41–42; among Roman Catholics, 42; among Yankees, 46–47, 351 (n. 72)

Plisch, Gottlieb, 142–43

Pluralism: among Norwegian Americans, 278; and electoral politics, 311

Polish Americans: and marital fertility, 195

Political movements: of centralization, 286; of school centralization, 286; regarding temperance, 286, 293; regarding women's rights, 286, 293; and religious backgrounds, 294; radical, 311; conservative, 311–16

Political parties: membership informed by ethnoculture, 309, 311; bringing stability into political debate, 311; building coalitions, 311; homogenizing issues, 311; informed by race, 311; informed by social class, 311; membership informed by economic program, 311; as lacking responsibility to society, 314

Polk County, Iowa, 194

Populism, 311

Poultry, 141, 148, 152, 202

Prepaid tickets: enabling emigration, 98, 351 (n. 74)

Presbyterians: in Middle West, 5; and particularism, 270; and temperance, 292

Preus, Herman Amberg, 72, 163–64, 278
Progressivism, 285
Public education, 156, 273; resistance
to, 177, 182, 230, 273–79; and cultural
diffusion, 181–82, 226, 233, 235, 239;
and promotion of English language,
233, 235; cultural conflict in, 233–34;
as agent of moral weakness, 253, 255,
275, 276, 280, 281, 308; debate among
Roman Catholics about, 273–76, 294;
and failure to prevent crime, 275–76;
broadening influence of, 276, 291; and
failure to emphasize family authority,
278, 297, 308; Norwegian American
support of, 278–79; immigrants' control of, 283; political movements and,
286, 290–91, 296, 297–98, 307, 320;
as central to citizenship, 289; attempts
to make mandatory, 291; attempts to
systematize, 291; parental rights in, 291
Puchner, R., 58

Quarles, Joseph V., 90
Quick, Herbert, 18, 88, 140, 142, 146, 149,
162, 171, 173, 174–75, 178–79, 193–94,
204, 214, 225–26, 228, 230–31, 233, 237

Racine County, Wisconsin, 91
Radicalism, 311
Radio, 238
Rasmussen, Karl, 319
Rationalism, 10, 14, 277
Reconstruction, 291
Red River Valley, 96, 98
Reiersen, Johan R., 58
Religious freedom, 323; praised, 19, 66–
67, 74, 130, 272, 274, 325, 342 (n. 54),
346 (n. 101), 358 (n. 65), 399 (n. 130);
concerns about, 71, 74; and clerical
authority, 116–17, 122, 125, 127, 128, 279
Republicanism: associated with Protestantism, 12–13, 36–37, 47–48, 73–74,
160, 285, 291, 335 (n. 49); associated
with "progress," 36; associated with
"freedom," 36, 335 (n. 49); fragility
of, 43; and homogeneity, 45–46; and
family, 160; classical forms of, 315
Republican Party: associated with Americans, 242, 288; and political patronage,
245; associated with specific ethnic

groups, 245–46, 298, 310; and educational reform movements, 298, 310;
and its membership's level of support
for women's suffrage referendum, 301;
political backlash against, 306; and
its membership's level of support for
temperance referendum, 306, 310; associated with "pietism," 309; associated
with "right behavior," 309; associated
with "subjective piety," 309; associated
with state activism, 309, 310, 311; associated with liberalism, 310; electoral
failures, 310; associated with centralization, 310, 311; associated with economic
centralization, 311
Rerum novarum, 267, 300
Retirement contracts, 205; and "bonds of
maintenance," 206
Richland County, Ohio: migrants from,
92
Riots: between ethnic groups, 243
Roman Catholicism, 230, 286, 317; attacks
on, 12–13, 284–85; and corporatism,
15, 269; "Americanism" within, 16, 65,
67, 270, 294; and clerical authority,
115, 123–24, 126; and justice, 126; and
family, 252, 267; liberalism within,
255, 270, 274, 294, 309; and Social
Catholicism, 262–63; and state, 265;
and United States, 291, 294; and Cahensly movement, 294; in opposition to
liberalism, 406 (n. 102)
Roman Catholics, 22, 61, 69, 277; as proportion of immigrants, 5; in Middle
West, 5, 27, 52, 130, 163, 271; clergy of,
51–52; acculturation of, 65; settlements
comprised of, 104–6, 111; church conflict
among, 122–28; and political party allegiance, 246; and family, 253, 266–67;
and public schools, 273–76, 279, 280,
294; and public school political debate,
297–98; as opponents of educational
reform, 298; women's groups among,
300; as opponents to temperance, 303;
and level of support for temperance
referenda, 306, 307
Rosenius, Carl Olof, 330 (n. 50)
Rousseau, Jean-Jacques, 8
Ruggles, Steven, 196, 379 (n. 40)
Rural life: as symbol of morality, 260
Rynning, Ole, 56

Ræder, Ole Munch, 56, 60–61, 68–69, 113, 230
Rölvaag, O. E., 117

Sac County, Iowa, 100
St. Anthony Falls (Minnesota) Democrat, 93, 98
St. Dominic's Catholic Church, 122, 123, 125, 128, 130
St. Donatus, Iowa, 238
St. Joseph community, Iowa, 242
St. Louis, Missouri, 106
St. Paul Daily Press, 93
Salter, William, 47, 91
Sampson, Magnus W., 93
Sandoz, Mari, 171
Santa Claus, 257
Sarna, Jonathan D., 242
Sassel, Reverend, 251, 252
Satellite communities, 95
Saunders, Frederick, 34–36, 38
Scandinavian Americans: and women's work, 257; in politics, 280; and support of temperance, 295, 405 (n. 76); as adherents of Republican Party, 310
Scandinavian Lutheranism, 17; and family, 252–53; and corporatism, 263, 269–70; and acceptance of liberal forms, 269–70, 272, 280, 310; and cultural diffusion, 273, 280; membership in American Protective Association, 295; pietism in, 330 (n. 50)
Schafer, Joseph, 167, 234, 237
Schmidt, F. A., 278
Schmucker, Samuel Simon, 396 (n. 84)
Schoolland, Klass, 268
Schurz, Carl, 61
Scots Americans, 234; stereotypes of, 236
Scott County, Iowa, 92
Seaton, Emma, 83
Second Great Awakening, 12, 164
Sectarianism: in American religious life, 70–71
"Sect-types": defined, 354 (n. 16)
Secularization, 155, 277; and public education, 277
Sensuality: increasing in American society, 258–59
Sewing machines, 231
Sheboygan County, Wisconsin, 62, 231
Sheep, 145

Simeoni, Cardinal, 126
Sinsinawa Mound, Wisconsin, 122, 124, 125, 128
Sioux City, Iowa, 242
Sipma, Sjoerd Aukes, 30, 86–87, 139, 143
Skandinaven, 278
Slavery, 36
Smith, Daniel Scott, 192, 193, 194
Smith, John Talbot, 54
Smith, Timothy L., 14
Smyth, Clement, 65
Social Catholicism, 262–63, 264, 270, 312
Social class: in relation to work and leisure, 256; and women's rights advocates, 299; and class warfare, 315
Social Darwinism, 265
Social Gospel, 279
Social mobility: as threat to family, 253; desire for associated with Americans, 254–55
Social problems: and state intervention, 288
Society of the Army of the Tennessee, 290
Sollors, Werner, 329 (n. 24), 344 (n. 74)
Somersetshire, England: emigrants from, 92–93
Sorokin, Pitirim A., 370 (n. 21)
South Dakota: defeat of women's suffrage amendment in, 301
Southerners, 32
Spaulding, John Lancaster (archbishop), 260, 273, 294
Spring Prairie, Wisconsin, settlement, 210
Ständeorganisation, 264
State: as an institution, 252–53, 280; as threat to religious belief, 254; in relation to individualism, 265; and education, 274, 289; as force threatening local communities, 284, 305; efforts to extend influence of, 284–86, 287–88, 288–90, 305, 316, 320, 322; positive role of, 289–90; as activist institution, 289–90, 316, 324; as "artificial," 395 (n. 74)
Stearns County, Minnesota, 98, 99
Steele County, Minnesota, 243
Stem household, 205–8; incidence of in United States, 210, 215–16, 217–18; in relation to opportunities for children, 210–15; increasing female influence in, 216–17; associated with parental authority, 266

Stillwater (Minnesota) Gazette, 54
Stord, Norway: emigrants from, 119
Strong, Josiah, 285, 288, 317, 325
Stub, H. G., 267
Stuttgard [sic] Universal Gazette, 41
"Subjective piety," 118
Suckow, Ruth, 88, 162, 173, 178
Suicide, 276
Sully, Iowa, 321
Svenska Amerikanaren, 295
Sweden: emigrants from, 93, 97, 98, 152, 241
Swedish Americans, 228; and public education, 233; as participants in riots, 243; and political patronage, 245; and political party allegiance, 246; and attitudes toward a national state, 272–73; and anti-Catholicism, 295; and concern about Yankee influence, 295; and support for public schools, 295; and levels of support for women's suffrage referendum, 301
Swedish Lutheranism, 271–72; and pietism, 272, 332 (n. 65); and parochial schools, 398 (n. 119)
Swensson, Carl, 398 (n. 119)
Swiss Americans, 61
Swisshelm, Jane G., 175
Switzerland, 173
Syllabus of Errors, 15
Sändebudet, 295

Tama County, Iowa, 99
Telemark, Norway, 99
Temperance, 252, 256, 320; identified with Yankees, 242–43, 292; taught in public schools, 275; political movements regarding, 286, 296; and amendments to state constitutions, 292; identified with Protestant churches, 292; and nativism, 292, 293; and family, 292, 293, 296; and extralegal violence, 292, 303; support for among women, 292, 303; opposition against among Irish and Germans, 293, 302; support carried from European homelands, 294; opposition identified with invasion of family, 297, 302, 308; support for among Dutch Calvinists, 301–2, 405 (n. 78); identified with governmental intrusion, 303; and Iowa constitutional referenda, 303, 305–6,

307, 308; its supporters identified with excess and fanaticism, 303–5, 308
Tennessee: migrants from, 111
Texas: planned immigrant colonization in, 337 (n. 66)
Theater: immorality of, 257
Thomas William I., 13–14, 15, 18, 150
Thomson, John and Mary, 30, 86
Thorpe, T. B., 34–36, 38
Threshing ring, 141
Tobacco: production of, 244; sale of to minors, 290
Tocqueville, Alexis de, 55, 68, 165, 198, 199
"Tramps," 147
Transportation: improvements in, 136, 138, 148
Traynor, W. J. H., 287, 288, 317
Trägårdh, Lars, 272
Troeltsch, Ernst, 67, 354 (n. 16)
"True love," 170; purported lack of among Europeans, 174–75; and marriage, 198–99, 259, 378 (n. 31); and weakened parental power, 259
Turner, Asa, 48
Turner, Frederick Jackson, 2, 4, 5, 6, 18, 226

Undantag, 205
Underwood, Myranda, 30, 85
United Brethren Church: and temperance, 292
Unonius, Gustav, 187
Urbanization, 150, 258

Valley City, North Dakota, 242
Vermont: migrants from, 82, 85, 87, 92, 110
Vernon County, Wisconsin, 94, 95, 212, 213
Violin: associated with the devil, 114
Virginia: migrants from, 80
Volksverein für Amerika, 315
Voluntary associations: churches as, 67, 115, 127. See also Ethnic churches
Voting behavior: resulting from attempts at education reform, 298; in Iowa constitution women's suffrage amendment referendum, 301; in Iowa constitution temperance amendment referenda, 305–8

Walburg, Anton H., 69, 254–55, 308
Walker, Mack, 353 (n. 3)
Walker, Robert J., 29
Wallace, Michael, 11
Walther, C. F. W, 116, 263, 264, 271, 272, 276, 277, 303, 346 (n. 101)
Wapello County, Iowa, 26
Waples, Eliot O., 207
Washington, George, 61
Waushara County, Wisconsin, 182
Wehrwein, Carl F., 206
Welfare maternalism, 289–90
Welsh Americans, 237
"West," the: ethnocultural diversity in, 1, 4, 27, 35, 74; as locus of economic opportunity, 2, 7, 26, 27–31, 44–45, 79, 227; as setting for cultural conflict, 3, 39, 45, 48; as setting of cultural fragmentation, 7, 43–44, 80, 285; as site of ethnocultural separation, 8, 35, 40, 43–44, 75, 279, 285, 289, 316; idea of, 9, 18; as immature society, 26, 33–35, 80, 289; as threat to national stability, 27, 44–45, 289; social equality in, 30, 80; as site of creation of new "races," 32; and its political importance to United States, 34; as a site of assimilation, 39, 45, 75, 280; as a new Canaan, 79, 82; as center of European American culture, 285
Westphalia, Germany: emigrants from, 98, 99, 105
Westward migration: and its role in weakening former ties, 79–80; and tactics to temper separation, 81, 101; sense of loss stemming from, 82–88; and shared information, 86. *See also* Chain migration
Wheat, 135, 136; and frontier, 139; production of, 139, 140; attraction to, 140; planting of, 140–41; threshing of, 141; harvest of, 141, 147; marketing of, 142; declining harvests of, 144; and natural pests, 144
"Wheat period," 139
Whitney, Thomas R., 35, 36, 38, 55
Wild Rose community, Wisconsin, 182, 240
Wilson, Charles (Wilhelm Bedø), 256
Wisconsin, 70, 153, 191, 291; immigrants in, 5, 62–63, 86, 119, 181, 195, 206, 230, 231, 234, 283; migrants to, 85, 87, 93, 96; farming in, 136, 142, 144; transfer

of estates in, 206–7; ethnic conflict in, 241–42; political debate in, 297, 310
Wisconsin Banner, 57
Wisconsin Synod, 17, 298
Wohlin, Nils, 14
Women: work responsibilities of, 151–52, 160, 171–74, 178, 179–80, 182–83, 210, 218–19; and leisure, 256–57; as elected officials, 299; as school teachers, 299; excluded from theological politics, 396 (n. 79)
Women's Christian Temperance Union, 292, 305
Women's rights: political movements supporting, 286, 290, 293, 296, 298–301; and temperance, 293; and "natural" roles for women, 298, 300, 308; and "natural" order of family, 298, 308
Women's rights organizations, 267, 289
Women's suffrage, 255; advocated by immigrants, 255; political movements favoring, 286, 290, 293, 296; and its influence on family, 297, 298, 299; referendum for amendment to Iowa constitution on, 301
Wood, Gordon S., 11
Wood, Grant, 145
Woodward, Mary, 179
World War I, 316, 319–25; and ethnic groups, 320, 324; increased power of national government during, 321; extralegal activities supporting, 321, 324; English-only language laws during, 322–23; increased power of state governments during, 322–23; violations of civil rights during, 322–23, 324; protests against in ethnic communities, 324
Wyman, Roger, 298

Yale Band, 338 (n. 87)
Yankee household: typology defined, 163–66; and contractualism, 164, 189; and individualism, 164–65, 170, 188, 198, 200; and importance of lateral ties, 165–66, 170, 189; and importance of conjugal ties, 166, 182–84, 188, 191, 197; and intergenerational discontinuity, 167–68, 184, 188, 189, 197, 199, 200–203; and tendency to forsake farming, 169, 198, 199; and conjugal affect, 170, 183, 184, 198–99; and critique of Euro-

pean household, 171, 174–77, 178–79, 182–83; size of, 189–90, 198; marital fertility of, 192–94, 198; and departure of children from home, 199–203; and affection between mother and child, 201–3; and conjugal conflict, 201–3; loneliness within, 202–3

Yankees (northeastern Americans), 32, 234; migration westward, 26–27, 79, 80, 87, 90, 91, 104, 110; ethnic settlements among, 98, 104, 110–11; gendered division of labor among, 152, 155, 160, 171, 173, 218; family patterns among, 158, 160, 163, 200–202; and their view of European American families, 159; intergenerational relationships among, 162, 168, 188, 198–203; farming patterns among, 167; and self-made personhood, 167, 168, 256; and land speculation, 167, 372 (n. 44); and shrinking rural communities, 169, 195; as proponents of education, 182, 199; household tensions among, 188, 199–203; and declining marital fertility, 193–94, 195, 198; age at first marriage among, 195–96; rates of marriage among, 196, 198; and social mobility, 202; interaction with immigrants, 226, 230; dislike of immigrants, 241–42; admired by immigrants, 256; associated with commerce, 260; as advocates of activist state, 288; identified as supporters of temperance, 293; voting as supporters of educational reform, 298; associated with excess and fanaticism, 304–5, 405 (n. 85); planned colonies among, 339 (n. 89); as "un-American," 343 (n. 58)

Znaniecki, Florian, 13–14, 15, 18, 150

Årdal, Norway, 95